Conferences of John Cassian

by
John Cassian

Printed on acid free ANSI archival quality paper.
ISBN: 978-1-78139-116-7

Contents

Part I   1
Preface   3
Conference 1.   6
Conference 2.   34
Conference 3.   59
Conference 4.   85
Conference 5.   105
Conference 6.   132
Conference 7.   154
Conference 8.   186
Conference 9.   213
Conference 10.   245

Part II.   265
Preface   267
Conference 11.   269
Conference 13.   287
Conference 14.   315
Conference 15.   338
Conference 16.   348
Conference 17.   372

Part III.   403
Preface   405
Conference 18.   407
Conference 19.   429
Conference 20.   445
Conference 21.   459
Conference 23.   495
Conference 24.   522

Part I.

Containing Conferences I.-X.

PREFACE

THE obligation, which was promised to the blessed Pope Castor in the preface to those volumes which with God's help I composed in twelve books on the Institutes of the Coenobia, and the remedies for the eight principal faults, has now been, as far as my feeble ability permitted, satisfied. I should certainly like to see what was the opinion fairly arrived at on this work both by his judgment and yours, whether, on a matter so profound and so lofty, and one which has never yet been made the subject of a treatise, we have produced anything worthy of your notice, and of the eager desire of all the holy brethren. But now as the aforesaid Bishop has left us and departed to Christ, meanwhile these ten Conferences of the grandest of the Fathers, viz., the Anchorites who dwelt in the desert of Scete, which he, fired with an incomparable desire for saintliness, had bidden me write for him in the same style (not considering in the greatness of his affection, what a burden he placed on shoulders too weak to bear it)--these Conferences I have thought good to dedicate to you in particular, O blessed Pope, [1] Leontius, [2] and holy brother Helladius. [3] For one of you was united to him whom I have mentioned, by the ties of brotherhood, and the rank of the priesthood, and (what is more to the point) by fervour in sacred study, and so has an hereditary right to demand the debt due to his brother: while the other has ventured to follow the sublime customs of the Anchorites, not like some others, presumptuously on his own account, but seizing, at the inspiration of the Holy Ghost, on the right path of doctrine almost before he had been taught and choosing to learn not so much from his own ideas as from their traditions. Wherein just as I had anchored in the harbour of Silence, a wide sea opens out before me, so that I must venture to hand down for posterity some of the Institutes and teaching of these great men. For the bark of my slender abilities will be exposed to the dangers of a longer voyage on the deep, in proportion as the Anchorite's life is grander than that of the Coenobium, and the contemplation of God, to which those inestimable men ever devoted themselves, more sublime than ordinary practical life. It is yours therefore to assist our efforts by your pious prayers for fear lest so sacred a subject that is to be treated in an untried but faithful manner, should be imperilled by us, or lest by our simplicity should lose itself in the depths of the subject matter. Let us therefore pass from what is visible to the eye and the external mode of life of the monks, of which we treated in the former books, to the life of the inner man, which is hidden from view; and from the system of the canonical prayers, let our discourse mount to that continuance in unceasing prayer, which the Apostle enjoins, that whoever has through reading our former work already spiritually gained the name of Jacob by ousting his carnal faults, may now by the reception of the Institutes which are not mine but the fathers', mount by a pure insight to the merits and (so to speak) the dignity of Israel, and in the same way be taught what it is that he should observe on these lofty heights of perfection. [4] And so may your prayers gain from Him, Who has deemed us worthy both to see them and to learn from them and to dwell with them, that He will vouchsafe to grant us a perfect recollection of their teaching, and a ready tongue to tell it, that we may explain them as beautifully and as exactly as we received them from them and may succeed in setting before you the men themselves incorporated, as it were, in their own Institutes, and what is more to the point, speaking in the Latin tongue. Of this however we wish above all to advertise the reader of these Conferences as well as of our earlier works, that if there chances to be anything herein which by reason of his condition and the character of his profession, or owing to custom and the common mode of life seems to him either impossible or very difficult, he should measure it not by the limits of his own powers but by the worth and perfection of the speakers, whose zeal and purpose he should first consider, as they were truly dead to this worldly life, and so hampered by no feelings for their kinsmen according to the flesh, and by no ties of worldly occupations. Next let him bear in mind the character of the country in which they dwelt, how they lived in a vast desert, and were cut off from intercourse with all their fellow-men, and thus were able to have their minds enlightened, and to contemplate, and utter those things which perhaps will seem impossibilities to the uninitiated and uninstructed, because of their way of life and the commonplace character of their habits. But if any one wants to give a true opinion on this matter, and is anxious to try whether such perfection can be attained, let him first endeavour to make his purpose their own, with the same zeal and the same mode of life, and then in the end he will find that those things which used to seem beyond the powers of men, are not only possible, but really delightful. But now let us proceed at once to their Conferences and Institutes.

NOTES:
[1] Papa. See note 3 on the Preface to the Institutes.

[2] The see of which Leontius was Bishop is uncertain, possibly Frejus.

[3] Helladius was afterwards raised to the Episcopate, but of what see is unknown. See the Preface to Conf. XVIII.

[4] The allusion is rather forced and strained. But Cassian means to say that those who have got the better of their carnal sins by perusing his former work, are already fit to be named Jacob (the supplanter), who got the better of his brother: and he hopes that this new work of his will give them such a view of God and insight into His dealings that they may be worthy to have their name changed, as Jacob's was, to Israel, which he takes to mean the man seeing God. Cf. the note on Against Nestorius, VII. ix. (intelligibilis here = spiritualis, cf. intellectualis. Conf. XII. xi., and elsewhere).

CONFERENCE 1.

First Conference of Abbot Moses
on the Goal or the Aim of the Monk

CHAPTER I.

Of our stay in Scete, and that which we proposed to Abbot Moses.

WHEN I was in the desert of Scete, where are the most excellent monastic fathers and where all perfection flourishes, in company with the holy father Germanus (who had since the earliest days and commencement of our spiritual service been my closest companion both in the coenobium and in the desert, so that to show the harmony of our friendship and aims, everybody would say that a single heart and soul existed in our two bodies), I sought out Abbot Moses, [5] who was eminent amid those splendid flowers, not only in practical but also in contemplative excellence, in my anxiety to be grounded by his instruction: and together we implored him to give us a discourse for our edification; not without tears, for we knew full well his determination never to consent to open the gate of perfection, except to those who desired it with all faithfulness, and sought it with all sorrow of heart; for fear lest if he showed it at random to those who cared nothing for it, or only desired it in a half-hearted way, by opening what is necessary, and what ought only to be discovered to those seeking perfection, to unworthy persons, and such as accepted it with scorn, he might appear to lay himself open either to the charge of bragging, or to the sin of betraying his trust; and at last being overcome by our prayers he thus began.

NOTES:
[5] On this Moses see the note on the Institutes, Book X. xxv.

CHAPTER II.

Of the question of Abbot Moses, who asked what was the goal and what the end of the monk.

ALL the arts and sciences, said he, have some goal or mark; and end or aim of their own, on which the diligent pursuer of each art has his eye, and so endures all sorts of toils and dangers and losses, cheerfully and with equanimity, e.g., the farmer, shunning neither at one time the scorching heat of the sun, nor at another the frost and cold, cleaves the earth unweariedly, and again and again subjects the clods of his field to his ploughshare, while he keeps before him his goal; viz., by diligent labour to break it up small like fine sand, and to clear it of all briers, and free it from all weeds, as he believes that in no other way can he gain his ultimate end, which is to secure a good harvest, and a large crop; on which he can either live himself free from care, or can increase his possessions. Again, when his barn is well stocked he is quite ready to empty it, and with incessant labour to commit the seed to the crumbling furrow, thinking nothing of the present lessening of his stores in view of the future harvest. Those men too who are engaged in mercantile pursuits, have no dread of the uncertainties and chances of the ocean, and fear no risks, while an eager hope urges them forward to their aim of gain. Moreover those who are inflamed with the ambition of military life, while they look forward to their aim of honours and power take no notice of danger and destruction in their wanderings, and are not crushed by present losses and wars, while they are eager to obtain the end of some honour held out to them. And our profession too has its own goal and end, for which we undergo all sorts of toils not merely without weariness but actually with delight; on account of which the want of food in fasting is no trial to us, the weariness of our vigils becomes a delight; reading and constant meditation on the Scriptures does not pall upon us; and further incessant toil, and self-denial, and the privation of all things, and the horrors also of this vast desert have no terrors for us. And doubtless for this it was that you yourselves despised the love of kinsfolk, and scorned your fatherland, and the delights of this world, and passed through so many countries, in order that you might come to us, plain and simple folk as we are, living in this wretched state in the desert. Wherefore, said he, answer and tell me what is the goal and end, which incite you to endure all these things so cheerfully.

7

CHAPTER III.

Of our reply.

AND when he insisted on eliciting an opinion from us on this question, we replied that we endured all this for the sake of the kingdom of heaven.

CHAPTER IV.

Of Abbot Moses' question on the aforesaid statement.

TO which he replied: Good, you have spoken cleverly of the (ultimate) end. But what should be our (immediate) goal or mark, by constantly sticking close to which we can gain our end, you ought first to know. And when we frankly confessed our ignorance, he proceeded: The first thing, as I said, in all the arts and sciences is to have some goal, i.e., a mark for the mind, and constant mental purpose, for unless a man keeps this before him with all diligence and persistence, he will never succeed in arriving at the ultimate aim and the gain which he desires. For, as I said, the farmer who has for his aim to live free from care and with plenty, while his crops are springing has this as his immediate object and goal; viz., to keep his field clear from all brambles, and weeds, and does not fancy that he can otherwise ensure wealth and a peaceful end, unless he first secures by some plan of work and hope that which he is anxious to obtain. The business man too does not lay aside the desire of procuring wares, by means of which he may more profitably amass riches, because he would desire gain to no purpose, unless he chose the road which leads to it: and those men who are anxious to be decorated with the honours of this world, first make up their minds to what duties and conditions they must devote themselves, that in the regular course of hope they may succeed in gaining the honours they desire. And so the end of our way of life is indeed the kingdom of God. But what is the (immediate) goal you must earnestly ask, for if it is not in the same way discovered by us, we shall strive and wear ourselves out to no purpose, because a

8

man who is travelling in a wrong direction, has all the trouble and gets none of the good of his journey. And when we stood gaping at this remark, the old man proceeded: The end of our profession indeed, as I said, is the kingdom of God or the kingdom of heaven: but the immediate aim or goal, is purity of heart, without which no one can gain that end: fixing our gaze then steadily on this goal as if on a definite mark, let us direct our course as straight towards it as possible, and if our thoughts wander somewhat from this, let us revert to our gaze upon it, and check them accurately as by a sure standard, which will always bring back all our efforts to this one mark, and will show at once if our mind has wandered ever so little from the direction marked out for it.

CHAPTER V.

A comparison with a man who is trying to hit a mark.

AS those, whose business it is to use weapons of war, whenever they want to show their skill in their art before a king of this world, try to shoot their arrows or darts into certain small targets which have the prizes painted on them; for they know that they cannot in any other way than by the line of their aim secure the end and the prize they hope for, which they will only then enjoy when they have been able to hit the mark set before them; but if it happens to be withdrawn from their sight, however much in their want of skill their aim may vainly deviate from the straight path, yet they cannot perceive that they have strayed from the direction of the intended straight line because they have no distinct mark to prove the skilfulness of their aim, or to show up its badness: and therefore while they shoot their missiles idly into space, they cannot see how they have gone wrong or how utterly at fault they are, since no mark is their accuser, showing how far they have gone astray from the right direction; nor can an unsteady look help them to correct and restore the straight line enjoined on them. So then the end indeed which we have set before us is, as the Apostle says, eternal life, as he declares, "having indeed your fruit unto holiness, and the end eternal life;" [6] but the immediate goal is purity of heart, which he not unfairly terms "sanctification," without which the afore-mentioned end cannot be gained; as if he had said in other words, having your immediate goal in purity of heart, but the end life eternal. Of which goal the same blessed Apostle teaches us, and significantly uses the very term, i.e., skopos, saying as follows, "Forgetting those things which are behind and reaching forward to those that are before, I press toward the mark, for the prize of the high calling of the Lord:" [7] which is more clearly put in Greek kata skopon diwkw, i.e., "I press toward the mark, as if he said, "With this aim, with which I forget those things that are behind, i.e., the faults of earlier life, I strive to reach as the end the heavenly prize." Whatever then can help to guide us to this object; viz., purity of heart, we must follow with all our might, but whatever hinders us from it, we must shun as a dangerous and hurtful thing. For, for this we do and endure all things, for this we make light of our kinsfolk, our country, honours, riches, the delights of this world, and all kinds of pleasures, namely in order that we may retain a lasting purity of heart. And so when this object is set before us, we shall always direct our actions and thoughts straight towards the attainment of it; for if it be not constantly fixed before our eyes, it will not only make all our toils vain and useless, and force them to be endured to no purpose and without any reward, but it will also excite all kinds of thoughts opposed to one another. For the mind, which has no fixed point to which it may return, and on which it may chiefly fasten, is sure to rove about from hour to hour and minute to minute in all sorts of wandering thoughts, and from those things which come to it from outside, to be constantly changed into that state which first offers itself to it.

NOTES:
[6] Rom. 6:22.
[7] Phil. 3:13, 14.

CHAPTER VI.

Of those who in renouncing the world, aim at perfection without love.

FOR hence it arises that in the case of some who have despised the greatest possessions of this world, and not only large sums of gold and silver, but also large properties, we have seen them afterwards disturbed and excited over a knife, or pencil, or pin, or pen. Whereas if they kept their gaze steadily fixed out of a pure heart they would certainly never allow such a thing to happen for trifles, while in order that they might not suffer it in the case of great and precious riches they chose rather to renounce them altogether. For often too some guard their books so jealously that they will not allow them to be even slightly moved or touched by any one else, and from this fact they meet with occasions of impatience and death, which give them warning of the need of acquiring the requisite patience and love; and when they have given up all their wealth for the love of Christ, yet as they preserve their former disposition in the matter of trifles, and are sometimes quickly upset about them, they become in all points barren and unfruitful, as those who are without the charity of which the Apostle speaks: and this the blessed Apostle foresaw in spirit, and "though," says he, "I give all my goods to feed the poor, and give my body to be burned, but have not charity, it profiteth me nothing."[8] And from this it clearly follows that perfection is not arrived at simply by self-denial, and the giving up of all our goods, and the casting away of honours, unless there is that charity, the details of which the Apostle describes, which consists in purity of heart alone. For "not to be envious," "not to be puffed up, not to be angry, not to do any wrong, not to seek one's own, not to rejoice in iniquity, not to think evil" etc., what is all this except ever to offer to God a perfect and clean heart, and to keep it free from all disturbances?

NOTES:
[8] 1 Cor. 13:3.

CHAPTER VII.

How peace of mind should be sought.

EVERYTHING should be done and sought after by us for the sake of this. For this we must seek for solitude, for this we know that we ought to submit to fastings, vigils, toils, bodily nakedness, reading, and all other virtues that through them we may be enabled to prepare our heart and to keep it unharmed by all evil passions, and resting on these steps to mount to the perfection of charity, and with regard to these observances, if by accident we have been employed in some good and useful occupation and have been unable to carry out our customary discipline, we should not be overcome by vexation or anger, or passion, with the object of overcoming which, we were going to do that which we have omitted. For the gain from fasting will not balance the loss from anger, nor is the profit from reading so great as the harm which results from despising a brother. Those things which are of secondary importance, such as fastings, vigils, withdrawal from the world, meditation on Scripture, we ought to practise with a view to our main object, i.e., purity of heart, which is charity, and we ought not on their account to drive away this main virtue, for as long as it is still found in us intact and unharmed, we shall not be hurt if any of the things which are of secondary importance are necessarily omitted; since it will not be of the slightest use to have done everything, if this main reason of which we have spoken be removed, for the sake of which everything is to be done. For on this account one is anxious to secure and provide for one's self the implements for any branch of work, not simply to possess them to no purpose, nor as if one made the profit and advantage, which is looked for from them, to consist in the bare fact of possession but that by using them, one may effectually secure practical knowledge and the end of that particular art of which they are auxiliaries. Therefore fastings, vigils, meditation on the Scriptures, self-denial, and the abnegation of all possessions are not perfection, but aids to perfection: because the end of that science does not lie in these, but by means of these we arrive at the end. He then will practise these exercises to no purpose, who is contented with these as if they were the highest good, and has fixed the purpose of his heart simply on them, and does not extend his efforts towards reaching the end, on account of which these should be sought: for he possesses indeed the implements of his art, but is ignorant of the end, in which all that is valuable resides. Whatever then can disturb that purity and peace of mind--even though it may seem useful and valuable--should be shunned as really hurtful, for by this rule we shall succeed in escaping harm from mistakes and vagaries, and make straight for the desired end and reach it.

CHAPTER VIII.

Of the main effort towards the contemplation of heavenly things and an illustration from the case of Martha and Mary.

THIS then should be our main effort: and this steadfast purpose of heart we should constantly aspire after; viz., that the soul may ever cleave to God and to heavenly things. Whatever is alien to this, however great it may be, should be given the second place, or even treated as of no consequence, or perhaps as hurtful. We have an excellent illustration of this state of mind and condition in the gospel in the case of Martha and Mary: for when Martha was performing a service that was certainly a sacred one, since she was ministering to the Lord and His disciples, and Mary being intent only on spiritual instruction was clinging close to the feet of Jesus which she kissed and anointed with the ointment of a good confession, she is shown by the Lord to have chosen the better part, and one which should not be taken away from her: for when Martha was toiling with pious care, and was cumbered about her service, seeing that of herself alone she was insufficient for such service she asks for the help of her sister from the Lord, saying: "Carest Thou not that my sister has left me to serve alone: bid her therefore that she help me"--certainly it was to no unworthy work, but to a praiseworthy service that she summoned her: and yet what does she hear from the Lord? "Martha, Martha, thou art anxious and troubled about many things: but few things are needful, or only one. Mary hath chosen the good part, which shall not be taken away from her."[9] You see then that the Lord makes the chief good consist in meditation, i.e., in divine contemplation: whence we see that all other virtues should be put in the second place, even though we admit that they are necessary, and useful, and excellent, because they are all performed for the sake of this one thing. For when the Lord says: "Thou art careful and troubled about many things, but few things are needful or only one," He makes the chief good consist not in practical work however praiseworthy and rich in fruits it may be, but in contemplation of Him, which indeed is simple and "but one"; declaring that "few things" are needful for perfect bliss, i.e., that contemplation which is first secured by reflecting on a few saints: from the contemplation of whom, he who has made some progress rises and attains by God's help to that which is termed "one thing," i.e., the consideration of God alone, so as to get beyond those actions and services of saints, and feed on the beauty and knowledge of God alone. "Mary" therefore "chose the good part, which shall not be taken away from her." And this must be more carefully considered. For when He says that Mary chose the good part, although He says nothing of Martha, and certainly does not appear to blame her, yet in praising the one, He implies that the other is inferior. Again when He says "which shall not be taken away from her" He shows that from the other her portion can be taken away (for a bodily ministry cannot last forever with a man), but teaches that this one's desire can never have an end.

NOTES:
[9] S. Luke 10:40-42. The reading which Cassian here follows is found in ['aleph = the Sinaiticus]BC,^2 but has not much Latin authority. It is however followed by Jerome Ep: ad Eustochium, xxii. 24, though the Vulgate has simply Porro unum est necessarium. For Mary as the type of the contemplative life, and Martha of the practical, compare S. Gregory the Great. Moralia VI. c. xxviii.

CHAPTER IX.

A question how it is that the practice of virtue cannot remain with a man.

TO which we, being deeply moved, replied what then? will the effort of fasting, diligence in reading, works of mercy, justice, piety, and kindness, be taken away from us, and not continue with the doers of them, especially since the Lord Himself promises the reward of the kingdom of heaven to these works, when He says: "Come, ye blessed of My Father, inherit the kingdom prepared for you from the beginning of the world. For I was an hungred, and ye gave Me to eat; I was thirsty and ye gave Me to drink:" etc.[10] How then shall these works be taken away, which admit the doers of them into the kingdom of heaven?

NOTES:
[10] S. Matt. 25:34, 35.

CHAPTER X.

The answer that not the reward, but the doing of them will come to an end.

MOSES. I did not say that the reward for a good work would be taken away, as the Lord Himself says: "Whosoever shall give to one of the least of these, a cup of cold water only in the name of a disciple, verily I say unto you, he shall not lose his reward:"[11] but I maintain that the doing of a thing, which either bodily necessity, or the onslaught of the flesh, or the inequalities of this world, compel to be done, will be taken away. For diligence in reading, and self-denial in fasting, are usefully practised for purifying the heart and chastening the flesh in this life only, as long as "the flesh lusteth against the spirit,"[12] and sometimes we see that even in this life they are taken away from those men who are worn out with excessive toil, or bodily infirmity or old age, and cannot be practised by them. How much more then will they come to an end hereafter, when "this corruptible shall have put on incorruption,"[13] and the body which is now "a natural body" shall have risen "a spiritual body"[14] and the flesh shall have begun to be such that it no longer lusts against the spirit? And of this the blessed Apostle also clearly speaks, when he says that "bodily exercise is profitable for a little: but godliness" (by which he certainly means love) "is profitable for all things, having the promise of the life that now is and of that which is to come."[15] This clearly shows that what is said to be useful for a little, is not to be practised for all time, and cannot possibly by itself alone confer the highest state of perfection on the man who slaves at it. For the term "for a little" may mean either of the two things, i.e., it may refer to the shortness of the time, because bodily exercise cannot possibly last on with man both in this life and in the world to come: or it may refer to the smallness of the profit which results from exercising the flesh, because bodily austerities produce some sort of beginnings of progress, but not the actual perfection of love, which has the promise of the life that now is and of that which is to come: and therefore we deem that the practice of the aforesaid works is needful, because without them we cannot climb the heights of love. For what you call works of religion and mercy are needful in this life while these inequalities and differences of conditions still prevail; but even here we should not look for them to be performed, unless such a large proportion of poor, needy, and sick folk abounded, which is brought about by the wickedness of men; viz., of those who have grasped and kept for their own use (without however using them) those things which were granted to all by the Creator of all alike. As long then as this inequality lasts in this world, this sort of work will be needful and useful to the man that practises it, as it brings to a good purpose and pious will the reward of an eternal inheritance: but it will come to an end in the life to come, where equality will reign, when there will be no longer inequality, on account of which these things must be done, but all men will pass from these manifold practical works to the love of God, and contemplation of heavenly things in continual purity of heart: to which those men who are urgent in devoting themselves to knowledge and purifying the heart, have chosen to give themselves up with all their might and main, betaking themselves, while they are still in the flesh, to that duty, in which they are to continue, when they have laid aside corruption, and when they come to that promise of the Lord the Saviour, which says "Blessed are the pure in heart for they shall see God." [16]

NOTES:
[11] S. Matt. 10:42.
[12] Gal. 5:17.
[13] 1 Cor. 15:53.
[14] 1 Cor. 15:44.
[15] 1 Tim. 4:8.
[16] S. Matt. 5:8.

CHAPTER XI.

On the abiding character of love.

AND why do you wonder that those duties enumerated above will cease, when the holy Apostle tells us that even the higher gifts of the Holy Spirit will pass away: and points out that charity alone will abide without end, saying "whether there be prophecies, they shall fail; whether there be tongues, they shall cease: whether there be knowledge, it will come to an end," but of this he says "Charity never faileth." For all gifts are given for a time as use and need require, but when the dispensation is ended they will without doubt presently pass away: but love will never be destroyed. For not only does it work usefully in us in this world; but also in that to come, when the burden of bodily needs is cast off, it will continue in far greater vigour and excellence, and will never be weakened by any defect, but by means of its perpetual incorruption will cling to God more intently and earnestly. [17]

NOTES:
[17] 1 Cor. 13:8.

CHAPTER XII.

A question on perseverance in spiritual contemplation.

GERMANUS. Who then, while he is burdened with our frail flesh, can be always so intent on this contemplation, as never to think about the arrival of a brother, or visiting the sick, or manual labour, or at least about showing kindness to strangers and visitors? And lastly, who is not interrupted by providing for the body, and looking after it? Or how and in what way can the mind cling to the invisible and incomprehensible God, this we should like to learn.

CHAPTER XIII.

The answer concerning the direction of the heart towards God, and concerning the kingdom of God and the kingdom of the devil.

MOSES. To cling to God continually, and as you say inseparably to hold fast to meditation on Him, is impossible for a man while still in this weak flesh of ours. But we ought to be aware on what we should have the purpose of our mind fixed, and to what goal we should ever recall the gaze of our soul: and when the mind can secure this it may rejoice; and grieve and sigh when it is withdrawn from this, and as often as it discovers itself to have fallen away from gazing on Him, it should admit that it has lapsed from the highest good, considering that even a momentary departure from gazing on Christ is fornication. And when our gaze has wandered ever so little from Him, let us turn the eyes of the soul back to Him, and recall our mental gaze as in a perfectly straight direction. For everything depends on the inward frame of mind, and when the devil has been expelled from this, and sins no longer reign in it, it follows that the kingdom of God is founded in us, as the Evangelist says "The kingdom of God cometh not with observation, nor shall men say Lo here, or lo there: for verily I say unto you that the kingdom of God is within you."[18] But nothing else can be "within you," but knowledge or ignorance of truth, and delight either in vice or in virtue, through which we prepare a kingdom for the devil or for Christ in our heart: and of this kingdom the Apostle describes

17

the character, when he says "For the kingdom of God is not meat and drink, but righteousness and peace and joy in the Holy Ghost."[19] And so if the kingdom of God is within us, and the actual kingdom of God is righteousness and peace and joy, then the man who abides in these is most certainly in the kingdom of God, and on the contrary those who live in unrighteousness, and discord, and the sorrow that worketh death, have their place in the kingdom of the devil, and in hell and death. For by these tokens the kingdom of God and the kingdom of the devil are distinguished: and in truth if lifting up our mental gaze on high we would consider that state in which the heavenly powers live on high, who are truly in the kingdom of God, what should we imagine it to be except perpetual and lasting joy? For what is so specially peculiar and appropriate to true blessedness as constant calm and eternal joy? And that you may be quite sure that this, which we say, is really so, not on my own authority but on that of the Lord, hear how very clearly He describes the character and condition of that world: "Behold," says He, "I create new heavens and a new earth: and the former things shall not be remembered nor come into mind. But ye shall be glad and rejoice forever in that which I create."[20] And again "joy and gladness shall be found therein: thanksgiving and the voice of praise, and there shall be month after month, and Sabbath after Sabbath."[21] And again: "they shall obtain joy and gladness; and sorrow and sighing shall flee away."[22] And if you want to know more definitely about that life and the city of the saints, hear what the voice of the Lord proclaims to the heavenly Jerusalem herself: "I will make," says He, "thine officers peace and thine overseers righteousness. Violence shall no more be heard in thy land, desolation nor destruction within thy borders. And salvation shall take possession of thy walls, and praise of thy gates. The sun shall be no more thy light by day, neither shall the brightness of the moon give light to thee: but the Lord shall be thine everlasting light, and thy God thy glory. Thy sun shall no more go down, neither shall thy moon withdraw itself: but the Lord shall be thine everlasting light, and the days of thy mourning shall be ended:"[23] and therefore the holy Apostle does not say generally or without qualification that every joy is the kingdom of God, but markedly and emphatically that joy alone which is "in the Holy Ghost."[24] For he was perfectly aware of another detestable joy, of which we hear "the world shall rejoice,"[25] and "woe unto you that laugh, for ye shall mourn."[26] In fact the kingdom of heaven must be taken in a threefold sense, either that the heavens shall reign, i.e., the saints over other things subdued, according to this text, "Be thou over five cities, and thou over ten;"[27]

18

and this which is said to the disciples: "Ye shall sit upon twelve thrones judging the twelve tribes of Israel:"[28] or that the heavens themselves shall begin to be reigned over by Christ, when "all things are subdued unto Him," and God begins to be "all in all:"[29] or else that the saints shall reign in heaven with the Lord.

NOTES:
[18] S. Luke 17:20, 21.
[19] Rom. 14:17.
[20] Is. 45:17, 18.
[21] Is. 51:3; 66:23.
[22] Is. 35:10.
[23] Is. 60:17-20.
[24] Cf. Rom. 14:17.
[25] S. John 16:20.
[26] S. Luke 6:25.
[27] S. Luke 19:17, 19.
[28] S. Matt. 19:28.
[29] 1 Cor. 15:28.

CHAPTER XIV.

Of the continuance of the soul.

WHEREFORE every one while still existing in this body should already be aware that he must be committed to that state and office, of which he made himself a sharer and an adherent while in this life, nor should he doubt that in that eternal world he will be partner of him, whose servant and minister he chose to make himself here: according to that saying of our Lord which says "If any man serve Me, let him follow Me, and where I am, there shall My servant also be."[30] For as the kingdom of the devil is gained by consenting to sin, so the kingdom of God is attained by the practice of virtue in purity of heart and spiritual knowledge. But where the kingdom of God is, there most certainly eternal life is enjoyed, and where the kingdom of the devil is, there without doubt is death and the grave. And the man who is in this condition, cannot praise the Lord, according to the saying of the prophet which tells us: "The dead cannot praise Thee, O Lord; neither all they that go down into the grave (doubtless of sin). But we," says he, "who live (not forsooth to sin nor I to this world but to God) will bless the Lord, from this time forth for evermore: for in death no man remembereth God: but in the grave (of sin) who will confess to the Lord?"[31] i.e., no one will. For no man even though he were to call himself a Christian a thousand times over, or a monk, confesses God when he is sinning: no man who allows those things which the Lord hates, remembereth God, nor calls himself with any truth the servant of Him, whose commands he scorns with obstinate rashness: in which death the blessed Apostle declares that the widow is involved, who gives herself to pleasure, saying "a widow who giveth herself to pleasure is dead while she liveth."[32] There are then many who while still living in this body are dead, and lying in the grave cannot praise God; and on the contrary there are many who though they are dead in the body yet bless God in the spirit, and praise Him, according to this: "O ye spirits and souls of the righteous, bless ye the Lord:"[33] and "every spirit shall praise the Lord."[34] And in the Apocalypse the souls of them that are slain are not only said to praise God but to address Him also.[35] In the gospel too the Lord says with still greater clearness to the Sadducees: "Have ye not read that which was spoken by God, when He said to you: I am the God of Abraham, and the God of Isaac and the God of Jacob. He is not the God of the dead but of the living: for all do live unto Him."[36] Of whom also the Apostle says: "wherefore God is not ashamed to be called their God: for He hath prepared for them a city."[37] For that they are not idle after the separation from this body, and are not incapable of feeling, the parable in the gospel shows, which tells us of the beggar Lazarus and Dives clothed in purple, one of whom obtained a position of bliss, i.e., Abraham's bosom, the other is consumed with the dreadful heat of eternal fire.[38] But if you care too to understand the words spoken to the thief "To-day thou shalt be with Me in Paradise,"[39] what do they clearly show but that not only does their former intelligence continue with the souls, but also that in their changed condition they partake of some state which corresponds to their actions and deserts? For the Lord would certainly never have promised him this, if He had known that his soul after being separated from the flesh would either have been deprived of perception or have been resolved into nothing. For it was not his flesh but his soul which was to enter Paradise with Christ. At least we must avoid, and shun with the utmost horror, that wicked punctuation of the heretics, who, as they do not believe that Christ could be found in Paradise on the same day on which He descended into hell, thus punctuate "Verily, I say unto you to-day," and making a stop apply "thou shall be with Me in Paradise," in such a way that they imagine that this promise was not fulfilled at once after he departed from this life, but that it will be fulfilled after the resurrection,[40] as they do not understand what before the time of His resurrection He declared to the Jews, who fancied that He was hampered by human difficulties and weakness of the flesh as they were: "No man hath ascended into heaven, but He who came down from heaven, even the Son of man who is in heaven:"[41] by which He clearly shows that the souls of the departed are not only not deprived of their reason, but that they are not even without such feelings as hope and sorrow, joy and fear, and that they already are beginning to taste beforehand something of what is reserved for them at the last judgment, and that they are not as some unbelievers hold resolved into nothing after their departure from this life:[42] but that they live a more real life, and are still more earnest in waiting on the praises of God. And indeed to put aside for a little Scripture proofs, and to discuss, as far as our ability permits us, a little about the nature of the soul itself, is it not beyond the bounds of I will not say the folly, but the madness of all stupidity, even to have the slightest suspicion that the nobler part of man, in which as the blessed Apostle shows, the image and likeness of God consists,[43] will, when the burden of the body with which it is oppressed in this world is laid aside, become insensible, when, as it contains in itself all the power of reason, it makes the dumb and senseless material flesh sensible, by participation with it: especially when it follows, and the order of reason itself demands that when the mind has put off the grossness of the flesh with which it is now weighed down, it will restore its intellectual powers better than ever, and receive them in a purer and finer condition than it lost them. But so far did the blessed Apostle recognize that what we say is true, that he actually wished to depart from this flesh; that by separation from it, he might be able to be joined more earnestly to the Lord; saying: "I desire to be dissolved and to be with Christ, which is far better, for while we are in the body we are absent from the Lord:" and therefore "we are bold and have our desire always to be absent from the body, and present with the Lord. Wherefore also we strive, whether absent or present, to be pleasing to Him;"[44] and he declares indeed that the continuance of the soul which is in the flesh is distance from the Lord, and absence from Christ, and trusts with entire faith that its separation and departure from this flesh involves presence with Christ. And again still more clearly the same Apostle speaks of this state of the souls as one that is very full of life: "But ye are come to Mount Sion, and the city of the living God, the heavenly Jerusalem, and to an innumerable company of angels, and the church of the first born, who are written in heaven, and the spirits of just men made perfect."[45] Of which spirits he speaks in another passage, "Furthermore we have had instructors of our flesh, and we reverenced them: shall we not much more be subject to the Father of spirits and live?" [46]

NOTES:

[30] S. John 12:26.

[31] Ps. 113:17, 18; 6:6.

[32] 1 Tim. 5:6.

[33] Dan. 3:86 (LXX).

[34] Ps. 150:6.

[35] Cf. Rev. 6:9, 10.

[36] S. Matt. 22:31, 32.

[37] Heb. 11:16.

[38] Cf. S. Luke 16:19 sq.

[39] S. Luke 23:43.

[40] The punctuation which Cassian here mentions only to reject, and which is rightly characterized by Alford as "worse than silly," is also mentioned by Theophylact. Com. in loc.

[41] S. John 3:13.

[42] Augustine (De Haeres. c. lix.) speaks of "Seleuciani" or "Hermiani" as denying a visible Paradise, and a future resurrection; and again in c. lxxxiii. he speaks of some Arabian heretics, as teaching that the soul died and was dissolved (dissolvi) with the body, and that it would at the end of the world be revived and rise again. These were the heretics of whom Eusebius speaks in his Eccl. History Book VI. c. xxxvii., where he tells us that they were successfully refuted by Origen. It is probably to this last error that Cassian is here making allusion.

[43] Cf. 1 Cor. 11:7; Col. 3:10.

[44] Phil. 1:23; 2 Cor. 5:6.

[45] Heb. 12:22, 23.

[46] Heb. 12:9

CHAPTER XV.

How we must meditate on God.

BUT the contemplation of God is gained in a variety of ways. For we not only discover God by admiring His incomprehensible essence, a thing which still lies hid in the hope of the promise, but we see Him through the greatness of His creation, and the consideration of His justice, and the aid of His daily providence: when with pure minds we contemplate what He has done with His saints in every generation, when with trembling heart we admire His power with which He governs, directs, and rules all things, or the vastness of His knowledge, and that eye of His from which no secrets of the heart can lie hid, when we consider the sand of the sea, and the number of the waves measured by Him and known to Him, when in our wonder we think that the drops of rain, the days and hours of the ages, and all things past and future are present to His knowledge; when we gaze in unbounded admiration on that ineffable mercy of His, which with unwearied patience endures countless sins which are every moment being committed under His very eyes, or the call with which from no antecedent merits of ours, but by the free grace of His pity He receives us; or again the numberless opportunities of salvation which He grants to those whom He is going to adopt--that He made us be born in such a way as that from our very cradles His grace and the knowledge of His law might be given to us, that He Himself, overcoming our enemy in us simply for the pleasure of His good will, rewards us with eternal bliss and everlasting rewards, when lastly He undertook the dispensation of His Incarnation for our salvation, and extended the marvels of His sacraments[47] to all nations. But there are numberless other considerations of this sort, which arise in our minds according to the character of our life and the purity of our heart, by which God is either seen by pure eyes or embraced: which considerations certainly no one will preserve lastingly, if anything of carnal affections still survives in him, because "thou canst not," saith the Lord, "see My face: for no man shall see Me and live;"[48] viz., to this world and to earthly affections.

NOTES:
[47] Mysteriorum.
[48] Exod. 33:20.

CHAPTER XVI.

A question on the changing character of the thoughts.

GERMANUS. How is it then, that even against our will, aye and without our knowledge idle thoughts steal upon us so subtilely and secretly that it is fearfully hard not merely to drive them away, but even to grasp and seize them? Can then a mind sometimes be found free from them, and never attacked by illusions of this kind?

CHAPTER XVII.

The answer what the mind can and what it cannot do with regard to the state of its thoughts.

MOSES. It is impossible for the mind not to be approached by thoughts, but it is in the power of every earnest man either to admit them or to reject them. As then their rising up does not entirely depend on ourselves, so the rejection or admission of them lies in our own power. But because we said that it is impossible for the mind not to be approached by thoughts, you must not lay everything to the charge of the assault, or to those spirits who strive to instil them into us, else there would not remain any free will in man, nor would efforts for our improvement be in our power: but it is, I say, to a great extent in our power to improve the character of our thoughts and to let either holy and spiritual thoughts or earthly ones grow up in our hearts. For for this purpose frequent reading and continual meditation on the Scriptures is employed that from thence an opportunity for spiritual recollection may be given to us, therefore the frequent singing of Psalms is used, that thence constant feelings of compunction may be provided, and earnest vigils and fasts and prayers, that the mind may be brought low and not mind earthly things, but contemplate things celestial, for if these things are dropped and carelessness creeps on us, the mind being hardened with the foulness of sin is sure to incline in a carnal direction and fall away.

CHAPTER XVIII.

Comparison of a soul and a millstone.

AND this movement of the heart is not unsuitably illustrated by the comparison of a mill wheel, which the headlong rush of water whirls round, with revolving impetus, and which can never stop its work so long as it is driven round by the action of the water: but it is in the power of the man who directs it, to decide whether he will have wheat or barley or darnel ground by it. That certainly must be crushed by it which is put into it by the man who has charge of that business. So then the mind also through the trials of the present life is driven about by the torrents of temptations pouring in upon it from all sides, and cannot be free from the flow of thoughts: but the character of the thoughts which it should either throw off or admit for itself, it will provide by the efforts of its own earnestness and diligence: for if, as we said, we constantly recur to meditation on the Holy Scriptures and raise our memory towards the recollection of spiritual things and the desire of perfection and the hope of future bliss, spiritual thoughts are sure to rise from this, and cause the mind to dwell on those things on which we have been meditating. But if we are overcome by sloth or carelessness and spend our time in idle gossip, or are entangled in the cares of this world and unnecessary anxieties, the result will be that a sort of species of tares will spring up, and afford an injurious occupation for our hearts, and as our Lord and Saviour says, wherever the treasure of our works or purpose may be, there also our heart is sure to continue. [49]

NOTES:
[49] Cf. S. Matt. 6:21.

CHAPTER XIX.

Of the three origins of our thoughts.

ABOVE all we ought at least to know that there are three origins of our thoughts, i.e., from God, from the devil, and from ourselves. They come from God when He vouchsafes to visit us with the illumination of the Holy Ghost, lifting us up to a higher state of progress, and where we have made but little progress, or through acting slothfully have been overcome, He chastens us with most salutary compunction, or when He discloses to us heavenly mysteries, or turns our purpose and will to better actions, as in the case where the king Ahasuerus, being chastened by the Lord, was prompted to ask for the books of the annals, by which he was reminded of the good deeds of Mordecai, and promoted him to a position of the highest honour and at once recalled his most cruel sentence concerning the slaughter of the

Jews.[50] Or when the prophet says: "I will hearken what the Lord God will say in me."[51] Another too tells us "And an angel spoke, and said in me,"[52] or when the Son of God promised that He would come with His Father, and make His abode in us,[53] and "It is not ye that speak, but the Spirit of your Father which speaketh in you."[54] And the chosen vessel: "Ye seek a proof of Christ that speaketh in me."[55] But a whole range of thoughts springs from the devil, when he endeavours to destroy us either by the pleasures of sin or by secret attacks, in his crafty wiles deceitfully showing us evil as good, and transforming himself into an angel of light to us:[56] as when the evangelist tells us: "And when supper was ended, when the devil had already put it into the heart of Judas Iscariot, Simon's son, to betray"[57] the Lord: and again also "after the sop," he says, "Satan entered into him."[58] Peter also says to Ananias: "Why hath Satan tempted thine heart, to lie to the Holy Ghost?"[59] And that which we read in the gospel much earlier as predicted by Ecclesiastes: "If the spirit of the ruler rise up against thee, leave not thy place."[60] That too which is said to God against Ahab in the third book of Kings, in the character of an unclean spirit: "I will go forth and will be a lying spirit in the mouth of all his prophets."[61] But they arise from ourselves, when in the course of nature we recollect what we are doing or have done or have heard. Of which the blessed David speaks: "I thought upon the ancient days, and had in mind the years from of old, and I meditated, by night I exercised myself with my heart, and searched out my spirit."[62] And again: "the Lord knoweth the thoughts of man, that they are vain:"[63] and "the thoughts of the righteous are judgments."[64] In the gospel too the Lord says to the Pharisees: "why do ye think evil in your hearts?" [65]

NOTES:
[50] Cf. Esth. 6:1 sq.
[51] Ps. 84 (85):9.
[52] Zech. 1:14.
[53] Cf. S. John 14:23.
[54] S. Matt. 10:20.
[55] 2 Cor. 13:3.
[56] Cf. 2 Cor. 11:4.
[57] S. John 13:2.
[58] S. John 13:27.
[59] Acts 5:3.
[60] Eccl. 10:4.
[61] 1 Kings 22:22.

[62] Ps. 76 (77):6, 7. Scobebam (which Petschenig edits from the MSS.) = scopebam, which is found in the Gallican Psalter as in the old Latin in this passage. It is clearly a Latinized form of skopein.
[63] Ps. 93 (94):11.
[64] Prov. 12:5.
[65] S. Matt. 9:4.

CHAPTER XX.

About discerning the thoughts, with an illustration from a good money-changer.

WE ought then carefully to notice this threefold order, and with a wise discretion to analyse the thoughts which arise in our hearts, tracking out their origin and cause and author in the first instance, that we may be able to consider how we ought to yield ourselves to them in accordance with the desert of those who suggest them so that we may, as the Lord's command bids us, become good money-changers,[66] whose highest skill and whose training is to test what is perfectly pure gold and what is commonly termed tested,[67] or what is not sufficiently purified in the fire; and also with unerring skill not to be taken in by a common brass denarius, if by being coloured with bright gold it is made like some coin of great value; and not only shrewdly to recognize coins stamped with the heads of usurpers, but with a still shrewder skill to detect those which have the image of the right king, but are not properly made, and lastly to be careful by the test of the balance to see that they are not under proper weight. All of which things the gospel saying, which uses this figure, shows us that we ought also to observe spiritually; first that whatever has found an entrance into our hearts, and whatever doctrine has been received by us, should be most carefully examined to see whether it has been purified by the divine and heavenly fire of the Holy Ghost, or whether it belongs to Jewish superstition, or whether it comes from the pride of a worldly philosophy and only externally makes a show of religion. And this we can do, if we carry out the Apostle's advice, "Believe not every spirit, but prove the spirits whether they are of God."[68] But by this kind those men also are deceived, who after having been professed as monks are enticed by the grace of style, and certain doctrines of philosophers, which at the first blush, owing to some pious meanings not out of harmony with religion, deceive as with the glitter of gold their hearers, whom they have superficially attracted, but render them poor and miserable for ever, like men deceived by false money made of copper: either bringing them back to the bustle of this world, or enticing them into the errors of heretics, and bombastic conceits: a thing which we read of as happening to Achan in the book of Joshua the son of Nun,[69] when he coveted a golden weight from the camp of the Philistines, and stole it, and was smitten with a curse and condemned to eternal death. In the second place we should be careful to see that no wrong interpretation fixed on to the pure gold of Scripture deceives us as to the value of the metal: by which means the devil in his craft tried to impose upon our Lord and Saviour as if He was a mere man, when by his malevolent interpretation he perverted what ought to be understood generally of all good men, and tried to fasten it specially on to Him, who had no need of the care of the angels: saying, "For He shall give His angels charge concerning Thee, to keep Thee in all Thy ways: and in their hands they shall bear Thee up, lest at any time Thou dash Thy foot against a stone"[70] by a skilful assumption on his part giving a turn to the precious sayings of Scripture and twisting them into a dangerous sense, the very opposite of their true meaning, so as to offer to us the image and face of an usurper under cover of the gold colour which may deceive us. Or whether he tries to cheat us with counterfeits, for instance by urging that some work of piety should be taken up which as it does come from the true minds of the fathers, leads under the form of virtue to vice; and, deceiving us either by immoderate or impossible fasts, or by too long vigils, or inordinate prayers, or unsuitable reading, brings us to a bad end. Or, when he persuades us to give ourselves up to mixing in the affairs of others, and to pious visits, by which he may drive us away from the spiritual cloisters of the monastery, and the secrecy of its friendly peacefulness, and suggests that we take on our shoulders the anxieties and cares of religious women who are in want, that when a monk is inextricably entangled in snares of this sort he may distract him with most injurious occupations and cares. Or else when he incites a man to desire the holy office of the clergy under the pretext of edifying many people, and the love of spiritual gain, by which to draw us away from the humility and strictness of our life. All of which things, although they are opposed to our salvation and to our profession, yet when covered with a sort of veil of compassion and religion, easily deceive those who are lacking in skill and care. For they imitate the coins of the true king, because they seem at first full of piety, but are not stamped by those who have the right to coin, i.e., the approved Catholic fathers, nor do they proceed from the head public office for receiving them, but are made by stealth and by the fraud of the devil, and palmed off upon the unskilful and ignorant not without serious harm. And even although they seem to be useful and needful at first, yet if afterwards they begin to interfere with the soundness of our profession, and as it were to weaken in some sense the whole body of our purpose, it is well that they should be cut off and cast away from us like a member which may be necessary, but yet offends us and which seems to perform the office of the right hand or foot. For it is better, without one member of a command, i.e., its working or result, to continue safe and sound in other parts, and to enter as weak into the kingdom of heaven rather than with the whole mass of commands to fall into some error which by an evil custom separates us from our strict rule and the system purposed and entered upon, and leads to such loss, that it will never outweigh the harm that will follow, but will cause all our past fruits and the whole body of our work to be burnt in hell fire.[71] Of which kind of illusions it is well said in the Proverbs: "There are ways which seem to be right to a man, but their latter end will come into the depths of hell,"[72] and again "An evil man is harmful when he attaches himself to a good man,"[73] i.e., the devil deceives when he is covered with an appearance of sanctity: "but he hates the sound of the watchman,"[74] i.e., the power of discretion which comes from the words and warnings of the fathers.

NOTES:

[66] Ut efficiamur secundum praeceptum Domini probabiles trapezitae. The saying to which Cassian here alludes, ginesqe trapexitai dokimoi, is not found anywhere in the Gospels, but "is the most commonly quoted of all Apocryphal sayings, and seems to be genuine." Westcott, Introd. to the Gospels, p. 454. It is quoted among others by Origen in Joann. xix., and in Jerome Ep. 152. See these and other reff. in Anger's Synopsis, p. 274; and cf. the note of Gazaeus here.

[67] Obrizum. The word occurs in the Vulgate five times for "pure gold." See 2 Chr. 3:5; Job 28:15; 31:24; Isa. 13:12; Dan. 10:5; and is akin to the Greek obruzon. Cf. Pliny Nat. Hist. xxxiii. c. 3, And Jerome De Nom. Hebr. s. v. Ophaz.

[68] 1 John 4:1.

[69] Cf. Josh. 7.

[70] S. Matt. 4:6; Ps. 90:11, 12.

[71] Cf. S. Matt. 18:8.

[72] Prov. 16:25 (LXX).

[73] Prov. 11:15 (LXX).

[74] Prov. 11:15 (LXX).

CHAPTER XXI.

Of the illusion of Abbot John.

IN this manner we have heard that Abbot John who lived at Ly-con,[75] was recently deceived. For when his body was exhausted and failing as he had put off taking food during a fast of two days, on the third day while he was on his way to take some refreshment the devil came in the shape of a filthy Ethiopian, and falling at his feet, cried "Pardon me because I appointed this labour for you." And so that great man, who was so perfect in the matter of discretion, understood that under pretence of an abstinence practised unsuitably, he was deceived by the craft of the devil, and engaged in a fast of such a character as to affect his worn out body with a weariness that was unnecessary, indeed that was harmful to the spirit; as he was deceived by a counterfeit coin, and, while he paid respect to the image of the true king upon it, was not sufficiently alive to the question whether it was rightly cut and stamped. But the last duty of this "good money-changer," which, as we mentioned before, concerns the examination of the weight, will be fulfilled, if whenever our thoughts suggest that anything is to be done, we scrupulously think it over, and, laying it in the scales of our breast, weigh it with the most exact balance, whether it be full of good for all, or heavy with the fear of God: or entire and sound in meaning; or whether it be light with human display or some conceit of novelty, or whether the pride of foolish vain glory has not diminished or lessened the weight of its merit. And so straightway weighing them in the public balance, i.e., testing them by the acts and proofs of the Apostles and Prophets let us hold them as it were entire and perfect and of full weight, or else with all care and diligence reject them as imperfect and counterfeit, and of insufficient weight.

NOTES:

[75] On this John of Lycon or Lycopolis see the note on Inst. IV. xxiii.

CHAPTER XXII.

Of the fourfold method of discrimination.

THIS power of discriminating will then be necessary for us in the fourfold manner of which we have spoken; viz., first that the material does not escape our notice whether it be of true or of painted gold: secondly, that those thoughts which falsely promise works of religion should be rejected by us as forged and counterfeit coins, as they are those which are not rightly stamped, and which bear an untrue image of the king; and that we may be able in the same way to detect those which in the case of the precious gold of Scripture, by means of a false and heretical meaning, show the image not of the true king but of an usurper; and that we refuse those whose weight and value the rust of vanity has depreciated and not allowed to pass in the scales of the fathers, as coins that are too light, and are false and weigh too little; so that we may not incur that which we are warned by the Lord's command to avoid with all our power, and lose the value and reward of all our labour. "Lay not up for yourselves treasures on the earth, where rust and moth corrupt and where thieves break through and steal."[76] For whenever we do anything with a view to human glory we know that we are, as the Lord says, laying up for ourselves treasure on earth, and that consequently being as it were hidden in the ground and buried in the earth it must be destroyed by sundry demons or consumed by the biting rust of vain glory, or devoured by the moths of pride so as to contribute nothing to the use and profits of the man who has hidden it. We should then constantly search all the inner chambers of our hearts, and trace out the footsteps of whatever enters into them with the closest investigation lest haply some beast, if I may say so, relating to the understanding, either lion or dragon, passing through has furtively left the dangerous marks of his track, which will show to others the way of access into the secret recesses of the heart, owing to a carelessness about our thoughts. And so daily and hourly turning up the ground of our heart with the gospel plough, i.e., the constant recollection of the Lord's cross, we shall manage to stamp out or extirpate from our hearts the lairs of noxious beasts and the lurking places of poisonous serpents.

NOTES:
[76] S. Matt. 6:19.

CHAPTER XXIII.

Of the discourse of the teacher in regard to the merits of his hearers.

AT this the old man seeing that we were astonished, and inflamed at the words of his discourse with an insatiable desire, stopped his speech for a little in consequence of our admiration and earnestness, and presently added: Since your zeal, my sons, has led to so long a discussion, and a sort of fire supplies keener zest to our conference in proportion to your earnestness, as from this very thing I can clearly see that you are truly thirsting after teaching about perfection, I want still to say something to you on the excellence of discrimination and grace which rules and holds the field among all virtues, and not merely to prove its value and usefulness by daily instances of it, but also from former deliberations and opinions of the fathers. For I remember that frequently when men were asking me with sighs and tears for a discourse of this kind, and I myself was anxious to give them some teaching I could not possibly manage it, and not merely my thoughts but even my very power of speech failed me so that I could not find how to send them away with even some slight consolation. And by these signs we clearly see that the grace of the Lord inspires the speakers with words according to the deserts and zeal of the hearers. And because the very short night which is before us does not allow me to finish the discourse, let us then rather give it up to bodily rest, in which the whole of it will have to be spent, if a reasonable portion is refused, and let us reserve the complete scheme of the discourse for unbroken consideration on a future day or night. For it is right for the best counsellors on discretion to show the diligence of their minds in the first place in this, and to prove whether they are or can be possessors of it by this evidence and patience, so that in treating of that virtue which is the mother of moderation they may by no means fall into the vice which is opposite to it; viz., that of undue length, by their actions and deeds destroying the force of the system and nature which they recommend in word. In regard then to this most excellent discretion, on which we still propose to inquire, so far as the Lord gives us power, it may in the first instance be a good thing, when we are disputing about its excellence and the moderation which we know exists in it as the first of virtues, not to allow ourselves to exceed the due limit of the discussion and of our time.

And so with this the blessed Moses put a stop to our talk, and urged us, eager though we were and hanging on his lips, to go off to bed for a little, advising us to lie down on the same mats on which we were sitting, and to put our bundles[77] under our heads instead of pillows, as these being tied evenly to thicker leaves of papyrus collected in long and slender bundles, six feet apart, at one time provide the brethren when sitting at service with a very low seat instead of a footstool, at another time being put under their necks when they go to bed furnish a support for their heads, that is not too hard, but comfortable and just right. For which uses of the monks these things are considered especially fit and suitable not only because they are somewhat soft, and prepared at little cost of money and labour, as the papyrus grows everywhere along the banks of the Nile, but also because they are of a convenient stuff and light enough to be removed or fetched as need may require. And so at last at the bidding of the old man we settled ourselves down to sleep in deep stillness, both excited with delight at the conference we had held, and also buoyed up with hope of the promised discussion.

NOTES:

[77] Embrimium. The word is possibly of Egyptian origin. It occurs also in Cyril in Vita S. Euthymii Abbati, n. 90, and in Apophthegm. Patrum num. 7, and is possibly the same word as "Ebymium," which occurs in the Rule of Pachomius, c. xiv. See Ducange, sub voce.

CONFERENCE 2.

Second Conference of Abbot Moses
on Discretion

CHAPTER I.

Abbot Moses' introduction on the grace of discretion.

AND so when we had enjoyed our morning sleep, when to our delight the dawn of light again shone upon us, and we had begun to ask
once more for his promised talk, the blessed Moses thus began: As I
see you inflamed with such an eager desire, that I do not believe that
that very short interval of quiet which I wanted to subtract from our
spiritual conference and devote to bodily rest, has been of any use for
the repose of your bodies, on me too a greater anxiety presses when I
take note of your zeal. For I must give the greater care and devotion in
paying my debt, in proportion as I see that you ask for it the more earnestly, according to that saying: "When thou sittest to eat with a ruler
consider diligently what is put before thee, and put forth thine hand,
knowing that thou oughtest to prepare such things."[78] Wherefore as we
are going to speak of the excellent quality of discretion and the virtue
of it, on which subject our discourse of last night had entered at the
termination of our discussion, we think it desirable first to establish its
excellence by the opinions of the fathers, that when it has been shown
what our predecessors thought and said about it, then we may bring
forward some ancient and modern shipwrecks and mischances of various people, who were destroyed and hopelessly ruined because they
paid but little attention to it, and then as well as we can we must treat
of its advantages and uses: after a discussion of which we shall know
better how we ought to seek after it and practise it, by the consideration of the importance of its value and grace. For it is no ordinary
virtue nor one which can be freely gained by merely human efforts,

unless they are aided by the Divine blessing, for we read that this is also reckoned among the noblest gifts of the Spirit by the Apostle: "To one is given by the Spirit the word of wisdom, to another the word of knowledge by the same Spirit, to another faith by the same Spirit, to another the gift of healing by the same Spirit," and shortly after, "to another the discerning of spirits." Then after the complete catalogue of spiritual gifts he subjoins: "But all these worketh one and the selfsame Spirit, dividing to every man severally as He will."[79] You see then that the gift of discretion is no earthly thing and no slight matter, but the greatest prize of divine grace. And unless a monk has pursued it with all zeal, and secured a power of discerning with unerring judgment the spirits that rise up in him, he is sure to go wrong, as if in the darkness of night and dense blackness, and not merely to fall down dangerous pits and precipices, but also to make frequent mistakes in matters that are plain and straightforward.

NOTES:
[78] Prov. 23:1, 2 (LXX).
[79] 1 Cor. 12:8-11.

CHAPTER II.

What discretion alone can give a monk; and a discourse of the blessed Antony on this subject.

AND so I remember that while I was still a boy, in the region of Thebaid, where the blessed Antony lived,[80] the elders came to him to inquire about perfection: and though the conference lasted from evening till morning, the greatest part of the night was taken up with this question. For it was discussed at great length what virtue or observance could preserve a monk always unharmed by the snares and deceits of the devil, and carry him forward on a sure and right path, and with firm step to the heights of perfection. And when each one gave his opinion according to the bent of his own mind, and some made it consist in zeal in fasting and vigils, because a soul that has been brought low by these, and so obtained purity of heart and body will be the more easily united to God, others in despising all things, as, if the mind were utterly deprived of them, it would come the more freely to God, as if henceforth there were no snares to entangle it: others thought that withdrawal from the world was the thing needful, i.e., solitude and the secrecy of the hermit's life; living in which a man may more readily commune with God, and cling more especially to Him; others laid down that the duties of charity, i.e., of kindness should be practised, because the Lord in the gospel promised more especially to give the kingdom to these; when He said "Come ye blessed of My Father, inherit the kingdom prepared for you from the foundation of the world. For I was an hungred and ye gave Me to eat, I was thirsty and ye gave Me to drink, etc.:"[81] and when in this fashion they declared that by means of different virtues a more certain approach to God could be secured, and the greater part of the night had been spent in this discussion, then at last the blessed Antony spoke and said: All these things which you have mentioned are indeed needful, and helpful to those who are thirsting for God, and desirous to approach Him. But countless accidents and the experience of many people will not allow us to make the most important of gifts consist in them. For often when men are most strict in fasting or in vigils, and nobly withdraw into solitude, and aim at depriving themselves of all their goods so absolutely that they do not suffer even a day's allowance of food or a single penny to remain to them, and when they fulfil all the duties of kindness with the utmost devotion, yet still we have seen them suddenly deceived, so that they could not bring the work they had entered upon to a suitable close, but brought their exalted fervour and praiseworthy manner of life to a terrible end. Wherefore we shall be able clearly to recognize what it is which mainly leads to God, if we trace out with greater care the reason of their downfall and deception. For when the works of the above mentioned virtues were abounding in them, discretion alone was wanting, and allowed them not to continue even to the end. Nor can any other reason for their falling off be discovered except that as they were not sufficiently instructed by their elders they could not obtain judgment and discretion, which passing by excess on either side, teaches a monk always to walk along the royal road, and does not suffer him to be puffed up on the right hand of virtue, i.e., from excess of zeal to transgress the bounds of due moderation in foolish presumption, nor allows him to be enamoured of slackness and turn aside to the vices on the left hand, i.e., under pretext of controlling the body, to grow slack with the opposite spirit of lukewarmness. For this is discretion, which is termed in the gospel the "eye," "and light of the body," according to the Saviour's saying: "The light of thy body is thine eye: but if thine eye be single, thy whole body will be full of light, but if thine eye be evil, thy whole body will be full of darkness:"[82] because as it discerns all the thoughts and actions of men, it sees and overlooks all things which should be done. But if in any man this is "evil," i.e., not fortified by sound judgment and knowledge, or deceived by some error and presumption, it will make our whole body "full of darkness," i.e., it will darken all our mental vision and our actions, as they will be involved in the darkness of vices and the gloom of disturbances. For, says He, "if the light which is in thee be darkness, how great will that darkness be!"[83] For no one can doubt that when the judgment of our heart goes wrong, and is overwhelmed by the night of ignorance, our thoughts and deeds, which are the result of deliberation and discretion, must be involved in the darkness of still greater sins.

NOTES:
[80] Cf. the note on the Institutes, V. iv.
[81] S. Matt. 25:36, 35.
[82] S. Matt. 6:22, 23.
[83] S. Matt. 6:22, 23.

CHAPTER III.

Of the error of Saul and of Ahab, by which they were deceived through lack of discretion.

LASTLY, the man who in the judgment of God was the first to be worthy of the kingdom of His people Israel, because he was lacking in this "eye" of discretion, was, as if his whole body were full of darkness, actually cast down from the kingdom while, being deceived by the darkness of this "light," and in error, he imagined that his own offerings were more acceptable to God than obedience to the command of Samuel, and met with an occasion of falling in that very matter in which he had hoped to propitiate the Divine Majesty.[84] And ignorance, I say, of this discretion led Ahab the king of Israel after a triumph and splendid victory which had been granted to him by the favour of God to fancy that mercy on his part was better than the stern execution of the divine command, and, as it seemed to him, a cruel rule: and moved by this consideration, while he desired to temper a bloody victory with mercy, he was on account of his indiscriminating clemency rendered full of darkness in his whole body, and condemned irreversibly to death.[85]

NOTES:
[84] Cf. 1 Sam. 15.
[85] Cf. 1 Kings 20.

CHAPTER IV.

What is said of the value of discretion in Holy Scripture.

SUCH is discretion, which is not only the "light of the body," but also called the sun by the Apostle, as it said "Let not the sun go down upon your wrath."[86] It is also called the guidance of our life: as it said "Those who have no guidance, fall like leaves."[87] It is most truly named counsel, without which the authority of Scripture allows us to do nothing, so that we are not even permitted to take that spiritual "wine which maketh glad the heart of man"[88] with out its regulating control: as it is said "Do everything with counsel, drink thy wine with counsel,"[89] and again "like a city that has its walls destroyed and is not fenced in, so is a man who does anything without counsel."[90] And how injurious the absence of this is to a monk, the illustration and figure in the passage quoted shows, by comparing it to a city that is destroyed and without walls. Herein lies wisdom, herein lies intelligence and understanding without which our inward house cannot be built, nor can spiritual riches be gathered together, as it is said: "A house is built with wisdom, and again it is set up with intelligence. With understanding the storehouses are filled with all precious riches and good things."[91] This I say is "solid food," which can only be taken by those who are full grown and strong, as it is said: "But solid food is for full grown men, who by reason of use have their senses exercised to discern good and evil."[92] And it is shown to be useful and necessary for us, only in so far as it is in accordance with the word of God and its powers, as is said "For the word of God is quick and powerful, and sharper than any two-edged sword, and reaching even to the dividing asunder of soul and spirit, of both joints and marrow, and a discerner of the thoughts and intents of the heart:"[93] and by this it is clearly shown that no virtue can possibly be perfectly acquired or continue without the grace of discretion. And so by the judgment of the blessed Antony as well as of all others it has been laid down that it is discretion which leads a fearless monk by fixed stages to God, and preserves the virtues mentioned above continually intact, by means of which one may ascend with less weariness to the extreme summit of perfection, and without which even those who toil most willingly cannot reach the heights of perfection. For discretion is the mother of all virtues, as well as their guardian and regulator.

NOTES:
[86] Eph. 4:26.
[87] Prov. 11:14 (LXX).
[88] Ps. 103 (104):15.
[89] Prov. 31:3 (LXX).
[90] Prov. 25:28 (LXX).
[91] Prov. 24:3, 4 (LXX).
[92] Heb. 5:14.
[93] Heb. 4:12.

CHAPTER V.

Of the death of the old man Heron.

AND to support this judgment delivered of old by the blessed Antony and the other fathers by a modern instance, as we promised to do, remember what you lately saw happen before your very eyes, I mean, how the old man Heron,[94] only a very few days ago was cast down by an illusion of the devil from the heights to the depths, a man whom we remember to have lived for fifty years in this desert and to have preserved a strict continence with especial severity, and who aimed at the secrecy of solitude with marvellous fervour beyond all those who dwell here. By what device then or by what method was he deluded by the deceiver after so many labours, and falling by a most grievous downfall struck with profound grief all those who live in this desert? Was it not because, having too little of the virtue of discretion he preferred to be guided by his own judgment rather than to obey the counsels and conference of the brethren and the regulations of the elders? Since he ever practised incessant abstinence and fasting with such severity, and persisted in the secrecy of solitude and a monastic cell so constantly that not even the observance of the Easter festival could ever persuade him to join in the feast with the brethren: when in accordance with the annual observance, all the brethren remained in the church and he alone would not join them for fear lest he might seem to relax in some degree from his purpose by taking only a little pulse.

And deceived by this presumption he received with the utmost reverence an angel of Satan as an angel of light and with blind slavishness obeyed his commands and cast himself down a well, so deep that the eye could not pierce its depths, nothing doubting of the promise of the angel who had assured him that the merits of his virtues and labours were such that he could not possibly run any risk. And that he might prove the truth of this most certainly by experimenting on his own safety, in the dead of night he was deluded enough to cast himself into the above mentioned well, to prove indeed the great merit of his virtue if he should come out thence unhurt. And when by great efforts on the part of the brethren he had been got out already almost dead, on the third day afterward he expired, and what was still worse, persisted in his obstinate delusion so that not even the experience of his death could persuade him that he had been deceived by the craft of devils. Wherefore in spite of the merits of his great labours and the number of years which he had spent in the desert those who with compassion and the greatest kindness pitied his end, could hardly obtain from Abbot Paphnutius[95] that he should not be reckoned among suicides, and be deemed unworthy of the memorial and oblation for those at rest. [96]

NOTES:

[94] Gazaeus thinks that this is a different person from the man of the same name mentioned by Palladius, Hist. Laus. c. xxxii.

[95] On Paphnutius see the note on III. i.

[96] Pausantium, i.e., those at rest. The word is used for the departed in a similar way in the 6th Canon of the Council of Aurelia (Orleans) A.D. 511. "Quando recitantur pausantium nomina." And the phrase "Pausat in pace" is occasionally found in sepulchral inscriptions. Inscr. Boldetti Cimeter. p. 399; Inscr. Maff. Gall. Antiq. p. 55.

CHAPTER VI.

Of the destruction of two brethren for lack of discretion.

WHAT shall I say of those two brethren who lived beyond that desert of the Thebaid where once the blessed Antony dwelt, and, not being sufficiently influenced by careful discrimination, when they were going through the vast and extended waste determined not to take any food with them, except such as the Lord Himself might provide for them. And when as they wandered through the deserts and were already fainting from hunger they were spied at a distance by the Mazices[97] (a race which is even more savage and ferocious than almost all wild tribes, for they are not driven to shed blood, as other tribes are, from desire of spoil but from simple ferocity of mind), and when these acting contrary to their natural ferocity, met them with bread, one of the two as discretion came to his aid, received it with delight and thankfulness as if it were offered to him by the Lord, thinking that the food had been divinely provided for him, and that it was God's doing that those who always delighted in bloodshed had offered the staff of life to men who were already fainting and dying; but the other refused the food because it was offered to him by men and died of starvation. And though this sprang in the first instance from a persuasion that was blameworthy yet one of them by the help of discretion got the better of the idea which he had rashly and carelessly conceived, but the other persisting in his obstinate folly, and being utterly lacking in discretion, brought upon himself that death which the Lord would have averted, as he would not believe that it was owing to a Divine impulse that the fierce barbarians forgot their natural ferocity and offered them bread instead of a sword.

NOTES:
[97] Mazices: a people of Mauritania Caesariensis, who joined in the revolt of Firmus, but submitted to Theodosius in 373. See Ammianus Marcellinus XXIX. v. S: 17

CHAPTER VII.

Of an illusion into which another fell for lack of discretion.

WHY also should I speak of one (whose name we had rather not mention as he is still alive), who for a long while received a devil in the brightness of an angelic form, and was often deceived by countless revelations from him and believed that he was a messenger of right-eousness: for when these were granted, every night he provided a light in his cell without the need of any lamp. At last he was ordered by the devil to offer up to God his own son who was living with him in the monastery, in order that his merits might by this sacrifice be made equal to those of the patriarch Abraham. And he was so far seduced by his persuasion that he would really have committed the murder unless his son had seen him getting ready the knife and sharpening it with unusual care, and looking for the chains with which he meant to tie him up for the sacrifice when he was going to offer him up; and had fled away in terror with a presentiment of the coming crime.

CHAPTER VIII.

Of the fall and deception of a monk of Mesopotamia.

IT is a long business too to tell the story of the deception of that monk of Mesopotamia, who observed an abstinence that could be imitated by but few in that country, which he had practised for many years concealed in his cell, and at last was so deceived by revelations and dreams that came from the devil that after so many labours and good deeds, in which he had surpassed all those who dwelt in the same parts, he actually relapsed miserably into Judaism and circumcision of the flesh. For when the devil by accustoming him to visions through the wish to entice him to believe a falsehood in the end, had like a messenger of truth revealed to him for a long while what was perfectly true, at length he showed him Christian folk together with the leaders of our religion and creed; viz., Apostles and Martyrs, in darkness and filth, and foul and disfigured with all squalor, and on the other hand the Jewish people with Moses, the patriarchs and prophets, dancing with all joy and shining with dazzling light; and so persuaded him that if he wanted to share their reward and bliss, he must at once submit to circumcision. And so none of these would have been so miserably deceived, if they had endeavoured to obtain a power of discretion. Thus the mischances and trials of many show how dangerous it is to be without the grace of discretion.

CHAPTER IX.

A question about the acquirement of true discretion.

TO this Germanus: It has been fully and completely shown both by recent instances and by the decisions of the ancients how discretion is in some sense the fountain head and the root of all virtues. We want then to learn how it ought to be gained, or how we can tell whether it is genuine and from God, or whether it is spurious and from the devil: so that (to use the figure of that gospel parable which you discussed on a former occasion, in which we are bidden to become good money changers[98]) we may be able to see the figure of the true king stamped on the coin and to detect what is not stamped on coin that is current, and that, as you said in yesterday's talk using an ordinary expression, we may reject it as counterfeit, under the teaching of that skill which you treated of with sufficient fulness and detail, and showed ought to belong to the man who is spiritually a good money changer of the gospel. For of what good will it be to have recognized the value of that virtue and grace if we do not know how to seek for it and to gain it?

NOTES:
[98] Cf. I. xx.

CHAPTER X.

The answer how true discretion may be gained.

THEN MOSES: True discretion, said he, is only secured by true humility. And of this humility the first proof is given by reserving everything (not only what you do but also what you think), for the scrutiny of the elders, so as not to trust at all in your own judgment but to acquiesce in their decisions in all points, and to acknowledge what ought to be considered good or bad by their traditions.[99] And this habit will not only teach a young man to walk in the right path through the true way of discretion, but will also keep him unhurt by all the crafts and deceits of the enemy. For a man cannot possibly be deceived, who lives not by his own judgment but according to the example of the elders, nor will our crafty foe be able to abuse the ignorance of one who is not accustomed from false modesty to conceal all the thoughts which rise in his heart, but either checks them or suffers them to remain, in accordance with the ripened judgment of the elders. For a wrong thought is enfeebled at the moment that it is discovered: and even before the sentence of discretion has been given, the foul serpent is by the power of confession dragged out, so to speak, from his dark under-ground cavern, and in some sense shown up and sent away in disgrace. For evil thoughts will hold sway in us just so long as they are hidden in the heart: and that you may gather still more effectually the power of this judgment I will tell you what Abbot Serapion did,[100] and what he used often to tell to the younger brethren for their edification.

NOTES:
[99] Cf. what is said on this subject in the Institutes, Book IV. c. ix.
[100] Probably the author of Conference V., where see the note on c. i.

CHAPTER XI.

The words of Abbot Serapion on the decline of thoughts that are exposed to others, and also on the danger of self- confidence.

WHILE, said he, I was still a lad, and stopping with Abbot Theonas,[101] this habit was forced upon me by the assaults of the enemy, that after I had supped with the old man at the ninth hour, I used every day secretly to hide a biscuit in my dress, which I would eat on the sly later on without his knowing it. And though I was constantly guilty of the theft with the consent of my will, and the want of restraint that springs from desire that has grown inveterate, yet when my unlawful desire was gratified I would come to myself and torment myself over the theft committed in a way that overbalanced the pleasure I had enjoyed in the eating. And when I was forced not without grief of heart to fulfil day after day this most heavy task required of me, so to speak, by Pharaoh's taskmasters, instead of bricks, and could not escape from this cruel tyranny, and yet was ashamed to disclose the secret theft to the old man, it chanced by the will of God that I was delivered from the yoke of this voluntary captivity, when certain brethren had sought the old man's cell with the object of being instructed by him. And when after supper the spiritual conference had begun to be held, and the old man in answer to the questions which they had propounded was speaking about the sin of gluttony and the dominion of secret thoughts, and showing their nature and the awful power which they have so long as they are kept secret, I was overcome by the power of the discourse and was conscience stricken and terrified, as I thought that these things were mentioned by him because the Lord had revealed to the old man my bosom secrets; and first I was moved to secret sighs, and then my heart's compunction increased and I openly burst into sobs and tears, and produced from the folds of my dress which shared my theft and received it, the biscuit which I had carried off in my bad habit to eat on the sly; and I laid it in the midst and lying on the ground and begging for forgiveness confessed how I used to eat one every day in secret, and with copious tears implored them to intreat the Lord to free me from this dreadful slavery. Then the old man: "Have faith, my child," said he, "Without any words of mine, your confession frees you from this slavery. For you have today triumphed over your victorious adversary, by laying him low by your confession in a manner which more than makes up for the way in which you were overthrown by him through your former silence, as when, never confuting him with your own answer or that of another, you had allowed him to lord it over you, according to that saying of Solomon's: `Because sentence is not speedily pronounced against the evil, the heart of the children of men is full within them to do evil:'[102] and therefore after this exposure of him that evil spirit will no longer be able to vex you, nor will that foul serpent henceforth make his lurking place in you, as he has been dragged out into light from the darkness by your life-giving confession." The old man had not finished speaking when lo! a burning lamp proceeding from the folds of my dress filled the cell with a sulphureous smell so that the pungency of the odour scarcely allowed us to stay there: and the old man resuming his admonition said Lo! the Lord has visibly confirmed to you the truth of my words, so that you can see with your eyes how he who was the author of His Passion has been driven out from your heart by your life-giving confession, and know that the enemy who has been exposed will certainly no longer find a home in you, as his expulsion is made manifest. And so, as the old man declared, said he, the sway of that diabolical tyranny over me has been destroyed by the power of this confession and stilled for ever so that the enemy has never even tried to force upon me any more the recollection of this desire, nor have I ever felt myself seized with the passion of that furtive longing. And this meaning we see is neatly expressed in a figure in Ecclesiastes. "If" says he "a serpent bite without hissing there is no sufficiency for the charmer,"[103] showing that the bite of a serpent in silence is dangerous, i.e., if a suggestion or thought springing from the devil is not by means of confession shown to some charmer, I mean some spiritually minded person who knows how to heal the wound at once by charms from the Scripture, and to extract the deadly poison of the serpent from the heart, it will be impossible to help the sufferer who is already in danger and must soon die. In this way therefore we shall easily arrive at the knowledge of true discretion, so as by following the steps of the

Elders never to do anything novel nor to decide anything by or on our own responsibility, but to walk in all things as we are taught by their tradition and upright life. And the man who is strengthened by this system will not only arrive at the perfect method of discretion, but also will remain perfectly safe from all the wiles of the enemy: for by no other fault does the devil drag down a monk so precipitately and lead him away to death, as when he persuades him to despise the counsel of the Elders and to rely on his own opinion and judgment: for if all the arts and contrivances discovered by man's ingenuity and those which are only useful for the conveniences of this temporary life, though they can be felt with the hand and seen with the eye, can yet not be understood by anyone, without lessons from a teacher, how foolish it is to fancy that there is no need of an instructor in this one alone which is invisible and secret and can only be seen by the purest heart, a mistake in which brings about no mere temporary loss or one that can easily be repaired, but the destruction of the soul and everlasting death: for it is concerned with a daily and nightly conflict against no visible foes, but invisible and cruel ones, and a spiritual combat not against one or two only, but against countless hosts, failure in which is the more dangerous to all, in proportion as the foe is the fiercer and the attack the more secret. And therefore we should always follow the footsteps of the Elders with the utmost care, and bring to them everything which rises in our hearts, by removing the veil of shame.

NOTES:
[101] See the note on Conference XXI. i.
[102] Eccl. 8:11 (LXX).
[103] Eccl. 10:11 (LXX).

CHAPTER XII.

A confession of the modesty which made us ashamed to reveal our thoughts to the elders.

GERMANUS: The ground of that hurtful modesty, through which we endeavour to hide bad thoughts, is especially owing to this reason; viz., that we have heard of a superior of the Elders in the region of Syria, as it was believed, who, when one of the brethren had laid bare his thoughts to him in a genuine confession, was afterwards extremely indignant and severely chid him for them. Whence it results that while we press them upon ourselves and are ashamed to make them known to the Elders, we cannot obtain the remedies that would heal them.

CHAPTER XIII.

The answer concerning the trampling down of shame, and the danger of one without contrition.

MOSES: Just as all young men are not alike in fervour of spirit nor equally instructed in learning and good morals, so too we cannot find that all old men are equally perfect and excellent. For the true riches of old men are not to be measured by grey hairs but by their diligence in youth and the rewards of their past labours. "For," says one, "the things that thou hast not gathered in thy youth, how shall thou find them in thy old age?" "For venerable old age is not that of long time, nor counted by the number of years: but the understanding of a man is grey hairs, and a spotless life is old age."[104] And therefore we are not to follow in the steps or embrace the traditions and advice of every old man whose head is covered with grey hairs, and whose age is his sole claim to respect, but only of those whom we find to have distinguished themselves in youth in an approved and praiseworthy manner, and to have been trained up not on self-assurance but on the traditions of the Elders. For there are some, and unhappily they form the majority, who pass their old age in a lukewarmness which they contracted in youth, and in sloth, and so obtain authority not from the ripeness of their character but simply from the number of their years. Against whom that reproof of the Lord is specially aimed by the prophet: "Strangers have devoured his strength and he knew it not: yea, grey hairs also are spread about upon him, and he is ignorant of it."[105] These men, I say, are not pointed out as examples to youth from the uprightness of their lives, nor from the strictness of their profession, which would be worthy of praise and imitation, but simply from the number of their years; and so the subtle enemy uses their grey hairs to deceive the younger men, by a wrongful appeal to their authority, and endeavours in his cunning craftiness to upset and deceive by their example those who might have been urged into the way of perfection by their advice or that of others; and drags them down by means of their teaching and practice either into a baneful indifference, or into deadly despair. And as I want to give you an instance of this, I will tell you a fact which may supply us with some wholesome teaching, without giving the name of the actor, lest we might be guilty of something of the same kind as the man who published abroad the sins of the brother which had been disclosed to him. When this one, who was not the laziest of young men, had gone to an old man, whom we know very well, for the sake of the profit and health of his soul, and had candidly confessed that he was troubled by carnal appetites and the spirit of fornication, fancying that he would receive from the old man's words consolation for his efforts, and a cure for the wounds inflicted on him, the old man attacked him with the bitterest reproaches, and called him a miserable and disgraceful creature, and unworthy of the name of monk, while he could be affected by a sin and lust of this character, and instead of helping him so injured him by his reproaches that he dismissed him from his cell in a state of hopeless despair and deadly despondency. And when he, oppressed with such a sorrow, was plunged in deep thought, no longer how to cure his passion, but how to gratify his lust, the Abbot Apollos,[106] the most skilful of the Elders, met him, and seeing by his looks and gloominess his trouble and the violence of the assault which he was secretly revolving in his heart, asked him the reason of this upset; and when he could not possibly answer the old man's gentle inquiry, the latter perceived more and more clearly that it was not without reason that he wanted to hide in silence the cause of a gloom so deep that he could not conceal it by his looks, and so began to ask him still more earnestly the reasons for his hidden grief. And by this he was forced to confess that he was on his way to a village to take a wife, and leave the monastery and return to the world, since, as the old man had told him, he could not be a monk, if he was unable to control the desires of the flesh and to cure his passion. And then the old man smoothed him down with kindly consolation, and told him that he himself was daily tried by the same pricks of desire and lust, and that therefore he ought not to give way to despair, nor be surprised at the violence of the attack of which he would get the better not so much by zealous efforts, as by the mercy and grace of the Lord; and he begged him to put off his intention just for one day, and having implored him to return to his cell, went as fast as he could to the monastery of the above mentioned old man--and when he had drawn near to him he stretched forth his hands and prayed with tears, and said "O Lord, who alone art the righteous judge and unseen Physician of secret strength and human weakness, turn the assault from the young man upon the old one, that he may learn to condescend to the weakness of sufferers, and to sympathize even in old age with the frailties of youth." And when he had ended his prayer with tears, he sees a filthy Ethiopian standing over against his cell and aiming fiery darts at him, with which he was straightway wounded, and came out of his cell and ran about hither and thither like a lunatic or a drunken man, and going in and out could no longer restrain himself in it, but began to hurry off in the same direction in which the young man had gone. And when Abbot Apollos saw him like a madman driven wild by the furies, he knew that the fiery dart of the devil which he had seen, had been fixed in his heart, and had by its intolerable heat wrought in him this mental aberration and confusion of the understanding; and so he came up to him and asked "Whither are you hurrying, or what has made you forget the gravity of years and disturbed you in this childish way, and made you hurry about so rapidly"? And when he owing to his guilty conscience and confused by this disgraceful excitement fancied that the lust of his heart was discovered, and, as the secrets of his heart were known to the old man, did not venture to return any answer to his inquiries, "Return," said he, "to your cell, and at last recognize the fact that till now you have been ignored or despised by the devil, and not counted in the number of those with whom he is daily roused to fight and struggle against their efforts and earnestness,--you who could not--I will not say ward off, but not even postpone for one day, a single dart of his aimed at you after so many years spent in this profession of yours. And with this the Lord has suffered you to be wounded that you may at least learn in your old age to sympathize with infirmities to which you are a stranger, and may know from your own case and experience how to condescend to the frailties of the young, though when you received a young man troubled by an attack from the devil, you did not encourage him with any consolation, but gave him up in dejection and destructive despair into the hands of the enemy, to be, as far as you were concerned, miserably destroyed by him. But the enemy would certainly never have attacked him with so fierce an onslaught, with which he has up till now scorned to attack you, unless in his jealousy at the progress he was to make, he had endeavoured to get the better of that virtue which he saw lay in his disposition, and to destroy it with his fiery darts, as he knew without the shadow of a doubt that he was the stronger, since he deemed it worth his while to attack him with such vehemence. And so learn from your own experience to sympathize with those in trouble, and never to terrify with destructive despair those who are in danger, nor harden them with severe speeches, but rather restore them with gentle and kindly consolations, and as the wise Solomon says, "Spare not to deliver those who are led forth to death, and to redeem those who are to be slain,"[107] and after the example of our Saviour, break not the bruised reed, nor quench the smoking flax,[108] and ask of the Lord that grace, by means of which you yourself may faithfully learn both in deed and power to sing: "the Lord hath given me a learned tongue that I should know how to uphold by word him that is weary:"[109] for no one could bear the devices of the enemy, or extinguish or repress those carnal fires which burn with a sort of natural flame, unless God's grace assisted our weakness, or protected and supported it. And therefore, as the reason for this salutary incident is over, by which the Lord meant to set that young man free from dangerous desires and to teach you something of the violence of their attack, and of the feeling of compassion, let us together implore Him in prayer, that He may be pleased to remove that scourge, which the Lord thought good to lay upon you for your good (for "He maketh sorry and cureth: he striketh and his hands heal. He humbleth and exalteth, he killeth and maketh alive: he bringeth down to the grave and bringeth up")[110], and may extinguish with the abundant dew of His Spirit the fiery darts of the devil, which at my desire He allowed to wound you. And although the Lord removed this temptation at a single prayer of the old man with the same speed with which He had suffered it to come upon him, yet He showed by a clear proof that a man's faults when laid bare were not merely not to be scolded, but that the grief of one in trouble ought not to be lightly despised. And therefore never let the clumsiness or shallowness of one old man or of a few deter you and keep you back from that life-giving way, of which we spoke earlier, or from the tradition of the Elders, if our crafty enemy makes a wrongful use of their grey hairs in order to deceive younger men: but without any cloak of shame everything should be disclosed to the Elders, and remedies for wounds be faithfully received from them together with examples of life and conversation: from which we shall find like help and the same sort of result, if we try to do nothing at all on our own responsibility and judgment.

NOTES:
[104] Ecclus. 25:5; Wisdom 4:8, 9.
[105] Hos. 7:9.
[106] Apollos or Apollonius was a most celebrated hermit of the fourth century, who finally became the head of a monastery of five hundred brethren in the Thebaid. Some account of him is given by Palladius (Hist. Laus. c. lii.) and

Rufinus (Hist. Monach. c. vii.). Cf. also Sozomen III. xiv.; and VI. xx., whence we learn that his life was written by Timothy, Bishop of Alexandria. Cassian relates another story of him in XXIV. ix.
[107] Prov. 24:11.
[108] Cf. S. Matt. 12:20.
[109] Is. 50:4.
[110] Job 5:18; 1 Sam. 2:6, 7.

CHAPTER XIV.

Of the call of Samuel.
LASTLY SO far has this opinion been shown to be pleasing to God that we see that this system not without reason finds a place in holy Scripture, so that the Lord would not of Himself instruct by the method of a Divine colloquy the lad Samuel, when chosen for judgment, but suffered him to run once or twice to the old man, and willed that one whom He was calling to converse with Him should be taught even by one who had offended God, as he was an old man, and preferred that he whom He had deemed worthy to be called by Him should be trained by the Elder in order to test the humility of him who was called to a Divine office, and to set an example to the younger men by the manner of his subjection.

CHAPTER XV.

Of the call of the Apostle Paul.
AND when Christ in His own Person called and addressed Paul, although He might have opened out to him at once the way of perfection, yet He chose rather to direct him to Ananias and commanded him to learn the way of truth from him, saying: "Arise and go into the city and there it shall be told thee what thou oughtest to do."[111] So He sends him to an older man, and thinks good to have him instructed by his teaching rather than His own, lest what might have been rightly done in the case of Paul might set a bad example of self-sufficiency, if each one were to persuade himself that he also ought in like manner to be trained by the government and teaching of God alone rather than by

the instruction of the Elders. And this self-sufficiency the apostle himself teaches, not only by his letters but by his acts and deeds, ought to be shunned with all possible care, as he says that he went up to Jerusalem solely for this reason; viz., to communicate in a private and informal conference with his co-apostles and those who were before him that Gospel which he preached to the Gentiles, the grace of the Holy Spirit accompanying him with powerful signs and wonders: as he says "And I communicated with them the Gospel which I preach among the Gentiles lest perhaps I had run or should run in vain."[112] Who then is so self-sufficient and blind as to dare to trust in his own judgment and discretion when the chosen vessel confesses that he had need of conference with his fellow apostles. Whence we clearly see that the Lord does not Himself show the way of perfection to anyone who having the opportunity of learning despises the teaching and training of the Elders, paying no heed to that saying which ought most carefully to be observed: "Ask thy father and he will show it to thee: thine Elders and they will tell thee." [113]

NOTES:
[111] Acts 9:6.
[112] Gal. 2:2.
[113] Deut. 32:7.

CHAPTER XVI.

How to seek for discretion.

WE ought then with all our might to strive for the virtue of discretion by the power of humility, as it will keep us uninjured by either extreme, for there is an old saying akrothtes isothtes, i.e., extremes meet. For excess of fasting and gluttony come to the same thing, and an unlimited continuance of vigils is equally injurious to a monk as the torpor of a deep sleep: for when a man is weakened by excessive abstinence he is sure to return to that condition in which a man is kept through carelessness and negligence, so that we have often seen those who could not be deceived by gluttony, destroyed by excessive fasting and by reason of weakness liable to that passion which they had before overcome. Unreasonable vigils and nightly watchings have also been the ruin of some whom sleep could not get the better of: wherefore as the apostle says "with the arms of righteousness on the right hand and on the left,"[114] we pass on with due moderation, and walk between the two extremes, under the guidance of discretion, that we may not consent to be led away from the path of continence marked out for us, nor fall by undue carelessness into the pleasures of the palate and belly.

NOTES:
[114] 2 Cor. 6:7.

CHAPTER XVII.

On excessive fasts and vigils.

FOR I remember that I had so often resisted the desire for food, that having abstained from taking any for two or three days, my mind was not troubled even by the recollection of any eatables and also that sleep was by the assaults of the devil so far removed from my eyes, that for several days and nights I used to pray the Lord to grant a little sleep to my eyes; and then I felt that I was in greater peril from the want of food and sleep than from struggling against sloth and gluttony. And so as we ought to be careful not to fall into dangerous effeminacy through desire for bodily gratification, nor indulge ourselves with eating before the right time nor take too much, so also we ought to refresh ourselves with food and sleep at the proper time even if we dislike it. For the struggle in each case is caused by the devices of the enemy; and excessive abstinence is still more injurious to us than careless satiety: for from this latter the intervention of a healthy compunction will raise us to the right measure of strictness, and not from the former.

CHAPTER XVIII.

A question on the right measure of abstinence and refreshment.

GERMANUS: What then is the measure of abstinence by keeping which with even balance we shall succeed in passing unharmed between the two extremes?

CHAPTER XIX.

Of the best plan for our daily food.

MOSES: On this matter we are aware that there have been frequent discussions among our Elders. For in discussing the abstinence of some who supported their lives continually on nothing but beans or only on vegetables and fruits, they proposed to all of them to partake of bread alone, the right measure of which they fixed at two biscuits, so small that they assuredly scarcely weighed a pound.

CHAPTER XX.

An objection on the ease of that abstinence in which a man is sustained by two biscuits.

AND this we gladly embraced, and answered that we should scarcely consider this limit as abstinence, as we could not possibly reach it entirely.

CHAPTER XXI.

The answer concerning the value and measure of well-proved abstinence.

MOSES: If you want to test the force of this rule, keep to this limit continually, never departing from it by taking any cooked food even on Sunday or Saturday, or on the occasions of the arrival of any of the brethren; for the flesh, refreshed by these exceptions, is able not only to support itself through the rest of the week on a smaller quantity, but can also postpone all refreshment without difficulty, as it is sustained by the addition of that food which it has taken beyond the limit; while the man who has always been satisfied with the full amount of the above-mentioned measure will never be able to do this, nor to put off breaking his fast till the morrow. For I remember that our Elders (and I recollect that we ourselves also often had the same experience) found it so hard and difficult to practise this abstinence, and observed the rule laid down with such pain and hunger that it was almost against their will and with tears and lamentation that they set this limit to their meals.

CHAPTER XXII.

What is the usual limit both of abstinence and of partaking food.

BUT this is the usual limit of abstinence; viz., for everyone to allow himself food according to the requirements of his strength or bodily frame or age, in such quantity as is required for the support of the flesh, and not for the satisfactory feeling of repletion. For on both sides a man will suffer the greatest injury, if having no fixed rule at one time he pinches his stomach with meagre food and fasts, and at another stuffs it by over-eating himself; for as the mind which is enfeebled for lack of food loses vigour in praying, while it is worn out with excessive weakness of the flesh and forced to doze, so again when weighed down with over-eating it cannot pour forth to God pure and free prayers: nor will it succeed in preserving uninterruptedly the purity of its chastity, while even on those days on which it seems to chastise the flesh with severer abstinence, it feeds the fire of carnal desire with the fuel of the food that it has already taken.

CHAPTER XXIII.

Quemadmodum abundantia umorum genitalium castigetur. [115]

NAM quod semel per escarum abundantian concretus fuerit in medullis, necesse est egeri atque ab ipsa naturae lege propelli, quae exuberantiam cujuslibet umoris superflui velut noxiam sibi atque contrariam in semet ipsa residere non patitur ideoque rationabili semper et aequali est corpus nostrum parsimonia castigandum, ut si naturali hac necessitate commorantes in carne omnimodis carere non possumus, saltim rarius nos et non amplius quamtrina vice ista conluvione respersos totius anni cursus inveniat, quod tamen sine ullo pruritu quietus egerat sopor, non fallax imago index occultae voluptatis eliciat.

55

PART 1

Wherefore this is the moderate and even allowance and measure of abstinence, of which we spoke, which has the approval also of the judgment of the fathers; viz., that daily hunger should go hand in hand with our daily meals, preserving both body and soul in one and the same condition, and not allowing the mind either to faint through weariness from fasting, nor to be oppressed by over-eating, for it ends in such a sparing diet that sometimes a man neither notices nor remembers in the evening that he has broken his fast.

NOTES:
[115] It has been thought best to leave the first part of the following chapter untranslated.

CHAPTER XXIV.

Of the difficulty of uniformity in eating; and of the gluttony of brother Benjamin.

AND so far is this not done without difficulty, that those who know nothing of perfect discretion would rather prolong their fasts for two days, and reserve for tomorrow what they should have eaten today, so that when they come to partake of food they may enjoy as much as they can desire. And you know that lastly your fellow citizen Benjamin most obstinately stuck to this: as he would not every day partake of his two biscuits, nor, continually take his meagre fare with uniform self-discipline, but preferred always to continue his fasts for two days that when he came to eat he might fill his greedy stomach with a double portion, and by eating four biscuits enjoy a comfortable sense of repletion, and manage to fill his belly by means of a two days' fast. And you doubtless remember what sort of an end there was to the life of this man who obstinately and pertinaciously relied on his own judgment rather than on the traditions of the Elders, for he forsook the desert and returned back to the vain philosophy of this world and earthly vanities, and so confirmed the above mentioned opinion of the Elders by the example of his downfall, and by his destruction teaches a lesson that no one who trusts in his own opinion and judgment can possibly climb the heights of perfection, nor fail to be deceived by the dangerous wiles of the devil.

CHAPTER XXV.

A question how is it possible always to observe one and the same measure.

GERMANUS: How then can we observe this measure without ever breaking it? for sometimes at the ninth hour when the Station fast[116] is over, brethren come to see us and then we must either for their sakes add something to our fixed and customary portion, or certainly fail in that courtesy which we are told to show to everybody.

NOTES:
[116] On the Statio see the note on the Institutes V. xx.

CHAPTER XXVI.

The answer how we should not exceed the proper measure of food.

MOSES: Both duties must be observed in the same way and with equal care: for we ought most scrupulously to preserve the proper allowance of food for the sake of our abstinence, and in like manner out of charity to show courtesy and encouragement to any of the brethren who may arrive; because it is absolutely ridiculous when you offer food to a brother, nay, to Christ Himself, not to partake of it with him, but to make yourself a stranger to his repast. And so we shall keep clear of guilt on either hand if we observe this plan; viz., at the ninth hour to partake of one of the two biscuits which form our proper canonical allowance, and to keep back the other to the evening, in expectation of something like this, that if any of the brethren comes to see us we may partake of it with him, and so add nothing to our own customary allowance: and by this arrangement the arrival of our brother which ought to be a pleasure to us will cause us no inconvenience: since we shall show him the civilities which courtesy requires in such a way as to relax nothing of the strictness of our abstinence. But if no one should come, we may freely take this last biscuit as belonging to us according to our canonical rule, and by this frugality of ours as a single biscuit was taken at the ninth hour, our stomach will not be overloaded at eventide, a thing which is often the case with those who under the idea that they are observing a stricter abstinence put off all their repast till evening; for the fact that we have but recently taken food hinders our intellect from being bright and keen both in our evening and in our nocturnal prayers, and so at the ninth hour a convenient and suitable time has been allowed for food, in which a monk can refresh himself and so find that he is not only fresh and bright during his nocturnal vigils, but also perfectly ready for his evening prayers, as his food is already digested.

With such a banquet of two courses, as it were, the holy Moses feasted us, showing us not only the grace and power of discretion by his present learned speech, but also the method of renunciation and the end and aim of the monastic life by the discussion previously held; so as to make clearer than daylight what we had hitherto pursued simply with fervour of spirit and zeal for God but with closed eyes, and to make us feel how far we had up till then wandered from purity of heart and the straight line of our course, since the practice of all visible arts belonging to this life cannot possibly stand without an understanding of their aim, nor can it be taken in hand without a clear view of a definite end.

CONFERENCE 3.

Conference of Abbot Paphnutius
on the Three Sorts of Renunciations

CHAPTER I.

Of the life and conduct of Abbot Paphnutius.

IN that choir of saints who shine like brilliant stars in the night of this world, we have seen the holy. Paphnutius,[117] like some great luminary, shining with the brightness of knowledge. For he was a presbyter of our company, I mean of those whose abode was in the desert of Scete, where he lived to extreme old age, without ever moving from his cell, of which he had taken possession when still young, and which was five miles from the church, even to nearer districts; nor was he when worn out with years hindered by the distance from going to Church on Saturday or Sunday. But not wanting to return from thence empty handed he would lay on his shoulders a bucket of water to last him all the week, and carry it back to his cell, and even when he was past ninety would not suffer it to be fetched by the labour of younger men. He then from his earliest youth threw himself into the monastic discipline with such fervour that when he had spent only a short time in it, he was endowed with the virtue of submission, as well as the knowledge of all good qualities. For by the practice of humility and obedience he mortified all his desires, and by this stamped out all his faults and acquired every virtue which the monastic system and the teaching of the ancient fathers produces, and, inflamed with desire for still further advances, he was eager to penetrate into the recesses of the desert, so that, with no human companions to disturb him, he might be more readily united to the Lord, to whom he longed to be inseparably joined, even while he still lived in the society of the brethren. And there once more in his excessive fervour he outstripped the virtues of the Anchorites, and in his eager desire for continual divine meditation avoided the sight of them: and he plunged into solitary places yet wilder and more inaccessible, and hid himself for a long while in them, so that, as the Anchorites themselves only with great difficulty caught a glimpse of him every now and then, the belief was that he enjoyed and delighted in the daily society of angels, and because of this remarkable characteristic of his[118] he was surnamed by them the Buffalo.

NOTES:

[117] Paphnutius. The name is not uncommon in the annals of the fourth century: (1) A Deacon who bore it suffered in the persecution of Diocletian; and (2) a Bishop of the same name, who had been a confessor, was mainly instrumental in preventing the rule of celibacy being forced on the clergy by the Council of Nicaea; (3) another was a prominent member of the Meletian schism; while (4) a fourth was present, as Bishop of Sais in Lower Egypt, at the Council of Alexandria in 362; and (5) the life of a fifth is given by Palladius (Hist. Laus. lxii.-lxv.) and Rufinus (Hist. Monach. c. xvi.). The one whom Cassian here mentions, surnamed the Buffalo, is apparently a different person from the last mentioned. Further details of his history are given in the Institutes IV. c. xxx. xxxi., and in Conference X. ii., iii. Cassian tells the interesting story of his share in the Anthropomorphite controversy, and the beneficial influence which he then exercised.

[118] I.e., his solitariness.

CHAPTER II.

Of the discourse of the same old man, and our reply to it.

AS then we were anxious to learn from his teaching, we came in some agitation to his cell towards evening. And after a short silence he began to commend our undertaking, because we had left our homes, and had visited so many countries out of love for the Lord, and were endeavouring with all our might to endure want and the trials of the desert, and to imitate their severe life, which even those who had been born and bred in the same state of want and penury, could scarcely put up with; and we replied that we had come for his teaching and instruction in order that we might be to some extent initiated in the customs of so great a man, and in that perfection which we had known from many evidences to exist in him, not that we might be honoured by any commendations to which we had no right, or be puffed up with any elation of mind, (with which we were sometimes exercised in our own cells at the suggestion of our enemy) in consequence of any words of his. Wherefore we begged him rather to lay before us what would make us humble and contrite, and not what would flatter us and puff us up.

CHAPTER III.

The statement of Abbot Paphnutius on the three kinds of vocations, and the three sorts of renunciations.

THEN THE BLESSED PAPHNUTIUS: There are, said he, three kinds of vocations. And we know that there are three sorts of renunciations as well, which are necessary to a monk, whatever his vocation may be. And we ought diligently to examine first the reason for which we said that there were three kinds of vocations, that when we are sure that we are summoned to God's service in the first stage of our vocation, we may take care that our life is in harmony with the exalted height to which we are called, for it will be of no use to have made a good beginning if we do not show forth an end corresponding to it. But if we feel that only in the last resort have we been dragged away from a worldly life, then, as it appears that we rest on a less satisfactory beginning as regards religion, so must we proportionately make the more earnest endeavours to rouse ourselves with spiritual fervour to make a better end. It is well too on every ground for us to know secondly the manner of the threefold renunciations because we shall never be able to attain perfection, if we are ignorant of it or if we know it, but do not attempt to carry it out in act.

CHAPTER IV.

An explanation of the three callings.

TO make clear therefore the main differences between these three kinds of calling, the first is from God, the second comes through man, the third is from compulsion. And a calling is from God whenever some inspiration has taken possession of our heart, and even while we are asleep stirs in us at desire for eternal life and salvation, and bids us follow God and cleave to His commandments with life-giving contrition: as we read in Holy Scripture that Abraham was called by the voice of the Lord from his native country, and all his dear relations, and his father's house; when the Lord said "Get thee out from thy country and from thy kinsfolk and from thy father's house."[119] And in this way we have heard that the blessed Antony also was called,[120] the occasion of whose conversion was received from God alone. For on entering a church he there heard in the Gospel the Lord saying: "Whoever hateth not father and mother and children and wife and lands, yea and his own soul also, cannot be my disciple;" and "if thou wilt be perfect, go sell all that thou hast, and give to the poor, and thou shalt have treasure in heaven, and come, follow me:"[121] And with heartfelt contrition he took this charge of the Lord as if specially aimed at him, and at once gave up everything and followed Christ, without any incitement thereto from the advice and teaching of men. The second kind of calling is that which we said took place through man; viz., when we are stirred up by the example of some of the saints, and their advice, and thus inflamed with the desire of salvation: and by this we never forget that by the grace of the Lord we ourselves were summoned, as we were aroused by the advice and good example of the above-mentioned saint, to give ourselves up to this aim and calling; and in this way also we find in Holy Scripture that it was through Moses that the children of Israel were delivered from the Egyptian bondage. But the third kind of calling is that which comes from compulsion, when we have been involved in the riches and pleasures of this life, and temptations suddenly come upon us and either threaten us with peril of death, or smite us with the loss and confiscation of our goods, or strike us down with the death of those dear to us, and thus at length even against our will we are driven to turn to God whom we scorned to follow in the days of our wealth. And of this compulsory call we often find instances in Scripture, when we read that on account of their sins the children of Israel were given up by the Lord to their enemies; and that on account of their tyranny and savage cruelty they turned again, and cried to the Lord. And it says: "The Lord sent them a Saviour, called Ehud, the son of Gera, the son of Jemini, who used the left hand as well as the right:" and again we are told, "they cried unto the Lord, who raised them up a Saviour and delivered them, to wit, Othniel, the son of Kenaz, Caleb's younger brother."[122] And it is of such that the Psalm speaks: "When He slew them, then they sought Him: and they returned and came to Him early in the morning: and they remembered that God was their helper, and the most High God their redeemer." And again: "And they cried unto the Lord when they were troubled, and He delivered them out of their distress." [123]

NOTES:

[119] Gen. 12:7.

[120] The story, to which allusion is here made, is given in the Vita Antonii of Athanasius. We are there told that six months after the death of his parents Antony, the a young man of eighteen, chanced to enter a church just as the gospel for the day was being read: and hearing the words, "If thou wilt be perfect," etc., he took them as addressed specially to himself, and at once proceeded to act upon them, selling all that he had except a small portion which he reserved for his sister's maintenance. Shortly after he was struck by the words, "Take the thought for the morrow," which he heard in church, and acting upon this, made away with the little property which was left, committed his sister to the care of certain faithful virgins, and betook himself to the ascetic life.

[121] S. Luke 14:26; S. Matt. 19:21.

[122] Judg. 3:15, 9.

[123] Ps. 77 (78):34, 35; 106 (107):19.

CHAPTER V.

How the first of these calls is of no use to a sluggard, and the last is no hindrance to one who is in earnest.

OF these three calls then, although the two former may seem to rest on better principles, yet sometimes we find that even by the third grade, which seems the lowest and the coldest, men have been made perfect and most earnest in spirit, and have become like those who made an admirable beginning in approaching the Lord's service, and passed the rest of their lives also in most laudable fervour of spirit: and again we find that from the higher grade very many have grown cold, and often have come to a miserable end. And just as it was no hindrance to the former class that they seemed to be converted not of their own free will, but by force and compulsion, in as much as the loving kindness of the Lord secured for them the opportunity for repentance, so too to the latter it was of no avail that the early days of their conversion were so bright, because they were not careful to bring the remainder of their life to a suitable end. For in the case of Abbot

Moses,[124] who lived in a spot in the wilderness called Calamus,[125] nothing was wanting to his merits and perfect bliss, in consequence of the fact that he was driven to flee to the monastery through fear of death, which was hanging over him because of a murder; for he made such use of his compulsory conversion that with ready zeal he turned it into a voluntary one and climbed the topmost heights of perfection. As also on the other hand; to very many, whose names I ought not to mention, it has been of no avail that they entered on the Lord's service with better beginning than this, as afterwards sloth and hardness of heart crept over them, and they fell into a dangerous state of torpor, and the bottomless pit of death, an instance of which we see clearly indicated in the call of the Apostles. For of what good was it to Judas that he had of his own free will embraced the highest grade of the Apostolate in the same way in which Peter and the rest of the Apostles had been summoned, as he allowed the splendid beginning of his call to terminate in a ruinous end of cupidity and covetousness, and as a cruel murderer even rushed into the betrayal of the Lord? Or what hindrance was it to Paul that he was suddenly blinded, and seemed to be drawn against his will into the way of salvation, as afterwards he followed the Lord with complete fervour of soul, and having begun by compulsion completed it by a free and voluntary devotion, and terminated with a magnificent end a life that was rendered glorious by such great deeds? Everything therefore depends upon the end; in which one who was consecrated by a noble conversion at the outset may through carelessness turn out a failure, and one who was compelled by necessity to adopt the monastic life may through fear of God and earnestness be made perfect.

NOTES:

[124] Moses. This Abbot is possibly a different person from the author of the first two Conferences, who had in his youth been a pupil of Antony; whereas the one here mentioned only took the monastic life out of fear of death on a charge of murder. He is mentioned again in Conferences VII. xxvi.; XIX. xi., and some account of him is given in Sozomen H. E. VI. xxix.

[125] Calamus, mentioned again in the Institutes X. xxiv. (where see note), and cf. Conf. VII. xxvi.; XXIV. iv.

CHAPTER VI.

An account of the three sorts of renunciations.

WE must now speak of the renunciations, of which tradition and the authority of Holy Scripture show us three, and which every one of us ought with the utmost zeal to make complete. The first is that by which as far as the body is concerned we make light of all the wealth and goods of this world; the second, that by which we reject the fashions and vices and former affections of soul and flesh; the third, that by which we detach our soul from all present and visible things, and contemplate only things to come, and set our heart on what is invisible. And we read that the Lord charged Abraham to do all these three at once, when He said to him "Get thee out from thy country, and thy kinsfolk, and thy father's house."[126] First He said "from thy country," i.e., from the goods of this world, and earthly riches: secondly, "from thy kinsfolk," i.e., from this former life and habits and sins, which cling to us from our very birth and are joined to us as it were by ties of affinity and kinship: thirdly, "from thy father's house," i.e., from all the recollection of this world, which the sight of the eyes can afford. For of the two fathers, i.e., of the one who is to be forsaken, and of the one who is to be sought, David thus speaks in the person of God: "Hearken, O daughter, and consider, and incline thine ear: forget also thine own people and thy father's house:"[127] for the person who says "Hearken, O daughter," is certainly a Father; and yet he bears witness that the one, whose house and people he urges should be forgotten, is none the less father of his daughter. And this happens when being dead with Christ to the rudiments of this world, we no longer, as the Apostle says, regard "the things which are seen, but those which are not seen, for the things which are not seen are eternal,"[128] and going forth in heart from this temporal and visible home, turn our eyes and heart towards that in which we are to remain for ever. And this we shall succeed in doing when, while we walk in the flesh, we are no longer at war with the Lord according to the flesh, proclaiming in deed and actions the truth of that saying of the blessed Apostle "Our conversation is in heaven."[129] To these three sorts of renunciations the three books of Solomon suitably correspond. For Proverbs answers to the first renunciation, as in it the desires for carnal things and earthly sins are repressed; to the second Ecclesiastes corresponds, as there everything which is done under the sun is declared to be vanity; to the third the

Song of Songs, in which the soul soaring above all things visible, is actually joined to the word of God by the contemplation of heavenly things.

NOTES:
[126] Gen. 12:1.
[127] Ps. 44 (45):11.
[128] 2 Cor. 4:18.
[129] Phil. 3:20.

CHAPTER VII.

How we can attain perfection in each of these sorts of renunciations.

WHEREFORE it will not be of much advantage to us that we have made our first renunciation with the utmost devotion and faith, if we do not complete the second with the same zeal and ardour. And so when we have succeeded in this, we shall be able to arrive at the third as well, in which we go forth from the house of our former parent, (who, as we know well, was our father from our very birth, after the old man, when we were "by nature children of wrath, as others also,"[130]) and fix our whole mental gaze on things celestial. And of this father Scripture says to Jerusalem which had despised God the true Father, "Thy father was an Amorite, and thy mother a Hittite;"[131] and in the gospel we read "Ye are of your father the devil and the lusts of your father ye love to do."[132] And when we have left him, as we pass from things visible to things unseen we shall be able to say with the Apostle: "But we know that if our earthly house of this tabernacle is dissolved we have a habitation from God, a house not made with hands, eternal in the heavens,"[133] and this also, which we quoted a little while ago: "But our conversation is in heaven, whence also we look for the Saviour, the Lord Jesus, who will reform the body of our low estate made like to the body of His glory,"[134] and this of the blessed David: "For I am a sojourner upon the earth," and "a stranger as all my fathers were;"[135] so that we may in accordance with the Lord's word be made like those of whom the Lord speaks to His Father in the gospel as follows: "They are not of the world, as I am not of the world,"[136] and again to the Apostles themselves: "If ye were of this world, the world would love its own: but because ye are not of this world, therefore the world hateth you."[137] Of this third renunciation then we shall succeed in reaching the perfection, whenever our soul is sullied by no stain of carnal coarseness, but, all such having been carefully eliminated, it has been freed from every earthly quality and desire, and by constant meditation on things Divine, and spiritual contemplation has so far passed on to things unseen, that in its earnest seeking after things above and things spiritual it no longer feels that it is prisoned in this fragile flesh, and bodily form, but is caught up into such an ecstasy as not only to hear no words with the outward ear, or to busy itself with gazing on the forms of things present, but not even to see things close at hand, or large objects straight before the very eyes. And of this no one can understand the truth and force, except one who has made trial of what has been said, under the teaching of experience; viz., one, the eyes of whose soul the Lord has turned away from all things present, so that he no longer considers them as things that will soon pass away, but as things that are already done with, and sees them vanish into nothing, like misty smoke; and like Enoch, "walking with God," and "translated" from human life and fashions, not "be found" amid the vanities of this life. And that this actually happened corporeally in the case of Enoch the book of Genesis thus tells us. "And Enoch walked with God, and was not found, for God translated him." And the Apostle also says: "By faith Enoch was translated that he should not see death," the death namely of which the Lord says in the gospel: "He that liveth and believeth in me shall not die eternally."[138] Wherefore, if we are anxious to attain true perfection, we ought to look to it that as we have outwardly with the body made light of parents, home, the riches and pleasures of the world, we may also inwardly with the heart forsake all these things and never be drawn back by any desires to those things which we have forsaken, as those who were led up by Moses, though they did not literally go back, are yet said to have returned in heart to Egypt; viz., by forsaking God who had led them forth with such mighty signs, and by worshipping the idols of Egypt of which they had thought scorn, as Scripture says: "And in their hearts they turned back into Egypt, saying to Aaron: Make us gods to go before us,"[139] for we should fall into like condemnation with those who, while dwelling in the wilderness, after they had tasted manna from heaven, lusted after the filthy food of sins, and of mean baseness, and should seem together with them to murmur in the same way: "It was well with us in Egypt, when we sat over the flesh pots and ate the onions, and garlic, and cucumbers, and melons:"[140] A form of speech, which, although it referred primarily to that people, we yet see fulfilled today in our own case and mode of life: for everyone who after renouncing this world turns back to his old desires, and reverts to his former likings asserts in heart and act the very same thing that they did, and says "It was well with me in Egypt," and I am afraid that the number of these will be as large as that of the multitudes of backsliders of whom we read under Moses, for though they were reckoned as six hundred and three thousand armed men who came out of Egypt, of this number not more than two entered the land of promise. Wherefore we should be careful to take examples of goodness from those who are few and far between, because according to that figure of which we have spoken in the gospel "Many are called but few" are said to be "chosen."[141] A renunciation then in body alone, and a mere change of place from Egypt will not do us any good, if we do not succeed in achieving that renunciation in heart, which is far higher and more valuable. For of that mere bodily renunciation of which we have spoken the apostle declares as follows: "Though I bestow all my goods to feed the poor, and give my body to be burned, but have not charity, it profiteth me nothing."[142] And the blessed Apostle would never have said this had it not been that he foresaw by the spirit that some who had given all their goods to feed the poor would not be able to attain to evangelical perfection and the lofty heights of charity, because while pride or impatience ruled over their hearts they were not careful to purify themselves from their former sins, and unrestrained habits, and on that account could never attain to that love of God which never faileth, and these, as they fall short in this second stage of renunciation, can still less reach that third stage which is most certainly far higher. But consider too in your minds with great care the fact that he did not simply say "If I bestow my goods." For it might perhaps be thought that he spoke of one who had not fulfilled the command of the gospel, but had kept back something for himself, as some half-hearted persons do. But he says "Though I bestow all my goods to feed the poor," i.e., even if my renunciation of those earthly riches be perfect. And to this renunciation he adds something still greater: "And though I give my body to be burned, but have not charity, I am nothing:" As if he had said in other words, though I bestow all my goods to feed the poor in accordance with that command in the gospel, where we are told "If thou wilt be perfect, go sell all that thou hast, and give to the poor, and thou shalt have treasure in heaven,"[143] renouncing them so as to keep back nothing at all for myself, and though to this distribution (of my goods) I should by the burning of my flesh add martyrdom so as to give up my body for Christ, and yet be impatient, or passionate or envious or proud, or excited by wrongs done by others, or seek what is mine, or indulge in evil thoughts, or not be ready and patient in bearing all that can be inflicted on me, this renunciation and the burning of the outer man will profit me nothing, while the inner man is still involved in the former sins, because, while in the fervour of the early days of my conversion I made light of the mere worldly substance, which is said to be not good or evil in itself but indifferent, I took no care to cast out in like manner the injurious powers of a bad heart, or to attain to that love of the Lord which is patient, which is "kind, which envieth not, is not puffed up, is not soon angry, dealeth not perversely, seeketh not her own, thinketh no evil," which "beareth all things, endureth all things,"[144] and which lastly never suffers him who follows after it to fall by the deceitfulness of sin.

NOTES:
[130] Eph. 2:3.
[131] Ezek. 16:3.
[132] S. John 8:44.
[133] 2 Cor. 5:1.
[134] Phil. 3:20, 21.
[135] Ps. 118 (119):19; Ps. 38 (39):13.
[136] S. John 17:16.
[137] S. John 15:19.
[138] Gen. 5:24 (LXX); Heb. 11:5; S. John 11:26.
[139] Acts 7:39, 40.
[140] Numb. 11:18; Exod. 16:3; Numb. 11:5.
[141] S. Matt. 22:14.
[142] 1 Cor. 13:3.
[143] S. Matt. 19:21.
[144] 1 Cor. 13:4-7.

CHAPTER VIII.

Of our very own possessions in which the beauty of the soul is seen or its foulness.

WE ought then to take the utmost care that our inner man as well may cast off and make away with all those possessions of its sins, which it acquired in its former life: which as they continually cling to body and soul are our very own, and, unless we reject them and cut them off while we are still in the flesh, will not cease to accompany us after death. For as good qualities, or charity itself which is their source, may be gained in this world, and after the close of this life make the man who loves it lovely and glorious, so our faults transmit to that eternal remembrance a mind darkened and stained with foul colours. For the beauty or ugliness of the soul is the product of its virtues or its vices, the colour it takes from which either makes it so glorious, that it may well hear from the prophet "And the king shall have pleasure in thy beauty,"[145] or so black, and foul, and ugly, that it must surely acknowledge the stench of its shame, and say "My wounds stink and are corrupt because of my foolishness,"[146] and the Lord Himself says to it "Why is not the wound of the daughter of my people closed?"[147] And therefore these are our very own possessions, which continually remain with the soul, which no king and no enemy can either give or take away from us. These are our very own possessions which not even death itself can part from the soul, but by renouncing which we can attain to perfection, and by clinging to which we shall suffer the punishment of eternal death.

NOTES:
[145] Ps. 44 (45):12.
[146] Ps. 37 (38):6.
[147] Jer. 8:22.

CHAPTER IX.

Of three sorts of possessions.

RICHES and possessions are taken in Holy Scripture in three different ways, i.e., as good, bad, and indifferent. Those are bad, of which it is said: "The rich have wanted and have suffered hunger,"[148] and "Woe unto you that are rich, for ye have received your consolation:"[149] and to have cast off these riches is the height of perfection; and a distinction which belongs to those poor who are commended in the gospel by the Lord's saying: "Blessed are the poor in spirit, for theirs is the kingdom of heaven;"[150] and in the Psalm: "This poor man cried, and the Lord heard him,"[151] and again: "The poor and needy shall praise thy name."[152] Those riches are good, to acquire which is the work of great virtue and merit, and the righteous possessor of which is praised by David who says "The generation of the righteous shall be blessed: glory and riches are in his house, and his righteousness remaineth for ever:"[153] and again "the ransom of a man's life are his riches."[154] And of these riches it is said in the Apocalypse to him who has them not and to his shame is poor and naked: "I will begin," says he, "to vomit thee out of my mouth. Because thou sayest I am rich and wealthy and have need of nothing: and knowest not that thou art wretched and miserable and poor and blind and naked, I counsel thee to buy of me gold fire-tried, that thou mayest be made rich, and mayest be clothed in white garments, and that the shame of thy nakedness may not appear."[155] There are some also which are indifferent, i.e., which may be made either good or bad: for they are made either one or the other in accordance with the will and character of those who use them: of which the blessed, Apostle says "Charge the rich of this world not to be high-minded nor to trust in the uncertainty of riches, but in God (who giveth us abundantly all things to enjoy), to do good, to give easily, to communicate to others, to lay up in store for themselves a good foundation that they may lay hold on the true life."[156] These are what the rich man in the gospel kept, and never distributed to the poor,-- while the beggar Lazarus was lying at his gate and desiring to be fed with his crumbs; and so he was condemned to the unbearable flames and everlasting heat of hell-fire. [157]

NOTES:
[148] Ps. 33 (34):11.
[149] S. Luke 6:24.
[150] S. Matt. 5:3.
[151] Ps. 33 (34):7.
[152] Ps. 73 (74):21.
[153] Ps. 111 (112):2, 3.
[154] Prov. 13:8.
[155] Rev. 3:16-18.
[156] 1 Tim. 6:17-19.
[157] Cf. S. Luke 14:19 sq.

CHAPTER X.

That none can become perfect merely through the first grade of renunciation.

IN leaving then these visible goods of the world we forsake not our own wealth, but that which is not ours, although we boast of it as either gained by our own exertions or inherited by us from our forefathers. For as I said nothing is our own, save this only which we possess with our heart, and which cleaves to our soul, and therefore cannot be taken away from us by any one. But Christ speaks in terms of censure of those visible riches, to those who clutch them as if they were their own, and refuse to share them with those in want. "If ye have not been faithful in what is another's, who will give to you what is your own?"[158] Plainly then it is not only daily experience which teaches us that these riches are not our own, but this saying of our Lord also, by the very title which it gives them. But concerning visible[159] and worthless riches Peter says to the Lord: "Lo, we have left all and followed thee. What shall we have therefore?"[160] when it is clear that they had left nothing but their miserable broken nets. And unless this expression "all" is understood to refer to that renunciation of sins which is really great and important, we shall not find that the Apostles had left anything of any value, or that the Lord had any reason for bestowing on them the blessing of so great glory, that they were allowed to hear from Him that "in the regeneration, when the Son of Man shall sit on the throne of His glory, ye also shall sit upon twelve thrones judging the twelve tribes of Israel."[161] If then those, who have completely renounced their earthly and visible goods, cannot for sufficient reason attain to Apostolic charity, nor climb with readiness and vigour to that third stage of renunciation which is still higher and belongs to but few, what should those think of themselves, who do not even make that first step (which is very easy) a thorough one, but keep together with their old want of faith, their former sordid riches, and fancy that they can boast of the mere name of monks? The first renunciation then of which we spoke is of what is not our own, and therefore is not enough of itself to confer perfection on the renunciant, unless he advances to the second, which is really and truly a renunciation of what belongs to us. And when we have made sure of this by the expulsion of all our faults, we shall mount to the heights of the third renunciation also, whereby we rise above not merely all those things which are done in this world or specially belong to men, but even that whole universe around us which is esteemed so glorious, and shall with heart and soul look down upon it as subject to vanity and destined soon to pass away; as we look, as the Apostle says, "not on those things which are seen, but on those which are not seen: for the things that are seen, are temporal, and the things which are not seen are eternal;"[162] that so we may be found worthy to hear that highest utterance, which was spoken to Abraham: "and come into a land which I will show thee,"[163] which clearly shows that unless a man has made those three former renunciations with all earnestness of mind, he cannot attain to this fourth, which is granted as a reward and privilege to one whose renunciation is perfect, that he may be found worthy to enter the land of promise which no longer bears for him the thorns and thistles of sins; which after all the passions have been driven out is acquired by purity of heart even in the body, and which no good deeds or exertions of man's efforts (can gain), but which the Lord Himself promises to show, saying "And come into the land which I will show to thee:" which clearly proves that the beginning of our salvation results from the call of the Lord, Who says "Get thee out from thy country," and that the completion of perfection and purity is His gift in the same way, as He says "And come into the land which I will show thee," i.e., not one you yourself can know or discover by your own efforts, but one which I will show not only to one who is ignorant of it, but even to one who is not looking for it. And from this we clearly gather that as we hasten to the way of salvation through being stirred up by the inspiration of the Lord, so too it is under the guidance of His direction and illumination that we attain to the perfection of the highest bliss.

NOTES:

[158] S. Luke 16:12.
[159] The MSS. vary between visibilibus and invisibilibus.
[160] S. Matt. 19:27.
[161] S. Matt. 19:28.
[162] 2 Cor. 4:18.
[163] Gen. 12:1.

CHAPTER XI.

A question on the free will of man and the grace of God.

GERMANUS: Where then is there room for free will, and how is it ascribed to our efforts that we are worthy of praise, if God both begins and ends everything in us which concerns our salvation?

CHAPTER XII.

The answer on the economy of Divine Grace, with free will still remaining in us.

PAPHNUTIUS: This would fairly influence us, if in every work and practice, the beginning and the end were everything, and there were no middle in between. And so as we know that God creates opportunities of salvation in various ways, it is in our power to make use of the opportunities granted to us by heaven more or less earnestly. For just as the offer came from God Who called him "get thee out of thy country," so the obedience was on the part of Abraham who went forth; and as the fact that the saying "Come into the land" was carried into action, was the work of him who obeyed, so the addition of the words "which I will show thee" came from the grace of God Who commanded or promised it. But it is well for us to be sure that although we practise every virtue with unceasing efforts, yet with all our exertions and zeal we can never arrive at perfection, nor is mere human diligence and toil of itself sufficient to deserve to reach the splendid reward of bliss, unless we have secured it by means of the co-operation of the Lord, and His directing our heart to what is right. And so we ought every moment to pray and say with David "Order my steps in thy paths that my footsteps slip not:"[164] and "He hath set my feet upon a rock and ordered my goings:"[165] that He Who is the unseen ruler of the human heart may vouchsafe to turn to the desire of virtue that will of ours, which is more readily inclined to vice either through want of knowledge of what is good, or through the delights of passion. And we read this in a verse in which the prophet sings very plainly: "Being pushed I was overturned that I might fall," where the weakness of our free will is shown. And "the Lord sustained me:"[166] again this shows that the Lord's help is always joined to it, and by this, that we may not be altogether destroyed by our free will, when He sees that we have stumbled, He sustains and supports us, as it were by stretching out His hand. And again: "If I said my foot was moved;" viz., from the slippery character of the will, "Thy mercy, O Lord, helped me."[167] Once more he joins on the help of God to his own weakness, as he confesses that it was not owing to his own efforts but to the mercy of God, that the foot of his faith was not moved. And again: "According to the multitude of the sorrows which I had in my heart," which sprang most certainly from my free will, "Thy comforts have refreshed my soul,"[168] i.e., by coming through Thy inspiration into my heart, and laying open the view of future blessings which Thou hast prepared for them who labour in Thy name, they not only removed all anxiety from my heart, but actually conferred upon it he greatest delight. And again: "Had it not been that the Lord helped me, my soul had almost dwelt in hell."[169] He certainly shows that through the depravity of this free will he would have dwelt in hell, had he not been saved by the assistance and protection of the Lord. For "By the Lord," and not by free-will, "are a man's steps directed," and "although the righteous fall" at least by free will, "he shall not be cast away." And why? because "the Lord upholdeth him with His hand:"[170] and this is to say with the utmost clearness: None of the righteous are sufficient of themselves to acquire righteousness, unless every moment when they stumble and fall the Divine mercy supports them with His hands, that they may not utterly collapse and perish, when they have been cast down through the weakness of free will.

NOTES:
[164] Ps. 16 (17):5.
[165] Ps. 39 (40):3.
[166] Ps. 117 (118):13.
[167] Ps. 93 (94):18.
[168] Ps. 93 (94):19.
[169] Ps. 93 (94):17.
[170] Ps. 36 (37):23, 24.

CHAPTER XIII.

That the ordering of our way comes from God.

AND truly the saints have never said that it was by their own efforts that they secured the direction of the way in which they walked in their course towards advance and perfection of virtue, but rather they prayed for it from the Lord, saying "Direct me in Thy truth," and "direct my way in thy sight."[171] But someone else declares that he discovered this very fact not only by faith, but also by experience, and as it were from the very nature of things: "I know, O Lord, that the way of man is not his: neither is it in a man to walk and to direct his steps."[172] And the Lord Himself says to Israel: "I will direct him like a green fir-tree: from Me is thy fruit found." [173]

NOTES:
[171] Ps. 24 (25):5; 6:9.
[172] Jer. 10:23.
[173] Hos. 14:9.

CHAPTER XIV.

That knowledge of the law is given by the guidance and illumination of the Lord.

THE knowledge also of the law itself they daily endeavour to gain not by diligence in reading, but by the guidance and illumination of God as they say to Him: "Show me Thy ways, O Lord, and teach me Thy paths:" and "open Thou mine eyes: and I shall see the wondrous things of Thy law:" and "teach me to do Thy will, for Thou art my God;" and again: "Who teacheth man knowledge." [174]

NOTES:
[174] Ps. 24 (25):4; 118 (119):18; 142 (143):10; 93 (94):10.

CHAPTER XV.

That the understanding, by means of which we can recognize God's commands, and the performance of a good will are both gifts from the Lord.

FURTHER the blessed David asks of the Lord that he may gain that very understanding, by which he can recognize God's commands which, he well knew, were written in the book of the law, and he says "I am Thy servant: O give me understanding that I may learn Thy commandments."[175] Certainly he was in possession of understanding, which had been granted to him by nature, and also had at his fingers' ends a knowledge of God's commands which were preserved in writing in the law: and still he prayed the Lord that he might learn this more thoroughly as he knew that what came to him by nature would never be sufficient for him, unless his understanding was enlightened by the Lord by a daily illumination from Him, to understand the law spiritually and to recognize His commands more clearly, as the "chosen vessel" also declares very plainly this which we are insisting on. "For it is God which worketh in you both to will and to do according to good will."[176] What could well be clearer than the assertion that both our good will and the completion of our work are fully wrought in us by the Lord? And again "For it is granted to you for Christ's sake, not only to believe in Him but also to suffer for Him."[177] Here also he declares that the beginning of our conversion and faith, and the endurance of suffering is a gift to us from the Lord. And David too, as he knows this, similarly prays that the same thing may be granted to him by God's mercy. "Strengthen, O God, that which Thou hast wrought in us:"[178] showing that it is not enough for the beginning of our salvation to be granted by the gift and grace of God, unless it has been continued and ended by the same pity and continual help from Him. For not free will but the Lord "looseth them that are bound." No strength of ours, but the Lord "raiseth them that are fallen:" no diligence in reading, but "the Lord enlightens the blind:" where the Greeks have kurios sofoi tuflous, i.e., "the Lord maketh wise the blind:" no care on our part, but "the Lord careth for the stranger:" no courage of ours, but "the Lord assists (or supports) all those who are down."[179] But this we say, not to slight our zeal and efforts and diligence, as if they were applied unnecessarily and foolishly, but that we may know that we cannot strive without the help of God, nor can our efforts be of any use in securing the great reward of purity, unless it has been granted to us by the assistance and mercy of the Lord: for "a horse is prepared for the day of battle: but help cometh from the Lord,"[180] "for no man can prevail by strength."[181] We ought then always to sing with the blessed David: "My strength and my praise is" not my free will, but "the Lord, and He is become my salvation."[182] And the teacher of the Gentiles was not ignorant of this when he declared that he was made capable of the ministry of the New Testament not by his own merits or efforts but by the mercy of God. "Not" says he, "that we are capable of thinking anything of ourselves as of ourselves, but our sufficiency is of God," which can be put in less good Latin but more forcibly, "our capability is of God," and then there follows: "Who also made us capable ministers of the New Testament." [183]

NOTES:
[175] Ps. 118 (119):125.
[176] Phil. 2:13.
[177] Phil. 1:29.
[178] Ps. 67 (68):29.
[179] Ps. 145 (146):7, 8, 9; 144 (145):16.
[180] Prov. 21:31.
[181] 1 Sam. 2:9.
[182] Ps. 117 (118):14.
[183] 2 Cor. 3:5, 6.

CHAPTER XVI.

That faith itself must be given us by the Lord.

BUT so thoroughly did the Apostles realize that everything which concerns salvation was given them by the Lord, that they even asked that faith itself should be granted from the Lord, saying: "Add to us faith"[184] as they did not imagine that it could be gained by free will, but believed that it would be bestowed by the free gift of God. Lastly the Author of man's salvation teaches us how feeble and weak and insufficient our faith would be unless it were strengthened by the aid of the Lord, when He says to Peter "Simon, Simon, behold Satan hath desired to have you that he may sift you as wheat. But I have prayed to my Father that thy faith fail not."[185] And another finding that this was happening in his own case, and seeing that his faith was being driven by the waves of unbelief on the rocks which would cause a fearful shipwreck, asks of the same Lord an aid to his faith, saying "Lord, help mine unbelief."[186] So thoroughly then did those Apostles and men in the gospel realize that everything which is good is brought to perfection by the aid of the Lord, and not imagine that they could preserve their faith unharmed by their own strength or free will that they prayed that it might be helped or granted to them by the Lord. And if in Peter's case there was need of the Lord's help that it might not fail, who will be so presumptuous and blind as to fancy that he has no need of daily assistance from the Lord in order to preserve it? Especially as the Lord Himself has made this clear in the gospel, saying: "As the branch cannot bear fruit of itself except it abide in the vine, so no more can ye, except ye abide in me."[187] And again: "for without me ye can do nothing."[188] How foolish and wicked then it is to attribute any good action to our own diligence and not to God's grace and assistance, is clearly shown by the Lord's saying, which lays down that no one can show forth the fruits of the Spirit without His inspiration and co-operation. For "every good gift and every perfect boon is from above, coming down from the Father of lights."[189] And Zechariah too says, "For whatever is good is His, and what is excellent is from Him."[190] And so the blessed Apostle consistently says: "What hast thou which thou didst not receive? But if thou didst receive it, why boastest thou as if thou hadst not received it?" [191]

NOTES:
[184] S. Luke 17:5.
[185] S. Luke 22:31, 32.
[186] S. Mark 9:23.
[187] S. John 15:4.
[188] S. John 15:5.
[189] S. James 1:17.
[190] Zech. 9:17 (LXX).
[191] 1 Cor. 4:7.

CHAPTER XVII.

That temperateness and the endurance of temptations must be given to us by the Lord.

AND that all the endurance, with which we can bear the temptations brought upon us, depends not so much on our own strength as on the mercy and guidance of God, the blessed Apostle thus declares: "No temptation hath come upon you but such as is common to man. But God is faithful, who will not suffer you to be tempted above that ye are able, but will with the temptation make also a way of escape, that ye may be able to bear it."[192] And that God fits and strengthens our souls for every good work, and worketh in us all those things which are pleasing to Him, the same Apostle teaches: "May the God of peace who brought out of darkness the great Shepherd of the sheep, Jesus Christ, in the blood of the everlasting Testament, fit you in all goodness, working in you what is well-pleasing in His sight."[193] And that the same thing may happen to the Thessalonians he prays as follows, saying: "Now our Lord Jesus Christ Himself and God our Father who hath loved us and hath given us everlasting consolation and good hope in grace, exhort your hearts, and confirm you in every good word and work." [194]

NOTES:
[192] 1 Cor. 10:13.
[193] Heb. 13:20, 21.
[194] 2 Thess. 2:15, 16.

CHAPTER XVIII.

That the continual fear of God must be bestowed on us by the Lord.

AND lastly the prophet Jeremiah, speaking in the person of God, clearly testifies that even the fear of God, by which we can hold fast to Him, is shed upon us by the Lord: saying as follows: "And I will give them one heart, and one way, that they may fear Me all days: and that it may be well with them and with their children after them. And I will make an everlasting covenant with them and will not cease to do them good: and I will give My fear in their hearts that they may not revolt from Me."[195] Ezekiel also says: "And I will give them one heart, and will put a new spirit in their bowels: and I will take away the stony heart out of their flesh and will give them a heart of flesh: that they may walk in My commandments, and keep My judgments and do them: and that they may be My people, and I may be their God." [196]

NOTES:
[195] Jer. 32:39, 40.
[196] Ezek. 11:19, 20.

CHAPTER XIX.

That the beginning of our good will and its completion comes from God.

AND this plainly teaches us that the beginning of our good will is given to us by the inspiration of the Lord, when He draws us towards the way of salvation either by His own act, or by the exhortations of some man, or by compulsion; and that the consummation of our good deeds is granted by Him in the same way: but that it is in our own power to follow up the encouragement and assistance of God with more or less zeal, and that accordingly we are rightly visited either with reward or with punishment, because we have been either careless or careful to correspond to His design and providential arrangement made for us with such kindly regard. And this is clearly and plainly described in Deuteronomy. "When," says he, "the Lord thy God shall have brought thee into the land which thou art going to possess, and shall have destroyed many nations before thee, the Hittite, and the Gergeshite, and the Amorite, the Canaanite, and the Perizzite, the Hivite, and the Jebusite, seven nations much more numerous than thou art and stronger than thou, and the Lord thy God shall have delivered them to thee, thou shalt utterly destroy them. Thou shalt make no league with them. Neither shalt thou make marriage with them."[197] So then Scripture declares that it is the free gift of God that they are brought into the land of promise, that many nations are destroyed before them, that nations more numerous and mightier than the people of Israel are given up into their hands. But whether Israel utterly destroys them, or whether it preserves them alive and spares them, and whether or no it makes a league with them, and makes marriages with them or not, it declares lies in their own power. And by this testimony we can clearly see what we ought to ascribe to free will, and what to the design and daily assistance of the Lord, and that it belongs to divine grace to give us opportunities of salvation and prosperous undertakings and victory: but that it is ours to follow up the blessings which God gives us with earnestness or indifference. And this same fact we see is plainly taught in the healing of the blind men. For the fact that Jesus passed by them, was a free gift of Divine providence and condescension. But the fact that they cried out and said "Have mercy on us, Lord, thou son of David,"[198] was an act of their own faith and belief. That they received the sight of their eyes was a gift of Divine pity. But that after the reception of any blessing, the grace of God, and the use of free will both remain, the case of the ten lepers, who were all healed alike, shows us. For when one of them through goodness of will returned thanks, the Lord looking for the nine, and praising the one, showed that He was ever anxious to help even those who were unmindful of His kindness. For even this is a gift of His visitation; viz., that he receives and commends the grateful one, and looks for and censures those who are thankless.

NOTES:
[197] Deut. 7:1-3.
[198] S. Matt. 20:31.

CHAPTER XX.

That nothing can be done in this world without God.

BUT it is right for us to hold with unswerving faith that nothing whatever is done in this world without God. For we must acknowledge that everything is done either by His will or by His permission, i.e., we must believe that whatever is good is carried out by the will of God and by His aid, and whatever is the reverse is done by His permission, when the Divine Protection is withdrawn from us for our sins and the hardness of our hearts, and suffers the devil and the shameful passions of the body to lord it over us. And the words of the Apostle most assuredly teach us this, when he says: "For this cause God delivered them up to shameful passions:" and again: "Because they did not like to have God in their knowledge, God delivered them up to a reprobate sense, to do those things which are not convenient."[199] And the Lord Himself says by the prophet: "But My people did not hear My voice and Israel did not obey me: Wherefore I gave them up unto their own hearts' lusts. They shall walk after their own inventions." [200]

NOTES:
[199] Rom. 1:26, 28.
[200] Ps. 80 (81):12, 13.

CHAPTER XXI.

An objection on the power of free will.

GERMANUS: This passage very clearly shows the freedom of the will, where it is said "If My people would have hearkened unto Me," and elsewhere "But My people would not hear My voice."[201] For when He says "If they would have heard" He shows that the decision to yield or not to yield lay in their own power. How then is it true that our salvation does not depend upon ourselves, if God Himself has given us the power either to hearken or not to hearken?

NOTES:
[201] Ps. 80 (81):12, 13.

CHAPTER XXII.

The answer; viz., that our free will always has need of the help of the Lord.

PAPHNUTIUS: You have shrewdly enough noticed how it is said "If they would have hearkened to Me:" but have not sufficiently considered either who it is who speaks to one who does or does not hearken; or what follows: "I should soon have put down their enemies, and laid My hand on those that trouble them."[202] Let no one then try by a false interpretation to twist that which we brought forward to prove that nothing can be done without the Lord, nor take it in support of free will, in such a way as to try to take away from man the grace of God and His daily oversight, through this test: "But My people did not hear My voice," and again: "If My people would have hearkened unto Me, and if Israel would have walked in My ways, etc.:" but let him consider that just as the power of free will is evidenced by the disobedience of the people, so the daily oversight of God who declares and admonishes him is also shown. For where He says "If My people would have hearkened unto Me" He clearly implies that He had spoken to them before. And this the Lord was wont to do not only by means of the written law, but also by daily exhortations, as this which is given by Isaiah: "All day long have I stretched forth My hands to a disobedient and gain-saying people."[203] Both points then can be supported from this passage, where it says: "If My people would have hearkened, and if Israel had walked in My ways, I should soon have put down their enemies, and laid My hand on those that trouble them." For just as free will is shown by the disobedience of the people, so the government of God and His assistance is made clear by the beginning and end of the verse, where He implies that He had spoken to them before, and that afterwards He would put down their enemies, if they would have hearkened unto Him. For we have no wish to do away with man's free will by what we have said, but only to establish the fact that the assistance and grace of God are necessary to it every day and hour. When he had instructed us with this discourse Abbot Paphnutius dismissed us from his cell before midnight in a state of contrition rather than of liveliness; insisting on this as the chief lesson in his discourse; viz., that when we fancied that by making perfect the first renunciation (which we were endeavouring to do with all our powers), we could climb the heights of perfection, we should make the discovery that we had not yet even begun to dream of the heights to which a monk can rise, since after we had learnt some few things about the second renunciation, we should find out that we had not before this even heard a word of the third stage, in which all perfection is comprised, and which in many ways far exceeds these lower ones.

NOTES:
[202] Ps. 80 (81):15.
[203] Is. 65:2.

CONFERENCE 4.

Conference of Abbot Daniel
on the Lust of the Flesh and of the Spirit

CHAPTER I.

Of the life of Abbot Daniel.

AMONG the other heroes of Christian philosophy we also knew
Abbot Daniel, who was not only the equal of those who dwelt in the
desert of Scete in every sort of virtue, but was specially marked by the
grace of humility. This man on account of his purity and gentleness,
though in age the junior of most, was preferred to the office of the diaconate by the blessed Paphnutius, presbyter in the same desert: for
the blessed Paphnutius was so delighted with his excellent qualities,
that, as he knew that he was his equal in virtue and grace of life, he
was anxious also to make him his equal in the order of the priesthood.
And since he could not bear that he should remain any longer in an
inferior office, and was also anxious to provide a worthy successor to
himself in his lifetime, he promoted him to the dignity of the priesthood.[204] He however relinquished nothing of his former customary
humility, and when the other was present, never took upon himself
anything from his advance to a higher order, but when Abbot Paphnutius was offering spiritual sacrifices, ever continued to act as a
deacon in the office of his former ministry. However, the blessed
Paphnutius though so great a saint as to possess the grace of foreknowledge in many matters, yet in this case was disappointed of his
hope of the succession and the choice he had made, for he himself
passed to God no long time after him whom he had prepared as his
successor.

PART 1

NOTES:

[204] Nothing further appears to be known of Daniel than what is here told us by Cassian. There has been some discussion as to the action of Paphnutius in having him raised to the priesthood, as Cassian here narrates. Was Paphnutius really a bishop, or is it a case of presbyterian orders, or do Cassian's expressions merely mean that Paphnutius procured his ordination first to the Diaconate and then to the Priesthood? Probably the latter, for (1) all the evidence goes to show that presbyters had not the power of ordination; and (2) there are many instances, in which it is said even of the laity that they "ordained" men to the ministry when all that can possibly be meant is that they "procured their ordination;" further (3) it will be noticed that it is not even said that Paphnutius ordained Daniel, but merely that he "promoted" him to the priesthood; an expression which might equally well be used of nomination as of actual ordination. See the subject discussed in Bingham's Antiquities, Book II. c. iii. S: 7, and C. Gore's "Church and the Ministry," p. 374.

CHAPTER II.

An investigation of the origin of a sudden change of feeling from inexpressible joy to extreme dejection of mind.

SO then we asked this blessed Daniel why it was that as we sat in the cells we were sometimes filled with the utmost gladness of heart, together with inexpressible delight and abundance of the holiest feelings, so that I will not say speech, but feeling could not follow it, and pure prayers were readily breathed, and the mind being filled with spiritual fruits, praying to God even in sleep could feel that its petitions rose lightly and powerfully to God: and again, why it was that for no reason we were suddenly filled with the utmost grief, and weighed down with unreasonable depression, so that we not only felt as if we ourselves were, overcome with such feelings, but also our cell grew dreadful, reading palled upon us, aye and our very prayers were offered up unsteadily and vaguely, and almost as if we were intoxicated: so that while we were groaning and endeavouring to restore ourselves to our former disposition, our mind was unable to do this, and the more earnestly it sought to fix again its gaze upon God, so was it the more vehemently carried away to wandering thoughts by shifting aberrations and so utterly deprived of all spiritual fruits, as not to be capable of being roused from this deadly slumber even by the desire of the kingdom of heaven, or by the fear of hell held out to it. To this he replied.

CHAPTER III.

His answer to the question raised.

A THREEFOLD account of this mental dryness of which you speak has been given by the Elders. For it comes either from carelessness on our part, or from the assaults of the devil, or from the permission and allowance of the Lord. From carelessness on our part, when through our own faults, coldness has come upon us, and we have behaved carelessly and hastily, and owing to slothful idleness have fed on bad thoughts, and so make the ground of our heart bring forth thorns and thistles; which spring up in it, and consequently make us sterile, and powerless as regards all spiritual fruit and meditation. From the assaults of the devil when, sometimes, while we are actually intent on good desires, our enemy with crafty subtilty makes his way into our heart, and without our knowledge and against our will we are drawn away from the best intentions.

CHAPTER IV.

How there is a twofold reason for the permission and allowance of God.

BUT for God's permission and allowance there is a twofold reason. First, that being for a short time forsaken by the Lord, and observing with all humility the weakness of our own heart, we may not be puffed up on account of the previous purity of heart granted to us by His visitation; and that by proving that when we are forsaken by Him we cannot possibly recover our former state of purity and delight by any groanings and efforts of our own, we may also learn that our previous gladness of heart resulted not from our own earnestness but from His gift, and that for the present time it must be sought once more from His grace and enlightenment. But a second reason for this allowance, is to prove our perseverance, and steadfastness of mind, and real desires, and to show in us, with what purpose of heart, or earnestness in prayer we seek for the return of the Holy Spirit, when He leaves us, and also in order that when we discover with what efforts we must seek for that spiritual gladness--when once it is lost--and the joy of purity, we may learn to preserve it more carefully, when once it is secured, and to hold it with firmer grasp. For men are generally more careless about keeping whatever they think can be easily replaced.

CHAPTER V.

How our efforts and exertions are of no use without God's help.

AND by this it is clearly shown that God's grace and mercy always work in us what is good, and that when it forsakes us, the efforts of the worker are useless, and that however earnestly a man may strive, he cannot regain his former condition without His help, and that this saying is constantly fulfilled in our case: that it is "not of him that willeth or runneth but of God which hath mercy."[205] And this grace on the other hand sometimes does not refuse to visit with that holy inspiration of which you spoke, and with an abundance of spiritual thoughts, even the careless and indifferent; but inspires the unworthy, arouses the slumberers, and enlightens those who are blinded by ignorance, and mercifully reproves us and chastens us, shedding itself abroad in our hearts, that thus we may be stirred by the compunction which He excites, and impelled to rise from the sleep of sloth. Lastly we are often filled by His sudden visitation with sweet odours, beyond the power of human composition--so that the soul is ravished with these delights, and caught up, as it were, into an ecstasy of spirit, and becomes oblivious of the fact that it is still in the flesh.

NOTES:
[205] Rom. 9:16.

CHAPTER VI.

How it is sometimes to our advantage to be left by God.

BUT the blessed David recognizes that sometimes this departure of which we have spoken, and (as it were) desertion by God may be to some extent to our advantage, so that he was unwilling to pray, not that he might not be absolutely forsaken by God in anything (for he was aware that this would have been disadvantageous both to himself and to human nature in its course towards perfection) but he rather entreated that it might be in measure and degree, saying "Forsake me not utterly"[206] as if to say in other words: I know that thou dost forsake thy saints to their advantage, in order to prove them, for in no other way could they be tempted by the devil, unless they were for a little forsaken by Thee. And therefore I ask not that Thou shouldest never forsake me, for it would not be well for me not to feel my weakness and say "It is good for me that Thou hast brought me low"[207] nor to have no opportunity of fighting. And this I certainly should not have, if the Divine protection shielded me incessantly and unbrokenly. For the devil will not dare to attack me while supported by Thy defence, as he brings both against me and Thee this objection and complaint, which he ever slanderously brings against Thy champions, "Does Job serve God for nought? Hast not Thou made a fence for him and his house and all his substance round about?"[208] But I rather entreat that Thou forsake me not utterly--what the Greeks call ἕως σφόδρα, i.e., too much. For, first, as it is advantageous to me for Thee to forsake me a little, that the steadfastness of my love may be tried, so it is dangerous if Thou suffer me to be forsaken excessively in proportion to my faults and what I deserve, since no power of man, if in temptation it is forsaken for too long a time by Thine aid, can endure by its own steadfastness, and not forthwith give in to the power of the enemy's side, unless Thou Thyself, as Thou knowest the strength of man, and moderatest his struggles, "Suffer us not to be tempted above that we are able, but makest with the temptation a way of escape that we may be able to bear it."[209] And something of this sort we read in the book of Judges was mystically designed in the matter of the extermination of the spiritual nations which were opposed to Israel: "These are the nations, which the Lord left that by them He might instruct Israel, that they might learn to fight with their enemies," and again shortly after:

"And the Lord left them that He might try Israel by them, whether they would hear the commandments of the Lord, which He had commanded their fathers by the hand of Moses, or not."[210] And this conflict God reserved for Israel, not from envy of their peace, or from a wish to hurt them, but because He knew that it would be good for them that while they were always oppressed by the attacks of those nations they might not cease to feel themselves in need of the aid of the Lord, and for this reason might ever continue to meditate on Him and invoke His aid, and not grow careless through lazy ease, and lose the habit of resisting, and the practice of virtue. For again and again, men whom adversity could not overcome, have been cast down by freedom from care and by prosperity.

NOTES:
[206] Ps. 118 (119):8.
[207] Ps. 118 (119):71.
[208] Job 1:9, 10.
[209] 1 Cor. 10:13.
[210] Judg. 3:1-4.

CHAPTER VII.

Of the value of the conflict which the Apostle makes to consist in the strife between the flesh and the spirit.

THIS conflict too we read in the Apostle has for our good been placed in our members: "For the flesh lusteth against the spirit: and the spirit against the flesh. But these two are opposed to each other so that ye should not do what ye would."[211] You have here too a contest as it were implanted in our bodies, by the action and arrangement of the Lord. For when a thing exists in everybody universally and without the slightest exception, what else can you think about it except that it belongs to the substance of human nature, since the fall of the first man, as it were naturally: and when a thing is found to be congenital with everybody, and to grow with their growth, how can we help believing that it was implanted by the will of the Lord, not to injure them but to help them? But the reason of this conflict; viz., of flesh and spirit, he tells us is this: "that ye should not do what ye would." And so, if we fulfil what God arranged that we should not fulfil, i.e., that we should not do what we liked, how can we help believing that it is bad for us?

And this conflict implanted in us by the arrangement of the Creator is in a way useful to us, and calls and urges us on to a higher state: and if it ceased, most surely there would ensue on the other hand a peace that is fraught with danger.

NOTES:
[211] Gal. 5:17.

CHAPTER VIII.

A question, how it is that in the Apostle's chapter, after he has spoken of the lusts of the flesh and spirit opposing one another, he adds a third thing; viz., man's will.

GERMANUS: Although some glimmer of the sense now seems clear to us, yet as we cannot thoroughly grasp the Apostle's meaning, we want you to explain this more clearly to us. For the existence of three things seems to be indicated here: first, the struggle of the flesh against the spirit, secondly the desire of the spirit against the flesh, and thirdly our own free will, which seems to be placed between the two, and of which it is said: "Ye should not do what ye will." And on this subject though as I said we can gather some hints, from what you have explained of the meaning, yet--since this conference gives the opportunity--we are anxious to have it more fully explained to us.

CHAPTER IX.

The answer on the understanding of one who asks rightly.

DANIEL: It belongs to the understanding to discern the distinctions and the drift of questions; and it is a main part of knowledge to understand how ignorant you are. Wherefore it is said that "if a fool asks questions, it will be accounted wisdom,"[212] because, although one who asks questions is ignorant of the answer to the question raised, yet as he wisely asks, and learns what he does not know, this very fact will be counted as wisdom in him, because he wisely discovers what he was ignorant of. According then to this division of yours, it seems that in this passage the Apostle mentions three things, the lust of the flesh against the spirit, and of the spirit against the flesh, the mutual struggle of which against each other appears to have this as its cause and reason; viz., "that," says he, "we should not do what we would." There remains then a fourth case, which you have overlooked; viz., that we should do what we would not. Now then, we must first discover the meaning of those two desires, i.e., of the flesh and spirit, and so next learn to discuss our free will, which is placed between the two, and then lastly in the same way we can see what cannot belong to our free will.

NOTES:
[212] Prov. 17:28 (LXX).

CHAPTER X.

That the word flesh is not used with one single meaning only.

WE find that the word flesh is used in holy Scripture with many different meanings: for sometimes it stands for the whole man, i.e., for that which consists of body and soul, as here "And the Word was made flesh,"[213] and "All flesh shall see the salvation of our God."[214] Sometimes it stands for sinful and carnal men, as here "My spirit shall not remain in those men, because they are flesh."[215] Sometimes it is used for sins themselves, as here: "But ye are not in the flesh but in the spirit,"[216] and again "Flesh and blood shall not inherit the kingdom of God:" lastly there follows, "Neither shall corruption inherit incorruption."[217] Sometimes it stands for consanguinity and relationship, as here: "Behold we are thy bone and thy flesh,"[218] and the Apostle says: "If by any means I may provoke to emulation them who are my flesh, and save some of them."[219] We must therefore inquire in which of these four meanings we ought to take the word flesh in this place, for it is clear that it cannot possibly stand as in the passage where it is said "The Word was made flesh," and "All flesh shall see the salvation of God." Neither can it have the same meaning as where it is said "My Spirit shall not remain in those men because they are flesh," because the word flesh is not used here as it is there where it stands simply for a sinful man--when he says" The flesh lusteth against the spirit and the spirit against the flesh."[220] Nor is he speaking of things material, but of realities which in one and the same man struggle either at the same time or separately, with the shifting and changing of time.

NOTES:
[213] S. John 1:14.
[214] S. Luke 3:6.
[215] Gen. 6:3.
[216] Rom. 8:9.
[217] 1 Cor. 15:50.
[218] 2 Sam. 5:1.
[219] Rom. 11:14.
[220] Gal. 5:17.

CHAPTER XI.

What the Apostle means by flesh in this passage, and what the lust of the flesh is.

WHEREFORE in this passage we ought to take "flesh" as meaning not man, i.e., his material substance, but the carnal will and evil desires, just as "spirit" does not mean anything material, but the good and spiritual desires of the soul: a meaning which the blessed Apostle has clearly given just before, where he begins: "But I say, walk in the spirit, and ye shall not fulfil the desires of the flesh; for the flesh lusteth against the spirit and the spirit against the flesh: but these are contrary the one to the other, that ye may not do what ye would." And since these two; viz., the desires of the flesh and of the spirit co-exist in one and the same man, there arises an internal warfare daily carried on within us, while the lust of the flesh which rushes blindly towards sin, revels in those delights which are connected with present ease. And on the other hand the desire of the spirit is opposed to these, and wishes to be entirely absorbed in spiritual efforts, so that it actually wants to be rid of even the necessary uses of the flesh, longing to be so constantly taken up with these things as to desire to have no share of anxiety about the weakness of the flesh. The flesh delights in wantonness and lust: the spirit does not even tolerate natural desires. The one wants to have plenty of sleep, and to be satiated with food: the other is nourished with vigils and fasting, so as to be unwilling even to admit of sleep and food for the needful purposes of life. The one longs to be enriched with plenty of everything, the other is satisfied even without the possession of a daily supply of scanty food. The one seeks to look sleek by means of baths, and to be surrounded every day by crowds of flatterers, the other delights in dirt and filth, and the solitude of the inaccessible desert, and dreads the approach of all mortal men. The one lives on the esteem and applause of men, the other glories in injuries offered to it, and in persecutions.

CHAPTER XII.

What is our free will, which stands in between the lust of the flesh and the spirit.

BETWEEN these two desires then the free will of the soul stands in an intermediate position somewhat worthy of blame, and neither delights in the excesses of sin, nor acquiesces in the sorrows of virtue. Seeking to restrain itself from carnal passions in such a way as not nevertheless to be willing to undergo the requisite suffering, and wanting to secure bodily chastity without chastising the flesh, and to acquire purity of heart without the exertion of vigils, and to abound in spiritual virtues together with carnal ease, and to attain the grace of patience without the irritation of contradiction, and to practise the humility of Christ without the loss of worldly honour, to aim at the simplicity of religion in conjunction with worldly ambition, to serve Christ not without the praise and favour of men, to profess the strictness which truth demands without giving the slightest offence to anybody: in a word, it is anxious to pursue future blessings in such a way as not to lose present ones. And this free will would never lead us to attain true perfection, but would plunge us into a most miserable condition of lukewarmness, and make us like those who are rebuked by the Lord's remonstrance in the Apocalypse: "I know thy works, that thou art neither hot nor cold. I would that thou wert hot or cold. But now thou art lukewarm, and I will forthwith spue thee out of my mouth;"[221] were it not that these contentions which rise up on both sides disturb and destroy this condition of lukewarmness. For when we give in to this free will of ours and want to let ourselves go in the direction of this slackness, at once the desires of the flesh start up, and injure us with their sinful passions, and do not suffer us to continue in that state of purity in which we delight, and allure us to that cold and thorny path of pleasure which we have to dread. Again, if inflamed with fervour of spirit, we want to root out the works of the flesh, and without any regard to human weakness try to raise ourselves altogether to excessive efforts after virtue, the frailty of the flesh comes in, and recalls us and restrains us from that over excess of spirit which is bad for us: and so the result is that as these two desires are contradicting each other in a struggle of this kind, the soul's free will, which does not like either to give itself up entirely to carnal desires, nor to throw itself into the exertions which virtue calls for, is tempered as it were by a fair balance, while this struggle between the two hinders that more dangerous free will of the soul, and makes a sort of equitable balance in the scales of our body, which marks out the limits of flesh and spirit most accurately, and does not allow the mind inflamed with fervour of spirit to sway to the right hand, nor the flesh to incline through the pricks of sin, to the left. And while this struggle goes on day after day in us to our profit, we are driven most beneficially to come to that fourth stage which we do not like, so as to gain purity of heart not by ease and carelessness, but by constant efforts and contrition of spirit; to retain our chastity, of the flesh by prolonged fastings, hunger, thirst, and watchfulness; to acquire purpose of heart by reading, vigils, constant prayer and the wretchedness of solitude; to preserve patience by the endurance of tribulation; to serve our Maker in the midst of blasphemies and abounding insults; to follow after truth if need be amid the hatred of the world and its enmity; and while, with such a struggle going on in our body, we are secured from slothful carelessness, and incited to that effort which is against the gain, and to the desire for virtue, our proper balance is admirably secured, and on one side the languid choice of our free will is tempered by fervour of spirit, and on the other the frigid coldness of the flesh is moderated by a gentle warmth, and while the desire of the spirit does not allow the mind to be dragged into unbridled licence, neither does the weakness of the flesh allow the spirit to be drawn on to unreasonable aspirations after holiness, lest in the one case incentives to all kinds of sins might arise, or in the other the earliest of all sins might lift its head and wound us with a yet more fatal dart of pride: but a due equilibrium will result from this struggle, and open to us a safe and secure path of virtue between the two, and teach the soldier of Christ ever to walk on the King's highway. And thus the result will be that when, in consequence of the lukewarmness arising from this sluggish will of which we have spoken, the mind has been more easily entangled in carnal desires, it is checked by the desire of the spirit, which by no means acquiesces in earthly sins; and again, if through over much feeling our spirit has been carried in unbounded fervour and towards ill-considered and impossible heights, it is recalled by the weakness of the flesh to sounder considerations and rising above the lukewarm condition of our free will with due proportion and even course proceeds along the way of perfection. Something of this sort we hear that the Lord ordained in the case of the building of that tower in the book of Genesis, where a confusion of tongues suddenly sprang up, and put a stop to the blasphemous and wicked attempts of men. For there would have remained there in opposition to God, aye and against the interest of those who had begun to assail His Divine Majesty, an agreement boding no good, unless by God's providence the difference of languages, raising disturbances among them, had forced them because of the variations of their words to go on to a better condition, and a happy and valuable discord had recalled to salvation those whom a ruinous union had driven to destruction, as when divisions arose they began to experience human weakness of which when puffed up by their wicked plots they had hitherto known nothing.

NOTES:
[221] Rev. 3:15, 16.

CHAPTER XIII.

Of the advantage of the delay which results from the struggle between flesh and spirit.

BUT from the differences which this conflict causes, there arises a delay that is so far advantageous to us, and from this struggle an adjournment that is for our good, so that while through the resistance of the material body we are hindered from carrying out those things which we have wickedly conceived with our minds, we are sometimes recalled to a better mind either by penitence springing up, or by some better thoughts which usually come to us when delay in carrying out things, and time for reflection intervene. Lastly, those who, as we know, are not prevented from carrying out the desires of their free will by any hindrances of the flesh, I mean devils and spiritual wickednesses, these, since they have fallen from a higher and angelical state, we see are in a worse plight than men, in as much as (owing to the fact that opportunity is always present to gratify their desires) they are not delayed from irrevocably performing whatever evil they have imagined because as their mind is quick to conceive it, so their substance is ready and free to carry it out; and while a short and easy method is given them of doing what they wish, no salutary second thoughts come in to amend their wicked intention.

CHAPTER XIV.

Of the incurable depravity of spiritual wickednesses.

FOR a spiritual substance and one that is not tied to any material flesh has no excuse for an evil thought which arises within, and also shuts out forgiveness for its sin, because it is not harassed as we are by incentives of the flesh without, to sin, but is simply inflamed by the fault of a perverse will. And therefore its sin is without forgiveness and its weakness without remedy. For as it falls through the allurements of no earthly matter, so it can find no pardon or place for repentance. And from this we can clearly gather that this struggle which arises in us of the flesh and spirit against each other is not merely harmless, but actually extremely useful to us.

CHAPTER XV.

Of the value of the lust of the flesh against the spirit in our case.

TO begin with, because it is an immediate reproof of our sloth and carelessness, and like some energetic schoolmaster who never allows us to deviate from the line of strict discipline, and if our carelessness has ever so little exceeded the limits of due gravity which become it, it immediately excites us by the stimulus of desire, and chides us and recalls us to due moderation. Secondly, because, in the matter of chastity and perfect purity, when by God's grace we see that we have been for some time kept from carnal pollution, in order that we may not imagine that we can no longer be disturbed by the motions of the flesh and thereby be elated and puffed up in our secret hearts as if we no longer bore about the corruption of the flesh, it humbles and checks us, and reminds us by its pricks that we are but men.[222] For as we ordinarily fall without much thought into other kinds of sins and those worse and more harmful, and are not so easily ashamed of committing them, so in this particular one the conscience is especially humbled, and by means of this illusion it is stung by the recollection of passions that have been neglected, as it sees clearly that it is rendered unclean by natural emotions, of which it knew nothing while it was still more unclean through spiritual sins; and so coming back at once to the cure of its former sluggishness, it is warned both that it ought not to trust in the attainments of purity in the past, which it sees to be lost by ever so small a falling away from the Lord, and also that it cannot attain the gift of this purity except by God's grace alone, since actual experience somehow or other teaches us that if we are anxious to reach abiding perfection of heart we must constantly endeavour to obtain the virtue of humility.

NOTES:
[222] Suo nos rursum quamvis quieto ac simplici visitans fluxu.

CHAPTER XVI.

Of the excitements of the flesh, without the humiliation of which we should fall more grievously.

TO the fact then that the pride which results from this purity would be more dangerous than all sins and wickednesses, and that we should on that account gain no reward for any height of perfect chastity, we may call as witnesses those powers of which we spoke before, which since it is believed that they experience no such fleshly lusts, were cast down from their high and heavenly estate in everlasting destruction simply from pride of heart. And so we should be altogether hopelessly lukewarm, since we should have no warning of carelessness on our part implanted either in our body or in our mind, nor should we ever strive to reach the glow of perfection, or even keep to strict frugality and abstinence, were it not that this excitement of the flesh springs up and humbles us and baffles us and makes us keen and anxious about purifying ourselves from spiritual sins.

CHAPTER XVII.

Of the lukewarmness of eunuchs.

LASTLY, on this account in those who are Eunuchs, we often detect the existence of this lukewarmness of mind, because, as they are so to speak free from the needs of the flesh, they fancy that they have no need either of the trouble of bodily abstinence, or of contrition of heart; and being rendered slack by this freedom from anxiety, they make no efforts either truly to seek or to acquire perfection of heart or even purity from spiritual faults. And this condition which is the result of their state in the flesh, becomes natural, which is altogether a worse state. For he who passes from the state of coldness to that of lukewarmness is branded by the Lord's words as still more hateful.

CHAPTER XVIII.

The question what is the difference between the carnal and natural man.

GERMANUS: You have, it seems to us, very clearly shown the value of the struggle which is raised between the flesh and spirit, so that we can believe that it can in a sort of way be grasped by us; and therefore we want to have this also explained to us in the same way; viz., what is the difference between the carnal and the natural man, or how the natural man can be worse than the carnal.

CHAPTER XIX.

The answer concerning the threefold condition of souls.

DANIEL: There are, according to the statements of Scripture, three kinds of souls; the first is the carnal, the second the natural, and the third the spiritual: which we find are thus described by the Apostle. For of the carnal he says: "I gave you milk to drink, not meat: for you were not able as yet. But neither indeed are you now able; for you are yet carnal." And again: "For whereas there is among you envying and contention, are you not carnal?"[223] Concerning the natural he also speaks as follows: "But the natural man perceiveth not the things that are of the spirit of God; for it is foolishness to him." But concerning the spiritual: "But the spiritual man judgeth all things: and he himself is judged by no man."[224] And again "You who are spiritual instruct such ones in the spirit of meekness."[225] And so, though at our renunciation we ceased to be carnal, i.e., we began to separate ourselves from intercourse with those in the world, and to have nothing to do with open pollution of the flesh, we must still be careful to strive with all our might to attain forthwith a spiritual condition, lest haply we flatter ourselves because we seem as far as the outer man is concerned to have renounced this world and got rid of the defilement of carnal fornication, as if by this we had reached the heights of perfection; and thence become careless and indifferent about purifying ourselves from other affections, and so being kept back between these two, become unable to reach the stage of spiritual advancement; either because we think that it is amply sufficient for our perfection if we seem to separate ourselves, as regards the outward man, from intercourse with this world and from its pleasure, or because we are free from corruption and carnal intercourse, and thus we find ourselves in that lukewarm condition which is considered the worst of all, and discover that we are spued out of the mouth of the Lord, in accordance with these words of His: "I would that thou wert hot or cold. But now thou art lukewarm and I will begin to spue thee out of My mouth."[226] And not without good reason does the Lord declare that those whom he has previously received in the bowels of His love, and who have become shamefully lukewarm, shall be spued out and rejected from His bosom: in as much as, though they might have yielded Him some health-giving subsistence, they preferred to be torn away from His heart: thus becoming far worse than those who had never found their way into the Lord's mouth as food, just as we turn away with loathing from that which nausea compels us to bring up. For whatever is cold is warmed when received into the mouth and is received with satisfaction and good results. But whatever has been once rejected owing to its miserable lukewarmness, we cannot--I will not say touch with the lips--but even look on from a distance without the greatest disgust. Rightly then is he said to be worse, because the carnal man, i.e., the worldly man and the heathen, is more readily brought to saving conversion and to the heights of perfection than one who has been professed as a monk, but has not, as his rule directs, laid hold on the way of perfection, and so has once for all drawn back from that fire of spiritual fervour. For the former is at last broken down by the sins of the flesh, and acknowledges his uncleanness, and in his compunction hastens from carnal pollution to the fountain of true cleansing, and the heights of perfection, and in his horror at that cold state of infidelity in which he finds himself, he is kindled with the fire of the spirit and flies the more readily to perfection. For one who has, as we said, once started with a lukewarm beginning, and has begun to abuse the name of monk, and who has not laid hold on the way of this profession with the humility and fervour that he ought, when once he is infected by this miserable plague, and is as it were unstrung by it, can no longer of himself discern what is perfect nor learn from the admonitions of another. For he says in his heart that which the Lord tells us: "Because I am rich and wealthy and want nothing;" and so this which follows is at once applied to him: "But thou art wretched, and miserable, and poor, and blind, and naked:"[227] and he is so far in a worse condition than a worldly man, because he has no idea that he is wretched or blind or naked or requires cleansing, or needs to be directed and taught by any one; and on this account he receives no sound advice as he does not realise that he is weighted with the name of monk, and is lowered in the judgment of all, whereas, though everybody believes him to be a saint and regards him as a servant of God, he must hereafter be subjected to a stricter judgment and punishment. Lastly, why should we any longer linger over those things which we have sufficiently discovered and proved by experience? We have often seen those who were cold and carnal, i.e., worldly men and heathen, attain spiritual warmth: but lukewarm and "natural" men never. And these too we read in the prophet are hated of the Lord, so that a charge is given to spiritual and learned men to desist from warning and teaching them, and not to sow the seed of the life-giving word in ground that is barren and unfruitful and choked by noxious thorns; but that they should scorn this, and rather cultivate fallow ground, i.e., that they should transfer all their care and teaching, and their zeal in the life-giving word to pagans and worldly men: as we thus read: "Thus saith the Lord to the men of Judah and inhabitants of Jerusalem: break up your fallow ground, and sow not among thorns." [228]

NOTES:
[223] 1 Cor. 3:2, 3.
[224] 1 Cor. 2:14, 15.
[225] Gal. 6:1.

[226] Rev. 3:15, 16.
[227] Rev. 3:17.
[228] Jer. 4:3.

CHAPTER XX.

Of those who renounce the world but ill.

IN the last place I am ashamed to say how we find that a large number have made their renunciation in such a way that we find that they have altered nothing of their former sins and habits, but only their state of life and worldly garb. For they are eager in amassing wealth which they never had before, or else do not give up that which they had, or which is still sadder, they actually strive to augment it under this excuse; viz., that they assert that it is right that they should always support with it their relations or the brethren, or they hoard it under pretence of starting congregations which they imagine that they can preside over as Abbots. But if only they would sincerely seek after the way of perfection, they would rather endeavour with all their might and main to attain to this: viz., that they might strip themselves not only of their wealth but of all their former likings and occupations, and place themselves unreservedly and entirely under the guidance of the Elders so as to have no anxiety not merely about others, but even about themselves. But on the contrary we find that while they are eager to be set over their brethren, they are never subject to their Elders themselves, and, with pride for their starting point, while they are quite ready to teach others they take no trouble to learn themselves or to practise what they are to teach: and so it is sure to end in their becoming, as the Saviour said, "blind leaders of the blind" so that "both fall into the ditch."[229] And this pride though there is only one kind of it, yet takes a twofold form. One form continually puts on the appearance of seriousness and gravity, the other breaks out with unbridled freedom into silly giggling and laughing. The former delights in not talking: the latter thinks it hard to be kept to the restraint of silence, and has no scruples about talking freely on matters that are unsuitable and foolish, while it is ashamed to be thought inferior to or less well informed than others. The one on account of pride seeks clerical office, the other looks down upon it, since it fancies that it is unsuitable or beneath its former dignity and life and the deserts of its birth. And which of these two should be accounted the worse each man must consider and decide for himself. At any rate the kind of disobedience is one and the same, if a man breaks the Elder's commands whether it be owing to zeal in work, or to love of ease: and it is as hurtful to upset the rules of the monastery for the sake of sleep, as it is for the sake of vigilance, and it is just the same to transgress the Abbot's orders in order to read, as it is to slight them in order to sleep: nor is there any difference in the incentive to pride if you neglect a brother, whether it is because of your fast or because of your breakfast: except that those faults which seem to show themselves under the guise of virtues and in the form of spirituality are worse and less likely to be cured than those which arise openly and from carnal pleasures. For these latter, like sicknesses which are perfectly plain and visible, are grappled with and cured, while the former, since they are covered under the cloak of virtue, remain uncured, and cause their victims to fall into a more dangerous and deadly state of ill health.

NOTES:
[229] Cf. S. Matt. 15:14.

CHAPTER XXI.

Of those who having made light of great things busy themselves about trifles.

FOR how can we show how absurd it is that we see that some men after their first enthusiasm of renunciation in which they forsook their estates and vast wealth and the service of the world, and betook themselves to the monasteries, are still earnestly devoted to those things which cannot altogether be cut off, and which we cannot do without in this state of life, even though they are small and trifling things; so that in their case the anxiety about these trifles is greater than their love of all their property. And it certainly will not profit them much that they have disregarded greater riches and property, if they have only transferred their affections (on account of which they were to make light of them) to small and trifling things. For the sin of covetousness and avarice of which they cannot be guilty in the matter of really valuable things, they retain with regard to commoner matters, and so show that they have not got rid of their former greed but only changed its object. For if they are too careful about their mats, baskets, blankets, books, and other trifles such as these, the same passion holds them captive as before. And they actually guard and defend their rights over them so jealously as to get angry with their brethren about them, and, what is worse, they are not ashamed to quarrel over them. And being still troubled by the bad effects of their former covetousness, they are not content to possess those things which the needs and requirements of the body compel a monk to have, according to the common number and measure, but here too they show the greediness of their heart, as they try to have those things which they are obliged to use, better got up than the others; or, exceeding all due bounds, keep as their special and peculiar property and guard from the touch of others that which ought to belong to all the brethren alike. As if the difference of metals, and not the passion of covetousness was what mattered; and as if it was wrong to be angry about big things, while one might innocently be about trifling matters: and as if we had not given up all our precious things just in order that we might learn more readily to think nothing about trifles! For what difference does it make whether one gives way to covetousness in the matter of large and splendid things, or in the matter of the merest trifles, except that we ought to think a man so far worse if he has made light of great things and then is a slave to little things? And so that sort of renunciation of the world does not attain perfection of heart, because though it ranks as poverty it still keeps the mind of wealth.

CONFERENCE 5.

Conference of Abbot Serapion
on the Eight Principal Faults

CHAPTER I.

Our arrival at Abbot Serapion's cell, and inquiry on the different kinds of faults and the way to overcome them.

IN that assembly of Ancients and Elders was a man named Serapion,[230] especially endowed with the grace of discretion, whose Conference I think it is worth while to set down in writing. For when we entreated him to discourse of the way to overcome our faults, so that their origin and cause might be made clearer to us, he thus began.

NOTES:

[230] Serapion when young was a pupil of Theonas, and an anecdote of his youthful indulgence in good things in secret has already been told in Conference II. c. xi. Another story of him is given in XVIII. xi. One of this name is mentioned by Palladius in the Lausiac History, c. lxxvi., and by Rufinus in the History of the Monks, c. xviii., where we are told that he lived at Arsinoee, and that he had ten thousand monks subject to his rule; a number which Sozomen also gives (H. E. VI. xxviii.). It is, however, doubtful whether this Serapion of Arsinoee is the person whose Conference Cassian here gives. Gazet identifies, Tillemont distinguishes the two. Jerome, it should be noticed, speaks in Ep. cviii. (Epistaphium Paulae) as if there was not only one of this name famous among the monks of Egypt at that time.

CHAPTER II.

Abbot Serapion's enumeration of eight principal faults.

THERE are eight principal faults which attack mankind; viz., first gastrimargia, which means gluttony, secondly fornication, thirdly philargyria, i.e., avarice or the love of money, fourthly anger, fifthly dejection, sixthly acedia, i.e., listlessness or low spirits, seventhly cenodoxia, i.e., boasting or vain glory; and eighthly pride.

CHAPTER III.

Of the two classes of faults and their fourfold manner of acting on us.

OF these faults then there are two classes. For they are either natural to us as gluttony, or arise outside of nature as covetousness. But their manner of acting on us is fourfold. For some cannot be consummated without an act on the part of the flesh, as gluttony and fornication, while some can be completed without any bodily act, as pride and vainglory. Some find the reasons for their being excited outside us, as covetousness and anger; others are aroused by internal feelings, as accidie[231] and dejection.

NOTES:
[231] For this word see the note on the Institutes V. i.

CHAPTER IV.

A review of the passions of gluttony and fornication and their remedies.

AND to make this clearer not only by a short discussion to the best of my ability, but by Scripture proof as well, gluttony and fornication, though they exist in us naturally (for sometimes they spring up without any incitement from the mind, and simply at the motion and allurement of the flesh) yet if they are to be consummated, must find an external object, and thus take effect only through bodily acts. For "every man is tempted of his own lust. Then lust when it has conceived beareth sin, and sin when it is consummated begets death."[232] For the first Adam could not have fallen a victim to gluttony unless he had had material food at hand, and had used it wrongly, nor could the second Adam be tempted without the enticement of some object, when it was said to Him: "If Thou art the Son of God, command that these stones be made bread."[233] And it is clear to everybody that fornication also is only completed by a bodily act, as God says of this spirit to the blessed Job: "And his force is in his loins, and his strength in the navel of his belly."[234] And so these two faults in particular, which are carried into effect by the aid of the flesh, especially require bodily abstinence as well as spiritual care of the soul; since the determination of the mind is not in itself enough to resist their attacks (as is sometimes the case with anger or gloominess or the other passions, which an effort of the mind alone can overcome without any mortification of the flesh); but bodily chastisement must be used as well, and be carried out by means of fasting and vigils and acts of contrition; and to this must be added change of scene, because since these sins are the results of faults of both mind and body, so they can only be overcome by the united efforts of both. And although the blessed Apostle says generally that all faults are carnal, since he enumerates enmities and anger and heresies among other works of the flesh,[235] yet in order to cure them and to discover their nature more exactly we make a twofold division of them: for we call some of them carnal, and some spiritual. And those we call carnal, which specially have to do with pampering the appetites of the flesh, and with which it is so charmed and satisfied, that sometimes it excites the mind when at rest and even drags it against its will to consent to its desire. Of which the blessed Apostle says: "In which also we all walked in time past in the desires of our flesh, fulfilling the will of the flesh and of our thoughts, and were by nature children of wrath even as the rest."[236] But we call those spiritual which spring only from the impulse of the mind and not merely contribute no pleasure to the flesh, but actually bring on it a weakness that is harmful to it, and only feed a diseased mind with the food of a most miserable pleasure. And therefore these need a single medicine for the heart: but those which are carnal can only be cured, as we said, by a double remedy. Whence it is extremely useful for those who aspire to purity, to begin by withdrawing from themselves the material which feeds these carnal passions, through which opportunity for or recollection of these same desires can arise in a soul that is still affected by the evil. For a complicated disease needs a complicated remedy. For from the body the object and material which would allure it must be withdrawn, for fear lest the lust should endeavour to break out into act; and before the mind we should no less carefully place diligent meditation on Scripture and watchful anxiety and the withdrawal into solitude, lest it should give birth to desire even in thought. But as regards other faults intercourse with our fellows is no obstacle, or rather it is of the greatest possible use, to those who truly desire to get rid of them, because in mixing with others they more often meet with rebuke, and while they are more frequently provoked the existence of the faults is made evident, and so they are cured with speedy remedies.

NOTES:
[232] S. James 1:14, 15.
[233] S. Matt. 4:3.
[234] Job 40:16.
[235] Cf. Gal. 5:19.
[236] Eph. 2:3.

CHAPTER V.

How our Lord alone was tempted without sin.

AND so our Lord Jesus Christ, though declared by the Apostle's word to have been tempted in all points like as we are, is yet said to have been "without sin,"[237] i.e., without the infection of this appetite, as He knew nothing of incitements of carnal lust, with which we are sure to be troubled even against our will and without our knowledge;[238] for the archangel thus describes the manner of His conception: "The Holy Ghost shall come upon thee and the power of the Most High shall overshadow thee: therefore that which shall be born of thee shall be called holy, the Son of God." [239]

NOTES:
[237] Heb. 4:15.
[238] The following from D. Mozley's profound work on the Augustinian Theory of Predestination may serve to illustrate the remarks in the text: "Scripture says that our Lord was in all points tempted like as we are. But the Church has not considered it consistent with piety to interpret this text to mean that our Lord had the same direct propension to sin that we have,

or that which is called by divines concupiscence. Such direct appetite for what is sinful is the characteristic of our fallen and corrupt nature; and our Lord did not assume a corrupt, but a sound humanity. Indeed, concupiscence, even prior to and independent of its gratification, has of itself the nature of sin; and therefore could not belong to a perfect Being. Our Lord had all the passions and affections that legitimately belong to man; which passions and affections, tending as they do in their own natures to become inordinate, constituted of themselves a state of trial; but the Church has regarded our Lord's trial as consisting in preserving ordinate affections from becoming inordinate, rather than in restraining desire proximate to sin from gratification" (p. 97).

[239] S. Luke 1:35.

CHAPTER VI.

Of the manner of the temptation in which our Lord was attacked by the devil.

FOR it was right that He who was in possession of the perfect image and likeness of God should be Himself tempted through those passions, through which Adam also was tempted while he still retained the image of God unbroken, that is, through gluttony, vainglory, pride; and not through those in which he was by his own fault entangled and involved after the transgression of the commandment, when the image and likeness of God was marred. For it was gluttony through which he took the fruit of the forbidden tree, vainglory through which it was said "Your eyes shall be opened," and pride through which it was said "Ye shall be as gods, knowing good and evil."[240] With these three sins then we read that the Lord our Saviour was also tempted; with gluttony when the devil said to Him: "Command these stones that they be made bread:" with vainglory: "If Thou art the Son of God cast Thyself down:" with pride, when he showed him all the kingdoms of the world and the glory of them and said: "All this will I give to Thee if Thou wilt fall down and worship me:"[241] in order that He might by His example teach us how we ought to vanquish the tempter when we are attacked on the same lines of temptation as He was. And so both the former and the latter are spoken of as Adam; the one being the first for destruction and death, and the other the first for resurrection and life. Through the one the whole race of mankind is brought into condemnation, through the other the whole race of mankind is set free. The one was fashioned out of raw and unformed earth, the other was born of the Virgin Mary. In His case then though it was fitting that He should undergo temptation, yet it was not necessary that He should fail under it. Nor could He who had vanquished gluttony be tempted by fornication, which springs from superfluity and gluttony as its root, with which even the first Adam would not have been destroyed unless before its birth he had been deceived by the wiles of the devil and fallen a victim to passion. And therefore the Son of God is not said absolutely to have come "in the flesh of sin," but "in the likeness of the flesh of sin," because though His was true flesh and He ate and drank and slept, and truly received the prints of the nails, there was in Him no true sin inherited from the fall, but only what was something like it. For He had no experience of the fiery darts of carnal lust, which in our case arise even against our will, from the constitution of our natures, but He took upon Him something like this, by sharing in our nature. For as He truly fulfilled every function which belongs to us, and bore all human infirmities, He has consequently been considered to have been subject to this feeling also, that He might appear through these infirmities to bear in His own flesh the state even of this fault and sin. Lastly the devil only tempted Him to those sins, by which he had deceived the first Adam, inferring that He as man would similarly be deceived in other matters if he found that He was overcome by those temptations by which he had overthrown His predecessor. But as he was overthrown in the first encounter he was not able to bring upon Him the second infirmity which had shot up as from the root of the first fault. For he saw that He had not even admitted anything from which this infirmity might take its rise, and it was idle to hope for the fruit of sin from Him, as he saw that He in no sort of way received into Himself seeds or roots of it. Yet according to Luke, who places last that temptation in which he uses the words "If Thou art the Son of God, cast Thyself down,"[242] we can understand this of the feeling of pride, so that that earlier one, which Matthew places third, in which, as Luke the evangelist says, the devil showed Him all the kingdoms of the world in a moment of time and promised them to Him, may be taken of the feeling of covetousness, because after His victory over gluttony, he did not venture to tempt Him to fornication, but passed on to covetousness, which he knew to be the root of all evils,[243] and when again vanquished in this, he did not dare attack Him with any of those sins which follow, which, as he knew full well, spring from this as a root and source; and so he passed on to the last passion; viz., pride, by which he knew that those who are perfect and have overcome all other sins, can be affected, and owing to which he remembered that he himself in his character of Lucifer, and many others too, had fallen from their heavenly estate, without temptation from any of the preceding passions. In this order then which we have mentioned, which is the one given by the evangelist Luke, there is an exact agreement between the allurements and forms of the temptations by which that most crafty foe attacked both the first and the second Adam. For to the one he said "Your eyes shall be opened;" to the other "he showed all the kingdoms of the world and the glory of them." In the one case he said "Ye shall be as gods;" in the other, "If Thou art the Son of God." [244]

NOTES:
[240] Gen. 3:5.
[241] Imaginarium.
[242] S. Luke 4:9.
[243] 1 Tim. 6:10.
[244] Cf. Gen. 3:5 with S. Matt. 4:6, 8.

CHAPTER VII.

How vainglory and pride can be consummated without any assistance from the body.

AND to go on in the order which we proposed, with our account of the way in which the other passions act (our analysis of which was obliged to be interrupted by this account of gluttony and of the Lord's temptation) vainglory and pride can be consummated even without the slightest assistance from the body. For in what way do those passions need any action of the flesh, which bring ample destruction on the soul they take captive simply by its assent and wish to gain praise and glory from men? Or what act on the part of the body was there in that pride of old in the case of the above mentioned Lucifer; as he only conceived it in his heart and mind, as the prophet tells us: "Who saidst in thine heart: I will ascend into heaven, I will set my throne above the stars of God. I will ascend above the heights of the clouds, I will be like the most High."[245] And just as he had no one to stir him up to this pride, so his thoughts alone were the authors of the sin when complete and of his eternal fall; especially as no exercise of the dominion at which he aimed followed.

NOTES:
[245] Is. 14:13, 14.

CHAPTER VIII.

Of covetousness, which is something outside our nature, and of the difference between it and those faults which are natural to us.

COVETOUSNESS and anger, although they are not of the same character (for the former is something outside our nature, while the latter seems to have as it were its seed plot within us) yet they spring up in the same way, as in most instances they find the reasons for their being stirred in something outside of us. For often men who are still rather weak complain that they have fallen into these sins through irritation and the instigation of others, and are plunged headlong into the passions of anger and covetousness by the provocation of other people. But that covetousness is something outside our nature, we can clearly see from this; viz., that it is proved not to have its first starting point inside us, nor does it originate in what contributes to keeping body and soul together, and to the existence of life. For it is plain that nothing belongs to the actual needs and necessities of our common life except our daily meat and drink: but everything else, with whatever zeal and care we preserve it, is shown to be something distinct from the wants of man by the needs of life itself. And so this temptation, as being something outside our nature, only attacks those monks who are but lukewarm and built on a bad foundation, whereas those which are natural to us do not cease from troubling even the best of monks and those who dwell in solitude. And so far is this shown to be true, that we find that there are some nations who are altogether free from this passion of covetousness, because they have never by use and custom received into themselves this fault and infirmity. And we believe that the old world before the flood was for long ages ignorant of the madness of this desire. And in the case of each one of us who makes his renunciation of the world a thorough one, we know that it is extirpated without any difficulty, if, that is, a man gives up all his property, and seeks the monastic discipline in such a way as not to allow himself to keep a single farthing. And we can find thousands of men to bear witness to this, who in a single moment have given up all their property, and have so thoroughly eradicated this passion as not to be in the slightest degree troubled by it afterwards, though all their life long they have to fight against gluttony, and cannot be safe from it without striving with the utmost watchfulness of heart and bodily abstinence.

CHAPTER IX.

How dejection and accidie generally arise without any external provocation, as in the case of other faults. [246]

DEJECTION and accidie generally arise without any external provocation, like those others of which we have been speaking: for we are well aware that they often harass solitaries, and those who have settled themselves in the desert without any intercourse with other men, and this in the most distressing way. And the truth of this any one who has lived in the desert and made trial of the conflicts of the inner man, can easily prove by experience.

NOTES:
[246] Such is the heading which Gazet gives. Petschenig edits "De ira atque tristitia, quod inter accedentia vitia plerumque [non] inveniantur;" where "non" is his own insertion, and as he frankly tells us, the heading does not suit the chapter.

CHAPTER X.

How six of these faults are related, and the two which differ from them are akin to one another.

OF these eight faults then, although they are different in their origin and in their way of affecting us, yet the six former; viz., gluttony, fornication, covetousness, anger, dejection, accidie, have a sort of connexion with each other, and are, so to speak, linked together in a chain, so that any excess of the one forms a starting point for the next. For from superfluity of gluttony fornication is sure to spring, and from fornication covetousness, from covetousness anger, from anger, dejection, and from dejection, accidie. And so we must fight against them in the same way, and with the same methods: and having overcome one, we ought always to enter the lists against the next. For a tall and spreading tree of a noxious kind will the more easily be made to wither if the roots on which it depends have first been laid bare or cut; and a pond of water which is dangerous will be dried up at once if the spring and flowing channel which produce it are carefully stopped up. Wherefore in order to overcome accidie, you must first get the better of dejection: in order to get rid of dejection, anger must first be expelled: in order to quell anger, covetousness must be trampled under foot: in order to root out covetousness, fornication must be checked: and in order to destroy fornication, you must chastise the sin of gluttony. But the two remaining faults; viz., vainglory and pride, are connected together in a somewhat similar way as the others of which we have spoken, so that the growth of the one makes a starting point for the other (for superfluity of vainglory produces an incentive to pride); but they are altogether different from the six former faults, and are not joined in the same category with them, since not only is there no opportunity given for them to spring up from these, but they are actually aroused in an entirely different way and manner. For when these others have been eradicated these latter flourish the more vigorously, and from the death of the others they shoot forth and grow up all the stronger: and therefore we are attacked by these two faults in quite a different way. For we fall into each one of those six faults at the moment when we have been overcome by the ones that went before them; but into these two we are in danger of falling when we have proved victorious, and above all after some splendid triumph. In the cases then of all faults just as they spring up from the growth of those that go before them, so are they eradicated by getting rid of the earlier ones. And in this way in order that pride may be driven out vainglory must be stifled, and so if we always overcome the earlier ones, the later ones will be checked; and through the extermination of those that lead the way, the rest of our passions will die down without difficulty. And though these eight faults of which we have spoken are connected and joined together in the way which we have shown, yet they may be more exactly divided into four groups and sub-divisions. For to gluttony fornication is linked by a special tie: to covetousness anger, to dejection accidie, and to vainglory pride is closely allied.

CHAPTER XI.

Of the origin and character of each of these faults.

AND now, to speak about each kind of fault separately: of gluttony there are three sorts: (1) that which drives a monk to eat before the proper and stated times; (2) that which cares about filling the belly and gorging it with all kinds of food, and (3) that which is on the look-out for dainties and delicacies. And these three sorts give a monk no little trouble, unless he tries to free himself from all of them with the same care and scrupulousness. For just as one should never venture to break one's fast before the right time so we must utterly avoid all greediness in eating, and the choice and dainty preparation of our food: for from these three causes different but extremely dangerous conditions of the soul arise. For from the first there springs up dislike of the monastery, and thence there grows up disgust and intolerance of the life there, and this is sure to be soon followed by withdrawal and speedy departure from it. By the second there are kindled the fiery darts of luxury and lasciviousness. The third also weaves the entangling meshes of covetousness for the nets of its prisoners, and ever hinders monks from following the perfect self-abnegation of Christ. And when there are traces of this passion in us we can recognize them by this; viz., if we are kept to dine by one of the brethren we are not content to eat our food with the relish which he has prepared and offers to us, but take the unpardonable liberty of asking to have something else poured over it or added to it, a thing which we should never do for three reasons: (1) because the monastic mind ought always to be accustomed to practise endurance and abstinence, and like the Apostle, to learn to be content in whatever state he is.[247] For one who is upset by taking an unsavoury morsel once and in a way, and who cannot even for a short time overcome the delicacy of his appetite will never succeed in curbing the secret and more important desires of the body; (2) because it sometimes happens that at the time our host is out of that particular thing which we ask for, and we make him feel ashamed of the wants and bareness of his table, by exposing his poverty which he would rather was only known to God; (3) because sometimes other people do not care about the relish which we ask for, and so it turns out that we are annoying most of them while intent on satisfying the desires of our own palate. And on this account we must by all means avoid such a liberty. Of fornication there are three sorts:

(1) that which is accomplished by sexual intercourse; (2) that which takes place without touching a woman, for which we read that Onan the son of the patriarch Judah was smitten by the Lord; and which is termed by Scripture uncleanness: of which the Apostle says: "But I say to the unmarried and to widows, that it is good for them if they abide even as I. But if they do not contain let them marry: for it is better to marry than to burn;"[248] (3) that which is conceived in heart and mind, of which the Lord says in the gospel: "Whosoever looketh on a woman to lust after her hath already committed adultery with her in his heart."[249] And these three kinds the blessed Apostle tells us must be stamped out in one and the same way. "Mortify," says he, "your members which are upon the earth, fornication, uncleanness, lust, etc."[250] And again of two of them he says to the Ephesians: "Let fornication and uncleanness be not so much as named among you:" and once more: "But know this that no fornicator or unclean person, or covetous person who is an idolater hath inheritance in the kingdom of Christ and of God."[251] And just as these three must be avoided by us with equal care, so they one and all shut us out and exclude us equally from the kingdom of Christ. Of covetousness there are three kinds: (1) That which hinders renunciants from allowing themselves of be stripped of their goods and property; (2) that which draws us to resume with excessive eagerness the possession of those things which we have given away and distributed to the poor; (3) that which leads a man to covet and procure what he never previously possessed. Of anger there are three kinds: one which rages within, which is called in Greek qumos; another which breaks out in word and deed and action, which they term orgh: of which the Apostle speaks, saying "But now do ye lay aside all anger and indignation;"[252] the third, which is not like those in boiling over and being done with in an hour, but which lasts for days and long periods, which is called mhnis. And all these three must be condemned by us with equal horror. Of dejection there are two kinds: one, that which springs up when anger has died down, or is the result of some loss we have incurred or of some purpose which has been hindered and interfered with; the other, that which comes from unreasonable anxiety of mind or from despair. Of accidie there are two kinds: one of which sends those affected by it to sleep; while the other makes them forsake their cell and flee away. Of vainglory, although it takes various forms and shapes, and is divided into different classes, yet there are two main kinds: (1) when we are puffed up about carnal things and things visible, and (2) when we are inflamed with the desire of vain praise for things spiritual and unseen.

NOTES:
[247] Cf. Phil. 4:11.
[248] 1 Cor. 7:8, 9.
[249] S. Matt. 5:28.
[250] Col. 3:5.
[251] Eph. 5:3-5.
[252] Col. 3:8.

CHAPTER XII.

How vainglory may be useful to us.

BUT in one matter vainglory is found to be a useful thing for beginners. I mean by those who are still troubled by carnal sins, as for instance, if, when they are troubled by the spirit of fornication, they formed an idea of the dignity of the priesthood, or of reputation among all men, by which they may be thought saints and immaculate: and so with these considerations they repel the unclean suggestions of lust, as deeming them base and at least unworthy of their rank and reputation; and so by means of a smaller evil they overcome a greater one. For it is better for a man to be troubled by the sin of vainglory than for him to fall into the desire for fornication, from which he either cannot recover at all or only with great difficulty after he has fallen. And this thought is admirably expressed by one of the prophets speaking in the person of God, and saying: "For My name's sake I will remove My wrath afar off: and with My praise I will bridle thee lest thou shouldest perish,"[253] i.e., while you are enchained by the praises of vainglory, you cannot possibly rush on into the depths of hell, or plunge irrevocably into the commission of deadly sins. Nor need we wonder that this passion has the power of checking anyone from rushing into the sin of fornication, since it has been again and again proved by many examples that when once a man has been affected by its poison and plague, it makes him utterly indefatigable, so that he scarcely feels a fast of even two or three days. And we have often known some who are living in this desert, confessing that when their home was in the monasteries of Syria they could without difficulty go for five days without food, while now they are so overcome with hunger even by the third hour, that they can scarcely keep on their daily fast to the ninth hour. And on this subject there is a very neat answer of Abbot

117

Macarius[254] to one who asked him why he was troubled with hunger as early as the third hour in the desert, when in the monastery he had often scorned food for a whole week, without feeling hungry. "Because," said he, "here there is nobody to see your fast, and feed and support you with his praise of you: but there you grew fat on the notice of others and the food of vainglory." And of the way in which, as we said, the sin of fornication is prevented by an attack of vainglory, there is an excellent and significant figure in the book of Kings, where, when the children of Israel had been taken captive by Necho, King of Egypt, Nebuchadnezzar, King of Assyria, came up and brought them back from the borders of Egypt to their own country, not indeed meaning to restore them to their former liberty and their native land, but meaning to carry them off to his own land and to transport them to a still more distant country than the land of Egypt in which they had been prisoners. And this illustration exactly applies to the case before us. For though there is less harm in yielding to the sin of vainglory than to fornication, yet it is more difficult to escape from the dominion of vainglory. For somehow or other the prisoner who is carried off to a greater distance, will have more difficulty in returning to his native land and the freedom of his fathers, and the prophet's rebuke will be deservedly aimed at him: "Wherefore art thou grown old in a strange country?[255] since a man is rightly said to have grown old in a strange country, if he has not broken up the ground of his faults. Of pride there are two kinds: (1) carnal, and (2) spiritual, which is the worse. For it especially attacks those who are seen to have made progress in some good qualities.

NOTES:
[253] Is. 48:9.
[254] Cf. note on the Institutes V. xli.
[255] Baruch 3:11.

CHAPTER XIII.

Of the different ways in which all these faults assault us.

ALTHOUGH then these eight faults trouble all sorts of men, yet they do not attack them all in the same way. For in one man the spirit of fornication holds the chief place: wrath rides rough shod over another: over another vainglory claims dominion: in an other pride holds the field: and though it is clear that we are all attacked by all of them, yet the difficulties come to each of us in very different ways and manners.

CHAPTER XIV.

Of the struggle into which we must enter against our faults, when they attack us.

WHEREFORE we must enter the lists against these faults in such a way that every one should discover his besetting sin, and direct his main attack against it, directing all his care and watchfulness of mind to guard against its assault, directing against it daily the weapons of fasting, and at all times hurling against it the constant darts of sighs and groanings from the heart, and employing against it the labours of vigils and the meditation of the heart, and further pouring forth to God constant tears and prayers and continually and expressly praying to be delivered from its attack. For it is impossible for a man to win a triumph over any kind of passion, unless he has first clearly understood that he cannot possibly gain the victory in the struggle with it by his own strength and efforts, although in order that he may be rendered pure he must night and day persist in the utmost care and watchfulness. And even when he feels that he has got rid of this fault, he should still search the inmost recesses of his heart with the same purpose, and single out the worst fault which he can see among those still there, and bring all the forces of the Spirit to bear against it in particular, and so by always overcoming the stronger passions, he will gain a quick and easy victory over the rest, because by a course of triumphs the soul is made more vigorous, and the fact that the next conflict is with weaker passion insures him a readier success in the struggle: as is generally the case with those who are wont to face all kinds of wild beasts in the presence of the kings of this world, out of consideration for the rewards--a kind of spectacle which is generally called "pancarpus."[256] Such men, I say, direct their first assault against whatever beasts they see to be the strongest and fiercest, and when they have despatched these, then they can more easily lay low the remaining ones, which are not so terrible and powerful. So too, by always overcoming the stronger passions, as weaker ones take their place, a perfect victory will be secured for us without any risk. Nor need we imagine that if any one grapples with one fault in particular, and seems too careless about guarding against the attacks of others, he will be easily wounded by a sudden assault, for this cannot possibly happen. For where a man is anxious to cleanse his heart, and has steeled his heart's purpose against the attack of any one fault, it is impossible for him not to have a general dread of all other faults as well, and take similar care of them. For if a man renders himself unworthy of the prize of purity by contaminating himself with other faults, how can he possibly succeed in gaining the victory over that one passion from which he is longing to be freed? But when the main purpose of our heart has singled out one passion as the special object of its attack, we shall pray about it more earnestly, and with special anxiety and fervour shall entreat that we may be more especially on our guard against it and so succeed in gaining a speedy victory. For the giver of the law himself teaches us that we ought to follow this plan in our conflicts and not to trust in our own power; as he says: "Thou shalt not fear them because the Lord thy God is in the midst of thee, a God mighty and terrible: He will consume these nations in thy sight by little and little and by degrees. Thou wilt not be able to destroy them altogether: lest perhaps the beasts of the earth should increase upon thee. But the Lord thy God shall deliver them in thy sight; and shall slay them until they be utterly destroyed." [257]

NOTES:

[256] Pancarpus (pagkarpos). The word was originally applied to an offering of all kinds of fruit. Cf. Tertullian ad Valent. xii. It is also used in the general sense "of all sorts" by Augustine, Adv. Secund. xxiii. Cassian here speaks as if it had become the popular name for the conflicts of gladiators with all kinds of beasts, though there is apparently no other authority for this.

[257] Deut. 7:21-23.

CHAPTER XV.

How we can do nothing against our faults without the help of God, and how we should not be puffed up by victories over them.

AND that we ought not to be puffed up by victories over them he likewise charges us; saying, "Lest after thou hast eaten and art filled, hast built goodly houses and dwelt in them, and shalt have herds of oxen and flocks of sheep, and plenty of gold and of silver, and of all things, thy heart be lifted up and thou remember not the Lord thy God, who brought thee out of the land of Egypt, out of the house of bondage; and was thy leader in the great and terrible wilderness."[258] Solomon also says in Proverbs: "When thine enemy shall fall be not glad, and in his ruin be not lifted up, lest the Lord see and it displease Him, and He turn away His wrath from him,"[259] i.e., lest He see thy pride of heart, and cease from attacking him, and thou begin to be forsaken by Him and so once more to be troubled by that passion which by God's grace thou hadst previously overcome. For the prophet would not have prayed in these words, "Deliver not up to beasts, O Lord, the soul that confesseth to Thee,"[260] unless he had known that because of their pride of heart some were given over again to those faults which they had overcome, in order that they might be humbled. Wherefore it is well for us both to be certified by actual experience, and also to be instructed by countless passages of Scripture, that we cannot possibly overcome such mighty foes in our own strength, and unless supported by the aid of God alone; and that we ought always to refer the whole of our victory each day to God Himself, as the Lord Himself also gives us instruction by Moses on this very point: "Say not in thine heart when the Lord thy God shall have destroyed them in thy sight: For my righteousness hath the Lord brought me in to possess this land, whereas these nations are destroyed for their wickedness. For it is not for thy righteousness, and the uprightness of thine heart, that thou shalt go in to possess their lands: but because they have done wickedly they are destroyed at thy coming in."[261] I ask what could be said clearer in opposition to that impious notion and impertinence of ours, in which we want to ascribe everything that we do to our own free will and our own exertions? "Say not," he tells us, "in thine heart, when the Lord thy God shall have destroyed them in thy sight: For my righteousness the Lord hath brought me in to possess this land." To those who have their eyes opened and their ears ready to hearken does not this plainly say: When your struggle with carnal faults has gone well for you, and you see that you are free from the filth of them, and from the fashions of this world, do not be puffed up by the success of the conflict and victory and ascribe it to your own power and wisdom, nor fancy that you have gained the victory over spiritual wickedness and carnal sins through your own exertions and energy, and free will? For there is no doubt that in all this you could not possibly have succeeded, unless you had been fortified and protected by the help of the Lord.

121

NOTES:
[258] Deut. 8:12-15.
[259] Prov. 24:17, 18 (LXX).
[260] Ps. 73 (74):19.
[261] Deut. 9:4, 5.

CHAPTER XVI.

Of the meaning of the seven nations of whose lands Israel took possession, and the reason why they are sometimes spoken of as "seven," and sometimes as "many."

THESE are the seven nations whose lands the Lord promised to give to the children of Israel when they came out of Egypt. And everything which, as the Apostle says, happened to them "in a figure"[262] we ought to take as written for our correction. For so we read: "When the Lord thy God shall have brought thee into the land, which thou art going in to possess, and shall have destroyed many nations before thee, the Hittite, and the Girgashites, and the Amorite, the Canaanite, and the Perizzite, and the Hivite, and the Jebusite, seven nations much more numerous than thou art and much stronger than thou: and the Lord thy God shall have delivered them to thee, thou shalt utterly destroy them."[263] And the reason that they are said to be much more numerous, is that faults are many more in number than virtues and so in the list of them the nations are reckoned as seven in number, but when the attack upon them is spoken of they are set down without their number being given, for thus we read "And shall have destroyed many nations before thee." For the race of carnal passions which springs from this sevenfold incentive and root of sin, is more numerous than that of Israel. For thence spring up murders, strifes, heresies, thefts, false witness, blasphemy, surfeiting, drunkenness, back-biting, buffoonery, filthy conversation, lies, perjury, foolish talking, scurrility, restlessness, greediness, bitterness, clamour, wrath, contempt, murmuring, temptation, despair, and many other faults, which it would take too long to describe. And if we are inclined to think these small matters, let us hear what the Apostle thought about them, and what was his opinion of them: "Neither murmur ye," says he, "as some of them murmured, and were destroyed of the destroyer:" and of temptation: "Neither let us tempt Christ as some of them tempted and perished by the serpents."[264] Of backbiting: "Love not backbiting lest thou be rooted out."[265] And of despair: "Who despairing have given themselves up to lasciviousness unto the working of all error, in uncleanness."[266] And that clamour is condemned as well as anger and indignation and blasphemy, the words of the same Apostle teach us as clearly as possible when he thus charges us: "Let all bitterness, and anger, and indignation, and clamour, and blasphemy be put away from you with all malice,"[267] and many more things like these. And though these are far more numerous than the virtues are, yet if those eight principal sins, from which we know that these naturally proceed, are first overcome, all these at once sink down, and are destroyed together with them with a lasting destruction. For from gluttony proceed surfeiting and drunkenness. From fornication filthy conversation, scurrility, buffoonery and foolish talking. From covetousness, lying, deceit, theft, perjury, the desire of filthy lucre, false witness, violence, inhumanity, and greed. From anger, murders, clamour and indignation. From dejection, rancor, cowardice, bitterness, despair. From accidie, laziness, sleepiness, rudeness, restlessness, wandering about, instability both of mind and body, chattering, inquisitiveness. From vainglory, contention, heresies, boasting and confidence in novelties. From pride, contempt, envy, disobedience, blasphemy, murmuring, backbiting. And that all these plagues are stronger than we, we can tell very plainly from the way in which they attack us. For the delight in carnal passions wars more powerfully in our members than does the desire for virtue, which is only gained with the greatest contrition of heart and body. But if you will only gaze with the eyes of the spirit on those countless hosts of our foes, which the Apostle enumerates where he says: "For we wrestle not against flesh and blood, but against principalities, against powers, against the world-rulers of this darkness, against spiritual wickedness in heavenly places,"[268] and this which we find of the righteous man in the ninetieth Psalm: "A thousand shall fall beside thee and ten thousand at thy right hand,"[269] then you will clearly see that they are far more numerous and more powerful than are we, carnal and earthly creatures as we are, while to them is given a substance which is spiritual and incorporeal.

NOTES:
[262] Cf. 1 Cor. 10:6.
[263] Deut. 7:1, 2.
[264] 1 Cor. 10:9, 10.
[265] Prov. 20:13 (LXX).
[266] Eph. 4:19.
[267] Eph. 4:31.

CHAPTER XVII.

A question with regard to the comparison of seven nations with eight faults.

GERMANUS: How then is it that there are eight faults which assault us, when Moses reckons the nations opposed to the people of Israel as seven, and how is it well for us to take possession of the territory of our faults?

CHAPTER XVIII.

The answer how the number of eight nations is made up in accordance with the eight faults.

SERAPION: Everybody is perfectly agreed that there are eight principal faults which affect a monk. And all of them are not included in the figure of the nations for this reason, because in Deuteronomy Moses, or rather the Lord through him, was speaking to those who had already gone forth from Egypt and been set free from one most powerful nation, I mean that of the Egyptians. And we find that this figure holds good also in our case, as when we have got clear of the snares of this world we are found to be free from gluttony, i.e., the sin of the belly and palate; and like them we have a conflict against these seven remaining nations, without taking account at all of the one which has been already overcome. And the land of this nation was not given to Israel for a possession, but the command of the Lord ordained that they should at once forsake it and go forth from it. And for this cause our fasts ought to be made moderate, that there may be no need for us through excessive abstinence, which results from weakness of the flesh and infirmity, to return again to the land of Egypt, i.e., to our former greed and carnal lust which we forsook when we made our renunciation of this world. And this has happened in a figure, in those who after having gone forth into the desert of virtue again hanker after the flesh pots over which they sat in Egypt.

CHAPTER XIX.

The reason why one nation is to be forsaken, while seven are commanded to be destroyed.

BUT the reason why that nation in which the children of Israel were born, was bidden not to be utterly destroyed but only to have its land forsaken, while it was commanded that these seven nations were to be completely destroyed, is this: because however great may be the ardour of spirit, inspired by which we have entered on the desert of virtues, yet we cannot possibly free ourselves entirely from the neighbourhood of gluttony or from its service and, so to speak, from daily intercourse with it. For the liking for delicacies and dainties will live on as something natural and innate in us, even though we take pains to cut off all superfluous appetites and desires, which, as they cannot be altogether destroyed, ought to be shunned and avoided. For of these we read "Take no care for the flesh with its desires."[270] While then we still retain the feeling for this care, which we are bidden not altogether to cut off, but to keep without its desires, it is clear that we do not destroy the Egyptian nation but separate ourselves in a sort of way from it, not thinking anything about luxuries and delicate feasts, but, as the Apostle says, being "content with our daily food and clothing."[271] And this is commanded in a figure in the law, in this way: "Thou shalt not abhor the Egyptian, because thou wast a stranger in his land."[272] For necessary food is not refused to the body without danger to it and sinfulness in the soul. But of those seven troublesome faults we must in every possible way root out the affections from the inmost recesses of our souls. For of them we read: "Let all bitterness and anger and indignation and clamour and blasphemy be put away from you with all malice:" and again: "But fornication and all uncleanness and covetousness let it not so much as be named among you, or obscenity or foolish talking or scurrility."[273] We can then cut out the roots of these faults which are grafted into our nature from without while we cannot possibly cut off occasions of gluttony. For however far we have advanced, we cannot help being what we were born. And that this is so we can show not only from the lives of little people like ourselves but from the lives and customs of all who have attained perfection, who even when they have got rid of incentives to all other passions, and are retiring to the desert with perfect fervour of spirit and bodily abnegation, yet still cannot do without thought for their daily meal and the preparation of their food from year to year.

NOTES:
[270] Rom. 13:14.
[271] Cf. 1 Tim. 6:8.
[272] Deut. 23:7.
[273] Eph. 4:31; 5:3, 4.

CHAPTER XX.

Of the nature of gluttony, which may be illustrated by the simile of the eagle.

AN admirable illustration of this passion, with which a monk, however spiritual and excellent, is sure to be hampered, is found in the simile of the eagle. For this bird when in its flight on high it has soared above the highest clouds, and has withdrawn itself from the eyes of all mortals and from the face of the whole earth, is yet compelled by the needs of the belly to drop down and descend to the earth and feed upon carrion and dead bodies. And this clearly shows that the spirit of gluttony cannot be altogether extirpated like all other faults, nor be entirely destroyed like them, but that we can only hold down and check by the power of the mind all incentives to it and all superfluous appetites.

CHAPTER XXI.

Of the lasting character of gluttony as described to some philosophers.

FOR the nature of this fault was admirably expressed under cover of the following puzzle by one of the Elders in a discussion with some philosophers, who thought that they might chaff him like a country bumpkin because of his Christian simplicity. "My father," said he, "left me in the clutches of a great many creditors. All the others I have paid in full, and have freed myself from all their pressing claims; but one I cannot satisfy even by a daily payment." And when they could not see the meaning of the puzzle, and urgently begged him to explain it: "I was," said he, "in my natural condition, encompassed by a great many faults. But when God inspired me with the longing to be free, I renounced this world, and at the same time gave up all my property which I had inherited from my father, and so I satisfied them all like pressing creditors, and freed myself entirely from them. But I was never able altogether to get rid of the incentives to gluttony. For though I reduce the quantity of food which I take to the smallest possible amount, yet I cannot avoid the force of its daily solicitations, but must be perpetually `dunned' by it, and be making as it were interminable payments by continually satisfying it, and pay never ending toll at its demand." Then they declared that this man, whom they had till now despised as a booby and a country bumpkin, had thoroughly grasped the first principles of philosophy, i.e., training in ethics, and they marvelled that he could by the light of nature have learnt that which no schooling in this world could have taught him, while they themselves with all their efforts and long course of training had not learnt this. This is enough on gluttony in particular. Now let us return to the discourse in which we had begun to consider the general relation of our faults to each other.

CHAPTER XXII.

How it was that God foretold to Abraham that Israel would have to drive out ten nations.

WHEN the Lord was speaking with Abraham about the future (a point which you did not ask about) we find that He did not enumerate seven nations, but ten, whose land He promised to give to his seed.[274] And this number is plainly made up by adding idolatry, and blasphemy, to whose dominion, before the knowledge of God and the grace of Baptism, both the irreligious hosts of the Gentiles and blasphemous ones of the Jews were subject, while they dwelt in a spiritual Egypt. But when a man has made his renunciation and come forth from thence, and having by God's grace conquered gluttony, has come into the spiritual wilderness, then he is free from the attacks of these

three, and will only have to wage war against those seven which
Moses enumerates.

NOTES:
[274] Cf. Gen. 15:18-21.

CHAPTER XXIII.

How it is useful for us to take possession of their lands.

BUT the fact that we are bidden for our good to take possession
of the countries of those most wicked nations, may be understood in
this way. Each fault has its own especial corner in the heart, which it
claims for itself in the recesses of the soul, and drives out Israel, i.e.,
the contemplation of holy and heavenly things, and never ceases to
oppose them. For virtues cannot possibly live side by side with faults.
"For what participation hath righteousness with unrighteousness? Or
what fellowship hath light with darkness?"[275] But as soon as these
faults have been overcome by the people of Israel, i.e., by those virtues
which war against them, then at once the place in our heart which the
spirit of concupiscence and fornication had occupied, will be filled by
chastity. That which wrath had held, will be claimed by patience. That
which had been occupied by a sorrow that worketh death, will be taken
by a godly sorrow and one full of joy. That which had been wasted by
accidie, will at once be tilled by courage. That which pride had trodden down will be ennobled by humility: and so when each of these
faults has been expelled, their places (that is the tendency towards
them) will be filled by the opposite virtues which are aptly termed the
children of Israel, that is, of the soul that seeth God:[276] and when these
have expelled all passions from the heart we may believe that they
have recovered their own possessions rather than invaded those of others.

NOTES:
[275] 2 Cor. 6:14.
[276] Cf. the note on Against Nestorius VII. ix.

CHAPTER XXIV.

How the lands from which the Canaanites were expelled, had been assigned to the seed of Shem.

FOR, as an ancient tradition tells us,[277] these same lands of the Canaanites into which the children of Israel were brought, had been formerly allotted to the children of Shem at the division of the world, and afterward the descendants of Ham wickedly invading them with force and violence took possession of them. And in this the righteous judgment of God is shown, as He expelled from the land of others these who had wrongfully taken possession of them, and restored to those others the ancient property of their fathers which had been assigned to their ancestors at the division of the world. And we can perfectly well see that this figure holds good in our own case. For by nature God's will assigned the possession of our heart not to vices but to virtues, which, after the fall of Adam were driven out from their own country by the sins which grew up, i.e., by the Canaanites; and so when by God's grace they are by our efforts and labour restored again to it, we may hold that they have not occupied the territory of another, but rather have recovered their own country.

NOTES:
[277] The "ancient tradition" to which Cassian here alludes is given in the Clementine Recognitions I. xxix., xxx.; and in Epiphanius "Heresies," c. lxvi. S: 83, sq., where it is given as an answer to the Manichaean objection against the cruelty and injustice of the extermination of the Canaanites by the Israelites.

CHAPTER XXV.

Different passages of Scripture on the meaning of the eight faults.

AND in reference to these eight faults we also have the following in the gospel: "But when the unclean spirit is gone out from a man, he walketh through dry places seeking rest and findeth none. Then he saith, I will return to my house from whence I came out: and coming he findeth it empty, swept, and garnished: then he goeth and taketh seven other spirits worse than himself, and they enter in and dwell there: and the last state of that man is made worse than the first."[278] Lo, just as in the former passages we read of seven nations besides that of the Egyptians from which the children of Israel had gone forth, so here too seven unclean spirits are said to return beside that one which we first hear of as going forth from the man. And of this sevenfold incentive of sins Solomon gives the following account in Proverbs: "If thine enemy speak loud to thee, do not agree to him because there are seven mischiefs in his heart;"[279] i.e., if the spirit of gluttony is overcome and begins to flatter you with having humiliated it, asking in a sort of way that you would relax something of the fervour with which you began, and yield to it something beyond what the due limits of abstinence, and measure of strict severity would allow, do not you be overcome by its submission, nor return in fancied security from its assaults, as you seem to have become for a time freed from carnal desires, to your previous state of carelessness or former liking for good things. For through this the spirit whom you have vanquished is saying "I will return to my house from whence I came out," and forthwith the seven spirits of sins which proceed from it will prove to you more injurious than that passion which in the first instance you overcame, and will presently drag you down to worse kinds of sins.

NOTES:
[278] S. Matt. 12:43-45.
[279] Prov. 26:25 (LXX).

CHAPTER XXVI.

How when we have got the better of the passion of gluttony we must take pains to gain all the other virtues.

WHEREFORE while we are practising fasting and abstinence, we must be careful when we have got the better of the passion of gluttony never to allow our mind to remain empty of the virtues of which we stand in need; but we should the more earnestly fill the inmost recesses of our heart with them for fear lest the spirit of concupiscence should return and find us empty and void of them, and should not be content to secure an entrance there for himself alone, but should bring in with him into our heart this sevenfold incentive of sins and make our last state worse than the first. For the soul which boasts that it has renounced this world with the eight faults that hold sway over it, will afterwards be fouler and more unclean and visited with severer punishments, than it was when formerly it was at home in the world, when it had taken upon itself neither the rules nor the name of monk. For these seven spirits are said to be worse than the first which went forth, for this reason; because the love of good things, i.e., gluttony would not be in itself harmful, were it not that it opened the door to other passions; viz, to fornication, covetousness, anger, dejection, and pride, which are clearly hurtful in themselves to the soul, and domineering over it. And therefore a man will never be able to gain perfect purity, if he hopes to secure it by means of abstinence alone, i.e., bodily fasting, unless he knows that he ought to practise it for this reason that when the flesh is brought low by means of fasting, he may with greater ease enter the lists against other faults, as the flesh has not been habituated to gluttony and surfeiting.

CHAPTER XXVII.

That our battles are not fought with our faults in the same order as that in which they stand in the list.

BUT you must know that our battles are not all fought in the same order, because, as we mentioned that the attacks are not always made on us in the same way, each one of us ought also to begin the battle with due regard to the character of the attack which is especially made on him so that one man will have to fight his first battle against the fault which stands third on the list, another against that which is fourth or fifth. And in proportion as faults hold sway over us, and the character of their attack may demand, so we too ought to regulate the order of our conflict, in such a way that the happy result of a victory and triumph succeeding may insure our attainment of purity of heart and complete perfection.

Thus far did Abbot Serapion discourse to us of the nature of the eight principal faults, and so clearly did he expound the different sorts of passions which are latent within us--the origin and connexion of which, though we were daily tormented by them, we could never before thoroughly understand and perceive--that we seemed almost to see them spread out before our eyes as in a mirror.

CONFERENCE 6.

Conference of Abbot Theodore [280]
on the Death of the Saints

CHAPTER I.

Description of the wilderness, and the question about the death of the saints.

IN the district of Palestine near the village of Tekoa which had the honour of producing the prophet Amos,[281] there is a vast desert which stretches far and wide as far as Arabia and the dead sea, into which the streams of Jordan enter and are lost, and where are the ashes of Sodom. In this district there lived for a long while monks of the most perfect life and holiness, who were suddenly destroyed by an incursion of Saracen robbers:[282] whose bodies we knew were seized upon with the greatest veneration[283] both by the Bishops of the neighbourhood and by the whole populace of Arabia, and deposited among the relics of the martyrs, so that swarms of people from two towns met, and made terrible war upon each other, and in their struggle actually came to blows for the possession of the holy spoil, while they strove among themselves with pious zeal as to which of them had the better claim to bury them and keep their relics--the one party boasting of their vicinity to the place of their abode, the other of the fact that they were near the place of their birth. But we were upset by this and being disturbed either on our own account or on account of some of the brethren who were in no small degree scandalized at it, inquired why men of such illustrious merits and of so great virtues should be thus slain by robbers, and why the Lord permitted such a crime to be committed against his servants, so as to give up into the hands of wicked men those who were the admiration of everybody: and so in our grief we came to the holy Theodore, a man who excelled in practical common sense. For he was living in Cellae,[284] a place that lies between Nitria and Scete, and is five miles distant from the monasteries of Nitria, and cut off by eighty intervening miles of desert from the wilderness of Scete where we were living. And when we had made our complaint to him about the death of the men mentioned above, and expressed our surprise at the great patience of God, because He suffered men of such worth to be killed in this way, so that those who ought to be able by the weight of their sanctity to deliver others from trials of this kind, could not save themselves from the hands of wicked men (and asked) why it was that God allowed so great a crime to be committed against his servants, then the blessed Theodore replied.

NOTES:

[281] Cf. Amos 1:1.

[282] Saraceni (Sarakhnoi): a name given by the classical geographers to a tribe of Arabia Felix, famous for its predatory propensities. Jerome speaks of the "mons et desertum Saracenorum quod vocatur Pharan" (Liber de situ nominibus sub voce Choreb) and elsewhere describes their predatory habits (Liber Heb.Quaest. in Genesim) "Saracenos vagos . . . qui universas gentes . . . incursant." By the seventh century the name had become a merely general name equivalent to Arab, and was accordingly adopted and applied indifferently to all the followers of Mohammed by the writers of the middle ages (cf. the Dictionary of Greek and Roman Geography, sub voce).

[283] There is no mention of these martyrs in the so-called Martyrologium Hieronymianum, but they are commemorated on May 28, in the Roman Martyrology.

[284] Cellae, which was, according to the passage before us, between the deserts of Scete and Nitria, apparently derived its name from the cells of the monks who congregated there. This at least is the explanation of the name given by Sozomen (H. E. VI. xxxi.) who speaks of a region called Kellia, throughout which numerous little dwellings (oikhmata) are dispersed, whence it obtains its name. Sozomen also speaks (c. xxix.) of Macarius as priest of Cellae, a fact which gives some ground for conjecturing that Cellae may be identified with Dair Abu Makar, one of the four monasteries still existing in the deserts of Nitria and Scete, probably founded by the saint whose name it bears (Macarius). See A. J. Butler's "Coptic Churches of Egypt," vol. i. c. vii.

CHAPTER II.

Abbot Theodore's answer to the question proposed to him.

THIS question often exercises the minds of those who have not much faith or knowledge, and imagine that the prizes and rewards of the saints (which are not given in this world, but laid up for the future) are bestowed in the short space of this mortal life. But we whose hope in Christ is not only in this life, for fear lest, as the Apostle says, we should be "of all men most miserable"[285] (because as we receive none of the promises in this world we should for our unbelief lose them also in that to come) ought not wrongly to follow their ideas, lest through ignorance of the true real explanation, we should hesitate and tremble and fail in temptation, if we find ourselves given up to such men; and should ascribe to God injustice or carelessness about the affairs of mankind--a thing which it is almost a sin to mention--because He does not protect in their temptations men who are living an upright and holy life, nor requite good men with good things and evil men with evil things in this world; and so we should deserve to fall under the con-demnation of those whom the prophet Zephaniah rebukes, saying "who say in their hearts the Lord will not do good, nor will He do evil:"[286] or at least be found among those of whom we are told that they blaspheme God with such complaints as this: "Every one that doeth evil is good in the sight of the Lord, and such please Him: for surely where is the God of judgment?"[287] Adding further that blas-phemy which is described in the same way in what follows: "He laboureth in vain that serveth God, and what profit is it that we have kept His ordinances, and walked sorrowful before the Lord? Where-fore now we call the proud happy, for they that work wickedness are enriched, and they have tempted God, and are preserved."[288] Where-fore that we may avoid this ignorance which is the root and cause of this most deadly error, we ought in the first place to know what is really good, and what is bad, and so finally if we grasp the true scrip-tural meaning of these words, and not the false popular one, we shall escape being deceived by the errors of unbelievers.

NOTES:
[285] 1 Cor. 15:19.
[286] Zeph. 1:12.
[287] Mal. 2:17.
[288] Mal. 3:14, 15.

CHAPTER III.

Of the three kinds of things there are in the world; viz., good, bad, and indifferent.

ALTOGETHER there are three kinds of things in the world; viz., good, bad, and indifferent. And so we ought to know what is properly good, and what is bad, and what is indifferent, that our faith may be supported by true knowledge and stand firm in all temptations. We must then believe that in things which are merely human there is no real good except virtue of soul alone, which leads us with unfeigned faith to things divine, and makes us constantly adhere to that unchanging good. And on the other hand we ought not to call anything bad, except sin alone, which separates us from the good God, and unites us to the evil devil. But those things are indifferent which can be appropriated to either side according to the fancy or wish of their owner, as for instance riches, power, honour, bodily strength, good health, beauty, life itself, and death, poverty, bodily infirmities, injuries, and other things of the same sort, which can contribute either to good or to evil as the character and fancy of their owner directs. For riches are often serviceable for our good, as the Apostle says, who charges "the rich of this world to be ready to give, to distribute to the needy, to lay up in store for themselves a good foundation against the time to come, that" by this means "they may lay hold on the true life."[289] And according to the gospel they are a good thing for those who "make to themselves friends of the unrighteous mammon."[290] And again, they can be drawn in the direction of what is bad when they are amassed only for the sake of hoarding them or for a life of luxury, and are not employed to meet the wants of the poor. And that power also and honour and bodily strength and good health are indifferent and available for either (good or bad) can easily be shown from the fact that many of the Old Testament saints enjoyed all these things and were in positions of great wealth and the highest honour, and blessed with bodily strength, and yet are known to have been most acceptable to God. And on the contrary those who have wrongfully abused these things and perverted them for their own purposes are not without good reason punished or destroyed, as the Book of Kings shows us has often happened. And that even life and death are in themselves indifferent the birth of S. John and of Judas proves. For in the case of the one his life was so profitable to himself that we are told that his birth brought joy to others also, as we read "And many shall rejoice at his birth;"[291] but of the life of the other it is said: "It were good for that man if he had never been born."[292] Further it is said of the death of John and of all saints "Right dear in the sight of the Lord is the death of His saints:"[293] but of that of Judas and men like him "The death of the wicked is very evil."[294] And how useful bodily sickness sometimes may be the blessing on Lazarus, the beggar who was full of sores, shows us. For Scripture makes mention of no other good qualities or deserts of his, but it was for this fact alone; viz., that he endured want and bodily sickness with the utmost patience, that he was deemed worthy of the blessed lot of a place in Abraham's bosom.[295] And with regard to want and persecution and injuries which everybody thinks to be bad, how useful and necessary they are is clearly proved by this fact; viz., that the saints not only never tried to avoid them, but actually either sought them with all their powers or bravely endured them, and thus became the friends of God, and obtained the reward of eternal life, as the blessed Apostle chants: "For which cause I delight myself in my infirmities, in reproaches, in necessities, in persecutions, in distresses for Christ. For when I am weak, then I am strong, for power is made perfect in infirmity."[296] And therefore those who are exalted with the greatest riches and honours and powers of this world, should not be deemed to have secured their chief good out of them (for this is shown to consist only in virtue) but only something indifferent, because just as to good men who use them well and properly they will be found to be useful and convenient (for they afford them opportunities for good works and fruits which shall endure to eternal life), so to those who wrongfully abuse their wealth, they are useless and out of place, and furnish occasions of sin and death.

NOTES:
[289] 1 Tim. 6:17-19.
[290] S. Luke 16:9.
[291] S. Luke 1:14.
[292] S. Matt. 26:24.
[293] Ps. 115:6 (116:15).
[294] Ps. 33 (34):32.
[295] Cf. S. Luke 16:20.
[296] 2 Cor. 12:9, 10.

CHAPTER IV.

How evil cannot be forced on any one by another against his will.

PRESERVING then these distinctions clear and fixed, and knowing that there is nothing good except virtue alone, and nothing bad except sin alone and separation from God, let us now carefully consider whether God ever allows evil to be forced on his saints either by Himself or by some one else. And you will certainly find that this never happens. For another can never possibly force the evil of sin upon anyone, who does not consent and who resists, but only on one who admits it into himself through sloth and the corrupt desire of his heart. Finally, when the devil having exhausted all his wicked devices had tried to force upon the blessed Job this evil of sin, and had not only stripped him of all his worldly goods, but also after that terrible and utterly unlooked for calamity of bereavement through the death of his seven children, had heaped upon him dreadful wounds and intolerable tortures from the crown of his head to the sole of his foot, he tried in vain to fasten on him the stain of sin, because he remained steadfast through it all, never brought himself to consent to blasphemy.

CHAPTER V.

An objection, how God Himself can be said to create evil.

GERMANUS: We often read in holy Scripture that God has created evil or brought it upon men, as is this passage: "There is none beside Me. I am the Lord, and there is none else: I form the light and create darkness, I make peace, and create evil."[297] And again: "Shall there be evil in a city which the Lord hath not done?" [298]

NOTES:
[297] Is. 45:6, 7.
[298] Amos 3:6.

CHAPTER VI.

The answer to the question proposed.

THEODORE: Sometimes holy Scripture is wont by an improper use of terms to use "evils" for "affliction;" not that these are properly and in their nature evils, but because they are imagined to be evils by those on whom they are brought for their good. For when divine judgment is reasoning with men it must speak with the language and feelings of men. For when a doctor for the sake of health with good reason either cuts or cauterizes those who are suffering from the inflammation of ulcers, it is considered an evil by those who have to bear it. Nor are the spur and the whip pleasant to a restive horse. Moreover all chastisement seems at the moment to be a bitter thing to those who are chastised, as the Apostle says: "Now all chastisement for the present indeed seemeth not to bring with it joy but sorrow; but afterwards it will yield to them that are exercised by it most peaceable fruits of righteousness," and "whom the Lord loveth He chasteneth, and scourgeth every son whom He receiveth: for what son is there whom the father doth not correct?"[299] And so evils are sometimes wont to stand for afflictions, as where we read: "And God repented of the evil which He had said that He would do to them and He did it not."[300] And again: "For Thou, Lord, are gracious and merciful, patient and very merciful and ready to repent of the evil,"[301] i.e., of the sufferings and losses which Thou art forced to bring upon us as the reward of our sins. And another prophet, knowing that these are profitable to some men, and certainly not through any jealousy of their safety, but with an eye to their good, prays thus: "Add evils to them, O Lord, add evils to the haughty ones of the earth;"[302] and the Lord Himself says "Lo, I will bring evils upon them,"[303] i.e., sorrows, and losses, with which they shall for the present be chastened for their soul's health, and so shall be at length driven to return and hasten back to Me whom in their prosperity they scorned. And so that these are originally evil we cannot possibly assert: for to many they conduce to their good and offer the occasions of eternal bliss, and therefore (to return to the question raised) all those things, which are thought to be brought upon us as evils by our enemies or by any other people, should not be counted as evils, but as things indifferent. For in the end they will not be what he thinks, who brought them upon us in his rage and fury, but what he makes them who endures them. And so when death has been brought upon a saint, we ought not to think that an evil has happened to him but a thing indifferent; which is an evil to a wicked man, while to the good it is rest and freedom from evils. "For death is rest to a man whose way is hidden."[304] And so a good man does not suffer any loss from it, because he suffers nothing strange, but by the crime of an enemy he only receives (and not without the reward of eternal life) that which would have happened to him in the course of nature, and pays the debt of man's death, which must be paid by an inevitable law, with the interest of a most fruitful passion, and the recompense of a great reward.

NOTES:
[299] Heb. 12:6-11.
[300] Jonah 3:10 (LXX).
[301] Joel 2:13 (LXX).
[302] Is. 26:15 (LXX).
[303] Jer. 11:11.
[304] Job 3:23 (LXX).

CHAPTER VII.

A question whether the man who causes the death of a good man is guilty, if the good man is the gainer by his death.

GERMANUS: Well then, if a good man does not only suffer no evil by being killed, but actually gains a reward from his suffering, how can we accuse the man who has done him no harm but good by killing him?

CHAPTER VIII.

The answer to the foregoing question.

THEODORE: We are talking about the actual qualities of things good and bad, and what we call indifferent; and not about the characters of the men who do these things. Nor ought any bad or wicked man to go unpunished because his evil deed was not able to do harm to a good man. For the endurance and goodness of a righteous man are of no profit to the man who is the cause of his death or suffering, but only to him who patiently endures what is inflicted on him. And so the one is justly punished for savage cruelty, because he meant to injure him, while the other nevertheless suffers no evil, because in the goodness of his heart he patiently endures his temptation and sufferings, and so causes all those things, which were inflicted upon him with evil intent, to turn out to his advantage, and to conduce to the bliss of eternal life.

CHAPTER IX.

The case of Job who was tempted by the devil; and of the Lord who was betrayed by Judas: and how prosperity as well as adversity is advantageous to a good man.

FOR the patience of Job did not bring any gain to the devil, through making him a better man by his temptations, but only to Job himself who endured them bravely; nor was Judas granted freedom from eternal punishment, because his act of betrayal contributed to the salvation of mankind. For we must not regard the result of the deed, but the purpose of the doer. Wherefore we should always cling to this assertion; viz., that evil cannot be brought upon a man by another, unless a man has admitted it by his sloth or feebleness of heart: as the blessed Apostle confirms this opinion of ours in a verse of Scripture: "But we know that all things work together for good to them that love God."[305] But by saying "All things work together for good," he includes everything alike, not only things fortunate, but also those which seem to be misfortunes: through which the Apostle tells us in another place that he himself has passed, when he says: "By the armour of righteousness on the right hand and on the left," i.e., "Through honour and dishonour, through evil report and good report, as deceivers and yet true, as sorrowful but always rejoicing, as needy and yet enriching many:"[306] All those things then which are considered fortunate, and are called those "on the right hand," which the holy Apostle designates by the terms honour and good report; and those too which are counted misfortunes, which he clearly means by dishonour and evil report, and which he describes as "on the left hand," become to the perfect man "the armour of righteousness," if when they are brought upon him, he bears them bravely: because, as he fights with these, and uses those very weapons with which he seems to be attacked, and is protected by them as by bow and sword and stout shield against those who bring these things upon him, he secures the advantage of his patience and goodness, and obtains a grand triumph of steadfastness by means of those very weapons of his enemies which are hurled against him to kill him; and if only he is not elated by success or cast down by failure, but ever marches straightforward on the king's highway, and does not swerve from that state of tranquillity as it were to the right hand, when joy overcomes him, nor let himself be driven so to speak to the left hand, when misfortunes overwhelm him, and sorrow holds sway. For "Much peace have they that love Thy law, and to them there is no stumbling block."[307] But of those who shift about according to the character and changes of the several chances which happen to them, we read: "But a fool will change like the moon."[308] For just as it is said of men who are perfect and wise: "To them that love God all things work together for good,"[309] so of those who are weak and foolish it is declared that "everything is against a foolish man,"[310] for he gets no profit out of prosperity, nor does adversity make him any better. For it requires as much goodness to bear sorrows bravely, as to be moderate in prosperity: and it is quite certain that one who fails in one of these, will not bear up under the other. But a man can be more easily overcome by prosperity than by misfortunes: for these sometimes restrain men against their will and make them humble and through most salutary sorrow cause them to sin less, and make them better: while prosperity puffs up the mind with soothing but most pernicious flatteries and when men are secure in the prospect of their happiness dashes them to the ground with a still greater destruction.

NOTES:
[305] Rom. 8:28.
[306] 2 Cor. 6:7-10.
[307] Ps. 118 (119):165.
[308] Ecclus. 27:11.
[309] Rom. 8:28.
[310] Prov. 14:7 (LXX).

CHAPTER X.

Of the excellence of the perfect man who is figuratively spoken of as ambidextrous.

THOSE are they then who are figurately spoken of in holy Scripture as amfoterodexion, i.e., ambidextrous, as Ehud is described in the book of Judges "who used either hand as the right[311] hand." And this power we also can spiritually acquire, if by making a right and proper use of those things which are fortunate, and which seem to be "on the right hand," as well as of those which are unfortunate and as we call it "on the left hand," we make them both belong to the right side, so that whatever turns up proves in our case, to use the words of the Apostle, "the armour of righteousness." For we see that the inner man consists of two parts, and if I may be allowed the expression, two hands, nor can any of the saints do without that which we call the left hand: but by means of it the perfection of virtue is shown, where a man by skilful use can turn both hands into right hands. And in order to make our meaning clearer, the saint has for his right hand his spiritual achievements, in which he is found when with fervent spirit he gets the better of his desires and passions, when he is free from all attacks of the devil, and without any effort or difficulty rejects and cuts off all carnal sins, when he is exalted above the earth and regards all things present and earthly as light smoke or vain shadows, and scorns them as what is about to vanish away, when with an overflowing heart he not only longs most intensely for the future but actually sees it the more clearly, when he is more effectually fed on spiritual contemplations, when he sees heavenly mysteries more brightly laid open to him, when he pours forth his prayers to God with greater purity and readiness, when he is so inflamed with fervent of spirit as to pass with the utmost readiness of soul to things invisible and eternal, so as scarcely to believe that he any longer remains in the flesh. He has also a left hand, when he is entangled in the toils of temptation, when he is inflamed with the heat of desire for carnal lusts, when he is set on fire by emotion towards rage and anger, when he is overcome by being puffed up with pride or vainglory, when he is oppressed by a sorrow that worketh death, when he is shaken to pieces by the contrivances and attacks of accidie, and when he has lost all spiritual warmth, and grows indifferent with a sort of lukewarmness and unreasonable grief so that not only is he forsaken by good and kindling thoughts, but actually Psalms, prayer, reading, and retirement in his cell all pall upon him, and all virtuous exercises seem by an intolerable and horrible loathing to have lost their savour. And when a monk is troubled in this way, then he knows that he is attacked "on the left hand." Anyone therefore who is not at all puffed up through the aid of vainglory by any of those things on the right hand which we have mentioned, and who struggles manfully against those on the left hand, and does not yield to despair and give in, but rather on the other hand seizes the armour of patience to practise himself in virtue--this man can use both hands as right hands, and in each action he proves triumphant and carries off the prize of victory from that condition on the left hand as well as that on the right. Such, we read, was the reward which the blessed Job obtained who was certainly crowned (for a victory) on the right hand, when he was the father of seven sons and walked as a rich and wealthy man, and yet offered daily sacrifices to the Lord for their purification, in his anxiety that they might prove acceptable and dear to God rather than to himself, when his gates stood open to every stranger, when he was "feet to lame and eyes to blind,"[312] when the shoulders of the suffering were kept warm by the wool of his sheep, when he was a father to orphans and a husband to widows, when he did not even in his heart rejoice at the fall of his enemy. And again it was the same man who with still greater virtue triumphed over adversity on the left hand, when deprived in one moment of his seven sons he was not as a father overcome with bitter grief but as a true servant of God rejoiced in the will of his Creator. When instead of being a wealthy man he became poor, naked instead of rich, pining away instead of strong, despised and contemptible instead of famous and honourable, and yet preserved his fortitude of mind unshaken, when, lastly, bereft of all his wealth and substance he took up his abode on the dunghill, and like some stern executioner of his own body scraped with a potsherd the matter that broke out, and plunging his fingers deep into his wounds dragged out on every side masses of worms from his limbs. And in all this he never fell into despair and blasphemy, nor murmured at all against his Creator. Moreover also so little was he overcome by such a weight of bitter temptations that the cloak which out of all his former property remained to cover his body, and which alone could be saved from destruction by the devil because he was clothed with it, he rent and cast off, and covered with it his nakedness which he voluntarily endured, which the terrible robber had brought upon him. The hair of his head too, which was the only thing left untouched out of all the remains of his former glory, he shaved and cast to his tormentor, and cutting off even that which his savage foe had left to him he exulted over him and mocked him with that celestial cry of his: "If we have received good at the hand of the Lord, should we not also receive evil? Naked came I out of my mother's womb, and naked shall I return thither. The Lord gave and the Lord hath taken away; as it hath pleased the Lord, so is it done; blessed be the name of the Lord."[313] I should also with good reason call Joseph ambidextrous, as in prosperity he was very dear to his father, affectionate to his brethren, acceptable to God; and in adversity was chaste, and faithful to the Lord, in prison most kind to the prisoners, forgetful of wrongs, generous to his enemies; and to his brethren who were envious of him and as far as lay in their powers, his murderers, he proved not only affectionate but actually munificent. These men then and those who are like them are rightly termed amfoterodexion, i.e., ambidextrous. For they can use either hand as the right hand, and passing through those things which the Apostle enumerates can fairly say: "Through the armour of righteousness on the right hand and on the left, through honour and dishonour, through evil report and good report etc." And of this right and left hand Solomon speaks as follows in the Song of songs, in the person of the bride: "His left hand is under my head, and his right hand shall embrace me."[314] And while this passage shows that both are useful, yet it puts one under the head, because misfortunes ought to be subject to the control of the heart, since they are only useful for this; viz., to train us for a time and discipline us for our salvation and make us perfect in te matter of patience. But the right hand she hopes will ever cling to her to cherish her and hold her fast in the blessed embrace of the Bridegroom, and unite her to him indissolubly. We shall then be ambidextrous, when neither abundance nor want affects us, and when the former does not entice us to the luxury of a dangerous carelessness, while the latter does not draw us to despair, and complaining; but when, giving thanks to God in either case alike, we gain one and the same advantage out of good and bad fortune. And such that truly ambidextrous man, the teacher of the Gentiles, testifies that he himself was, when he says: "For I have learnt in whatsoever state I am, to be content therewith. I know both how to be brought low and I know how to abound: everywhere and in all things I am instructed both to be full and to be hungry, both to abound and to suffer need. I can do all things in Him which strengtheneth me."[315]

NOTES:

[311] Judg. 3:15, where the LXX has amfoterodexion.

[312] Job 29:15.
[313] Job 2:10; 1:21.
[314] Cant. 2:6.
[315] Phil. 4:11-13.

CHAPTER XI.

Of the two kinds of trials, which come upon us in a threefold way.

WELL then, though we say that trial is twofold, i.e., in prosperity and in adversity, yet you must know that all men are tried in three different ways. Often for their probation, sometimes for their improvement, and m some cases because their sins deserve it. For their probation indeed, as we read that the blessed Abraham and Job and many of the saints endured countless tribulations; or this which is said to the people in Deuteronomy by Moses: "And thou shalt remember all the way through which the Lord thy God hath brought thee for forty years through the desert, to afflict thee and to prove thee, and that the things that were in thy heart might be made known, whether thou wouldst keep His Commandments or no:"[316] and this which we find in the Psalms: "I proved thee at the waters of strife."[317] To Job also: "Thinkest thou that I have spoken for any other cause than that thou mightest be seen to be righteous?"[318] But for improvement, when God chastens his righteous ones for some small and venial sins, or to raise them to a higher state of purity, and delivers them over to various trials, that He may purge away all their unclean thoughts, and, to use the prophet's word, the "dross," which he sees to have collected in their secret parts, and may thus transmit them like pure gold, to the judgment to come, as He allows nothing to remain in them for the fire of judgment to discover when hereafter it searches them with penal torments according to this saying: "Many are the tribulations of the righteous."[319] And: "My son, neglect not the discipline of the Lord, neither be thou wearied whilst thou art rebuked by Him. For whom the Lord loveth He chastiseth, and scourgeth every son whom He receiveth. For what son is there whom the father doth not correct? But if ye are without chastisement, whereof all are partakers, then are ye bastards, and not sons."[320] And in the Apocalypse: "Those whom I love, I reprove and chasten."[321] To whom under the figure of Jerusalem the following words are spoken by Jeremiah, in the person of God: "For I will utterly consume all the nations among which I scattered thee: but I

145

will not utterly consume thee: but I will chastise thee in judgment, that thou mayest not seem to thyself innocent."[322] And for this life-giving cleansing David prays when he says: "Prove me, O Lord, and try me; turn my reins and my heart."[323] Isaiah also, well knowing the value of this trial, says "O Lord, correct us but with judgment: not in Thine anger."[324] And again: "I will give thanks to thee, O Lord, for thou wast angry with me: Thy wrath is turned away, and Thou hast comforted me."[325] But as a punishment for sins, the blows of trial are inflicted, as where the Lord threatens that He will send plagues upon the people of Israel: "I will send the teeth of beasts upon them, with the fury of creatures that trail upon the ground:"[326] and "In vain have I struck your children: they have not received correction."[327] In the Psalms also: "Many are the scourges of the sinners:"[328] and in the gospel: "Behold thou art made whole: now sin no more, lest a worse thing happen unto thee."[329] We find, it is true, a fourth way also in which we know on the authority of Scripture that some sufferings are brought upon us simply for the manifestation of the glory of God and His works, according to these words of the gospel: "Neither did this man sin nor his parents, but that the works of God might be manifested in him:"[330] and again: "This sickness is not unto death, but for the glory of God that the Son of God may be glorified by it."[331] There are also other sorts of vengeance, with which some who have overpassed the bounds of wickedness are smitten in this life, as we read that Dathan and Abiram or Korah were punished, or above all, those of whom the Apostle speaks: "Wherefore God gave them up to vile passions and a reprobate mind:"[332] and this must be counted worse than all other punishments. For of these the Psalmist says: "They are not in the labours of men; neither shall they be scourged like other men."[333] For they are not worthy of being healed by the visitation of the Lord which gives life, and by plagues in this world, as "in despair they have given themselves over to lasciviousness, unto the working of all error unto uncleanness,"[334] and as by hardening their hearts, and by growing accustomed and used to sin they have got beyond cleansing in this brief life and punishment in the present world: men, who are thus reproved by the holy word of the prophet: "I destroyed some of you, as God destroyed Sodom and Gomorrah, and you were as a firebrand plucked out of the burning: yet you returned not to Me, saith the Lord,"[335] and Jeremiah: "I have killed and destroyed thy people, and yet they are not returned from their ways."[336] And again: "Thou hast smitten them and they have not grieved: Thou hast bruised them and they refused to receive correction: they have made their faces harder than the rock, they have refused to return."[337] And the prophet seeing that all the remedies of this life will have been applied in vain for their healing, and already as it were despairing of their life, declares: "The bellows have failed in the fire, the founder hath melted in vain: for their wicked deeds are not consumed. Call them reprobate silver, for the Lord hath rejected them."[338] And the Lord thus laments that to no purpose has He applied this salutary cleansing by fire to those who are hardened in their sins, in the person of Jerusalem crusted all over with the rust of her sins, when He says: "set it empty upon burning coals, that it may be hot, and the brass thereof may be melted; and let the filth of it be melted in the midst thereof. Great pains have been taken, and the great rust thereof is not gone out, no not even by fire. Thy uncleanness is execrable: because I desired to cleanse thee, and thou art not cleansed from thy filthiness."[339] Wherefore like a skilful physician, who has tried all saving cures, and sees there is no remedy left which can be applied to their disease, the Lord is in a manner overcome by their iniquities and is obliged to desist from that kindly chastisement of His, and so denounces them saying: "I will no longer be angry with thee, and thy jealousy has departed from thee."[340] But of others, whose heart has not grown hard by continuance in sin, and who do not stand in need of that most severe and (if I may so call it) caustic remedy, but for whose salvation the instruction of the life-giving word is sufficient--of them it is said: "I will improve them by hearing of their suffering."[341] We are well aware that there are other reasons also of the punishment and vengeance which is inflicted on those who have sinned grievously--not to expiate their crimes, nor wipe out the deserts of their sins, but that the living may be put in fear and amend their lives. And these we plainly see were inflicted on Jeroboam the son of Nebat, and Baasha the son of Ahiah, and Ahab and Jezebel, when the Divine reproof thus declares: "Behold, I will bring evil upon thee, and will cut down thy posterity, and will kill of Ahab every male, and him that is shut up and the last in Israel. And I will make thy house like the house of Jeroboam the son of Nebat and like the house of Baasha the son of Ahiah: for that which thou hast done to provoke Me to anger, and for making Israel to sin. The dogs also shall eat Jezebel in the field of Jezreel. If Ahab die in the city, the dogs shall eat him: but if he die in the field the birds of the air shall eat him,"[342] and this which is threatened as the greatest threat of all: "Thy dead body shall not be brought to the sepulchre of thy fathers."[343] It was not that this short and momentary punishment would suffice to purge away the blasphemous inventions of him who first made the golden calves and led to the lasting sin of the people, and their wicked separation from the Lord,--or the countless and disgraceful profanities of those others, but it was that by their example the fear of those punishments which they dreaded might fall on others also, who, as they thought little of the future or even disbelieved in it altogether, would only be moved by consideration of things present; and that owing to this proof of His severity they might acknowledge that there is no lack of care for the affairs of men, and for their daily doings, in the majesty of God on high, and so through that which they greatly feared might the more clearly see in God the rewarder of all their deeds. We find, it is true, that even for lighter faults some men have received the same sentence of death in this world, as that with which those men were punished who, as we said before, were the authors of a blasphemous falling away: as happened in the case of the man who gathered sticks on the Sabbath,[344] and in that of Ananias and Sapphira, who through the sin of unbelief kept back some portion of their goods: not that the guilt of their sins was equal, but because they were the first found out in a new kind of transgression, and so it was right that as they had given to others an example of sin, so also they should give them an example of punishment and of fear, that anyone, who should attempt to copy them, might know that (even if his punishment were postponed in this life) he would be punished in the same way that they were at the trial of the judgment hereafter. And, since in our desire to run through the different kinds of trials and punishments we seem to have wandered somewhat from our subject, on which we were saying that the perfect man will always remain steadfast in either kind of trial, now let us return to it once more.

NOTES:
[316] Deut. 8:2.
[317] Ps. 80 (81):7.
[318] Job 40:3 (LXX).
[319] Ps. 33 (34):19.
[320] Heb. 12:5-8.
[321] Rev. 3:19.
[322] Jer. 30:11.
[323] Ps. 25 (26):2.
[324] The passage is not from Isaiah, but from Jer. 10:24.
[325] Is. 12:1.
[326] Deut. 32:24.
[327] Jer. 2:30.
[328] Ps. 31 (32):10.

329 S. John 5:14.
330 S. John 9:3.
331 S. John 11:4.
332 Rom. 1:26, 28.
333 Ps. 72 (73):5.
334 Eph. 4:19.
335 Amos 4:11.
336 Jer. 15:7.
337 Jer. 5:3.
338 Jer. 6:29, 30.
339 Ezek. 24:11-13.
340 Ezek. 16:42.
341 Hos. 7:12 (LXX).
342 1 Kings 21:21-24.
343 1 Kings 13:22.
344 Cf. Numb. 15:32.

CHAPTER XII.

How the upright man ought to be like a stamp not of wax but of hard steel.

AND so the mind of the upright man ought not to be like wax or any other soft material which always yields to the shape of what presses on it, and is stamped with its form and impress and keeps it until it takes another shape by having another seal stamped upon it; and so it results that it never retains its own form but is turned and twisted about to correspond to whatever is pressed upon it. But he should rather be like some stamp of hard steel, that the mind may always keep its proper form and shape inviolate, and may stamp and imprint on everything which occurs to it the marks of its own condition, while upon it itself nothing that happens can leave any mark.

CHAPTER XIII.

A question whether the mind can constantly continue in one and the same condition.

GERMANUS: But can our mind constantly preserve its condition unaltered, and always continue in the same state?

CHAPTER XIV.

The answer to the point raised by the questioner.

THEODORE: It is needful that one must either, as the Apostle says, "be renewed in the spirit of the mind,"[345] and daily advance by "pressing forward to those things which are before,"[346] or, if one neglects to do this, the sure result will be to go back, and become worse and worse. And therefore the mind cannot possibly remain in one and the same state. Just as when a man, by pulling hard, is trying to force a boat against the stream of a strong current he must either stem the rush of the torrent by the force of his arms, and so mount to what is higher up, or letting his hands slacken be whirled headlong down stream. Wherefore it will be a clear proof of our failure if we find that we have gained nothing more, nor should we doubt but that we have altogether gone back, whenever we find that we have not advanced upwards, because, as I said, the mind of man cannot possibly continue in the same condition, nor so long as he is in the flesh will any of the saints ever reach the height of all virtues, so that they continue unalterable. For something must either be added to them or taken away from them, and in no creature can there be such perfection, as not to be subject to the feeling of change; as we read in the book of Job: "What is man that he should be without spot, and he that is born of a woman that he should appear just? Behold among His saints none is unchangeable, and the heavens are not pure in His sight."[347] For we confess that God only is unchangeable, who alone is thus addressed by the prayer of the holy prophet "But Thou art the same,"[348] and who says of Himself "I am God, and I change not,"[349] because He alone is by nature always good, always full and perfect, and one to whom nothing can ever be added, or from whom nothing can be taken away. And so we ought always with incessant care and anxiety to give ourselves up to the acquirement of virtue, and constantly to occupy ourselves with the practice of it, lest, if we cease to go forward, the result should immediately be a going back. For, as we said, the mind cannot continue in one and the same condition, I mean without receiving addition to or diminution of its good qualities. For to fail to gain new ones, is to lose them, because when the desire of making progress ceases, there the danger of going back is present.

NOTES:
[345] Eph. 4:23.
[346] Phil. 3:13.
[347] Job 15:14, 15.
[348] Ps. 101 (102):27.
[349] Mal. 3:6.

CHAPTER XV.

How one loses by going away from one's cell.

AND so we ought always to remain shut up in our cell. For whenever a man has strayed from it and returns fresh to it and begins again to live there he will be upset and disturbed. For if he has let it go he cannot without difficulty and pains recover that fixed purpose of mind, which he had gained when he remained in his cell; and as through this he has gone back, he will not think anything of the advance which he has missed, and which he would have secured if he had not allowed himself to leave his cell, but he will rather congratulate himself if he finds that he has regained that condition from which he fell away. For just as time once lost and gone cannot any more be recovered, so neither can those advantages which have been missed be restored: for whatever earnest purpose of the mind there may be afterwards, it will be the profit of the day then present, and the gain that belongs to the time that then is, and will not make up for the gain that has been once for all lost.

CHAPTER XVI.

How even celestial powers above are capable of change.

BUT that even the powers above are, as we said, subject to change is shown by those who fell from their ranks through the fault of a corrupt will. Wherefore we ought not to think that the nature of those is unchangeable, who remain in the blessed condition in which they were created, simply because they were not in like manner led astray to choose the worse part. For it is one thing to have a nature incapable of change, and another thing for a man through the efforts of his virtue, and by guarding what is good through the grace of the unchangeable God, to be kept from change. For everything that is secured or preserved by care, can also be lost by carelessness. And so we read: "Call no man blessed before his death,"[350] because so long as a man is still engaged in the struggle, and if I may use the expression, still wrestling--even though he generally conquers and carries off many prizes of victory,--yet he can never be free from fear, and from the suspicion of an uncertain issue. And therefore God alone is called unchangeable and good, as His goodness is not the result of effort, but a natural possession, and so He cannot be anything but good. No virtue then can be acquired by man without the possibility of change, but in order that when it once exists it may be continually preserved, it must be watched over with the same care and diligence with which it was acquired.

NOTES:
[350] Ecclus. 11:30.

CHAPTER XVII.

That no one is dashed to the ground by a sudden fall.

BUT we must not imagine that anyone slips and comes to grief by a sudden fall, but that he falls by a hopeless collapse either from being deceived by beginning his training badly, or from the good qualities of his soul failing through a long course of carelessness of mind, and so his faults gaining ground upon him little by little. For "loss goeth before destruction, and an evil thought before a fall,"[351] just as no house ever fails to the ground by a sudden collapse, but only when there is some flaw of long standing in the foundation, or when by long continued neglect of its inmates, what was at first only a little drip finds its way through, and so the protecting walls are by degrees ruined, and in consequence of long standing neglect the gap becomes larger, and break away, and in time the drenching storm and rain pours in like a river: for "by slothfulness a building is cast down, and through the weakness of hands the house shall drop through."[352] And that the same thing happens spiritually to the soul the same Solomon thus tells us in other words, when he says: "water dripping drives a man out of the house on a stormy day."[353] Elegantly then does he compare carelessness of mind to a roof, and to tiles that have not been looked after, through which in the first instance only very slight drippings (so to speak) of the passions make their way to the soul: but if these are not heeded, as being but small and trifling, then the beams of virtues will decay and be carried away by a great tempest of sins, through which "on a stormy day," i.e., in the time of temptation, the devil's attack will assail us, and the soul will be driven forth from the abode of virtue, in which, as long as it preserved all watchful diligence, it had remained as in a house that belonged to it.

And so when we had heard this, we were so immensely delighted with our spiritual repast, that the mental pleasure with which we were filled by this conference outweighed the sorrow which we had experienced before from the death of the saints. For not only were we instructed in things about which we had been puzzled, but we also learnt from the raising of that question some things, which our understanding had been too small for us to ask about.

NOTES:
[351] Prov. 16:8 (LXX).
[352] Eccl. 10:18 (LXX).
[353] Prov. 27:15 (LXX).
[280] This Abbot Theodore is probably the same person as the one mentioned in the Institutes, Book V. cc. xxxiii.-xxxv.; but nothing further is known of him, and there is no reason for identifying him with any of the other monks of this name of the fourth century.

153

CONFERENCE 7.

First Conference of Abbot Serenus
on Inconstancy of Mind, and Spiritual Wickedness

CHAPTER I.

On the chastity of Abbot Serenus. [354]

AS we desire to introduce to earnest minds the Abbot Serenus, a man of the greatest holiness and continence, and one who answers like a mirror to his name, whom we admired above all others with peculiar veneration, we think that we only carry out our desire by the attempt to insert his conferences in our book. To this man beyond all other virtues, which shone forth not merely in his actions and manners, but by God's grace in his very look as well, there was granted by a special blessing the gift of continence, so that he never felt himself disturbed even by natural incitements even in sleep. And how it was that by the assistance of God's grace he attained such wondrous purity of the flesh, as it seems beyond the conditions of human nature, I think that I ought first of all to explain.

NOTES:
[354] Very little is known of Serenus but what is here told. Cf. the Vitae Patrum, c. l.

CHAPTER II.

The question of the aforesaid old man on the state of our thoughts.

THIS man then in his prayers by day and night, and in fasts and vigils unweariedly entreated for inward chastity of heart and soul, and seeing that he had obtained what he wished and prayed for, and that all the passions of carnal concupiscence in his heart were dead, was roused as it were by the sweetest taste of purity, and inflamed by his zeal for chastity towards a yet more ardent desire, and began to apply himself to stricter fasts and prayers that the mortification of this passion which by God's grace had been granted to his inner man, might be extended also so as to include external purity, to such an extent that he might no longer be affected by any simple and natural movement, such as is excited even in children and infants. And by the experience of the gift he had obtained, which he knew he had secured by no merit of his labours, but by the grace of God, he was the more ardently stimulated to obtain this also in like manner, as he believed that God could much more easily tear up by the roots this incitement of the flesh, (which even by man's art and skill is sometimes destroyed by potions and remedies or by the use of the knife) since He had of His own free gift conferred that purity of spirit which is a still greater thing, and which cannot be acquired by human efforts and exertions. And when with unceasing supplications and tears he was applying himself unweariedly to the petition he had commenced, there came to him an angel in a vision by night, and seemed to open his belly, and to remove from his bowels a sort of fiery fleshly humour, and to cast it away, and restore everything to its place as before; and "lo" he said, "the incitements of your flesh are removed, and you may be sure that you have this day obtained that lasting purity of body for which you have faithfully asked." It will be enough thus briefly to have told this of the grace of God which was granted to this famous man in a special way. But I deem it unnecessary to say anything of those virtues which he possessed in common with other good men, for fear lest that particular narrative on this man's name might seem to deprive others of that which is specially mentioned of him. Him therefore, as we were inflamed with the greatest eagerness for conference with and instruction from him, we arranged to visit in Lent; and when he had very quietly inquired of us of the character of our thoughts and the state of our in-

ner man, and what help we had got towards its purity from our long
stay in the desert, we approached him with these complaints:

CHAPTER III.

Our answer on the fickle character of our thoughts.

THE time spent here, and the dwelling in solitude, and meditation, through which you think that we ought to have attained
perfection of the inner man, has only done this for us; viz., teach us
that which we are unable to be, without making us what we are trying
to be. Nor do we feel that by this knowledge we have acquired any
fixed steadfastness of the purity which we long for, or any strength and
firmness; but only an increase of confusion and shame: for though our
meditation in all our discipline aims at this in our daily studies, and
endeavours from trembling beginnings to reach a sure and unwavering
skill, and to begin to know something of what originally it knew but
vaguely or was altogether ignorant of, and by advancing by sure steps
(so to speak) towards the condition of that discipline, to habituate itself
perfectly to it without any difficulty, I find on the contrary that while I
am struggling in this desire for purity, I have only got far enough to
know what I cannot be. And hence I feel that nothing but trouble results to me from all this contrition of heart, so that matter for tears is
never wanting, and yet I do not cease to be what I ought not to be. And
so what is the good of having learnt what is best, if it cannot be attained even when known? for when we have been feeling that the aim
of our heart was directed towards what we purposed, insensibly the
mind returns to its previous wandering thoughts and slips back with a
more violent rush, and is taken up with daily distractions and incessantly drawn away by numberless things that take it captive, so that we
almost despair of the improvement which we long for, and all these
observances seem useless. Since the mind which every moment wanders off vaguely, when it is brought back to the fear of God or spiritual
contemplation, before it is established in it, darts off and strays; and
when we have been roused and have discovered that it has wandered
from the purpose set before it, and want to recall it to the meditation
from which it has strayed, and to bind it fast with the firmest purpose
of heart, as if with chains, while we are making the attempt it slips
away from the inmost recesses of the heart swifter than a snake.

Wherefore we being inflamed by daily exercises of this kind, and yet not seeing that we gain from them any strength and stability in heart are overcome and in despair driven to this opinion; viz., to believe that it is from no fault of our own but from a fault of our nature that these wanderings of mind are found in mankind.

CHAPTER IV.

The discourse of the old man on the state of the soul and its excellence.

SERENUS: It is dangerous to jump to a conclusion and lay down the law hastily on the nature of anything before you have properly discussed the subject and considered its true character. Nor should you, looking only at your own weakness, hazard a conjecture instead of pronouncing a judgment based on the character and value of the practice itself, and others' experience of it. For if anyone, who was ignorant of swimming but knew that the weight of his body could not be supported by water, wished from the proof which his inexperience afforded, to lay down that no one composed of solid flesh could possibly be supported on the liquid element, we ought not therefore to think his opinion a true one, which he seemed to bring forward in accordance with his own experience, since this can be shown to be not merely not impossible but actually extremely easily done by others, by the clearest proofs and ocular demonstration. And so the nous, i.e., the mind, is defined as aeikinhtos kai polukinhtos, i.e., ever shifting and very shifting: as it is thus described in the so called wisdom of Solomon in other words: kai gewdes skhnos briqei noun polufrontida, i.e., "And the earthly tabernacle weigheth down the mind that museth on many things."[355] This then in accordance with its nature can never remain idle, but unless provision is made where it may exercise its motions and have what will continually occupy it, it must by its own fickleness wander about and stray over all kinds of things until, accustomed by long practice and daily use--in which you say that you have toiled without result--it tries and learns what food for the memory it ought to prepare, toward which it may bring back its unwearied flight and acquire strength for remaining, and thus may succeed in driving away the hostile suggestion of the enemy by which it is distracted, and in persisting in that state and condition which it yearns for. We ought not then to ascribe this wandering inclination of our heart either to human nature or to God its Creator. For it is a true statement of Scripture, that "God made man upright; but they themselves found out many thoughts."[356] The character of these then depends on us ourselves, for it says "a good thought comes near to those that know it, but a prudent man will find it."[357] For where anything is subject to our prudence and industry so that it can be found out, there if it is not found out, we ought certainly to set it down to our own laziness or carelessness and not to the fault of our nature. And with this meaning the Psalmist also is in agreement, when he says: "Blessed is the man whose help is from Thee: in his heart he hath disposed his ascents."[358] You see then that it lies in our power to dispose in our hearts either ascents, i.e., thoughts that belong to God, or descents; viz., those that sink down to carnal and earthly things. And if this was not in our power the Lord would not have rebuked the Pharisees, saying "Why do ye think evil in your hearts?"[359] nor would He have given this charge by the prophet, saying: "Take away the evil of your thoughts from mine eyes;" and "How long shall wicked thoughts remain in you?"[360] Nor would the character of them as of our works be taken into consideration in the day of judgment in our case as the Lord threatens by Isaiah: "Lo, I come to gather together their works and thoughts together with all nations and tongues;"[361] nor would it be right that we should be condemned or defended by their evidence in that terrible and dreadful examination, as the blessed Apostle says: "Their thoughts between themselves accusing or also defending one another, in the day when God shall judge the secrets of men according to my gospel." [362]

NOTES:
[355] Wisdom 9:15.
[356] Eccl. 7:29 (LXX).
[357] Prov. 19:7 (LXX).
[358] Ps. 83 (84):6.
[359] S. Matt. 9:4.
[360] Is. 1:16; Jer. 4:24.
[361] Is. 66:18.
[362] Rom. 2:15, 16.

CHAPTER V.

On the perfection of the soul, as drawn from the comparison of the Centurion in the gospel.

OF this perfect mind then there is an excellent figure drawn in the case of the centurion in the gospel; whose virtue and consistency, owing to which he was not led away by the rush of thoughts, but in accordance with his own judgment either admitted such as were good, or easily drove away those of the opposite character, are described in this tropical form: "For I also am a man under authority, having soldiers under me: and I say to this man, Go, and he goeth; and to another, Come, and he cometh; and to my servant, Do this, and he doeth it."[363] If then we too strive manfully against disturbances and sins and can bring them under our own control and discretion, and fight and destroy the passions in our flesh, and bring under the sway of reason the swarm of our thoughts, and drive back from our breast the terrible hosts of the powers opposed to us by the life-giving standard of the Lord's cross, we shall in reward for such triumphs be promoted to the rank of that centurion spiritually understood, who, as we read in Exodus, was mystically pointed to by Moses: "Appoint for thee rulers of thousands, and of hundreds, and of fifties and of tens."[364] And so we too when raised to the height of this dignity shall have the same right and power to command, so that we shall not be carried away by thoughts against our will, but shall be able to continue in and cling to those which spiritually delight us, commanding the evil suggestions to depart, and they will depart, while to good ones we shall say "Come," and they will come: and to our servant also, i.e., the body we shall in like manner enjoin what belongs to chastity and continence, and it will serve us without any gainsaying, no longer arousing in us the hostile incitements of concupiscence, but showing all subservience to the spirit. And what is the character of the arms of this centurion, and for what use in battle they are, hear the blessed Apostle declaring: "The arms," he says "of our warfare are not carnal, but mighty to God." He tells us their character; viz., that they are not carnal or weak, but spiritual and mighty to God. Then he next suggests in what struggles they are to be used: "Unto the pulling down of fortifications, purging the thoughts, and every height that exalteth itself against the knowledge of God, and bringing into captivity every understanding unto the obedience of Christ, and having in readiness to avenge all disobedience, when your obedience shall be first fulfilled."[365] And since though useful, it yet belongs to another time to run through these one by one, I only want you to see the different sorts of these arms and their characteristics, as we also ought always to walk with them girt upon us if we mean to fight the Lord's battles and to serve among the centurions of the gospel. "Take," he says "the shield of faith, wherewith ye may be able to quench all the fiery darts of the evil one."[366] Faith then is that which intercepts the flaming darts of lust, and destroys them by the fear of future judgment, and belief in the heavenly kingdom. "And the breastplate," he says, "of charity."[367] This indeed is that which going round the vital parts of the breast and protecting what is exposed to the deadly wounds of swelling thoughts, keeps off the blows opposed to it, and does not allow the darts of the devil to penetrate to our inner man. For it "endureth all things, suffereth all things, beareth all things."[368] "And for an helmet the hope of salvation."[369] The helmet is what protects the head. As then Christ is our head, we ought always in all temptations and persecutions to protect it with the hope of future good things to come, and especially to keep faith in Him whole and undefiled. For it is possible for one who has lost other parts of the body, weak as he may be, still to survive: but even a short time of living is extended to no one without a head. "And the sword of the Spirit which is the word of God."[370] For it is "sharper than any two-edged sword, and piercing even to the dividing of soul and spirit, and of the joints and marrow, and is a discerner of the thoughts and intents of the heart:"[371] as it divides and cuts off whatever carnal and earthly things it may find in us. And whosoever is protected by these arms will ever be defended from the weapons and ravages of his foes, and will not be led away bound in the chains of his spoilers, a captive and a prisoner, to the hostile land of vain thoughts, nor hear the words of the prophet: "Why art thou grown old in a strange country?"[372] But he will stand like a triumphant conqueror in the land of thoughts which he has chosen. Would you understand too the strength and courage of this centurion, by which he bears these arms of which we spoke before as not carnal but mighty to God? Hear of the selection by which the King himself marks and approves brave men when he summons them to the spiritual combat. "Let," says He, "the weak say that I am strong;" and: "Let him who is the sufferer become a warrior."[373] You see then that none but sufferers and weak people can fight the Lord's battles, weak indeed with that weakness, founded on which that centurion of ours in the gospel said with confidence: "For when I am weak, then am I strong," and again, "for strength is made perfect in weakness."[374] Of which weakness one of the prophets says: "And he that is weak among them shall be as the house of David."[375] For the patient sufferer shall fight these wars, with that patience of which it is said "patience is necessary for you that doing the will of God you may receive the reward."[376]

NOTES:
[363] S. Matt. 8:9.
[364] Exod. 8:21.
[365] 1 Cor. 10:4-6.
[366] Eph. 6:16.
[367] 1 Thess. 5:8.
[368] 1 Cor. 13:7.
[369] 1 Thess. 5:8.
[370] Eph. 6:17.
[371] Heb. 4:12.
[372] Baruch 3:11.
[373] Joel 2:10, 11 (LXX).
[374] 2 Cor. 12:9, 10.
[375] Zech. 12:8.
[376] Heb. 10:36.

CHAPTER VI.

Of perseverance as regards care of the thoughts.

BUT we shall find out by our own experience that we can and ought to cling to the Lord if we have our wills mortified and the desires of this world cut off, and we shall be taught by the authority of those who in converse with the Lord say in all confidence: "My soul hath stuck close to Thee;" and: "I have stuck unto Thy testimonies, O Lord;" and: "It is good for me to stick fast to God;" and: "He who cleaveth to the Lord, is one spirit."[377] We ought not then to be wearied out by these wanderings of mind and relax from our fervour: for "he that tilleth his ground shall be filled with bread: but he that followeth idleness shall be filled with poverty."[378] Nor should we be drawn away from being intent on this watchfulness through a dangerous despair, for "in every one who is anxious there is abundance, for he who is pleasant and free from grief will be in want;" and again: "a man in grief labours for himself, and forcibly brings about his own destruction."[379] Moreover also: "the kingdom of heaven suffereth violence and

161

the violent take it by force,"[380] for no virtue is acquired without effort, nor can anyone attain to that mental stability which he desires without great sorrow of heart, for "man is born to trouble,"[381] and in order that he may be able to attain to "the perfect man, the measure of the stature of the fulness of Christ"[382] he must ever be on the watch with still greater intentness, and toil with ceaseless carefulness. But to the fulness of this measure no one will ever attain, but one who has considered it beforehand and been trained to it now and has had some foretaste of it while still in this world, and being marked a most precious member of Christ, has possessed in the flesh an earnest of that "joint"[383] by which he can be united to His body: desiring one thing alone, thirsting for but one thing, ever bringing not only his acts but even his thoughts to bear on one thing alone; viz., that he may even now keep as an earnest that which is said of the blessed life of the saints hereafter; viz., that "God may be" to him "all in all." [384]

NOTES:
[377] Ps. 42 (43):9; 118 (119):31; 71 (72):28; 1 Cor. 6:17.
[378] Prov. 28:19.
[379] Prov. 14:23; 16:26 (LXX).
[380] S. Matt. 11:12.
[381] Job 5:7.
[382] Eph. 4:13.
[383] Eph. 4:13.
[384] 1 Cor. 15:28.

CHAPTER VII.

A question on the roving tendency of the mind and the attacks of spiritual wickedness.

GERMANUS: Perhaps this tendency of the mind to rove might to some extent be checked were it not that so great a swarm of enemies surrounded it, and ceaselessly urged it toward what it has no wish for, or rather whither the roving character of its own nature drives it. And since such numberless foes, and those so powerful and terrible, surround it, we should not fancy that it was possible for them to be withstood especially by this weak flesh of ours, were we not encouraged to this view by your words as if by oracles from heaven.

CHAPTER VIII.

The answer on the help of God and the power of free will.

SERENUS: No one who has experienced the conflicts of the inner man, can doubt that our foes are continually lying in wait for us. But we mean that they oppose our progress in such a way that we can think of them as only inciting to evil things and not forcing. But no one could altogether avoid whatever sin they were inclined to imprint upon our hearts, if a strong impulse was present to force (evil) upon us, just as it is to suggest it. Wherefore as there is in them ample power of inciting, so in us there is a supply of power of rejection, and of liberty of acquiescing. But if we are afraid of their power and assaults, we may also claim the protection and assistance of God against them, of which we read: "For greater is He who is in us than he who is in this world:"[385] and His aid fights on our side with much greater power than their hosts fight against us; for God is not only the suggester of what is good, but the maintainer and insister of it, so that sometimes He draws us towards salvation even against our will and without our knowing it. It follows then that no one can be deceived by the devil but one who has chosen to yield to him the consent of his own will: as Ecclesiastes clearly puts it in these words: "For since there is no gainsaying by those who do evil speedily, therefore the heart of the children of men is filled within them to do evil."[386] It is therefore clear that each man goes wrong from this; viz., that when evil thoughts assault him he does not immediately meet them with refusal and contradiction, for it says: "resist him, and he will flee from you." [387]

NOTES:
[385] 1 John 4:4.
[386] Eccl. 8:11 (LXX).
[387] S. James 4:7.

CHAPTER IX.

A question on the union of the soul with devils.

GERMANUS: What, I pray you, is that indiscriminate and common union of the soul with those evil spirits, by which it is possible for them to be (I will not say joined with but) united to it in such a way that they can imperceptibly talk with it, and find their way into it and suggest to it whatever they want, and incite it to whatever they like, and look into and see its thoughts and movements; and the result is so close a union between them and the soul that it is almost impossible without God's grace to distinguish between what results from their instigation, and what from our free will.

CHAPTER X.

The answer how unclean spirits are united with human souls.

SERENUS: It is no wonder that spirit can be imperceptibly joined with spirit, and exercise an unseen power of persuasion toward what is allowed to it. For there is between them (just as between men) some sort of similarity and kinship of substance, since the description which is given of the nature of the soul, applies equally well to their substance. But it is impossible for spirits to be implanted in spirits inwardly or united with them in such a way that one can hold the other; for this is the true prerogative of Deity alone, which is the only simple and incorporeal nature.

CHAPTER XI.

An objection whether unclean spirits can be present in or united with the souls of those whom they have filled.

GERMANUS: To this idea we think that what we see happen in the case of those possessed is sufficiently opposed, when they say and do what they know not under the influence of the spirits. How then are we to refuse to believe that their souls are not united to those spirits, when we see them made their instruments, and (forsaking their natural condition) yielding to their movements and moods, in such a way that they give expression no longer to their own words and actions and wishes, but to those of the demons?

CHAPTER XII.

The answer how it is that unclean spirits can lord it over those possessed.

SERENUS: What you speak of as taking place in the case of demoniacs is not opposed to our assertion; viz., that those possessed by unclean spirits say and do what they do not want to, and are forced to utter what they know not; for it is perfectly clear that they are not subject to the entrance of the spirits all in the same way: for some are affected by them in such a way as to have not the slightest conception of what they do and say, while others know and afterwards recollect it. But we must not imagine that this is done by the infusion of the spirit in such a way that it penetrates into the actual substance of the soul and, being as it were united to it and somehow clothed with it, utters words and sayings through the mouth of the sufferer. For we ought not to believe that this can possibly be done by them. For we can clearly see that this results from no loss of the soul but from weakness of the body, when the unclean spirit seizes on those members in which the vigour of the soul resides, and laying on them an enormous and intolerable weight overwhelms it with foulest darkness, and interferes with its intellectual powers: as we see sometimes happen also from the fault of wine and fever or excessive cold, and other indispositions affecting men from without; and it was this which the devil was forbidden to attempt to inflict on the blessed Job, though he had received power over his flesh, when the Lord commanded him saying: "Lo, I give him into thine hands: only preserve his soul,"[388] i.e., do not weaken the seat of his soul and make him mad, and overpower the understanding and wisdom of what remains, by smothering the ruling power in his heart with your weight.

NOTES:
[388] Job 2:6 (LXX).

CHAPTER XIII.

How spirit cannot be penetrated by spirit, and how God alone is incorporeal.

FOR even if spirit is mingled with this crass and solid matter; viz., flesh (as very easily happens), should we therefore believe that it can be united to the soul, which is in like manner spirit, in such a way as to make it also receptive in the same way of its own nature: a thing which is possible to the Trinity alone, which is so capable of pervading every intellectual nature, that it cannot only embrace and surround it but even insert itself into it and, incorporeal though it is, be infused into a body? For though we maintain that some spiritual natures exist, such as angels, archangels and the other powers, and indeed our own souls and the thin air, yet we ought certainly not to consider them incorporeal. For they have in their own fashion a body in which they exist, though it is much finer than our bodies are, in accordance with the Apostle's words when he says: "And there are bodies celestial, and bodies terrestrial:" and again: "It is sown a natural body, it is raised a spiritual body;"[389] from which it is clearly gathered that there is nothing incorporeal but God alone, and therefore it is only by Him that all spiritual and intellectual substances can be pervaded, because He alone is whole and everywhere and in all things, in such a way as to behold and see the thoughts of men and their inner movements and all the recesses of the soul; since it was of Him alone that the blessed Apostle spoke when he said: "For the word of God is quick and powerful and sharper than any two-edged sword, and piercing even to the dividing of soul and spirit and of the joints and marrow; and is a discerner of the thoughts and intents of the heart; and there is no creature invisible in His sight, but all things are naked and open to His eyes."[390] And the blessed David says: "Who fashioneth their hearts one by one;" and again: "For He knoweth the secrets of the heart;"[391] and Job too: "Thou who alone knowest the hearts of men." [392]

NOTES:
[389] 1 Cor. 15:40, 44.
[390] Heb. 4:12, 13.
[391] Ps. 32 (33):15; 43 (44):22.
[392] 2 Chron. 6:30.

CHAPTER XIV.

An objection, as to how we ought to believe that devils see into the thoughts of men.

GERMANUS: In this way, which you describe, those spirits cannot possibly see into our thoughts. But we think it utterly absurd to hold such an opinion, when Scripture says: "If the spirit of him that hath power ascend upon thee;"[393] and again: "When the devil had put it into the heart of Simon Iscariot to betray the Lord."[394] How then can we believe that our thoughts are not open to them, when we feel that for the most part they spring up and are nursed by their suggestions and instigation?

NOTES:
[393] Eccl. 10:4.
[394] S. John 13:2.

CHAPTER XV.

The answer what devils can and what they cannot do in regard to the thoughts of men.

SERENUS: Nobody doubts that unclean spirits can influence the character of our thoughts, but this is by affecting them from without by sensible influences, i.e., either from our inclinations or from our words, and those likings to which they see that we are especially disposed. But they cannot possibly come near to those which have not yet come forth from the inmost recesses of the soul. And the thoughts too, which they suggest, whether they are actually or in a kind of way embraced, are discovered by them not from the nature of the soul itself, i.e., that inner inclination which lies concealed so to speak in the very marrow, but from motions and signs given by the outward man, as for example, when they suggest gluttony, if they have seen a monk raising his eyes anxiously to the window or to the sun, or inquiring eagerly what o'clock it is, they know that he has admitted the feeling of greediness. If when they suggest fornication they find him calmly submitting to the attack of lust, or see him perturbed in body, or at any rate not groaning as he ought under the wantonness of an impure suggestion, they know that the dart of lust is already fixed in his very soul. If they stir up incitements to grief, or anger, or rage, they can tell whether they have taken root in the heart by the movements of the body, and visible disturbances, when, for instance, they have noticed him either groaning silently, or panting with indignation or changing colour; and so they cunningly discover the fault to which he is given over. For they know that every one of us is enticed in a regular way by that one, to the incitement of which they see, by a sort of assenting motion of the body, that he has yielded his consent and agreement. And it is no wonder that this is discovered by those powers of the air, when we see that even clever men can often discover the state of the inner man from his mien and look and external bearing. How much more surely then can this be discovered by those who as being of a spiritual nature are certainly much more subtle and cleverer than men.

CHAPTER XVI.

An illustration showing how we are taught that unclean spirits know the thoughts of men.

FOR just as some thieves are in the habit of examining the concealed treasures of the men in those houses which they mean to rob, and in the dark shades of night sprinkle with careful hands little grains of sand and discover the hidden treasures which they cannot see by the tinkling sound with which they answer to the fall of the sand, and so arrive at certain knowledge of each thing and metal, which betrays itself in a way by the voice elicited from it; so these too, in order to explore the treasures of our heart, scatter over us the sand of certain evil suggestions, and when they see some bodily affection arise corresponding to their character, they recognize as if by a sort of tinkling sound proceeding from the inmost recesses, what it is that is stored up in the secret chamber of the inner man.

CHAPTER XVII.

On the fact that not every devil has the power of suggesting every passion to men.

BUT we ought to know this, that not all devils can implant all the passions in men, but that certain spirits brood over each sin, and that some gloat over uncleanness and filthy lusts, others over blasphemy, others are more particularly devoted to anger and wrath, others thrive on gloominess, others are pacified with vainglory and pride; and each one implants in the hearts of men that sin, in which he himself revels, and they cannot implant their special vices all at one time, but in turn, according as the opportunity of time or place, or a man, who is open to their suggestions, excites them.

CHAPTER XVIII.

A question whether among the devils there is any order observed in the attack, or system in its changes.

GERMANUS: Must we then believe that wickedness is arranged and so to speak systematized among them in such a way that there is some order in the changes observed by them, and a regular plan of attack carried out, though it is clear that method and system can only exist among good and upright men, as Scripture says: "Thou shalt seek wisdom among the ungodly and shalt not find it; and: "our enemies are senseless;" and this: "There is neither wisdom, nor courage, nor counsel among the ungodly." [395]

NOTES:
[395] Prov. 14:6; Deut. 32:31; Prov. 21:30 (LXX).

169

CHAPTER XIX.

The answer how far an agreement exists among devils about the attack and its changes.

SERENUS: It is a true assertion that there is no lasting concord among bad men, and that perfect harmony cannot exist even in regard to those particular faults which have attractions for them all in common. For, as you have said, it can never be that system and discipline are preserved among undisciplined things. But in some matters, where community of interests, and necessity enforces it, or participation in some gain recommends it, they must arrange for some agreement for the time being. And we see very clearly that this is so in the case of this war of spiritual wickedness; so that not only do they observe times and changes among themselves, but actually are known specially to occupy some particular spots and to haunt them persistently: for since they must make their attacks through certain fixed temptations and well defined sins, and at particular times, we clearly infer from this that no one can at one and at the same time be deluded by the emptiness of vainglory and inflamed by the lust of fornication, nor at one and the same time be puffed up by the outrageous haughtiness of spiritual pride, and subject to the humiliation of carnal gluttony. Nor can anyone be overcome by silly giggling and laughter and at the same time be excited by the stings of anger, or at any rate filled with the pains of gnawing grief: but all the spirits must one by one advance to attack the soul, in such a way that when one has been vanquished and retreated, he must make way for another spirit to attack it still more vehemently, or if he has come forth victorious, he will none the less hand it over to be deceived by another.

CHAPTER XX.

Of the fact that opposite powers are not of the same boldness, and that the occasions of temptation are not under their control.

WE ought also not to be ignorant of this, that they have not all the same fierceness and energy, nor indeed the same boldness and malice, and that with beginners and feeble folk only the weaker spirits join battle, and when these spiritual wickednesses are beaten, then gradually the assaults of stronger ones are made against the athlete of Christ. For in proportion to a man's strength and progress, is the difficulty of the struggle made greater: for none of the saints could possibly be equal to the endurance of the malice of so many and so great foes, or meet their attacks, or even bear their cruelty and savagery, were it not that the merciful judge of our contest, and president of the games, Christ Himself, equalized the strength of the combatants, and repelled and checked their excessive attacks, and made with the temptation a way of escape as well that we might be able to bear it. [396]

NOTES:
[396] 1 Cor. 10:13.

CHAPTER XXI.

Of the fact that devils struggle with men not without effort on their part.

BUT our belief is that they undertake this struggle not without effort on their part. For in their conflict they themselves have some sort of anxiety and depression, and especially when they are matched with stronger rivals, i.e., saints and perfect men. Otherwise no contest or struggle, but only a simple deception of men, and one free from anxiety on their part would be assigned to them. And how then would the Apostle's words stand, where he says: "We wrestle not against flesh and blood, but against principalities, against powers, against world-rulers of this darkness, against spiritual wickedness in heavenly places;" and this too: "So fight I, not as one that beateth the air;" and again: "I have fought a good fight"?[397] For where it is spoken of as a fight, and conflict, and battle, there must be effort and exertion and anxiety on both sides, and equally there must either be in store for them chagrin and confusion for their failure, or delight consequent upon their victory. But where one fights with ease and security against another who struggles with great effort, and in order to overthrow his rival makes use of his will alone as his strength, there it ought not to be called a battle, struggle, or strife, but a sort of unfair and unreasonable assault and attack. But they certainly have to labour, and when

they attack men, exert themselves in no lesser degree in order to secure
from each one that victory which they want to obtain, and there is
hurled back upon them the same confusion which was awaiting us had
we been worsted by them; as it is said: "The head of their compassing
me about, the labour of their own lips shall overwhelm them;" and:
"His sorrow shall be turned on his own head;" and again: "Let the
snare which he knoweth not come upon him, and let the net which he
hath hidden catch him, and into that very snare let him fall;"[398] viz.,
that which he contrived for the deception of men. They then themselves also come to grief, and as they damage us so are they also in
like manner damaged by us, nor when they are worsted do they depart
without confusion, and seeing these defeats of theirs and their struggles, one who had good eyes in his inner man, seeing also that they
gloated over the downfall and mischances of individuals, and fearing
lest his own case might furnish them with this kind of delight, prayed
to the Lord saying: "Lighten mine eyes that I sleep not in death: lest
mine enemy say, I have prevailed against him. They that trouble me
will rejoice if I be moved;" and: "O My God, let them not rejoice over
me; let them not say in their hearts, Aha, Aha, our very wish; neither
let them say; we have devoured him." and: "They gnashed their teeth
upon me. Lord, how long wilt Thou look on this?" for: "he lieth in
wait secretly as a lion in his den: he lieth in wait to ravish the poor;"
and: "He seeketh from God his meat."[399] And again when all their efforts are exhausted, and they have failed to secure our deception, they
must "be confounded and blush" at the failure of their efforts, "who
seek our souls to destroy them: and let them be covered with shame
and confusion who imagine evil against us."[400] Jeremiah also says:
"Let them be confounded, and let not me be confounded: let them be
afraid, and let not me be afraid: bring upon them the fury of Thy
wrath, and with a double destruction destroy them."[401] For no one can
doubt that when they are vanquished by us they will be destroyed with
a double destruction: first, because while men are seeking after holiness, they, though they possessed it, lost it, and became the cause of
man's ruin; secondly, because being spiritual existences, they have
been vanquished by carnal and earthly ones. Each one then of the
saints when he looks on the destruction of his foes and his own triumphs, exclaims with delight: "I will follow after mine enemies and
overtake them: and I will not turn until they are destroyed. I will break
them and they shall not be able to stand: they shall fall under my
feet,"[402] and in his prayers against them the same prophet says: "Judge
thou, O Lord, them that wrong me: overthrow them that fight against

me. Take hold of arms and shield: and rise up to help me. Bring out
the sword and shut up the way against them that persecute me: say to
my soul, I am thy salvation."[403] And when by subduing and destroying
all our passions we have vanquished these, we shall then be permitted
to hear those words of blessing: "Thy hand shall be exalted over thine
enemies, and all thine enemies shall perish."[404] And so when we read
or chant all these and such like passages found in holy writ, unless we
take them as written against those spiritual wickednesses which lie in
wait for us night and day, we shall not only fail to draw from them any
edification to make us gentle and patient, but shall actually meet with
some dreadful consequence and one that is quite contrary to evangelical perfection. For we shall not only not be taught to pray for or to
love our enemies, but actually shall be stirred up to hate them with an
implacable hatred, and to curse them and incessantly to pour forth
prayers against them. And it is terribly wrong and blasphemous to
think that these words were uttered in such a spirit by holy men and
friends of God, on whom before the coming of Christ the law was not
imposed for the very reason that they went beyond its commands, and
chose rather to obey the precepts of the gospel and to aim at apostolical perfection, though they lived before the dispensation of the time.

NOTES:
[397] Eph. 6:12; 1 Cor. 9:26; 2 Tim. 4:7.
[398] Ps. 139 (140):10; 7:17; 34 (35):8.
[399] Ps. 12 (13):4, 5; 34 (35):24, 28, 16, 17; 9 (10):9; 103 (104):21.
[400] Ps. 39 (40):15; 34 (35):26; 39 (40):15.
[401] Jer. 17:18.
[402] Ps. 17 (18):38, 39.
[403] Ps. 34 (35):1-3.
[404] Micah 5:9.

CHAPTER XXII.

On the fact that the power to hurt does not depend upon the will
of the devils.

BUT that they have not the power of hurting any man is shown in
a very clear way by the instance of the blessed Job, where the enemy
did not venture to try him beyond what was allowed to him by the Divine permission; and it is evidenced by the confession of the same

spirits contained in the records of the gospel, where they say: "If Thou cast us out, suffer us to go into the herd of swine."[405] And far more must we hold that they cannot of their own free will enter into any one of men who are created in the image of God, if they have not power to enter into dumb and unclean animals without the permission of God. But no one--I will not say of the younger men, whom we see living most steadfastly in this desert, but even of those who are perfect-- could live alone in the desert, surrounded by such swarms of foes of this kind, if they had unlimited power and freedom to hurt and tempt us: and still more clearly is this supported by the words of our Lord and Saviour, which in the lowliness of the manhood He had assumed, He uttered to Pilate, when He said: "Thou couldest have no power against Me at all, unless it were given thee from above." [406]

NOTES:
[405] S. Matt. 8:31.
[406] S. John 19:11.

CHAPTER XXIII.

Of the diminished power of the devils.

BUT we have thoroughly discovered both by our own experience and by the testimony of the Elders that the devils have not now the same power as they had formerly during the early days of the ancho- rites, when yet there were only a few monks living in the desert. For such was their fierceness that it was with difficulty that a few very steadfast men, and those advanced in years were able to endure a life of solitude. Since in the actual monasteries where eight or ten men used to live, their violence attacked them so and their assaults were experienced so frequently, and so visibly, that they did not dare all to go to bed at once by night, but took turns and while some snatched a little sleep, others kept watch and devoted themselves to Psalms and prayer and reading. And when the wants of nature compelled them to sleep, they awoke the others, and committed to them in like manner the duty of keeping watch over those who were going to bed. Whence we cannot doubt that one of two things has brought about this result not only in the case of us who seem to be fairly strong from the ex- perience which our age gives us, but also in the case of younger men as well. For either the malice of the devils has been beaten back by the power of the cross penetrating even to the desert, and by its grace which shines everywhere; or else our carelessness makes them relax something of their first onslaught, as they scorn to attack us with the same energy with which they formerly raged against those most admirable soldiers of Christ; and by this deceit and ceasing from open attacks they do us still more damage. For we see that some have fallen into so sluggish a condition that they have to be coaxed by too gentle exhortations for fear lest they should forsake their cells and fall into more dangerous troubles, and wander and stray about and be entangled in what I would call grosser sins; and it is thought that a great thing is got from them if they can even with some listlessness remain in the desert, and the Elders often say to them as a great relief: Stop in your cells, and eat and drink and sleep as much as you like,[407] if only you will stay in them always.

NOTES:
[407] So centuries later it is told of a Jesuit father that when one wanted to relax the strictness of his fast, he replied, "Eat an ox, but be a Christian."

CHAPTER XXIV.

Of the way in which the devils prepare for themselves an entrance into the bodies of those whom they are going to possess.

IT is clear then that unclean spirits cannot make their way into those whose bodies they are going to seize upon, in any other way than by first taking possession of their minds and thoughts. And when they have robbed them of fear and the recollection of God and spiritual meditation, they boldly advance upon them, as if they were dispossessed of all protection and Divine safeguard, and could easily be bound, and then take up their dwelling in them as if in a possession given over to them.

CHAPTER XXV.

On the fact that those men are more wretched who are possessed by sins than those who are possessed by devils.

PART 1

ALTHOUGH it is a fact that those men are more grievously and severely troubled, who, while they seem to be very little affected by them in the body, are yet possessed in spirit in a far worse way, as they are entangled in their sins and lusts. For as the Apostle says: "Of whom a man is overcome, of him he is also the servant." Only that in this respect they are more dangerously ill, because though they are their slaves, yet they do not know that they are assaulted by them, and under their dominion. But we know that even saintly men have been given over in the flesh to Satan and to great afflictions for some very slight faults, since the Divine mercy will not suffer the very least spot or stain to be found in them on the day of judgment, and purges away in this world every spot of their filth, as the prophet, or rather God Himself says, in order that He may commit them to eternity as gold or silver refined and needing no penal purification. "And," says He, "I will clean purge away thy dross, and I will take away all thy tin; and after this thou shall be called the city of the just, a faithful city." And again: "Like as silver and gold are tried in the furnace, so the Lord chooseth the hearts;" And again: "The fire tries gold and silver; but man is tried in the furnace of humiliation;" and this also: "For whom the Lord loveth He chasteneth, and scourgeth every son whom He receiveth." [408]

NOTES:
[408] Is. 1:25, 26; Prov. 17:3 (LXX); Ecclus. 2:5; Heb. 12:6.

CHAPTER XXVI.

Of the death of the prophet who was led astray, and of the infirmity of the Abbot Paul, with which he was visited for the sake of his cleansing.

AND we see clear instance of this in the case of that prophet and man of God in the third book of Kings, who was straightway destroyed by a lion for a single fault of disobedience, in which he was implicated not of set purpose nor by the fault of his own will but by the enticement of another, as the Scripture speaks thus of him: "It is the man of God, who was disobedient to the mouth of the Lord, and the Lord delivered him to the lion, and it tare him according to the word of the Lord, which He spake."[409] In which case the punishment of the present offence and carelessness together with the reward of his righteousness, for which the Lord gave over his prophet in this world to the destroyer, are shown by the moderation and abstinence of the beast of prey, as that most savage creature did not dare even to taste the carcass that was given over to him. And of the same thing a very clear and plain proof has been given in our own days in the case of the Abbots Paul and Moses who lived in a spot in this desert called Calamus,[410] for the former had formerly dwelt in the wilderness which is hard by the city of Panephysis,[411] which we know had only recently been made a wilderness by an inundation of salt water; which whenever the north wind blew, was driven from the marshes and spreading over the adjacent fields covered the face of the whole district, so as to make the ancient villages, which on this very account had been deserted by all their inhabitants, look like islands. Here, then, the Abbot Paul had made such progress in purity of heart in the stillness and silence of the desert, that he did not suffer, I will not say a woman's face, but even the clothes of one of that sex to appear in his sight. For when as he was going to the cell of one of the Elders together with Abbot Archebius[412] who lived in the same desert, by accident a woman met him, he was so disgusted at meeting her that he dropped the business of his friendly visit which he had taken in hand and dashed back again to his own monastery with greater speed than a man would flee from the face of a lion or terrible dragon; so that he was not moved even by the shouts and prayers of the aforesaid Abbot Archebius who called him back to go on with the journey they had undertaken to ask the old man what they had proposed to do. But though this was done in his eagerness for chastity and desire for purity, yet because it was done not according to knowledge, and because the observance of discipline, and the methods of proper strictness were overstrained, for he imagined that not merely familiarity with a woman (which is the real harm,) but even the very form of that sex was to be execrated, he was forthwith overtaken by such a punishment that his whole body was struck with paralysis, and none of his limbs were able to perform their proper functions, since not merely his hands and feet, but even the movements of the tongue, which enables us to frame our words, (were affected) and his very ears lost the sense of hearing, so that there was left in him nothing more of his manhood than an immovable and insensible figure. But he was reduced to such a condition that the utmost care of men was unable to minister to his infirmity, but only the tender service of women could attend to his wants: for when he was taken to a convent of holy virgins, food and drink, which he could not ask for even by signs, were brought to him by female attendants, and for the performance of all that nature required he was ministered to by the same service for nearly four years, i.e., to the end of his life. And though he was affected by such weakness of all his members that none of his limbs retained their keen power of motion and feeling, nevertheless such grace of goodness proceeded from him that when sick persons were anointed with the oil which had touched what should be called his corpse rather than his body, they were instantly healed of all diseases, so that as regards his own malady it was made clearly and plainly evident even to unbelievers that the infirmity of all his limbs was caused by the providence and love of the Lord, and that the grace of these healings was granted by the power of the Holy Ghost as a witness of his purity and a manifestation of his merits.

NOTES:
[409] 1 Kings 13:26.
[410] Cf. [note] on the Institutes X. xxiv.
[411] Cf. [note] on the Institutes IV. xxx.
[412] On Archebius cf. the note on XI. ii.

CHAPTER XXVII.

On the temptation of Abbot Moses.

BUT the second person whom we mentioned as living in this desert, although he was also a remarkable and striking man, yet, in order to punish a single word, to which in a dispute with Abbot Macarius,[413] he had given utterance somewhat too sharply, as he was anticipated in some opinion, he was instantly delivered to so dreadful a demon that he filled his mouth with filth[414] which he supplied, and the Lord showed by the quickness of his cure, and the author of his healing, that He had brought this scourge upon him to purify him, that there might not remain in him any stain from his momentary error: for as soon as Abbot Macarius committed himself to prayer, quicker than a word the evil spirit fled away from him and departed.

NOTES:
[413] On Macarius see the note on the Institutes V. xli.
[414] Humanas egestiones.

CHAPTER XXVIII.

How we ought not to despise those who are delivered up to unclean spirits.

FROM which it plainly results that we ought not to hate or despise those whom we see to be delivered up to various temptations or to those spirits of evil, because we ought firmly to hold these two points: first, that none of them can be tempted at all by them without God's permission, and secondly that all things which are brought upon us by God, whether they seem to us at the present time to be sad or joyful, are inflicted for our advantage as by a most kind father and most compassionate physician, and that therefore men are, as it were, given into the charge of schoolmasters, and humbled in order that when they depart out of this world they may be removed in a state of greater purity to the other life, or have a lighter punishment inflicted on them, as they have been, as the Apostle says, delivered over at the present time "to Satan for the destruction of the flesh that the spirit may be saved in the day of the Lord Jesus." [415]

NOTES:
[415] 1 Cor. 5:5.

CHAPTER XXIX.

An objection, asking why those who are tormented by unclean spirits are separated from the Lord's communion.

GERMANUS: And how is it that we see them not only scorned and shunned by everybody, but actually always kept away from the Lord's communion in our provinces, in accordance with these words of the gospel: "Give not that which is holy to the dogs, neither cast your pearls before swine;"[416] while you tell us that somehow we ought to hold that the humiliation of this temptation is brought upon them with a view to their purification and profit?

CHAPTER XXX.

The answer to the question raised.

SERENUS: If we had this knowledge. or rather faith, of which I treated above; viz., to believe that all things were brought about by God, and ordered for the good of our souls, we should not only never despise them, but rather pray without ceasing for them as our own members, and sympathize with them with all our hearts and the fullest affection (for "when one member suffers, all the members suffer with it"[417]), as we know that we cannot possibly be perfected without them inasmuch as they are members of us, just as we read that our predecessors could not attain the fulness of promise without us, as the Apostle speaks of them as follows: "And these all being approved by the testimony of faith, received not the promise, God providing some better thing for us that they should not be perfected without us."[418] But we never remember that holy communion was forbidden them; nay rather if it were possible, they thought that it ought to be given to them daily; nor indeed according to the words of the gospel which you incongruously apply in this sense "Give not that which is holy to dogs,"[419] ought we to believe that holy communion becomes food for the demon, and not a purification and safeguard of body and soul; for when it is received by a man it, so to speak, burns out and puts to flight the spirit which has its seat in his members or is trying to lurk in them. For in this way we have lately seen Abbot Andronicus and many others cured. For the enemy will more and more abuse the man who is possessed, if he sees him cut off from the heavenly medicine, and will tempt him more often and more fearfully, as he sees him removed the further from this spiritual remedy. [420]

NOTES:
[417] 1 Cor. 12:26.
[418] Heb. 11:39, 40.
[419] S. Matt. 7:6.
[420] The question whether the Holy Communion should ever be given to those possessed is discussed by S. Thomas Aquinas, in the Summa III. Q. lxxx. Art. 9, and answered in the affirmative, the authorities quoted in its favour

being this passage from Cassian, and the third Canon of the 1st Council of Orange (A.D. 441).

CHAPTER XXXI.

On the fact that those men are more to be pitied to whom it is not given to be subjected to those temporal temptations.

BUT we ought to consider those men truly wretched and miserable in whose case, although they defile themselves with all kinds of sins and wickedness, yet not only is there no visible sign of the devil's possession shown in them, nor is any temptation proportionate to their actions, nor any scourge of punishment brought to bear upon them. For they are vouchsafed no swift and immediate remedy in this world, whose "hardness and impenitent heart," being too much for punishment in this life, "heapeth up for itself wrath and indignation in the day of wrath and revelation of the righteous judgment of God," "where their worm dieth not, and their fire is not quenched."[421] Against whom the prophet as if perplexed at the affliction of the saints, when he sees them subject to various losses and temptations, and on the other hand sees sinners not only passing through the course of this world without any scourge of humiliation, but even rejoicing in great riches, and the utmost prosperity in everything, inflamed with uncontrollable indignation and fervour of spirit, exclaims: "But as for me, my feet had almost gone, my treadings had well nigh slipped. For I was grieved at the wicked, when I saw the peace of sinners. For there is no regard to their death, nor is there strength in their stripes. They are not in the labour of men, neither shall they be scourged like other men,"[422] since hereafter they shall be punished with the devils, to whom in this world it was not vouchsafed to be scourged in the lot and discipline of sons, together with men. Jeremiah also, when conversing with God on this prosperity of sinners, although he never professes to doubt about the justice of God, as he says "for Thou art just, O Lord, if I dispute with Thee," yet in his inquiry as to the reasons of this inequality, proceeds to say: "But yet I will speak what is just to Thee. Why doth the way of the wicked prosper? Why is it well with all them that transgress and do wickedly? Thou hast planted them and they have taken root: they prosper and bring forth fruit. Thou art near in their mouth and far from their reins."[423] And when the Lord mourns for their destruction by the prophet, and anxiously directs doctors and physicians to heal them, and in a manner urges them on to a similar lamentation and says: "Babylon is suddenly fallen: she is destroyed. Howl for her: take balm for her pain, if so she may be healed;" then, in their despair, the angels, to whom is entrusted the care of man's salvation, make reply; or at any rate the prophet in the person of the Apostles and spiritual men and doctors who see the hardness of their soul, and their impenitent heart: "We have healed Babylon: but she is not cured. Let us forsake her, and let us go every man to his own land because her judgment hath reached even to the heavens, and is lifted up to the clouds."[424] Of their desperate feebleness then Isaiah speaks in the Person of God to Jerusalem: "From the sole of the foot unto the top of the head there is no soundness therein: wounds and bruises and swelling sores: they are not bound up nor dressed nor fermented with oil." [425]

NOTES:
[421] Rom. 2:5; Is. 66:24.
[422] Ps. 72 (73):2-5.
[423] Jer. 12:1-2.
[424] Jer. 51:8, 9.
[425] Is. 1:6.

CHAPTER XXXII.

Of the different desires and wishes which exist in the powers of the air.

BUT it is clearly proved that there exist in unclean spirits as many desires as there are in men. For some of them, which are commonly called Plani,[426] are shown to be so seductive and sportive that, when they have taken continual possession of certain places or roads, they delight themselves not indeed with tormenting the passers by whom they can deceive, but, contenting themselves merely with laughing at them and mocking them, try to tire them out rather than to injure them: while some spend the night merely by harmlessly taking possession of men, though others are such slaves to fury and ferocity that they are not simply content with hurting the bodies of those, of whom they have taken possession, by tearing them in a dreadful manner, but actually are eager to rush upon those who are passing by at a distance, and to attack them with most savage slaughter: like those described in the gospel, for fear of whom no man dared to pass by that way. And there is no doubt that these and such as these in their insatiable fury delight in wars and bloodshed. Others we find affect the hearts of those whom they have seized with empty pride, (and these are commonly called Bacucei[427]) so that they stretch themselves up beyond their proper height and at one time puff themselves up with arrogance and pomposity, and at another time condescend in an ordinary and bland manner, to a state of calmness and affability: and as they fancy that they are great people and the wonder of everybody, at one time show by bowing their body that they are worshipping higher powers, while at another time they think that they are worshipped by others, and so go through all those movements which express true service either proudly or humbly. Others we find are not only keen for lies, but also inspire men with blasphemies. And of this we ourselves can testify as we have heard a demon openly confessing that he had proclaimed a wicked and impious doctrine by the mouths of Arius and Eunomius. And the same thing we read that one of them openly proclaimed in the fourth book of Kings: "I will go forth," he said, "and will be a lying spirit in the mouth of all his prophets."[428] On which the Apostle, when reproving those who are deceived by them, adds as follows: "giving heed to seducing spirits and doctrines of devils speaking lies in hypocrisy."[429] And that there are other kinds of devils which are deaf and dumb the gospels testify. And that some spirits incite to lust and wantonness the prophet maintains saying: "The spirit of fornication deceived them and they went astray from their God."[430] In the same way the authority of Scripture teaches us that there are demons of the night and of the day and of the noonday:[431] But it would take too long to search through the whole of Scripture and run through the different kinds of them, as they are termed by the prophets onocentaurs, satyrs, sirens, witches, howlers, ostriches, urchins; and asps and basilisks in the Psalms; and are called lions, dragons, scorpions in the gospel, and are named by the Apostle the prince of this world, rulers of this darkness, and spirits of wickedness.[432] And all these names we ought not to take as given at random or hap-hazard, but as alluding to their fierceness and madness under the sign of those wild beasts which are more or less harmful and dangerous among us, and by comparing them to the poisonous wickedness or power which among other beasts or serpents, some preeminence in evil confers on them, they are called by their names, in such a way that to one is assigned the name of lion because of the fury of his rage and the madness of his anger, to another that of basilisk because of his deadly poison, which kills a person before it is perceived, and to another that of onocentaur or urchin or ostrich because of his sluggish malice.

NOTES:
[426] "Planoi," "Seducers," if the reading be correct: but some MSS. have "Fauni."
[427] The origin of this term is obscure.
[428] 1 Kings 22:22.
[429] 1 Tim. 4:1, 2.
[430] Hos. 4:12.
[431] Ps. 90 (91):5, 6.
[432] Cf. Is. 13:21, 22; 34:13, 15; Ps. 90 (91):13; S. Luke 10:19; S. John 14:30; Eph. 6:12.

CHAPTER XXXIII.

A question as to the origin of such differences in powers of evil in the sky.

GERMANUS: We certainly do not doubt that those orders which the Apostle enumerates refer to them: "For we wrestle not against flesh and blood, but against principalities, against powers, against the world-rulers of this darkness, against spirits of wickedness in heavenly places:"[433] but we want to know whence comes such a difference between them, or how such grades of wickedness exist? Were they created for this, to meet with these orders of evil, and in some way to serve this wickedness?

NOTES:
[433] Eph. 6:12.

CHAPTER XXXIV.

The postponement of the answer to the question raised.

SERENUS: Although your proposals would rob us of our whole night's rest, so that we should not notice the approach of the rising dawn, and should be tempted greedily to prolong our conference till sunrise, yet since the solving of the question raised, if we began to trace it out, would launch us on a wide and deep sea of questions, which the shortness of the time at our disposal would not permit us to traverse, I think it will be more convenient to reserve it for consideration another night, when by the raising of this question I shall receive from your very ready converse some spiritual joy and richer fruit, and we shall be able if the Holy Spirit grants us a prosperous breeze to penetrate more freely into the intricacies of the questions raised. Wherefore let us enjoy a little sleep, and so shake off the drowsiness that steals over our eyes, as the dawn approaches, and then we will go together to church, for the observance of Sunday bids us do this, and after service will come back, and as you wish, discuss with redoubled delight what the Lord may have given to us for our common improvement.

CONFERENCE 8.

The Second Conference of Abbot Serenus
on Principalities

CHAPTER I.

Of the hospitality of Abbot Serenus.

WHEN we had finished the duties of the day, and the congregation had been dismissed from Church we returned to the old man's cell, and enjoyed a most sumptuous repast. For instead of the sauce which with a few drops of oil spread over it was usually set on the table for his daily meal, he mixed a little decoction and poured over it a somewhat more liberal allowance of oil than usual; for each of them when he is going to partake of his daily repast, pours those drops of oil on, not that he may receive any enjoyment from the taste of it (for so limited is the supply that it is hardly enough I will not say to line the passage of his throat and jaws, but even to pass down it) but that using it, he may keep down the pride of his heart (which is certain to creep in stealthily and surely if his abstinence is any stricter) and the incitements to vainglory, for as his abstinence is practised with the greater secrecy, and is carried on without anyone to see it, so much the more subtly does it never cease to tempt the man who conceals it. Then he set before us table salt, and three olives each: after which he produced a basket containing parched vetches which they call trogalia,[434] from which we each took five grains, two prunes and a fig apiece. For it is considered wrong for anyone to exceed that amount in that desert. And when we had finished this repast and had begun to ask him again for his promised solution of the question, "Let us hear," said the old man, "your question, the consideration of which we postponed till the present time."

CHAPTER II.

Statements on the different kinds of spiritual wickednesses.

THEN GERMANUS: We want to know what is the origin of the great variety of hostile powers opposed to men, and the difference between them, which the blessed Apostle sums up as follows: "We wrestle not against flesh and blood, but against principalities, against powers, against the world-rulers of this darkness, against spiritual wickedness in heavenly places:"[435] and again: "Neither angels nor principalities nor powers nor any other creature, can separate us from the love of God which is in Christ Jesus our Lord."[436] Whence then arises the enmity of all this malice jealous of us? Are we to believe that those powers were created by the Lord for this; viz., to fight against men in these grades and orders?

NOTES:
[435] Eph. 6:12.
[436] Rom. 8:38, 39.

CHAPTER III.

The answer on the many kinds of food provided in holy Scripture.

SERENUS: The authority of holy Scripture says on those points on which it would inform us some things so plainly and clearly even to those who are utterly void of understanding, that not only are they not veiled in the obscurity of any hidden meaning, but do not even require the help of any explanation, but carry their meaning and sense on the surface of the words and letters: but some things are so concealed and involved in mysteries as to offer us an immense field for skill and care in the discussion and explanation of them. And it is clear that God has so ordered it for many reasons: first for fear lest the holy mysteries, if they were covered by no veil of spiritual meaning, should be exposed equally to the knowledge and understanding of everybody, i.e., the profane as well as the faithful and thus there might be no difference in the matter of goodness and prudence between the lazy and the earnest: next that among those who are indeed of the household of faith, while immense differences of intellectual power open out before them, there might be the opportunity of reproving the slothfulness of the idle, and of proving the keenness and diligence of the earnest. And so holy Scripture is fitly compared to a rich and fertile field, which, while bearing and producing much which is good for man's food without being cooked by fire, produces some things which are found to be unsuitable for man's use or even harmful unless they have lost all the roughness of their raw condition by being tempered and softened down by the heat of fire. But some are naturally fit for use in both states, so that even when uncooked they are not unpleasant from their raw condition, but still are rendered more palatable by being cooked and heated by fire. Many more things too are produced only fit for the food of irrational creatures, and cattle, and wild animals and birds, but utterly useless as food for men, which while still in their rough state without being in any way touched by fire, conduce to the health and life of cattle. And we can clearly see that the same system holds good in that most fruitful garden of the Scriptures of the Spirit, in which some things shine forth clear and bright in their literal sense, in such a way that while they have no need of any higher interpretation, they furnish abundant food and nourishment in the simple sound of the words, to the hearers: as in this passage: "Hear, O Israel, the Lord thy God is one Lord;" and: "Thou shalt love the Lord thy God with all thy heart, and with all thy soul, and with all thy strength."[437] But there are some which, unless they are weakened down by an allegorical interpretation, and softened by the trial of the fire of the spirit cannot become wholesome food for the inner man without injury and loss to him; and damage rather than profit will accrue to him from receiving them: as with this passage: "But let your loins be girded up and your lights burning;" and: "whosoever has no sword, let him sell his coat and buy himself a sword;" and: "whosoever taketh not up his cross and followeth after Me is not worthy of Me;"[438] a passage which some most earnest monks, having "indeed a zeal for God, but not according to knowledge"[439] understood literally, and so made themselves wooden crosses, and carried them about constantly on their shoulders, and so were the cause not of edification but of ridicule on the part of all who saw them. But some are capable of being taken suitable and properly in both ways, i.e., the historical and allegorical, so that either explanation furnishes a healing draught to the soul; as this passage: "If any one shall smite thee on the right cheek, turn to him the other also;" and: "when they persecute you in one city, flee to another;" and: "if thou wilt be perfect, go, sell all that thou hast and give to the poor, and thou shalt have treasure in heaven, and come follow Me."[440] It produces indeed "grass for the cattle" also, (and of this food all the fields of Scripture are full); viz., plain and simple narratives of history, by which simple folk, and those who are incapable of perfect and sound understanding (of whom it is said "Thou, Lord, wilt save both man and beast")[441] may be made stronger and more vigorous for their hard work and the labour of actual life, in accordance with the state and measure of their capacity.

NOTES:
[437] Deut. 6:4, 5.
[438] S. Luke 12:35; 22:36; S. Matt. 10:38.
[439] Rom. 10:2.
[440] S. Matt. 5:39; 10:23; 19:21.
[441] Ps. 35 (36):7.

CHAPTER IV.

Of the double sense in which Holy Scripture may be taken.

WHEREFORE on those passages which are brought forward with a clear explanation we also can constantly lay down the meaning and boldly state our own opinions. But those which the Holy Spirit, reserving for our meditation and exercise, has inserted in holy Scripture with veiled meaning, wishing some of them to be gathered from various proofs and conjectures, ought to be step by step and carefully brought together, so that their assertions and proofs may be arranged by the discretion of the man who is arguing or supporting them. For sometimes when a difference of opinion is expressed on one and the same subject, either view may be considered reasonable and be held without injury to the faith either firmly, or doubtfully, i.e., in such a way that neither is full belief nor absolute rejection accorded to it, and the second view need not interfere with the former, if neither of them is found to be opposed to the faith: as in this case: where Elias came in the person of John,[442] and is again to be the precursor of the Lord's Advent: and in the matter of the "Abomination of desolation" which "stood in the holy place," by means of that idol of Jupiter which, as we read,

189

was placed in the temple in Jerusalem, and which is again to stand in the Church through the coming of Antichrist,[443] and all those things which follow in the gospel, which we take as having been fulfilled before the captivity of Jerusalem and still to be fulfilled at the end of this world. In which matters neither view is opposed to the other, nor does the first interpretation interfere with the second.

NOTES:
[442] Cf. S. Matt. 11:14.
[443] See Dan. 9:27; 2 Macc. 6:2; S. Matt. 24:15 sq.

CHAPTER V.

Of the fact that the question suggested ought to be included among those things to be held in a neutral or doubtful way.

AND therefore since the question raised by us, does not seem to have been sufficiently or often ventilated among men, and is clear to most people, and from this fact what we bring forward may perhaps appear to some to be doubtful, we ought to regulate our own view (since it does not interfere with faith in the Trinity) so that it may be included among those things which are to be held doubtfully; although they rest not on mere opinions such as are usually given to guesses and conjectures, but on clear Scripture proof.

CHAPTER VI.

Of the fact that nothing is created evil by God.

GOD forbid that we should admit that God has created anything which is substantially evil, as Scripture says "everything that God had made was very good."[444] For if they were created by God such as they are now, or made for this purpose; viz., to occupy these positions of malice, and ever to be ready for the deception and ruin of men, we should in opposition to the view of the above quoted Scripture slander God as the Creator and author of evil, as having Himself formed utterly evil wills and natures, creating them for this very purpose; viz., that they might ever persist in their wickedness and never pass over to the feeling of a good will. The following reason then of this diversity is what we received from the tradition of the fathers, being drawn from the fount of Holy Scripture.

NOTES:
[444] Gen. 1:31.

CHAPTER VII.

Of the origin of principalities or powers.

NONE of the faithful question the fact that before the formation of this visible creation God made spiritual and celestial powers, in order that owing to the very fact that they knew that they had been formed out of nothing by the goodness of the Creator for such glory and bliss, they might render to Him continual thanks and ceaselessly continue to praise Him. For neither should we imagine that God for the first time began to originate His creation and work with the formation of this world, as if in those countless ages beforehand He had taken no thought of Providence and the divine ordering of things, and as if we could believe that having none towards whom to show the blessings of His goodness, He had been solitary, and a stranger to all bountifulness; a thing which is too poor and unsuitable to fancy of that boundless and eternal and incomprehensible Majesty; as the Lord Himself says of these powers: "When the stars were made together, all my angels praised Me with a loud voice."[445] Those then who were present at the creation of the stars, are most clearly proved to have been created before that "beginning" in which it is said that heaven and earth were made, inasmuch as they are said with loud voices and admiration to have praised the Creator because of all those visible creatures which, as they saw, proceeded forth from nothing. Before then that beginning in time which is spoken of by Moses, and which according to the historic and Jewish interpretation denotes the age of this world (without prejudice to our interpretation, according to which we explain that the "beginning," of all things is Christ, in whom the Father created all things, as it is said "All things were made by him, and without Him was not anything made,")[446] before, I say, that beginning of Genesis in time there is no question that God had already created all those powers and heavenly virtues; which the Apostle enumerates in order and thus describes: "For in Christ were created all things both in heaven and on earth, visible and invisible, whether they be angels or archangels, whether they be thrones or dominions, whether they be principalities or powers. All things were made by Him and in Him." [447]

NOTES:
[445] Job 38:7 (LXX).
[446] S. John 1:3.
[447] Col. 1:16.

CHAPTER VIII.

Of the fall of the devil and the angels.

AND so we are clearly shown that out of that number of them some of the leaders fell, by the lamentations of Ezekiel and Isaiah, in which we know that the prince of Tyre or that Lucifer who rose in the morning is lamented with a doleful plaint: and of him the Lord speaks as follows to Ezekiel: "Son of man, take up a lamentation over the prince of Tyre, and say to him: Thus saith the Lord God: Thou wast the seal of resemblance, full of wisdom, perfect in beauty. Thou wast in the pleasures of the paradise of God: every precious stone was thy covering: the sardius, the topaz and the jasper, the chrysolyte and the onyx and the beryl, the sapphire and the carbuncle and the emerald: gold the work of thy beauty, and thy pipes were prepared in the day that thou wast created. Thou wast a cherub stretched out and protecting, and I set thee in the holy mountain of God, thou hast walked in the midst of the stones of fire. Thou wast perfect in thy ways from the day of thy creation, until iniquity was found in thee. By the multitude of thy merchandise thy inner parts were filled with iniquity and thou hast sinned; and I cast thee out from the mountain of God, and destroyed thee, O covering cherub, out of the midst of the stones of fire. And thy heart was lifted up with thy beauty: thou hast lost thy wisdom in thy beauty, I have cast thee to the ground: I have set thee before the face of kings, that they might behold thee. Thou hast defiled thy sanctuaries by the multitude of thy iniquities and by the iniquity of thy traffic."[448] Isaiah also says of another: "How art thou fallen from heaven, O Lucifer, who didst rise in the morning? how art thou fallen to the ground, that didst wound the nations? and thou saidst in thine heart, I will ascend into heaven, I will exalt my throne above the stars of God, I will sit in the mountain of the covenant, in the sides of the north. I will ascend above the heights of the clouds. I will be like the Most High."[449] But Holy Scripture relates that these fell not alone from that summit of their station in bliss, as it tells us that the dragon dragged down together with himself the third part of the stars.[450] One of the Apostles too says still more plainly: "But the angels who kept not their first estate, but left their own dwelling, He hath reserved in everlasting chains under darkness to the judgment of the great day."[451] This too which is said to us: "But ye shall die like men and fall like one of the princes,"[452] what does it imply but that many princes have fallen? And by these testimonies we can gather the reason for this diversity; viz., either that they still retain those differences of rank (which adverse powers are said to possess, after the manner of holy and heavenly virtues) from the station of their former rank in which they were severally created, or else that, though themselves cast down from heavenly places, yet, as a reward for that wickedness of theirs in which they have graduated in evil, they claim in perversity these grades and titles of rank among themselves, by way of copying those virtues which have stood firm there.

NOTES:
[448] Ezek. 28:11-18.
[449] Is. 14:12-14.
[450] Cf. Rev. 12:4.
[451] S. Jude 6.
[452] Ps. 81 (80):7.

CHAPTER IX.

An objection stating that the fall of the devil took its origin from the deception of Eve.

GERMANUS: Up till now we used to believe that the reason and commencement of the ruin and fall of the devil, in which he was cast out from his heavenly estate, was more particularly envy, when in his spiteful subtlety he deceived Adam and Eve.

CHAPTER X.

The answer about the beginning of the devil's fall.

SERENUS: The passage in Genesis shows that that was not the beginning of his fall and ruin, as before their deception it takes the view that he had already been branded with the ignominy of the name of the serpent, where it says: "But the serpent was wiser" or as the Hebrew copies express it, "more subtle than all the beasts of the earth, which the Lord God had made."[453] You see then that he had fallen away from his angelic holiness even before he deceived the first man, so that he not only deserved to be stamped with the ignominy of this title, but actually excelled all other beasts of the earth in the subterfuges of wickedness. For Holy Scripture would not have designated a good angel by such a term, nor would it say of those who were still continuing in that state of bliss: "But the serpent was wiser than all the beasts of the earth." For this title could not possibly be applied I say not to Gabriel or Michael, but it would not even be suitable to any good man. And so the title of serpent and the comparison to beasts most clearly suggests not the dignity of an angel but the infamy of an apostate. Finally the occasion of the envy and seduction, which led him to deceive man, arose from the ground of his previous fall, in that he saw that man, who had but recently been formed out of the dust of the ground, was to be called to that glory, from which he remembered that he himself, while still one of the princes, had fallen. And so that first fall of his, which was due to pride, and which obtained for him the name of the serpent, was followed by a second owing to envy: and as this one found him still in the possession of something upright so that he could enjoy some interchange of conference and counsel with man, by the Lord's sentence he was very properly cast down to the lowest depth, that he might no longer walk as before erect, and looking up on high, but should cleave to the ground and creep along, and be brought low upon his belly and feed upon the earthly food and works of sins, and henceforward proclaim his secret hostility, and put between himself and man an enmity that is to our advantage, and a discord that is to our profit, so that while men are on their guard against him as a dangerous enemy, he can no longer injure them by a deceptive show of friendship.

NOTES:
[453] Gen. 3:1.

CHAPTER XI.

The punishment of the deceiver and the deceived.

BUT we ought in this matter, in order that we may shun evil counsels, to learn a special lesson from the fact that though the author of the deception was visited with a fitting punishment and condemnation, yet still the one who was led astray did not go scot free from punishment, although it was somewhat lighter than that of him who was the author of the deception. And this we see was very plainly expressed. For Adam who was deceived, or rather (to use the Apostle's words) "was not deceived" but, acquiescing in the wishes of her who was deceived, seems to have come to yield a consent that was deadly, is only condemned to labour and the sweat of his brow, which is assigned to him not by means of a curse upon himself, but by means of a curse upon the ground, and its barrenness. But the woman, who persuaded him to this, is visited with an increase of anguish, and pains and sorrow, and also given over to the yoke of perpetual subjection. But the serpent who was the first to incite them to this offence, is punished by a lasting curse. Wherefore we should with the utmost care and circumspection be on our guard against evil counsels, for as they bring punishment upon their authors, so too they do not suffer those who are deceived by them to go free from guilt and punishment.

CHAPTER XII.

Of the crowd of the devils, and the disturbance which they always raise in our atmosphere.

BUT the atmosphere which extends between heaven and earth is ever filled with a thick crowd of spirits, which do not fly about in it quietly or idly, so that most fortunately the divine providence has withdrawn them from human sight. For through fear of their attacks, or horror at the forms, into which they transform and turn themselves at will, men would either be driven out of their wits by an insufferable

195

dread, and faint away, from inability to look on such things with bodily eyes, or else would daily grow worse and worse, and be corrupted by their constant example and by imitating them, and thus there would arise a sort of dangerous familiarity and deadly intercourse between men and the unclean powers of the air, whereas those crimes which are now committed among men, are concealed either by walls and enclosures or by distance and space, or by some shame and confusion: but if they could always look on them with open face, they would be stimulated to a greater pitch of insanity, as there would not be a single moment in which they would see them desist from their wickedness, since no bodily weariness, or occupation in business or care for their daily food (as in our case) forces them sometimes even against their will to desist from the purposes they have begun to carry out.

CHAPTER XIII.

Of the fact that opposing powers turn the attack, which they aim at men, even against each other.

FOR it is quite clear that they aim these attacks, with which they assault men, even against each other, for in like manner they do not cease to promote with unwearied strife the discords and struggles which they have undertaken for some peoples because of a sort of innate love of wickedness which they have: and this we read of as being very clearly set forth in the vision of Daniel the prophet, where the angel Gabriel speaks as follows: "Fear not, Daniel: for from the first day that thou didst set thy heart to understand, to afflict thyself in the sight of thy God, thy words have been heard: and I am come for thy words. But the prince of the kingdom of the Persians resisted me one and twenty days: and behold Michael one of the chief princes came to help me, and I remained there by the king of the Persians. But I am come to teach thee what things shall befall thy people in the latter days."[454] And we can not possibly doubt that this prince of the kingdom of the Persians was a hostile power, which favoured the nation of the Persians an enemy of God's people; for in order to hinder the good which it saw would result from the solution of the question for which the prophet prayed the Lord, by the archangel, in its jealousy it opposed itself to prevent the saving comfort of the angel from reaching Daniel too speedily, and from strengthening the people of God, over which the archangel Gabriel was: and the latter said that even then, owing to the fierceness of his assaults, he would not have been able to come to him, had not Michael the archangel come to help him, and met the prince of the kingdom of the Persians, and joined battle with him, and intervened, and defended him from his attack, and so enabled him to come to instruct the prophet after twenty-one days. And a little later on it says: "And the angel said: Dost thou know wherefore I am come to thee? And now I will return to fight against the prince of the Persians. For when I went forth, there appeared the prince of the Greeks coming. But I will tell thee what is written down in the Scriptures of truth: and none is my helper in all these things but Michael your prince."[455] And again: "At that time shall Michael rise up, the great prince, who standeth for the children of thy people."[456] So then we read that in the same way another was called the prince of the Greeks, who since he was patron of that nation which was subject to him seems to have been opposed to the nation of the Persians as well as to the people of Israel. From which we clearly see that antagonistic powers raise against each other those quarrels of nations, and conflicts and dissensions, which they show among themselves at their instigation, and that they either exult at their victories or are cast down at their defeats, and thus cannot live in harmony among themselves, while each of them is always striving with restless jealousy on behalf of those whom he presides over, against the patron of some other nation.

NOTES:
[454] Dan. 10:12-14.
[455] Dan. 10:20, 21.
[456] Dan. 12:1.

CHAPTER XIV.

How it is that spiritual wickednesses obtained the names of powers or principalities.

WE can then see clear reasons, in addition to those ideas which we expounded above, why they are called principalities or powers; viz., because they rule and preside over different nations, and at least hold sway over inferior spirits and demons, of which the gospels give us evidence by their own confession that there exist legions. For they could not be called lords unless they had some over whom to exercise the sway of lordship; nor could they be called powers or principalities, unless there were some over whom they could claim power: and this we find pointed out very clearly in the gospel by the Pharisees in their blasphemy: "He casteth out devils by Beelzebub the prince of the devils,"[457] for we find that they are also called "rulers of darkness,"[458] and that one of them is styled "the prince of this world."[459] But the blessed Apostle declares that hereafter, when all things shall be subdued to Christ, these orders shall be destroyed, saying: "When He shall have delivered up the kingdom to God even the Father, when He shall have destroyed all principalities and powers and dominions."[460] And this certainly can only take place if they are removed from the sway of those over whom we know that powers and dominions and principalities take charge in this world.

NOTES:
[457] S. Luke 11:15.
[458] Eph. 6:12.
[459] S. John 14:30.
[460] 1 Cor. 15:24.

CHAPTER XV.

Of the fact that it is not without reason that the names of angels and archangels are given to holy and heavenly powers.

FOR no one doubts that not without cause or reason are the same titles of rank assigned to the better sort, and that they are names of office and of worth or dignity, for it is plain that they are termed angels, i.e., messengers from their office of bearing messages, and the appropriateness of the name teaches that they are "archangels" because the preside over angels, "dominions" because they hold dominion over certain persons, and "principalities" because they have some to be princes over, and "thrones" because they are so near to God and so privy and close to Him that the Divine Majesty specially rests in them as in a Divine throne, and in a way reclines surely on them.

CHAPTER XVI.

Of the subjection of the devils, which they show to their own princes, as seen in a brother's vision.

BUT that unclean spirits are ruled over by worse powers and are subject to them we not only find from those passages of Scripture, recorded in the gospels when the Pharisees maligned the Lord, and He answered "If I by Beelzebub the prince of the devils cast out devils,"[461] but we are also taught this by clear visions and many experiences of the saints, for when one of our brethren was making a journey in this desert, as day was now declining he found a cave and stopped there meaning to say his evening office in it, and there midnight passed while he was still singing the Psalms. And when after he had finished his office he sat down a little before refreshing his wearied body, on a sudden he began to see innumerable troops of demons gathering together on all sides, who came forward in an immense crowd, and a long line, some preceding and others following their prince; who at length arrived, being taller and more dreadful to look at than all the others; and, a throne having been placed, he sat down as on some lofty tribunal, and began to investigate by a searching examination the actions of each one of them; and those who said that they had not yet been able to circumvent their rivals, he commanded to be driven out of his sight with shame and ignominy as idle and slothful, rebuking them with angry wrath for the waste of so much time, and for their labour thrown away: but those who reported that they had deceived those assigned to them, he dismissed before all with the highest praise amidst the exultation and applause of all, as most brave warriors, and most renowned as an example to all the rest: and when in this number some most evil spirit had presented himself, in delight at having to relate some magnificent triumph, he mentioned the name of a very well known monk, and declared that after having incessantly attacked him for fifteen years, he had at last got the better of him, so as to destroy him that very same night by the sin of fornication, for that he had not only impelled him to commit adultery with some consecrated maid, but had actually persuaded him to keep her and marry her. And when there arose shouts of joy at this narrative, he was extolled with the highest praise by the prince of darkness, and departed crowned with great honours. And so when at break of day the whole swarm of demons had vanished from his eyes, the brother being doubtful about the assertion of the unclean spirit, and rather thinking that he had desired to entice him by an ancient customary deceit, and to brand an innocent brother with the crime of incest, being mindful of those words of the gospel; viz., that "he abode not in the truth because there is no truth in him. When he speaketh a lie, he speaketh of his own, for he is a liar, and its father,"[462] he made his way to Pelusium, where he knew that the man lived, whom the evil spirit declared to be destroyed: for the brother was very well known to him, and when he had asked him, he found that on the same night on which that foul demon had announced his downfall to his company and prince, he had left his former monastery, and sought the town, and had gone astray by a wretched fall with the girl mentioned.

NOTES:
[461] S. Luke 11:19.
[462] S. John 8:44.

CHAPTER XVII.

Of the fact that two angels always cling to every man.

FOR Holy Scripture bears witness that two angels, a good and a bad one, cling to each one of us. And of the good ones the Saviour says: "Do not despise one of these little ones; for I say unto you that their angels in heaven do always behold the face of thy Father which is in heaven:"[463] and this also: "the angel of the Lord shall encamp round about them that fear Him, and deliver them."[464] Moreover this also which is said in the Acts of the Apostles, of Peter, that "it is his angel."[465] But of both sorts the book of the Shepherd teaches us very fully.[466] But if we consider about him who attacked the blessed Job we shall clearly learn that it was he who always plotted against him but never could entice him to sin, and that therefore he asked for power from the Lord, as he was worsted not by his (Job's) virtue but by the Lord's protection which ever shielded him. Of Judas also it is said: "And let the devil stand at his right hand." [467]

NOTES:
[463] S. Matt. 18:10.
[464] Ps. 33 (34):8.
[465] Acts 12:15.

[466] The reference is to the Pastor or Shepherd of Hermas, a work of the second century. The passage to which Cassian alludes is found in Book II. Commandm. vi.; where it is said that "there are two angels with a man, one of righteousness and the other of iniquity," and suggestions are given how to recognize each of them and to distinguish the suggestions of the one from those of the other. The passage is also alluded to by Origen, De Principiis, Book III. c. ii. and Hom. xxxv. in (Lucam); and Cassian refers to it again in Conf. XIII. c. xii.

[467] Ps. 108 (109):6.

CHAPTER XVIII.

Of the degrees of wickedness which exist in hostile spirits, as shown in the case of two philosophers.

BUT of the difference that there is between demons we have learnt a great deal by means of those two philosophers who formerly by acts of magic had oftentimes great experience both of their laziness and of their courage and savage wickedness. For these looking down on the blessed Antony as a boor and rustic, and wanting, if they could not injure him any further, at least to drive him from his cell by illusions of magic and the devices of demons, despatched against him most foul spirits, for they were impelled to this attack upon him by the sting of jealousy because enormous crowds came daily to him as the servant of God. And when these most savage demons did not even venture to approach him as he was now signing his breast and forehead with the sign of the cross, and, now devoting himself to prayer and supplication, they returned without any result to those who had directed them; and these again sent against him others more desperate in wickedness, and when these too had spent their strength in vain, and returned without having accomplished anything, and others still more powerful were nevertheless told off against the victorious soldier of Christ, and could prevail nothing against him, all these great plots of theirs devised with all the arts of magic were only useful in proving the great value that there is in the profession of Christians, so that those fierce and powerful shadows, which they thought would veil the sun and moon if they were directed towards them, could not only not injure him, but not even draw him forth from his monastery for a single instant.

CHAPTER XIX.

Of the fact that devils cannot prevail at all against men unless they have first secured possession of their minds.

AND when in their astonishment at this they came straight to Abbot Antony and disclosed the extent of their attacks and the reason of them and their plots, they dissembled their jealousy and asked that they might forthwith be made Christians. But when he had asked of them the day when the assault was made, he declared that at that time he had been afflicted with the most bitter pangs of thought. And by this experience the blessed Antony proved and established the opinion which we expressed yesterday in our Conference, that demons cannot possibly find an entrance into the mind or body of anyone, nor have they the power of overwhelming the soul of anyone, unless they have first deprived it of all holy thoughts, and made it empty and free from spiritual meditation. But you must know that unclean spirits are obedient to men in two ways. For either they are by divine grace and power subject to the holiness of the faithful, or they are captivated by the sacrifices of sinners, and certain charms, and are flattered by them as their worshippers. And the Pharisees too were led astray by this notion and fancied that by this device even the Lord the Saviour gave commands to devils, and said "By Beelzebub the prince of the devils He casteth out devils," in accordance with that plan by which they knew that their own magicians and enchanters--by invoking his name and offering sacrifices, with which they know he is pleased and delighted--have as his servants power even over the devils who are subject to him.

CHAPTER XX.

A question about the fallen angels who are said in Genesis to have had intercourse with the daughters of men.

GERMANUS: Since a passage of Genesis was a little while ago by the providence of God brought forward in our midst, and happily reminded us that we can now conveniently ask about a point which we have always longed to learn, we want to know what view we ought to take about those fallen angels who are said to have had intercourse with the daughters of men, and whether such a thing can literally take place with a spiritual nature. And also with regard to this passage of the gospel which you quoted of the devil a little while back, "for he is a liar and his father,"[468] we should like in the same way to hear who is to be understood by "his father."

NOTES:
[468] S. John 8:44. We find from Augustine (Tract. xxiv. in Johan.) that the Manichees interpreted this text as implying that the devil had a father, translating it "For he is a liar, and so is his father." Augustine himself explains it as Abbot Serenus does below in c. xxv.; viz., that the devil is not only a liar himself but the parent of lies.

CHAPTER XXI.

The answer to the question raised.

SERENUS: You have propounded two not unimportant questions, to which I will reply, to the best of my ability, in the order in which you have raised them. We cannot possibly believe that spiritual existences can have carnal intercourse with women. But if this could ever have literally happened how is it that it does not now also sometimes take place, and that we do not see some in the same way born of women by the agency of demons without intercourse with men? especially when it is clear that they delight in the pollution of lust, which they would certainly prefer to bring about through their own agency rather than through that of men, if they could possibly manage it, as Ecclesiastes declares: "What is it that hath been? The same that is. And what is it that hath been done? The same that is done. And there is nothing new that can be said under the sun, so that a man can say: Behold this is new; for it hath already been in the ages which were before us."[469] But the question raised may be resolved in this way. After the death of righteous Abel, in order that the whole human race might not spring from a wicked fratricide, Seth was born in the place of his brother who was slain, to take the place of his brother not only as regards posterity, but also as regards justice and goodness. And his offspring, following the example of their father's goodness, always remained separate from intercourse with and the society of their kin-

dred descended from the wicked Cain, as the difference of the genealogy very clearly tells us, where it says: "Adam begat Seth, Seth begat
Enos, Enos begat Cainan, but Cainan begat Mahalaleel, but Mahalaleel
begat Jared, Jared begat Enoch, Enoch begat Methuselah, Methuselah
begat Lamech, Lamech begat Noah."[470] And the genealogy of Cain is
given separately as follows: "Cain begat Enoch, Enoch begat Cainan,
Cainan begat Mahalaleel, Mahalaleel begat Methuselah, Methuselah
begat Lamech, Lamech begat Jabal and Jubal."[471] And so the line
which sprang from the seed of righteous Seth always mixed with its
own kith and kin, and continued for a long while in the holiness of its
fathers and ancestors, untouched by the blasphemies and the wickedness of an evil offspring, which had implanted in it a seed of sin as it
were transmitted by its ancestors. As long then as there continued that
separation of the lines between them, the seed of Seth, as it sprang
from an excellent root, was by reason of its sanctity termed "angels of
God," or as some copies have it "sons of God;"[472] and on the contrary
the others by reason of their own and their fathers' wickedness and
their earthly deeds were termed "children of men." Though then there
was up to this time that holy and salutary separation between them, yet
after this the sons of Seth who were the sons of God saw the daughters
of those who were born of the line of Cain, and inflamed with the desire for their beauty took to themselves from them wives who taught
their husbands the wickedness of their fathers, and at once led them
astray from their innate holiness and the single-mindedness of their
forefathers. To whom this saying applies with sufficient accuracy: "I
have said: Ye are Gods, and ye are all the children of the Most High.
But ye shall die like men, and fall like one of the princes;"[473] who fell
away from that true study of natural philosophy, handed down to them
by their ancestors, which the first man who forthwith traced out the
study of all nature, could clearly attain to, and transmit to his descendants on sure grounds, inasmuch as he had seen the infancy of this
world, while still as it were tender and throbbing and unorganized; and
as there was in him not only such fulness of wisdom, but also the grace
of prophecy given by the Divine inspiration, so that while he was still
an untaught inhabitant of this world he gave names to all living creatures, and not only knew about the fury and poison of all kinds of
beasts and serpents, but also distinguished between the virtues of
plants and trees and the natures of stones, and the changes of seasons
of which he had as yet no experience, so that he could well say: "The
Lord hath given me the true knowledge of the things that are, to know
the disposition of the whole world, and the virtues of the elements, the

beginning and the ending and the midst of times, the alterations of their courses and the changes of their seasons, the revolutions of the year and the disposition of the stars, the natures of living creatures and the rage of wild beasts, the force of winds, and the reasonings of men, the diversities of plants and the virtues of roots, and all such things as are hid and open I have learnt."[474] This knowledge then of all nature the seed of Seth received through successive generations, handed down from the fathers, so long as it remained separate from the wicked line, and as it had received it in holiness, so it made use of it to promote the glory of God and the needs of everyday life. But when it had been mingled with the evil generation, it drew aside at the suggestion of devils to profane and harmful uses what it had innocently learnt, and audaciously taught by it the curious arts of wizards and enchantments and magical superstitions, teaching its posterity to forsake the holy worship of the Divinity and to honour and worship either the elements or fire or the demons of the air. How it was then that this knowledge of curious arts of which we have spoken, did not perish in the deluge, but became known to the ages that followed, should, I think, be briefly explained, as the occasion of this discussion suggests, although the answer to the question raised scarcely requires it. And so, as ancient traditions tell us, Ham the son of Noah, who had been taught these superstitions and wicked and profane arts, as he knew that he could not possibly bring any handbook on these subjects into the ark, into which he was to enter with his good father and holy brothers, inscribed these nefarious arts and profane devices on plates of various metals which could not be destroyed by the flood of waters, and on hard rocks, and when the flood was over he hunted for them with the same inquisitiveness with which he had concealed them, and so transmitted to his descendants a seed-bed of profanity and perpetual sin. In this way then that common notion, according to which men believe that angels delivered to men enchantments and diverse arts, is in truth fulfilled. From these sons of Seth then and daughters of Cain, as we have said, there were I born still worse children who became mighty hunters, violent and most fierce men who were termed giants by reason of the size of their bodies and their cruelty and wickedness. For these first began to harass their neighbours and to practise pillaging among men, getting their living rather by rapine than by being contented with the sweat and labour of toil, and their wickedness increased to such a pitch that the world could only be purified by the flood and deluge. So then when the sons of Seth at the instigation of their lust had transgressed that command which had been for a long while kept by a natural instinct from the beginning of the world, it was needful that it should afterwards be restored by the letter of the law: "Thou shalt not give thy daughter to his son to wife, nor shalt thou take a wife of his daughters to thy son; for they shall seduce your hearts to depart from your God, and to follow their gods and serve them." [475]

NOTES:
[469] Eccl. 1:9, 10.
[470] Gen. 5:4-40.
[471] Gen. 4:17-21.
[472] In Gen. 6:2 the MSS. of the LXX. fluctuate between aggeloi tou Qeou and `uioi tou Qeou. The interpretation of the passage which Cassian here rejects is adopted by Philo and Josephus, the book of Enoch, and several of the early fathers, including Justin Martyr, Tertullian, Clement of Alexandria, Lactantius and others. The explanation, which Cassian here gives, taking the "sons of God" of the Sethites, and the "daughters of men" of the line of Cain, is apparently first found in Julius Africanus (`oi apo tou Shq dikaioi), and is adopted among others by Augustine, De Civitate Dei, Book XV. xxiii., where the passage is fully discussed.
[473] Ps. 81 (82):6, 7.
[474] Wis. 7:17-21.
[475] Deut. 8:3; Exod. 34:16; cf. 1 Kings 11:2.

CHAPTER XXII.

An objection, as to how an unlawful intermingling with the daughters of Cain could be charged against the line of Seth before the prohibition of the law.

GERMANUS: If that command had been given to them, then the sin of breaking it might fairly have been brought against them for their audacity in so marrying. But since the observance of that separation had not yet been established by any rule, how could that intermingling of races be counted wrong in them, as it had not been forbidden by any command? For a law does not ordinarily forbid crimes that are past, but those that are future.

CHAPTER XXIII.

The answer, that by the law of nature men were from the beginning liable to judgment and punishment.

SERENUS: God at man's creation implanted in him naturally complete knowledge of the law, and if this had been kept by man, as at the beginning, according to the Lord's purposes, there would not have been any need for another law to be given, which He afterwards proclaimed in writing: for it were superfluous for an external remedy to be offered, where an internal one was still implanted and vigorous. But since this had been, as we have said, utterly corrupted by freedom and the opportunity of sinning, the severe restrictions of the law of Moses were added as the executor and vindicator of this (earlier law) and to use the expressions of Scripture, as its helper, that through fear of immediate punishment men might be kept from altogether losing the good of natural knowledge, according to the word of the prophet who says "He gave the law to help them:"[476] and it is also described by the Apostle as having been given as a schoolmaster[477] to little children, as it instructs and guards them to prevent them from departing through sheer forgetfulness from the teaching in which they had been instructed by the light of nature: for that the complete knowledge of the law was implanted in man at his first creation, is clearly proved from this; viz., that we know that before the law, aye, and even before the flood, all holy men observed the commands of the law without having the letter to read. For how could Abel, without the command of the law, have known that he ought to offer to God a sacrifice of the firstlings of his flock and of the fat thereof,[478] unless he had been taught by the law which was naturally implanted in him? How could Noah have distinguished what animals were clean and what were unclean,[479] when the commandment of the law had not yet made a distinction, unless he had been taught by a natural knowledge? Whence did Enoch learn how to "walk with God,"[480] having never acquired any light of the law from another? Where had Shem and Japheth read "Thou shalt not uncover the nakedness of thy father," so that they went backwards and covered the shame of their father?[481] How was Abraham taught to abstain from the spoils of the enemy which were offered to him, that he might not receive any recompense for his toil, or to pay to the priest Melchizedec the tithes which are ordered by the law of Moses?[482] How was it too that the same Abraham and Lot also humbly offered to passers by and strangers offices of kindness and the washing of their feet, while yet the Evangelic command had not shone forth?[483] Whence did Job obtain such earnestness of faith, such purity of chastity, such knowledge of humility, gentleness, pity and kindness, as we now see shown not even by those who know the gospels by heart? Which of the saints do we read of as not having observed some commandment of the law before the giving of the law? Which of them failed to keep this: "Hear, O Israel, the Lord thy God is one Lord?"[484] Which of them did not fulfil this: "Thou shalt not make to thyself any graven image, nor the likeness of anything which is in heaven or in the earth or under the earth?" Which of them did not observe this: "Honour thy father and thy mother," or what follows in the Decalogue: "Thou shalt do no murder; Thou shalt not commit adultery; Thou shalt not steal; Thou shalt not bear false witness; Thou shalt not covet thy neighbour's wife,"[485] and many other things besides, in which they anticipated the commands not only of the law but even of the gospel?

NOTES:
[476] Is. 8:20 (LXX).
[477] Cf. Gal. 3:24.
[478] Gen. 4:4.
[479] Gen. 7:2.
[480] Gen. 5:22.
[481] Gen. 9:23; Lev. 18:7.
[482] Gen. 14:20, 22.
[483] Gen. 18, 19; cf. S. John 13:34.
[484] Deut. 4:4.
[485] Exod. 20:4-17.

CHAPTER XXIV.

Of the fact that they were justly punished, who sinned before the flood.

AND so then we see that from the beginning God created everything perfect, nor would there have been need for anything to have been added to His original arrangement--as if it were shortsighted and imperfect--if everything had continued in that state and condition in which it had been created by Him. And therefore in the case of those who sinned before the law and even before the flood we see that God visited them with a righteous judgment, because they deserved to be punished without any excuse, for having transgressed the law of nature; nor should we fall into the blasphemous slanders of those who are ignorant of this reason, and so depreciate the God of the Old Testament, and run down our faith, and say with a sneer: Why then did it please your God to will to promulgate the law after so many thousand years, while He suffered such long ages to pass without any law? But if He afterwards discovered something better, then it appears that at the beginning of the world His wisdom was inferior and poorer, and that afterwards as if taught by experience He began to provide for something better, and to amend and improve His original arrangements. A thing which certainly cannot happen to the infinite foreknowledge of God, nor can these assertions be made about Him by the mad folly of heretics without grievous blasphemy, as Ecclesiastes says: "I have learnt that all the words which God hath made from the beginning shall continue forever: nothing can be added to them, and nothing can be taken away from them,"[486] and therefore "the law is not made for the righteous, but for the unrighteous, and insubordinate, for the ungodly and sinners, for the wicked and profane."[487] For as they had the sound and complete system of natural laws implanted in them they had no need of this external law in addition, and one committed to writing, and what was given as an aid to that natural law. From which we infer by the clearest of reasonings that that law committed to writing need not have been given at the beginning (for it was unnecessary for this to be done while the natural law still remained, and was not utterly violated) nor could evangelical perfection have been granted before the law had been kept. For they could not have listened to this saying: "If a man strikes thee on the right cheek, turn to him the other also,"[488] who were not content to avenge wrongs done to them with the even justice of the lex talionis, but repaid a very slight touch with deadly kicks and wounds with weapons, and for a single truth sought to take the life of those who had struck them. Nor could it be said to them, "love your enemies,"[489] among whom it was considered a great thing and most important if they loved their friends, but avoided their enemies and dissented from them only in hatred without being eager to oppress and kill them.

NOTES:
[486] Eccl. 3:14 (LXX).
[487] 1 Tim. 1:9.

488 S. Matt. 5:39.
489 S. Matt. 5:44.

CHAPTER XXV.

How this that is said of the devil in the gospel is to be understood; viz., that "he is a liar, and his father."

BUT as for this which disturbed you about the devil, that "he is a liar and his father,"490 as if it seemed that he and his father were pronounced by the Lord to be liars, it is sufficiently ridiculous to imagine this even cursorily. For as we said a little while ago spirit does not beget spirit just as soul cannot procreate soul, though we do not doubt that the compacting of flesh is formed from man's seed, as the Apostle clearly distinguishes in the case of both substances; viz., flesh and spirit, what should be ascribed to whom as its author, and says: "Moreover we have had fathers of our flesh for instructors, and we reverenced them: shall we not much more be in subjection to the Father of spirits and live?"491 What could show more clearly than this distinction, that he laid down that men were the fathers of our flesh, but always taught that God alone was the Father of souls. Although even in the actual compacting of this body a ministerial office alone must be attributed to men, but the chief part of its formation to God the Creator of all, as David says: "Thy hands have made me and fashioned me:"492 And the blessed Job: "Hast thou not milked me as milk, and curdled me as cheese? Thou hast put me together with bones and sinews;"493 and the Lord to Jeremiah: "Before I formed thee in the womb, I knew thee."494 But Ecclesiastes very clearly and accurately gathers the nature of either substance, and its beginning, by an examination of the rise and commencement, from which each originated, and by a consideration of the end to which each is tending, and decides also of the division of this body and soul, and discourses as follows: "Before the dust returns to the earth as it was, and the spirit returns unto God who gave it."495 But what could be said with greater plainness than that he declares that the matter of the flesh which he styled dust, because it springs from the seed of man, and seems to be sown by his ministration, must, as it was taken from the earth, again return to the earth, while he points out that the spirit which is not begotten by intercourse between the sexes, but belongs to God alone in a special way, returns to its creator? And this also is clearly implied in that breathing by God, through which Adam in the first instance received his life. And so from these passages we clearly infer that no one can be called the Father of spirits but God alone, who makes them out of nothing whenever He pleases, while men can only be termed the fathers of our flesh. So then the devil also in as much as he was created a spirit or an angel and good, had no one as his Father but God his Maker. But when he had become puffed up by pride and had said in his heart: "I will ascend above the heights of the clouds, I will be like the Most High,"[496] he became a liar, and "abode not in the truth;"[497] but brought forth a lie from his own storehouse of wickedness and so became not only a liar, but also the father of the actual lie, by which when he promised Divinity to man and said "Ye shall be as gods,"[498] he abode not in the truth, but from the beginning became a murderer, both by bringing Adam into a state of mortality, and by slaying Abel by the hand of his brother at his suggestion. But already the approach of dawn is bringing to a close our discussion, which has occupied nearly two whole nights, and our brief and simple words have drawn our bark of this Conference from the deep sea of questions to a safe harbour of silence, in which deep indeed, as the breath of the Divine Spirit drives us further in, so is there ever opened out a wider and boundless space reaching beyond the sight of our eye, and, as Solomon says, "It will become much further from us than it was, and a great depth; who shall find it out?"[499] Wherefore let us pray the Lord that both His fear and His love, which cannot fail, may continue steadfast in us, and make us wise in all things, and ever shield us unharmed, from the darts of the devil. For with these guards it is impossible for anyone to fall into the snares of death. But there is this difference between the perfect and imperfect, that in the case of the former love is steadfast, and so to speak riper and lasts more abidingly and so makes them persevere in holiness more steadfastly and more easily, while in the case of the latter its position is weaker and it more easily grows cold, and so quickly and more frequently allows them to be entangled in the snares of sin. And when we heard this, the words of this Conference so fired us that when we went away from the old man's cell we longed with a keener ardour of soul than when we first came, for the fulfilment of his teaching.

NOTES:
[490] S. John 8:44.
[491] Heb. 12:9.

PART 1

[492] Ps. 118 (119):73.
[493] Job 10:10, 11.
[494] Jer. 1:5.
[495] Eccl. 12:7.
[496] Is. 14:14.
[497] S. John 8:44.
[498] Gen. 3:5.
[499] Eccl. 7:25.

CONFERENCE 9.

The First Conference of Abbot Isaac
on Prayer

CHAPTER I.

Introduction to the Conference.

WHAT was promised in the second book of the Institutes[500] on continual and unceasing perseverance in prayer, shall be by the Lord's help fulfilled by the Conferences of this Elder, whom we will now bring forward; viz., Abbot Isaac:[501] and when these have been propounded I think that I shall have satisfied the commands of Pope Castor of blessed memory, and your wishes, O blessed Pope Leontius and holy brother Helladius, and the length of the book in its earlier part may be excused, though, in spite of our endeavour not only to compress what had to be told into a brief discourse, but also to pass over very many points in silence, it has been extended to a greater length than we intended. For having commenced with a full discourse on various regulations which we have thought it well to curtail for the sake of brevity, at the close the blessed Isaac spoke these words.

NOTES:
[500] See the Institutes Book II. c. ix.
[501] Isaac was, as we gather from c. xxxi., a disciple of St. Antony, and is mentioned by Palladius Dial. de vita Chrysost. There are also a few stories of him in the Apophthegmata Patrum (Migne, Vol. lxv. p. 223); and see the Dictionary of Christian Biography, Vol. iii. p. 294.

CHAPTER II.

The words of Abbot Isaac on the nature of prayer.

THE aim of every monk and the perfection of his heart tends to continual and unbroken perseverance in prayer, and, as far as it is allowed to human frailty, strives to acquire an immovable tranquillity of mind and a perpetual purity, for the sake of which we seek unweariedly and constantly to practise all bodily labours as well as contrition of spirit. And there is between these two a sort of reciprocal and inseparable union. For just as the crown of the building of all virtues is the perfection of prayer, so unless everything has been united and compacted by this as its crown, it cannot possibly continue strong and stable. For lasting and continual calmness in prayer, of which we are speaking, cannot be secured or consummated without them, so neither can those virtues which lay its foundations be fully gained without persistence in it. And so we shall not be able either to treat properly of the effect of prayer, or in a rapid discourse to penetrate to its main end, which is acquired by labouring at all virtues, unless first all those things which for its sake must be either rejected or secured, are singly enumerated and discussed, and, as the Parable in the gospel teaches,[502] whatever concerns the building of that spiritual and most lofty tower, is reckoned up and carefully considered beforehand. But yet these things when prepared will be of no use nor allow the lofty height of perfection to be properly placed upon them unless a clearance of all faults be first undertaken, and the decayed and dead rubbish of the passions be dug up, and the strong foundations of simplicity and humility be laid on the solid and (so to speak) living soil of our breast, or rather on that rock of the gospel,[503] and by being built in this way this tower of spiritual virtues will rise, and be able to stand unmoved, and be raised to the utmost heights of heaven in full assurance of its, stability. For if it rests on such foundations, then though heavy storms of passions break over it, though mighty torrents of persecutions beat against it like a battering ram, though a furious tempest of spiritual foes dash against it and attack it, yet not only will no ruin overtake it, but the onslaught will not injure it even in the slightest degree.

NOTES:
[502] Cf. S. Luke 14:28.
[503] Cf. S. Luke 6:48.

CHAPTER III.

How pure and sincere prayer can be gained.

And therefore in order that prayer may be offered up with that earnestness and purity with which it ought to be, we must by all means observe these rules. First all anxiety about carnal things must be entirely got rid of; next we must leave no room for not merely the care but even the recollection of any business affairs, and in like manner also must lay aside all backbitings, vain and incessant chattering, and buffoonery; anger above all and disturbing moroseness must be entirely destroyed, and the deadly taint of carnal lust and covetousness be torn up by the roots. And so when these and such like faults which are also visible to the eyes of men, are entirely removed and cut off, and when such a purification and cleansing, as we spoke of, has first taken place, which is brought about by pure simplicity and innocence, then first there must be laid the secure foundations of a deep humility, which may be able to support a tower that shall reach the sky; and next the spiritual structure of the virtues must be built up upon them, and the soul kept free from all conversation and from roving thoughts that thus it may by little and little begin to rise to the contemplation of God and to spiritual insight. For whatever our mind has been thinking of before the hour of prayer, is sure to occur to us while we are praying through the activity of the memory. Wherefore what we want to find ourselves like while we are praying, that we ought to prepare ourselves to be before the time for prayer. For the mind in prayer is formed by its previous condition, and when we are applying ourselves to prayer the images of the same actions and words and thoughts will dance before our eyes, and make us either angry, as in our previous condition, or gloomy, or recall our former lust and business, or make us shake with foolish laughter (which I am ashamed to speak of) at some silly joke, or smile at some action, or fly back to our previous conversation. And therefore if we do not want anything to haunt us while we are praying, we should be careful before our prayer, to exclude it from the shrine of our heart, that we may thus fulfill the Apostle's injunction: "Pray without ceasing;" and: "In every place lifting up holy hands without wrath or disputing."[504] For otherwise we shall not be able to carry out that charge unless our mind, purified from all stains of sin, and given over to virtue as to its natural good, feed on the continual contemplation of Almighty God.

NOTES:
[504] 1 Thess. 5:17; 1 Tim. 2:8.

CHAPTER IV.

Of the lightness of the soul which may be compared to a wing or feather.

FOR the nature of the soul is not inaptly compared to a very fine feather or very light wing, which, if it has not been damaged or affected by being spoilt by any moisture falling on it from without, is borne aloft almost naturally to the heights of heaven by the lightness of its nature, and the aid of the slightest breath: but if it is weighted by any moisture falling upon it and penetrating into it, it will not only not be carried away by its natural lightness into any aerial flights but will actually be borne down to the depths of earth by the weight of the moisture it has received. So also our soul, if it is not weighted with faults that touch it, and the cares of this world, or damaged by the moisture of injurious lusts, will be raised as it were by the natural blessing of its own purity and borne aloft to the heights by the light breath of spiritual meditation; and leaving things low and earthly will be transported to those that are heavenly and invisible. Wherefore we are well warned by the Lord's command: "Take heed that your hearts be not weighed down by surfeiting and drunkenness and the cares of this world."[505] And therefore if we want our prayers to reach not only the sky, but what is beyond the sky, let us be careful to reduce our soul, purged from all earthly faults and purified from every stain, to its natural lightness, that so our prayer may rise to God unchecked by the weight of any sin.

NOTES:
[505] S. Luke 21:34.

CHAPTER V.

Of the ways in which our soul is weighed down.

BUT we should notice the ways in which the Lord points out that the soul is weighed down: for He did not mention adultery, or fornication, or murder, or blasphemy, or rapine, which everybody knows to be deadly and damnable, but surfeiting and drunkenness, and the cares or anxieties of this world: which men of this world are so far from avoiding or considering damnable that actually some who (I am ashamed to say) call themselves monks entangle themselves in these very occupations as if they were harmless or useful. And though these three things, when literally given way to weigh down the soul, and separate it from God, and bear it down to things earthly, yet it is very easy to avoid them, especially for us who are separated by so great a distance from all converse with this world, and who do not on any occasion have anything to do with those visible cares and drunkenness and surfeiting. But there is another surfeiting which is no less dangerous, and a spiritual drunkenness which it is harder to avoid, and a care and anxiety of this world, which often ensnares us even after the perfect renunciation of all our goods, and abstinence from wine and all feastings and even when we are living in solitude--and of such the prophet says: "Awake, ye that are drunk but not with wine;"[506] and another: "Be astonished and wonder and stagger: be drunk and not with wine: be moved, but not with drunkenness."[507] And of this drunkenness the wine must consequently be what the prophet calls "the fury of dragons": and from what root the wine comes you may hear: "From the vineyard of Sodom," he says, "is their vine, and their branches from Gomorrha." Would you also know about the fruit of that vine and the seed of that branch? "Their grape is a grape of gall, theirs is a cluster of bitterness"[508] for unless we are altogether cleansed from all faults and abstaining from the surfeit of all passions, our heart will without drunkenness from wine and excess of any feasting be weighed down by a drunkenness and surfeiting that is still more dangerous. For that worldly cares can sometimes fall on us who mix with no actions of this world, is clearly shown according to the rule of the Elders, who have laid down that anything which goes beyond the necessities of daily food, and the unavoidable needs of the flesh, belongs to worldly cares and anxieties, as for example if, when a job bringing in a penny would satisfy the needs of our body, we try to extend it by a longer toil and work in order to get twopence or threepence; and when a covering of two tunics would be enough for our use both by night and day, we manage to become the owners of three or four, or when a hut containing one or two cells would be sufficient, in the pride of worldly ambition and greatness we build four or five cells, and these splendidly decorated, and larger than our needs required, thus showing the passion of worldly lusts whenever we can.

NOTES:
[506] Joel 1:5.
[507] Is. 29:9.
[508] Deut. 32:32, 33.

CHAPTER VI.

Of the vision which a certain Elder saw concerning the restless work of a brother.

AND that this is not done without the prompting of devils we are taught by the surest proofs, for when one very highly esteemed Elder was passing by the cell of a certain brother who was suffering from this mental disease of which we have spoken, as he was restlessly toiling in his daily occupations in building and repairing what was unnecessary, he watched him from a distance breaking a very hard stone with a heavy hammer, and saw a certain Ethiopian standing over him and together with him striking the blows of the hammer with joined and clasped hands, and urging him on with fiery incitements to diligence in the work: and so he stood still for a long while in astonishment at the force of the fierce demon and the deceitfulness of such an illusion. For when the brother was worn out and tired and wanted to rest and put an end to his toil, he was stimulated by the spirit's prompting and urged on to resume his hammer again and not to cease from devoting himself to the work which he had begun, so that being unweariedly supported by his incitements he did not feel the harm that so great labour was doing him. At last then the old man, disgusted at such a horrid mystification by a demon, turned aside to the brother's cell and saluted him, and asked "what work is it, brother, that you are doing?" and he replied: "We are working at this awfully hard stone, and we can hardly break it at all." Whereupon the Elder replied: "You were

218

right in saying 'we can,' for you were not alone, when you were striking it, but there was another with you whom you did not see, who was
standing over you not so much to help you as urge you on with all his
force." And thus the fact that the disease of worldly vanity has not got
hold of our hearts, will be proved by no mere abstinence from those
affairs which even if we want to engage in, we cannot carry out, nor
by the despising of those matters which if we pursued them would
make us remarkable in the front rank among spiritual persons as well
as among worldly men, but only when we reject with inflexible firmness of mind whatever ministers to our power and seems to be veiled
in a show of right. And in reality these things which seem trivial and
of no consequence, and which we see to be permitted indifferently by
those who belong to our calling, none the less by their character affect
the soul than those more important things, which according to their
condition usually intoxicate the senses of worldly people and which do
not allow[509] a monk to lay aside earthly impurities and aspire to God,
on whom his attention should ever be fixed; for in his case even a
slight separation from that highest good must be regarded as present
death and most dangerous destruction. And when the soul has been
established in such a peaceful condition, and has been freed from the
meshes of all carnal desires, and the purpose of the heart has been
steadily fixed on that which is the only highest good, he will then fulfil
this Apostolic precept: "Pray without ceasing;" and: "in every place
lifting up holy hands without wrath and disputing:"[510] for when by this
purity (if we can say so) the thoughts of the soul are engrossed, and are
re-fashioned out of their earthly condition to bear a spiritual and angelic likeness, whatever it receives, whatever it takes in hand,
whatever it does, the prayer will be perfectly pure and sincere.

NOTES:
[509] Sinentes, though the reading of almost all MSS. must be an error either of
the author or of a copyist for sinentia.
[510] 1 Thess. 5:17; 1 Tim. 2:8.

CHAPTER VII.

A question how it is that it is harder work to preserve than to
originate good thoughts.

PART 1

GERMANUS: If only we could keep as a lasting possession those spiritual thoughts in the same way and with the same ease with which we generally conceive their germs! for when they have been conceived in our hearts either through the recollection of the Scriptures or by the memory of some spiritual actions, or by gazing upon heavenly mysteries, they vanish all too soon and disappear by a sort of unnoticed flight. And when our soul has discovered some other occasions for spiritual emotions, different ones again crowd in upon us, and those which we had grasped are scattered, and lightly fly away so that the mind retaining no persistency, and keeping of its own power no firm hand over holy thoughts, must be thought, even when it does seem to retain them for a while, to have conceived them at random and not of set purpose. For how can we think that their rise should be ascribed to our own will, if they do not last and remain with us? But that we may not owing to the consideration of this question wander any further from the plan of the discourse we had commenced, or delay any longer the explanation promised of the nature of prayer, we will keep this for its own time, and ask to be informed at once of the character of prayer, especially as the blessed Apostle exhorts us at no time to cease from it, saying "Pray without ceasing." And so we want to be taught first of its character, i.e., how prayer ought always to be offered up, and then how we can secure this, whatever it is, and practise it without ceasing. For that it cannot be done by any light purpose of heart both daily experience and the explanation of your holiness show us, as you have laid it down that the aim of a monk, and the height of all perfection consist in the consummation of prayer.

CHAPTER VIII.

Of the different characters of prayer.

ISAAC: I imagine that all kinds of prayers cannot be grasped without great purity of heart and soul and the illumination of the Holy Spirit. For there are as many of them as there can be conditions and characters produced in one soul or rather in all souls. And so although we know that owing to our dulness of heart we cannot see all kinds of prayers, yet we will try to relate them in some order, as far as our slender experience enables us to succeed. For according to the degree of the purity to which each soul attains, and the character of the state in which it is sunk owing to what happens to it, or is by its own efforts renewing itself, its very prayers will each moment be altered: and therefore it is quite clear that no one can always offer up uniform prayers. For every one prays in one way when he is brisk, in another when he is oppressed with a weight of sadness or despair, in another when he is invigorated by spiritual achievements, in another when cast down by the burden of attacks, in another when he is asking pardon for his sins, in another when he asks to obtain grace or some virtue or else prays for the destruction of some sin, in another when he is pricked to the heart by the thought of hell and the fear of future judgment, in another when he is aglow with the hope and desire of good things to come, in another when he is taken up with affairs and dangers, in another when he is in peace and security, in another when he is enlightened by the revelation of heavenly mysteries, and in another when he is depressed by a sense of barrenness in virtues and dryness in feeling.

CHAPTER IX.

Of the fourfold nature of prayer.

AND therefore, when we have laid this down with regard to the character of prayer, although not so fully as the importance of the subject requires, but as fully as the exigencies of time permit, and at any rate as our slender abilities admit, and our dulness of heart enables us,--a still greater difficulty now awaits us; viz., to expound one by one the different kinds of prayer, which the Apostle divides in a fourfold manner, when he says as follows: "I exhort therefore first of all that supplications, prayers, intercessions, thanksgivings be made."[511] And we cannot possibly doubt that this division was not idly made by the Apostle. And to begin with we must investigate what is meant by supplication, by prayer, by intercession, and by thanksgiving. Next we must inquire whether these four kinds are to be taken in hand by him who prays all at once, i.e., are they all to be joined together in every prayer,--or whether they are to be offered up in turns and one by one, as, for instance, ought at one time supplications, at another prayers, at another intercessions, and at another thanksgivings to be offered, or should one man present to God supplications, another prayers, another intercessions, another thanksgivings, in accordance with that measure of age, to which each soul is advancing by earnestness of purpose?

NOTES:
[511] 1 Tim. 2:1.

CHAPTER X.

Of the order of the different kinds laid down with regard to the character of prayer.

AND so to begin with we must consider the actual force of the names and words, and discuss what is the difference between prayer and supplication and intercession; then in like manner we must investigate whether they are to be offered separately or all together; and in the third place must examine whether the particular order which is thus arranged by the Apostle's authority has anything further to teach the hearer, or whether the distinction simply is to be taken, and it should be considered that they were arranged by him indifferently in such a way: a thing which seems to me utterly absurd. For one must not believe that the Holy Spirit uttered anything casually or without reason through the Apostle. And so we will, as the Lord grants us, consider them in the same order in which we began.

CHAPTER XI.

Of Supplications.

"I EXHORT therefore first of all that supplications be made." Supplication is an imploring or petition concerning sins, in which one who is sorry for his present or past deeds asks for pardon.

CHAPTER XII.

Of Prayer.

PRAYERS are those by which we offer or vow something to God, what the Greeks call euch, i.e., a vow. For where we read in Greek `ias eucas mou tw Kuriw apodwsw, in Latin we read: "I will pay my vows unto the Lord;"[512] where according to the exact force of the words it may be thus represented: "I will pay my prayers unto the Lord." And this which we find in Ecclesiastes: "If thou vowest a vow unto the Lord do not delay to pay it," is written in Greek likewise: ean euxe euchn tw Kuriw, i.e., "If thou prayest a prayer unto the Lord, do not delay to pay it,"[513] which will be fulfilled in this way by each one of us. We pray, when we renounce this world and promise that being dead to all worldly actions and the life of this world we will serve the Lord with full purpose of heart. We pray when we promise that despising secular honours and scorning earthly riches we will cleave to the Lord in all sorrow of heart and humility of spirit. We pray when we promise that we will ever maintain the most perfect purity of body and steadfast patience, or when we vow that we will utterly root out of our heart the roots of anger or of sorrow that worketh death. And if, enervated by sloth and returning to our former sins we fail to do this we shall be guilty as regards our prayers and vows, and these words will apply to us: "It is better not to vow, than to vow and not to pay," which can be rendered in accordance with the Greek: "It is better for thee not to pray than to pray and not to pay." [514]

CHAPTER XIII.

Of Intercession.

IN the third place stand intercessions, which we are wont to offer up for others also, while we are filled with fervour of spirit, making request either for those dear to us or for the peace of the whole world, and to use the Apostle's own phrase, we pray "for all men, for kings and all that are in authority." [515]

NOTES:
[512] Ps. 115:4 (116:14).

513 Eccl. 5:3.
514 Eccl. 5:4.
515 1 Tim. 2:1, 2.

CHAPTER XIV.

Of Thanksgiving.

THEN in the fourth place there stand thanksgivings which the mind in ineffable transports offers up to God, either when it recalls God's past benefits or when it contemplates His present ones, or when it looks forward to those great ones in the future which God has prepared for them that love Him. And with this purpose too sometimes we are wont to pour forth richer prayers, while, as we gaze with pure eyes on those rewards of the saints which are laid up in store hereafter, our spirit is stimulated to offer up unspeakable thanks to God with boundless joy.

CHAPTER XV.

Whether these four kinds of prayers are necessary for everyone to offer all at once or separately and in turns.

AND of these four kinds, although sometimes occasions arise for richer and fuller prayers (for from the class of supplications which arises from sorrow for sin, and from the kind of prayer which flows from confidence in our offerings and the performance of our vows in accordance with a pure conscience, and from the intercession which proceeds from fervour of love, and from the thanksgiving which is born of the consideration of God's blessings and His greatness and goodness, we know that oftentimes there proceed most fervent and ardent prayers so that it is clear that all these kinds of prayer of which we have spoken are found to be useful and needful for all men, so that in one and the same man his changing feelings will give utterance to pure and fervent petitions now of supplications, now of prayers, now of intercessions) yet the first seems to belong more especially to beginners, who are still troubled by the stings and recollection of their sins; the second to those who have already attained some loftiness of

mind in their spiritual progress and the quest of virtue; the third to
those who fulfil the completion of their vows by their works, and are
so stimulated to intercede for others also through the consideration of
their weakness, and the earnestness of their love; the fourth to those
who have already torn from their hearts the guilty thorns of conscience, and thus being now free from care can contemplate with a
pure mind the beneficence of God and His compassions, which He has
either granted in the past, or is giving in the present, or preparing for
the future, and thus are borne onward with fervent hearts to that ardent
prayer which cannot be embraced or expressed by the mouth of men.
Sometimes however the mind which is advancing to that perfect state
of purity and which is already beginning to be established in it, will
take in all these at one and the same time, and like some incomprehensible and all-devouring flame, dart through them all and offer up to
God inexpressible prayers of the purest force, which the Spirit Itself,
intervening with groanings that cannot be uttered, while we ourselves
understand not, pours forth to God, grasping at that hour and ineffably
pouring forth in its supplications things so great that they cannot be
uttered with the mouth nor even at any other time be recollected by the
mind. And thence it comes that in whatever degree any one stands, he
is found sometimes to offer up pure and devout prayers; as even in that
first and lowly station which has to do with the recollection of future
judgment, he who still remains under the punishment of terror and the
fear of judgment is so smitten with sorrow for the time being that he is
filled with no less keenness of spirit from the richness of his supplications than he who through the purity of his heart gazes on and
considers the blessings of God and is overcome with ineffable joy and
delight. For, as the Lord Himself says, he begins to love the more, who
knows that he has been forgiven the more. [516]

NOTES:
[516] Cf. S. Luke 7:47.

CHAPTER XVI.

Of the kinds of prayer to which we ought to direct ourselves.
YET we ought by advancing in life and attaining to virtue to aim
rather at those kinds of prayer which are poured forth either from the

contemplation of the good things to come or from fervour of love, or which at least, to speak more humbly and in accordance with the measure of beginners, arise for the acquirement of some virtue or the extinction of some fault. For otherwise we shall not possibly attain to those sublimer kinds of supplication of which we spoke, unless our mind has been little by little and by degrees raised through the regular course of those intercessions.

CHAPTER XVII.

How the four kinds of supplication were originated by the Lord.

THESE four kinds of supplication the Lord Himself by His own example vouchsafed to originate for us, so that in this too He might fulfil that which was said of Him: "which Jesus began both to do and to teach."[517] For He made use of the class of supplication when He said: "Father, if it be possible, let this cup pass from me;" or this which is chanted in His Person in the Psalm: "My God, My God, look upon Me, why hast Thou forsaken me,"[518] and others like it. It is prayer where He says: "I have magnified Thee upon the earth, I have finished the work which Thou gavest Me to do," and this: "And for their sakes I sanctify Myself that they also may be sanctified in the truth."[519] It is intercession when He says: "Father, those Whom Thou hast given me, I will that they also may be with Me that they may see My glory which Thou hast given Me;" or at any rate when He says: "Father, forgive them for they know not what they do."[520] It is thanksgiving when He says: "I confess to Thee, Father, Lord of heaven and earth, that Thou hast hid these things from the wise and prudent, and hast revealed them unto babes. Even so, Father, for so it seemed good in Thy sight:" or at least when He says: "Father, I thank Thee that Thou hast heard Me. But I knew that Thou hearest Me always."[521] But though our Lord made a distinction between these four kinds of prayers as to be offered separately and one by one according to the scheme which we know of, yet that they can all be embraced in a perfect prayer at one and the same time He showed by His own example in that prayer which at the close of S. John's gospel we read that He offered up with such fulness. From the words of which (as it is too long to repeat it all) the careful inquirer can discover by the order of the passage that this is so. And the Apostle also in his Epistle to the Philippians has expressed the same meaning, by putting these four kinds of prayers in a slightly different order, and has shown that they ought sometimes to be offered together in the fervour of a single prayer, saying as follows: "But in everything by prayer and supplication with thanksgiving let your requests be made known unto God."[522] And by this he wanted us especially to understand that in prayer and supplication thanksgiving ought to be mingled with our requests.

NOTES:
[517] Acts 1:1.
[518] S. Matt. 26:39; Ps. 21 (22):2.
[519] S. John 17:4, 19.
[520] S. John 17:24; S. Luke 23:34.
[521] S. Matt. 11:25, 26; S. John 11:41, 42.
[522] Phil. 4:6.

CHAPTER XVIII.

Of the Lord's Prayer.

AND so there follows after these different kinds of supplication a still more sublime and exalted condition which is brought about by the contemplation of God alone and by fervent love, by which the mind, transporting and flinging itself into love for Him, addresses God most familiarly as its own Father with a piety of its own. And that we ought earnestly to seek after this condition the formula of the Lord's prayer teaches us, saying "Our Father." When then we confess with our own mouths that the God and Lord of the universe is our Father, we profess forthwith that we have been called from our condition as slaves to the adoption of sons, adding next "Which art in heaven," that, by shunning with the utmost horror all lingering in this present life, which we pass upon this earth as a pilgrimage, and what separates us by a great distance from our Father, we may the rather hasten with all eagerness to that country where we confess that our Father dwells, and may not allow anything of this kind, which would make us unworthy of this our profession and the dignity of an adoption of this kind, and so deprive us as a disgrace to our Father's inheritance, and make us incur the wrath of His justice and severity. To which state and condition of sonship when we have advanced, we shall forthwith be inflamed with the piety which belongs to good sons, so that we shall bend all our energies to the advance not of our own profit, but of our Father's glory, saying to Him: "Hallowed be Thy name," testifying that our desire and our joy is His glory, becoming imitators of Him who said: "He who speaketh of himself, seeketh his own glory. But He who seeks the glory of Him who sent Him, the same is true and there is no unrighteousness in Him."[523] Finally the chosen vessel being filled with this feeling wished that he could be anathema from Christ[524] if only the people belonging to Him might be increased and multiplied, and the salvation of the whole nation of Israel accrue to the glory of His Father; for with all assurance could he wish to die for Christ as he knew that no one perished for life. And again he says: "We rejoice when we are weak but ye are strong."[525] And what wonder if the chosen vessel wished to be anathema from Christ for the sake of Christ's glory and the conversion of His own brethren and the privilege of the nation, when the prophet Micah wished that he might be a liar and a stranger to the inspiration of the Holy Ghost, if only the people of the Jews might escape those plagues and the going forth into captivity which he had announced in his prophecy, saying: "Would that I were not a man that hath the Spirit, and that I rather spoke a lie;"[526] --to pass over that wish of the Lawgiver, who did not refuse to die together with his brethren who were doomed to death, saying: "I beseech Thee, O Lord; this people hath sinned a heinous sin; either forgive them this trespass, or if Thou do not, blot me out of Thy book which Thou hast written."[527] But where it is said "Hallowed be Thy name," it may also be very fairly taken in this way: "The hallowing of God is our perfection." And so when we say to Him" Hallowed be Thy name" we say in other words, make us, O Father, such that we maybe able both to understand and take in what the hallowing of Thee is, or at any rate that Thou mayest be seen to be hallowed in our spiritual converse. And this is effectually fulfilled in our case when "men see our good works, and glorify our Father Which is in heaven." [528]

NOTES:
[523] S. John 7:18.
[524] Cf. Rom. 9:3.
[525] 2 Cor. 13:9.
[526] Micah 2:11.
[527] Exod. 32:31, 32.
[528] S. Matt. 5:16.

CHAPTER XIX.

Of the clause "Thy kingdom come."

THE second petition of the pure heart desires that the kingdom of its Father may come at once; viz., either that whereby Christ reigns day by day in the saints (which comes to pass when the devil's rule is cast out of our hearts by the destruction of foul sins, and God begins to hold sway over us by the sweet odour of virtues, and, fornication being overcome, charity reigns in our hearts together with tranquillity, when rage is conquered; and humility, when pride is trampled under foot) or else that which is promised in due time to all who are perfect, and to all the sons of God, when it will be said to them by Christ: "Come ye blessed of My Father, inherit the kingdom prepared for you from the foundation of the world;"[529] (as the heart) with fixed and steadfast gaze, so to speak, yearns and longs for it and says to Him "Thy kingdom come." For it knows by the witness of its own conscience that when He shall appear, it will presently share His lot. For no guilty person would dare either to say or to wish for this, for no one would want to face the tribunal of the Judge, who knew that at His coming he would forthwith receive not the prize or reward of his merits but only punishment.

NOTES:
[529] S. Matt. 25:34.

CHAPTER XX.

Of the clause "Thy will be done."

THE third petition is that of sons: "Thy will be done as in heaven so on earth." There can now be no grander prayer than to wish that earthly things may be made equal with things heavenly: for what else is it to say "Thy will be done as in heaven so on earth," than to ask that men may be like angels and that as God's will is ever fulfilled by them in heaven, so also all those who are on earth may do not their own but His will? This too no one could say from the heart but only one who believed that God disposes for our good all things which are seen, whether fortunate or unfortunate, and that He is more careful and provident for our good and salvation than we ourselves are for our-selves. Or at any rate it may be taken in this way: The will of God is the salvation of all men, according to these words of the blessed Paul: "Who willeth all men to be saved and to come to the knowledge of the truth."[530] Of which will also the prophet Isaiah says in the Person of God the Father: "And all Thy will shall be done."[531] When we say then "Thy will be done as in heaven so on earth," we pray in other words for this; viz., that as those who are in heaven, so also may all those who dwell on earth be saved, O Father, by the knowledge of Thee.

NOTES:
[530] 1 Tim. 2:4.
[531] Is. 46:10.

CHAPTER XXI.

Of our supersubstantial or daily bread.

NEXT: "Give us this day our bread which is epiousion," i.e., "su-persubstantial," which another Evangelist calls "daily."[532] The former indicates the quality of its nobility and substance, in virtue of which it is above all substances and the loftiness of its grandeur and holiness exceeds all creatures, while the latter intimates the purpose of its use and value. For where it says "daily" it shows that without it we cannot live a spiritual life for a single day. Where it says "today" it shows that it must be received daily and that yesterday's supply of it is not enough, but at it must be given to us today also in like manner. And our daily need of it suggests to us that we ought at all times to offer up this prayer, because there is no day on which we have no need to strengthen the heart of our inner man, by eating and receiving it, al-though the expression used, "today" may be taken to apply to his present life, i.e., while we are living in this world supply us with this bread. For we know that it will be given to those who deserve it by Thee hereafter, but we ask that Thou wouldest grant it to us today, be-cause unless it has been vouchsafed to a man to receive it in this life he will never be partaker of it in that.

NOTES:

[532] Here Cassian is relying entirely on Jerome's revised text of the Latin, which has supersubstantialis in S. Matt. 6:11, as the rendering of epiousios but translates the same word by quotidianum in the parallel passage in S. Luke 11:3. It is curious that Cassian should have been thus misled, with his knowledge of Greek, as well as his acquaintance with the old Latin version which has quotidianum in both gospels. Cf. Bishop Lightfoot "On a Fresh Revision of the New Testament," p. 219.

CHAPTER XXII.

Of the clause: "Forgive us our debts, etc."

"AND forgive us our debts as we also forgive our debtors." O unspeakable mercy of God, which has not only given us a form of prayer and taught us a system of life acceptable to Him, and by the requirements of the form given, in which He charged us always to pray, has torn up the roots of both anger and sorrow, but also gives to those who pray an opportunity and reveals to them a way by which they may move a merciful and kindly judgment of God to be pronounced over them and which somehow gives us a power by which we can moderate the sentence of our Judge, drawing Him to forgive our offences by the example of our forgiveness: when we say to Him: "Forgive us as we also forgive." And so without anxiety and in confidence from this prayer a man may ask for pardon of his own offences, if he has been forgiving towards his own debtors, and not towards those of his Lord. For some of us, which is very bad, are inclined to show ourselves calm and most merciful in regard to those things which are done to God's detriment, however great the crimes may be, but to be found most hard and inexorable exactors of debts to ourselves even in the case of the most trifling wrongs. Whoever then does not from his heart forgive his brother who has offended him, by this prayer calls down upon himself not forgiveness but condemnation, and by his own profession asks that he himself may be judged more severely, saying: Forgive me as I also have forgiven. And if he is repaid according to his own request, what else will follow but that he will be punished after his own example with implacable wrath and a sentence that cannot be remitted? And so if we want to be judged mercifully, we ought also to be merciful towards those who have sinned against us. For only so much will be remitted to us, as we have remitted to those who have injured us however spitefully. And some dreading this, when this prayer is chanted by all the people in church, silently omit this clause, for fear lest they may seem by their own utterance to bind themselves rather than to excuse themselves, as they do not understand that it is in vain that they try to offer these quibbles to the Judge of all men, who has willed to show us beforehand how He will judge His suppliants. For as He does not wish to be found harsh and inexorable towards them, He has marked out the manner of His judgment, that just as we desire to be judged by Him, so we should also judge our brethren, if they have wronged us in anything, for "he shall have judgment without mercy who hath shown no mercy." [533]

NOTES:
[533] S. James 2:13.

CHAPTER XXIII.

Of the clause: "Lead us not into temptation."

NEXT there follows: "And lead us not into temptation," on which there arises no unimportant question, for if we pray that we may not be suffered to be tempted, how then will our power of endurance be proved, according to this text: "Every one who is not tempted is not proved;"[534] and again: "Blessed is the man that endureth temptation"?[535] The clause then, "Lead us not into temptation," does not mean this; viz., do not permit us ever to be tempted, but do not permit us when we fall into temptation to be overcome. For Job was tempted, but was not led into temptation. For he did not ascribe folly to God nor blasphemy, nor with impious mouth did he yield to that wish of the tempter toward which he was drawn. Abraham was tempted, Joseph was tempted, but neither of them was led into temptation for neither of them yielded his consent to the tempter. Next there follows: "But deliver us from evil," i.e., do not suffer us to be tempted by the devil above that we are able, but "make with the temptation a way also of escape that we may be able to bear it." [536]

NOTES:
[534] Ecclus. 34:11.
[535] S. James 1:12.
[536] 1 Cor. 10:13.

CHAPTER XXIV.

How we ought not to ask for other things, except only those which are contained in the limits of the Lord's Prayer.

YOU see then what is the method and form of prayer proposed to us by the Judge Himself, who is to be prayed to by it, a form in which there is contained no petition for riches, no thought of honours, no request for power and might, no mention of bodily health and of temporal life. For He who is the Author of Eternity would have men ask of Him nothing uncertain, nothing paltry, and nothing temporal. And so a man will offer the greatest insult to His Majesty and Bounty, if he leaves on one side these eternal petitions and chooses rather to ask of Him something transitory and uncertain; and will also incur the indignation rather than the propitiation of the Judge by the pettiness of his prayer.

CHAPTER XXV.

Of the character of the sublimer prayer.

THIS prayer then though it seems to contain all the fulness of perfection, as being what was originated and appointed by the Lord's own authority, yet lifts those to whom it belongs to that still higher condition of which we spoke above, and carries them on by a loftier stage to that ardent prayer which is known and tried by but very few, and which to speak more truly is ineffable; which transcends all human thoughts, and is distinguished, I will not say by any sound of the voice, but by no movement of the tongue, or utterance of words, but which the mind enlightened by the infusion of that heavenly light describes in no human and confined language, but pours forth richly as from copious fountain in an accumulation of thoughts, and ineffably utters to God, expressing in the shortest possible space of time such great things that the mind when it returns to its usual condition cannot easily utter or relate. And this condition our Lord also similarly prefigured by the form of those supplications which, when he retired alone in the mountain He is said to have poured forth in silence, and when being in an agony of prayer He shed forth even drops of blood, as an example of a purpose which it is hard to imitate.

CHAPTER XXVI.

Of the different causes of conviction.

BUT who is able, with whatever experience he may be endowed, to give a sufficient account of the varieties and reasons and grounds of conviction, by which the mind is inflamed and set on fire and incited to pure and most fervent prayers? And of these we will now by way of specimen set forth a few, as far as we can by God's enlightenment recollect them. For sometimes a verse of any one of the Psalms gives us an occasion of ardent prayer while we are singing. Sometimes the harmonious modulation of a brother's voice stirs up the minds of dullards to intense supplication. We know also that the enunciation and the reverence of the chanter adds greatly to the fervour of those who stand by. Moreover the exhortation of a perfect man, and a spiritual conference has often raised the affections of those present to the richest prayer. We know too that by the death of a brother or some one dear to us, we are no less carried away to full conviction. The recollection also of our coldness and carelessness has sometimes aroused in us a healthful fervour of spirit. And in this way no one can doubt that numberless opportunities are not wanting, by which through God's grace the coldness and sleepiness of our minds can be shaken off.

CHAPTER XXVII.

Of the different sorts of conviction.

BUT how and in what way those very convictions are produced from the inmost recesses of the soul it is no less difficult to trace out. For often through some inexpressible delight and keenness of spirit the fruit of a most salutary conviction arises so that it actually breaks forth into shouts owing to the greatness of its incontrollable joy; and the delight of the heart and greatness of exultation makes itself heard even in the cell of a neighbour. But sometimes the mind hides itself in complete silence within the secrets of a profound quiet, so that the amazement of a sudden illumination chokes all sounds of words and the overawed spirit either keeps all its feelings to itself or loses[537] them and pours forth its desires to God with groanings that cannot be uttered. But sometimes it is filled with such overwhelming conviction and grief that it cannot express it except by floods of tears.

NOTES:
[537] Petschenig's text reads "amittat." v. l. emittat.

CHAPTER XXVIII.

A question about the fact that a plentiful supply of tears is not in our own power.

GERMANUS: My own poor self indeed is not altogether ignorant of this feeling of conviction. For often when tears arise at the recollection of my faults, I have been by the Lord's visitation so refreshed by this ineffable joy which you describe that the greatness of the joy has assured me that I ought not to despair of their forgiveness. Than which state of mind I think there is nothing more sublime if only it could be recalled at our own will. For sometimes when I am desirous to stir myself up with all my power to the same conviction and tears, and place before my eyes all my faults and sins, I am unable to bring back that copiousness of tears, and so my eyes are dry and hard like some hardest flint, so that not a single tear trickles from them. And so in proportion as I congratulate myself on that copiousness of tears, just so do I mourn that I cannot bring it back again whenever I wish.

CHAPTER XXIX.

The answer on the varieties of conviction which spring from tears.

ISAAC: Not every kind of shedding of tears is produced by one feeling or one virtue. For in one way does that weeping originate which is caused by the pricks of our sins smiting our heart, of which we read: "I have laboured in my groanings, every night I will wash my

235

bed; I will water my couch with my tears."[538] And again: "Let tears run down like a torrent day and night: give thyself no rest, and let not the apple of thine eye cease."[539] In another, that which arises from the contemplation of eternal good things and the desire of that future glory, owing to which even richer well-springs of tears burst forth from uncontrollable delights and boundless exultation, while our soul is athirst for the mighty Living God, saying, "When shall I come and appear before the presence of God? My tears have been my meat day and night,"[540] declaring with daily crying and lamentation: "Woe is me that my sojourning is prolonged;" and: "Too long hath my soul been a sojourner."[541] In another way do the tears flow forth, which without any conscience of deadly sin, yet still proceed from the fear of hell and the recollection of that terrible judgment, with the terror of which the prophet was smitten and prayed to God, saying: "Enter not into judgment with Thy servant, for in Thy sight shall no man living be justified."[542] There is too another kind of tears, which are caused not by knowledge of one's self but by the hardness and sins of others; whereby Samuel is described as having wept for Saul, and both the Lord in the gospel and Jeremiah in former days for the city of Jerusalem, the latter thus saying: "Oh, that my head were water and mine eyes a fountain of tears! And I will weep day and night for the slain of the daughter of my people."[543] Or also such as were those tears of which we hear in the hundred and first Psalm: "For I have eaten ashes for my bread, and mingled my cup with weeping."[544] And these were certainty not caused by the same feeling as those which arise in the sixth Psalm from the person of the penitent, but were due to the anxieties of this life and its distresses and losses, by which the righteous who are living in this world are oppressed. And this is clearly shown not only by the words of the Psalm itself, but also by its title, which runs as follows in the character of that poor person of whom it is said in the gospel that "blessed are the poor in spirit, for theirs is the kingdom of heaven:"[545] "A prayer of the poor when he was in distress and poured forth his prayer to God." [546]

NOTES:
[538] Ps. 6:7.
[539] Lam. 2:18.
[540] Ps. 42 (43):3, 4.
[541] Ps. 119 (120):5, 6.
[542] Ps. 142 (143):2.
[543] Jer. 9:1.
[544] Ps. 101 (102):10.

CHAPTER XXX.

How tears ought not to be squeezed out, when they do not flow spontaneously.

FROM these tears those are vastly different which are squeezed out from dry eyes while the heart is hard: and although we cannot believe that these are altogether fruitless (for the attempt to shed them is made with a good intention, especially by those who have not yet been able to attain to perfect knowledge or to be thoroughly cleansed from the stains of past or present sins), yet certainly the flow of tears ought not to be thus forced out by those who have already advanced to the love of virtue, nor should the weeping of the outward man be with great labour attempted, as even if it is produced it will never attain the rich copiousness of spontaneous tears. For it will rather cast down the soul of the suppliant by his endeavours, and humiliate him, and plunge him in human affairs and draw him away from the celestial heights, wherein the awed mind of one who prays should be steadfastly fixed, and will force it to relax its hold on its prayers and grow sick from barren and forced tears.

CHAPTER XXXI.

The opinion of Abbot Antony on the condition of prayer.

AND that you may see the character of true prayer I will give you not my own opinion but that of the blessed Antony: whom we have known sometimes to have been so persistent in prayer that often as he was praying in a transport of mind, when the sunrise began to appear, we have heard him in the fervour of his spirit declaiming: Why do you hinder me, O sun, who art arising for this very purpose; viz., to withdraw me from the brightness of this true light? And his also is this heavenly and more than human utterance on the end of prayer: That is not, said he, a perfect prayer, wherein a monk understands himself and the words which he prays. And if we too, as far as our slender ability allows, may venture to add anything to this splendid utterance, we will bring forward the marks of prayer which are heard from the Lord, as far as we have tried them.

CHAPTER XXXII.

Of the proof of prayer being heard.

WHEN, while we are praying, no hesitation intervenes and breaks down the confidence of our petition by a sort of despair, but we feel that by pouring forth our prayer we have obtained what we are asking for, we have no doubt that our prayers have effectually reached God. For so far will one be heard and obtain an answer, as he believes that he is regarded by God, and that God can grant it. For this saying of our Lord cannot be retracted: "Whatsoever ye ask when ye pray, believe that you shall receive, and they shall come to you." [547]

NOTES:
[547] S. Mark 11:24.

CHAPTER XXXIII.

An objection that the confidence of being thus heard as described belongs only to saints.

GERMANUS: We certainly believe that this confidence of being heard flows from purity of conscience, but for us, whose heart is still smitten by the pricks of sins, how can we have it, as we have no merits to plead for us, whereby we might confidently presume that our prayers would be heard?

CHAPTER XXXIV.

Answer on the different reasons for prayer being heard.

ISAAC: That there are different reasons for prayer being heard in accordance with the varied and changing condition of souls the words of the gospels and of the prophets teach us. For you have the fruits of an answer pointed out by our Lord's words in the case of the agreement of two persons; as it is said: "If two of you shall agree upon earth touching anything for which they shall ask, it shall be done for them of my Father which is in heaven."[548] You have another in the fulness of faith, which is compared to a grain of mustard-seed. "For," He says, "if you have faith as a grain of mustard seed, ye shall say unto this mountain: Be thou removed, and it shall be removed; and nothing shall be impossible to you."[549] You have it in continuance in prayer, which the Lord's words call, by reason of unwearied perseverance in petitioning, importunity: "For, verily, I say unto you that if not because of his friendship, yet because of his importunity he will rise and give him as much as he needs."[550] You have it in the fruits of almsgiving: "Shut up alms in the heart of the poor and it shall pray for thee in the time of tribulation."[551] You have it in the purifying of life and in works of mercy, as it is said: "Loose the bands of wickedness, undo the bundles that oppress;" and after a few words in which the barrenness of an unfruitful fast is rebuked, "then," he says, "thou shall call and the Lord shall hear thee; thou shalt cry, and He shall say, Here am I."[552] Sometimes also excess of trouble causes it to be heard, as it is said: "When I was in trouble I called unto the Lord, and He heard me;"[553] and again: "Afflict not the stranger for if he crieth unto Me, I will hear him, for I am merciful."[554] You see then in how many ways the gift of an answer may be obtained, so that no one need be crushed by the despair of his conscience for securing those things which are salutary and eternal. For if in contemplating our wretchedness I admit that we are utterly destitute of all those virtues which we mentioned above, and that we have neither that laudable agreement of two persons, nor that faith which is compared to a grain of mustard seed, nor those works of piety which the prophet describes, surely we cannot be without that importunity which He supplies to all who desire it, owing to which alone the Lord promises that He will give whatever He has been prayed to give. And therefore we ought without unbelieving hesitation to persevere, and not to have the least doubt that by continuing in them we shall obtain all those things which we have asked according to the mind of God. For the Lord, in His desire to grant what is heavenly and eternal, urges us to constrain Him as it were by our importunity, as He not only does not despise or reject the importunate, but actually welcomes and praises them, and most graciously promises to grant whatever they have perseveringly hoped for; saying, "Ask and ye shall receive: seek and ye shall find: knock and it shall be opened unto you. For every one that asketh receiveth, and he that seeketh findeth, and to him that knocketh it shall be opened;"[555] and again: "All things whatsoever ye shall ask in prayer believing ye shall receive, and nothing shall be impossible to you."[556] And therefore even if all the grounds for being heard which we have mentioned are altogether wanting, at any rate the earnestness of importunity may animate us, as this is placed in the power of any one who wills without the difficulties of any merits or labours. But let not any suppliant doubt that he certainly will not be heard, so long as he doubts whether he is heard. But that this also shall be sought from the Lord unweariedly, we are taught by the example of the blessed Daniel, as, though he was heard from the first day on which he began to pray, he only obtained the result of his petition after one and twenty days.[557] Wherefore we also ought not to grow slack in the earnestness of the prayers we have begun, if we fancy that the answer comes but slowly, for fear lest perhaps the gift of the answer be in God's providence delayed, or the angel, who was to bring the Divine blessing to us, may when he comes forth from the Presence of the Almighty be hindered by the resistance of the devil, as it is certain that he cannot transmit and bring to us the desired boon, if he finds that we slack off from the earnestness of the petition made. And this would certainly have happened to the above mentioned prophet unless he had with incomparable steadfastness prolonged and persevered in his prayers until the twenty-first day. Let us then not be at all cast down by despair from the confidence of this faith of ours, even when we fancy that we are far from having obtained what we prayed for, and let us not have any doubts about the Lord's promise where He says: "All things, whatsoever ye shall ask in prayer believing, ye shall receive."[558] For it is well for us to consider this saying of the blessed Evangelist John, by which the ambiguity of this question is clearly solved: "This is," he says, "the confidence which we have in Him, that whatsoever we ask according to His will, He heareth us."[559] He bids us then have a full and undoubting confidence of the answer only in those things which are not for our own advantage or for temporal comforts, but are in conformity to the Lord's will. And we are also taught to put this into our prayers by the Lord's Prayer, where we say "Thy will be done,"--Thine not ours. For if we also remember these words of the Apostle that "we know not what to pray for as we ought"[560] we shall see that we sometimes ask for things opposed to our salvation and that we are most providentially refused our requests by Him who sees what is good for us with greater right and truth than we can. And it is clear that this also happened to the teacher of the Gentiles when he prayed that the messenger of Satan who had been for his good allowed by the Lord's will to buffet him, might be removed, saying: "For which I besought the Lord thrice that he might depart from me. And He said unto me, My grace is sufficient for thee, for strength is made perfect in weakness."[561] And this feeling even our Lord expressed when He prayed in the character[562] of man which He had taken, that He might give us a form of prayer as other things also by His example; saying thus: "Father, if it be possible, let this cup pass from me: nevertheless not as I will but as Thou wilt,"[563] though certainly His will was not discordant with His Father's will, "For He had come to save what was lost and to give His life a ransom for many;"[564] as He Himself says: "No man taketh my life from Me, but I lay it down of Myself. I have power to lay it down and I have power to take it again."[565] In which character there is in the thirty-ninth Psalm the following sung by the blessed David, of the Unity of will which He ever maintained with the Father: "To do Thy will: O My God, I am willing."[566] For even if we read of the Father: "For God so loved the world that He gave His only begotten Son,"[567] we find none the less of the Son: "Who gave Himself for our sins."[568] And as it is said of the One: "Who spared not His own Son, but gave Him for all of us,"[569] so it is written of the other: "He was offered because He Himself willed it."[570] And it is shown that the will of the Father and of the Son is in all things one, so that even in the actual mystery of the Lord's resurrection we are taught that there was no discord of operation. For just as the blessed Apostle declares that the Father brought about the resurrection of His body, saying: "And God the Father, who raised Him from the dead,"[571] so also the Son testifies that He Himself will raise again the Temple of His body, saying: "Destroy this temple, and in three days I will raise it up again."[572] And therefore we being instructed by all these examples of our Lord which have been enumerated ought to end our supplications also with the same prayer, and always to subjoin this clause to all our petitions: "Nevertheless not as I will, but as Thou wilt."[573] But it is clear enough that one who does not[574] pray with attention of mind cannot observe

that threefold reverence[575] which is usually practised in the assemblies
of the brethren at the close of service.

NOTES:
[548] S. Matt. 18:19.
[549] S. Matt. 17:19.
[550] S. Luke 11:8.
[551] Ecclus. 29:15.
[552] Is. 58:6, 9.
[553] Ps. 119 (120):1.
[554] Exod. 22:21, 27.
[555] S. Luke 9:9, 10.
[556] S. Matt. 21:22; 17:20.
[557] Cf. Dan. 10:2 sq.
[558] S. Matt. 21:22.
[559] 1 John 5:16.
[560] Rom. 8:26.
[561] 2 Cor. 12:8, 9.
[562] Ex persona hominis assumpti. The language is scarcely accurate, but it
must be remembered that the Conferences were written before the rise of
the Nestorian heresy had shown the need of exactness of expression on the
subject of the Incarnation. Compare the note on Against Nestorius, Book
III. c. iii.
[563] S. Matt. 26:39.
[564] S. Matt. 18:11; 20:28.
[565] S. John 10:18.
[566] Ps. 39 (40):9.
[567] 1 John 3:16.
[568] Gal. 1:4.
[569] Rom. 8:32.
[570] Is. 53:7 (Lat.).
[571] Gal. 1:1.
[572] S. John 2:19.
[573] S. Matt. 26:39.
[574] "Non" though wanting in most MSS. must be read in the text.
[575] Reading "curvationis" with Petschenig: the text of Gazaeus has "orationis."

CHAPTER XXXV.

Of prayer to be offered within the chamber and with the door shut.

BEFORE all things however we ought most carefully to observe the Evangelic precept, which tells us to enter into our chamber and shut the door and pray to our Father, which may be fulfilled by us as follows: We pray within our chamber, when removing our hearts inwardly from the din of all thoughts and anxieties, we disclose our prayers in secret and in closest intercourse to the Lord. We pray with closed doors when with closed lips and complete silence we pray to the searcher not of words but of hearts. We pray in secret when from the heart and fervent mind we disclose our petitions to God alone, so that no hostile powers are even able to discover the character of our petition. Wherefore we should pray in complete silence, not only to avoid distracting the brethren standing near by our whispers or louder utterances, and disturbing the thoughts of those who are praying, but also that the purport of our petition may be concealed from our enemies who are especially on the watch against us while we are praying. For so we shall fulfil this injunction: "Keep the doors of thy mouth from her who sleepeth in thy bosom." [576]

NOTES:
[576] Micah 7:5.

CHAPTER XXXVI.

Of the value of short and silent prayer.

WHEREFORE we ought to pray often but briefly, lest if we are long about it our crafty foe may succeed in implanting something in our heart. For that is the true sacrifice, as "the sacrifice of God is a broken spirit." This is the salutary offering, these are pure drink offerings, that is the "sacrifice of righteousness," the "sacrifice of praise," these are true and fat victims, "holocausts full of marrow," which are offered by contrite and humble hearts, and which those who practise this control and fervour of spirit, of which we have spoken, with effectual power can sing: "Let my prayer be set forth in Thy sight as the incense: let the lifting up of my hands be an evening sacrifice."[577] But the approach of the right hour and of night warns us that we ought with fitting devotion to do this very thing, of which, as our slender ability allowed, we seem to have propounded a great deal, and to have prolonged our conference considerably, though we believe that we have discoursed very little when the magnificence and difficulty of the subject are taken into account.

With these words of the holy Isaac we were dazzled rather than satisfied, and after evening service had been held, rested our limbs for a short time, and intending at the first dawn again to return under promise of a fuller discussion departed, rejoicing over the acquisition of these precepts as well as over the assurance of his promises. Since we felt that though the excellence of prayer had been shown to us, still we had not yet understood from his discourse its nature, and the power by which continuance in it might be gained and kept.

NOTES:
[577] Ps. 50 (51):19, 21; 49 (50):23; 65 (66):15; 140 (141):2.

CONFERENCE 10.

The Second Conference of Abbot Isaac
on Prayer

CHAPTER I.

Introduction.

AMONG the sublime customs of the anchorites which by God's help have been set forth although in plain and unadorned style, the course of our narration compels us to insert and find a place for something, which may seem so to speak to cause a blemish on a fair body: although I have no doubt that by it no small instruction on the image of Almighty God of which we read in Genesis will be conferred on some of the simpler sort, especially when the grounds are considered of a doctrine so important that men cannot be ignorant of it without terrible blasphemy and serious harm to the Catholic faith.

CHAPTER II.

Of the custom which is kept up in the Province of Egypt for signifying the time of Easter.

IN the country of Egypt this custom is by ancient tradition observed that--when Epiphany is past, which the priests of that province regard as the time, both of our Lord's baptism and also of His birth in the flesh, and so celebrate the commemoration of either mystery not separately as in the Western provinces but on the single festival of this day,[578] --letters are sent from the Bishop of Alexandria through all the Churches of Egypt, by which the beginning of Lent, and the day of

Easter are pointed out not only in all the cities but also in all the monasteries.[579] In accordance then with this custom, a very few days after the previous conference had been held with Abbot Isaac, there arrived the festal letters of Theophilus[580] the Bishop of the aforesaid city, in which together with the announcement of Easter he considered as well the foolish heresy of the Anthropomorphites[581] at great length, and abundantly refuted it. And this was received by almost all the body of monks residing in the whole province of Egypt with such bitterness owing to their simplicity and error, that the greater part of the Elders decreed that on the contrary the aforesaid Bishop ought to be abhorred by the whole body of the brethren as tainted with heresy of the worst kind, because he seemed to impugn the teaching of holy Scripture by the denial that Almighty God was formed in the fashion of a human figure, though Scripture teaches with perfect clearness that Adam was created in His image. Lastly this letter was rejected also by those who were living in the desert of Scete and who excelled all who were in the monasteries of Egypt, in perfection and in knowledge, so that except Abbot Paphnutius the presbyter of our congregation, not one of the other presbyters, who presided over the other three churches in the same desert, would suffer it to be even read or repeated at all in their meetings.

NOTES:

[578] The observance of Epiphany can be traced back in the Christian Church to the second century, and, as Cassian tells us here, in the East (in which its observance apparently originated) it was in the first instance a double festival, commemorating both the Nativity and the Baptism of our Lord. From the East its observance passed over to the West, where however the Nativity was already observed as a separate festival, and hence the special reference of Epiphany was somewhat altered, and the manifestation to the Magi was coupled with that at the Baptism: hence the plural Epiphaniorum dies. Meanwhile, as the West adopted the observance of this festival from the East, so the East followed the West in observing a separate feast of the Nativity. Cassian's words show us that when he wrote the two festivals were both observed separately in the West, though apparently not yet (to the best of his belief) in the East, but the language of a homily by S. Chrysostom (Vol. ii. p.354 Ed. Montfaucon) delivered in A.D. 386 shows that the separation of the two festivals had already begun at Antioch, and all the evidence goes to show that "the Western plan was being gradually adopted in the period which we may roughly define as the last quarter of the 4th and the first quarter of the 5th century." Dictionary of Christian Antiquities, Vol. i. p. 361. See further Origines de Culte Chretien, par L'Abbe Duchesne, p. 247 sq.

[579] The "Festal letters" (`eortastikai epistolai, Euseb. VII. xx., xxi.) were de-
livered by the Bishop of Alexandria as Homilies, and then put into the form
of an Epistle and sent round to all the churches of Egypt; and, according to
some late writers, to the Bishops of all the principal sees, in accordance
with a decision of the Council of Nicaea, in order to inform them of the
right day on which Easter should be celebrated. Cassian here speaks of
them as sent immediately after Epiphany, and this was certainly the time at
which the announcement of the date of Easter was made in the West shortly
after his day (so the Council of Orleans, Canon i., A.D. 541; that of Braga
A.D. 572, Canon ix.; and that of Auxerre A.D. 572, Canon ii.), but there is
ample evidence in the Festal letters both of S. Athanasius and of S. Cyril
that at Alexandria the homilies were preached on the previous Easter, and it
is difficult to resist the inference that Cassian's memory is here at fault as to
the exact time at which the incident related really occurred, and that he is
transferring to Egypt the custom with which he was familiar in the West,
assigning to the festival of Epiphany what really must have taken place at
Easter.

[580] Theophilus succeeded Timothy as Bishop of Alexandria in the summer of
385. The festal letters of which Cassian here speaks were issued by him in
the year 399.

[581] The Anthropomorphite heresy, into which the monks of Egypt had fallen,
"supposed that God possesses eyes, a face, and hands and other members of
a bodily organization." It arose from taking too literally those passages of
the Old Testament in which God is spoken of in human terms, out of condescension to man's limited powers of grasping the Divine nature and
appears historically to have been a recoil from the allegorism of Origen and
others of the Alexandrian school. The Festal letter of Theophilus in which
he condemned these views, and maintained the incorporeal nature of God is
no longer extant, but is alluded to also by Sozomen, H. E. VIII. xi., where
an account is given of the Origenistic controversy, of which it was the occasion, and out of which Theophilus came so badly. On the heresy see also
Epiphanius, Haer. lxx.; Augustine, Haer. l. and lxxvi.; and Theodoret, H. E.
IV. x.

CHAPTER III.

Of Abbot Sarapion and the heresy of the Anthropomorphites into
which he fell in the error of simplicity.

AMONG those then who were caught by this mistaken notion
was one named Sarapion, a man of long-standing strictness of life, and
one who was altogether perfect in actual discipline, whose ignorance

with regard to the view of the doctrine first mentioned was so far a stumbling block to all who held the true faith, as he himself outstripped almost all the monks both in the merits of his life and in the length of time (he had been there). And when this man could not be brought back to the way of the right faith by many exhortations of the holy presbyter Paphnutius, because this view seemed to him a novelty, and one that was not ever known to or handed down by his predecessors, it chanced that a certain deacon, a man of very great learning, named Photinus, arrived from the region of Cappadocia with the desire of visiting the brethren living in the same desert: whom the blessed Paphnutius received with the warmest welcome, and in order to confirm the faith which had been stated in the letters of the aforesaid Bishop, placed him in the midst and asked him before all the brethren how the Catholic Churches throughout the East interpreted the passage in Genesis where it says "Let us make man after our image and likeness."[582] And when he explained that the image and likeness of God was taken by all the leaders of the churches not according to the base sound of the letters, but spiritually, and supported this very fully and by many passages of Scripture, and showed that nothing of this sort could happen to that infinite and incomprehensible and invisible glory, so that it could be comprised in a human form and likeness, since its nature is incorporeal and uncompounded and simple, and what can neither be apprehended by the eyes nor conceived by the mind, at length the old man was shaken by the numerous and very weighty assertions of this most learned man, and was drawn to the faith of the Catholic tradition. And when both Abbot Paphnutius and all of us were filled with intense delight at his adhesion, for this reason; viz, that the Lord had not permitted a man of such age and crowned with such virtues, and one who erred only from ignorance and rustic simplicity, to wander from the path of the right faith up to the very last, and when we arose to give thanks, and were all together offering up our prayers to the Lord, the old man was so bewildered in mind during his prayer because he felt that the Anthropomorphic image of the Godhead which he used to set before himself in prayer, was banished from his heart, that on a sudden he burst into a flood of bitter tears and continual sobs, and cast himself down on the ground and exclaimed with strong groanings: "Alas! wretched man that I am! they have taken away my God from me, and I have now none to lay hold of; and whom to worship and address I know not." By which scene we were terribly disturbed, and moreover with the effect of the former Conference still remaining in our hearts, we returned to Abbot Isaac, whom when we saw close at hand, we addressed with these words.

NOTES:
[582] Gen. 1:26.

CHAPTER IV.

Of our return to Abbot Isaac and question concerning the error into which the aforesaid old man had fallen.

ALTHOUGH even besides the fresh matter which has lately arisen, our delight in the former conference which was held on the character of prayer would summon us to postpone everything else and return to your holiness, yet this grievous error of Abbot Sarapion, conceived, as we fancy, by the craft of most vile demons, adds somewhat to this desire of ours. For it is no small despair by which we are cast down when we consider that through the fault of this ignorance he has not only utterly lost all those labours which he has performed in so praiseworthy a manner for fifty years in this desert, but has also incurred the risk of eternal death. And so we want first to know why and wherefore so grievous an error has crept into him. And next we should like to be taught how we can arrive at that condition in prayer, of which you discoursed some time back not only fully but splendidly. For that admirable Conference has had this effect upon us, that it has only dazzled our minds and has not shown us how to perform or secure it.

CHAPTER V.

The answer on the heresy described above.

ISAAC: We need not be surprised that a really simple man who had never received any instruction on the substance and nature of the Godhead could still be entangled and deceived by an error of simplicity and the habit of a longstanding mistake, and (to speak more truly) continue in the original error which is brought about, not as you suppose by a new illusion of the demons, but by the ignorance of the

249

ancient heathen world, while in accordance with the custom of that erroneous notion, by which they used to worship devils formed in the figure of men, they even now think that the incomprehensible and ineffable glory of the true Deity should be worshipped under the limitations of some figure, as they believe that they can grasp and hold nothing if they have not some image set before them, which they can continually address while they are at their devotions, and which they can carry about in their mind and have always fixed before their eyes. And against this mistake of theirs this text may be used: "And they changed the glory of the incorruptible God into the likeness of the image of corruptible man."[583] Jeremiah also says: "My people have changed their glory for an idol."[584] Which error although by this its origin, of which we have spoken, it is engrained in the notions of some, yet none the less is it contracted in the hearts also of those who have never been stained with the superstition of the heathen world, under the colour of this passage where it is said "Let us make man after our image and our likeness,"[585] ignorance and simplicity being its authors, so that actually there has arisen owing to this hateful interpretation a heresy called that of the Anthropomorphites, which maintains with obstinate perverseness that the infinite and simple substance of the Godhead is fashioned in our lineaments and human configuration. Which however any one who has been taught the Catholic doctrine will abhor as heathenish blasphemy, and so will arrive at that perfectly pure condition in prayer which will not only not connect with its prayers any figure of the Godhead or bodily lineaments (which it is a sin even to speak of), but will not even allow in itself even the memory of a name, or the appearance of an action, or an outline of any character.

NOTES:
[583] Rom. 1:23.
[584] Jer. 2:11.
[585] Gen. 1:26.

CHAPTER VI.

Of the reasons why Jesus Christ appears to each one of us either in His humility or in His glorified condition.

FOR according to the measure of its purity, as I said in the former Conference, each mind is both raised and moulded in its prayers if it forsakes the consideration of earthly and material things so far as the condition of its purity may carry it forward, and enable it with the inner eyes of the soul to see Jesus either still in His humility and in the flesh, or glorified and coming in the glory of His Majesty: for those cannot see Jesus coming in His Kingdom who are still kept back in a sort of state of Jewish weakness, and cannot say with the Apostle: "And if we have known Christ after the flesh, yet now we know Him so no more;"[586] but only those can look with purest eyes on His Godhead, who rise with Him from low and earthly works and thoughts and go apart in the lofty mountain of solitude which is free from the disturbance of all earthly thoughts and troubles, and secure from the interference of all sins, and being exalted by pure faith and the heights of virtue reveals the glory of His Face and the image of His splendour to those who are able to look on Him with pure eyes of the soul. But Jesus is seen as well by those who live in towns and villages and hamlets, i.e., who are occupied in practical affairs and works, but not with the same brightness with which He appeared to those who can go up with Him into the aforesaid mount of virtues, i.e., Peter, James, and John. For so in solitude He appeared to Moses and spoke with Elias. And as our Lord wished to establish this and to leave us examples of perfect purity, although He Himself, the very fount of inviolable sanctity, had no need of external help and the assistance of solitude in order to secure it (for the fulness of purity could not be soiled by any stain from crowds, nor could He be contaminated by intercourse with men, who cleanses and sanctifies all things that are polluted) yet still He retired into the mountain alone to pray, thus teaching us by the example of His retirement that if we too wish to approach God with a pure and spotless affection of heart, we should also retire from all the disturbance and confusion of crowds, so that while still living in the body we may manage in some degree to adapt ourselves to some likeness of that bliss which is promised hereafter to the saints, and that "God may be" to us "all in all." [587]

NOTES:
[586] 2 Cor. 5:16.
[587] 1 Cor. 15:28.

251

CHAPTER VII.

What constitutes our end and perfect bliss.

FOR then will be perfectly fulfilled in our case that prayer of our Saviour in which He prayed for His disciples to the Father saying "that the love wherewith Thou lovedst Me may be in them and they in us;" and again: "that they all may be one as Thou, Father, in Me and I in Thee, that they also may be one in us,"[588] when that perfect love of God, wherewith "He first loved us"[589] has passed into the feelings of our heart as well, by the fulfilment of this prayer of the Lord which we believe cannot possibly be ineffectual. And this will come to pass when God shall be all our love, and every desire and wish and effort, every thought of ours, and all our life and words and breath, and that unity which already exists between the Father and the Son, and the Son and the Father, has been shed abroad in our hearts and minds, so that as He loves us with a pure and unfeigned and indissoluble love, so we also may be joined to Him by a lasting and inseparable affection, since we are so united to Him that whatever we breathe or think, or speak is God, since, as I say, we attain to that end of which we spoke before, which the same Lord in His prayer hopes may be fulfilled in us: "that they all may be one as we are one, I in them and Thou in Me, that they also may be made perfect in one;" and again: "Father, those whom Thou hast given Me, I will that where I am, they may also be with Me."[590] This then ought to be the destination of the solitary, this should be all his aim that it may be vouchsafed to him to possess even in the body an image of future bliss, and that he may begin in this world to have a foretaste of a sort of earnest of that celestial life and glory. This, I say, is the end of all perfection, that the mind purged from all carnal desires may daily be lifted towards spiritual things, until the whole life and all the thoughts of the heart become one continuous prayer.

NOTES:
[588] S. John 17:26, 21.
[589] 1 John 4:16.
[590] S. John 17:22-24.

CHAPTER VIII.

A question on the training in perfection by which we can arrive at perpetual recollection of God.

GERMANUS: The extent of our bewilderment at our wondering awe at the former Conference, because of which we came back again, increases still more. For in proportion as by the incitements of this teaching we are fired with the desire of perfect bliss, so do we fall back into greater despair, as we know not how to seek or obtain training for such lofty heights. Wherefore we entreat that you will patiently allow us (for it must perhaps be set forth and unfolded with a good deal of talk) to explain what while sitting in the cell we had begun to revolve in a lengthy meditation, although we know that your holiness is not at all troubled by the infirmities of the weak, which even for this reason should be openly set forth, that what is out of place in them may receive correction. Our notion then is that the perfection of any art or system of training must begin with some simple rudiments, and grow accustomed first to somewhat easy and tender beginnings, so that being nourished and trained little by little by a sort of reasonable milk, it may grow up and so by degrees and step by step mount up from the lowest depths to the heights: and when by these means it has entered on the plainer principles and so to speak passed the gates of the entrance of the profession, it will consequently arrive without difficulty at the inmost shrine and lofty heights of perfection. For how could any boy manage to pronounce the simplest union of syllables unless he had first carefully learnt the letters of the alphabet? Or how can any one learn to read quickly, who is still unfit to connect together short and simple sentences? But by what means will one who is ill instructed in the science of grammar attain eloquence in rhetoric or the knowledge of philosophy? Wherefore for this highest learning also, by which we are taught even to cleave to God, I have no doubt that there are some foundations of the system, which must first be firmly laid and afterwards the towering heights of perfection may be placed and raised upon them. And we have a light idea that these are its first principles; viz., that we should first learn by what meditations God may be grasped and contemplated, and next that we should manage to keep a very firm hold of this topic whatever it is which we do not doubt is the height of all perfection. And therefore we want you to show us some material for this recollection, by which we may conceive and ever keep the idea of God in the mind, so that by always keeping it before our eyes, when we find that we have dropped away from Him, we may at once be able to recover ourselves and return thither and may succeed in laying hold of it again without any delay from wandering around the subject and searching for it. For it happens that when we have wandered away from our spiritual speculations and have come back to ourselves as if waking from a deadly sleep, and, being thoroughly roused, look for the subject matter, by which we may be able to revive that spiritual recollection which has been destroyed, we are hindered by the delay of the actual search before we find it, and are once more drawn aside from our endeavour, and before the spiritual insight is brought about, the purpose of heart which had been conceived, has disappeared. And this trouble is certain to happen to us for this reason because we do not keep something special firmly set before our eyes like some principle to which the wandering thoughts may be recalled after many digressions and varied excursions; and, if I may use the expression, after long storms enter a quiet haven. And so it comes to pass that as the mind is constantly hindered by this want of knowledge and difficulty, and is always tossed about vaguely, and as if intoxicated, among various matters, and cannot even retain firm hold for any length of time of anything spiritual which has occurred to it by chance rather than of set purpose: while, as it is always receiving one thing after another, it does not notice either their beginning and origin or even their end.

CHAPTER IX.

The answer on the efficacy of understanding, which is gained by experience.

ISAAC: Your minute and subtle inquiry affords an indication of purity being very nearly reached. For no one would be able even to make inquiries on these matters,I will not say to look within and discriminate,--except one who had been urged to sound the depths of such questions by careful and effectual diligence of mind, and watchful anxiety, and one whom the constant aim after a well controlled life had taught by practical experience to attempt the entrance to this purity and to knock at its doors. And therefore as I see you, I will not say, standing before the doors of that true prayer of which we have been speaking, but touching its inner chambers and inward parts as it were with the hands of experience, and already laying hold of some parts of it, I do not think that I shall find any difficulty in introducing you now within what I may call its hall, for you to roam about its recesses, as the Lord may direct; nor do I think that you will be hindered from investigating what is to be shown you by any obstacles or difficulties. For he is next door to understanding who carefully recognizes what he ought to ask about, nor is he far from knowledge, who begins to understand how ignorant he is. And therefore I am not afraid of the charge of betraying secrets, and of levity, if I divulge what when speaking in my former discourse on the perfection of prayer I had kept back from discussing, as I think that its force was to be explained to us who are occupied with this subject and interest even without the aid of my words, by the grace of God.

CHAPTER X.

Of the method of continual prayer.

WHEREFORE in accordance with that system, which you admirably compared to teaching children (who can only take in the first lessons on the alphabet and recognize the shapes of the letters, and trace out their characters with a steady hand if they have, by means of some copies and shapes carefully impressed on wax, got accustomed to express their figures, by constantly looking at them and imitating them daily), we must give you also the form of this spiritual contemplation, on which you may always fix your gaze with the utmost steadiness, and both learn to consider it to your profit in unbroken continuance, and also manage by the practice of it and by meditation to climb to a still loftier insight. This formula then shall be proposed to you of this system, which you want, and of prayer, which every monk in his progress towards continual recollection of God, is accustomed to ponder, ceaselessly revolving it in his heart, having got rid of all kinds of other thoughts; for he cannot possibly keep his hold over it unless he has freed himself from all bodily cares and anxieties. And as this was delivered to us by a few of those who were left of the oldest fathers, so it is only divulged by us to a very few and to those who are really keen. And so for keeping up continual recollection of God this pious formula is to be ever set before you. "O God, make speed to save me: O Lord, make haste to help me,"[591] for this verse has not unreasonably been picked out from the whole of Scripture for this purpose. For it embraces all the feelings which can be implanted in human nature, and can be fitly and satisfactorily adapted to every condition, and all assaults. Since it contains an invocation of God against every danger, it contains humble and pious confession, it contains the watchfulness of anxiety and continual fear, it contains the thought of one's own weakness, confidence in the answer, and the assurance of a present and ever ready help. For one who is constantly calling on his protector, is certain that He is always at hand. It contains the glow of love and charity, it contains a view of the plots, and a dread of the enemies, from which one, who sees himself day and night hemmed in by them, confesses that he cannot be set free without the aid of his defender. This verse is an impregnable wall for all who are labouring under the attacks of demons, as well as impenetrable coat of mail and a strong shield. It does not suffer those who are in a state of moroseness and anxiety of mind, or depressed by sadness or all kinds of thoughts to despair of saving remedies, as it shows that He, who is invoked, is ever looking on at our struggles and is not far from His suppliants. It warns us whose lot is spiritual success and delight of heart that we ought not to be at all elated or puffed up by our happy condition, which it assures us cannot last without God as our protector, while it implores Him not only always but even speedily to help us. This verse, I say, will be found helpful and useful to every one of us in whatever condition we may be. For one who always and in all matters wants to be helped, shows that he needs the assistance of God not only in sorrowful or hard matters but also equally in prosperous and happy ones, that he may be delivered from the one and also made to continue in the other, as he knows that in both of them human weakness is unable to endure without His assistance. I am affected by the passion of gluttony. I ask for food of which the desert knows nothing, and in the squalid desert there are wafted to me odours of royal dainties and I find that even against my will I am drawn to long for them. I must at once say: "O God, make speed to save me: O Lord, make haste to help me." I am incited to anticipate the hour fixed for supper, or I am trying with great sorrow of heart to keep to the limits of the right and regular meagre fare. I must cry out with groans: "O God, make speed to save me: O Lord, make haste to help me." Weakness of the stomach hinders me when wanting severer fasts, on account of the assaults of the flesh, or dryness of the belly and constipation frightens me. In order that effect may be given to my wishes, or else that the fire of carnal lust may be quenched without the remedy of a stricter fast, I must pray: "O God, make speed to save me: O Lord, make haste to help me." When I come to supper, at the bidding of the proper hour I loathe taking food and am prevented from eating anything to satisfy the requirements of nature: I must cry with a sigh: "O God, make speed to save me: O Lord, make haste to help me." When I want for the sake of steadfastness of heart to apply myself to reading a headache interferes and stops me, and at the third hour sleep glues my head to the sacred page, and I am forced either to overstep or to anticipate the time assigned to rest; and finally an overpowering desire to sleep forces me to cut short the canonical rule for service in the Psalms: in the same way I must cry out: "O God, make speed to save me: O Lord, make haste to help me." Sleep is withdrawn from my eyes, and for many nights I find myself wearied out with sleeplessness caused by the devil, and all repose and rest by night is kept away from my eyelids; I must sigh and pray: "O God, make speed to save me: O Lord, make haste to help me." While I am still in the midst of a struggle with sin suddenly an irritation of the flesh affects me and tries by a pleasant sensation to draw me to consent while in my sleep. In order that a raging fire from without may not burn up the fragrant blossoms of chastity, I must cry out: "O God, make speed to save me: O Lord, make haste to help me." I feel that the incentive to lust is removed, and that the heat of passion has died away in my members: In order that this good condition acquired, or rather that this grace of God may continue still longer or forever with me, I must earnestly say: "O God, make speed to save me: O Lord, make haste to help me." I am disturbed by the pangs of anger, covetousness, gloominess, and driven to disturb the peaceful state in which I was, and which was dear to me: In order that I may not be carried away by raging passion into the bitterness of gall, I must cry out with deep groans: "O God, make speed to save me: O Lord, make haste to help me." I am tried by being puffed up by accidie, vainglory, and pride, and my mind with subtle thoughts flatters itself somewhat on account of the coldness and carelessness of others: In order that this dangerous suggestion of the enemy may not get the mastery over me, I must pray with all contrition of heart: "O God, make speed to save me: O Lord, make haste to help me." I have gained the grace of humility and simplicity, and by continually mortifying my spirit have got rid of the swellings of pride: In order that the "foot of pride" may not again "come against me," and "the hand of the sinner disturb me,"[592] and that I may not be more seriously damaged by elation at my success, I must cry with all my might, "O God, make speed to save me: O Lord, make haste to help me." I am on fire with innumerable and various wanderings of soul and shiftiness of heart, and cannot collect my scattered thoughts, nor can I even pour forth my prayer without interruption and images of vain figures, and the recollection of conversations and actions, and I feel myself tied down by such dryness and barrenness that I feel I cannot give birth to any offspring in the shape of spiritual ideas: In order that it may be vouchsafed to me to be set free from this wretched state of mind, from which I cannot extricate myself by any number of sighs and groans, I must full surely cry out: "O God, make speed to save me: O Lord, make haste to help me." Again, I feel that by the visitation of the Holy Spirit I have gained purpose of soul, steadfastness of thought, keenness of heart, together with an ineffable joy and transport of mind, and in the exuberance of spiritual feelings I have perceived by a sudden illumination from the Lord an abounding revelation of most holy ideas which were formerly altogether hidden from me: In order that it may be vouchsafed to me to linger for a longer time in them I must often and anxiously exclaim: "O God, make speed to save me: O Lord, make haste to help me." Encompassed by nightly horrors of devils I am agitated, and am disturbed by the appearances of unclean spirits, my very hope of life and salvation is withdrawn by the horror of fear. Flying to the safe refuge of this verse, I will cry out with all my might: "O God, make speed to save me: O Lord, make haste to help me." Again, when I have been restored by the Lord's consolation, and, cheered by His coming, feel myself encompassed as if by countless thousands of angels, so that all of a sudden I can venture to seek the conflict and provoke a battle with those whom a while ago I dreaded worse than death, and whose touch or even approach I felt with a shudder both of mind and body: In order that the vigour of this courage may, by God's grace, continue in me still longer, I must cry out with all my powers "O God, make speed to save me: O Lord, make haste to help me." We must then ceaselessly and continuously pour forth the prayer of this verse, in adversity that we may be delivered, in prosperity that we may be preserved and not puffed up. Let the thought of this verse, I tell you, be conned over in your breast without ceasing. Whatever work you are doing, or office you are holding, or journey you are going, do not cease to chant this. When you are going to bed, or eating, and in the last necessities of nature, think on this. This thought in your heart may be to you a saving formula, and not only keep you unharmed by all attacks of devils, but also purify you from all faults and earthly stains, and lead you to that invisible and celestial contemplation, and carry you on to that ineffable glow of prayer, of which so few have any experience. Let sleep come upon you still considering this verse, till having been moulded by the constant use of it, you grow accustomed to repeat it even in your sleep. When you wake let it be the first thing to come into your mind, let it anticipate all your waking thoughts, let it when you rise from your bed send you down on your knees, and thence send you forth to all your work and business, and let it follow you about all day long. This you should think about, according to the Lawgiver's charge, "at home and walking forth on a journey,"[593] sleeping and waking. This you should write on the threshold and door of your mouth, this you should place on the walls of your house and in the recesses of your heart so that when you fall on your knees in prayer this may be your chant as you kneel, and when you rise up from it to go forth to all the necessary business of life it may be your constant prayer as you stand.

NOTES:
[591] Ps. 69 (70):2. It is not improbable that this chapter suggested to S. Benedict the use of these words as the opening versicle of the hour services, a position which it has ever since occupied in the West. See the Rule of S. Benedict, cc. ix., xvii., and xviii.
[592] Ps. 35 (36):12.
[593] Deut. 6:7.

CHAPTER XI.

Of the perfection of prayer to which we can rise by the system described.

THIS, this is the formula which the mind should unceasingly cling to until, strengthened by the constant use of it and by continual meditation, it casts off and rejects the rich and full material of all manner of thoughts and restricts itself to the poverty of this one verse, and so arrives with ready ease at that beatitude of the gospel, which holds the first place among the other beatitudes: for He says "Blessed are the poor in spirit, for theirs is the kingdom of heaven."[594] And so one who becomes grandly poor by a poverty of this sort will fulfil this saying of the prophet: "The poor and needy shall praise the name of the Lord."[595] And indeed what greater or holier poverty can there be than that of one who knowing that he has no defence and no strength of his own, asks for daily help from another's bounty, and as he is aware that every single moment his life and substance depend on Divine assistance, professes himself not without reason the Lord's bedesman, and cries to Him daily in prayer: "But I am poor and needy: the Lord helpeth me."[596] And so by the illumination of God Himself he mounts to that manifold knowledge of Him and begins henceforward to be nourished on sublimer and still more sacred mysteries, in accordance with these words of the prophet: "The high hills are a refuge for the stags, the rocks for the hedgehogs,"[597] which is very fairly applied in the sense we have given, because whosoever continues in simplicity and innocence is not injurious or offensive to any one, but being content with his own simple condition endeavours simply to defend himself from being spoiled by his foes, and becomes a sort of spiritual hedgehog and is protected by the continual shield of that rock of the gospel, i.e., being sheltered by the recollection of the Lord's passion and by ceaseless meditation on the verse given above he escapes the snares of his opposing enemies. And of these spiritual hedgehogs we read in Proverbs as follows: "And the hedgehogs are a feeble folk, who have made their homes in the rocks."[598] And indeed what is feebler than a Christian, what is weaker than a monk, who is not only not permitted any vengeance for wrongs done to him but is actually not allowed to suffer even a slight and silent feeling of irritation to spring up within? But whoever advances from this condition and not only secures the simplicity of innocence, but is also shielded by the virtue of discretion, becomes an exterminator of deadly serpents, and has Satan crushed beneath his feet, and by his quickness of mind answers to the figure of the reasonable stag, this man will feed on the mountains of the prophets and Apostles, i.e., on their highest and loftiest mysteries. And thriving on this pasture continually, he will take in to himself all the thoughts of the Psalms and will begin to sing them in such a way that he will utter them with the deepest emotion of heart not as if they were the compositions of the Psalmist, but rather as if they were his own utterances and his very own prayer; and will certainly take them as aimed at himself, and will recognize that their words were not only fulfilled formerly by or in the person of the prophet, but that they are fulfilled and carried out daily in his own case. For then the Holy Scriptures lie open to us with greater clearness and as it were their very veins and marrow are exposed, when our experience not only perceives but actually anticipates their meaning, and the sense of the words is revealed to us not by an exposition of them but by practical proof. For if we have experience of the very state of mind in which each Psalm was sung and written, we become like their authors and anticipate the meaning rather than follow it, i.e., gathering the force of the words before we really know them, we remember what has happened to us, and what is happening in daily assaults when the thoughts of them come over us, and while we sing them we call to mind all that our carelessness has brought upon us, or our earnestness has secured, or Divine Providence has granted or the promptings of the foe have deprived us of, or slippery and subtle forgetfulness has carried off, or human weakness has brought about, or thoughtless ignorance has cheated us of. For all these feelings we find expressed in the Psalms so that by seeing whatever happens as in a very clear mirror we understand it better, and so instructed by our feelings as our teachers we lay hold of it as something not merely heard but actually seen, and, as if it were not committed to memory, but implanted in the very nature of things, we are affected from the very bottom of the heart, so that we get at its meaning not by reading the text but by experience anticipating it. And so our mind will reach that incorruptible prayer to which in our former treatise, as the Lord vouchsafed to grant, the scheme of our Conference mounted, and this is not merely not engaged in gazing on any image, but is actually distinguished by the use of no words or utterances; but with the purpose of the mind all on fire, is produced through ecstasy of heart by some unaccountable keenness of spirit, and the mind being thus affected without the aid of the senses or any visible material pours it forth to God with groanings and sighs that cannot be uttered.

NOTES:
[594] S. Matt. 5:3.
[595] Ps. 73 (74):21.
[596] Ps. 39 (40):17 (LXX).
[597] Ps. 103 (104):18.
[598] Prov. 30:26 (LXX).

CHAPTER XII.

A question as to how spiritual thoughts can be retained without losing them.

GERMANUS: We think that you have described to us not only the system of this spiritual discipline for which we asked, but perfection itself; and this with great clearness and openness. For what can be more perfect and sublime than for the recollection of God to be embraced in so brief a meditation, and for it, dwelling on a single verse, to escape from all the limitations of things visible, and to comprise in one short word the thoughts of all our prayers. And therefore we beg you to explain to us one thing which still remains; viz., how we can keep firm hold of this verse which you have given us as a formula, in such a way that, as we have been by God's grace set free from the trifles of worldly thoughts, so we may also keep a steady grasp on all spiritual ones.

CHAPTER XIII.

On the lightness of thoughts.

FOR when the mind has taken in the meaning of a passage in any Psalm, this insensibly slips away from it, and ignorantly and thoughtlessly it passes on to a text of some other Scripture. And when it has begun to consider this with itself, while it is still not thoroughly explored, the recollection of some other passage springs up, and shuts out the consideration of the former subject. From this too it is transferred to some other, by the entrance of some fresh consideration, and the soul always turns about from Psalm to Psalm and jumps from a passage in the Gospels to read one in the Epistles, and from this passes on to the prophetic writings, and thence is carried to some spiritual history, and so it wanders about vaguely and uncertainly through the whole body of the Scriptures, unable, as it may choose, either to reject or keep hold of anything, or to finish anything by fully considering and examining it, and so becomes only a toucher or taster of spiritual meanings, not an author and possessor of them. And so the mind, as it is always light and wandering, is distracted even in time of service by all sorts of things, as if it were intoxicated, and does not perform any office properly. For instance, while it is praying, it is recalling some Psalm or passage of Scripture. While it is chanting, it is thinking about something else besides what the text of the Psalm itself contains. When it repeats a passage of Scripture, it is thinking about something that has to be done, or remembering something that has been done. And in this way it takes in and rejects nothing in a disciplined and proper way, and seems to be driven about by random incursions, without the power either of retaining what it likes or lingering over it. It is then well for us before everything else to know how we can properly perform these spiritual offices, and keep firm hold of this particular verse which you have given us as a formula, so that the rise and fall of our feelings may not be in a state of fluctuation from their own lightness, but may lie under our own control.

CHAPTER XIV.

The answer how we can gain stability of heart or of thoughts.

ISAAC: Although, in our former discussion on the character of prayer, enough was, as I think, said on this subject, yet as you want it repeated to you again, I will give you a brief instruction on steadfastness of heart. There are three things which make a shifting heart steadfast, watchings, meditation, and prayer, diligence in which and constant attention will produce steadfast firmness of mind. But this cannot be secured in any other way unless all cares and anxieties of this present life have been first got rid of by indefatigable persistence in work dedicated not to covetousness but to the sacred uses of the monastery, that we may thus be able to fulfil the Apostle's command: "Pray without ceasing."[599] For he prays too little, who is accustomed only to pray at the times when he bends his knees. But he never prays, who even while on his bended knees is distracted by all kinds of wanderings of heart. And therefore what we would be found when at our prayers, that we ought to be before the time of prayer. For at the time of its prayers the mind cannot help being affected by its previous condition, and while it is praying, will be either transported to things heavenly, or dragged down to earthly things by those thoughts in which it had been lingering before prayer.

Thus far did Abbot Isaac carry on his Second Conference on the character of Prayer to us astonished hearers; whose instruction on the consideration of that verse quoted above (which he gave as a sort of outline for beginners to hold) we greatly admired, and wished to follow very closely, as we fancied that it would be a short and easy method; but we have found it even harder to observe than that system of ours by which we used formerly to wander here and there in varied meditations through the whole body of the Scriptures without being tied by any chains of perseverance. It is then certain that no one is kept away from perfection of heart by not being able to read, nor is rustic simplicity any hindrance to the possession of purity of heart and mind, which lies close at hand for all, if only they will by constant meditation on this verse keep the thoughts of the mind safe and sound towards God.

NOTES:
[599] 1 Thess. 5:17.

Part II.

Containing Conferences XI.-XVII
(except XII)

PREFACE

ALTHOUGH many of the saints who are taught by your example can scarcely emulate the greatness of your perfection, with which you shine like great luminaries with marvellous brightness in this world, yet still you, O holy brothers Honoratus and Eucherius,[600] are so stirred by the great glory of those splendid men from whom we received the first principles of monasticism, that one of you, presiding as he does over a large monastery of the brethren, is hoping that his congregation, which learns a lesson from the daily sight of your saintly life, may be instructed in the precepts of those fathers, while the other has been anxious to make his way to Egypt to be edified by the sight of these in the flesh, that he might leave this province that is frozen as it were with the cold of Gaul, and like some pure turtle dove fly to those lands on which the sun of righteousness looks and to which it approaches nearest, and which abound with the ripe fruits of virtues. As a matter of course the greatness of my love wrings this from me; viz., that considering the desire of the one and the labour of the other, I should not decline the danger and peril of writing, if only to the one there may be added authority among his children, and from the other may be removed the necessity for so risky a journey. Further since neither the Institutes of the coenobia which we wrote to the best of our ability in twelve books for Bishop Castor of blessed memory, nor the ten Conferences of the fathers living in the desert of Scete, which we composed somehow or other at the bidding of Saints Helladius and Leontius the Bishops,[601] were able to satisfy your faith and zeal, now in order that the reason for our journey may be also known, I have thought that seven Conferences of the three fathers whom we first saw living in another desert, might be written in the same style and dedicated to you, in which whatever has been in our previous works perhaps obscurely explained or even omitted on the subject of perfection, may be supplied. But if even this is not enough to satisfy the holy thirst of your desires, seven other Conferences, which are to be sent to

PART 2

the holy brethren living in the islands of the Stoechades,[602] will, I fancy, satisfy your wants and your ardour.

NOTES:

[600] On Honoratus and Eucherius, see the Introduction.

[601] Cf. the Preface to Conference I.

[602] A group of islands off the coast of France opposite Marseilles; mentioned by Pliny, H. N. III. V., now known as Les Isles d'Hieres.

CONFERENCE 11.

The First Conference of Abbot Chaeremon
on Perfection

CHAPTER I.

Description of the town of Thennesus.

WHEN we were living in a monastery in Syria after our first infancy in the faith, and when after we had grown somewhat we had begun to long for some greater grace of perfection, we determined straightway to seek Egypt and penetrating even to the remotest desert of the Thebaid,[603] to visit very many of the saints, whose glory and fame had spread abroad everywhere, with the wish if not to emulate them at any rate to know them. And so we came by a very lengthy voyage to a town of Egypt named Thennesus,[604] whose inhabitants are so surrounded either by the sea or by salt lakes that they devote themselves to business alone and get their wealth and substance by naval commerce as the land fails them, so that indeed when they want to build houses, there is no soil sufficient for this, unless it is brought by boat from a distance.

NOTES:
[603] It is very doubtful whether Cassian ever carried out the intention, of which he here speaks, of visiting the Thebaid. So far as we can trace the course of his wanderings, he does not seem to have penetrated farther into Egypt than the desert of Scete.
[604] Thennesus, a town at the Tanitic mouth of the Nile near Lake Menzaleh. For the description of the neighbouring country compare Conference VII. c. xxvi.

CHAPTER II.

Of Bishop Archebius.

AND when we arrived there, God gratified our wishes, and had brought about the arrival of that most blessed and excellent man Bishop Archebius,[605] who had been carried off from the assembly of anchorites and given as Bishop to the town of Panephysis,[606] and who kept all his life long to his purpose of solitude with such strictness that he relaxed nothing of the character of his former humility, nor flattered himself on the honour that had been added to him (for he vowed that he had not been summoned to that office as fit for it, but complained that he had been expelled from the monastic system as unworthy of it because though he had spent thirty-seven years in it he had never been able to arrive at the purity so high a profession demands); he then when he had received us kindly and most graciously in the aforesaid Thennesus whither the business of electing a Bishop there had brought him, as soon as he heard of our wish and desire to inquire of the holy fathers even in still more remote parts of Egypt: "Come," said he, "see in the meanwhile the old men who live not far from our monastery, the length of whose service is shown by their bent bodies, as their holiness shines forth in their appearance, so that even the mere sight of them will give a great lesson to those who see them: and from them you can learn not so much by their words as by the actual example of their holy life, what I grieve that I have lost, and having lost cannot give to you. But I think that my poverty will be somewhat lessened by this zeal of mine, if when you are seeking that pearl of the Gospel which I have not, I at least provide where you can conveniently procure it."

NOTES:

[605] Archebius has already been mentioned in Conference VII. xxvi.; and in the Institutes V. xxxvii., xxxviii., two stories are told illustrative of his kindness and goodness of disposition; but he is not known to us from any other source except Cassian's writings.

[606] For the situation of Panephysis, see the note on the Institutes, Book IV. c. xxx.

CHAPTER III.

Description of the desert where Chaeremon, Nesteros, and Joseph lived.

AND so he took his staff and scrip, as is there the custom for all monks starting on a journey, and himself led us as guide of our road to his own city, i.e., Panephysis, the lands of which and indeed the greater part of the neighbouring region (formerly an extremely rich one since from it, as report says, everything was supplied for the royal table), had been covered by the sea which was disturbed by a sudden earthquake and overflowed its banks, and so (almost all the villages being in ruins) covered what were formerly rich lands with salt marshes, so that you might think that what is spiritually sung in the psalm was a literal prophecy of that region. "He hath turned rivers into a wilderness; and the springs of waters into a thirsty land: a fruitful land into saltness for the wickedness of them that dwell therein."[607] In these districts then many towns perched in this way on the higher hills were deserted by their inhabitants and turned by the inundation into islands, and these afforded the desired solitude to the holy anchorites, among whom three old men; viz., Chaeremon, Nesteros and Joseph, stood out as anchorites of the longest standing.

NOTES:
[607] Ps. 106 (107):33 sq.

CHAPTER IV.

Of Abbot Chaeremon and his excuse about the teaching which we asked for.

AND so the blessed Archebius thought it best to take us first to Chaeremon,[608] because he was nearer to his monastery, and because he was more advanced than the other two in age: for he had passed the hundredth year of his life, vigorous only in spirit, but with his back bowed with age and constant prayer, so that, as if he were once more in his childhood he crawled with his hands hanging down and resting on the ground. Gazing then at one and the same time on this man's wonderful face and on his walk (for though all his limbs had already

271

failed and were dead yet he had lost none of the severity of his previous strictness) when we humbly asked for the word and doctrine, and declared that longing for spiritual instruction was the only reason for our coming, he sighed deeply and said: What doctrine can I teach you, I in whom the feebleness of age has relaxed my former strictness, as it has also destroyed my confidence in speaking? For how could I presume to teach what I do not do, or instruct another in what I know I now practise but feebly and coldly? Wherefore I do not allow any of the younger men to live with me now that I am of such an advanced age, lest the other's strictness should be relaxed owing to my example. For the authority of a teacher will never be strong unless he fixes it in the heart of his hearer by the actual performance of his duty.

NOTES:
[608] Chaeremon is perhaps the same person of whom a short account is given in the Lausiac History of Palladius, c. xcii.

CHAPTER V.

Of our answer to his excuse.

AT this we were overwhelmed with no slight confusion and replied as follows: Although both the difficulty of the place and the solitary life itself, which even a robust youth could scarcely put up with, ought to be sufficient to teach us everything (and indeed without your saying anything they do teach and impress us a very great deal) yet still we ask you to lay aside your silence for a little and in a more worthy manner implant in us those principles by which we may be able to embrace, not so much by imitating it as by admiring it, that goodness which we see in you. For even if our coldness is known to you, and does not deserve to obtain what we are asking for, yet at least the trouble of so long a journey ought to be repaid by it, as we made haste to come here after our first beginning in the monastery of Bethlehem, owing to a longing for your instruction, and a yearning for our own good.

CHAPTER VI.

Abbot Chaeremon's statement that faults can be overcome in three ways.

THEN the blessed CHAEREMON: There are, said he, three things which enable men to control their faults; viz., either the fear of hell or of laws even now imposed; or the hope and desire of the kingdom of heaven; or a liking for goodness itself and the love of virtue. For then we read that the fear of evil loathes contamination: "The fear of the Lord hateth evil."[609] Hope also shuts out the assaults of all faults: for "all who hope in Him shall not fail."[610] Love also fears no destruction from sins, for "love never faileth;"[611] and again: "love covers a multitude of sins."[612] And therefore the blessed Apostle confines the whole sum of salvation in the attainment of those three virtues, saying "Now abideth faith, hope, love, these three."[613] For faith is what makes us shun the stains of sin from fear of future judgment and punishment; hope is what withdraws our mind from present things, and despises all bodily pleasures from its expectation of heavenly rewards; love is what inflames us with keenness of heart for the love of Christ and the fruit of spiritual goodness, and makes us hate with a perfect hatred whatever is opposed to these. And these three things although they all seem to aim at one and the same end (for they incite us to abstain from things unlawful) yet they differ from each other greatly in the degrees of their excellence. For the two former belong properly to those men who in their aim at goodness have not yet acquired the love of virtue, and the third belongs specially to God and to those who have received into themselves the image and likeness of God. For He alone does the things that are good, with no fear and no thanks or reward to stir Him up, but simply from the love of goodness. For, as Solomon says, "The Lord hath made all things for Himself."[614] For under cover of His own goodness He bestows all the fulness of good things on the worthy and the unworthy because He cannot be wearied by wrongs, nor be moved by passions at the sins of men, as He ever remains perfect goodness and unchangeable in His nature.

NOTES:
[609] Prov. 8:13.
[610] Ps. 33 (34):23.
[611] 1 Cor. 13:8.
[612] 1 Pet. 4:8.

CHAPTER VII.

By what steps we can ascend to the heights of love and what permanence there is in it.

IF then any one is aiming at perfection, from that first stage of fear which we rightly termed servile (of which it is said: "When ye have done all things say: we are unprofitable servants,"[615]) he should by advancing a step mount to the higher path of hope--which is compared not to a slave but to a hireling, because it looks for the payment of its recompense, and as if it were free from care concerning absolution of its sins and fear of punishment, and conscious of its own good works, though it seems to look for the promised reward, yet it cannot attain to that love of a son who, trusting in his father's kindness and liberality, has no doubt that all that the father has is his, to which also that prodigal who together with his father's substance had lost the very name of son, did not venture to aspire, when he said: "I am no more worthy to be called thy son;" for after those husks which the swine ate, satisfaction from which was denied to him, i.e., the disgusting food of sin, as he "came to himself," and was overcome by a salutary fear, he already began to loathe the uncleanness of the swine, and to dread the punishment of gnawing hunger, and as if he had already been made a servant, desires the condition of a hireling and thinks about the remuneration, and says: "How many hired servants of my father have abundance of bread, and I perish here with hunger. I will then return to my father and will say unto him, `Father I have sinned against heaven and before thee, and am no more worthy to be called thy son: make me as one of thy hired servants.'"[616] But those words of humble penitence his father who ran to meet him received with greater affection than that with which they were spoken, and was not content to allow him lesser things, but passing through the two stages without delay restored him to his former dignity of sonship. We also ought forthwith to hasten on that by means of the indissoluble grace of love we may mount to that third stage of sonship, which believes that all that the father has is its own, nd so we may be counted worthy to receive the image and likeness of our heavenly Father, and be able to say after the likeness of

274

the true son: "All that the Father hath is mine."[617] Which also the blessed Apostle declares of us, saying: "All things are yours, whether Paul or Apollos or Cephas, or the world, or life, or death, or things present, or things to come; all are yours."[618] And to this likeness the commands of our Saviour also summon us: "Be ye," says He, "perfect, even as your Father in heaven is perfect."[619] For in these persons sometimes the love of goodness is found to be interrupted, when the vigour of the soul is relaxed by some coldness or joy or delight, and so loses either the fear of hell for the time, or the desire of future blessings. And there is indeed in these a stage leading to some advance, which affects us so that when from fear of punishment or from hope of reward we begin to avoid sin we are enabled to pass on to the stage of love, for "fear," says one, "is not in love, but perfect love casteth out fear: for fear hath torment, but he who fears is not perfect in love. We therefore love because God first loved us."[620] We can then only ascend to that true perfection when, as He first loved us for the grace of nothing but our salvation, we also have loved Him for the sake of nothing but His own love alone. Wherefore we must do our best to mount with perfect ardour of mind from this fear to hope, from hope to the love of God, and the love of the virtues themselves, that as we steadily pass on to the love of goodness itself, we may, as far as it is possible for human nature, keep firm hold of what is good.

NOTES:
[615] S. Luke 17:10.
[616] S. Luke 15:17-19.
[617] S. John 16:15.
[618] 1 Cor. 3:22.
[619] St. Matt. 5:48.
[620] 1 John 4:18, 19.

CHAPTER VIII.

How greatly those excel who depart from sin through the feeling of love.

FOR there is a great difference between one who puts out the fire of sin within him by fear of hell or hope of future reward, and one who from the feeling of divine love has a horror of sin itself and of uncleanness, and keeps hold of the virtue of purity simply from the love and longing for purity, and looks for no reward from a promise for the future, but, delighted with the knowledge of good things present, does everything not from regard to punishment but from delight in virtue. For this condition can neither abuse an opportunity to sin when all human witnesses are absent, nor be corrupted by the secret allurements of thoughts, while, keeping in its very marrow the love of virtue itself, it not only does not admit into the heart anything that is opposed to it, but actually hates it with the utmost horror. For it is one thing for a man in his delight at some present good to hate the stains of sins and of the flesh, and another thing to check unlawful desires by contemplating the future reward; and it is one thing to fear present loss and another to dread future punishment. Lastly it is a much greater thing to be unwilling to forsake good for good's own sake, than it is to withhold consent from evil for fear of evil. For in the former case the good is voluntary, but in the latter it is constrained and as it were violently forced out of a reluctant party either by fear of punishment or by greed of reward. For one who abstains from the allurements of sin owing to fear, will whenever the obstacle of fear is removed, once more return to what he loves and thus will not continually acquire any stability in good, nor will he ever rest free from attacks because he will not secure the sure and lasting peace of chastity. For where there is the disturbance of warfare there cannot help being the danger of wounds. For one who is in the midst of the conflict, even though he is a warrior and by fighting bravely inflicts frequent and deadly wounds on his foes, must still sometimes be pierced by the point of the enemy's sword. But one who has defeated the attack of sins and is now in the enjoyment of the security of peace, and has passed on to the love of virtue itself, will keep this condition of good continually, as he is entirely wrapped up in it, because he believes that nothing can be worse than the loss of his inmost chastity. For he deems nothing dearer or more precious than present purity, to whom a dangerous departure from virtue or a poisonous stain of sin is a grievous punishment. To such an one, I say, neither will regard for the presence of another add anything to his goodness nor will solitude take anything away from it: but as always and everywhere he bears about with him his conscience as a judge not only of his actions but also of his thoughts, he will especially try to please it, as he knows that it cannot be cheated nor deceived, and that he cannot escape it.

CHAPTER IX.

That love not only makes sons out of servants, but also bestows the image and likeness of God.

AND if to anyone relying on the help of God and not on his own efforts, it has been vouchsafed to acquire this state, from the condition of a servant, wherein is fear, and from a mercenary greed of hope, whereby there is sought not so much the good of the donor as the recompense of reward, he will begin to pass on to the adoption of sons, where there is no longer fear, nor greed, but that love which never faileth continually endures. Of which fear and love the Lord in chiding some shows what is befitting for each one: "A son knoweth his own father, and a servant feareth his lord: And if I be a Father, where is My honour: and if I be a Lord, where is my fear?"[621] For one who is a servant must needs fear because "if knowing his lord's will he has done things worthy of stripes, he shall be beaten with many stripes."[622] Whoever then by this love has attained the image and likeness of God, will now delight in goodness for the pleasure of goodness itself, and having somehow a like feeling of patience and gentleness will henceforth be angered by no faults of sinners, but in his compassion and sympathy will rather ask for pardon for their infirmities, and, remembering that for so long he himself was tried by the stings of similar passions till by the Lord's mercy he was saved, will feel that, as he was saved from carnal attacks not by the teaching of his own exertions but by God's protection, not anger but pity ought to be shown to those who go astray; and with full peace of mind will he sing to God the following verse: "Thou hast broken my chains. I will offer to Thee the sacrifice of praise;" and: "except the Lord had helped me, my soul had almost dwelt in hell."[623] And while he continues in this humility of mind he will be able even to fulfil this Evangelic command of perfection: "Love your enemies, do good to them that hate you, and pray for them that persecute you and slander you."[624] And so it will be vouchsafed to us to attain that reward which is subjoined, whereby we shall not only bear the image and likeness of God, but shall even be called sons: "that ye may be," says He "sons of your Father which is in heaven, Who maketh His sun to rise on the good and evil, and sends rain on the just and on the unjust:"[625] and this feeling the blessed John knew that he had attained when he said: "that we may have confidence in the day of judgment, because as He is so are we also in this world."[626] For in what can a weak and fragile human nature be like Him, except in always showing a calm love in its heart towards the good and evil, the just and the unjust, in imitation of God, and by doing good for the love of goodness itself, arriving at that true adoption of the sons of God, of which also the blessed Apostle speaks as follows: "Every one that is born of God doeth not sin, for His seed is in him, and he cannot sin, because he is born of God;" and again: "We know that every one who is born of God sinneth not, but his birth of God preserves him, and the wicked one toucheth him not"?[627] And this must be understood not of all kinds of sins, but only of mortal sins: and if any one will not extricate and cleanse himself from these, for him the aforesaid Apostle tells us in another place that we ought not even to pray, saying: "If a man knows his brother to be sinning a sin not unto death, let him ask, and He will give him life for them that sin not unto death. There is a sin unto death: I do not say that he should ask for it."[628] But of those which he says are not unto death, from which even those who serve Christ faithfully cannot, with whatever care they keep themselves, be free, of these he says: "If we say that we have no sin we deceive ourselves and the truth is not in us;" and again: "If we say that we have not sinned, we make Him a liar, and His word is not in us."[629] For it is an impossibility for any one of the saints not to fall into those trivial faults which are committed by word, and thought, and ignorance, and forgetfulness, and necessity, and will, and surprise: which though quite different from that sin which is said to be unto death, still cannot be free from fault and blame.

NOTES:
[621] Mal. 1:6.
[622] S. Luke 12:47.
[623] Ps. 115:7, 8 (116:16, 17); 93 (94):17.
[624] S. Matt. 5:44.
[625] S. Matt. 5:45.
[626] 1 John 4:17.
[627] 1 John 3:9; 5:18.
[628] 1 John 5:16.
[629] 1 John 1:8, 10.

CHAPTER X.

How it is the perfection of love to pray for one's enemies and by what signs we may recognize a mind that is not yet purified.

WHEN then any one has acquired this love of goodness of which we have been speaking, and the imitation of God, then he will be endowed with the Lord's heart of compassion, and will pray also for his persecutors, saying in like manner: "Father, forgive them, for they know not what they do."[630] But it is a clear sign of a soul that is not yet thoroughly purged from the dregs of sin, not to sorrow with a feeling of pity at the offences of others, but to keep to the rigid censure of the judge: for how will he be able to obtain perfection of heart, who is without that by which, as the Apostle has pointed out, the full requirements of the law can be fulfilled, saying: "Bear one another's burdens and so fulfil the law of Christ,"[631] and who has not that virtue of love, which "is not grieved, is not puffed up, thinketh no evil," which "endureth all things, beareth all things."[632] For "a righteous man pitieth the life of his beasts: but the heart of the ungodly is without pity."[633] And so a monk is quite certain to fall into the same sins which he condemns in another with merciless and inhuman severity, for "a stern king will fall into misfortunes," and "one who stops his ears so as not to hear the weak, shall himself cry, and there shall be none to hear him." [634]

NOTES:
[630] S. Luke 23:34.
[631] Gal. 6:2.
[632] 1 Cor. 13:4-7.
[633] Prov. 12:10 (LXX).
[634] Prov. 13:17; 21:13.

CHAPTER XI.

A question why he has called the feeling of fear and hope imperfect.

GERMANUS: You have indeed spoken powerfully and grandly of the perfect love of God. But still this fact disturbs us; viz., that while you were exalting it with such praise, you said that the fear of God and the hope of eternal reward were imperfect, though the prophet seems to have thought quite differently about them, where he said: "Fear the Lord, all ye His saints, for they that fear Him lack nothing."[635] And again in the matter of observing God's righteous acts he admits that he has done them from consideration of the reward, saying: "I have inclined my heart to do thy righteous acts forever, for the reward."[636] And the Apostle says: "By faith Moses when he was grown up, denied himself to be the son of Pharaoh's daughter; choosing rather to be afflicted with the people of God than to have the pleasure of sin for a season, esteeming the reproach of Christ greater riches than the treasure of the Egyptians; for he looked unto the reward."[637] How then can we think that they are imperfect, if the blessed David boasted that he did the righteous acts of God in hope of a recompense, and the giver of the Law is said to have looked for a future reward and so to have despised the adoption to royal dignity, and to have preferred the most terrible affliction to the treasures of the Egyptians?

NOTES:
[635] Ps. 33 (34):10.
[636] Ps. 118 (119):112.
[637] Heb. 11:24-26.

CHAPTER XII.

The answer on the different kinds of perfection.

CHAEREMON: In accordance with the condition and measure of every mind Holy Scripture summons our free wills to different grades of perfection. For no uniform crown of perfection can be offered to all men, because all have not the same virtue, or purpose, or fervour, and so the Divine Word has in some way appointed different ranks and different measures of perfection itself. And that this is so the variety of beatitudes in the gospel clearly shows. For though they are called blessed, whose is the kingdom of heaven, and blessed are they who shall possess the earth, and blessed are they who shall receive their consolation, and blessed are they who shall be filled, yet we believe that there is a great difference between the habitations of the kingdom of heaven, and the possession of the earth, whatever it be, and also between the reception of consolation and the fulness and satisfaction of righteousness; and that there is a great distinction between those who shall obtain mercy, and those who shall be deemed worthy to enjoy the most glorious vision of God. "For there is one glory of the sun, and another glory of the moon, and another glory of the stars: for star differeth from star in glory, so also is the resurrection of the dead."[638] While therefore in accordance with this rule holy Scripture praises those who fear God, and says "Blessed are all they that fear the Lord,"[639] and promises them for this a full measure of bliss, yet it says again: "There is no fear in love, but perfect love casteth out fear: for fear hath torment. But he that feareth is not yet perfect in love."[640] And again, though it is a grand thing to serve God, and it is said: "Serve the Lord in fear;" and: "It is a great thing for thee to be called My servant;" and: "Blessed is that servant whom his Lord, when He cometh, shall find so doing,"[641] yet it is said to the Apostles: "I no longer call you servants, for the servant knoweth not what his Lord doeth: but I call you friends, for all things whatsoever I have heard from my Father, I have made known unto you."[642] And once more: "Ye are My friends, if ye do whatever I command you."[643] You see then that there are different stages of perfection, and that we are called by the Lord from high things to still higher in such a way that he who has become blessed and perfect in the fear of God; going as it is written "from strength to strength,"[644] and from one perfection to another, i.e., mounting with keenness of soul from fear to hope, is summoned in the end to that still more blessed stage, which, is love, and he who has been "a faithful and wise servant"[645] will pass to the companionship of friendship and to the adoption of sons. So then our saying also must be understood according to this meaning: not that we say that the consideration of that enduring punishment or of that blessed recompense which is promised to the saints is of no value, but because, though they are useful and introduce those who pursue them to the first beginning of blessedness, yet again love, wherein is already fuller confidence, and a lasting joy, will remove them from servile fear and mercenary hope to the love of God, and carry them on to the adoption of sons, and somehow make them from being perfect still more perfect. For the Saviour says that in His Father's house are "many mansions,"[646] and although all the stars seem to be in the sky, yet there is a mighty difference between the brightness of the sun and of the moon, and between that of the morning star and the rest of the stars. And therefore the blessed Apostle prefers it not only above fear and hope but also above all gifts which are counted great and wonderful, and shows the way of love still more excellent than all. For when after finishing his list of spiritual gifts of virtues he wanted to describe its members, he began as follows: "And yet I show unto you a still more excellent way. Though I speak with the tongues of men and angels, and though I have the gift of prophecy and know all mysteries and all knowledge, and though I have all faith so that I can remove mountains, and though I bestow all my goods to feed the poor, and give my body to be burned, but have not love, it profiteth me nothing." You see then that nothing more precious, nothing more perfect, nothing more sublime, and, if I may say so, nothing more enduring can be found than love. For "whether there be prophecies, they shall fail, whether there be tongues, they shall cease, whether there be knowledge, it shall be destroyed," but "love never faileth,"[647] and without it not only those most excellent kinds of gifts, but even the glory of martyrdom itself will fail.

NOTES:
[638] 1 Cor. 15:41, 42.
[639] Ps. 127 (128):1.
[640] 1 John 4:18.
[641] Ps. 2:11; Is. 49:6; S. Matt. 24:46.
[642] S. John 15:14, 15.
[643] S. John 15:13.
[644] Ps. 83 (84):8.
[645] S. Matt. 24:45.
[646] S. John 14:2.
[647] 1 Cor. 12:31; 13:1-8.

CHAPTER XIII.

Of the fear which is the outcome of the greatest love.

WHOEVER then has been established in this perfect love is sure to mount by a higher stage to that still more sublime fear belonging to love, which is the outcome of no dread of punishment or greed of reward, but of the greatest love; whereby a son fears with earnest affection a most indulgent father, or a brother fears his brother, a friend his friend, or a wife her husband, while there is no dread of his blows or reproaches, but only of a slight injury to his love, and while in every word as well as act there is ever care taken by anxious affection lest the warmth of his love should cool in the very slightest degree towards the object of it. And one of the prophets has finely described the grandeur of this fear, saying: "Wisdom and knowledge are the riches of salvation: the fear of the Lord is his treasure."[648] He could not describe with greater clearness the worth and value of that fear than by saying that the riches of our salvation, which consist in true wisdom and knowledge of God, can only be preserved by the fear of the Lord. To this fear then not sinners but saints are invited by the prophetic word where the Psalmist says: "O fear the Lord, all ye His Saints: for they that fear Him lack nothing."[649] For where a man fears the Lord with this fear it is certain that nothing is lacking to his perfection. For it was clearly of that other penal fear that the Apostle John said that "He who feareth is not made perfect in love, for fear hath punishment."[650] There is then a great difference between this fear, to which nothing is lacking, which is the treasure of wisdom and knowledge, and that imperfect fear which is called "the beginning of wisdom,"[651] and which has in it punishment and so is expelled from the hearts of those who are perfect by the incoming of the fulness of love. For "there is no fear in love, but perfect love casteth out fear."[652] And in truth if the beginning of wisdom consists in fear, what will its perfection be except in the love of Christ which, as it contains in it the fear which belongs to perfect love, is called not the beginning but the treasure of wisdom and knowledge? And therefore there is a twofold stage of fear. The one for beginners, i.e., for those who are still subject to the yoke and to servile terror; of which we read: "And the servant shall fear his Lord;"[653] and in the gospel: "I no longer call you servants, for the servant knoweth not what his Lord doeth;" and therefore "the servant," He tells us, "abideth not in the house for ever, but the Son abideth for ever."[654] For He is instructing us to pass on from that penal fear to the fullest freedom of love, and the confidence of the friends and sons of God. Finally the blessed Apostle, who had by the power of the Lord's love already passed through the servile stage of fear, scorns lower things and declares that he has been enriched with good things by the Lord, "for God hath not given us" he says "a spirit of fear but of power and of love and of a sound mind."[655] Those also who are inflamed with a perfect love of their heavenly Father, and whom the Divine adoption has already made sons instead of servants, he addresses in these words: "For ye have not received the spirit of bondage again to fear, but ye received the spirit of adoption, whereby we cry, Abba, Father."[656] It is of this fear too, that the prophet spoke when he would describe that sevenfold spirit, which according to the mystery of the Incarnation, full surely descended on the God man:[657] "And there shall rest upon Him the Spirit of the Lord: the Spirit of wisdom and of understanding, the Spirit of counsel and of might, the Spirit of knowledge and of true godliness," and in the last place he adds as something special these words: "And the Spirit of the fear of the Lord shall fill Him."[658] Where we must in the first place notice carefully that he does not say "and there shall rest upon Him the Spirit of fear," as he said in the earlier cases, but he says "there shall fill Him the Spirit of the fear of the Lord." For such is the greatness of its richness that when once it has seized on a man by its power, it takes possession not of a portion but of his whole mind. And not without good reason. For as it is closely joined to that love which "never faileth," it not only fills the man, but takes a lasting and inseparable and continual possession of him in whom it has begun, and is not lessened by any allurements of temporal joy or delights, as is sometimes the case with that fear which is cast out. This then is the fear belonging to perfection, with which we are told that the God-man,[659] who came not only to redeem mankind, but also to give us a pattern of perfection and example of goodness, was filled. For the true Son of God "who did no sin neither was guile found in His mouth,"[660] could not feel that servile fear of punishment.

NOTES:
[648] Is. 33:6.
[649] Ps. 33 (34):10.
[650] 1 John 4:18.
[651] Ps. 110 (111):10.

[652] 1 John 4:18.
[653] Mal. 1:6 (LXX).
[654] S. John 15:15; 8:35.
[655] 2 Tim. 1:7.
[656] Rom. 8:15.
[657] Homo Dominicus. See the note on Against Nestorius, V. v.
[658] Is. 11:2, 3.
[659] Homo Dominicus.
[660] 1 Pet. 2:22.

CHAPTER XIV.

A question about complete chastity.

GERMANUS: Now that you have finished your discourse on per-fect chastity, we want also to ask somewhat more freely about the end of chastity. For we do not doubt that those lofty heights of love, by which, as you have hitherto explained, we mount to the image and likeness of God, cannot possibly exist without perfect purity. But we should like to know whether a lasting grant of it can be secured so that no incitement to lust may ever disturb the serenity of our heart, and that thus we may be enabled to pass the time of our sojourneying in the flesh free from this carnal passion, so as never to be inflamed by the fire of excitement.

CHAPTER XV.

The postponement of the explanation which is asked for.

CHAEREMON: It is indeed a sign of the utmost blessedness and of singular goodness both continually to learn and to teach that love by which we cling to the Lord, so that meditation on Him may, as the Psalmist says, occupy all the days and nights of our life,[661] and may support our soul, which insatiably hungers and thirsts after righteous-ness, by continually chewing the cud of this heavenly food. But we must also, in accordance with the kindly forethought of our Saviour, make some provision for the food of the body, that we faint not by the way,[662] for "the spirit indeed is willing, but the flesh is weak."[663] And

PART 2

this we must now secure by taking a little food, so that after supper, the mind may be rendered more attentive for the careful tracing out of what you want.

NOTES:
[661] Cf. Ps. 1:2.
[662] Cf. S. Matt. 15:32.
[663] S. Matt. 26:41.

CONFERENCE 13.

The Third Conference of Abbot Chaeremon.
on the Protection of God[665]

CHAPTER I.

Introduction.

WHEN after a short sleep we returned for morning service and were waiting for the old man, Abbot Germanus was troubled by great scruples because in the previous discussion, the force of which had inspired us with the utmost longing for this chastity which was till now unknown to us, the blessed old man had by the addition of a single sentence broken down the claims of man's exertions, adding that man even though he strive with all his might for a good result, yet cannot become master of what is good unless he has acquired it simply by the gift of Divine bounty and not by the efforts of his own toil. While then we were puzzling over this question the blessed Chaeremon arrived at the cell, and as he saw that we were whispering together about something, he cut the service of prayers and Psalms shorter than usual, and asked us what was the matter.

CHAPTER II.

A question why the merit of good deeds may not be ascribed to the exertions of the man who does them.

THEN GERMANUS: As we are almost shut out, so to speak, by the greatness of that splendid virtue, which was described in last night's discussion, from believing in the possibility of it, so, if you will

pardon my saying so, it seems to us absurd for the reward of our efforts, i.e., perfect chastity, which is gained by the earnestness of one's
own toil, not to be ascribed chiefly to the exertions of the man who
makes the effort. For it is foolish, if, when for example, we see a husbandman taking the utmost pains over the cultivation of the ground,
we do not ascribe the fruits to his exertions.

CHAPTER III.

The answer that without God's help not only perfect chastity but
all good of every kind cannot be performed.

CHAEREMON: By this very instance which you bring forward
we can still more clearly prove that the exertions of the worker can do
nothing without God's aid. For neither can the husbandman, when he
has spent the utmost pains in cultivating the ground, forthwith ascribe
the produce of the crops and the rich fruits to his own exertions, as he
finds that these are often in vain unless opportune rains and a quiet and
calm winter aids them, so that we have often seen fruits already ripe
and set and thoroughly matured snatched as it were from the hands of
those who were grasping them; and their continuous and earnest efforts were of no use to the workers because they were not under the
guidance of the Lord's assistance. As then the Divine goodness does
not grant these rich crops to idle husbandmen who do not till their
fields by frequent ploughing, so also toil all night long is of no use to
the workers unless the mercy of the Lord prospers it. But herein human pride should never try to put itself on a level with the grace of
God or to intermingle itself with it, so as to fancy that its own efforts
were the cause of Divine bounty, or to boast that a very plentiful crop
of fruits was an answer to the merits of its own exertions. For a man
should consider and with a most careful scrutiny weigh the fact that he
could not by his own strength apply those very efforts which he has
earnestly used in his desire for wealth, unless the Lord's protection and
pity had given him strength for the performance of all agricultural labours; and that his own will and strength would have been powerless
unless Divine compassion had supplied the means for the completion
of them, as they sometimes fail either from too much or from too little
rain. For when vigour has been granted by the Lord to the oxen, and
bodily health and the power to do all the work, and prosperity in un-

dertakings, still a man must pray lest there come to him, as Scripture says, "a heaven of brass and an earth of iron," and "the cankerworm eat what the locust hath left, and the palmerworm eat what the cankerworm hath left, and the mildew destroys what the palmerworm hath left."[666] Nor is it only in this that the efforts of the husbandman in his work need God's help, unless it also averts unlooked for accidents by which, even when the field is rich with the expected fruitful crops, not only is the man deprived of what he has vainly hoped and looked for, but actually loses the abundant fruits which he has already gathered and stored up in the threshing floor or in the barn. From which we clearly infer that the initiative not only of our actions but also of good thoughts comes from God, who inspires us with a good will to begin with, and supplies us with the opportunity of carrying out what we rightly desire: for "every good gift and every perfect gift cometh down from above, from the Father of lights,"[667] who both begins what is good, and continues it and completes it in us, as the Apostle says: "But He who giveth seed to the sower will both provide bread to eat and will multiply your seed and make the fruits of your righteousness to increase."[668] But it is for us, humbly to follow day by day the grace of God which is drawing us, or else if we resist with "a stiff neck," and (to use the words of Scripture) "uncircumcised ears,"[669] we shall deserve to hear the words of Jeremiah: "Shall he that falleth, not rise again? and he that is turned away, shall he not turn again? Why then is this people in Jerusalem turned away with a stubborn revolting? They have stiffened their necks and refused to return." [670]

NOTES:
[666] Deut. 28:23; Joel 1:4.
[667] S. James 1:17.
[668] 2 Cor. 9:10.
[669] Acts 7:51.
[670] Jer. 8:4, 5.

CHAPTER IV.

An objection, asking how the Gentiles can be said to have chastity without the grace of God.

GERMANUS: To this explanation, the excellence of which we cannot hastily disprove, it seems a difficulty that it tends to destroy free will. For as we see that many of the heathen to whom the assistance of Divine grace has certainly not been vouchsafed, are eminent not only in the virtues of frugality and patience, but (which is more remarkable) in that of chastity, how can we think that the freedom of their will is taken captive and that these virtues are granted to them by God's gift, especially as in following after the wisdom of this world, and in their utter ignorance not only of God's grace but even of the existence of the true God, as we have known Him by the course of our reading and the teaching of others--they are said to have gained the most perfect purity of chastity by their own efforts and exertions.

CHAPTER V.

The answer on the imaginary chastity of the philosophers.

CHAEREMON: I am pleased that, though you are fired with the greatest longing to know the truth, yet you bring forward some foolish points, as by your raising these objections the value of the Catholic faith may seem better established, and if I may use the expression, more thoroughly explored. For what wise man would make such contradictory statements as yesterday to maintain that the heavenly purity of chastity could not possibly even by God's grace be bestowed on any mortals, and now to hold that it was obtained even by the heathen by their own strength? But as you have certainly, as I said, made these objections from the desire of getting at the truth, consider what we hold on these points. First we certainly must not think that the philosophers attained such chastity of soul, as is required of us, on whom it is enjoined that not fornication only, but uncleanness be not so much as named among us. But they had a sort of merikh, i.e., some particle of chastity; viz. continence of the flesh, by which they could restrain their lust from carnal intercourse: but this internal purity of mind and continual purity of body they could not attain, I will not say, in act, but even in thought. Finally Socrates, the most famous of them all, as they themselves esteem him, was not ashamed to profess this of himself. For when one who judged a man's character by his looks (fusiognwmwn) looked at him, and said ommata paid erastou, i.e., "the eyes of a corrupter of boys," and his scholars rushed at him, and brought him to their master and wanted to avenge the insult, it is said that he checked their indignation with these words: pausaoqe, etairoi.

Eimi gar, epecw de, i.e., Stop, my friends, for I am, but I restrain my-self. It is then quite clearly shown not only by our assertions but actually by their own admissions that it was only the performance of indecent act, i.e., the disgrace of intercourse, that was by force of ne-cessity checked by them, and that the desire and delight in this passion was not shut out from their hearts. But with what horror must one bring forward this saying of Diogenes? For a thing which the philoso-phers of this world were not ashamed to bring forward as something remarkable, cannot be spoken or heard by us without shame: for to one to be punished for the crime of adultery they relate that he said to dwrean pwloumenon qanatw mh agoraze, i.e., you should not buy with your death what is sold for nothing.[671] It is clear then that they did not recognize the virtue of the true chastity which we seek for, and so it is quite certain that our circumcision which is in the spirit cannot be ac-quired save only by the gift of God, and that it belongs only to those who serve God with full contrition of their spirit.

NOTES:
[671] The source of these stories of Socrates and Diogenes has not been traced.

CHAPTER VI.

That without the grace of God we cannot make any diligent ef-forts.

AND therefore though in many things, indeed in everything, it can be shown that men always have need of God's help, and that hu-man weakness cannot accomplish anything that has to do with salvation by itself alone, i.e., without the aid of God, yet in nothing is this more clearly shown than in the acquisition and preservation of chastity. For as the discussion on the difficulty of its perfection is put off for so long, let us meanwhile discourse briefly on the instruments of it. Who, I ask, could, however fervent he might be in spirit, relying on his own strength with no praise from men endure the squalor of the desert, and I will not say the daily lack but the supply of dry bread? Who without the Lord's consolation, could put up with the continual thirst for water, or deprive his human eyes of that sweet and delicious morning sleep, and regularly compress his whole time of rest and re-pose into the limits of four hours? Who would be sufficient without

God's grace to give continual attendance to reading and constant earnestness in work, receiving no advantage of present gain? And all
these matters, as we cannot desire them continuously without divine
inspiration, so in no respect whatever can we perform them without
His help. And that we may ensure that these things are not only proved
to us by the teaching of experience, but also made still clearer by sure
proof and arguments, does not some weakness intervene in the case of
many things which we wish usefully to perform, and though the full
keenness of our desire and the perfection of our will be not wanting,
yet interfere with the wish we have conceived, so that there is no carrying out of our purpose, unless the power to perform it has been
granted by the mercy of the Lord, so that, although there are countless
swarms of people who are anxious to stick faithfully to the pursuit of
virtue, you can scarcely find any who are able to carry it out and endure it, to say nothing of the fact that, even when no weakness at all
hinders us, the opportunity for doing everything that we wish does not
lie in our own power. For it is not in our power to secure the silence of
solitude and severe fasts and undisturbed study even when we could
use such opportunities, but by a chapter of accidents we are often very
much against our will kept away from the salutary ordinances so that
we have to pray to the Lord for opportunities of place or time in which
to practise them. And it is clear that the ability for these is not sufficient for us unless there be also granted to us by the Lord an
opportunity of doing what we are capable of (as the Apostle also says:
"For we wanted to come to you once and again, but Satan hindered
us"[672]), so that sometimes we find for our advantage we are called
away from these spiritual exercises in order that while without our
own consent the regularity of our routine is broken and we yield something to weakness of the flesh, we may even against our will be
brought to a salutary patience. Of which providential arrangement of
God the blessed Apostle says something similar: "For which I besought the Lord thrice that it might depart from me. And He said to
me: My grace is sufficient for thee: for my strength is made perfect in
weakness:" and again: "For we know not what to pray for as we
ought." [673]

NOTES:
[672] 1 Thess. 2:18.
[673] 2 Cor. 12:8, 9; Rom. 8:26.

CHAPTER VII.

Of the main purpose of God and His daily Providence.

FOR the purpose of God whereby He made man not to perish but to live for ever, stands immovable. And when His goodness sees in us even the very smallest spark of good will shining forth, which He Himself has struck as it were out of the hard flints of our hearts, He fans and fosters it and nurses it with His breath, as He "willeth all men to be saved and to come to the knowledge of the truth," for as He says, "it is not the will of your Father which is in heaven that one of these little ones should perish," and again it says: "Neither will God have a soul to perish, but recalleth," meaning that he that is cast off should not altogether perish.[674] For He is true, and lieth not when He lays down with an oath: "As I live, saith the Lord God, for I will not the death of a sinner, but that he should turn from his way and live."[675] For if He willeth not that one of His little ones should perish, how can we imagine without grievous blasphemy that He does not generally will all men, but only some instead of all to be saved? Those then who perish, perish against His will, as He testifies against each one of them day by day: "Turn from your evil ways, and why will ye die, O house of Israel?"[676] And again: "How often would I have gathered thy children together as a hen gathereth her chickens under her wings, and ye would not;" and: "Wherefore is this people in Jerusalem turned away with a stubborn revolting? They have hardened their faces and refused to return."[677] The grace of Christ then is at hand every day, which, while it "willeth all men to be saved and to come to the knowledge of the truth," calleth all without any exception, saying: "Come unto Me, all ye that labour and are heavy laden, and I will refresh you."[678] But if He calls not all generally but only some, it follows that not all are heavy laden either with original or actual sin, and that this saying is not a true one: "For all have sinned and come short of the glory of God;" nor can we believe that "death passed on all men."[679] And so far do all who perish, perish against the will of God, that God cannot be said to have made death, as Scripture itself testifies: "For God made not death, neither rejoiceth in the destruction of the living."[680] And hence it comes that for the most part when instead of good things we ask for the opposite, our prayer is either heard but tardily or not at all; and again the Lord vouchsafes to bring upon us even against our will, like some most beneficent physician, for our good what we think is opposed to it, and sometimes He delays and hinders our injurious purposes and deadly attempts from having their horrible effects, and, while we are rushing headlong towards death, draws us back to salvation, and rescues us without our knowing it from the jaws of hell.

NOTES:
[674] 1 Tim. 2:4; S. Matt. 18:14; 2 Sam. 14:14.
[675] Ezek. 33:11.
[676] Ezek. 33:11.
[677] S. Matt. 23:37; Jer. 8:5.
[678] S. Matt. 11:28.
[679] Rom. 3:23; 5:12.
[680] Wisdom 1:13.

CHAPTER VIII.

Of the grace of God and the freedom of the will.

AND this care of His and providence with regard to us the Divine word has finely described by the prophet Hosea under the figure of Jerusalem as an harlot, and inclining with disgraceful eagerness to the worship of idols, where when she says: "I will go after my lovers, who give me my bread, and my water, and my wool, and my flax, and my oil, and my drink;" the Divine consideration replies having regard to her salvation and not to her wishes: "Behold I will hedge up thy way with thorns, and I will stop it up with a wall, and she shall not find her paths. And she shall follow after her lovers, and shall not overtake them: and she shall seek them, and shall not find them, and shall say: I will return to my first husband, because it was better with me then than now."[681] And again our obstinacy, and scorn, with which we in our rebellious spirit disdain Him when He urges us to a salutary return, is described in the following comparison: He says: "And I said thou shalt call Me Father, and shalt not cease to walk after Me. But as a woman that despiseth her lover, so hath the house of Israel despised Me, saith the Lord."[682] Aptly then, as He has compared Jerusalem to an adulteress forsaking her husband, He compares His own love and persevering goodness to a man who is dying of love for a woman. For the goodness and love of God, which He ever shows to mankind,--since it is overcome by no injuries so as to cease from caring for our salvation, or be driven from His first intention, as if vanquished by our iniquities,--could not be more fitly described by any comparison than the case of a man inflamed with most ardent love for a woman, who is consumed by a more burning passion for her, the more he sees that he is slighted and despised by her. The Divine protection then is inseparably present with us, and so great is the kindness of the Creator towards His creatures, that His Providence not only accompanies it, but actually constantly precedes it, as the prophet experienced and plainly confessed, saying: "My God will prevent me with His mercy."[683] And when He sees in us some beginnings of a good will, He at once enlightens it and strengthens it and urges it on towards salvation, increasing that which He Himself implanted or which He sees to have arisen from our own efforts. For He says "Before they cry, I will hear them: While they are still speaking I will hear them;" and again: "As soon as He hears the voice of thy crying, He will answer thee."[684] And in His goodness, not only does He inspire us with holy desires, but actually creates occasions for life and opportunities for good results, and shows to those in error the direction of the way of salvation.

NOTES:
[681] Hosea 2:5-7.
[682] Jer. 3:19, 20.
[683] Ps. 58 (59):11.
[684] Is. 65:24; 30:19.

CHAPTER IX.

Of the power of our good will, and the grace of God.

WHENCE human reason cannot easily decide how the Lord gives to those that ask, is found by those that seek, and opens to those that knock, and on the other hand is found by those that sought Him not, appears openly among those who asked not for Him, and all the day long stretches forth His hands to an unbelieving and gainsaying people, calls those who resist and stand afar off, draws men against their will to salvation, takes away from those who want to sin the faculty of carrying out their desire, in His goodness stands in the way of those who are rushing into wickedness. But who can easily see how it is that the completion of our salvation is assigned to our own will, of which it is said: "If ye be willing, and hearken unto Me, ye shall eat the good things of the land,"[685] and how it is "not of him that willeth or runneth, but of God that hath mercy"?[686] What too is this, that God "will render to every man according to his works;"[687] and "it is God who worketh in you both to will and to do, of His good pleasure;"[688] and "this is not of yourselves but it is the gift of God: not of works, that no man may boast"?[689] What is this too which is said: "Draw near to the Lord, and He will draw near to you,"[690] and what He says elsewhere: "No man cometh unto Me except the Father who sent Me draw Him"?[691] What is it that we find: "Make straight paths for your feet and direct your ways,"[692] and what is it that we say in our prayers: "Direct my way in Thy sight," and "establish my goings in Thy paths, that my footsteps be not moved"?[693] What is it again that we are admonished: "Make you a new heart and a new spirit,"[694] and what is this which is promised to us: "I will give them one heart and will put a new spirit within them:" and "I will take away the stony heart from their flesh and will give them an heart of flesh that they may walk in Thy statutes and keep My judgments"?[695] What is it that the Lord commands, where He says: "Wash thine heart of iniquity, O Jerusalem, that thou mayest be saved,"[696] and what is it that the prophet asks for from the Lord, when he says "Create in me a clean heart, O God," and again: "Thou shalt wash me, and I shall be whiter than snow"?[697] What is it that is said to us: "Enlighten yourselves with the light of knowledge;"[698] and this which is said of God: "Who teacheth man knowledge;"[699] and: "the Lord enlightens the blind,"[700] or at any rate this, which we say in our prayers with the prophet: "Lighten mine eyes that I sleep not in death,"[701] unless in all these there is a declaration of the grace of God and the freedom of our will, because even of his own motion a man can be led to the quest of virtue, but always stands in need of the help of the Lord? For neither does anyone enjoy good health whenever he will, nor is he at his own will and pleasure set free from disease and sickness. But what good is it to have desired the blessing of health, unless God, who grants us the enjoyments of life itself, grant also vigorous and sound health? But that it may be still clearer that through the excellence of nature which is granted by the goodness of the Creator, sometimes first beginnings of a good will arise, which however cannot attain to the complete performance of what is good unless it is guided by the Lord, the Apostle bears witness and says: "For to will is present with me, but to perform what is good I find not." [702]

NOTES:
[685] Is. 1:19.
[686] Rom. 9:16.

[687] Rom. 2:6.
[688] Phil. 2:13.
[689] Eph. 2:8, 9.
[690] S. James 4:8.
[691] S. John 6:44.
[692] Prov. 4:26 (LXX).
[693] Ps. 5:9; 16 (17):5.
[694] Ezek. 18:31.
[695] Ezek. 1:19, 20.
[696] Jer. 4:14.
[697] Ps. 50 (51):12, 9.
[698] Hos. 10:12 (LXX).
[699] Ps. 93 (94):10.
[700] Ps. 145 (146):8.
[701] Ps. 12 (13):4.
[702] Rom. 7:18.

CHAPTER X.

On the weakness of free will.

FOR Holy Scripture supports the freedom of the will where it says: "Keep thy heart with all diligence,"[703] but the Apostle indicates its weakness by saying "The Lord keep your hearts and minds in Christ Jesus."[704] David asserts the power of free will, where he says "I have inclined my heart to do Thy righteous acts,"[705] but the same man in like manner teaches us its weakness, by praying and saying, "Incline my heart unto Thy testimonies and not to covetousness:"[706] Solomon also: "The Lord incline our hearts unto Himself that we may walk in all His ways and keep His commandments, and ordinances and judgments."[707] The Psalmist denotes the power of our will, where he says: "Keep thy tongue from evil, and thy lips that they speak no guile,"[708] our prayer testifies to its weakness, when we say: "O Lord, set a watch before my mouth, and keep the door of my lips."[709] The importance of our will is maintained by the Lord, when we find "Break the chains of thy neck, O captive daughter of Zion:"[710] of its weakness the prophet sings, when he says: "The Lord looseth them that are bound:" and "Thou hast broken my chains: To Thee will I offer the sacrifice of praise."[711] We hear in the gospel the Lord summoning us to come speedily to Him by our free will: "Come unto Me all ye that labour and are heavy laden, and I will refresh you,"[712] but the same Lord testifies

297

to its weakness, by saying: "No man can come unto Me except the Father which sent Me draw him."[713] The Apostle indicates our free will by saying: "So run that ye may obtain:"[714] but to its weakness John Baptist bears witness where he says: "No man can receive anything of himself, except it be given him from above."[715] We are commanded to keep our souls with all care, when the Prophet says: "Keep your souls,"[716] but by the same spirit another Prophet proclaims: "Except the Lord keep the city, the watchman waketh but in vain."[717] The Apostle writing to the Philippians, to show that their will is free, says "Work out your own salvation with fear and trembling," but to point out its weakness, he adds: "For it is God that worketh in you both to will and to do of His good pleasure." [718]

NOTES:
[703] Prov. 4:23.
[704] Phil. 4:7.
[705] Ps. 118 (119):112.
[706] Ps. 118 (119):36.
[707] 1 Kings 8:58.
[708] Ps. 33 (34):14.
[709] Ps. 140 (141):3.
[710] Is. 52:2.
[711] Ps. 145 (146):7; 115 (116):16, 17.
[712] S. Matt. 11:28.
[713] S. John 6:44.
[714] 1 Cor. 9:24.
[715] S. John 3:27.
[716] Jer. 17:21.
[717] Ps. 126 (127):1.
[718] Phil. 2:12, 13.

CHAPTER XI.

Whether the grace of God precedes or follows our good will.

AND so these are somehow mixed up and indiscriminately confused, so that among many persons, which depends on the other is involved in great questionings, i.e., does God have compassion upon us because we have shown the beginning of a good will, or does the beginning of a good will follow because God has had compassion upon us? For many believing each of these and asserting them more widely than is right are entangled in all kinds of opposite errors. For if we say that the beginning of free will is in our own power, what about Paul the persecutor, what about Matthew the publican, of whom the one was drawn to salvation while eager for bloodshed and the punishment of the innocent, the other for violence and rapine? But if we say that the beginning of our free will is always due to the inspiration of the grace of God, what about the faith of Zaccheus, or what are we to say of the goodness of the thief on the cross, who by their own desires brought violence to bear on the kingdom of heaven and so prevented the special leadings of their vocation? But if we attribute the performance of virtuous acts, and the execution of God's commands to our own will, how do we pray: "Strengthen, O God, what Thou hast wrought in us;" and "The work of our hands stablish Thou upon us"?[719] We know that Balaam was brought to curse Israel, but we see that when he wished to curse he was not permitted to. Abimelech is preserved from touching Rebecca and so sinning against God. Joseph is sold by the envy of his brethren, in order to bring about the descent of the children of Israel into Egypt, and that while they were contemplating the death of their brother provision might be made for them against the famine to come: as Joseph shows when he makes himself known to his brethren and says: "Fear not, neither let it be grievous unto you that ye sold me into these parts: for for your salvation God sent me before you;" and below: "For God sent me before that ye might be preserved upon the earth and might have food whereby to live. Not by your design was I sent but by the will of God, who has made me a father to Pharaoh and lord of all his house, and chief over all the land of Egypt." And when his brethren were alarmed after the death of his father, he removed their suspicions and terror by saying: "Fear not: Can ye resist the will of God? You imagined evil against me but God turned it into good, that He might exalt me, as ye see at the present time, that He might save much people."[720] And that this was brought about providentially the blessed David likewise declare saying in the hundred and fourth Psalm: "And He called for a dearth upon the land: and brake all the staff of bread. He sent a man before them: Joseph was sold for a slave."[721] These two then; viz., the grace of God and free will seem opposed to each other, but really are in harmony, and we gather from the system of goodness that we ought to have both alike, lest if we withdraw one of them from man, we may seem to have broken the rule of the Church's faith: for when God sees us inclined to will what is good, He meets, guides, and strengthens us: for "At the voice of thy cry, as soon as He shall hear, He will answer thee;" and: "Call upon

Me," He says, "in the day of tribulation and I will deliver thee, and thou shalt glorify Me."[722] And again, if He finds that we are unwilling or have grown cold, He stirs our hearts with salutary exhortations, by which a good will is either renewed or formed in us.

NOTES:
[719] Ps. 67 (68):29; 89 (90):17.
[720] Gen. 45:5-8; 50:19, 20.
[721] Ps. 104 (105):16, 17.
[722] Is. 30:19; Ps. 49 (50):15.

CHAPTER XII.

That a good will should not always be attributed to grace, nor always to man himself.

FOR we should not hold that God made man such that he can never will or be capable of what is good: or else He has not granted him a free will, if He has suffered him only to will or be capable of evil, but neither to will or be capable of what is good of himself. And, in this case how will that first statement of the Lord made about men after the fall stand: "Behold, Adam is become as one of us, knowing good and evil"?[723] For we cannot think that before, he was such as to be altogether ignorant of good. Otherwise we should have to admit that he was formed like some irrational and insensate beast: which is sufficiently absurd and altogether alien from the Catholic faith. Moreover as the wisest Solomon says: "God made man upright," i.e., always to enjoy the knowledge of good only, "But they have sought out many imaginations,"[724] for they came, as has been said, to know good and evil. Adam therefore after the fall conceived a knowledge of evil which he had not previously, but did not lose the knowledge of good which he had before. Finally the Apostle's words very clearly show that mankind did not lose after the fall of Adam the knowledge of good: as he says: "For when the Gentiles, which have not the law, do by nature the things of the law, these, though they have not the law, are a law to themselves, as they show the work of the law written in their hearts, their conscience bearing witness to these, and their thoughts within them either accusing or else excusing them, in the day in which God shall judge the secrets of men."[725] And with the same meaning the Lord rebukes by the prophet the unnatural but freely chosen blindness of the Jews, which they by their obstinacy brought upon themselves, saying: "Hear ye deaf, and ye blind, behold that you may see. Who is deaf but My servant? and blind, but he to whom I have sent My messengers?"[726] And that no one might ascribe this blindness of theirs to nature instead of to their own will, elsewhere He says: "Bring forth the people that are blind and have eyes: that are deaf and have ears;" and again: "having eyes, but ye see not; and ears, but ye hear not."[727] The Lord also says in the gospel: "Because seeing they see not, and hearing they hear not neither do they understand."[728] And in them is fulfilled the prophecy of Isaiah which says: "Hearing ye shall hear and shall not understand: and seeing ye shall see and shall not see. For the heart of this people is waxed fat, and their ears are dull of hearing: and they have closed their eyes, lest they should see with their eyes and hear with their ears and understand with their heart, and be turned and I should heal them."[729] Finally in order to denote that the possibility of good was in them, in chiding the Pharisees, He says: "But why of your own selves do ye not judge what is right?"[730] And this he certainly would not have said to them, unless He knew that by their natural judgment they could discern what was fair. Wherefore we must take care not to refer all the merits of the saints to the Lord in such a way as to ascribe nothing but what is evil and perverse to human nature: in doing which we are confuted by the evidence of the most wise Solomon, or rather of the Lord Himself, Whose words these are; for when the building of the Temple was finished and he was praying, he spoke as follows: "And David my father would have built a house to the name of the Lord God of Israel: and the Lord said to David my father: Whereas thou hast thought in thine heart to build a house to My name, thou hast well done in having this same thing in thy mind. Nevertheless thou shall not build a house to My name."[731] This thought then and this purpose of king David, are we to call it good and from God or bad and from man? For if that thought was good and from God, why did He by whom it was inspired refuse that it should be carried into effect? But if it is bad and from man, why is it praised by the Lord? It remains then that we must take it as good and from man. And in the same way we can take our own thoughts today. For it was not given only to David to think what is good of himself, nor is it denied to us naturally to think or imagine anything that is good. It cannot then be doubted that there are by nature some seeds of goodness in every soul implanted by the kindness of the Creator: but unless these are quickened by the assistance of God, they will not be able to attain to an increase of perfection, for, as the blessed Apostle says: "Neither is he that planteth anything nor he that watereth, but God that giveth the increase."[732] But that freedom of the will is to some degree in a man's own power is very clearly taught in the book termed the Pastor,[733] where two angels are said to be attached to each one of us, i.e., a good and a bad one, while it lies at a man's own option to choose which to follow. And therefore the will always remains free in man, and can either neglect or delight in the grace of God. For the Apostle would not have commanded saying: "Work out your own salvation with fear and trembling," had he not known that it could be advanced or neglected by us. But that men might not fancy that they had no need of Divine aid for the work of Salvation, he subjoins: "For it is God that worketh in you both to will and to do, of His good pleasure."[734] And therefore he warns Timothy and says: "Neglect not the grace of God which is in thee;" and again: "For which cause I exhort thee to stir up the grace of God which is in thee."[735] Hence also in writing to the Corinthians he exhorts and warns them not through their unfruitful works to show themselves unworthy of the grace of God, saying: "And we helping, exhort you that ye receive not the grace of God in vain:"[736] for the reception of saving grace was of no profit to Simon doubtless because he had received it in vain; for he would not obey the command of the blessed Peter who said: "Repent of thine iniquity, and pray God if haply the thoughts of thine heart may be forgiven thee; for I perceive that thou art in the gall of bitterness and the bonds of iniquity."[737] It prevents therefore the will of man, for it is said: "My God will prevent me with His mercy;"[738] and again when God waits and for our good delays, that He may put our desires to the test, our will precedes, for it is said: "And in the morning my prayer shall prevent Thee;" and again: "I prevented the dawning of the day and cried;" and: "Mine eyes have prevented the morning."[739] For He calls and invites us, when He says: "All the day long I stretched forth My hands to a disobedient and gainsaying people;"[740] and He is invited by us when we say to Him: "All the day long I have stretched forth My hands unto Thee."[741] He waits for us, when it is said by the prophet: "Wherefore the Lord waiteth to have compassion upon us;"[742] and He is waited for by us, when we say: "I waited patiently for the Lord, and He inclined unto me;" and: "I have waited for thy salvation, O Lord."[743] He strengthens us when He says: "And I have chastised them, and strengthened their arms; and they have imagined evil against me;"[744] and He exhorts us to strengthen ourselves when He says: "Strengthen ye the weak hands, and make strong the feeble knees."[745] Jesus cries: "If any man thirst let him come unto Me and drink;"[746] the prophet also cries to Him: "I have laboured with crying, my jaws are become hoarse: mine eyes have failed, whilst I hope in my God."[747] The Lord seeks us, when He says: "I sought and there was no man. I called, and there was none to answer;"[748] and He Himself is sought by the bride who mourns with tears: "I sought on my bed by night Him whom my soul loved: I sought Him and found Him not; I called Him, and He gave me no answer." [749]

NOTES:
[723] Gen. 3:22.
[724] Eccl. 7:29 (LXX).
[725] Rom. 2:14-16.
[726] Is. 42:18, 19.
[727] Is. 43:8; Jer. 5:21.
[728] S. Matt. 13:13.
[729] Is. 6:9, 10.
[730] S. Luke 12:57.
[731] 1 Kings 8:17-19.
[732] 1 Cor. 3:7.
[733] Cf. Conf. VIII. c. xvii.
[734] Phil. 2:12, 13.
[735] 1 Tim. 4:14; 2 Tim. 1:6.
[736] 2 Cor. 6:1.
[737] Acts 8:22, 23.
[738] Ps. 58 (59):11.
[739] Ps. 87 (88):14; 118 (119):147, 148.
[740] Rom. 10:21.
[741] Ps. 87 (88):10.
[742] Is. 30:18.
[743] Ps. 39 (40):2; 118 (119):166.
[744] Hosea 7:15.
[745] Is. 35:3.
[746] S. John 7:37.
[747] Ps. 68 (69):4.
[748] Cant. 5:6.
[749] Cant. 3:1.

CHAPTER XIII.

How human efforts cannot be set against the grace of God.

AND so the grace of God always co-operates with our will for its advantage, and in all things assists, protects, and defends it, in such a way as sometimes even to require and look for some efforts of good will from it that it may not appear to confer its gifts on one who is asleep or relaxed in sluggish ease, as it seeks opportunities to show that as the torpor of man's sluggishness is shaken off its bounty is not unreasonable, when it bestows it on account of some desire and efforts to gain it. And none the less does God's grace continue to be free grace while in return for some small and trivial efforts it bestows with priceless bounty such glory of immortality, and such gifts of eternal bliss. For because the faith of the thief on the cross came as the first thing, no one would say that therefore the blessed abode of Paradise was not promised to him as a free gift, nor could we hold that it was the penitence of King David's single word which he uttered: "I have sinned against the Lord," and not rather the mercy of God which removed those two grievous sins of his, so that it was vouchsafed to him to hear from the prophet Nathan: "The Lord also hath put away thine iniquity: thou shalt not die."[750] The fact then that he added murder to adultery, was certainly due to free will: but that he was reproved by the prophet, this was the grace of Divine Compassion. Again it was his own doing that he was humbled and acknowledged his guilt; but that in a very short interval of time he was granted pardon for such sins, this was the gift of the merciful Lord. And what shall we say of this brief confession and of the incomparable infinity of Divine reward, when it is easy to see what the blessed Apostle, as he fixes his gaze on the greatness of future remuneration, announced on those countless persecutions of his? "for," says he, "our light affliction which is but for a moment worketh in us a far more exceeding and eternal weight of glory,"[751] of which elsewhere he constantly affirms, saying that "the sufferings of this present time are not worthy to be compared with the future glory which shall be revealed in us."[752] However much then human weakness may strive, it cannot come up to the future reward, nor by its efforts so take off from Divine grace that it should not always remain a free gift. And therefore the aforesaid teacher of the Gentiles, though he bears his witness that he had obtained the grade of the Apostolate by the grace of God, saying: "By the grace of God I am what I am," yet also declares that he himself had corresponded to Divine Grace, where he says: "And His Grace in me was not in vain; but I laboured more abundantly than they all: and yet not I, but the Grace of God with me."[753] For when he says: "I laboured," he shows the effort of his own will; when he says: "yet not I, but the grace of God," he points out the value of Divine protection; when he says: "with me," he affirms that it cooperates with him when he was not idle or careless, but working and making an effort.

NOTES:
[750] 2 Sam. 12:13.
[751] 2 Cor. 4:17.
[752] Rom. 8:18.
[753] 1 Cor. 15:10.

CHAPTER XIV.

How God makes trial of the strength of man's will by means of his temptations.

AND this too we read that the Divine righteousness provided for in the case of Job His well tried athlete, when the devil had challenged him to single combat. For if he had advanced against his foe, not with his own strength, but solely with the protection of God's grace; and, supported only by Divine aid without any virtue of patience on his own part, had borne that manifold weight of temptations and losses, contrived with all the cruelty of his foe, how would the devil have repeated with some justice that slanderous speech which he had previously uttered: "Doth Job serve God for nought? Hast Thou not hedged him in, and all his substance round about? but take away thine hand," i.e., allow him to fight with me in his own strength, "and he will curse Thee to Thy face."[754] But as after the struggle the slanderous foe dare not give vent to any such murmur as this, he admired that he was vanquished by his strength and not by that of God; although too we must not hold that the grace of God was altogether wanting to him, which gave to the tempter a power of tempting in proportion to that which it knew that he had of resisting, without protecting him from his attacks in such a way as to leave no room for human virtue, but only providing for this; viz., that the most fierce foe should not drive him out of his mind and overwhelm him when weakened, with unequal thoughts and in an unfair contest. But that the Lord is sometimes wont to tempt our faith that it maybe made stronger and more glorious, we are taught by the example of the centurion in the gospel, in whose case though the Lord knew that He would cure his servant by the power of His word, yet He chose to offer His bodily presence, saying: "I will come and heal him:" but when the centurion overcame this offer of His by the ardour of still more fervent faith, and said: "Lord, I am not worthy that Thou shouldest come under my roof: but speak the word only and my servant shall be healed," the Lord marvelled at him and praised him, and put him before all those of the people of Israel who had believed, saying: "Verily, I say unto you, I have not found so great faith in Israel."[755] For there would have been no ground for praise or merit, if Christ had only preferred in him what He Himself had given. And this searching trial of faith we read that the Divine righteousness brought about also in the case of the grandest of the patriarchs; where it is said: "And it came to pass after these things that God did tempt Abraham."[756] For the Divine righteousness wished to try not that faith with which the Lord had inspired him, but that which when called and enlightened by the Lord he could show forth by his own free will. Wherefore the firmness of his faith was not without reason proved, and when the grace of God, which had for a while left him to prove him, came to his aid, it was said: "Lay not thine hand on the lad, and do nothing unto him: for now I know that thou fearest the Lord, and for my sake hast not spared thy beloved son."[757] And that this kind of temptation can befall us, for the sake of proving us, is sufficiently clearly foretold by the giver of the Law in Deuteronomy: "If there rise in the midst of you a prophet or one that saith he hath seen a dream, and foretell a sign and wonder; and that come to pass which he spoke, and he say to thee: Let us go and serve strange gods which ye know not, thou shalt not hear the words of that prophet or dreamer; for the Lord your God surely trieth thee, whether thou lovest Him with all thine heart, and keepest His Commandments, or no."[758] What then follows? When God has permitted that prophet or dreamer to arise, must we hold that He will protect those whose faith He is purposing to try, in such a way as to leave no place for their own free will, where they can fight with the tempter with their own strength? And why is it necessary for them even to be tried if He knows them to be so weak and feeble as not to be able by their own power to resist the tempter? But certainly the Divine righteousness would not have permitted them to be tempted, unless it knew that there was within them an equal power of resistance, by which they could by an equitable judgment be found in either result either guilty or worthy of praise. To the same effect also is this which the Apostle says: "Therefore let him that thinketh he standeth, take heed lest he fall. There hath no temptation taken you but such as is common to man. But God is faithful, who will not suffer you to be tempted above that ye are able, but will with the temptation make also a way of escape that ye may be able to bear it."[759] For when he says "Let him that standeth take heed lest he fall" he sets free will on its guard, as he certainly knew that, after grace had been received, it could either stand by its exertions or fall through carelessness. But when he adds: "there hath no temptation taken you but what is common to man" he chides their weakness and the frailty of their heart that is not yet strengthened, as they could not yet resist the attacks of the hosts of spiritual wickedness, against which he knew that he and those who were perfect daily fought; of which also he says to the Ephesians: "For we wrestle not against flesh and blood, but against principalities, against powers, against the world-rulers of this darkness, against spiritual wickedness in heavenly places."[760] But when he subjoins: "But God is faithful who will not suffer you to be tempted above that ye are able," he certainly is not hoping that the Lord will not suffer them to be tempted, but that they may not be tempted above what they are able to bear. For the one shows the power of man's will, the other denotes the grace of the Lord who moderates the violence of temptations. In all these phrases then there is proof that Divine grace ever stirs up the will of man, not so as to protect and defend it in all things in such a way as to cause it not to fight by its own efforts against its spiritual adversaries, the victor over whom may set it down to God's grace, and the vanquished to his own weakness, and thus learn that his hope is always not in his own courage but in the Divine assistance, and that he must ever fly to his Protector. And to prove this not by our own conjecture but by still clearer passages of Holy Scripture let us consider what we read in Joshuah the son of Nun: "The Lord," it says, "left these nations and would not destroy them, that by them He might try Israel, whether they would keep the commandments of the Lord their God, and that they might learn to fight with their enemies."[761] And if we may illustrate the incomparable mercy of our Creator from something earthly, not as being equal in kindness, but as an illustration of mercy: if a tender and anxious nurse carries an infant in her bosom for a long time in order sometime to teach it to walk, and first allows it to crawl, then supports it that by the aid of her right hand it may lean on its alternate steps, presently leaves it for a little and if she sees it tottering at all, catches hold of it, and grabs at it when falling, when down picks it up, and either shields it from a fall, or allows it to fall lightly, and sets it up again after a tumble, but when she has brought it up to boyhood or the strength of youth or early manhood, lays upon it some burdens or labours by which it may be not overwhelmed but exercised, and allows it to vie with those of its own age; how much more does the heavenly Father of all know whom to carry in the bosom of His grace, whom to train to virtue in His sight by the exercise of free will, and yet He helps him in his efforts, hears him when he calls, leaves him not when he seeks Him, and sometimes snatches him from peril even without his knowing it.

NOTES:
[754] Job 1:9-11.
[755] S. Matt. 8:7-10.
[756] Gen. 22:1.
[757] Gen. 22:12.
[758] Deut. 13:1-3.
[759] 1 Cor. 10:12, 13.
[760] Eph. 6:12.
[761] Judg. 3:1, 2; 2:22.

CHAPTER XV.

Of the manifold grace of men's calls.

AND by this it is clearly shown that God's "judgments are inscrutable and His ways past finding out,"[762] by which He draws mankind to salvation. And this too we can prove by the instances of calls in the gospels. For He chose Andrew and Peter and the rest of the apostles by the free compassion of His grace when they were thinking nothing of their healing and salvation. Zacchaeus, when in his faithfulness he was struggling to see the Lord, and making up for his littleness of stature by the height of the sycamore tree, He not only received, but actually honoured by the blessing of His dwelling with him. Paul even against his will and resisting He drew to Him. Another He charged to cleave to Him so closely that when he asked for the shortest possible delay in order to bury his father He did not grant it. To Cornelius when constantly attending to prayers and alms the way of salvation was shown by way of recompense, and by the visitation of an angel he was bidden to summon Peter, and learn from him the words of salvation, whereby he might be saved with all his. And so the manifold wisdom of God grants with manifold and inscrutable kindness salvation to men; and imparts to each one according to his capacity the grace of His bounty, so that He wills to grant His healing not according to the uniform power of His Majesty but according to the measure of the faith in which He finds each one, or as He Himself has imparted it to each one. For when one believed that for the cure of his leprosy the will of Christ alone was sufficient He healed him by the simple consent of His will, saying: "I will, be thou clean."[763] When another prayed that He would come and raise his dead daughter by laying His hands on her, He entered his house as he had hoped, and granted what was asked of Him. When another believed that what was essential for his salvation depended on His command, and answered: "Speak the word only, and my servant shall be healed,"[764] He restored to their former strength the limbs that were relaxed, by the power of a word, saying: "Go thy way, and as thou hast believed so be it unto thee."[765] To others hoping for restoration from the touch of His hem, He granted rich gifts of healing. To some, when asked, He bestowed remedies for their diseases. To others He afforded the means of healing unasked: others He urged on to hope, saying: "Willest thou to be made whole?"[766] to others when they were without hope He brought help spontaneously. The desires of some He searched out before satisfying their wants, saying: "What will ye that I should do for you?"[767] To another who knew not the way to obtain what he desired, He showed it in His kindness, saying: "If thou believest thou shalt see the glory of God."[768] Among some so richly did He pour forth the mighty works of His cures that of them the Evangelist says: "And He healed all their sick."[769] But among others the unfathomable depth of Christ's beneficence was so stopped up, that it was said: "And Jesus could do there no mighty works because of their unbelief."[770] And so the bounty of God is actually shaped according to the capacity of man's faith, so that to one it is said: "According to thy faith be it unto thee:"[771] and to another: "Go thy way, and as thou hast believed so be it unto thee;"[772] to another "Be it unto thee according as thou wilt,"[773] and again to another: "Thy faith hath made thee whole." [774]

NOTES:
[762] Rom. 11:33.
[763] S. Matt. 8:3.
[764] S. Matt. 8:8.

[765] S. Matt. 8:13.
[766] S. John 5:6.
[767] S. Matt. 20:32.
[768] S. John 11:40.
[769] S. Matt. 14:14.
[770] S. Mark 6:5, 6.
[771] S. Matt. 9:29.
[772] S. Matt. 8:13.
[773] S. Matt. 15:28.
[774] S. Luke 18:42.

CHAPTER XVI.

Of the grace of God; to the effect that it transcends the narrow limits of human faith.

BUT let no one imagine that we have brought forward these instances to try to make out that the chief share in our salvation rests with our faith, according to the profane notion of some who attribute everything to free will and lay down that the grace of God is dispensed in accordance with the desert of each man: but we plainly assert our unconditional opinion that the grace of God is superabounding, and sometimes overflows the narrow limits of man's lack of faith. And this, as we remember, happened in the case of the ruler in the gospel, who, as he believed that it was an easier thing for his son to be cured when sick than to be raised when dead, implored the Lord to come at once, saying: "Lord, come down ere my child die;" and though Christ reproved his lack of faith with these words: "Except ye see signs and wonders ye will not believe," yet He did not manifest the grace of His Divinity in proportion to the weakness of his faith, nor did He expell the deadly disease of the fever by His bodily presence, as the man believed he would, but by the word of His power, saying: "Go thy way, thy son liveth."[775] And we read also that the Lord poured forth this superabundance of grace in the case of the cure of the paralytic, when, though he only asked for the healing of the weakness by which his body was enervated, He first brought health to the soul by saying: "Son, be of good cheer, thy sins be forgiven thee." After which, when the scribes did not believe that He could forgive men's sins, in order to confound their incredulity, He set free by the power of His word the man's limb, and put an end to his disease of paralysis, by saying: "Why

310

think ye evil in your hearts? Whether is easier to say, thy sins be forgiven thee, or to say, arise and walk? But that ye may know that the Son of man hath power on earth to forgive sins, then saith He to the sick of the palsy: Arise, take up thy bed, and go unto thine house."[776] And in the same way in the case of the man who had been lying for thirty-eight years near the edge of the pool, and hoping for a cure from the moving of the water, He showed the princely character of His bounty unasked. For when in His wish to arouse him for the saving remedy, He had said to him: "willest thou to be made whole," and when the man complained of his lack of human assistance and said: "I have no man to put me into the pool when the water is troubled," the Lord in His pity granted pardon to his unbelief and ignorance, and restored him to his former health, not in the way which he expected, but in the way which He Himself willed, saying: "Arise, take up thy bed and go unto thine house."[777] And what wonder if these acts are told of the Lord's power, when Divine grace has actually wrought similar works by means of His servants! For when Peter and John were entering the temple, when the man who was lame from his mother's womb and had no idea how to walk, asked an alms, they gave him not the miserable coppers which the sick man asked for, but the power to walk, and when he was only expecting the smallest of gifts to console him, enriched him with the prize of unlooked for health, as Peter said: "Silver and gold have I none: but such as I have, give I unto thee. In the name of Jesus Christ of Nazareth, rise up and walk." [778]

NOTES:
[775] S. John 4:48-50.
[776] S. Matt. 9:2-6.
[777] S. John 5:6-8.
[778] Acts 3:6.

CHAPTER XVII.

Of the inscrutable providence of God.

BY those instances then which we have brought forward from the gospel records we can very clearly perceive that God brings salvation to mankind in diverse and innumerable methods and inscrutable ways, and that He stirs up the course of some, who are already wanting it, and thirsting for it, to greater zeal, while He forces some even against their will, and resisting. And that at one time He gives his assistance for the fulfilment of those things which he sees that we desire for our good, while at another time He puts into us the very beginnings of holy desire, and grants both the commencement of a good work and perseverance in it. Hence it comes that in our prayers we proclaim God as not only our Protector and Saviour, but actually as our Helper and Sponsor. For whereas He first calls us to Him, and while we are still ignorant and unwilling, draws us towards salvation, He is our Protector and Saviour, but whereas when we are already striving, He is wont to bring us help, and to receive and defend those who fly to Him for refuge, He is termed our Sponsor and Refuge. Finally the blessed Apostle when revolving in his mind this manifold bounty of God's providence, as he sees that he has fallen into some vast and boundless ocean of God's goodness, exclaims: "O the depth of the riches of the wisdom and knowledge of God! How inscrutable are the judgments of God and His ways past finding out! For who hath known the mind of the Lord?"[779] Whoever then imagines that he can by human reason fathom the depths of that inconceivable abyss, will be trying to explain away the astonishment at that knowledge, at which that great and mighty teacher of the gentiles was awed. For if a man thinks that he can either conceive in his mind or discuss exhaustively the dispensation of God whereby He works salvation in men, he certainly impugns the truth of the Apostle's words and asserts with profane audacity that His judgments can be scrutinized, and His ways searched out. This providence and love of God therefore, which the Lord in His unwearied goodness vouchsafes to show us, He compares to the tenderest heart of a kind mother, as He wishes to express it by a figure of human affection, and finds in His creatures no such feeling of love, to which he could better compare it. And He uses this example, because nothing dearer can be found in human nature, saying: "Can a mother forget her child, that she should not have compassion on the son of her womb?" But not content with this comparison He at once goes beyond it, and subjoins these words: "And though she may forget, yet will not I forget thee." [780]

NOTES:
[779] Rom. 11:33, 34.
[780] Is. 49:15.

CHAPTER XVIII.

The decision of the fathers that free will is not equal to save a man.

AND from this it is clearly gathered by those who, led not by chattering words but by experience, measure the magnitude of grace, and the paltry limits of man's will, that "the race is not to the swift nor the battle to the strong, nor food to the wise, nor riches to the prudent, nor grace to the learned," but that "all these worketh that one and the selfsame Spirit, dividing to every man severally as He will."[781] And therefore it is proved by no doubtful faith but by experience which can (so to speak) be laid hold of, that God the Father of all things worketh indifferently all things in all, as the Apostle says, like some most kind father and most benign physician; and that now He puts into us the very beginnings of salvation, and gives to each the zeal of his free will; and now grants the carrying out of the work, and the perfecting of goodness; and now saves men, even against their will and without their knowledge, from ruin that is close at hand, and a headlong fall; and now affords them occasions and opportunities of salvation, and wards off headlong and violent attacks from purposes that would bring death; and assists some who are already willing and running, while He draws others who are unwilling and resisting, and forces them to a good will. But that, when we do not always resist or remain persistently unwilling, everything is granted to us by God, and that the main share in our salvation is to be ascribed not to the merit of our own works but to heavenly grace, we are thus taught by the words of the Lord Himself: "And you shall remember your ways and all your wicked doings with which you have been defiled; and you shall be displeased with yourselves in your own sight for all your wicked deeds which you have committed. And you shall know that I am the Lord, when I shall have done well by you for My own name's sake, not according to your evil ways, nor according to your wicked deeds, O house of Israel."[782] And therefore it is laid down by all the Catholic fathers who have taught perfection of heart not by empty disputes of words, but in deed and act, that the first stage in the Divine gift is for each man to be inflamed with the desire of everything that is good, but in such a way that the choice of free will is open to either side: and that the second stage in Divine grace is for the aforesaid practices of virtue to be able to be performed, but in such a way that the possibili-

313

ties of the will are not destroyed: the third stage also belongs to the gifts of God, so that it may be held by the persistence of the goodness already acquired, and in such a way that the liberty may not be surrendered and experience bondage. For the God of all must be held to work in all, so as to incite, protect, and strengthen, but not to take away the freedom of the will which He Himself has once given. If however any more subtle inference of man's argumentation and reasoning seems opposed to this interpretation, it should be avoided rather than brought forward to the destruction of the faith (for we gain not faith from understanding, but understanding from faith, as it is written: "Except ye believe, ye will not understand"[783]) for how God works all things in us and yet everything can be ascribed to free will, cannot be fully grasped by the mind and reason of man.

Strengthened by this food the blessed Chaeremon prevented us from feeling the toil of so difficult a journey.

NOTES:
[781] Eccl. 9:11 (LXX); 1 Cor. 12:11.
[782] Ezek. 20:43, 44.
[783] Is. 7:9.
[665] Of the Semi-Pelagianism of this Conference and the erroneous passages from it extracted by Prosper, see the Introduction.

CONFERENCE 14.

The First Conference of Abbot Nesteros
on Spiritual Knowledge

CHAPTER I.

The words of Abbot Nesteros on the knowledge of the religious.

THE order of our promise and course demands that there should follow the instruction of Abbot Nesteros,[784] a man of excellence in all points and of the greatest knowledge: who when he had seen that we had committed some parts of Holy Scripture to memory and desired to understand them, addressed us in these words. There are indeed many different kinds of knowledge in this world, since there is as great a variety of them as there is of the arts and sciences. But, while all are either utterly useless or only useful for the good of this present life, there is yet none which has not its own system and method for learning it, by which it can be grasped by those who seek it. If then those arts are guided by certain special rules for their publication, how much more does the system and expression of our religion, which tends to the contemplation of the secrets of invisible mysteries, and seeks no present gain but the reward of an eternal recompense, depend on a fixed order and scheme. And the knowledge of this is twofold: first, praktikh, i.e., practical, which is brought about by an improvement of morals and purification from faults: secondly, qewretikh, which consists in the contemplation of things Divine and the knowledge of most sacred thoughts.

NOTES:
[784] Nesteros. In the Vitae Patrum there are some stories of one or two of this name (for it is not quite clear whether they are distinct persons or one and the same to whom the stories refer). One was known as `o megas, and was

a friend of St. Antony, and is supposed by some to be the same whose Conferences Cassian here relates, but nothing certain is known of him.

CHAPTER II.

On grasping the knowledge of spiritual things.

WHOEVER then would arrive at this theoretical knowledge must first pursue practical knowledge with all his might and main. For this practical knowledge can be acquired without theoretical, but theoretical cannot possibly be gained without practical. For there are certain stages, so distinct, and arranged in such a way that man's humility may be able to mount on high; and if these follow each other in turn in the order of which we have spoken, man can attain to a height to which he could not fly, if the first step were wanting. In vain then does one strive for the vision of God, who does not shun the stains of sins: "For the spirit of God hates deception, and dwells not in a body subject to sins." [785]

NOTES:
[785] Wisdom 1:4, 5.

CHAPTER III.

How practical perfection depends on a double system.

BUT this practical perfection depends on a double system; for its first method is to know the nature of all faults and the manner of their cure. Its second, to discover the order of the virtues, and form our mind by their perfection so that it may be obedient to them, not as if it were forced and subject to some fierce sway, but as if it delighted in its natural good, and throve upon it, and mounted by that steep and narrow way with real pleasure. For in what way will one, who has neither succeeded in understanding the nature of his own faults, nor tried to eradicate them, be able to gain an understanding of virtues, which is the second stage of practical training, or the mysteries of spiritual and heavenly things, which exist in the higher stage of theoretical knowledge? For it will necessarily be maintained that he cannot advance to more lofty heights who has not surmounted the lower ones, and much less will he be able to grasp those things that are without, who has not succeeded in understanding what is within his comprehension. But you should know that we must make an effort with a twofold purpose in our exertion; both for the expulsion of vice, and for the attainment of virtue. And this we do not gather from our own conjecture, but are taught by the words of Him who alone knows the strength and method of His work: "Behold," He says: "I have set thee this day over the nations and over kingdoms, to root up, and to pull down, and to waste, and to destroy, and to build and to plant."[786] He points out that for getting rid of noxious things four things are requisite; viz., to root up, to pull down, to waste, and to destroy: but for the performance of what is good, and the acquisition of what pertains to righteousness only to build and to plant. Whence it is perfectly evident that it is a harder thing to tear up and eradicate the inveterate passions of body and soul than to introduce and plant spiritual virtues.

NOTES:
[786] Jer. 1:10.

CHAPTER IV.

How practical life is distributed among many different professions and interests.

THIS practical life then, which as has been said rests on a double system, is distributed among many different professions and interests. For some make it their whole purpose to aim at the secrecy of an anchorite and purity of heart, as we know that in the past Elijah and Elisha, and in our own day the blessed Antony and others who followed with the same object, were joined most closely to God by the silence of solitude. Some have given all their efforts and interests towards the system of the brethren and the watchful care of the coenobium; as we remember that recently Abbot John, who presided over a big monastery in the neighbourhood of the city Thmuis,[787] and some other men of like merits were eminent with the signs of Apostles. Some are pleased with the kindly service of the guest house and reception, by which in the past the patriarch Abraham and Lot pleased the Lord, and recently the blessed Macarius,[788] a man of singular courtesy and patience who presided over the guest house at Alexandria in such a way as to be considered inferior to none of those who aimed at the retirement of the desert. Some choose the care of the sick, others devote themselves to intercession, which is offered up for the oppressed and afflicted, or give themselves up to teaching, or give alms to the poor, and flourish among men of excellence and renown, by reason of their love and goodness.

NOTES:

[787] It is doubtful whether this is the same John who was mentioned in the Institutes V. xxviii. and to whom the xixth Conference is assigned. Thmuis is the coptic Thmoui, a little to the south of the Mendesian branch of the Nile. See Rawlinson's note to Herod. ii. c. 166 and cf. Ptolemy IV. v. S: 51.

[788] On the two Macarii see the note on the Institutes V. xli.

CHAPTER V.

On perseverance in the line that has been chosen.

WHEREFORE it is good and profitable for each one to endeavour with all his might and main to attain perfection in the work that has been begun, according to the line which he has chosen as the grace which he has received; and while he praises and admires the virtues of others, not to swerve from his own line which he has once for all chosen, as he knows that, as the Apostle says, the body of the Church indeed is one, but the members many, and that it has "gifts differing according to the grace which is given us, whether prophecy, according to the proportion of the faith, whether ministry, in ministering, or he that teacheth, in doctrine, or he that exhorteth in exhortation, he that giveth, in simplicity, he that ruleth, with carefulness, he that showeth mercy, with cheerfulness."[789] For no members can claim the offices of other members, because the eyes cannot perform the duties of the hands, nor the nostrils of the ears. And so not all are Apostles, not all prophets, not all doctors, not all have the gifts of healing, not all speak with tongues, not all interpret. [790]

NOTES:

[789] Rom. 12:4-8.

[790] Cf. 1 Cor. 12:28.

CHAPTER VI.

How the weak are easily moved.

FOR those who are not yet settled in the line which they have taken up are often, when they hear some praised for different interests and virtues, so excited by the praise of them that they try forthwith to imitate their method: and in this human weakness is sure to expend its efforts to no purpose. For it is an impossibility for one and the same man to excel at once in all those good deeds which I enumerated above. And if anyone is anxious equally to affect them all, he is quite sure to come to this; viz., that while he pursues them all, he will not thoroughly succeed in any one, and will lose more than he will gain from this changing and shifting about. For in many ways men advance towards God, and so each man should complete that one which he has once fixed upon, never changing the course of his purpose, so that he may be perfect in whatever line of life his may be.

CHAPTER VII.

An instance of chastity which teaches us that all men should not be emulous of all things.

FOR apart from that loss, which we have said that a monk incurs who wants in light-mindedness to pass from one pursuit to another, there is a risk of death that is hence incurred, because at times things which are rightly done by some are wrongly taken by others as an example, and things which turned out well for some, are found to be injurious to others. For, to give an instance, it is as if one wished to imitate the good deed of that man, which Abbot John is wont to bring forward, not for the sake of imitating him but simply out of admiration for him; for one came to the aforesaid old man in a secular dress and when he had brought him some of the first fruits of his crops, he found some one there possessed by a most fierce devil. And this one though he scorned the adjurations and commands of Abbot John, and vowed that he would never at his bidding leave the body which he had occupied, yet was terrified at the coming of this other, and departed with a most humble utterance of his name. And the old man marvelled not a little at his so evident grace and was the more astonished at him because he saw that he had on a secular dress; and so began carefully to ask of him the manner of his life and pursuit. And when he said that he was living in the world and bound by the ties of marriage, the blessed John, considering in his mind the greatness of his virtue and grace, searched out still more carefully what his manner of life might be. He declared that he was a countryman, and that he sought his food by the daily toil of his hands, and was not conscious of anything good about him except that he never went forth to his work in the fields in the morning nor came home in the evening without having returned thanks in Church for the food of his daily life, to God Who gave it; and that he had never used any of his crops without having first offered to God their first fruits and tithes; and that he had never driven his oxen over the bounds of another's harvest without having first muzzled them that his neighbour might not sustain the slightest loss through his carelessness. And when these things did not seem to Abbot John sufficient to procure such grace as that with which he saw that he was endowed, and he inquired of him and investigated what it was which could be connected with the merits of such grace, he was induced by respect for such anxious inquiries to confess that, when he wanted to be professed as a monk, he had been compelled by force and his parents' command, twelve years before to take a wife, who, without any body to that day being aware of it, was kept by him as a virgin in the place of a sister. And when the old man heard this, he was so overcome with admiration that he announced publicly in his presence that it was not without good reason that the devil who had scorned him himself, could not endure the presence of this man, whose virtue he himself, not only in the ardour of youth, but even now, would not dare to aim at without risk of his chastity. And though Abbot John would tell this story with the utmost admiration, yet he never advised any monk to try this plan as he knew that many things which are rightly done by some involved others who imitate them in great danger, and that that cannot be tried by all, which the Lord bestowed upon a few by a special gift.

CHAPTER VIII.

Of spiritual knowledge.

BUT to return to the explanation of the knowledge from which our discourse took its rise. Thus, as we said above, practical knowledge is distributed among many subjects and interests, but theoretical is divided into two parts, i.e., the historical interpretation and the spiritual sense. Whence also Solomon when he had summed up the manifold grace of the Church, added: "for all who are with her are clothed with double garments."[791] But of spiritual knowledge there are three kinds, tropological, allegorical, anagogical,[792] of which we read as follows in Proverbs: "But do you describe these things to yourself in three ways according to the largeness of your heart."[793] And so the history embraces the knowledge of things past and visible, as it is repeated in this way by the Apostle: "For it is written that Abraham had two sons, the one by a bondwoman, the other by a free: but he who was of the bondwoman was born after the flesh, but he who was of the free was by promise." But to the allegory belongs what follows, for what actually happened is said to have prefigured the form of some mystery "For these," says he, "are the two covenants the one from Mount Sinai, which gendereth into bondage, which is Agar. For Sinai is a mountain in Arabia, which is compared to Jerusalem which now is, and is in bondage with her children." But the anagogical sense rises from spiritual mysteries even to still more sublime and sacred secrets of heaven, and is subjoined by the Apostle in these words: "But Jerusalem which is above is free, which is the mother of us. For it is written, Rejoice, thou barren that bearest not, break forth and cry, thou that travailest not, for many are the children of the desolate more than of her that hath an husband."[794] The tropological sense is the moral explanation which has to do with improvement of life and practical teaching, as if we were to understand by these two covenants practical and theoretical instruction, or at any rate as if we were to want to take Jerusalem or Sion as the soul of man, according to this: "Praise the Lord, O Jerusalem: praise thy God, O Sion."[795] And so these four previously mentioned figures coalesce, if we desire, in one subject, so that one and the same Jerusalem can be taken in four senses: historically as the city of the Jews; allegorically as Church of Christ, anagogically as the heavenly city of God "which is the mother of us all," tropologically, as the soul of man, which is frequently subject to praise or blame from the Lord under this title. Of these four kinds of interpretation the blessed Apostle speaks as follows: "But now, brethren, if I come to you speaking with tongues what shall I profit you unless I speak to you either by revelation or by knowledge or by prophecy or by doctrine?"[796] For "revelation" belongs to allegory whereby what is concealed under the historical narrative is revealed in its spiritual sense and interpretation, as for instance if we tried to expound how "all our fathers were under the cloud and were all baptized unto Moses in the cloud and in the sea," and how they "all ate the same spiritual meat and drank the same spiritual drink from the rock that followed them. But the rock was Christ."[797] And this explanation where there is a comparison of the figure of the body and blood of Christ which we receive daily, contains the allegorical sense. But the knowledge, which is in the same way mentioned by the Apostle, is tropological, as by it we can by a careful study see of all things that have to do with practical discernment whether they are useful and good, as in this case, when we are told to judge of our own selves "whether it is fitting for a woman to pray to God with her head uncovered."[798] And this system, as has been said, contains the moral meaning. So "prophecy" which the Apostle puts in the third place, alludes to the anagogical sense by which the words are applied to things future and invisible, as here: "But we would not have you ignorant, brethren, concerning those that sleep: that ye be not sorry as others also who have no hope. For if we believe that Christ died and rose again, even so them also which sleep in Jesus will God bring with Him. For this we say to you by the word of God, that we which are alive at the coming of the Lord shall not prevent those that sleep in Christ, for the Lord Himself shall descend from heaven with a shout, with the voice of the archangel and with the trump of God; and the dead in Christ shall rise first."[799] In which kind of exhortation the figure of anagoge is brought forward. But "doctrine" unfolds the simple course of historical exposition, under which is contained no more secret sense, but what is declared by the very words: as in his passage: "For I delivered unto you first of all what I also received, how that Christ died for our sins according to the Scriptures, and that He was buried, and that He rose again on the third day, and that he was seen of Cephas;"[800] and: "God sent His Son, made of a woman, made under the law, to redeem them that were under the law;"[801] or this: "Hear, O Israel, the Lord the God is one Lord." [802]

NOTES:

[791] Prov. 31:21 (LXX).

[792] The meaning of the four senses of Scripture here spoken of; viz., the historical, tropological, allegorical, ana anagogical, is well summed up in these lines: Litera, gesta docet; quid credas, allegoria; Moralis, quid agas; quo tendas anagogia. Or, as the lines are sometimes given: Litera scripta docet; quod credas, allegoria; Quod speres, anagoge; quid agas, tropologia. Both Origen and Jerome had spoken of the threefold sense of Scripture, referring to the LXX. rendering of Prov. 22:20 (which Cassian quotes below): but in general the Latin Fathers, and the Schoolmen after them, separated the third of Origen's senses; viz., the spiritual, into two, the allegorical and the anagogical: and so the "fourfold" sense became the established method of interpretation in the West.

[793] Prov. 22:20 (LXX).

[794] Gal. 4:22-27.

[795] Ps. 147:12.

[796] 1 Cor. 14:6.

[797] 1 Cor. 10:1-4.

[798] 1 Cor. 11:13.

[799] 1 Thess. 4:12-15.

[800] 1 Cor. 15:3-5.

[801] Gal. 4:4, 5.

[802] Deut. 6:4.

CHAPTER IX.

How from practical knowledge we must proceed to spiritual.

WHEREFORE if you are anxious to attain to the light of spiritual knowledge, not wrongly for an idle boast but for the sake of being made better men, you are first inflamed with the longing for that blessedness, of which we read: "blessed are the pure in heart for they shall see God,"[803] that you may also attain to that of which the angel said to Daniel: "But they that are learned shall shine as the splendor of the firmament: and they that turn many to righteousness as the stars for ever and ever;" and in another prophet: "Enlighten yourselves with the light of knowledge while there is time."[804] And so keeping up that diligence in reading, which I see that you have, endeavour with all eagerness to gain in the first place a thorough grasp of practical, i.e., ethical knowledge. For without this that theoretical purity of which we have spoken cannot be obtained, which those only, who are perfected not by the words of others who teach them, but by the excellence of their own actions, can after much expenditure of effort and toil attain as a reward for it. For as they gain their knowledge not from meditation on the law but from the fruit of their labour, they sing with the Psalmist: "From Thy commandments I have understanding;" and having overcome all their passions, they say with confidence: "I will sing, and I will understand in the undefiled way."[805] For he who is striving in an undefiled way in the course of a pure heart, as he sings the Psalm, understands the words which are chanted. And therefore if you would prepare in your heart a holy tabernacle of spiritual knowledge, purge yourselves from the stain of all sins, and rid yourselves of the cares of this world. For it is an impossibility for the soul which is taken up even to a small extent with worldly troubles, to gain the gift of knowledge or to become an author of spiritual interpretation, and diligent in reading holy things. Be careful therefore in the first place, and especially you, John, as your more youthful age requires you the rather to be careful about what I am going to say--that you may enjoin absolute silence on your lips, in order that your zeal for reading and the efforts of your purpose may not be destroyed by vain pride. For this is the first practical step towards learning, to receive the regulations and opinions of all the Elders with an earnest heart, and with lips that are dumb; and diligently to lay them up in your heart, and endeavour rather to perform than to teach them. For from teaching, the dangerous arrogance of vainglory, but from performing, the fruit of spiritual knowledge will flourish. And so you should never venture to say anything in the conference of the Elders unless some ignorance that might be injurious, or a matter which it is important to know leads you to ask a question; as some who are puffed up with vainglory, pretend that they ask, in order really to show off the knowledge which they perfectly possess. For it is an impossibility for one, who takes to the pursuit of reading with the purpose of gaining the praise of men, to be rewarded with the gift of true knowledge. For one who is bound by the chain of this passion, is sure to be also in bondage to other faults, and especially to that of pride: and so if he is baffled by his encounter with practical and ethical knowledge, he will certainly not attain that spiritual knowledge which springs from it. Be then in all things "swift to hear, but slow to speak,"[806] lest there come upon you that which is noted by Solomon: "If thou seest a man who is quick to speak, know that there is more hope of a fool than of him;[807] and do not presume to teach any one in words what you have not already performed in deed. For our Lord taught us by His own example that we ought to keep to this order, as of Him it is said: "what Jesus began to do and to teach."[808] Take care then that you do not rush into teaching before doing, and so be reckoned among the number of those of whom the Lord speaks in the gospel to the disciples: "What they say unto you, that observe and do, but not after their words: for they say and do not. But they bind heavy burdens and grievous to be borne, and lay them on men's shoulders; but they themselves will not move them with one of their fingers."[809] For if he who shall "break one of these commands, and shall teach men so, shall be called least in the kingdom of heaven,"[810] it follows that one who has dared to despise many and greater commands and to teach men so, shall certainly be considered not least in the kingdom of heaven, but greatest in the punishment of hell. And therefore you must be careful not to be led on to teach by the example of those who have attained some skill in discussion and readiness in speech and because they can discourse on what they please elegantly and fully, are imagined to possess spiritual knowledge, by those who do not know how to distinguish its real force and character. For it is one thing to have a ready tongue and elegant language, and quite another to penetrate into the very heart and marrow of heavenly utterances and to gaze with pure eye of the soul on profound and hidden mysteries; for this can be gained by no learning of man's, nor condition of this world, only by purity of soul, by means of the illumination of the Holy Ghost.

NOTES:
[803] S. Matt. 5:8.
[804] Dan. 12:3; Hos. 10:12.
[805] Ps. 118 (119):104; 100 (101):1, 2.
[806] S. James 1:19.
[807] Prov. 29:20 (LXX).
[808] Acts 1:1.
[809] S. Matt. 23:3, 4.
[810] S. Matt. 5:19.

CHAPTER X.

How to embrace the system of true knowledge.

YOU must then, if you want to get at the true knowledge of the Scriptures, endeavour first to secure steadfast humility of heart, to carry you on by the perfection of love not to the knowledge which puffeth up, but to that which enlightens. For it is an impossibility for an impure mind to gain the gift of spiritual knowledge. And therefore with every possible care avoid this, lest through your zeal for reading there arise in you not the light of knowledge nor the lasting glory which is promised through the light that comes from learning but only the instruments of your destruction from vain arrogance. Next you must by all means strive to get rid of all anxiety and worldly thoughts, and give yourself over assiduously or rather continuously, to sacred reading, until continual meditation fills your heart, and fashions you so to speak after its own likeness, making of it, in a way, an ark of the testimony,[811] which has within it two tables of stone, i.e., the constant assurance of the two testaments;[812] and a golden pot, i.e., a pure and undefiled memory which preserves by a constant tenacity the manna stored up in it, i.e., the enduring and heavenly sweetness of the spiritual sense and the bread of angels; moreover also the rod of Aaron, i.e., the saving standard of Jesus Christ our true High Priest, that ever buds with the freshness of immortal memory. For this is the rod which after it had been cut from the root of Jesse, died and flourished again with a more vigorous life. But all these are guarded by two Cherubim, i.e., the fulness of historical and spiritual knowledge. For the Cherubim mean a multitude of knowledge: and these continually protect the mercy seat of God, i.e., the peace of your heart, and overshadow it from all the assaults of spiritual wickedness. And so your soul will be carried forward not only to the ark of the Divine Covenant, but also to the priestly kingdom, and owing to its unbroken love of purity being as it were engrossed in spiritual studies, will fulfil the command given to the priests, enjoined as follows by the giver of the Law: "And he shall not go forth from the sanctuary, lest he pollute the Sanctuary of God,"[813] i.e., his heart, in which the Lord promised that he would ever dwell, saying: "I will dwell in them and will walk among them."[814] Wherefore the whole series of the Holy Scriptures should be diligently committed to memory and ceaselessly repeated. For this continual meditation will bring us a twofold fruit: first, that while the attention of the mind is taken up in reading and preparing the lessons it cannot possibly be taken captive in any snares of bad thoughts: next that those things which were conned over and frequently repeated and which while we were trying to commit them to memory we could not understand as the mind was at that time taken up, we can afterward see more clearly, when we are free from the distraction of all acts and visions, and especially when we reflect on them in silence in our meditation by night. So that when we are at rest, and as it were plunged in the stupor of sleep, there is revealed to us the understanding of the most secret meanings, of which in our waking hours we had not the remotest conception.

NOTES:
[811] Cf. Heb. 9:4, 5.
[812] Instrumentum is a favourite word with Tertullian, who uses it more than once of the two Testaments, e.g., Apol. xix.; and, Against Marcion iv. where he speaks of the "Two Instruments, or as it is usual to speak, of the Two Testaments."
[813] Lev. 21:12.
[814] 2 Cor. 5:16.

CHAPTER XI.

Of the manifold meaning of the Holy Scriptures.

BUT as the renewal of our soul grows by means of this study, Scripture also will begin to put on a new face, and the beauty of the holier meanings will somehow grow with our growth. For their form is adapted to the capacity of man's understanding, and will appear earthly to carnal people, and divine to spiritual ones, so that those to whom it formerly appeared to be involved in thick clouds, cannot apprehend its subtleties nor endure its light. But to make this which we are aiming at somewhat clearer by an instance, it will be enough to produce a single passage of the law, by which we can prove that all the heavenly commands as well are applied to men in accordance with the measure of our state. For it is written in the law: "Thou shalt not commit adultery."[815] This is rightly observed according to the simple meaning of the letter, by a man who is still in bondage to foul passions. But by one who has already forsaken these dirty acts and impure affections, it must be observed in the spirit, so that he may forsake not only the worship of idols but also all heathen superstitions and the observance of auguries and omens and all signs and days and times, or at any rate that he be not entangled in the conjectures of words and names which destroy the simplicity of our faith. For by fornication of this kind we read that Jerusalem was defiled, as she committed adultery "on every high hill and under every green tree,"[816] whom also the Lord rebuked by the prophet, saying: "Let now the astrologers stand and save thee, they that gazed at the stars and counted the months, that from them they might tell the things that shall come to thee,"[817] of which fornication elsewhere also the Lord says in rebuking them: "The spirit of fornication deceived them, and they went a whoring from their God."[818] But one who has forsaken both these kinds of fornication, will have a third kind to avoid, which is contained in the superstitions of the law and of Judaism; of which the Apostle says: "Ye observe days and months and times and years;" and again: "Touch not, taste not, handle not."[819] And there is no doubt that this is said of the superstitions of the law, into which one who has fallen has certainly gone a whoring from Christ, and is not worthy to hear this from the Apostle: "For I have espoused you to one husband, to exhibit you as a chaste virgin to Christ."[820] But this that follows will be directed to him by the words of the same Apostle: "But I am afraid lest as the serpent by his cunning deceived Eve, so your minds should be corrupted and fall from the simplicity which is in Christ Jesus."[821] But if one has escaped the uncleanness even of this fornication there will still be a fourth, which is committed by adulterous intercourse with heretical teaching. Of which too the blessed Apostle speaks: "I know that after my departure grievous wolves shall enter in among you, not sparing the flock, and of yourselves also shall arise men speaking perverse things so as to lead astray the disciples after them."[822] But if a man has succeeded in avoiding even this, let him beware lest he fall by a more subtle sin into the guilt of fornication. I mean that which consists in wandering thoughts, because every thought which is not only shameful but even idle, and departing in however small a degree from God is regarded by the perfect man as the foulest fornication.

NOTES:
[815] Exod. 20:14.
[816] Jer. 3:6.
[817] Is. 47:13.
[818] Hos. 4:12.
[819] Gal. 4:10; Col. 2:21.
[820] 2 Cor. 11:2.
[821] 2 Cor. 11:3.
[822] Acts 20:29, 30.

CHAPTER XII.

A question how we can attain to forgetfulness of the cares of this world.

UPON this I was at first moved by a secret emotion, and then groaned deeply and said, All these things which you have set forth so fully have affected me with still greater despair than that which I had previously endured: as besides those general captivities of the soul whereby I doubt not that weak people are smitten from without, a special hindrance to salvation is added by that knowledge of literature which I seem already to have in some slight measure attained, in which the efforts of my tutor, or my attention to continual reading have so weakened me that now my mind is filled with those songs of the poets so that even at the hour of prayer it is thinking about those trifling fables, and the stories of battles with which from its earliest infancy it was stored by its childish lessons: and when singing Psalms or asking forgiveness of sins either some wanton recollection of the poems intrudes itself or the images of heroes fighting presents itself before the eyes, and an imagination of such phantoms is always tricking me and does not suffer my soul to aspire to an insight into things above, so that this cannot be got rid of by my daily lamentations.

CHAPTER XIII.

Of the method by which we can remove the dross from our memory.

NESTEROS: From this very fact, from which there springs up for you the utmost despair of your purification, a speedy and effectual remedy may arise if only you will transfer to the reading of and meditation upon the writings of the Spirit, the same diligence and earnestness which you say that you showed in those secular studies of yours. For your mind is sure to be taken up with those poems until it is gaining with the same zeal and assiduity other matters for it to reflect upon, and is in labour with spiritual and divine things instead of unprofitable earthly ones. But when these are thoroughly and entirely conceived and it has been nourished upon them, then by degrees the former thoughts can be expelled and utterly got rid of. For the mind of man cannot be emptied of all thoughts, and so as long as it is not taken up with spiritual interests, is sure to be occupied with what it learnt long since. For as long as it has nothing to recur to and exercise itself upon unweariedly, it is sure to fall back upon what it learnt in child-hood, and ever to think about what it took in by long use and meditation. In order then that this spiritual knowledge may be strengthened in you with a lasting steadfastness, and that you may not enjoy it only for a time like those who just touch it not by their own exertions but at the recital of another, and if I may use the expression, perceive its scent in the air; but that it may be laid up in your heart, and deeply noted in it, and thoroughly seen and handled, it is well for you to use the utmost care in securing that, even if perhaps you hear things that you know very well produced in the Conference, you do not regard them in a scornful and disdainful way because you already know them, but that you lay them to your heart with the same eager-ness, with which the words of salvation which we are longing for ought to be constantly poured into our ears or should ever proceed from our lips. For although the narration of holy things be often re-peated, yet in a mind that feels a thirst for true knowledge the satiety will never create disgust, but as it receives it every day as if it were something new and what it wanted however often it may have taken it in, it will so much the more eagerly either hear or speak, and from the repetition of these things will gain confirmation of the knowledge it already possesses, rather than weariness of any sort from the frequent Conference. For it is a sure sign of a mind that is cold and proud, if it receives with disdain and carelessness the medicine of the words of salvation, although it be offered with the zeal of excessive persistence. For "a soul that is full jeers at honeycomb: but to a soul that is in want even little things appear sweet."[823] And so if these things have been carefully taken in and stored up in the recesses of the soul and stamped with the seal of silence, afterwards like some sweet scented wine that maketh glad the heart of man, they will, when mellowed by the antiq-uity of the thoughts and by long-standing patience, be brought forth from the jar of your heart with great fragrance, and like some perennial fountain will flow abundantly from the veins of experience and irrigat-ing channels of virtue and will pour forth copious streams as if from some deep well in your heart. For that will happen in your case, which is spoken in Proverbs to one who has achieved this in his work: "Drink waters from your own cisterns and from the fount of your own wells. Let waters from your own fountain flow in abundance for you, but let your waters pass through into your streets."[824] And according to the prophet Isaiah: "Thou shalt be like a watered garden, and like a fountain of water whose waters shall not fail. And the places that have been desolate for ages shall be built in thee; thou shalt raise up the foundations of generation and generation; and thou shalt be called the repairer of the fences, turning the paths into rest."[825] And that blessedness shall come upon thee which the same prophet promises: "And the Lord will not cause thy teacher to flee away from thee any more, and thine eyes shall see thy teacher. And thine ears shall hear the word of one admonishing thee behind thy back: This is the way, walk ye in it, and go not aside either to the right hand or to the left."[826] And so it will come to pass that not only every purpose and thought of your heart, but also all the wanderings and rovings of your imagination will become to you a holy and unceasing pondering of the Divine law.

NOTES:
[823] Prov. 27:7.
[824] Prov. 5:15, 16.
[825] Is. 58:11, 12.
[826] Is. 30:20, 21.

CHAPTER XIV.

How an unclean soul can neither give nor receive spiritual knowledge.

BUT it is, as we have already said, impossible for a novice either to understand or to teach this. For if one is incapable of receiving it how can he be fit to pass it on to another? But if he has had the audacity to teach anything on these matters, most certainly his words will be idle and useless and only reach the ears of his hearers, without being able to touch their hearts, uttered as they were in sheer idleness and unfruitful vanity, for they do not proceed from the treasure of a good conscience, but from the empty impertinence of boastfulness. For it is impossible for an impure soul (however earnestly it may devote itself to reading) to obtain spiritual knowledge. For no one pours any rich ointment or fine honey or any precious liquid into a dirty and stinking vessel. For a jar that has once been filled with foul odours spoils the sweetest myrrh more readily than it receives any sweetness or grace from it, for what is pure is corrupted much more quickly than what is corrupt is purified. And so the vessel of our bosom unless it has first been purified from all the foul stains of sin will not be worthy to receive that blessed ointment of which it is said by the prophet: "Like the ointment upon the head, which ran down upon the beard of Aaron, which ran down upon the edge of his garment,"[827] nor will it keep undefiled that spiritual knowledge and the words of Scripture which are "sweeter than honey and the honeycomb."[828] "For what share hath righteousness with iniquity? or what agreement hath light with darkness? or what concord has Christ with Belial?" [829]

NOTES:
[827] Ps. 132 (133):2.
[828] Ps. 18 (19):11.
[829] 2 Cor. 6:14, 15.

CHAPTER XV.

An objection owing to the fact that many impure persons have knowledge while saints have not.

GERMANUS: This assertion does not seem to us founded on truth, or based on solid reasoning. For if it is clear that all who either never receive the faith of Christ at all or who corrupt it by the wicked sin of heresy, are of unclean hearts, how is it that many Jews and heretics, and Catholics also who are entangled in various sins, have acquired perfect knowledge of the Scriptures and boast of the greatness of their spiritual learning, and on the other hand countless swarms of saintly men, whose heart has been purified from all stain of sin, are content with the piety of simple faith and know nothing of the mysteries of a deeper knowledge? How then will that opinion stand, which attributes spiritual knowledge solely to purity of heart?

CHAPTER XVI.

The answer to the effect that bad men cannot possess true knowledge.

NESTEROS: One who does not carefully weigh every word of the opinions uttered cannot rightly discover the value of the assertion. For we said to begin with that men of this sort only possess skill in disputation and ornaments of speech; but cannot penetrate to the very heart of Scripture and the mysteries of its spiritual meanings. For true knowledge is only acquired by true worshippers of God; and certainly this people does not possess it to whom it is said: "Hear, O, foolish people, thou who hast no heart: ye who having eyes see not, and having ears, hear not." And again: "Because thou hast rejected knowledge, I also will reject thee from acting as My priest."[830] For as it is said that in Christ "all the treasures of wisdom and knowledge are hid,"[831] how can we hold that he who has scorned to find Christ, or, when He is found blasphemes Him with impious lips, or at least defiles the Catholic faith by his impure deeds, has acquired spiritual knowledge? "For the Spirit of God will avoid deception, and dwelleth not in a body that is subject to sin."[832] There is then no way of arriving at spiritual knowledge but this which one of the prophets has finely described: "Sow to yourselves for righteousness: reap the hope of life. Enlighten yourselves with the light of knowledge."[833] First then we must sow for righteousness, i.e., by works of righteousness we must extend practical perfection; next we must reap the hope of life, i.e., by the expulsion of carnal sins must gather the fruits of spiritual virtues: and so we shall succeed in enlightening ourselves with the light of knowledge. And the Psalmist also sees that this system ought to be followed, when he says: "Blessed are they that are undefiled in the way: who walk in the law of the Lord. Blessed are they that seek His testimonies."[834] For he does not say in the first place: "Blessed are they that seek His testimonies," and afterwards add: "Blessed are they that are undefiled in the way;" but he begins by saying: "Blessed are they that are undefiled in the way;" and by this clearly shows that no one can properly come to seek God's testimonies unless he first walks undefiled in the way of Christ by his practical life. Those therefore whom you mentioned do not possess that knowledge which the impure cannot attain, but yeudwnumon, i.e., what is falsely so called, of which the blessed Apostle speaks: "O Timothy, keep that which is committed to thee, avoiding profane novelties of words, and oppositions of the knowledge that is falsely so called;"[835] which is in the Greek tas antiqeseis ths yeudwnumou gnwsews. Of those then who seem to acquire some show of knowledge or of those who while they devote themselves diligently to reading the sacred volume and to committing the Scriptures to memory, yet forsake not carnal sins, it is well said in Proverbs: "Like as a golden ring in a swine's snout so is the beauty of an evil-disposed woman."[836] For what does it profit a man to gain the ornaments of heavenly eloquence and the most precious beauty of the Scriptures if by clinging to filthy deeds and thoughts he destroys it by burying it in the foulest ground, or defiles it by the dirty wallowing of his own lusts? For the result will be that which is an ornament to those who rightly use it, is not only unable to adorn them, but actually becomes dirty by the increased filth and mud. For "from the mouth of a sinner praise is not comely;"[837] as to him it is said by the prophet: "Wherefore dost thou declare My righteous acts, and takest My covenant in thy lips?"[838] of souls like this, who never possess in any lasting fashion the fear of the Lord of which it is said: "the fear of the Lord is instruction and wisdom,"[839] and yet try to get at the meaning of Scripture by continual meditation on them, it is appropriately asked in Proverbs: "What use are riches to a fool? For a senseless man cannot possess wisdom."[840] But so far is this true and spiritual knowledge removed from that worldly erudition, which is defiled by te stains of carnal sins, that we know that it has sometimes flourished most grandly in some who were without eloquence and almost illiterate. And this is very clearly shown by the case of the Apostles and many holy men, who did not spread themselves out with an empty show of leaves, but were bowed down by the weight of the true fruits of spiritual knowledge: of whom it is written in the Acts of the Apostles: "But when they saw the boldness of Peter and John, and perceived that they were ignorant and unlearned men, they were astonished."[841] And therefore if you are anxious to attain to that never-failing fragrance, you must first strive with all your might to obtain from the Lord the purity of chastity. For no one, in whom the love of carnal passions and especially of fornication still holds sway, can acquire spiritual knowledge. For "in a good heart wisdom will rest;" and: "He that feareth the Lord shall find knowledge with righteousness."[842] But that we must attain to spiritual knowledge in the order of which we have already spoken, we are taught also by the blessed Apostle. For when he wanted not merely to draw up a list of all his own virtues, but rather to describe their order, that he might explain which follows what, and which gives birth to what, after some others he proceeds as follows: "In watchings, in fastings, in chastity, in knowledge, in long suffering, in gentleness, in the Holy Ghost, in love unfeigned."[843] And by this enumeration of virtues he evidently meant to teach us that we must come from watchings and fastings to chastity, from chastity to knowledge, from knowledge to long suffering, from long suffering to gentleness, from gentleness to the Holy Ghost, from the Holy Ghost to the rewards of love unfeigned. When then by this system and in this order you too have come to spiritual knowledge, you will certainly have, as we said, not barren or idle learning but what is vigorous and fruitful; and the seed of the word of salvation which has been committed by you to the hearts of your hearers, will be watered by the plentiful showers of the Holy Ghost that will follow; and, according to this that the prophet promised, "the rain will be given to your seed, wherever you shall sow in the land, and the bread of the corn of the land shall be most plentiful and fat." [844]

NOTES:
[830] Jer. 5:21; Hos. 4:6.
[831] Col. 2:3.
[832] Wisd. 1:4, 5.
[833] Hos. 10:12.
[834] Ps. 118 (119):1, 2.
[835] 1 Tim. 6:20.
[836] Prov. 11:22.
[837] Ecclus. 15:9.
[838] Ps. 49 (50):16.
[839] Prov. 15:33.
[840] Prov. 17:16.
[841] Acts 4:13.
[842] Prov. 14:33; Ecclus. 32:20.
[843] 2 Cor. 6:5, 6.
[844] Is. 30:23.

CHAPTER XVII.

To whom the method of perfection should be laid open.

TAKE care too, when your riper age leads you to teach, lest you be led astray by the love of vainglory, and teach at random to the most impure persons these things which you have learnt not so much by reading as by the effects of experience, and so incur what Solomon, that wisest of men, denounced: "Attach not a wicked man to the pastures of the just, and be not led astray by the fulness of the belly," for "delicacies are not good for a fool, nor is there room for wisdom where sense is wanting: for folly is the more led on, because a stubborn servant is not improved by words, for even though he understands, he will not obey." And "Do not say anything in the ears of an imprudent man, lest haply he mock at thy wise speeches."[845] And "give not that which is holy to dogs, neither cast ye your pearls before swine, lest haply they trample them under foot and turn again and rend you."[846] It is right then to hide the mysteries of spiritual meanings from men of this sort, that you may effectually sing: "Thy words have I hid within my heart: that I should not sin against Thee."[847] But you will perhaps say: And to whom are the mysteries of Holy Scripture to be dispensed? Solomon, the wisest of men, shall teach you: "Give, says he, strong drink to those who are in sorrow, and give wine to drink, to those who are in pain, that they may forget their poverty, and remember their pain no more,"[848] i.e., to those who in consequence of the punishment of their past actions are oppressed with grief and sorrow, supply richly the joys of spiritual knowledge like "wine that maketh glad the heart of man,"[849] and restore them with the strong drink of the word of salvation, lest haply they be plunged in continual sorrow and a despair that brings death, and so those who are of this sort be "swallowed up in overmuch sorrow."[850] But of those who remain in coldness and carelessness, and are smitten by no sorrow of heart we read as follows: "For one who is kindly and without sorrow, shall be in want."[851] With all possible care therefore avoid being puffed up with the love of vainglory, and so failing to become a partaker with him whom the prophet praises, "who hath not given his money upon usury."[852] For every one who, from love of the praise of men dispenses the words of God, of which it is said "the words of the Lord are pure words, as silver tried by the fire, purged from the earth, refined seven times,"[853] puts out his money upon usury, and will deserve for this not merely no reward, but rather punishment. For this reason he chose to use up his Lord's money that he might be the garner from a temporal profit, and not that the Lord, as it is written, might "when He comes, receive His own with usury." [854]

NOTES:
[845] Prov. 24:15; 19:10; 18:2; 29:19; 23:9 (LXX).
[846] S. Matt. 7:6.
[847] Ps. 118 (119):11.
[848] Prov. 31:6, 7.
[849] Ps. 103 (104):15.
[850] 2 Cor. 2:7.
[851] Prov. 19:23.
[852] Ps. 14 (15):5.
[853] Ps. 11 (12):7.
[854] S. Matt. 25:27.

CHAPTER XVIII.

Of the reasons for which spiritual learning is unfruitful.

BUT it is certain that for two reasons the teaching of spiritual things is ineffectual. For either the teacher is commending what he has no experience of, and is trying with empty-sounding words to instruct his hearer, or else the hearer is a bad man and full of faults and cannot receive in his hard heart the holy and saving doctrine of the spiritual man; and of these it is said by the prophet: "For the heart of this people is blinded, and their ears are dull of hearing and their eyes have they closed: lest at any time they should see with their eyes and hear with their ears, and understand with their heart and be converted and I should heal them." [855]

CHAPTER XIX.

How often even those who are not worthy can receive the grace of the saving word.

BUT sometimes in the lavish generosity of God in His Providence, "Who willeth all men to be saved and to come to the knowledge of the truth,"[856] it is granted that one who has not shown himself by an irreproachable life to be worthy of the preaching of the gospel attains the grace of spiritual teaching for the good of many. But by what means the gifts of healing are granted by the Lord for the expulsion of devils it follows that we must in a similar discussion explain, which as we are going to rise for supper we will keep for the evening, because that is always more effectually grasped by the heart which is taken in by degrees and without excessive bodily efforts.

NOTES:
[855] Is. 6:10.
[856] 1 Tim. 2:4.

337

CONFERENCE 15.

The Second Conference of Abbot Nesteros
on Divine Gifts

CHAPTER I.

Discourse of Abbot Nesteros on the threefold system of gifts.

AFTER evening service we sat down together on the mats as usual ready for the promised narration: and when we had kept silence for some little time out of reverence for the Elder, he anticipated the silence of our respect by such words as these. The previous order of our discourse had brought us to the exposition of the system of spiritual gifts, which we have learnt from the tradition of the Elders is a threefold one. The first indeed is for the sake of healing, when the grace of signs accompanies certain elect and righteous men on account of the merits of their holiness, as it is clear that the apostles and many of the saints wrought signs and wonders in accordance with the authority of the Lord Who says: "Heal the sick, raise the dead, cleanse the lepers, cast out devils: freely ye have received, freely give."[857] The second when for the edification of the church or on account of the faith of those who bring their sick, or of those who are to be cured, the virtue of health proceeds even from sinners and men unworthy of it. Of whom the Saviour says in the gospel: "Many shall say to Me in that day, Lord, Lord, have we not prophesied in Thy name, and in Thy name cast out devils, and in Thy name done many mighty works? And then I will confess to them, I never knew you: Depart from Me, ye workers of iniquity."[858] And on the other hand, if the faith of those who bring them or of the sick is wanting, it prevents those on whom the gifts of healing are conferred from exercising their powers of healing. On which subject Luke the Evangelist says: "And Jesus could not there do any mighty work because of their unbelief."[859] Whence also

the Lord Himself says: "Many lepers were in Israel in the days of Elisha the prophet, and none of them was cleansed but Naaman the
Syrian."[860] The third method of healing is copied by the deceit and
contrivance of devils, that, when a man who is enslaved to evident sins
is out of admiration for his miracles regarded as a saint and a servant
of God, men may be persuaded to copy his sins and thus an opening
being made for cavilling, the sanctity of religion may be brought into
disgrace, or else that he, who believes that he possesses the gift of
healing, may be puffed up by pride of heart and so fall more grievously. Hence it is that invoking the names of those, who, as they know,
have no merits of holiness or any spiritual fruits, they pretend that by
their merits they are disturbed and made to flee from the bodies they
have possessed. Of which it says in Deuteronomy: "If there rise up in
the midst of thee a prophet, or one who says that he has seen a dream,
and declare a sign and a wonder, and that which he hath spoken
cometh to pass, and he say to thee: Let us go and follow after other
gods whom thou knowest not, and let us serve them: thou shalt not
hear the words of that prophet or of that dreamer, for the Lord thy God
is tempting thee that it may appear whether thou lovest Him or not,
with all thy heart and with all thy soul."[861] And in the gospel it says:
"There shall arise false Christs and false prophets, and shall give great
signs and wonders, so that, if it were possible, even the elect should be
led astray." [862]

NOTES:
[857] S. Matt. 10:8.
[858] S. Matt. 7:22, 23.
[859] S. Mark 6:5, 6.
[860] S. Luke 4:27.
[861] Deut. 13:1-3.
[862] S. Matt 24:24.

CHAPTER II.

Wherein one ought to admire the saints.

WHEREFORE we never ought to admire those who affect these
things, for these powers, but rather to look whether they are perfect in
driving out all sins, and amending their ways, for this is granted to
each man not for the faith of some other, or for a variety of reasons,

but for his own earnestness, by the action of God's grace. For this is practical knowledge which is termed by another name by the Apostle; viz., love, and is by the authority of the Apostle preferred to all tongues of men and of angels, and to full assurance of faith which can even remove mountains, and to all knowledge, and prophecy, and to the distribution of all one's goods, and finally to the glory of martyrdom itself. For when he had enumerated all kinds of gifts and had said: "To one is given by the Spirit the word of wisdom, to another the word of knowledge, to another faith, to another the gift of healing, to another the working of miracles, etc.:"[863] when he was going to speak about love notice how in a few words he put it before all gifts: "And yet," he says, "I show unto you a still more excellent way."[864] By which it is clearly shown that the height of perfection and blessedness does not consist in the performance of those wonderful works but in the purity of love. And this not without good reason. For all those things are to pass away and be destroyed, but love is to abide for ever. And so we have never found that those works and signs were affected by our fathers: nay, rather when they did possess them by the grace of the Holy Spirit they would never use them, unless perhaps extreme and unavoidable necessity drove them to do so.

NOTES:
[863] 1 Cor. 12:8-10.
[864] 1 Cor. 12:31.

CHAPTER III.

Of a dead man raised to life by Abbot Macarius.

AS also we remember that a dead man was raised to life by Abbot Macarius who was the first to find a home in the desert of Scete.[865] For when a certain heretic who followed the error of Eunomius was trying by dialectic subtlety to destroy the simplicity of the Catholic faith, and had already deceived a large number of men, the blessed Macarius was asked by some Catholics, who were terribly disturbed by the horror of such an upset, to set free the simple folk of all Egypt from the peril of infidelity, and came for this purpose. And when the heretic had approached him with his dialectic art, and wanted to drag him away in his ignorance to the thorns of Aristotle, the blessed Macarius put a stop to his chatter with apostolic brevity, saying: "the kingdom of God is not in word but in power."[866] Let us go therefore to the tombs, and let us invoke the name of the Lord over the first dead man we find, and let us, as it is written, "show our faith by our works,"[867] that by His testimony the manifest proofs of a right faith may be shown, and we may prove the clear truth not by an empty discussion of words but by the power of miracles and that judgment which cannot be deceived. And when he heard this the heretic was overwhelmed with shame before the people who were present, and pretended for the moment that he consented to the terms proposed, and promised that he would come on the morrow, but the next day when they were all in expectation who had come together with greater eagerness to the appointed place, owing to their desire for the spectacle, he was terrified by the consciousness of his want of faith, and fled away, and at once escaped out of all Egypt. And when the blessed Macarius had waited together with the people till the ninth hour, and saw that he had owing to his guilty conscience avoided him, he took the people, who had been perverted by him and went to the tombs determined upon. Now in Egypt the overflow of the river Nile has introduced this custom that, since the whole breadth of that country is covered for no small part of the year by the regular flood of waters like a great sea so that there is no means of getting about except by a passage in boats, the bodies of the dead are embalmed and stored away in cells an good height up. For the soil of that land being damp from the continual moisture prevents them from burying them. For if it receives any bodies buried in it, it is forced by the excessive inundations to cast them forth on its surface. When then the blessed Macarius had taken up his position by a most ancient corpse, he said "O man, if that heretic and son of perdition had come hither with me, and, while he was standing by, I had exclaimed and invoked the name of Christ my God, say in the presence of these who were almost perverted by his fraud, whether you would have arisen." Then he arose and replied with words of assent. And then Abbot Macarius asked him what he had formerly been when he enjoyed life here, or in what age of men he had lived, or if he had then known the name of Christ, and he replied that he had lived under kings of most ancient date, and declared that in those days he had never heard the name of Christ. To whom once more Abbot Macarius: "Sleep," said he, "in peace with the others in your own order, to be roused again by Christ in the end." All this power then and grace of his which was in him would perhaps have always been hidden, unless the needs of the whole province which was endangered, and his entire devotion to

Christ, and unfeigned love, had forced him to perform this miracle. And certainly it was not the ostentation of glory but the love of Christ and the good of all the people that wrung from him the performance of it. As the passage in the book of Kings shows us that the blessed Elijah also did, who asked that fire might descend from heaven on the sacrifices laid on the pyre, for this reason that he might set free the faith of the whole people which was endangered by the tricks of the false prophets.

NOTES:

[865] This was the "Egyptian," not the "Alexandrian" Macarius. See the note on the Institutes, V. xli. The story is also given by Rufinus, History of the Monks, c. xxviii.; as well as Sozomen, H. E. III. xiv., and by both of these writers is expressly ascribed to the Egyptian Macarius.

[866] 1 Cor. 4:20.

[867] Cf. S. James 2:14.

CHAPTER IV.

Of the miracle which Abbot Abraham wrought on the breasts of a woman.

WHY also need I mention the acts of Abbot Abraham,[868] who was surnamed `aplous, i.e., the simple, from the simplicity of his life and his innocence. This man when he had gone from the desert to Egypt for the harvest in the season of Quinquagesima[869] was pestered with tears and prayers by a woman who brought her little child, already pining away and half dead from lack of milk; he gave her a cup of water to drink signed with the sign of the cross; and when she had drunk it at once most marvellously her breasts that had been till then utterly dry flowed with a copious abundance of milk.

NOTES:

[868] Possibly the same person as the author of Conference xxiv., but nothing further appears to be known of him.

[869] I.e., the fifty days from Easter to Whitsuntide; cf. the note on the Institutes, II. xviii.

CHAPTER V.

Of the cure of a lame man which the same saint wrought.

OR when the same man as he went to a village was surrounded by mocking crowds, who sneered at him and showed him a man who was for many years deprived of the power of walking from a contracted knee, and crawled from a weakness of long standing, they tempted him and said, "Show us, father Abraham, if you are the servant of God, and restore this man to his former health, that we may believe that the name of Christ, whom you worship, is not vain." Then he at once invoked the name of Christ, and stooped down and laid hold of the man's withered foot and pulled it. And immediately at his touch the dried and bent knee was straightened, and he got back the use of his legs, which he had forgotten how to use in his long years of weakness, and went away rejoicing.

CHAPTER VI.

How the merits of each man should not be judged by his miracles.

AND so these men gave no credit to themselves for their power of working such wonders, because they confessed that they were done not by their own merits but by the compassion of the Lord and with the words of the Apostle they refused the human honour offered out of admiration for their miracles: "Men and brethren, why marvel ye at this, or why look ye on us as though by our own power or holiness we had caused this man to walk."[870] Nor did they think that any one should be renowned for the gifts and marvels of God, but rather for the fruits of his own good deeds, which are brought about by the efforts of his mind and the power of his works. For often, as was said above, men of corrupt minds, reprobate concerning the truth, both cast out devils and perform the greatest miracles in the name of the Lord. Of whom when the Apostles complained and said: "Master, we saw one casting out devils in Thy name, and we forbade him because he followeth not with us," though for the present Christ replied to them "Forbid him not, for he that is not against you is for you,"[871] still when they say at the end: "Lord, Lord, have we not in Thy name prophesied, and in Thy name cast out devils, and in Thy name done many mighty works?" He testifies that then He will answer: "I never knew you: depart from me, ye workers of iniquity."[872] And therefore He actually warns those, to whom He Himself has given this glory of miracles and mighty works because of their holiness, that they be not puffed up by them, saying: "Rejoice not because the devils are subject to you, but rejoice rather because your names are written in heaven." [873]

NOTES:
[870] Acts 3:12.
[871] S. Luke 9:49, 50.
[872] S. Matt. 7:22, 23.
[873] **S. Luke 10:20.**

CHAPTER VII.

How the excellence of gifts consists not in miracles but in humility.

FINALLY the Author Himself of all miracles and mighty works, when He called His disciples to learn His teaching, clearly showed what those true and specially chosen followers ought chiefly to learn from Him, saying: "Come and learn of Me," not chiefly to cast out devils by the power of heaven, not to cleanse the lepers, not to give sight to the blind, not to raise the dead: for even though I do these things by some of My servants, yet man's estate cannot insert itself into the praises of God, nor can a minister and servant gather hereby any portion for himself there where is the glory of Deity alone. But do ye, says He, learn this of Me, "for I am meek and lowly of heart."[874] For this it is which it is possible for all men generally to learn and practise, but the working of miracles and signs is not always necessary, nor good for all, nor granted to all. Humility therefore is the mistress of all virtues, it is the surest foundation of the heavenly building, it is the special and splendid gift of the Saviour. For he can perform all the miracles which Christ wrought, without danger of being puffed up, who follows the gentle Lord not in the grandeur of His miracles, but in the virtues of patience and humility. But he who aims at commanding unclean spirits, or bestowing gifts of healing, or showing some wonderful miracle to the people, even though when he is showing off he invokes the name of Christ, yet he is far from Christ, because in his pride of heart he does not follow his humble Teacher.

For when He was returning to the Father, He prepared, so to speak, His will and left this to His disciples: "A new commandment," said He, "give I unto you that ye love one another; as I have loved you, so do ye also love one another:" and at once He subjoined: "By this shall all men know that ye are My disciples, if ye have love to one another."[875] He says not: "if ye do signs and miracles in the same way," but "if ye have love to one another;" and this it is certain that none but the meek and humble can keep. Wherefore our predecessors never reckoned those as good monks or free from the fault of vainglory, who professed themselves exorcists among men, and proclaimed with boastful ostentation among admiring crowds the grace which they had either obtained or which they claimed. But in vain, for "he who trusteth in lies feedeth the winds: and the same runneth after birds that fly away."[876] For without doubt that will happen to them which we find in Proverbs: "As the winds and clouds and rain are very clear so are these who boast of a fictitious gift."[877] And so if any one does any of these things in our presence, he ought to meet with commendation from us not from admiration of his miracles, but from the beauty of his life, nor should we ask whether the devils are subject to him, but whether he possesses those features of love which the Apostle describes.

NOTES:
[874] S. Matt. 11:28, 29.
[875] S. John 13:34, 35.
[876] Prov. 10:4.
[877] Prov. 35:14.

CHAPTER VIII.

How it is more wonderful to have cast out one's faults from one's self than devils from another.

AND in truth it is a greater miracle to root out from one's own flesh the incentives to wantonness than to cast out unclean spirits from the bodies of others, and it is a grander sign to restrain the fierce passions of anger by the virtue of patience than to command the powers of the air, and it is a greater thing to have shut out the devouring pangs of gloominess from one's own heart than to have expelled the sickness of another and the fever of his body. Finally it is in many ways a grander

345

virtue and a more splendid achievement to cure the weaknesses of one's own soul than those of the body of another. For just as the soul is higher than the flesh, so is its salvation of more importance, and as its nature is more precious and excellent, so is its destruction more grievous and dangerous.

CHAPTER IX.

How uprightness of life is of more importance than the working of miracles.

AND of those cures it was said to the blessed Apostles: "Rejoice not that the devils are subject to you."[878] For this was wrought not by their own power, but by the might of the name invoked. And therefore they are warned not to presume to claim for themselves any blessedness or glory on this account as it was done simply by the power and might of God, but only on account of the inward purity of their life and heart, for which it was vouchsafed to them to have their names written in heaven.

NOTES:
[878] S. Luke 10:20.

CHAPTER X.

A revelation on the trial of perfect chastity.

AND to prove this that we have said both by the testimony of the ancients and divine oracles, we had better bring forward in his own words and experience what the blessed Paphnutius[879] felt on the subject of admiration of miracles and the grace of purity, or rather what he learnt from the revelation of an angel. For this man had been famous for many years for his signal strictness so that he fancied that he was completely free from the snares of carnal concupiscence because he felt himself superior to all the attacks of the demons with whom he had fought openly and for a long while; and when some holy men had come to him, he was preparing for them a porridge of lentiles which they call Athera,[880] and his hand, as it happened, was burnt in the oven, by a flame that darted up. And when this happened he was much mortified and began silently to consider with himself, and ask why was not the fire at peace with me, when my more serious contests with demons have ceased? or how will that unquenchable fire which searches out the deserts of all pass me by in that dread day of judgment, and fail to detain me, if this trivial temporal fire from without has not spared me? And as he was troubled by thoughts of this kind and vexation a sudden sleep overcame him and an angel of the Lord came to him and said: "Paphnutius, why are you vexed because that earthly fire is not yet at peace with you, while there still remains in your members some disturbance of carnal motions that is not completely removed? For as long as the roots of this flourish within you, they will not suffer that material fire to be at peace with you. And certainly you could not feel it harmless unless you found by such proofs as these that all these internal motions within you were destroyed. Go, take a naked and most beautiful virgin, and if while you hold her you find that the peace of your heart remains steadfast, and that carnal heat is still and quiet within you, then the touch of this visible flame also shall pass over you gently and without harming you as it did over the three children in Babylon." And so the Elder was impressed by this revelation and did not try the dangers of the experiment divinely shown to him, but asked his own conscience and examined the purity of his heart; and, guessing that the weight of purity was not yet sufficient to outweigh the force of this trial, it is no wonder, said he, if when the battles with unclean spirits come upon me, I still feel the flames of the fire, which I used to think of less importance than the savage attacks of demons, still raging against me. Since it is a greater virtue and a grander grace to extinguish the inward lust of the flesh than by the sign of the Lord[881] and the power of the might of the Most High to subdue the wicked demons which rush upon one from without, or to drive them by invoking the Divine name from the bodies which they have possessed. So far Abbot Nesteros, finishing the account of the true working of the gifts of grace accompanied us to the cell of the Elder Joseph which was nearly six miles distant from his, as we were eager for instruction in his doctrine.

NOTES:
[879] Cf. the note on Conferences III. i.
[880] Athera. This is noticed by Pliny (Hist. Nat. xxii. 25, 57, S: 121) as the Egyptian name for a decoction made from grain.
[881] I.e., the sign of the cross.

CONFERENCE 16.

The First Conference of Abbot Joseph
on Friendship

CHAPTER I.

What Abbot Joseph asked us in the first instance.

THE blessed Joseph,[882] whose instructions and precepts are now to be set forth, and who was one of the three whom we mentioned in the first Conference,[883] belonged to a most illustrious family, and was the chief man of his city in Egypt, which was named Thmuis,[884] and so was carefully trained in the eloquence of Greece as well as Egypt, so that he could talk admirably with us or with those who were utterly ignorant of Egyptian, not as the others did through an interpreter, but in his own person. And when he found that we were anxious for instruction from him, he first inquired whether we were own brothers, and when he heard that we were united in a tie of spiritual and not carnal brotherhood, and that from the first commencement of our renunciation of the world we had always been joined together in an unbroken bond as well in our travels, which we had both undertaken for the sake of spiritual service, as also in the pursuits of the monastery, he began his discourse as follows.

NOTES:
[882] Nothing further appears to be known of this Joseph than what Cassian here states.
[883] Viz., the first of the Second Part of the Conferences, i.e., Conference XI.
[884] See [note 188, above] on Conference XIV. c. iv.

CHAPTER II.

Discourse of the same elder on the untrustworthy sort of friendship.

THERE are many kinds of friendship and companionship which unite men in very different ways in the bonds of love. For some a previous recommendation makes to enter upon an intercourse first of acquaintance and afterwards even of friendship. In the case of others some bargain or an agreement to give and take something has joined them in the bonds of love. Others a similarity and union of business or science or art or study has united in the chain of friendship, by which even fierce souls become kindly disposed to each other, so that those, who in forests and mountains delight in robbery and revel in human bloodshed, embrace and cherish the partners of their crimes. But there is another kind of love, where the union is from the instincts of nature and the laws of consanguinity, whereby those of the same tribe, wives and parents, and brothers and children are naturally preferred to others, a thing which we find is the case not only with mankind but with all birds and beasts. For at the prompting of a natural instinct they protect and defend their offspring and their young ones so that often they are not afraid to expose themselves to danger and death for their sakes. Indeed those kinds of beasts and serpents and birds, which are cut off and separated from all others by their intolerable ferocity or deadly poison, as basilisks, unicorns and vultures, though by their very look they are said to be dangerous to every one, yet among themselves they remain peaceful and harmless owing to community of origin and fellow-feeling. But we see that all these kinds of love of which we have spoken, as they are common both to the good and bad, and to beasts and serpents, certainly cannot last for ever. For often separation of place interrupts and breaks them off, as well as forgetfulness from lapse of time, and the transaction of affairs and business and words. For as they are generally due to different kinds of connexions either of gain, or desires, or kinship, or business, so when any occasion for separation intervenes they are broken off.

CHAPTER III.

How friendship is indissoluble.

AMONG all these then there is one kind of love which is indissoluble, where the union is owing not to the favour of a recommendation, or some great kindness or gifts, or the reason of some bargain, or the necessities of nature, but simply to similarity of virtue. This, I say, is what is broken by no chances, what no interval of time or space can sever or destroy, and what even death itself cannot part. This is true and unbroken love which grows by means of the double perfection and goodness of friends, and which, when once its bonds have been entered, no difference of liking and no disturbing opposition of wishes can sever. But we have known many set on this purpose, who though they had been joined together in companionship out of their burning love for Christ, yet could not maintain it continually and unbrokenly, because although they relied on a good beginning for their friendship, yet they did not with one and the same zeal maintain the purpose on which they had entered, and so there was between them a sort of love only for a while, for it was not maintained by the goodness of both alike, but by the patience of the one party, and so although it is held to by the one with unwearied heroism, yet it is sure to be broken by the pettiness of the other. For the infirmities of those who are somewhat cold in seeking the healthy condition of perfection, however patiently they may be borne by the strong, are yet not put up with by those who are weaker themselves. For they have implanted within them causes of disturbance which do not allow them to be at ease, just as those, who are affected by bodily weakness, generally impute the delicacy of their stomach and weak health to the carelessness of their cooks and servants, and however carefully their attendants may serve them, yet nevertheless they ascribe the grounds of their upset to those who are in good health, as they do not see that they are really due to the failure of their own health. Wherefore this, as we said, is the sure and indissoluble union of friendship, where the tie consists only in likeness in goodness. For "the Lord maketh men to be of one mind in an house."[885] And therefore love can only continue undisturbed in those in whom there is but one purpose and mind to will and to refuse the same things. And if you also wish to keep this unbroken, you must be careful that having first got rid of your faults, you mortify your own desires, and with united zeal and purpose diligently fulfil that in which the prophet specially delights: "Behold how good and joyful a thing it is for brethren to dwell together in unity."[886] Which should be taken of unity of spirit rather than of place. For it is of no use for those who differ in character and purpose to be united in one dwelling, nor is it an hindrance for those who are grounded on equal goodness to be separated by distance of place. For with God the union of character, not of place, joins brethren together in a common dwelling, nor can unruffled peace ever be maintained where difference of will appears.

NOTES:
[885] Ps. 67 (68):7.
[886] Ps. 132 (133):1.

CHAPTER IV.

A question whether anything that is really useful should be performed even against a brother's wish.

GERMANUS: What then? If when one party wants to do something which he sees is useful and profitable according to the mind of God, the other does not give his consent, ought it to be performed even against the wish of the brother, or should it be thrown on one side as he wants?

CHAPTER V.

The answer, how a lasting friendship can only exist among those who are perfect.

JOSEPH: For this reason we said that the full and perfect grace of friendship can only last among those who are perfect and of equal goodness, whose likemindedness and common purpose allows them either never, or at any rate hardly ever, to disagree, or to differ in those matters which concern their progress in the spiritual life. But if they begin to get hot with eager disputes, it is clear that they have never been at one in accordance with the rule which we gave above. But be-

351

cause no one can start from perfection except one who has begun from the very foundation, and your inquiring is not with regard to its greatness, but as to how you can attain to it, I think it well to explain to you, in a few words, the rule for it and the sort of path along which your steps should be directed, that you may be able more easily to secure the blessing of patience and peace.

CHAPTER VI.

By what means union can be preserved unbroken.

THE first foundation then, of true friendship consists in contempt for worldly substance and scorn for all things that we possess. For it is utterly wrong and unjustifiable if, after the vanity of the world and all that is in it has been renounced, whatever miserable furniture remains is more regarded than what is most valuable; viz., the love of a brother. The second is for each man so to prune his own wishes that he may not imagine himself to be a wise and experienced person, and so prefer his own opinions to those of his neighbour. The third is for him to recognize that everything, even what he deems useful and necessary, must come after the blessing of love and peace. The fourth for him to realize that he should never be angry for any reason good or bad. The fifth for him to try to cure any wrath which a brother may have conceived against him however unreasonably, in the same way that he would cure his own, knowing that the vexation of another is equally bad for him, as if he himself were stirred against another, unless he removes it, to the best of his ability, from his brother's mind. The last is what is undoubtedly generally decisive in regard to all faults; viz., that he should realize daily that he is to pass away from this world; as the realization of this not only permits no vexation to linger in the heart, but also represses all the motions of lusts and sins of all kinds. Whoever then has got hold of this, can neither suffer nor be the cause of bitter wrath and discord. But when this fails, as soon as he who is jealous of love has little by little infused the poison of vexation in the hearts of friends, it is certain that owing to frequent quarrels love will gradually grow cool, and at sometime or other he will part the hearts of the lovers, that have been for a long while exasperated. For if one is walking along the course previously marked out, how can he ever differ from his friend, for if he claims nothing for himself, he entirely cuts off the first cause of quarrel (which generally springs from trivial things and most unimportant matters), as he observes to the best of his power what we read in the Acts of the Apostles on the unity of believers: "But the multitude of believers was of one heart and soul; neither did any of them say that any of the things which he possessed was his own, but they had all things common."[887] Then how can any seeds of discussion arise from him who serves not his own but his brother's will, and becomes a follower of his Lord and Master, who speaking in the character[888] of man which He had taken, said: "I am not come to do Mine own will, but the will of Him that sent Me"?[889] But how can he arouse any incitement to contention, who has determined to trust not so much to his own judgment as to his brother's decision, on his own intelligence and meaning, in accordance with his will either approving or disapproving his discoveries, and fulfilling in the humility of a pious heart these words from the Gospel: "Nevertheless, not as I will, but as Thou wilt."[890] Or in what way will he admit anything which grieves the brother, who thinks that nothing is more precious than the blessing of peace, and never forgets these words of the Lord: "By this shall all men know that ye are My disciples, that ye love one another;"[891] for by this, as by a special mark, Christ willed that the flock of His sheep should be known in this world, and be separated from all others by this stamp, so to speak? But on what grounds will he endure either to admit the rancour of vexation in himself or for it to remain in another, if his firm decision is that there cannot be any good ground for anger, as it is dangerous and wrong, and that when his broker is angry with him he cannot pray, in just the same way as when he himself is angry with his brother, as he ever keeps in an humble heart these words of our Lord and Saviour: "If thou bring thy gift to the altar and there remember that thy brother hath aught against thee, leave there thy gift at the altar, and go thy way; first be reconciled to thy brother, and then come and offer thy gift."[892] For it will be of no use for you to declare that you are not angry, and to believe that you are fulfilling the command which says: "Let not the sun go down upon thy wrath;" and: "Whosoever is angry with his brother, shall be in danger of the judgment,"[893] if you are with obstinate heart disregarding the vexation of another which you could smooth down by kindness on your part. For in the same way you will be punished for violating the Lord's command. For He who said that you should not be angry with another, said also that you should not disregard the vexations of another, for it makes no difference in the sight of God, "Who willeth all men to be saved,"[894] whether you destroy yourself or someone else.

Since the death of any one is equally a loss to God, and at the same time it is equally a gain to him to whom all destruction is delightful, whether it is acquired by your death or by the death of your brother. Lastly, how can he retain even the least vexation with his brother, who realizes daily that he is presently to depart from this world?

NOTES:
887 Acts 4:32.
888 Ex persona. See note on IX. xxxiv.
889 S. John 6:38.
890 S. Matt. 26:39.
891 S. John 13:35.
892 S. Matt. 5:23, 24.
893 Eph. 4:26; S. Matt. 5:22.
894 1 Tim. 2:4.

CHAPTER VII.

How nothing should be put before love, or after anger.

AS then nothing should be put before love, so on the other hand nothing should be put below rage and anger. For all things, however useful and necessary they seem, should yet be disregarded that disturbing anger may be avoided, and all things even which we think are unfortunate should be undertaken and endured that the calm of love and peace may be preserved unimpaired, because we should reckon nothing more damaging than anger and vexation, and nothing more advantageous than love.

CHAPTER VIII.

On what grounds a dispute can arise among spiritual persons.

FOR as our enemy separates brethren who are still weak and carnal by a sudden burst of rage on account of some trifling and earthly matter, so he sows the seeds of discord even between spiritual persons, on the ground of some difference of thoughts, from which certainly those contentions and strifes about words, which the Apostle condemns, for the most part arise: whereby consequently our spiteful and malignant enemy sows discord between brethren who were of one mind. For these words of wise Solomon are true: "Contention breeds hatred: but friendship will be a defence to all who do not strive." [895]

NOTES:
[895] Prov. 10:12.

CHAPTER IX.

How to get rid even of spiritual grounds of discord.

WHEREFORE for the preservation of lasting and unbroken love, it is of no use to have removed the first ground of discord, which generally arises from frail and earthly things, or to have disregarded all carnal things, and to have permitted to our brethren an unrestricted share in everything which our needs require, unless too we cut off in like manner the second, which generally arises under the guise of spiritual feelings; and unless we gain in everything humble thoughts and harmonious wills.

CHAPTER X.

On the best tests of truth.

FOR I remember, that when my youthful age suggested to me to cling to a partner, thoughts of this sort often mingled with our moral training and the Holy Scriptures, so that we fancied that nothing could be truer or more reasonable: but when we came together and began to produce our ideas, in the general discussion which was held, some things were first noted by the others as false and dangerous, and then presently were condemned and pronounced by common consent to be injurious; though before they had seemed to shine as if with a light infused by the devil, so that they would easily have caused discord, had not the charge of the Elders, observed like some divine oracle, restrained us from all strife, that charge; namely, whereby it was ordered by them almost with the force of a law, that neither of us should trust to his own judgments more than his brother's, if he wanted never to be deceived by the craft of the devil.

CHAPTER XI.

How it is impossible for one who trusts to his own judgment to escape being deceived by the devil's illusions.

FOR often it has been proved that what the Apostle says really takes place. "For Satan himself transforms himself into an angel of light,"[896] so that he deceitfully sheds abroad a confusing and foul obscuration of the thoughts instead of the true light of knowledge. And unless these thoughts are received in a humble and gentle heart, and kept for the consideration of some more experienced brother or approved Elder, and when thoroughly sifted by their judgment, either rejected or admitted by us, we shall be sure to venerate in our thoughts an angel of darkness instead of an angel of light, and be smitten with a grievous destruction: an injury which it is impossible for any one to avoid who trusts in his own judgment, unless he becomes a lover and follower of true humility and with all contrition of heart fulfils what the Apostle chiefly prays for: "If then there be any consolation in Christ, if any comfort of love, if any bowels of compassion, fulfil ye my joy, that you be of one mind, having the same love, being of one accord, doing nothing by contention, neither by vainglory; but in humility each esteeming others better than themselves;" and this: "in honour preferring one another,"[897] that each may think more of the knowledge and holiness of his partner, and hold that the better part of true discretion is to be found in the judgment of another rather than in his own.

CHAPTER XII.

Why inferiors should not be despised in Conference.

FOR it often happens either by an illusion of the devil or by the occurrence of a human mistake (by which every man in this life is liable to be deceived) that sometimes one who is keener in intellect and more learned, gets some wrong notion in his head, while he who is duller in wits and of less worth, conceives the matter better and more truly. And therefore no one, however learned he may be, should persuade himself in his empty vanity that he cannot require conference with another. For even if no deception of the devil blinds his judgment, yet he cannot avoid the noxious snares of pride and conceit. For who can arrogate this to himself without great danger, when the chosen vessel in whom, as he maintained, Christ Himself spoke, declares that he went up to Jerusalem simply and solely for this reason, that he might in a secret discussion confer with his fellow-Apostles on the gospel which he preached to the gentiles by the revelation and co-operation of the Lord? By which fact we are shown that we ought not only by these precepts to preserve unanimity and harmony, but that we need not fear any crafts of the devil opposing us, or snares of his illusions.

NOTES:
[896] 2 Cor. 11:14.
[897] Phil. 2:1-3; Rom. 12:10.

CHAPTER XIII.

How love does not only belong to God but is God.

FINALLY so highly is the virtue of love extolled that the blessed Apostle John declares that it not only belongs to God but that it is God, saying: "God is love: he therefore that abideth in love, abideth in God, and God in him."[898] For so far do we see that it is divine, that we find that what the Apostle says is plainly a living truth in us: "For the love of God is shed abroad in our hearts by the Holy Ghost Who dwelleth in us."[899] For it is the same thing as if he said that God is shed abroad

357

in our hearts by the Holy Ghost Who dwelleth in us: who also, when we know not what we should pray for, "makes intercession for us with groanings that cannot be uttered: But He that searcheth the hearts knoweth what the Spirit desireth, for He asketh for the saints according to God." [900]

NOTES:
[898] 1 John 4:16.
[899] Rom. 5:5.
[900] Rom. 8:26, 27.

CHAPTER XIV.

On the different grades of love.

IT is possible then for all to show that love which is called agaph, of which the blessed Apostle says: "While therefore we have time, let us do good unto all men, but specially to them that are of the household of faith."[901] And this should be shown to all men in general to such an extent that we are actually commanded by our Lord to yield it to our enemies, for He says: "Love your enemies."[902] But diaqesis, i.e., affection is shown to but a few and those who are united to us by kindred dispositions or by a tie of goodness; though indeed affection seems to have many degrees of difference. For in one way we love our parents, in another our wives, in another our brothers, in another our children, and there is a wide difference in regard to the claims of these feelings of affection, nor is the love of parents towards their children always equal. As is shown by the case of the patriarch Jacob, who, though he was the father of twelve sons and loved them all with a father's love, yet loved Joseph with deeper affection, as Scripture clearly shows: "But his brethren envied him, because his father loved him;"[903] evidently not that that good man his father failed in greatly loving the rest of his children, but that in his affection he clung to this one, because he was a type of the Lord, more tenderly and indulgently. This also, we read, was very clearly shown in the case of John the Evangelist, where these words are used of him: "that disciple whom Jesus loved,"[904] though certainly He embraced all the other eleven, whom He had chosen in the same way, with His special love, as this He shows also by the witness of the gospel, where He says: "As I have loved you, so do ye also love one another;" of whom elsewhere also it is said: "Loving His own who were in the world, He loved them even to the end."[905] But this love of one in particular did not indicate any coldness in love for the rest of the disciples, but only a fuller and more abundant love towards the one, which his prerogative of virginity and the purity of his flesh bestowed upon him. And therefore it is marked by exceptional treatment, as being something more sublime, because no hateful comparison with others, but a richer grace of superabundant love singled it out. Something of this sort too we have in the character of the bride in the Song of Songs, where she says: "Set in order love in me."[906] For this is true love set in order, which, while it hates no one, yet loves some still more by reason of their deserving it, and which, while it loves all in general, singles out for itself some from those, whom it may embrace with a special affection, and again among those, who are the special and chief objects of its love, singles out some who are preferred to others in affection.

NOTES:
[901] Gal. 6:10.
[902] S. Matt. 5:44.
[903] Gen. 37:4.
[904] S. John 13:23.
[905] S. John 13:34, 1.
[906] Cant. 2:4.

CHAPTER XV.

Of those who only increase their own or their brother's grievances by hiding them.

ON the other hand we know (and O! would that we did not know) some of the brethren who are so hard and obstinate, that when they know that their own feelings are aroused against their brother, or that their brother's are against them, in order to conceal their vexation of mind, which is caused by indignation at the grievance of one or the other, go apart from those whom they ought to smooth down by humbly making up to them and talking with them; and begin to sing some verses of the Psalms. And these while they fancy that they are softening the bitter thoughts which have arisen in their heart, increase by their insolent conduct what they could have got rid of at once if they had been willing to show more care and humility, for a well-timed expression of regret would cure their own feelings and soften their brother's heart. For by that plan they nourish and cherish the sin of meanness or rather of pride, instead of stamping out all inducement to quarrelling, and they forget the charge of the Lord which says: "Whosoever is angry with his brother, is in danger of the judgment;" and: "if thou remember that thy brother hath aught against thee, leave there thy gift before the altar, and go thy way, first be reconciled to thy brother, and then come and offer thy gift." [907]

NOTES:
[907] S. Matt. 5:22-24.

CHAPTER XVI.

How it is that, if our brother has any grudge against us, the gifts of our prayers are rejected by the Lord.

SO far therefore is our Lord anxious that we should not disregard the vexation of another that He does not accept our offerings if our brother has anything against us, i.e., He does not allow prayers to be offered by us to Him until by speedy amends we remove from his (our brother's) mind the vexation which he whether rightly or wrongly feels. For He does not say: "if thy brother hath a true ground for complaint against thee leave thy gift at the altar, and go thy way, first be reconciled to him;" but He says: "if thou remember that thy brother hath aught against thee," i.e., if there be anything however trivial or small, owing to which your brother's anger is roused against you, and this comes back to your recollection by a sudden remembrance, you must know that you ought not to offer the spiritual gift of your prayers until by kindly amends you have removed from your brother's heart the vexation arising from whatever cause. If then the words of the Gospel bid us make satisfaction to those who are angry for past and utterly trivial grounds of quarrel, and those which have arisen from the slightest causes, what will become of us wretches who with obstinate hypocrisy disregard more recent grounds of offence, and those of the utmost importance, and due to our own faults; and being puffed up with the devil's own pride, as we are ashamed to humble ourselves, deny that we are the cause of our brother's vexation and in a spirit of rebellion disdaining to be subject to the Lord's commands, contend that they never ought to be observed and never can be fulfilled? And so it comes to pass that as we make up our minds that He has commanded things which are impossible and unsuitable, we become, to use the Apostle's expression, "not doers but judges of the law." [908]

NOTES:
[908] S. James 4:11.

CHAPTER XVII.

Of those who hold that patience should be shown to worldly people rather than to the brethren.

THIS too should be bitterly lamented; namely, that some of the brethren, when angered by some reproachful words, if they are besieged by the prayers of some one else who wants to smooth them down, when they hear that vexation ought not to be admitted or retained against a brother, according to what is written: "Whoever is angry with his brother is in danger of the judgment;" and: "Let not the sun go down upon your wrath,"[909] instantly assert that if a heathen or one living in the world had said or done this, it rightly ought to be endured. But who could stand a brother who was accessory to so great a fault, or gave utterance to so insolent a reproach with his lips! As if patience were to be shown only to unbelievers and blasphemers, and not to all in general, or as if anger should be reckoned as bad when it is against a heathen, but good when it is against a brother; whereas certainly the obstinate rage of an angry soul brings about the same injury to one's self whoever may be the subject against whom it is aroused. But how terribly obstinate, aye and senseless is it for them, owing to the stupidity of their dull mind, not to be able to discern the meaning of these words, for it is not said: "Every one who is angry with a stranger shall be in danger of the judgment," which might perhaps according to their interpretation except those who are partners of our faith and life, but the word of the Gospel most significantly expresses it by saying: "Every one who is angry with his brother, shall be in danger of the judgment." And so though we ought according to the rule of truth to regard every man as a brother, yet in this passage one of the faithful and a partaker of our mode of life is denoted by the title of brother rather than a heathen.

361

909 Eph. 4:26.

CHAPTER XVIII.

Of those who pretend to patience but excite their brethren to anger by their silence.

BUT what sort of a thing is this, that sometimes we fancy that we are patient because when provoked we scorn to answer, but by sullen silence or scornful motions and gestures so mock at our angry brothers that by our silent looks we provoke them to anger more than angry reproaches would have excited them, meanwhile thinking that we are in no way guilty before God, because we have let nothing fall from our lips which could brand us or condemn us in the judgment of men. As if in the sight of God mere words, and not mainly the will was called in fault, and as if only the actual deed of sin, and not also the wish and purpose, was reckoned as wrong; or as if it would be asked in the judgment only what each one had done and not what he also purposed to do. For it is not only the character of the anger roused, but also the purpose of the man who provokes it which is bad, and therefore the true scrutiny of our judge will ask, not how the quarrel was stirred up but by whose fault it arose: for the purpose of the sin, and not the way in which the fault is committed must be taken into account. For what does it matter whether a man kills a brother with a sword by himself, or drives him to death by some fraud, when it is clear that he is killed by his wiles and crime? As if it were enough not to have pushed a blind man down with one's own hand, though he is equally guilty who scorned to save him, when it was in his power, when fallen and on the point of tumbling into the ditch: or as if he alone were guilty who had caught a man with the hand, and not also the one who had prepared and set the trap for him, or who would not set him free when he might have done so. So then it is of no good to hold one's tongue, if we impose silence upon ourselves for this reason that by our silence we may do what would have been done by an outcry on our part, simulating certain gestures by which he whom we ought to have cured, may be made still more angry, while we are commended for all this, to his loss and damage: as if a man were not for this very reason the more guilty, because he tried to get glory for himself out of his brother's fall. For such a silence will be equally bad for both because while it increases the vexation in the heart of another, so it prevents it from being removed from one's own: and against such persons the prophet's curse is with good reason directed: "Woe to him that giveth drink to his friend, and presenteth his gall, and maketh him drunk, that he may behold his nakedness. He is filled with shame instead of glory."[910] And this too which is said of such people by another: "For every brother will utterly supplant, and every friend will walk deceitfully. And a man shall mock his brother, and they will not speak the truth, for they have bent their tongue like a bow for lies and not for truth."[911] But often a feigned patience excites to anger more keenly than words, and, a spiteful silence exceeds the most awful insults in words, and the wounds of enemies are more easily borne than the deceitful blandishment of mockers, of which it is well said by the prophet: "Their words are smoother than oil, and yet they are darts:" and elsewhere "the words of the crafty are soft: but they smite within the belly:" to which this also may be finely applied: "With the mouth he speaks peace to his friend, but secretly he layeth snares for him;" with which however the deceiver is rather deceived, for "if a man prepares a net before his friend, it surrounds his own feet;" and: "if a man digs a pit for his neighbour, he shall fall into it himself."[912] Lastly when a great multitude had come with swords and staves to take the Lord, none of the murderers of the author of our life stood forth as more cruel than he who advanced before them all with a counterfeit respect and salutation and offered a kiss of feigned love; to whom the Lord said: "Judas, betrayest thou the Son of man with a kiss?"[913] i.e., the bitterness of thy persecution and hatred has taken as a cloke this which expresses the sweetness of true love. More openly too and more energetically does He emphasize the force of this grief by the prophet, saying: "For if mine enemy had cursed me, I would have borne it: and if he who hated me had spoken great things against me, I would have hid myself from him. But it was thou, a man of one mind, my guide, and my familiar friend: who didst take sweet meats together with me: in the house of God we walked with consent." [914]

NOTES:
[910] Hab. 2:15, 16.
[911] Jer. 9:4, 5.
[912] Ps. 54 (55):22; Prov. 26:22; Jer. 9:8; Prov. 29:5; 26:27.
[913] S. Luke 22:48.
[914] Ps. 54 (55):13-15.

CHAPTER XIX.

Of those who fast out of rage.

THERE is too another evil sort of vexation which would not be worth mentioning were it not that we know it is allowed by some of the brethren who, when they have been vexed or enraged actually abstain persistently from food, so that (a thing which we cannot mention without shame) those who when they are calm declare that they cannot possibly put off their refreshment to the sixth or at most the ninth hour, when they are filled with vexation and rage do not feel fasts even for two days, and support themselves, when exhausted by such abstinence, by a surfeit of anger. Wherein they are plainly guilty of the sin of sacrilege, as out of the devil's own rage they endure fasts which ought specially to be offered to God alone out of desire for humiliation of heart and purification from sin: which is much the same as if they were to offer prayers and sacrifices not to God but to devils, and so be worthy of hearing this rebuke of Moses: "They sacrificed to devils and not to God; to gods whom they knew not." [915]

NOTES:
[915] Deut. 32:17.

CHAPTER XX.

Of the feigned patience of some who offer the other cheek to be smitten.

WE are not ignorant also of another kind of insanity, which we find in some of the brethren under colour of a counterfeit patience, as in this case it is not enough to have stirred up quarrels unless they incite them with irritating words so as to get themselves smitten, and when they have been touched by the slightest blow, at once they offer another part of their body to be smitten, as if in this way they could fulfil to perfection that command which says: "If a man smite thee on the right cheek, offer him the other also;"[916] while they totally ignore the meaning and purpose of the passage. For they fancy that they are practising evangelical patience through the sin of anger, for the utter eradication of which not only was the exchange of retaliation and the irritation of strife forbidden, but the command was actually given us to mitigate the wrath of the striker by the endurance of a double wrong.

NOTES:
[916] S. Matt. 5:39.

CHAPTER XXI.

A question how if we obey the commands of Christ we can fail of evangelical perfection.

GERMANUS: How can we blame one who satisfies the command of the Gospel and not only does not retaliate, but is actually prepared to have a double wrong offered to him?

CHAPTER XXII.

The answer that Christ looks not only at the action but also at the will.

JOSEPH: As was said a little before, we must look not only at the thing which is done, but also at the character of the mind and the purpose of the doer. And therefore if you weigh with a careful scrutiny of heart what is done by each man and consider with what mind it is done or from what feeling it proceeds, you will see that the virtue of patience and gentleness cannot possibly be fulfilled in the opposite spirit, i.e., that of impatience and rage. Since our Lord and Saviour, when giving us a thorough lesson on the virtue of patience and gentleness (i.e., teaching us not only to profess it with our lips, but to store it up in the inmost recesses of the soul) gave us this summary of evangelical perfection, saying: "If any one smites thee on thy right cheek, offer him the other also"[917] (doubtless the "right" cheek is mentioned, as another "right" cheek cannot be found except in the face of the inner man, so to speak), as by this He desires entirely to remove all incitement to anger from the deepest recesses of the soul, i.e., that if your external right cheek has received a blow from the striker, the inner man also humbly consenting may offer its right cheek to be smitten, sympathizing with the suffering of the outward man, and in a way submitting and subjecting its own body to wrong from the striker, that

365

the inner man may not even silently be disturbed in itself at the blows of the outward man. You see then that they are very far from evangelical perfection, which teaches that patience must be maintained, not in words but in inward tranquillity of heart, and which bids us preserve it whatever evil happens, that we may not only keep ourselves always from disturbing anger, but also by submitting to their injuries compel those, who are disturbed by their own fault, to become calm, when they have had their fill of blows; and so overcome their rage by our gentleness. And so also we shall fulfil these words of the Apostle: "Be not overcome of evil, but overcome evil with good."[918] And it is quite clear that this cannot be fulfilled by those who utter words of gentleness and humility in such a spirit and rage that they not only fail to lessen the fire of wrath which has been kindled, but rather make it blaze up the more fiercely both in their own feelings and in those of their enraged brother. But these, even if they could in some way keep calm and quiet themselves, would yet not bear any fruits of righteousness, while they claim the glory of patience on their part by their neighbour's loss, and are thus altogether removed from that Apostolic love which "Seeketh not her own,"[919] but the things of others. For it does not so desire riches in such a way as to make profit for itself out of one's neighbour's loss, nor does it wish to gain anything if it involves the spoiling of another.

NOTES:
[917] S. Matt. 5:39.
[918] Rom. 12:21.
[919] 1 Cor. 13:5.

CHAPTER XXIII.

How he is the strong and vigorous man, who yields to the will of another.

BUT you must certainly know that in general he plays a stronger part who subjects his own will to his brother's, than he who is found to be the more pertinacious in defending and clinging to his own decisions. For the former by bearing and putting up with his neighbour gains the character of being strong and vigorous, while the latter gains that of being weak and sickly, who must be pampered and petted so that sometimes for the sake of his peace and quiet it is a good thing to relax something even in necessary matters. And indeed in this he need not fancy that he has lost anything of his own perfection, though by yielding he has given up something of his intended strictness, but on the contrary he may be sure that he has gained much more by his virtue of long-suffering and patience. For this is the Apostle's command: "Ye who are strong should bear the infirmities of the weak;" and: "Bear ye one another's burdens, and so fulfil the law of Christ."[920] For a weak man will never support a weak man, nor can one who is suffering in the same way, bear or cure one in feeble health, but one who is himself not subject to infirmity brings remedies to one in weak health. For it is rightly said to him: "Physician, heal thyself." [921]

NOTES:
[920] Rom. 15:1; Gal. 6:2.
[921] S. Luke 4:23.

CHAPTER XXIV.

How the weak are harmful and cannot bear wrongs.

WE must note too the fact that the nature of the weak is always such that they are quick and ready to offer reproaches and sow the seeds of quarrels, while they themselves cannot bear to be touched by the shadow of the very slightest wrong, and while they are riding roughshod over us and flinging about wanton charges, they are not able to bear even the slightest and most trivial ones themselves. And so according to the aforesaid opinion of the Elders love cannot last firm and unbroken except among men of the same purpose and goodness. For at some time or other it is sure to be broken, however carefully it may be guarded by one of them.

CHAPTER XXV.

A question how he can be strong who does not always support the weak.

GERMANUS: How then can the patience of a perfect man be worthy of praise if it cannot always bear the weak?

CHAPTER XXVI.

The answer that the weak does not always allow himself to be borne.

JOSEPH: I did not say that the virtue and endurance of one who is strong and robust would be overcome, but that the miserable condition of the weak, encouraged by the tolerance of the perfect, and daily growing worse, is sure to give rise to reasons on account of which he himself ought no longer to be borne; or else with a shrewd suspicion that the patience of his neighbour shows up and sets off his own impatience at some time or other he chooses to make off rather than always to be borne by the magnanimity of the other. This then we think should be above all else observed by those who want to keep the affection of their companions unimpaired; viz., that first of all when provoked by any wrongs, a monk should keep not only his lips but even the depth of his breast unmoved: but if he finds that they are even slightly disturbed, let him keep himself in by entire silence, and diligently observe what the Psalmist speaks of: "I was troubled and spake nothing;" and: "I said I will take heed to thy ways that I offend not with my tongue. I have set a guard to my mouth, when the sinner stood against me. I was dumb and was humbled, and kept silence from good things;"[922] and he should not pay any heed to his present state, nor give vent to what his violent rage suggests and his exasperated mind expresses at the moment, but should dwell on the grace of past love or look forward in his mind to the renewal and restoration of peace, and contemplate it even in the very hour of rage, as if it were sure presently to return. And while he is reserving himself for the delight of harmony soon to come, he will not feel the bitterness of the present quarrel and will easily make such answers that, when love is restored, he will not be able to accuse himself as guilty or be blamed by the other; and thus he will fulfil these words of the prophet: "In wrath remember mercy." [923]

NOTES:
[922] Ps. 86 (87):5; 38 (39):2, 3.
[923] Hab. 3:2.

CHAPTER XXVII.

How anger should be repressed.

WE ought then to restrain every movement of anger and moderate it under the direction of discretion, that we may not by blind rage be hurried into that which is condemned by Solomon: "The wicked man expends all his anger, but the wise man dispenses it bit by bit,"[924] i.e., a fool is inflamed by the passion of his anger to avenge himself; but a wise man, by the ripeness of his counsel and moderation little by little diminishes it, and gets rid of it. Something of the same kind too is this which is said by the Apostle: "Not avenging yourselves, dearly beloved: but give place to wrath,"[925] i.e., do not under the compulsion of wrath proceed to vengeance, but give place to wrath, i.e., do not let your hearts be confined in the straits of impatience and cowardice so that, when a fierce storm of passion rises, you cannot endure it; but be ye enlarged in your hearts, receiving the adverse waves of anger in the wide gulf of that love which "suffereth all things, beareth all things;"[926] and so your mind will be enlarged with wide long-suffering and patience, and will have within it safe recesses of counsel, in which the foul smoke of anger will be received and be diffused and forthwith vanish away; or else the passage may be taken in this way: we give place to wrath, as often as we yield with humble and tranquil mind to the passion of another, and bow to the impatience of the passionate, as if we admitted that we deserved any kind of wrong. But those who twist the meaning of the perfection of which the Apostle speaks so as to make out that those give place to anger, who go away from a man in a rage, seem to me not to cut off but rather to foment the incitement to quarrelling, for unless a neighbour's wrath is overcome at once by amends being humbly made, a man provokes rather than avoids it by his flight. And there is something like this that Solomon says: "Be not hasty in thy spirit to be wroth, for anger reposes in the bosom of fools;" and: "Be not quick to rush into a quarrel, lest thou repent thereof at the last."[927] For he does not blame a hasty exhibition of quarrelling and anger in such a way as to praise a tardy one. In the same way too must this be taken: "A fool declares his anger in the very same hour, but a prudent man hides his shame."[928] For he does not lay it down that a shameful outburst of anger ought to be hidden by wise men in such a way that while he blames a speedy outburst of anger he fails to forbid a tardy one, as certainly, if owing to human weakness it does burst forth, he means that it should be hidden for this reason, that while for the moment it is wisely covered up, it may be destroyed forever. For the nature of anger is such that when it is given room it languishes and perishes, but if openly exhibited, it burns more and more. The hearts then should be enlarged and opened wide, lest they be confined in the narrow straits of cowardice, and be filled with the swelling surge of wrath, and so we become unable to receive what the prophet calls the "exceeding broad" commandment of God in our narrow heart, or to say with the prophet: "I have run the way of thy commandments for thou hast enlarged my heart."[929] For that long-suffering is wisdom we are taught by very clear passages of Scripture: for "a man who is long-suffering is great in prudence; but a coward is very foolish."[930] And therefore Scripture says of him who to his credit asked the gift of wisdom from the Lord: "God gave Solomon wisdom and prudence exceeding much, and largeness of heart as the sand of the sea for multitude." [931]

NOTES:
[924] Prov. 29:11.
[925] Rom. 12:19.
[926] 1 Cor. 13:7.
[927] Eccl. 7:9; Prov. 25:8.
[928] Prov. 12:16.
[929] Ps. 118 (119):32.
[930] Prov. 14:29.
[931] 1 Kings 4:29.

CHAPTER XXVIII.

How friendships entered upon by conspiracy cannot be lasting ones.

THIS too has been often proved by many experiments; viz., that those who entered the bonds of friendship from a beginning of conspiracy, cannot possibly preserve their harmony unbroken; either because they tried to keep it not out of their desire for perfection nor because of the sway of Apostolic love, but out of earthly love, and because of their wants and the bonds of their agreement; or else because that most crafty foe of ours hurries them on the more speedily to break the chains of their friendship in order that he may make them breakers of their oath. This opinion then of the most prudent men is most certainly established; viz., that true harmony and undivided union can only exist among those whose life is pure, and who are men of the same goodness and purpose.

Thus much the blessed Joseph discoursed in his spiritual talk on friendship, and fired us with a more ardent desire to preserve the love of our fellowship as a lasting one.

CONFERENCE 17.

The Second Conference of Abbot Joseph
on Making Promises

CHAPTER I.

Of the vigils which we endured.

WHEN then the previous Conference was ended, and the inter-vening silence of night as well, as we had been conducted by the holy Abbot Joseph to a separate cell for the sake of quiet, but had passed the whole night without sleep (since owing to his words a fire was raging in our hearts), we came forth from the cell and retired about a hundred yards from it and sat down in a secluded spot. And so as an opportunity was given by the shades of night for secret and familiar converse together, as we sat there Abbot Germanus groaned heavily.

CHAPTER II.

Of the anxiety of Abbot Germanus at the recollection of our promise.

WHAT are we doing? said he. For we see that we are involved in a great difficulty and are in an evil plight, as reason itself and the life of the saints is effectually teaching us what is the best thing for our progress in the spiritual life, and yet our promise given to the Elders does not allow us to choose what is helpful. For we might, by the examples of such great men, be formed for a more perfect life and aim, were it not that the terms of our promise compelled us to return at once to the monastery. But if we return thither, we shall never get another chance of coming here again. But if we stay here and choose to carry out our wishes, what becomes of the faith of the oath which we are aware that we gave to our Elders promising a speedy return; that we might be allowed to make a hasty round of the monasteries and saints of this province? And when in this state of tumult we could not make up our minds what we ought to decide on the state of our salvation we simply testified by our groans the hard fate of our condition, upbraiding the audacity of our impudence, and yet hating the shame which was natural to us, weighed down by which we could not in any other way resist the prayers of those who kept us back against our profit and purpose, except by the promise of a speedy return, as we wept indeed that we laboured under the fault of that shame, of which it is said "There is a shame that bringeth sin." [932]

NOTES:
[932] Prov. 26:11.

CHAPTER III.

My ideas on this subject.

THEN I replied: The counsel or rather the authority of the Elder to whom we ought to refer our anxieties would make a short way out of our difficulties, and whatever is decided by his verdict, may, like a divine and heavenly reply, put an end to all our troubles. And we need not have any doubt of what is given to us by the Lord through the lips of this Elder, both for the sake of his merits and for our own faith. For by His gift believers have often obtained saving counsel from unworthy people, and unbelievers from saints, as the Lord grants this either on account of the merit of those who answer, or on account of the faith of those who ask advice. And so the holy Abbot Germanus caught eagerly at these words as if I had uttered them not of myself but at the prompting of the Lord, and when we had waited a little for the coming of the Elder and the approaching hour of the nocturnal service, after we had welcomed him with the usual greeting and finished reciting the right number of Psalms and prayers, we sat down again as usual on the same mats on which we had settled ourselves to sleep.

373

CHAPTER IV.

Abbot Joseph's question and our answer on the origin of our anxiety.

THEN the venerable Joseph saw that we were in rather low spirits, and, guessing that this was not the case without reason, addressed us in these words of the patriarch Joseph: "Why are your faces sad today?"[933] to whom we answered: We are not like those bond slaves of Pharaoh who have seen a dream and there is none to interpret it, but I admit that we have passed a sleepless night and there is no one to lighten the weight of our troubles unless the Lord may remove them by your wisdom. Then he, who recalled the excellence of the patriarch both by his merits and name, said: Does not the cure of man's perplexities come from the Lord? Let them be brought forward: for the Divine Compassion is able to give a remedy for them by means of our advice according to your faith.

NOTES:
[933] Gen. 40:7.

CHAPTER V.

The explanation of Abbot Germanus why we wanted to stay in Egypt, and were drawn back to Syria.

TO THIS GERMANUS: We used to think, said he, that we should go back to our monastery abundantly filled not only with spiritual joy but also with what is profitable by the sight of your holiness, and that after our return we should follow, though with but a feeble rivalry, what we had learnt from your teaching. For this our love for our Elders led us to promise them, while we fancied that we could in some degree follow in that monastery your sublime life and doctrine. Wherefore as we thought that by this means all joy would be bestowed upon us, so on the other hand we are overwhelmed with intolerable grief, as we find that we cannot possibly obtain in this way what we know to be good for us. On both sides then we are now hemmed in. For if we want to keep our promise which we made in the presence of all the brethren in the cave where our Lord Himself shone forth from

His chamber in the Virgin's womb,[934] and which He Himself witnessed, we shall incur the greatest loss in our spiritual life. But if we ignore our promise and stay in this district, and choose to consider that oath of ours as of less importance than our perfection, we are afraid of the awful dangers of falsehood and perjury. But not even by this plan can we lighten our burdens; viz., by fulfilling the terms of our oath by a very hasty return, and then coming back again as quickly as possible to these parts. For although even a small delay is dangerous and hurtful for those who are aiming at goodness and advance in spiritual things, yet still we would keep our faith and promise, though by an unwilling return, were it not that we felt sure that we should be so tightly bound down both by the authority and also by the love of the Elders, that we should henceforth have no opportunity at all to come back again to this place.

NOTES:
[934] Compare [notes] on the Institutes IV. c. xxxi.

CHAPTER VI.

Abbot Joseph's question whether we got more good in Egypt than in Syria.

TO this the blessed Joseph, after a short silence: Are you sure, said he, that you can get more profit in spiritual matters in this country?

CHAPTER VII.

The answer on the difference of customs in the two countries.

GERMANUS: Although we ought to be most grateful for the teaching of those men who taught us from our youth up to attempt great things, and, by giving us a taste of their excellence, implanted in our hearts a splendid thirst for perfection, yet if any reliance is to be placed on our judgment, we cannot draw any comparison between these customs and those which we learnt there, so as to hold our tongues about the inimitable purity of your life, which we believe is granted to you not only owing to the concentration of your mind and aim, but also owing to the aid and assistance of the place itself. Wherefore we do not doubt that for the following of your grand perfection this instruction which is given to us is not enough by itself, unless we have also the help of the life, and a long course of instruction somewhat dissolves the coldness of our heart by daily training.

CHAPTER VIII.

How those who are perfect ought not to make any promises absolutely, and whether decisions can be reversed without sin.

JOSEPH: It is good indeed and right and altogether in accordance with our profession, for us effectually to perform what we decided to do in the case of any promise. Wherefore a monk ought not to make any promise hastily, lest he may be forced to do what he incautiously promised, or if he is kept back by consideration of a sounder view, appear as a breaker of his promise. But because at the present moment our purpose is to treat not so much of a state of health as of the cure of sickness we must with salutary counsel consider not what you ought to have done in the first instance, but how you can escape from the rocks of this perilous shipwreck. When then no chains impede us and no conditions restrict us, in the case of a comparison of good things, if a choice is proposed, that which is most advantageous should be preferred: but when some detriment and loss stands in the way, in a comparison of things to our hurt, that should be sought which exposes us to the smallest loss. Further, as your assertion shows, when your heedless promise has brought you to this state that in either case some serious loss and inconvenience must result to you, the will in choosing should incline to that side which involves a loss that is more tolerable, or can be more easily made up for by the remedy of making amends. If then you think that you will get more good for your spirit by staying here than what accrued to you from your life in that monastery, and that the terms of your promise cannot be fulfilled without the loss of great good, it is better for you to undergo the loss from a falsehood and an unfulfilled promise (as it is done once for all, and need not any longer be repeated or be the cause of other sins) than for you to incur that loss, through which you say that your state of life would become colder, and which would affect you with a daily and unceasing injury. For a careless promise is changed in such a way that it may be pardoned or indeed praised, if it is turned into a better path, nor need we take it as a failure in consistency, but as a correction of rashness, whenever a promise that was faulty is corrected. And all this may be proved by most certain witness from Scripture, that for many the fulfilment of their promise has led to death, and on the other hand that for many it has been good and profitable to have refused it.

CHAPTER IX.

How it is often better to break one's engagements than to fulfil them.

AND both these points are very clearly shown by the cases of S. Peter the Apostle and Herod. For the former, because he departed from his expressed determination which he had as it were confirmed with an oath saying "Thou shalt never wash my feet,"[935] gained an immortal partnership with Christ, whereas he would certainly have been cut off from the grace of this blessedness, if he had clung obstinately to his word. But the latter, by clinging to the pledge of his ill-considered oath, became the bloody murderer of the Lord's forerunner, and through the vain fear of perjury plunged himself into condemnation and the punishment of everlasting death. In everything then we must consider the end, and must according to it direct our course and aim, and if when some wiser counsel supervenes, we see it diverging to the worse part, it is better to discard the unsuitable arrangement, and to come to a better mind rather than to cling obstinately to our engagements and so become involved in worse sins.

NOTES:
[935] S. John 13:8.

CHAPTER X.

Our question about our fear of the oath which we gave in the monastery in Syria.

GERMANUS: In so far as it concerns our desire, which we undertook to carry out for the sake of spiritual profit, we were hoping to be edified by continual intercourse with you. For if we were to return to our monastery it is certain that we should not only fail of so sublime a purpose, but that we should also suffer grievous loss from the mediocrity of the manner of life there. But that command of the gospel frightens us terribly: "Let your speech be yea, yea, nay, nay: but whatsoever is more than these, is from the evil one."[936] For we hold that we cannot compensate for transgressing so important a command by any righteousness, nor can that finally turn out well which has once been started with a bad beginning.

NOTES:
[936] S. Matt. 5:37.

CHAPTER XI.

The answer that we must take into account the purpose of the doer rather than the execution of the business.

JOSEPH: In every case, as we said, we must look not at the progress of the work but at the intention of the worker, nor must we inquire to begin with what a man has done, but with what purpose, so that we may find that some have been condemned for those deeds from which good has afterwards arisen, and on the other hand that some have arrived by means of acts in themselves reprehensible at the height of righteousness. And in the case of the former the good result of their actions was of no avail to them as they took the matter in and with an evil purpose, and wanted to bring about--not the good which actually resulted, but something of the opposite character; nor was the bad beginning injurious to the latter, as he put up with the necessity of a blameworthy start; not out of disregard for God, or with the purpose of doing wrong, but with an eye to a needful and holy end.

CHAPTER XII.

How a fortunate issue will be of no avail to evil doers, while bad deeds will not injure good men.

AND that we may make these statements clear by instances from Holy Scripture, what could be brought about that was more salutary and more to the good of the whole world, than the saving remedy of the Lord's Passion? And yet it was not only of no advantage, but was actually to the disadvantage of the traitor by whose means it is shown to have been brought about, so that it is absolutely said of him: "It were good for that man if he had never been born."[937] For the fruits of his labour will not be repaid to him according to the actual result, but according to what he wanted to do, and believed that he would accomplish. And again, what could there be more culpable than craft and deceit shown even to a stranger, not to mention one's brother and father? And yet the patriarch Jacob not only met with no condemnation or blame for such things but was actually dowered with the everlasting heritage of the blessing. And not without reason, for the last mentioned desired the blessing destined for the first-born not out of a greedy desire for present gain but because of his faith in everlasting sanctification; while the former (Judas) delivered the Redeemer of all to death, not for the sake of man's salvation, but from the sin of covetousness. And therefore in each case the fruits of their action are reckoned according to the intention of the mind and purpose of the will, according to which the object of the one was not to work fraud, nor was that of the other to work salvation. For justly is there repayment to each man as the recompense of reward, for what he conceived in the first instance in his mind, and not for what resulted from it either well or badly, against the wish of the worker. And so the most just Judge regarded him who ventured on such a falsehood as excusable and indeed worthy of praise, because without it he could not secure the blessing of the first-born; and that should not be reckoned as a sin, which arose from desire of the blessing. Otherwise the aforesaid patriarch would have been not only unfair to his brother, but also a cheat of his father and a blasphemer, if there had been any other way by which he could secure the gift of that blessing, and he had preferred to follow this which would damage and injure his brother. You see then that with God the inquiry is not into the carrying out of the act, but into the purpose of the mind. With this preparation then for a return to the question proposed (for which all this has been premised) I want you first to tell me for what reason you bound yourselves in the fetters of that promise.

NOTES:
[937] S. Matt. 26:24.

CHAPTER XIII.

Our answer as to the reason which demanded an oath from us.

GERMANUS: The first reason, as we said, was that we were afraid of vexing our Elders and resisting their orders; the second was that we very foolishly believed that, if we had learnt from you anything perfect or splendid to hear or look at, when we returned to the monastery, we should be able to perform it.

CHAPTER XIV.

The discourse of the Elder showing how the plan of action may be changed without fault provided that one keeps to the carrying out of a good intention.

JOSEPH: As we premised, the intent of the mind brings a man either reward or condemnation, according to this passage: "Their thoughts between themselves accusing or also defending one another, in the day when God shall judge the secrets of men;" and this too: "But I am coming to gather together their works and thoughts together with all nations and tongues."[938] Wherefore it was, as I see, from a desire for perfection that you bound yourselves with the chain of these oaths, as you then thought that by this plan it could be gained, while now that a riper judgment has supervened, you see that you cannot by this means scale its heights. And so any departure from that arrangement, which may seem to have happened, will be no hindrance, if only no change in that first purpose follows. For a change of instrument does not imply a desertion of the work, nor does the choice of a shorter and more direct road argue laziness on the path of the traveller. And so in this matter an improvement in a short-sighted arrangement is not to be reckoned a breach of a spiritual promise. For whatever is done out of the love of God and desire for goodness, which has "promise of the life that now is and of that which is to come,"[939] even though it may appear to commence with a hard and adverse beginning, is most worthy, not only of no blame, but actually of praise. And therefore the breaking of a careless promise will be no hindrance, if in every case the end, i.e., the proposed aim at goodness, be maintained. For we do all for this reason, that we may be able to show to God a clean heart, and if the attainment of this is considered to be easier in this country the alteration of the agreement extracted from you will be no hindrance to you, if only the perfection of that purity for the sake of which your promise was originally made, be the sooner secured according to the Lord's will.

NOTES:
[938] Rom. 2:15, 16; Is. 66:18.
[939] 1 Tim. 4:8.

CHAPTER XV.

A question whether it can be without sin that our knowledge affords to weak brethren an opportunity for lying.

GERMANUS: As far as the force of the words which have been reasonably and carefully considered, is concerned, our scruple about our promise would have easily been removed from us were it not that we were terribly alarmed lest by this example an opportunity for lying might be offered to certain weaker brethren, if they knew that the faith of an agreement could be in any way lawfully broken, whereas this very thing is forbidden in such vigorous and threatening terms by the prophet when he says: "Thou shall destroy all those who utter a lie;" and: "the mouth that speaketh a lie, shall slay the soul." [940]

NOTES:
[940] Ps. 5:7; Wisd. 1:11.

CHAPTER XVI.

The answer that Scripture truth is not to be altered on account of an offence given to the weak.

JOSEPH: Occasions and opportunities for destroying themselves cannot possibly be wanting to those who are on the road to ruin, or rather who are anxious to destroy themselves; nor are those passages of Scripture to be rejected and altogether torn out of the volume, by which the perversity of heretics is encouraged, or the unbelief of the Jews increased, or the pride of heathen wisdom offended; but surely they are to be piously believed, and firmly held, and preached according to the rule of truth. And therefore we should not, because of another's unbelief, reject the oikonomias, i.e., the "economy" of the prophets and saints which Scripture relates, lest while we are thinking that we ought to condescend to their infirmities, we stain ourselves with the sin not only of lying but of sacrilege. But, as we said, we ought to admit these according to the letter, and explain how they were rightly done. But for those who are wrongly disposed, the opening for lies will not be blocked up by this means, if we are trying either altogether to deny or to explain away by allegorical interpretations the truth of those things which we are going to bring forward or have already brought forward. For how will the authority of these passages injure them if their corrupt will is alone sufficient to lead them to sin?

CHAPTER XVII.

How the saints have profitably employed a lie like hellebore.

AND so we ought to regard a lie and to employ it as if its nature were that of hellebore; which is useful if taken when some deadly disease is threatening, but if taken without being required by some great danger is the cause of immediate death. For so also we read that holy men and those most approved by God employed lying, so as not only to incur no guilt of sin from it, but even to attain the greatest goodness; and if deceit could confer glory on them, what on the other hand would the truth have brought them but condemnation? Just as Rahab, of whom Scripture gives a record not only of no good deed but actually of unchastity, yet simply for the lie, by means of which she preferred to hide the spies instead of betraying them, had it vouchsafed to her to be joined with the people of God in everlasting blessing. But if she had preferred to speak the truth and to regard the safety of the citizens, there is no doubt that she and all her house would not have escaped the coming destruction, nor would it have been vouchsafed to her to be inserted in the progenitors of our Lord's nativity,[941] and reckoned in the list of the patriarchs, and through her descendants that

382

followed, to become the mother of the Saviour of all. Again Dalila, who to provide for the safety of her fellow citizens betrayed the truth she had discovered, obtained in exchange eternal destruction, and has left to all men nothing but the memory of her sin. When then any grave danger hangs on confession of the truth, then we must take to lying as a refuge, yet in such a way as to be for our salvation troubled by the guilt of a humbled conscience. But where there is no call of the utmost necessity present, there a lie should be most carefully avoided as if it were something deadly: just as we said of a cup of hellebore which is indeed useful if it is only taken in the last resort when a deadly and inevitable disease is threatening, while if it is taken when the body is in a state of sound and rude health, its deadly properties at once go to find out the vital parts. And this was clearly shown of Rahab of Jericho, and the patriarch Jacob; the former of whom could only escape death by means of this remedy, while the latter could not secure the blessing of the first-born without it. For God is not only the Judge and inspector of our words and actions, but He also looks into their purpose and aim. And if He sees that anything has been done or promised by some one for the sake of eternal salvation and shows insight into Divine contemplation, even though it may appear to men to be hard and unfair, yet He looks at the inner goodness of the heart and regards the desire of the will rather than the actual words spoken, because He must take into account the aim of the work and the disposition of the doer, whereby, as was said above, one man may be justified by means of a lie, while another may be guilty of a sin of everlasting death by telling the truth. To which end the patriarch Jacob also had regard when he was not afraid to imitate the hairy appearance of his brother's body by wrapping himself up in skins, and to his credit acquiesced in his mother's instigation of a lie for this object. For he saw that in this way there would be bestowed on him greater gains of blessing and righteousness than by keeping to the path of simplicity: for he did not doubt that the stain of this lie would at once be washed away by the flood of the paternal blessing, and would speedily be dissolved like a little cloud by the breath of the Holy Spirit; and that richer rewards of merit would be bestowed on him by means of this dissimulation which he put on than by means of the truth, which was natural to him.

NOTES:
[941] Cf. S. Matt. 1:5.

CHAPTER XVIII.

An objection that only those men employed lies with impunity, who lived under the law.

GERMANUS: It is no wonder that these schemes were properly employed in the Old Testament, and that some holy men laudably or at any rate venially told lies, as we see that many worse things were permitted to them owing to the rude character of the times. For why should we wonder that when the blessed David was fleeing from Saul, in answer to the inquiry of Abimelech the priest who said: "Why art thou alone, and is no man with thee?" he replied as follows: "The king hath commanded me a business, and said, Let no man know the thing for which thou art sent by me, for I have appointed my servants to such and such a place;" and again: "Hast thou here at hand a spear or a sword, for I brought not my own sword nor my own weapon with me, for the king's business required haste;" or this, when he was brought to Achish king of Gath, and feigned himself mad and frantic, "and changed his countenance before them, and slipped down between their hands; and stumbled against the doors of the gate and his spittle ran down on his beard;"[942] when they were even allowed to enjoy crowds of wives and concubines, and no sin was on this account imputed to them, and when moreover they often shed the blood of their enemies with their own hand, and this was thought not only worthy of no blame, but actually praiseworthy? And all these things we see by the light of the gospel are utterly forbidden, so that not one of them can be done without great sin and guilt. And in the same way we hold that no lie can be employed by any one, I will not say rightly, but not even venially, however it may be covered with the colour of piety, as the Lord says: "Let your speech be yea, yea, nay, nay: but whatsoever is more than these is of the evil one;" and the Apostle also agrees with this: "And lie not one to another." [943]

NOTES:
[942] 1 Sam. 21:1, 2, 8, 13.
[943] S. Matt. 5:37; Col. 3:9.

CHAPTER XIX.

The answer, that leave to lie, which was not even granted under the old Covenant, has rightly been taken by many.

JOSEPH: All liberty in the matter of wives and many concubines, as the end of time is approaching and the multiplying of the human race completed, ought rightly to be cut off by evangelical perfection, as being no longer necessary. For up to the coming of Christ it was well that the blessing of the original sentence should be in full vigour, whereby it was said: "Increase and multiply, and fill the earth."[944] And therefore it was quite right that from the root of human fecundity which happily flourished in the synagogue, in accordance with that dispensation of the times, the buds of angelical virginity should spring, and the fragrant flowers of continence be produced in the Church. But that lying was even then condemned the text of the whole Old Testament clearly shows, as it says: "Thou shall destroy all them that speak lies;" and again: "The bread of lying is sweet to a man, but afterwards his mouth is filled with gravel;" and the Giver of the law himself says: "Thou shalt avoid a lie."[945] But we said that it was then properly employed as a last resort when some need or plan of salvation was linked on to it, on account of which it ought not to be condemned. As is the case, which you mentioned, of king David when in his flight from the unjust persecution of Saul, to Abimelech the priest he used lying words, not with the object of getting any gain nor with the desire to injure anybody, but simply to save himself from that most iniquitous persecution; inasmuch as he would not stain his hands with the blood of the hostile king, so often delivered up to him by God; as he said: "The Lord be merciful to me that I may do no such thing to my master the Lord's anointed, as to lay my hand upon him, because he is the Lord's anointed."[946] And therefore these plans which we hear that holy men under the old covenant adopted either from the will of God, or for the prefiguring of spiritual mysteries or for the salvation of some people, we too cannot refuse altogether, when necessity constrains us, as we see that even apostles did not avoid them, where the consideration of something profitable required them: which in the meanwhile we will for a time postpone, while we first discuss those instances which we propose still to bring forward from the Old Testament, and afterwards we shall more suitably introduce them so as more readily to prove that good and holy men, both in the Old and in the New Testament, were entirely at one with each other in these contrivances. For what shall we say of that pious fraud of Hushai to Absalom for the salvation of king David, which though uttered with all appearance of good-will by the deceiver and cheat, and opposed to the good of him who asked advice, is yet commended by the authority of Holy Scripture, which says: "But by the will of the Lord the profitable counsel of Ahithophel was defeated that the Lord might bring evil upon Absalom"?[947] Nor could that be blamed which was done for the right side with a right purpose and pious intent, and was planned for the salvation and victory of one whose piety was pleasing to God, by a holy dissimulation. What too shall we say of the deed of that woman, who received the men who had been sent to king David by the aforesaid Hushai, and hid them in a well, and spread a cloth over its mouth, and pretended that she was drying pearl-barley, and said "They passed on after tasting a little water";[948] and by this invention saved them from the hands of their pursuers? Wherefore answer me, I pray you, and say what you would have done, if any similar situation had arisen for you, living now under the gospel; would you prefer to hide them with a similar falsehood, saying in the same way: "They passed on after tasting a little water," and thus fulfil the command: "Deliver those who are being led to death, and spare not to redeem those who are being killed;"[949] or by speaking the truth, would you have given up those in hiding to the men who would kill them? And what then becomes of the Apostle's words: "Let no man seek his own but the things of another:" and: "Love seeketh not her own, but the things of others;" and of himself he says: "I seek not mine own good but the good of many that they may be saved"?[950] For if we seek our own, and want obstinately to keep what is good for ourselves, we must even in urgent cases of this sort speak the truth, and so become guilty of the death of another: but if we prefer what is for another's advantage to our own good, and satisfy the demands of the Apostle, we shall certainly have to put up with the necessity of lying. And therefore we shall not be able to keep a perfect heart of love, or to seek, as Apostolic perfection requires, the things of others, unless we relax a little in those things which concern the strictness and perfection of our own lives, and choose to condescend with ready affection to what is useful to others, and so with the Apostle become weak to the weak, that we may be able to gain the weak.

NOTES:
[944] Ps. 5:7; Prov. 20:17; Exod. 23:7.

945 Gen. 1:28.
946 1 Sam. 24:7.
947 2 Sam. 17:14.
948 2 Sam. 17:20.
949 Prov. 24:11.
950 1 Cor. 10:24; 13:5; 1 Cor. 10:33.

CHAPTER XX.

How even Apostles thought that a lie was often useful and the truth injurious.

INSTRUCTED by which examples, the blessed Apostle James also, and all the chief princes of the primitive Church urged the Apostle Paul in consequence of the weakness of feeble persons to condescend to a fictitious arrangement and insisted on his purifying himself according to the requirements of the law, and shaving his head and paying his vows, as they thought that the present harm which would come from this hypocrisy was of no account, but had regard rather to the gain which would result from his still continued preaching. For the gain to the Apostle Paul from his strictness would not have counterbalanced the loss to all nations from his speedy death. And this would certainly have been then incurred by the whole Church unless this good and salutary hypocrisy had preserved him for the preaching of the Gospel. For then we may rightly and pardonably acquiesce in the wrong of a lie, when, as we said, a greater harm depends on telling the truth, and when the good which results to us from speaking the truth cannot counterbalance the harm which will be caused by it. And elsewhere the blessed Apostle testifies in other words that he himself always observed this disposition; for when he says: "To the Jews I became as a Jew that I might gain the Jews; to those who were under the law as being under the law, though not myself under the law, that I might gain those who were under the law; to those who were without law, I became as without law, though I was not without the law of God but under the law of Christ, that I might gain those who were without law; to the weak I became weak, that I might gain the weak: I became all things to all men, that I might save all;"951 what does he show but that according to the weakness and the capacity of those who were being instructed he always lowered himself and relaxed something of the vigour of perfection, and did not cling to what

387

his own strict life might seem to demand, but rather preferred that which the good of the weak might require? And that we may trace these matters out more carefully and recount one by one the glories of the good deeds of the Apostles, some one may ask how the blessed Apostle can be proved to have suited himself to all men in all things. When did he to the Jews become as a Jew? Certainly in the case where, while he still kept in his inmost heart the opinion which he had maintained to the Galatians saying: "Behold, I, Paul, say unto you that if ye be circumcised Christ shall profit you nothing,"[952] yet by circumcising Timothy he adopted a shadow as it were of Jewish superstition. And again, where did he become to those under the law, as under the law? There certainly where James and all the Elders of the Church, fearing lest he might be attacked by the multitude of Jewish believers, or rather of Judaizing Christians, who had received the faith of Christ in such a way as still to be bound by the rites of legal ceremonies, came to his rescue in his difficulty with this counsel and advice, and said: "Thou seest, brother, how many thousands there are among the Jews, who have believed, and they are all zealots for the law. But they have heard of thee that thou teachest those Jews who are among the Gentiles to depart from Moses, saying that they ought not to circumcise their children;" and below: "Do therefore this that we say unto thee: we have four men who have a vow on them. These take and sanctify thyself with them and bestow on them, that they may shave their heads; and all will know that the things which they have heard of thee are false, but that thou thyself also walkest keeping the law."[953] And so for the good of those who were under the law, he trode under foot for a while the strict view which he had expressed: "For I through the law am dead unto the law that I may live unto God;"[954] and was driven to shave his head, and be purified according to the law and pay his vows after the Mosaic rites in the Temple. Do you ask also where for the good of those who were utterly ignorant of the law of God, he himself became as if without law? Read the introduction to his sermon at Athens where heathen wickedness was flourishing: "As I passed by," he says, "I saw your idols and an altar on which was written: To the unknown God;" and when he had thus started from their superstition, as if he himself also had been without law, under the cloke of that profane inscription he introduced the faith of Christ, saying: "What therefore ye ignorantly worship, that declare I unto you." And after a little, as if he had known nothing whatever of the Divine law, he chose to bring forward a verse of a heathen poet rather than a saying of Moses or Christ, saying: "As some also of your own poets have said:

for we are also His offspring." And when he had thus approached them with their own authorities, which they could not reject, thus confirming the truth by things false, he added and said: "Since then we are the offspring of God we ought not to think that the Godhead is like to gold or silver or stone sculptured by the art and device of man."[955] But to the weak he became weak, when, by way of permission, not of command, he allowed those who could not contain themselves to return together again,[956] or when he fed the Corinthians with milk and not with meat, and says that he was with them in weakness and fear and much trembling.[957] But he became all things to all men that he might save all, when he says: "He that eateth let him not despise him that eateth not, and let not him that eateth not judge him that eateth:" and: "He that giveth his virgin in marriage doeth well, and he that giveth her not in marriage doeth better;" and elsewhere: "Who," says he, "is weak, and I am not weak? Who is offended, and I burn not?" and in this way he fulfilled what he had commanded the Corinthians to do when he said: "Be ye without offence to Jews and Greeks and the Church of Christ, as I also please all men in all things, not seeking mine own profit but that of the many, that they may be saved."[958] For it had certainly been profitable not to circumcise Timothy, not to shave his head, not to undergo Jewish purification, not to practice going barefoot,[959] not to pay legal vows; but he did all these things because he did not seek his own profit but that of the many. And although this was done with the full consideration of God, yet it was not free from dissimulation. For one who through the law of Christ was dead to the law that he might live to God, and who had made and treated that righteousness of the law in which he had lived blameless, as dung, that he might gain Christ, could not with true fervour of heart offer what belonged to the law; nor is it right to believe that he who had said: "For if I again rebuild what I have destroyed, I make myself a transgressor,"[960] would himself fall into what he had condemned. And to such an extent is account taken, not so much of the actual thing which is done as of the disposition of the doer, that on the other hand truth is sometimes found to have injured some, and a lie to have done them good. For when Saul was grumbling to his servants about David's flight, and saying: "Will the son of Jesse give you all fields and vineyards, and make you all tribunes and centurions: that all of you have conspired against me, and there is no one to inform me," did Doeg the Edomite say anything but the truth, when he told him: "I saw the son of Jesse in Nob, with Abimelech the son of Ahitub the priest, who consulted the Lord for him, and gave him victuals, and gave him also the sword of Goliath the Philistine"?[961] For which true story he deserved to be rooted up out of the land of the living, and it is said of him by the prophet: "Wherefore God shall destroy thee forever, and pluck thee up and tear thee out of thy tabernacle, and thy root from the land of the living:"[962] He then for showing the truth is forever plucked and rooted up out of that land in which the harlot Rahab with her family is planted for her lie: just as also we remember that Samson most injuriously betrayed to his wicked wife the truth which he had hidden for a long time by a lie, and therefore the truth so inconsiderately disclosed was the cause of his own deception, because he had neglected to keep the command of the prophet: "Keep the doors of thy mouth from her that sleepeth in thy bosom." [963]

NOTES:
[951] 1 Cor. 9:20-22.
[952] Gal. 5:2.
[953] Acts 21:20-24.
[954] Gal. 2:19.
[955] Acts 17:23, 29.
[956] Cf. 1 Cor. 7:5.
[957] Cf. 1 Cor. 3:2; 2:3.
[958] Rom. 14:3; 1 Cor. 8:38; 2 Cor. 11:29; 1 Cor. 10:32, 33.
[959] Nudipedalia non exercere. The expression is also used by Jerome of S. Paul's purification in Jerusalem (in Gal. Book II. c. iv.), though there is nothing in the account in the Acts about his going barefoot. Compare also Jerome against Jovinian, Book I. c. viii., and for the word, in connexion with the rites of the Christian Church, see Tertullian Apologeticum, c. xl.
[960] Gal. 2:18.
[961] 1 Sam. 22:7-10.
[962] Ps. 51 (52):7.
[963] Micah 2:7.

CHAPTER XXI.

Whether secret abstinence ought to be made known, without telling a lie about it, to those who ask, and whether what has once been declined may be taken in hand.

AND to bring forward some instances from our unavoidable and almost daily wants which with all our care we can never so guard against as not to be driven to incur them whether with or against our will: what, I ask you, is to be done when, while we are proposing to put off our supper, a brother comes and asks us if we have had it: is our fast to be concealed, and the good act of abstinence hidden, or is it to be proclaimed by telling the truth? If we conceal it, to satisfy the Lord's command which says: "Thou shalt not appear unto men to fast but unto thy Father Who is in secret;" and again: "Let not thy left hand know what thy right hand doeth,"[964] we must at once tell a lie. If we make manifest the good act of abstinence, the word of the gospel rightly discourages us: "Verily I say unto you, they have their reward."[965] But what if any one has refused with determination a cup offered to him by some brother, denying altogether that he will take what the other, rejoicing at his arrival, begs and intreats him to receive? Is it right that he should force himself to yield to his brother who goes on his knees and bows himself to the ground, and who thinks that he can only show his loving heart by this service, or should he obstinately cling to his own word and intention?

NOTES:
[964] S. Matt. 6:18, 3.
[965] S. Matt. 6:2.

CHAPTER XXII.

An objection, that abstinence ought to be concealed, but that things that have been declined should not be received.

GERMANUS: In the former instance we think there can be no doubt that it is better for our abstinence to be hidden than for it to be displayed to the inquirers, and in cases of this sort we also admit that a lie is unavoidable. But in the second there is no need for us to tell a lie, first because we can refuse what is offered by the service of a brother in such a way as to bind ourselves in no bond of determination, and next because when we once refuse we can keep our opinion unchanged.

CHAPTER XXIII.

The answer that obstinacy in this decision is unreasonable.

JOSEPH: There is no doubt that these are the decisions of those monasteries in which the infancy of your renunciation was, as you tell us, trained, as their leaders are accustomed to prefer their own will to their brother's supper, and most obstinately stick to what they have once intended. But our Elders, to whose faith the signs of Apostolical powers have borne witness, and who have treated everything with judgment and discretion of spirit rather than with stiff obstinacy of mind, have laid down that those men who give in to the infirmities of others, receive much richer fruits than those who persist in their determinations, and have declared that it is a better deed to conceal abstinence, as was said, by this needful and humble lie, rather than to display it with a proud show of truth.

CHAPTER XXIV.

How Abbot Piamun chose to hide his abstinence.

FINALLY Abbot Piamun[966] after twenty-five years did not hesitate to receive some grapes and wine offered to him by a certain brother, and at once preferred, against his rule, to taste what was brought him rather than to display his abstinence which was a secret from everybody. For if we would also bear in mind what we remember that our Elders always did, who used to conceal the marvels of their own good deeds, and their own acts, which they were obliged to bring forward in Conference for the instruction of the juniors, under cover of other persons, what else can we consider them but an open lie? And O that we too had anything worthy which we could bring forward for stirring up the faith of the juniors! Certainly we should have no scruples in following their fictions of that kind. For it is better under the colour of a figure like that to tell a lie than for the sake of maintaining that unreasonable truthfulness either hide in ill-advised silence what might be edifying to the hearers, or run into the display of an objectionable vanity by telling them truthfully in our own character. And the teacher of the Gentiles clearly teaches us the same lesson by his teaching, as he chose to bring forward the great revelations made to him, under the character of some one else, saying: "I know a man in Christ, whether in the body or out of the body I cannot tell, God knoweth, caught up even unto the third heaven: and I know such a man, that he was caught up into paradise and heard unspeakable words, which it is not lawful for man to utter." [967]

NOTES:
[966] On Piamun see the note on XVIII. i.
[967] 2 Cor. 12:2-4.

CHAPTER XXV.

The evidence of Scripture on changes of determination.

IT is impossible for us briefly to run through everything. For who could count up almost all the patriarchs and numberless saints, some of whom for the preservation of life, others out of desire for a blessing, others out of pity, others to conceal some secret, others out of zeal for God, others in searching for the truth, became, so to speak, patrons of lying? And as all cannot be enumerated, so all ought not to be altogether passed over. For piety forced the blessed Joseph to raise a false charge against his brethren even with an oath by the life of the king, saying: "Ye are spies: to see the nakedness of the land are ye come;" and below: "send," says he, "one of you, and bring your brothers hither: but ye shall be kept here until your words are made manifest whether ye speak the truth or no: but if not, by the life of Pharaoh, ye are spies."[968] For if he had not out of pity alarmed them by this lie, he would not have been able to see again his father and his brother, nor to preserve them in their great danger of starvation, nor to free the conscience of his brethren from the guilt of selling him. The act then of striking his brethren with fear by means of a lie was not so reprehensible as was it a holy and laudable act to urge his enemies and seekers to a salutary penitence by means of a feigned danger. Finally when they were weighed down by the odium of the very serious accusation, they were conscience-stricken not at the charge falsely raised against them, but at the thought of their earlier crime, and said to one another: "We suffer this rightly because we sinned against our brother, in that we saw the anguish of his soul when he asked us and we did not hearken to him: wherefore all this trouble hath come upon us."[969] And this con-

PART 2

fession, we think, expiated by most salutary humility their terrible sin
not only against their brother, against whom they had sinned with
wicked cruelty, but also against God. What about Solomon, who in his
first judgment manifested the gift of wisdom, which he had received of
God, only by making use of falsehood? For in order to get at the truth
which was hidden by the woman's lie, even he used the help of a lie
most cunningly invented, saying: "Bring me a sword and divide the
living child into two parts, and give the one half to the one and the
other half to the other." And when this pretended cruelty stirred the
heart of the true mother, but was received with approval by her who
was not the true mother, then at last by this most sagacious discovery
of the truth he pronounced the judgment which every one has felt to
have been inspired by God, saying: "Give her the living child and slay
it not: she is the mother of it."[970] Further we are more fully taught by
other passages of Scripture as well that we neither can nor should
carry out everything which we determine either with peace or disturbance of mind, as we often hear that holy men and angels and even
Almighty God Himself have changed what they had decided upon. For
the blessed David determined and confirmed it by an oath, saying:
"May God do so and add more to the foes of David if I leave of all that
belong unto Nabal until the morning a single male." And presently
when Abigail his wife interceded and intreated for him, he gave up his
threats, lightened the sentence, and preferred to be regarded as a
breaker of his word rather than to keep his pledged oath by cruelly
executing it, saying: "As the Lord liveth, if thou hadst not quickly
come to meet me there had not been left to Nabal by the morning light
a single male."[971] And as we do not hold that his readiness to take a
rash oath (which resulted from his anger and disturbance of mind)
ought to be copied by us, so we do think that the pardon and revision
of his determination is to be followed. The "chosen vessel," in writing
to the Corinthians, promises unconditionally to return, saying: "But I
will come to you when I pass through Macedonia: for I will pass
through Macedonia. But I will stay or even pass the winter with you
that you may conduct me whithersoever I shall go. For I do not want
only to see you in passing: for I hope to stay with you for some
time."[972] And this fact he remembers in the Second Epistle, thus: "And
in this confidence I was minded first to come unto you, that ye might
receive a second favour, and by you to pass into Macedonia and again
to come to you from Macedonia and by you be conducted to Judaea."
But a better plan suggested itself and he plainly admits that he is not
going to fulfil what he had promised. "When then," says he, "I pur-

394

posed this, did I use light-mindedness? or the things that I think, do I think after the flesh, that there should be with me yea, yea, and nay, nay?" Lastly, he declares even with the affirmation of an oath, why it was that he preferred to put on one side his pledged word rather than by his presence to bring a burden and grief to his disciples: "But I call God to witness against my soul that it was to spare you that I came not as far as Corinth. For I determined this with myself that I would not come unto you in sorrow."[973] Though when the angels had refused to enter the house of Lot at Sodom, saying to him: "We will not enter but will remain in the street," they were presently forced by his prayers to change their determination, as Scripture subjoins: "And Lot constrained them, and they turned in to him."[974] And certainly if they knew that they would turn in to him, they refused his request with a sham excuse: but if their excuse was a real one, then they are clearly shown to have changed their mind. And certainly we hold that the Holy Spirit inserted this in the sacred volume for no other reason but to teach us by their examples that we ought not to cling obstinately to our own determinations, but to subject them to our will, and so to keep our judgment free from all the chains of law that it may be ready to follow the call of good counsel in any direction, and may not delay or refuse to pass without any delay to whatever a sound discretion may find to be the better choice. And to rise to still higher instances, when king Hezekiah was lying on his bed and afflicted with grievous sickness the prophet Isaiah addressed him in the person of God, and said: "Thus saith the Lord: set thine house in order for thou shall die and not live. And Hezekiah," it says, "turned his face to the wall and prayed to the Lord and said: I beseech thee, O Lord, remember how I have walked before Thee in truth and with a perfect heart, and how I have done what was right in Thy sight. And Hezekiah wept sore." After which it was again said to him: "Go, return, and speak to Hezekiah king of Judah, saying: Thus saith the Lord God of David thy father: I have heard thy prayer, I have seen thy tears: and behold, I will add to thy days fifteen years: and I will deliver thee out of the hand of the king of the Assyrians, and I will defend this city for thy sake and for my servant David's sake."[975] What can be clearer than this proof that out of consideration for mercy and goodness the Lord would rather break His word and instead of the pre-arranged limit of death extend the life of him who prayed, for fifteen years, rather than be found inexorable because of His unchangeable decree? In the same way too the Divine sentence says to the men of Nineveh: "Yet three days, and Nineveh shall be overthrown;"[976] and presently this stern and abrupt sentence is softened by their penitence and fasting, and is turned to the side of mercy with goodness that is easy to be intreated. But if any one maintains that the Lord had threatened the destruction of their city (while He foreknew that they would be converted) for this reason, that He might incite them to a salutary penitence, it follows that those who are set over their brethren may, if need arises, without any blame for telling lies, threaten those who need improvement with severer treatment than they are really going to inflict. But if one says that God revoked that severe sentence in consideration of their penitence, according to what he says by Ezekiel: "If I say to the wicked, Thou shalt surely die: and he becomes penitent for his sin, and doeth judgment and justice, he shall surely live, he shall not die;"[977] we are similarly taught that we ought not obstinately to stick to our determination, but that we should with gentle pity soften down the threats which necessity called forth. And that we may not fancy that the Lord granted this specially to the Ninevites, He continually affirms by Jeremiah that He will do the same in general towards all, and promises that without delay He will change His sentence in accordance with our deserts; saying: "I will suddenly speak against a nation and against a kingdom to root out and to pull down and to destroy it. If that nation repent of the evil, which I have spoken against it, I also will repent of the evil which I thought to do to them. And I will suddenly speak of a nation and a kingdom, to build up and to plant it. If it shall do evil in My sight, that it obey not My voice: I will repent of the good that I thought to do to it." To Ezekiel also: "Leave out not a word, if so be they will hearken and be converted every one from his evil way: that I may repent Me of the evil that I thought to do to them for the wickedness of their doings."[978] And by these passages it is declared that we ought not obstinately to stick to our decisions, but to modify them with reason and judgment, and that better courses should always be adopted and preferred, and that we should turn without any delay to that course which is considered the more profitable. For this above all that invaluable sentence teaches us, because though each man's end is known beforehand to Him before his birth, yet somehow He so orders all things by a plan and method for all, and with regard to man's disposition, that He decides on everything not by the mere exercise of His power, nor according to the ineffable knowledge which His Prescience possesses, but according to the present actions of men, and rejects or draws to Himself each one, and daily either grants or withholds His grace. And that this is so the election of Saul also shows us, of whose miserable end the foreknowledge of God certainly could not be ignorant, and yet He chose him out of so many thousands of Israel and anointed him king, rewarding the then existing merits of his life, and not considering the sin of his coming fall, so that after he became reprobate, God complains almost in human terms and, with man's feelings, as if He repented of his choice, saying: "It repenteth Me that I have appointed Saul king: for he hath forsaken Me, and hath not performed My words;" and again: "But Samuel was grieved for Saul because the Lord repented that He had made Saul king over Israel."[979] Finally this that He afterwards executed, that the Lord also declares by the prophet Ezekiel that He will by His daily judgment do with all men, saying: "Yea, if I shall say to the righteous that he shall surely live, and he trusting in his righteousness commit iniquity: all his righteousness shall be forgotten, and in his iniquity which he hath committed, in the same he shall die. And if I shall say to the wicked: Thou shalt surely die; and if he repent of his sin and do judgment and righteousness, and if that wicked man restore the pledge and render what he hath robbed, and walk in the commandments of life, and do no righteous thing, he shall surely live, he shall not die. None of his sins which he hath committed shall be imputed unto him."[980] Finally, when the Lord would for their speedy fall turn away His merciful countenance from the people, whom He had chosen out of all nations, the giver of the law interposes on their behalf and cries out: "I beseech Thee, O Lord, this people have sinned a great sin; they have made for themselves gods of gold; and now if Thou forgivest their sin, forgive it; but if not, blot me out of Thy book which Thou hast written. To whom the Lord answered: If any man hath sinned before Me, I will blot him out of My book."[981] David also, when complaining in prophetic spirit of Judas and the Lord's persecutors, says: "Let them be blotted out of the book of the living;" and because they did not deserve to come to saving penitence because of the guilt of their great sin, he subjoins: "And let them not be written among the righteous."[982] Finally in the case of Judas himself the meaning of the prophetic curse was clearly fulfilled, for when his deadly sin as completed, he killed himself by hanging, that he might not after his name was blotted out be converted and repent and deserve to be once more written among the righteous in heaven. We must therefore not doubt that at the time when he was chosen by Christ and obtained a place in the Apostolate, the name of Judas was written in the book of the living, and that he heard as well as the rest the words: "Rejoice not because the devils are subject unto you, but rejoice because your names are written in heaven."[983] But because he was corrupted by the plague of covetousness and had his name struck out from that heavenly list, it is suitably said of him and of men like him by the prophet: "O Lord, let all those that forsake Thee be confounded. Let them that depart from Thee be written in the earth, because they have forsaken the Lord, the vein of living waters." And elsewhere: "They shall not be in the counsel of My people, nor shall they be written in the writing of the house of Israel, neither shall they enter into the land of Israel." [984]

NOTES:
[968] Gen. 42:9, 16.
[969] Gen. 42:21.
[970] 1 Kings 3:24-27.
[971] 1 Sam. 25:22, 34.
[972] 1 Cor. 16:5, 7.
[973] 2 Cor. 1:15-17, 23; 2:1.
[974] Gen. 19:2, 3.
[975] 2 Kings 20:1-6.
[976] Jonah 3:4 (LXX).
[977] Ezek. 33:14, 15.
[978] Jer. 18:7, 10; 26:2, 3.
[979] 1 Sam. 15:11, 35.
[980] Ezek. 33:13-16.
[981] Exod. 32:31-33.
[982] Ps. 68 (69):29.
[983] S. Luke 10:20.
[984] Jer. 17:13; Ezek. 13:9.

CHAPTER XXVI.

How saintly men cannot be hard and obstinate.

NOR must we omit the value of that command because even if we have bound ourselves by some oath under the influence of anger or some other passion, (a thing which ought never to be done by a monk) still the case for each side should be weighed by a thorough judgment of the mind, and the course on which we have determined should be compared to that which we are urged to adopt, and we should without hesitation adopt that which on the occurrence of sounder considerations is decided to be the best. For it is better to put our promise on one side than to undergo the loss of something good and more desirable. Finally we never remember that venerable and approved fathers were hard and unyielding in decisions of this sort, but as wax under the influence of heat, so they were modified by reason, and when sounder counsels prevailed, did not hesitate to give in to the better side. But those whom we have seen obstinately clinging to their determinations we have always set down as unreasonable and wanting in judgment.

CHAPTER XXVII.

A question whether the saying: "I have sworn and am purposed" is opposed to the view given above.

GERMANUS: So far as this consideration is concerned which has been clearly and fully treated of, a monk ought never to determine anything for fear lest he turn out a breaker of his word or else obstinate. And what then can we make of this saying of the Psalmist: "I have sworn and am purposed to keep Thy righteous judgments"?[985] What is "to swear and purpose" except to keep one's determinations fixedly?

NOTES:
[985] Ps. 118 (119):106.

CHAPTER XXVIII.

The answer telling in what cases the determination is to be kept fixedly, and in what cases it may be broken if need be.

JOSEPH: We do not lay this down with regard to those fundamental commands, without which our salvation cannot in any way exist, but with regard to those which we can either relax or hold fast to without endangering our state, as for instance, an unbroken and strict fast, or total abstinence from wine or oil, or entire prohibition to leave one's cell, or incessant attention to reading and meditation, all of which can be practised at pleasure, without damage to our profession and purpose, and, if need be, can be given up without blame. But we must most resolutely make up our minds to observe those fundamental commands, and not even, if need arise, to avoid death in their cause, with regard to which we must immovably assert: "I have sworn and am purposed." And this should be done for the preservation of love, for which all things else should be disregarded lest the beauty and perfection of its calm should suffer a stain. In the same way we must swear for the purity of our chastity, and we ought to do the same for faith, and sobriety and justice, to all of which we must cling with unchangeable persistence, and to forsake which even for a little is worthy of blame. But in the case of those bodily exercises, which are said to be profitable for a little,[986] we must, as we said, decide in such a way that, if there occurs any more decided opportunity for a good act, which would lead us to relax them, we need not be bound by any rule about them, but may give them up and freely adopt what is more useful. For in the case of those bodily exercises, if they are dropped for a time, there is no danger: but to have given up these others even for a moment is deadly.

NOTES:
[986] Cf. 1 Tim. 4:8.

CHAPTER XXIX.

How we ought to do those things which are to be kept secret.

YOU must also provide with the same care that if by chance some word has slipped out of your mouth which you want to be a secret, no injunction to secrecy may trouble the hearer. For it will be more likely to be unheeded if it is let pass carelessly and simply, because the brother, whoever he is, will not be tormented with such a temptation to divulge it, as he will take it as something trivial dropped in casual conversation, and as what is for this very reason of less account, because it was not committed to the hearer's mind with a strict injunction to silence. For even if you bind his faith by exacting an oath from him, you need not doubt that it will very soon be divulged; for a fiercer assault of the devil's power will be made upon him, both to annoy and betray you, and to make him break his oath as quickly as possible.

CHAPTER XXX.

That no determination should be made on those things which concern the needs of the common life.

AND therefore a monk ought not hastily to make any promise on those things which merely concern bodily exercise, for fear lest he may stir up the enemy still more to attack what he is keeping as it were under the observance of the law, and so he may be more readily compelled to break it. Since every one who lives under the grace of liberty, and sets himself a law, thereby binds himself in a dangerous slavery, so that if by chance necessity constrains him to do what he might have ventured on lawfully, and indeed laudably and with thanksgiving, he is forced to act as a transgressor, and to fall into sin: "for where there is no law there is no transgression." [987]

By this instruction and the teaching of the blessed Joseph we were confirmed as by a Divine oracle and made up our minds to stop in Egypt. But though henceforward we were but a little anxious about our promise, yet when seven years were over we were very glad to fulfil it. For we hastened to our monastery, at a time when we were confident of obtaining permission to return to the desert, and first paid our respects properly to our Elders; next we revived the former love in their minds as out of the ardour of their love they had not been at all softened by our very frequent letters to satisfy them, and in the last place, we entirely removed the sting of our broken promise and returned to the recesses of the desert of Scete, as they themselves forwarded us with joy.

This learning and doctrine of the illustrious fathers, our ignorance, O holy brother, has to the best of its ability made plain to you. And if perhaps our clumsy style has confused it instead of setting it in order, I trust that the blame which our clumsiness deserves will not interfere with the praise due to these grand men. Since it seemed to us a safer course in the sight of our Judge to state even in unadorned style this splendid doctrine rather than to hold our tongues about it, since if he considers the grandeur of the thoughts, the fact that the awkwardness of our style annoys him, need not be prejudicial to the profit of the reader, and for our part we are more anxious about its usefulness than its being praised. This at least I charge all those into whose hand this little book may fall; viz., that they must know that whatever in it pleases them belongs to the fathers, and whatever they dislike is all our own. [988]

NOTES:

[987] Rom. 4:15.

[988] In this last chapter Cassian certainly makes his own the sentiments of Abbot Joseph on the permissibility of lying; and is therefore not unreasonably attacked for the teaching of this Conference by Prosper. "Contra Collatorem," c. ix. John Cassian Index

Part III.

Containing Conferences XVIII.-XXIV.
(except XXII)

PREFACE

WHEN by the help of the grace of Christ I had published ten Conferences of the Fathers, which were composed at the urgent request of the most blessed Helladius and Leontius, I dedicated seven others to Honoratus a Bishop blessed in name as well as merits, and also to that holy servant of Christ, Eucherius. The same number also I have thought good to dedicate now to you, O holy brothers, Jovinianus, Minervius, Leontius, and Theodore.[989] Since the last named of you founded that holy and splendid monastic rule in the province of Gaul, with the strictness of ancient virtue, while the rest of you by your instructions have stirred up monks not only before all to seek the common life of the coenobia, but even to thirst eagerly for the sublime life of the anchorite. For those Conferences of the best of the fathers are arranged with such care, and so carefully considered in all respects, that they are suited to both modes of life whereby you have made not only the countries of the West, but even the isles to flourish with great crowds of brethren; i.e., I mean that not only those who still remain in congregations with praiseworthy subjection to rule, but those also who retire to no great distance from your monasteries, and try to carry out the rule of anchorites, may be more fully instructed, according as the nature of the place and the character of their condition may require. And to this your previous efforts and labours have especially contributed this, that, as they are already prepared and practised in these exercises, they can more readily receive the precepts and institutes of the Elders, and receiving into their cells the authors of the Conferences together with the actual volumes of the Conferences and talking with them after a fashion by daily questions and answers, they may not be left to their own resources to find that way which is difficult and almost unknown in this country, but full of danger even there where well-known paths and numberless instances of those who have gone before are not wanting, but may rather learn to follow the rule of the

PART 3

anchorite's life taught by their examples, whom ancient tradition and industry and long experience have thoroughly instructed.

NOTES:
[989] See the introduction.

CONFERENCE 18.

Conference of Abbot Piamun
on the Three Sorts of Monks

CHAPTER I.

How we came to Diolcos and were received by Abbot Piamun. [990]
AFTER visiting and conversing with those three Elders, whose Conferences we have at the instance of our brother Eucherius tried to describe, as we were still more ardently desirous to seek out the further parts of Egypt, in which a larger and more perfect company of saints dwelt, we came--urged not so much by the necessities of our journey as by the desire of visiting the saints who were dwelling there--to a village named Diolcos,[991] lying on one of the seven mouths of the river Nile. For when we heard of very many and very celebrated monasteries founded by the ancient fathers, like most eager merchants, at once we undertook the journey on an uncertain quest, urged on by the hope of greater gain. And when we wandered about there for some long time and fixed our curious eyes on those mountains of virtue conspicuous for their lofty height, the gaze of those around first singled out Abbot Piamun, the senior of all the anchorites living there and their presbyter, as if he were some tall lighthouse. For he was set on the top of a high mountain like that city in the gospel,[992] and at once shed his light on our faces, whose virtues and miracles, which were wrought by him under our very eyes, Divine Grace thus bearing witness to his excellence, if we are not to exceed the plan and limits of this volume, we feel we must pass over in silence. For we promised to commit to memory what we could recollect, not of the miracles of God, but of the institutes and pursuits of the saints, so as to supply our readers merely with necessary instruction for the perfect life, and not with matter for idle and useless admiration without any correction of

their faults. And so when Abbot Piamun had received us with welcome, and had refreshed us with becoming kindness, as he understood
that we were not of the same country, he first asked us anxiously
whence or why we had visited Egypt, and when he discovered that we
had come thither from a monastery in Syria out of desire for perfection
he began as follows: --

NOTES:
[990] Piamun, who has already been spoken of in XVII. xxiv., is also mentioned
by Rufinus (History of the Monks, c. xxxii), Palladius (the Lausiac History,
clxxii.), and Sozomen (H. E. VI. xxix.), all of whom tell, with slight variation, the same story, how that one day while he was officiating at the altar,
he saw an angel writing down the names of some of the brethren, and passing by the names of others, all of whom Piamun on subsequent inquiry
found to have been guilty of some grievous sin.
[991] On Diolcos see [note] on the Institutes V. xxxvi.
[992] Cf. S. Matt. 5:14.

CHAPTER II.

The words of Abbot Piamun, how monks who were novices ought
to be taught by the example of their elders.

WHATEVER man, my children, is desirous to attain skill in any
art, unless he gives himself up with the utmost pains and carefulness to
the study of that system which he is anxious to learn, and observes the
rules and orders of the best masters of that work or science, is indulg-
ing in a vain hope to reach by idle wishes any similarity to those
whose pains and diligence he avoids copying. For we know that some
have come from your country to these parts, only to go round the
monasteries for the sake of getting to know the brethren, not meaning
to adopt the rules and regulations, for the sake of which they travelled
hither, nor to retire to the cells and aim at carrying out in action what
they had learnt by sight or by teaching. And these people retained their
character and pursuits to which they had grown accustomed, and, as is
thrown in their teeth by some, are held to have changed their country
not for the sake of their profit, but owing to the need of escaping want.
For in the obstinacy of their stubborn mind, they not only could learn
nothing, but actually would not stay any longer in these parts. For if
they changed neither their method of fasting, nor their scheme of

Psalms, nor even the fashion of their garments, what else could we think that they were after in this country, except only the supply of their victuals.

CHAPTER III.

How the juniors ought not to discuss the orders of the seniors.

WHEREFORE if, as we believe, the cause of God has drawn you to try to copy our knowledge, you must utterly ignore all the rules by which your early beginnings were trained, and must with all humility follow whatever you see our Elders do or teach. And do not be troubled or drawn away and diverted from imitating it, even if for the moment the cause or reason of any deed or action is not clear to you, because if men have good and simple ideas on all things and are anxious faithfully to copy whatever they see taught or done by their Elders, instead of discussing it, then the knowledge of all things will follow through experience of the work. But he will never enter into the reason of the truth, who begins to learn by discussion, because as the enemy sees that he trusts to his own judgment rather than to that of the fathers' he easily urges him on so far till those things which are especially useful and helpful seem to him unnecessary or injurious, and the crafty foe so plays upon his presumption, that by obstinately clinging to his own opinion he persuades himself that only that is holy, which he himself in his pig-headed error thinks to be good and right.

CHAPTER IV.

Of the three sorts of monks which there are in Egypt.

WHEREFORE you should first hear how or whence the system and beginning of our order took its rise. For only then can a man at all effectually be trained in any art he may wish, and be urged on to practise it diligently, when he has learnt the glory of its authors and founders. There are three kinds of monks in Egypt, of which two are admirable, the third is a poor sort of thing and by all means to be avoided. The first is that of the coenobites, who live together in a congregation and are governed by the direction of a single Elder: and of this kind there is the largest number of monks dwelling throughout the whole of Egypt. The second is that of the anchorites, who were first trained in the coenobium and then being made perfect in practical life chose the recesses of the desert: and in this order we also hope to gain a place. The third is the reprehensible one of the Sarabaites.[993] And of these we will discourse more fully one by one in order. Of these three orders then you ought, as we said, first to know about the founders. For at once from this there may arise either a hatred for the order which is to be avoided, or a longing for that which is to be followed, because each way is sure to carry the man who follows it, to that end which its author and discoverer has reached.

NOTES:
[993] See the note on c. vii.

CHAPTER V.

Of the founders who originated the order of coenobites.

AND so the system of coenobites took its rise in the days of the preaching of the Apostles. For such was all that multitude of believers in Jerusalem, which is thus described in the Acts of the Apostles: "But the multitude of believers was of one heart and one soul, neither said any of them that any of the things which he possessed was his own, but they had all things common. They sold their possessions and property and divided them to all, as any man had need." And again: "For neither was there any among them that lacked; for as many as possessed fields or houses, sold them and brought the price of the things that they sold and laid them before the feet of the Apostles: and distribution was made to every man as he had need."[994] The whole Church, I say, was then such as now are those few who can be found with difficulty in coenobia. But when at the death of the Apostles the multitude of believers began to wax cold, and especially that multitude which had come to the faith of Christ from diverse foreign nations, from whom the Apostles out of consideration for the infancy of their faith and their ingrained heathen habits, required nothing more than that they should "abstain from things sacrificed to idols and from fornication, and from things strangled, and from blood,"[995] and so that liberty which was conceded to the Gentiles because of the weakness of their newly-born faith, had by degrees begun to mar the perfection of that Church which existed at Jerusalem, and the fervour of that early faith cooled down owing to the daily increasing number both of natives and foreigners, and not only those who had accepted the faith of Christ, but even those who were the leaders of the Church relaxed somewhat of that strictness. For some fancying that what they saw permitted to the Gentiles because of their weakness, was also allowable for themselves, thought that they would suffer no loss if they followed the faith and confession of Christ keeping their property and possessions. But those who still maintained the fervour of the apostles, mindful of that former perfection left their cities and intercourse with those who thought that carelessness and a laxer life was permissible to themselves and the Church of God, and began to live in rural and more sequestered spots, and there, in private and on their own account, to practise those things which they had learnt to have been ordered by the apostles throughout the whole body of the Church in general: and so that whole system of which we have spoken grew up from those disciples who had separated themselves from the evil that was spreading. And these, as by degrees time went on, were separated from the great mass of believers and because they abstained from marriage and cut themselves off from intercourse with their kinsmen and the life of this world, were termed monks or solitaries from the strictness of their lonely and solitary life. Whence it followed that from their common life they were called coenobites and their cells and lodgings coenobia. That then alone was the earliest kind of monks, which is first not only in time but also in grace, and which continued unbroken for a very long period up to the time of Abbot Paul and Antony; and even to this day we see its traces remaining in strict coenobia.

NOTES:
[994] Acts 4:32; 2:45; 4:34, 35.
[995] Acts 15:29.

CHAPTER VI.

Of the system of the Anchorites and its beginning.

OUT of this number of the perfect, and, if I may use the expression, this most fruitful root of saints, were produced afterwards the flowers and fruits of the anchorites as well. And of this order we have heard that the originators were those whom we mentioned just now; viz., Saint Paul[996] and Antony, men who frequented the recesses of the desert, not as some from faintheartedness, and the evil of impatience, but from a desire for loftier heights of perfection and divine contemplation, although the former of them is said to have found his way to the desert by reason of necessity, while during the time of persecution he was avoiding the plots of his neighbours. So then there sprang from that system of which we have spoken another sort of perfection, whose followers are rightly termed anchorites; i.e., withdrawers, because, being by no means satisfied with that victory whereby they had trodden under foot the hidden snares of the devil, while still living among men, they were eager to fight with the devils in open conflict, and a straightforward battle, and so feared not to penetrate the vast recesses of the desert, imitating, to wit, John the Baptist, who passed all his life in the desert, and Elijah and Elisha and those of whom the Apostle speaks as follows: "They wandered about in sheepskins and goatskins, being in want, distressed, afflicted, of whom the world was not worthy, wandering in deserts, in mountains and in dens and in caves of the earth." Of whom too the Lord speaks figuratively to Job: "But who hath sent out the wild ass free, and who hath loosed his bands? To whom I have given the wilderness for an house, and a barren land for his dwelling. He scorneth the multitude of the city and heareth not the cry of the driver; he looketh round about the mountains of his pasture, and seeketh for every green thing." In the Psalms also: "Let now the redeemed of the Lord say, those whom He hath redeemed from the hand of the enemy;" and after a little: "They wandered in a wilderness in a place without water: they found not the way of a city of habitation. They were hungry and thirsty: their soul fainted in them. And they cried unto the Lord in their trouble and He delivered them out of their distress;" whom Jeremiah too describes as follows: "Blessed is the man that hath borne the yoke from his youth. He shall sit solitary and hold his peace because he hath taken it up upon himself," and there sing in heart and deed these words of the Psalmist: "I am become like a pelican in the wilderness. I watched and am become like a sparrow alone upon the house-top." [997]

NOTES:
[996] Paul was from very early days celebrated as the first of the anchorites. Indeed, S. Jerome, who wrote his life (Works, Vol. ii. p.13 ed. Migne) calls him "auctor vitae monasticae" (Ep. xxii. ad Eustochium). He is said to have fled to the Thebaid from the terrors of the Decian persecution, and to have died there in extreme old age. Antony has already been several times mentioned by Cassian. See the Institutes V. iv.; Conference II. ii.; III. iv., etc.
[997] Heb. 11:37, 38; Job 39:5-8; Ps. 106 (107):2, 4-6; Lam. 3:27, 28; Ps. 101 (102):7, 8.

CHAPTER VII.

Of the origin of the Sarabaites and their mode of life.

AND while the Christian religion was rejoicing in these two orders of monks though this system had begun by degrees to deteriorate, there arose afterwards that disgusting and unfaithful kind of monks; or rather, that baleful plant revived and sprang up again which when it first shot up in the persons of Ananias and Sapphira in the early Church was cut off by the severity of the Apostle Peter--a kind which among monks has been for a long while considered detestable and execrable, and which was adopted by no one any more, so long as there remained stamped on the memory of the faithful the dread of that very severe sentence, in which the blessed Apostle not merely refused to allow the aforesaid originators of the novel crime to be cured by penitence or any amends, but actually destroyed that most dangerous germ by their speedy death. When then that precedent, which was punished with Apostolical severity in the case of Ananias and Sapphira had by degrees faded from the minds of some, owing to long carelessness and forgetfulness from lapse of time, there arose the race of Sarabaites, who owing to the fact that they have broken away from the congregations of the coenobites and each look after their own affairs, are rightly named in the Egyptian language Sarabaites,[998] and these spring from the number of those, whom we have mentioned, who wanted to imitate rather than truly to aim at Evangelical perfection, urged thereto by rivalry or by the praises of those who preferred the complete poverty of Christ to all manner of riches. These then while in their feeble mind they make a pretence of the greatest goodness and are forced by necessity to join this order, while they are anxious to be reckoned by the name of monks without emulating their pursuits, in no sort of way practise discipline, or are subject to the will of the Elders, or, taught by their traditions, learn to govern their own wills or take up and properly learn any rule of sound discretion; but making their renunciation only as a public profession, i.e., before the face of men, either continue in their homes devoted to the same occupations as before, though dignified by this title, or building cells for themselves and calling them monasteries remain in them perfectly free and their own masters, never submitting to the precepts of the gospel, which forbid them to be busied with any anxiety for the day's food, or troubles about domestic matters: commands which those alone fulfil with no unbelieving doubt, who have freed themselves from all the goods of this world and subjected themselves to the superiors of the coenobia so that they cannot admit that they are at all their own masters. But those who, as we said, shirk the severity of the monastery, and live two or three together in their cells, not satisfied to be under the charge and rule of an Abbot, but arranging chiefly for this; viz., that they may get rid of the yoke of the Elders and have liberty to carry out their wishes and go and wander where they will, and do what they like, these men are more taken up both day and night in daily business than those who live in the coenobia, but not with the same faith and purpose. For these Sarabaites do it not to submit the fruits of their labours to the will of the steward, but to procure money to lay by. And see what a difference there is between them. For the others think nothing of the morrow, and offer to God the most acceptable fruits of their toil: while these extend their faithless anxiety not only to the morrow, but even to the space of many years, and so fancy that God is either false or impotent as He either could not or would not grant them the promised supply of food and clothing. The one seek this in all their prayers; viz., that they may gain akthmosunhn, i.e., the deprivation of all things, and lasting poverty: the other that they may secure a rich quantity of all sorts of supplies. The one eagerly strive to go beyond the fixed rule of daily work that whatever is not wanted for the sacred purposes of the monastery, may be distributed at the will of the Abbot either among the prisons, or in the guest-chamber or in the infirmary or to the poor; the others that whatever the day's gorge leaves over, may be useful for extravagant wants or else laid by through the sin of covetousness. Lastly, if we grant that what has been collected by them with no good design, may be disposed of in better ways than we have mentioned, yet not even thus do they rise to the merits of goodness and perfection. For the others bring in such returns to the monastery, and daily report to them, and continue in such humility and subjection that they are deprived of their rights over what they gain by their own efforts, just as they are of their rights over themselves, as they constantly renew the fervour of their original act of renunciation, while they daily deprive themselves of the fruits of their labours: but these are puffed up by the fact that they are bestowing something on the poor, and daily fall headlong into sin. The one party are by patience and the strictness whereby they continue devoutly in the order which they have once embraced, so as never to fulfil their own will, crucified daily to this world and made living martyrs; the others are cast down into hell by the lukewarmness of their purpose. These two sorts of monks then vie with each other in almost equal numbers in this province; but in other provinces, which the need of the Catholic faith compelled me to visit, we have found that this third class of Sarabaites flourishes and is almost the only one, since in the time of Lucius who was a Bishop of Arian mis-belief[999] in the reign of Valens, while we carried alms[1000] to our brethren; viz., those from Egypt and the Thebaid, who had been consigned to the mines of Pontus and Armenia[1001] for their steadfastness in the Catholic faith, though we found the system of coenobia in some cities few and far between, yet we never made out that even the name of anchorites was heard among them.

NOTES:

[998] Sarabaites, this third sort of monks, whom Cassian here paints in such dark colours, are spoken of by S. Jerome (Ep. xxii. ad Eustochium) under the name of Remoboth. The origin of both names is obscure, but Jerome and Cassian are quite at one in their scorn for these pretended monks. S. Benedict begins his monastic rule by describing the four kinds of monks, coenobites, anchorites, sarabaites, and a fourth class to which he gives the name of "gyrovagi," i.e., wandering monks; these must be those of whom Cassian speaks below in c. viii. without giving them any definite name. See further Bingham, Antiquities VII. ii., and the Dictionary of Christian Antiquities, Art. Sarabaites.

[999] Lucius took the lead of the Arian party at Alexandria after the murder of George of Cappadocia in 361, and was put forward by his party as the candidate for the see which they regarded as vacant. In 373, after the death of Athanasius, he was forced upon the reluctant Church of Alexandria by the Arian Emperor Valens, and according to Gregory Nazianzen a fresh persecution of the orthodox party at once began; and to this it is that Piamun alludes in the text.

[1000] Diaconia. The word is used again by Cassian for almsgiving in Conf. XXI. i., viii., ix., and cf. Gregory the Great, Ep. xxii., and compare eis diakonian in Acts 11:29.

[1001] To work in the mines was a punishment to which the Confessors were frequently subjected in the time of persecution: Cf. the prayer in the Liturgy of S. Mark that God would have mercy on those in prison, or in the mines, etc. Hammond's Liturgies, p. 181.

CHAPTER VIII.

Of a fourth sort of monks.

THERE is however another and a fourth kind, which we have lately seen springing up among those who flatter themselves with the appearance and form of anchorites, and who in their early days seem in a brief fervour to seek the perfection of the coenobium, but presently cool off, and, as they dislike to put an end to their former habits and faults, and are not satisfied to bear the yoke of humility and patience any longer, and scorn to be in subjection to the rule of the Elders, look out for separate cells and want to remain by themselves alone, that as they are provoked by nobody they may be regarded by men as patient, gentle, and humble: and, this arrangement, or rather this lukewarmness never suffers those, of whom it has once got hold, to approach to perfection. For in this way their faults are not merely not rooted up, but actually grow worse, while they are excited by no one, like some deadly and internal poison which the more it is concealed, so much the more deeply does it creep in and cause an incurable disease to the sick person. For out of respect for each man's own cell no one ventures to reprove the faults of a solitary, which he would rather have ignored than cured. Moreover virtues are created not by hiding faults but by driving them out.

CHAPTER IX.

A question as to what is the difference between a coenobium and a monastery.

GERMANUS: Is there any distinction between a coenobium and a monastery, or is the same thing meant by either name?

CHAPTER X.

The answer.

PIAMUN: Although many people indifferently speak of monasteries instead of coenobia, yet there is this difference, that monastery is the title of the dwelling, and means nothing more than the place, i.e., the habitation of monks, while coenobium describes the character of the life and its system: and monastery may mean the dwelling of a single monk, while a coenobium cannot be spoken of except where dwells a united community of a large number of men living together. They are however termed monasteries in which groups of Sarabaites live.

CHAPTER XI.

Of true humility, and how Abbot Serapion exposed the mock humility of a certain man.

WHEREFORE as I see that you have learnt the first principles of this life from the best sort of monks, i.e., that starting from the excellent school of the coenobium you are aiming at the lofty heights of the anchorite's rule, you should with genuine feeling of heart pursue the virtue of humility and patience, which I doubt not that you learnt there; and not feign it, as some do, by mock humility in words, or by an artificial and unnecessary readiness for some duties of the body. And this sham humility Abbot Serapion[1002] once laughed to scorn most capitally. For when one had come to him making a great display of his lowliness by his dress and words, and the old man urged him, after his custom, to "collect the prayer"[1003] he would not consent to his request, but debasing himself declared that he was involved in such crimes that he did not deserve even to breathe the air which is common to all, and refusing even the use of the mat preferred to sit down on the bare ground. But when he had shown still less inclination for the washing of the feet, then Abbot Serapion, when supper was finished, and the customary Conference gave him an opportunity, began kindly and gently to urge him not to roam with shifty lightmindedness over the whole world, idly and vaguely, especially as he was young and strong, but to keep to his cell in accordance with the rule of the Elders and to elect to be supported by his own efforts rather than by the bounty of others; which even the Apostle Paul would not allow, and though when he was labouring in the cause of the gospel this provision might lightly have been made for him, yet he preferred to work night and day, to provide daily food for himself and for those who were ministering to him and could not do the work with their own hands. Whereupon the other was filled with such vexation and disgust that he could not hide by his looks the annoyance which he felt in his heart. To whom the Elder: Thus far, my son, you have loaded yourself with the weight of all kinds of crimes, not fearing lest by the confession of such awful sins you bring a reproach upon your reputation; how is it then, I pray, that now, at our simple admonition, which involved no reproof, but simply showed a feeling for your edification and love, I see that you are moved with such disgust that you cannot hide it by your looks, or conceal it by an appearance of calmness? Perhaps while you were humiliating yourself, you were hoping to hear from our lips this saying: "The righteous man is the accuser of himself in the opening of his discourse"?[1004] Further, true humility of heart must be preserved, which comes not from an affected humbling of body and in word, but from an inward humbling of the soul: and this will only then shine forth with clear evidences of patience when a man does not boast about sins, which nobody will believe, but, when another insolently accuses him of them, thinks nothing of it, and when with gentle equanimity of spirit he puts up with wrongs offered to him.

NOTES:
[1002] On Serapion see the note on Conf. V. i.
[1003] Orationem Colligere. See the notes on the Institutes II. vii.
[1004] Prov. 18:17.

CHAPTER XII.

A question how true patience can be gained.

GERMANUS: We should like to know how that calmness can be secured and maintained, that, as when silence is enjoined on us we shut the door of our mouth, and lay an embargo on speech, so also we may be able to preserve gentleness of heart, which sometimes even when the tongue is restrained loses its state of calmness within: and for this reason we think that the blessing of gentleness can only be preserved by one in a remote cell and solitary dwelling.

CHAPTER XIII.

The answer.

PIAMUN: True patience and tranquillity is neither gained nor retained without profound humility of heart: and if it has sprung from this source, there will be no need either of the good offices of the cell or of the refuge of the desert. For it will seek no external support from anything, if it has the internal support of the virtue of humility, its mother and its guardian. But if we are disturbed when attacked by anyone it is clear that the foundations of humility have not been securely laid in us, and therefore at the outbreak even of a small storm, our whole edifice is shaken and ruinously disturbed. For patience would not be worthy of praise and admiration if it only preserved its purposed tranquillity when attacked by no darts of enemies, but it is grand and glorious because when the storms of temptation beat upon it, it remains unmoved. For wherein it is believed that a man is annoyed and hurt by adversity, therein is he strengthened the more; and he is therein the more exercised, wherein he is thought to be annoyed. For everybody knows that patience gets its name from the passions and endurance, and so it is clear that no one can be called patient but one who bears without annoyance all the indignities offered to him, and so it is not without reason that he is praised by Solomon: "Better is the patient man than the strong, and he who restrains his anger than he who takes a city;" and again: "For a long-suffering man is mighty in prudence, but a faint-hearted man is very foolish."[1005] When then anyone is overcome by a wrong, and blazes up in a fire of anger, we should not hold that the bitterness of the insult offered to him is the cause of his sin, but rather the manifestation of secret weakness, in accordance with the parable of our Lord and Saviour which He spoke about the two houses,[1006] one of which was founded upon a rock, and the other upon the sand, on both of which He says that the tempest of rain and waters and storm beat equally: but that one which was founded on the solid rock felt no harm at all from the violence of the shock, while that which was built on the shifting and moving sand at once collapsed. And it certainly appears that it fell, not because it was struck by the rush of the storms and torrents, but because it was imprudently built upon the sand. For a saint does not differ from a sinner in this, that he is not himself tempted in the same way, but because he is not worsted even by a great assault, while the other is overcome even by a slight temptation. For the fortitude of any good man would not, as we said, be worthy of praise, if his victory was gained without his being tempted, as most certainly there is no room for victory where there is no struggle and conflict: for "Blessed is the man that endureth temptation, for when he has been proved he shall receive the crown of life which God hath promised to them that love Him."[1007] According to the Apostle Paul also "Strength is made perfect" not in ease and delights but "in weakness." "For behold," says He, "I have made thee this day a fortified city, and a pillar of iron, and a wall of brass, over all the land, to the kings of Judah, and to the princes thereof, and to the priests thereof, and to all the people of the land. And they shall fight against thee, and shall not prevail: for I am with thee, saith the Lord, to deliver thee." [1008]

NOTES:
[1005] Prov. 16:32; 14:29.
[1006] Cf. S. Matt. 7:24, 59.
[1007] S. James 1:12.
[1008] 2 Cor. 12:9; Jer. 1:18, 19.

CHAPTER XIV.

Of the example of patience given by a certain religious woman.

OF this patience then I want to give you at least two examples: one of a certain religious woman, who aimed at the virtue of patience so eagerly that she not only did not avoid the assaults of temptation, but actually made for herself occasions of trouble that she might not cease to be tried more often. For this woman as she was living at Alexandria and was born of no mean ancestors, and was serving the Lord religiously in the house which had been left to her by her parents, came to Athanasius the Bishop, of blessed memory, and entreated him to give her some other widow to support, who was being provided for at the expense of the Church. And, to give her petition in her own words: "Give me," she said, "one of the sisters to look after." When then the Bishop had commended the woman's purpose because he saw that she was very ready for a work of a mercy, he ordered a widow to be chosen out of the whole number, who was preferred to all the rest for the goodness of her character, and her grave and well-regulated life, for fear lest her wish to be liberal might be overcome by the fault of the recipient of her bounty, and she who sought gain out of the poor might be disgusted at her bad character and so suffer an injury to her faith. And when the woman was brought home, she ministered to her with all kinds of service, and found out her excellent modesty and gentleness, and saw that every minute she was honoured by thanks from her for her kind offices, and so after a few days she came back to the aforesaid Bishop, and said: I asked you to bid that a woman be given to me for me to support and to serve with obedient complaisance. And when he, not yet understanding the woman's object and desire, thought that her petition had been neglected by the deceitfulness of the superior, and inquired not without some anger in his mind, what was the reason of the delay, at once he discovered that a widow who was better than all the rest had been assigned to her, and so he secretly gave orders that the one who was the worst of all should be given to her, the one, I mean, who surpassed in anger and quarrelling and wine-bibbing and talkativeness all who were under the power of these faults. And when she was only too easily found and given to her, she began to keep her at home, and to minister to her with the same care as to the former widow, or even more attentively, and this was all the thanks which she got from her for her services; viz., to be constantly tried by unworthy wrongs and continually annoyed by her by reproaches and upbraiding, as she complained of her, and chid her with spiteful and disparaging remarks, because she had asked for her from the Bishop not for her refreshment but rather for her torment and annoyance, and had taken her away from rest to labour instead of from labour to rest. When then her continual reproaches broke out so far that the wanton woman did not restrain herself from laying hands on her, the other only redoubled her services in still humbler offices, and learnt to overcome the vixen not by resisting her, but by subjecting herself still more humbly, so that, when provoked by all kinds of indignities, she might smooth down the madness of the shrew by gentleness and kindness. And when she had been thoroughly strengthened by these exercises, and had attained the perfect virtue of the patience she had longed for, she came to the aforesaid Bishop to thank him for his decision and choice as well as for the blessing of her exercise, because he had at last as she wished provided her with a most worthy mistress for her patience, strengthened daily by whose constant annoyance as by some oil for wrestling, she had arrived at complete patience of mind; and, at last, said she, you have given me one to support, for the former one rather honoured and refreshed me by her services. This may be sufficient to have told about the female sex, that by this tale we may not only be edified, but even confounded, as we cannot maintain our patience unless we are like wild beasts removed in caves and cells.

CHAPTER XV.

Of the example of patience given by Abbot Paphnutius.

NOW let us give the other instance of Abbot Paphnutius, who always remained so zealously in the recesses of that renowned and far-famed desert of Scete, in which he is now Presbyter, so that the rest of the anchorites gave him the name of Bubalis,[1009] because he always delighted in dwelling in the desert as if with a sort of innate liking. And so as even in boyhood he was so good and full of grace that even the renowned and great men of that time admired his gravity and steadfast constancy, and although he was younger in age, yet put him on a level with the Elders out of regard for his virtues, and thought fit to admit him to their order, the same envy, which formerly excited the minds of his brethren against the patriarch Joseph, inflamed one out of the number of his brethren with a burning and consuming jealousy. And this man wanting to mar his beauty by some blemish or spot, hit on this kind of devilry, so as to seize an opportunity when Paphnutius had left his cell to go to Church on Sunday: and secretly entering his cell he slyly hid his own book among the boughs which he used to weave of palm branches, and, secure of his well-planned trick, himself went off as if with a pure and clean conscience to Church. And when the whole service was ended as usual, in the presence of all the brethren he brought his complaint to S. Isidore[1010] who was Presbyter of this desert before this same Paphnutius, and declared that his book had been stolen from his cell. And when his complaint had so disturbed the minds of all the brethren, and more especially of the Presbyter, so that they knew not what first to suspect or think, as all were overcome with the utmost astonishment at so new and unheard of a crime, such as no one remembered ever to have been committed in that desert before that time, and which has never happened since, he who had brought forward the matter as the accuser urged that they should all be kept in Church and certain selected men be sent to search the cells of the brethren one by one. And when this had been entrusted to three of the Elders by the Presbyter, they turned over the bed-chambers of them all, and at last found the book hidden in the cell of Paphnutius among the boughs of the palms which they call seira, just as the plotter had hidden it. And when the inquisitors at once brought it back to the Church and produced it before all, Paphnutius, although he was perfectly clear in the sincerity of his conscience, yet like one who acknowledged the guilt of thieving, gave himself up entirely to make amends and humbly asked for a plan of repentance, as he was so careful of his shame and modesty (and feared) lest if he tried to remove the stain of the theft by words, he might further be branded as a liar, as no one would believe anything but what had been found out. And when he had immediately left the Church not cast down in mind but rather trusting to the judgment of God, he continually shed tears at his prayers, and fasted thrice as often as before, and prostrated himself in the sight of men with all humility of mind. But when he had thus submitted himself with all contrition of flesh and spirit for almost a fortnight, so that he came early on the morning of Saturday and Sunday not to receive the Holy Communion[1011] but to prostrate himself on the threshold of the Church and humbly ask for pardon, He, Who is the witness of all secret things and knows them, suffered him to be no longer tried by Himself or defamed by others. For what the author of the crime, the wicked thief of his own property, the cunning defamer of another's credit, had done with no man there as a witness, that He made known by means of the devil who was himself the instigator of the sin. For possessed by a most fierce demon, he made known all the craft of his secret plot, and the same man who had conceived the accusation and the cheat betrayed it. But he was so long and grievously vexed by that unclean spirit that he could not even be restored by the prayers of the saints living there, who by means of divine gifts can command the devils, nor could the special grace of the Presbyter Isidore himself cast out from him his cruel tormentor, though by the Lord's bounty such power was given him that no one who was possessed was ever brought to his doors without being at once healed; for Christ was reserving this glory for the young Paphnutius, that the man should be cleansed only by the prayers of him against whom he had plotted, and that the jealous enemy should receive pardon for his offence and an end of his present punishment, only by proclaiming his name, from whose credit he had thought that he could detract. He then in his early youth already gave these signs of his future character, and even in his boyish years sketched the lines of that perfection which was to grow up in mature age. If then we want to attain to his height of virtue, we must lay the same foundation to begin with.

NOTES:

[1009] I.e., the Buffalo. On Paphnutius see the note on Conf. III.

[1010] Gazet thinks that this Isidore is the same person as the one mentioned in the Lausiac History c. i.; and Sozomen VI. xxviii., but doubts whether he is identical with the person of the same name mentioned in Rufinus: History of the Monks c. xvii., Sozomen VIII. xii., and Socrates VI. ix.

[1011] On the Saturday and Sunday celebration of the Holy Communion in Egypt compare the Institutes III. ii. In Gaul it was apparently received daily: Institutes VI. viii.

CHAPTER XVI.

On the perfection of patience.

A TWOFOLD reason however led me to relate this fact, first that we may weigh this steadfastness and constancy of the man, and as we are attacked by less serious wiles of the enemy, may the better secure a greater feeling of calmness and patience, secondly that we may with resolute decision hold that we cannot be safe from the storms of temptation and assaults of the devil if we make all the protection for our patience and all our confidence consist not in the strength of our inner man but in the doors of our cell or the recesses of the desert, and companionship of the saints, or the safeguard of anything else outside us. For unless our mind is strengthened by the power of His protection Who says in the gospel "the kingdom of God is within you,"[1012] in vain do we fancy that we can defeat the plots of our airy foe by the aid of men who are living with us, or that we can avoid them by distance of place, or exclude them by the protection of walls. For though none of these things was wanting to Saint Paphnutius yet the tempter did not fail to find a way of access against him to attack him; nor did the encircling walls, or the solitude of the desert or the merits of all those saints in the congregation repulse that most foul spirit. But because the holy servant of God had fixed the hope of his heart not on those external things but on Him Who is the judge of all secrets, he could not be moved even by the machinations of such an assault as that. On the other hand did not the man whom envy had hurried into so grievous a sin enjoy the benefit of solitude and the protection of a retired dwelling, and intercourse with the blessed Abbot and Presbyter Isidore and other saints? And yet because the storm raised by the devil found him upon the sand, it not only drove in his house but actually overturned it. We need not then seek for our peace in externals, nor fancy that another person's patience can be of any use to the faults of our impatience. For just as "the kingdom of God is within you," so "a man's foes are they of his own household."[1013] For no one is more my enemy than my own heart which is truly the one of my household closest to me. And therefore if we are careful, we cannot possibly be injured by intestine enemies. For where those of our own household are not opposed to us, there also the kingdom of God is secured in peace of heart. For if you diligently investigate the matter, I cannot be injured by any man however spiteful, if I do not fight against myself with warlike heart. But if I am injured, the fault is not owing to the other's attack, but to my own impatience. For as strong and solid food is good for a man in good health, so it is bad for a sick one. But it cannot hurt the man who takes it, unless the weakness of its recipient gives it its power to hurt. If then any similar temptation ever arises among brethren, we need never be shaken out of the even tenor of our ways and give an opening to the blasphemous snarls of men living in the world, nor wonder that some bad and detestable men have secretly found their way into the number of the saints, because so long as we are trodden down and trampled in the threshing floor of this world, the chaff which is destined for eternal fire is quite sure to be mingled with the choicest of the wheat. Finally if we bear in mind that Satan was chosen among the angels, and Judas among the apostles, and Nicholas the author of a detestable heresy among the deacons, it will be no wonder that the basest of men are found among the ranks of the saints. For although some maintain that this Nicholas was not the same man who was chosen for the work of the ministry by the Apostles,[1014] nevertheless they cannot deny that he was of the number of the disciples, all of whom were clearly of such a character and so perfect as those few whom we can now with difficulty discover in the coenobia. Let us then bring forward not the fall of the above-mentioned brother, who fell in the desert with so grievous a collapse, nor that horrible stain which he afterwards wiped out by the copious tears of his penitence, but the example of the blessed Paphnutius; and let us not be destroyed by the ruin of the former, whose ingrained sin of envy was increased and made worse by his affected piety, but let us imitate with all our might the humility of the latter, which in his case was no sudden production of the quiet of the desert, but had been gained among men, and was consummated and perfected by solitude. However you should know that the evil of envy is harder to be cured than other faults, for I should almost say that a man whom it has once tainted with the mischief of its poison is without a remedy. For it is the plague of which it is figuratively said by the prophet: "Behold I will send among you serpents, basilisks, against which there is no charm: and they shall bite you."[1015] Rightly then are the stings of envy compared by the prophet to the deadly poison of basilisks, as by it the first author of all poisons and their chief perished and died. For he slew himself before him of whom he was envious, and destroyed himself before that he poured forth the poison of death against man: for "by the envy of the devil death entered into the world: they therefore who are on his side follow him."[1016] For just as he who was the first to be corrupted by the plague of that evil, admitted no remedy of penitence, nor any healing plaster, so those also who have given themselves up to be smitten by the same pricks, exclude all the aid of the sacred charmer, because as they are tormented not by the faults but by the prosperity of those of whom they are jealous, they are ashamed to display the real truth and look out for some external unnecessary and trifling causes of offence: and of these, because they are altogether false, vain is the hope of cure, while the deadly poison which they will not produce is lurking in their veins. Of which the wisest of men has fitly said: "If a serpent bite

426

without hissing, there is no supply for the charmer."[1017] For those are silent bites, to which alone the medicine of the wise is no succour. For that evil is so far incurable that it is made worse by attentions, it is increased by services, is irritated by presents, because as the same Solomon says: "envy endures nothing."[1018] For just in proportion as another has made progress in humble submission or in the virtue of patience or in the merit of munificence, so is a man excited by worse pricks of envy, because he desires nothing less than the ruin or death of the man whom he envies. Lastly no submission on the part of their harmless brother could soften the envy of the eleven patriarchs, so that Scripture relates of them: "But his brothers envied him because his father loved him, and they could not speak peaceably unto him"[1019] until their jealousy, which would not listen to any entreaties on the part of their obedient and submissive brother, desired his death, and would scarcely be satisfied with the sin of selling a brother. It is plain then that envy is worse than all faults, and harder to get rid of, as it is inflamed by those remedies by which the others are destroyed. For, for example, a man who is grieved by a loss that has been caused to him, is healed by a liberal compensation: one who is sore owing to a wrong done to him, is appeased by humble satisfaction being made. What can you do with one who is the more offended by the very fact that he sees you humbler and kinder, who is not aroused to anger by any greed which can be appeased by a bribe; or by any injurious attack or love of vengeance, which is overcome by obsequious services; but is only irritated by another's success and happiness? But who is there who in order to satisfy one who envies him, would wish to fall from his good fortune, or to lose his prosperity or to be involved in some calamity? Wherefore we must constantly implore the divine aid, to which nothing is impossible, in order that the serpent may not by a single bite of this evil destroy whatever is flourishing in us, and animated as it were by the life and quickening power of the Holy Ghost. For the other poisons of serpents, i.e., carnal sins and faults, in which human frailty is easily entangled and from which it is as easily purified, show some traces of their wounds in the flesh, whereby although the earthly body is most dangerously inflamed, yet if any charmer well skilled in divine incantations applies a cure and antidote or the remedy of words of salvation, the poisonous evil does not reach to the everlasting death of the soul. But the poison of envy as if emitted by the basilisk, destroys the very life of religion and faith, even before the wound is perceived in the body. For he does not raise himself up against men, but, in his blasphemy, against God, who carps at nothing in his brother except his

427

felicity, and so blames no fault of man, but simply the judgment of God. This then is that "root of bitterness springing up"[1020] which raises itself to heaven and tends to reproaching the very Author Who bestows good things on man. Nor shall anyone be disturbed because God threatens to send "serpents, basilisks,"[1021] to bite those by whose crimes He is offended. For although it is certain that God cannot be the author of envy, yet it is fair and worthy of the divine judgment that, while good gifts are bestowed on the humble and refused to the proud and reprobate, those who, as the Apostle says, deserve to be given over "to a reprobate mind,"[1022] should be smitten and consumed by envy sent as it were by Him, according to this passage: "They have provoked me to jealousy by them that are no gods: and I will provoke them to jealousy by them that are no nation." [1023]

By this discourse the blessed Piamun excited still more keenly our desire in which we had begun to be promoted from the infant school of the coenobium to the second standard of the anchorites' life. For it was under his instruction that we made our first start in solitary living, the knowledge of which we afterwards followed up more thoroughly in Scete.

NOTES:
[1012] S. Luke 17:21.

[1013] S. Matt. 10:36.

[1014] As Cassian here implies, considerable doubt exists whether the Nicholas from whom the sect of the Nicolaitans (Rev. 2:15) derive their name was the same person as Nicholas the last of the seven "deacons" mentioned in Acts 6:5. According to Irenaeus (Haer. I. xxvi.) the Nicolaitans themselves claimed him as their founder, and the claim is allowed by Hippolytus (Philos. vii. S: 36), Epiphanius (Haer. I. ii. S: 25), and other writers of the fourth century. Clement of Alexandria however disputes the claim (Strom. III. iv. and cf. Euseb. H. E. III. xxix.), as does Theodoret (Haer. Tab. iii. 1).

[1015] Jer. 8:17.

[1016] Wisd. 2:24, 25.

[1017] Eccl. 10:2.

[1018] Prov. 27:4.

[1019] Gen. 37:4.

[1020] Heb. 12:15.

[1021] Jer. 8:17.

[1022] Rom. 1:28.

[1023] Deut. 32:21.

CONFERENCE 19.

Conference of Abbot John
on the Aim of the Coenobite and Hermit

CHAPTER I.

Of the coenobium of Abbot Paul and the patience of a certain brother.

AFTER only a few days we made our way once more with great alacrity, drawn by the desire for further instruction, to the coenobium of Abbot Paul, where though a greater number than two hundred of the brethren dwell there, yet, in honour of the festival which was then being held, an enormous collection of monks from other coenobia had come there as well: for the anniversary of the death[1024] of a former Abbot who had presided over the same monastery was being solemnly kept. And we have mentioned this assembly for this reason that we may briefly treat of the patience of a certain brother, which was remarkable for immovable gentleness on his part in the presence of all this congregation. For though the object of this work has regard to another person; viz., that we may produce the utterances of Abbot John[1025] who left the desert and submitted himself to that coenobium with the utmost goodness and humility, yet we think it not at all absurd to relate without any unnecessary verbiage, what we think is most instructive to those who are eager for goodness. And so when the whole body of the monks was seated in separate parties of twelve, in the large open court, when one of the brethren had been rather slow in fetching and bringing in a dish, the aforesaid Abbot Paul, who was busily hurrying about among the troops of brethren who were serving, saw it and struck him such a blow before them all on his open palm that the sound of the hand which was struck actually reached the ears of those whose backs were turned and who were sitting some way off.

But the youth of remarkable patience received it with such calmness of mind that not only did he let no word fall from his mouth or give the slightest sign of murmuring by the silent movements of his lips, but actually did not change colour in the slightest degree or (lose) the modest and peaceful look about his mouth. And this fact struck with astonishment not merely us, who had lately come from a monastery of Syria and had not learnt the blessing of this patience by such clear examples, but all those as well who were not without experience of such earnestness, so that by it a great lesson was taught even to those who were well advanced, because even if this paternal correction had not disturbed his patience, neither did the presence of so great a number bring the slightest sign of colour to his cheeks.

NOTES:
[1024] Depositio. A word frequently used for the day of the death (or burial) in Calendars and Martyrologies.
[1025] On this Abbot John compare the note on the Institutes V. xxvii.

CHAPTER II.

Of Abbot John's humility and our question.

IN this coenobium then we found a very old man named John, whose words and humility we think ought certainly not to be passed over in silence as in them he excelled all the saints, as we know that he was especially vigorous in this perfection, which though it is the mother of all virtues and the surest foundation of the whole spiritual superstructure, yet is altogether a stranger to our system. Wherefore it is no wonder that we cannot attain to the height of those men, as we cannot stand the training of the coenobium I will not say up to old age, but are scarcely content to endure the yoke of subjection for a couple of years, and at once escape to enjoy a dangerous liberty, while even for that short time we seem to be subject to the rule of the Elder not according to any strict rule, but as our free will directs. When then we had seen this old man in Abbot Paul's coenobium, we were struck, first by his age and the grace with which the man was endowed, and with looks fixed on the ground began to entreat him to vouchsafe to explain to us why he had forsaken the freedom of the desert and that exalted profession, in which his fame and celebrity had raised him above others who had adopted the same life, and why he had chosen to enter under the yoke of the coenobium. He said that as he was unequal to the system of the anchorites and unworthy of the heights of such perfection, he had gone back to the infant school, that he might learn to carry out the lessons taught there, according as the life demanded. And when our entreaties were not satisfied and we refused to take this humble answer, at last he began as follows.

CHAPTER III.

Abbot John's answer why he had left the desert.

THE system of the anchorites, which you are surprised at my leaving, I not only neither reject nor refuse, but rather embrace and regard with the utmost veneration: in which system, and after I had passed thirty years living in a coenobium, I rejoice that I have also spent twenty more, so that I can never be accused of sloth among those who tried it in a half-hearted way. But because its purity, of which I had had some slight experience, was sometimes soiled by the presence of anxiety about carnal matters, it seemed better to return to the coenobium to secure a readier attainment of an easier aim undertaken, and less danger from venturing on the higher life of the humble solitary.[1026] For it is better to seem earnest with smaller promises than careless in larger ones. And therefore if possibly I bring forward anything somewhat arrogantly and indeed somewhat too freely, I beg that you will not think it due to the sin of boasting but rather to my desire for your edification; and that, as I think that, when you ask so earnestly, nothing of the truth should be kept back from you, you will set it down to love rather than to boasting. For I think that some instruction may be given to you if I lay aside my humility, and simply lay bare the whole truth about my aim. For I trust that I shall not incur any reproach of vainglory from you because of the freedom of my words, nor any charge of falsehood from my conscience because of any suppression of the truth.

NOTES:

[1026] The true reading, as given by Petschenig, appears to be the following: Et minus de praesumptae sublimioris professionis humilitate periculum. It is probably on account of its difficulty that humilitate has been altered into difficultate, as in the text of Gazet (the two humilitate difficultate are found together in some MSS.). But the fact appears to be that humilitas is here

431

used for the life of an anchorite, as in Conference XXIV. ix., where Abbot Abraham uses the expression districtionem hujus humilitatis. The word is also used in a somewhat similar sense in Conf. I. xx. and XI. ii.

CHAPTER IV.

Of the excellence which the aforesaid old man showed in the system of the anchorites.

IF then anyone else delights in the recesses of the desert and would forget all human intercourse and say with Jeremiah: "I have not desired the day of man: Thou knowest,"[1027] I confess that by the blessing of God's grace, I also secured or at any rate tried to secure this. And so by the kind gift of the Lord I remember that I was often caught up into such an ecstasy as to forget that I was clothed with the burden of a weak body, and my soul on a sudden forgot all external notions and entirely cut itself off from all material objects, so that neither my eyes nor ears performed their proper functions. And my soul was so filled with divine meditations and spiritual contemplations that often in the evening I did not know whether I had taken any food and on the next day was very doubtful whether I had broken my fast yesterday. For which reason, a supply of food for seven days, i.e., seven sets of biscuits were set apart in a sort of hand-basket,[1028] and laid by on Saturday, that there might be no doubt when supper had been omitted; and by this plan another mistake also from forgetfulness was obviated, for when the number of cakes was finished it showed that the course of the week was over, and that the services of the same day had come round, and that the festival and holy day and services of the congregation could not escape the notice of the solitary. But even if that ecstasy of mind of which we have spoken should happen to interfere with this arrangement, yet still the method of the days' work would show the number of the days and check the mistake. And to pass over in silence the other advantages of the desert (for it is not our business to treat of their number and quantity, but rather of the aim of solitude and the coenobium) I will the rather briefly explain the reasons why I preferred to leave it, which you also wanted to know, and will in a concise discourse glance at all those fruits of solitude which I mentioned, and show to what greater advantages on the other side they ought to be held inferior.

NOTES:
[1027] Jer. 17:16.
[1028] In prochirio id est admanuensi sporta.

CHAPTER V.

Of the advantages of the desert.

SO long then as owing to the fewness of those who were then living in the desert, a greater freedom was afforded to us in a wider expanse of the wilderness, so long as in the seclusion of larger retreats we were caught up to those celestial ecstasies, and were not overwhelmed by a great quantity of brethren to visit us, and thus owing to the necessity of showing hospitality overburdened in our thoughts by the distractions of great cares, I frequented with insatiable desire and all my heart the peaceful retreats of the desert and that life which can only be compared to the bliss of the angels. But when, as I said, a larger number of the brethren began to seek a dwelling in that desert, and by cramping the freedom of the vast wilderness, not only caused that fire of divine contemplation to grow cold, but also entangled the mind in many ways in the chains of carnal matters, I determined to carry out my purpose in this system rather than to grow cold in that sublime mode of life, by providing for carnal wants; so that, if that liberty and those spiritual ecstasies are denied me, yet as all care for the morrow is avoided, I may console myself by fulfilling the precept of the gospel, and what I lose in sublimity of contemplation, may be made up to me by submission and obedience. For it is a wretched thing for a man to profess to learn any art or pursuit, and never to arrive at perfection in it.

CHAPTER VI.

Of the conveniences of the coenobium.

WHEREFORE I will briefly explain what advantages I now enjoy in this manner of life. You must consider my words and judge whether those advantages of the desert outweigh these comforts, and by this you will also be able to prove whether I chose to be cramped within the narrow limits of the coenobium from dislike or from desire of that purity of the solitary life. In this life then there is no providing for the day's work, no distractions of buying and selling, no unavoidable care for the year's food, no anxiety about bodily things, by which one has to get ready what is necessary not only for one's own wants but also for those of any number of visitors, finally no conceit from the praise of men, which is worse than all these things and sometimes in the sight of God does away with the good of even great efforts in the desert. But, to pass over those waves of spiritual pride and the deadly peril of vainglory in the life of the anchorite, let us return to this general burden which affects everybody, i.e., the ordinary anxiety in providing food, which has so far exceeded I say not the measure of that ancient strictness which altogether did without oil, but is beginning not to be content even with the relaxation of our own time according to which the requirements of all the supply of food for a year were satisfied by the preparation of a single pint of oil and a modius of lentils prepared for the use of visitors; but now the needful supply of food is scarcely met by two or three times that amount. And to such an extent has the force of this dangerous relaxation grown among some that, when they mix vinegar and sauce, they do not add that single drop of oil, which our predecessors who followed the rules of the desert with greater powers of abstinence, were accustomed to pour in simply for the sake of avoiding vainglory,[1029] but they break an Egyptian cheese for luxury and pour over it more oil than is required, and so take, under a single pleasant relish, two sorts of food which differ in their special flavour, each of which ought singly to be a pleasant refreshment at different times for a monk. To such a pitch however has this `ulikh kthsis, i.e., acquisition of material things grown, that actually under pretence of hospitality and welcoming guests anchorites have begun to keep a blanket in their cells--a thing which I cannot mention without shame-- to omit those things by which the mind that is awed by and intent on spiritual meditation is more especially hampered; viz., the concourse of brethren, the duties of receiving the coming and speeding the part- ing guest, visits to each other and the endless worry of various confabulations and occupations, the expectation of which owing to the continuous character of these customary interruptions keeps the mind on the stretch even during the time when these bothers seem to cease. And so the result is that the freedom of the anchorite's life is so hin- dered by these ties that it can never rise to that ineffable keenness of heart, and thus loses the fruits of its hermit life. And if this is now denied to me while I am living in the congregation and among others, at least there is no lack of peace of mind and tranquillity of heart that is freed from all business. And unless this is ready at hand for those also who live in the desert, they will indeed have to undergo the labours of the anchorite's life, but will lose its fruits which can only be gained in peaceful stability of mind. Finally even if there is any diminution of my purity of heart while I am living in the coenobium, I shall be satisfied by keeping in exchange that one precept of the Gospel, which certainly cannot be less esteemed than all those fruits of the desert; I mean that I should take no thought for the morrow, and submitting myself completely to the Abbot seem in some degree to emulate Him of whom it is said: "He humbled Himself, and became obedient unto death;" and so be able humbly to make use of His words: "For I came not to do mine own will, but the will of the Father which sent me." [1030]

NOTES:
[1029] Cf. Conference VIII.
[1030] Phil. 2:8; S. John 6:38.

CHAPTER VII.

A question on the fruits of the coenobium and the desert.

GERMANUS: Since it is evident that you have not, like so many, just touched the mere outskirts of each mode of life, but have ascended to the very heights, we should like to know what is the end of the coenobite's life and what the end of the hermit's. For no one can doubt that no man can discourse with greater fulness or fidelity, on these subjects than one who, taught by long use and experience, has followed them both, and so can by veracious teaching show us their value and aim.

CHAPTER VIII.

The answer to the question proposed.

JOHN: I should absolutely maintain that one and the same man could not attain perfection in both lives unless I was hindered by the example of some few. And since it is no small matter to find a man who is perfect in either of them, it is clear how much harder and I had almost said impossible it is for a man to be thoroughly efficient in both. And if this has ever happened, it cannot come under any general rule. For a general rule must be based not on exceptional instances, i.e., on the experience of a very few, but on what is within the power of the many or rather of all. But what is attained to here and there by but one or two, and is beyond the capacity of ordinary goodness, must be kept out of general rules as something permitted outside the condition and nature of human weakness, and should be brought forward as a miracle rather than as an example. Wherefore I will, as my slender ability allows, briefly intimate what you want to know. The aim indeed of the coenobite is to mortify and crucify all his desires and, according to that salutary command of evangelic perfection, to take no thought for the morrow. And it is perfectly clear that this perfection cannot be attained by any except a coenobite, such a man as the prophet Isaiah describes and blesses and praises as follows: "If thou turn away thy foot from the Sabbath, from doing thy own will in my holy day, and glorify Him, while thou dost not thine own ways, and thine own will is not found to speak a word: then shalt thou be delighted in the Lord, and I will lift thee up above the high places of the earth, and will feed thee with the inheritance of Jacob thy father. For the mouth of the Lord hath spoken it."[1031] But the perfection for a hermit is to have his mind freed from all earthly things, and to unite it, as far as human frailty allows, with Christ: and such a man the prophet Jeremiah describes when he says: "Blessed is the man who hath borne the yoke from his youth. He shall sit solitary and hold his peace, because he hath taken it upon himself;" the Psalmist also: "I am become like a pelican in the desert. I watched and became as a sparrow alone upon the housetop."[1032] To this aim then, which we have described as that of either life, unless each of them attains, in vain does the one adopt the system of the coenobium, and the other of the hermitage: for neither of them will get the good of his method of life.

NOTES:
[1031] Is. 58:13, 14.
[1032] Lam. 3:27, 28; Ps. 101 (102):7, 8.

CHAPTER IX.

Of true and complete perfection.

BUT this is merikh, i.e., no thorough and altogether complete perfection, but only a partial one. Perfection then is very rare and granted by God's gift to but a very few. For he is truly and not partially perfect who with equal imperturbability can put up with the squalor of the wilderness in the desert, as well as the infirmities of the brethren in the coenobium. And so it is hard to find one who is perfect in both lives, because the anchorite cannot thoroughly acquire akthmosunh, i.e., a disregard for and stripping oneself of material things, nor the coenobite purity in contemplation, although we know that Abbot Moses and Paphnutius and the two Macarii[1033] were masters of both in perfection. And so they were perfect in either life, and while they withdrew further than all the dwellers in the desert and delighted themselves unceasingly in the retirement of the wilderness, and as far as in them lay never sought intercourse with other men, yet they put up with the presence and the infirmities of those who came to them so that when a large number of the brethren came to them for the sake of seeing them and profiting by it, they endured this almost continuous trouble of receiving them with imperturbable patience, and men fancied that all the days of their life they had neither learnt nor practised anything but how to show common civility to those who came, so that it was a puzzle to all to say in which life their zeal was mainly shown, i.e., whether their greatness adapted itself more remarkably to the purity of the hermitage or to the common life.

NOTES:

[1033] Moses, Paphnutius, and the two Macarii have all been mentioned frequently before. On Moses (to whom the first two Conferences are assigned) see the note on the Institutes X. xxv.; on Paphnutius see [note] on Conference III. i.; and on the two Macarii, the [note on] Institutes V. xli.

CHAPTER X.

Of those who while still imperfect retire into the desert.

BUT some are sometimes so tantalized by the silence of the desert lasting all through the day that they altogether dread intercourse with men, and, when they have even for a little while broken through their habit of retirement owing to the accident of a visit from some of the brethren, boil over with marked vexation of mind, and show clear signs of annoyance. And this especially happens in the case of those who have betaken themselves to the solitary life without a well-matured purpose and without being thoroughly trained in the coenobium, as these men are always imperfect and easily upset, and incline to one side or the other, as the gales of trouble may drive them. For as they boil over impatiently at intercourse or conversation with the brethren, so while they are living in solitude they cannot stand the vastness of that silence which they themselves have courted, inasmuch as they themselves do not even know the reason why solitude ought to be wanted and sought for, but imagine that the value and the main part of this life consist in this; viz., in avoiding intercourse with the brethren and simply shunning and loathing the sight of a man.

CHAPTER XI.

A question how to cure those who have hastily left the congregation of the coenobium.

GERMANUS: By what treatment can any help be given to us or to others who are thus weak and only up to this; who had received but little instruction in the system of the coenobium when we began to aspire to dwell in solitude before we had got rid of our faults; or by what means shall we be able to acquire the constancy of an imperturbable mind, and immovable steadfastness of patience; we who all too soon gave up the common life in the coenobium, and forsook the schools and training ground for these exercises, in which our principles ought first to have been thoroughly schooled and perfected? How then can we now while we are living alone gain perfection in long-suffering and patience; or how can conscience, that searcher out of inward motives, discover whether these virtues exist in us or are wanting, so that because we are severed from intercourse with men, and not irritated by any of their provocations, we may not be deceived by false notions, and fancy that we have gained that imperturbable peace of mind?

CHAPTER XII.

The answer telling how a solitary can discover his faults.

JOHN: To those who are really seeking relief, healing remedies from the true Physician of souls will certainly not be wanting; and to those above all will they be given who do not disregard their ill-condition (either because they despair of it, or because they do not care about it), nor hide the danger they are in from their wound, nor in their wanton heart reject the remedy of penitence, but with an humble and yet careful heart flee to the heavenly Physician for the diseases they have contracted from ignorance or error or necessity. And so we ought to know that if we retire to solitude or secret places, without our faults being first cured, their operation is but repressed, while the power of feeling them is not extinguished. For the root of all sins not having been eradicated is still lying hid in us, or rather creeping up, and that it is still alive we can tell by these signs. For instance, if, when we are living in solitude we receive the approach of some brethren, or any very slight tarrying on their part, with any anxiety or fretfulness of mind, we should recognize that an incentive to the most hasty impatience is still existing in us. But if when we are hoping for the coming of a brother, and from some cause he perhaps delays a little, our mental indignation either silently blames his slowness, and annoyance at this inconvenient waiting disturbs our mind, the examination of our conscience will show that the sin of anger and vexation is plainly still remaining in us. Again, if when a brother asks for our book to read, or for some other article to use, his request annoys us, or a refusal on our part disgusts him, there can be no doubt that we are still entangled in the meshes of avarice or covetousness. But if a sudden thought or a passage of Holy Scripture brings up the recollection of a woman and we feel that we are at all attracted towards her, we should know that the fire of fornication is not yet extinguished in us. But if on a comparison of our own strictness with the laxity of another even th slightest conceit tries our mind, it is clear that we are affected with the dreadful plague of pride. When then we detect these signs of faults in our heart, we should clearly recognize that it is only the opportunity and not the passion of sin of which we are deprived. And certainly these passions, if at any time we were to mingle in the ordinary life of men, would at once start up from their lurking places in our thoughts and prove that they did not then for the first time come into existence when they broke out, but that they were then at last made public, because they had been long lying hid. And so even a solitary can detect by sure signs that the roots of each fault are still implanted in him, if he tries not to show his purity to men, but to maintain it inviolate in His sight, from whom no secrets of the heart can be hid.

CHAPTER XIII.

A question how a man can be cured who has entered on solitude without having his faults eradicated.

GERMANUS: We very clearly and plainly see the proofs by which the signs of infirmities are inferred, and the method of discerning diseases, i.e., how the faults which are concealed in us can be detected: for our every day experience and the daily motions of our thoughts show us all these as they have been stated. It remains then that as the proofs and causes of our maladies have been exposed to us in a most clear way so their remedies and cures may also be shown. For no one can doubt that one who has first discovered the grounds and beginnings of ailments, with the approving witness of the conscience of those affected, can best discourse on their remedies. And so though the teaching of your holiness has laid bare the secrets of our wounds whereby we venture to have some hope of a remedy, because so clear a diagnosis of the disease gives promise of the hope of a cure, yet because, as you say, the first elements of salvation are acquired in the coenobium, and men cannot be in a sound condition in solitude, unless they have first been healed by the medicine of the coenobium, we have fallen again into a dangerous state of despair lest as we left the coenobium in an imperfect condition we may not now that we are in the desert succeed in becoming perfect.

CHAPTER XIV.

The answer on their remedies.

JOHN: For those who are anxious for the cure of their ailments a saving remedy is sure not to be wanting, and therefore remedies should be sought by the same means that the signs of each fault are discovered. For as we have said that the faults of men's ordinary life are not wanting to solitaries, so we do not deny that all zeal for virtue, and all the means of healing are at the disposal of all those who are cut off from men's ordinary life. When then anyone discovers by those signs which we described above, that he is attacked by outbreaks of impatience or anger, he should always practise himself in the opposite and contrary things, and by setting before himself all sorts of injuries and wrongs, as if offered to him by somebody else, accustom his mind to submit with perfect humility to everything that wickedness can bring upon him; and by often representing to himself all kinds of rough and intolerable things, continually consider with all sorrow of heart with what gentleness he ought to meet them. And, by thus look-ing at the sufferings of all the saints, or indeed at those of the Lord Himself, he will admit that the various reproaches as well as punish-ments are less than he deserves, and prepare himself to endure all kinds of griefs. And when occasionally he has been recalled by some invitation to the assembly of the brethren--a thing which cannot but happen every now and then even to the strictest inmates of the desert,-- if he finds that his mind is silently disturbed even for trifles, he should like some stern censor of his secret emotions charge himself with all those various hard wrongs, to the perfect endurance of which he was training himself by his daily meditations, and blaming and chiding himself as follows, say My good man, are you the fellow who while training yourself in the practising ground of solitude, ventured most determinedly to think that you would get the better of all bad qualities, and who just now, when you were representing to yourself not only all sorts of bitter reproaches, but also intolerable punishments, fancied that you were pretty strong and able to stand against all storms? How is it that that unconquered patience of yours is upset by the first trial even of a light word? How is it that even a gentle breeze has shaken that house of yours which you fancied was built so strongly on the solid rock? Where is that which you announced when during a time of peace you were in your foolish confidence longing for war? "I am

ready, and am not troubled;" and this which you used often to say with
the prophet: "Prove me, O Lord, and try me: search out my reins and
my heart;" and: "prove me, O Lord, and know my heart: question me
and know my paths; and see if there be any way of wickedness in
me."[1034] How has a tiny ghost of an enemy frightened your grand
preparations for war? With such reproaches and remorse a man should
condemn himself and not allow the sudden temptation which has upset
him to go unpunished, but by chastising his flesh with a severer pen-
alty of fasting and vigils; and, by punishing his sin of lightness of
mind by continual pains of self-restraint, he should while living in
solitude consume in this fire of practice what he ought to have thoroughly driven out in the life of the coenobium. This at any rate we
must firmly and resolutely hold to in order to secure a lasting and unbroken patience; viz., that for us, to whom by the Divine law not
merely vengeance for, but even the recollection of injuries is forbidden, it is not permissible to be roused to anger because of some loss or
annoyance. For what greater injury can happen to the soul than for it,
owing to some sudden blindness from rage, to lose the brightness of
the true and eternal light and to fail of the sight of Him "Who is meek
and lowly of heart"?[1035] What I ask could be more dangerous or awk-
ward than for a man to lose his power of judging of goodness, and his
standard and rule of true discernment, and for one in his sober senses
to do what even a drunken man, and a fool would not be pardoned for
doing? One then who carefully considers these and other injuries of
the same kind, will readily endure and disregard not only all kinds of
losses, but also whatever wrongs and punishments can be inflicted by
the cruellest of men, as he will hold that there is nothing more damaging than anger, nor more valuable than peace of mind and unbroken
purity of heart, for the sake of which we should think nothing of the
advantages not merely of carnal matters but also of those things which
appear to be spiritual, if they cannot be gained or done without some
disturbance of this tranquillity.

NOTES:
[1034] Ps. 118 (119):60; 25 (26):2; 138 (139):23, 24.
[1035] S. Matt. 11:29.

CHAPTER XV.

A question whether chastity ought to be ascertained just as the other feelings.

GERMANUS: As the cure for other ailments, viz., anger, vexation, and impatience, has been shown to consist in opposing to them their contraries, so also we should like to learn what sort of treatment we ought to use against the spirit of fornication: I mean, whether the fire of lust can be quenched by the representation, as in those other cases, of greater inducements and things to excite it: because not merely to increase the incentives to lust within us, but even to touch them with a passing look of the mind, we believe to be utterly fatal to chastity.

CHAPTER XVI.

The answer giving the proofs by which it can be recognized.

JOHN: Your shrewd question has anticipated the subject, which even if you had said nothing must have arisen from our discourse, and therefore I do not doubt that it will be effectually grasped by your minds, since indeed your sharp wits have outstripped our instruction. For the puzzle of any question is easily removed, when the inquiry anticipates the answer, and is the first to travel along the road which it is to follow. And so to the treatment of those faults of which we have spoken above, intercourse with other men is not merely no hindrance, but a considerable help, for the more often that the outbursts of their impatience are exposed, the more thorough is the sorrow and compunction which they bring on those who have failed, and the speedier is the recovery of health which they confer on those who struggle against them. Wherefore even when we are living in solitude, though the incentive to irritation and matter for it cannot arise from men, yet we ought of set purpose to meditate on incitements to it, that as we are fighting against it with a continual struggle in our thoughts a speedier

443

cure for it may be found for us. But against the spirit of fornication the system is different, and the method an altered one. For as we must deprive the body of opportunities of lust, and contact with flesh, so we must deprive the mind of the recollection of it. For it is sufficiently dangerous for bosoms that are still weak and infirm even to tolerate the slightest recollection of this passion, in such a way that sometimes at the remembrance of holy women, or in reading a story in Holy Scripture a stimulus of dangerous excitement is aroused. For which reason our Elders used deliberately to omit passages of this kind when any of the juniors were present. However for those who are perfect and established in the feelings of chastity there can be no lack of proofs by which they may examine themselves, and establish their perfect uprightness of heart by the uncorrupted judgment of their own conscience. There will then be for the man who is thoroughly established a similar test even in regard to this passion, so that one who is sure that he has altogether exterminated the roots of this evil may for the sake of ascertaining his chastity, call up some picture as with a lascivious mind. But it is by no means proper for such a test to be attempted by those who are still weak (for to them it will be dangerous rather than useful), ut conjunctionem femineam et palpationem quodammodo teneram atque mollissimam corde pertractent. Cum ergo perfecta quis virtute fundatus ad illecebram blandissimorum tactuum, quos cogitando confinxerit, nullum mentis assensum, nullam commotionem carnis in se deprehenderit exagitatam, he will have a very sure proof of his purity, so that training himself to this steadfast purity he will not only possess the blessing of chastity and freedom from defilement in his heart, but even if he is obliged to touch the body of a woman, he will be horrified at it.

With this Abbot John brought his Conference to an end, as he saw that it was just time for the refreshment of the ninth hour.

CONFERENCE 20.

Conference of Abbot Pinufius
on the End of Penitence and the Marks of Satisfaction

CHAPTER I.

Of the humility of Abbot Pinufius, and of his hiding-place.

NOW that I am going to relate the precepts of that excellent and remarkable man, Abbot Pinufius, on the end of penitence, I fancy that I can dispose of a very large part of my material, if out of consideration lest I weary my reader, I here pass over in silence the praise of his humility, which I touched on in a brief discourse in the fourth book of the Institutes,[1036] which was entitled "Of the rules to be observed by renunciants," especially as many who have no knowledge of that work, may happen to read this, and then all the authority of the utterances will be weakened if there is no account of the virtues of the speaker. For this man when he was presiding as Abbot and Presbyter over a large coenobium not far from Panephysis, a city, as was there said, of Egypt, and when all that province had praised him to the skies for his virtues and miracles, so that he already seemed to himself to have received the reward of his labours in the remuneration of the praise of men, as he was afraid lest the emptiness of popular favour, which he especially disliked, might interfere with the fruits of an eternal reward, he secretly fled from his monastery and made his way to the furthest recesses of the monks of Tabennae,[1037] where he chose not the solitude of the desert, not that freedom from care of which the life of one alone affords, which even those who are imperfect and who cannot endure the effort which obedience requires in the coenobium, sometimes seek after with proud presumption, but he chose to submit himself to a most famous monastery. Where, however, that he might not be betrayed by any signs of his dress, he clothed himself in a secular garb, and lay before the doors with tears, as is the custom there, for many days, and clinging to the knees of all after being daily repulsed by those who to test his purpose said that now in extreme old age he was seeking this holy life not in sincerity, but driven by the lack of food, at last he obtained admission, and there he was told off to help a young brother who had been given the charge of a garden, and when he not only fulfilled with such marvellous and holy humility everything which his chief ordered him or which the care of the work entrusted to him demanded, but also performed in stealthy labour by night certain necessary offices which were avoided by the rest out of disgust for them, so that when morning dawned, all the congregation was delighted at such useful works but knew not their author; and when he had passed nearly three years there rejoicing in the labours, which he had desired, but to which he as so unfairly subjected, it happened that a certain brother known to him came there from the same parts of Egypt from which he himself had come. And this man for a time hesitated because the meanness of his clothes and of his office prevented him from readily recognizing him at once, but after looking very closely at him, fell at his feet, and first astonished all the brethren, and afterwards, when he betrayed his name, which the fame of his special sanctity had made known to them also, he smote them with sorrow and compunction because they had told off a man of his virtues and a priest to such mean offices. But he, shedding copious tears, and charging the accident of his betrayal to the serious envy of the devil, was brought in honourable custody by his brethren surrounding him to the monastery; and after that he had stayed there for a short time, he was once more troubled by the respect shown to his dignity and rank, and stealthily embarked on board ship and sailed to the Palestinian province of Syria, where he was received as a beginner and a novice in the house of that monastery in which we were living, and was charged by the Abbot to stop in our cell. But not even there could his virtues and merits long remain secret. For he was discovered and betrayed in the same way, and brought back to his own monastery with the utmost honour and respect.

NOTES:

[1036] Cf. Institutes IV. c. xxx., xxxi. Nothing further is known of Pinufius than what we gather from these passages of Cassian.

[1037] On Tabennae or Tabenna see the note on the Institutes IV. i.

CHAPTER II.

Of our coming to him.

WHEN then after no long time a desire for holy instruction had urged us also to visit Egypt, we sought him out with the utmost eagerness and devotion and were welcomed by him with such kindness and courtesy that he actually honoured us, as former sharers of the same cell with him, with a lodging in his own cell which he had built in the furthest corner of his garden. And there when in the presence of all the brethren at service he had delivered to one of the brethren who was submitting to the rule of the monastery sufficiently difficult and elevated precepts, which as we said, I summarized as briefly as I could in the fourth book of the Institutes, the heights of a true renunciation seemed to us so unattainable and so marvellous that we did not think that such humble folks as we could ever scale them. And therefore, cast down in despair, and not concealing in our looks the inner bitterness of our thoughts, we came back to the blessed old man with a tolerably anxious heart: and when he at once asked the reason why we were so sad, Abbot Germanus groaned deeply and replied as follows.

CHAPTER III.

A question on the end of penitence and the marks of satisfaction.

AS your grand and splendid exposition of a doctrine new to us has opened out to us a more difficult road to the most glorious renunciation, and has removed the scales from our eyes, and shown to us its summit raised in the heavens, so are we proportionately cast down with a greater weight of despair. Since, when we measure its vastness against our puny strength, and compare the excessively humble character of our ignorance with the boundless height of virtue shown to us, we feel that we are so small that we not only cannot attain to it, but that we are sure to fall short in what we have. For as we are weighed down by the burden of excessive despair, we fall away somehow from the lowest depths to still lower ones. Accordingly there is one and only one support which can provide a cure for our wounds; viz., for us to learn something of the end of penitence and especially on the marks of

447

satisfaction, that we may feel sure of the forgiveness of past sins, and so be spurred on to scale the heights of the perfection described above.

CHAPTER IV.

The answer on the humility shown by our request.

PINUFIUS: I am indeed delighted at the very plentiful fruits of your humility, which indeed I saw with no indifferent concern, when I was formerly received in the habitation of that cell of yours, and I am very glad that you welcome with such respect the charge given by us, the least of all Christians, and the words that I have taken the liberty of saying so that if I am not mistaken you carry them out as soon as ever they are spoken by us; and though, as I remember, the importance of the words scarcely deserves the efforts you bestow on them, yet you so conceal the merits of your virtue, as if no breath ever reached you of those things which you are daily practising. But because this fact is worthy of the highest praise; viz., that you declare that those institutes of the saints are still unknown to you as if you were still beginners we will, as briefly as possible, summarize what you so eagerly ask of us. For we must even beyond our powers and ability, obey the commands of such old friends as you. And so on the value and appeasing power of penitence many have published a great deal, not only in words but also in writing, showing how useful it is, how strong, and full of grace, so that when God is offended by our past sins, and on the point of inflicting a most just punishment for such offences, it somehow, if it is not wrong to say so, stops Him, and, if I may so say, stays the right hand of the Avenger even against His will. But I have no doubt that all this is well known to you, either from your natural wisdom, or from your unwearied study of Holy Scripture, so that from this the first shoots, so to speak, of your conversion sprang up. Finally, you are anxious not about the character of penitence but about its end, and the marks of satisfaction, and so by a very shrewd question ask what has been left out by others.

CHAPTER V.

Of the method of penitence and the proof of pardon.

WHEREFORE in order to satisfy as briefly and shortly as possible, your desire and question, the full and perfect description of penitence is, never again to yield to those sins for which we do penance, or for which our conscience is pricked. But the proof of satisfaction and pardon is for us to have expelled the love of them from our hearts. For each one may be sure that he is not yet free from his former sins as long as any image of those sins which he has committed or of others like them dances before his eyes, and I will not say a delight in--but the recollection of--them haunts his inmost soul while he is devoting himself to satisfaction for them and to tears. And so one who is on the watch to make satisfaction may then feel sure that he is free from his sins and that he has obtained pardon for past faults, when he never feels that his heart is stirred by the allurements and imaginations of these same sins. Wherefore the truest test of penitence and witness of pardon is found in our own conscience, which even before the day of judgment and of knowledge, while we are still in the flesh, discloses our acquittal from guilt, and reveals the end of satisfaction and the grace of forgiveness. And that what has been said may be more significantly expressed, then only should we believe that the stains of past sins are forgiven us, when the desires for present delights as well as the passions have been expelled from our heart.

CHAPTER VI.

A question whether our sins ought to be remembered out of contrition of heart.

GERMANUS: And whence can there be aroused in us this holy and salutary contrition from humiliation, which is described as follows in the person of the penitent: "I have acknowledged my sin, and mine unrighteousness have I not hid. I said: I will acknowledge against myself mine unrighteousness to the Lord," so that we may be able effectually to say also what follows: "And Thou forgavest the iniquity of my heart;"[1038] or how, when we kneel in prayer shall we be able to stir ourselves up to tears of confession, by which we may be able to obtain pardon for our offences, according to these words: "Every night will I wash my bed: I will water my couch with tears;"[1039] if we expel from our hearts all recollection of our faults, though on the contrary we are bidden carefully to preserve the remembrance of them, as the Lord says: "And thine iniquities I will not remember: but do thou recollect them"?[1040] Wherefore not only when I am at work, but also when I am at prayer I try of set purpose to recall to my mind the recollection of my sins, that I may be more effectually inclined to true humility and contrition of heart, and venture to say with the prophet: "Look upon my humility and my labour: and forgive me all my sins." [1041]

NOTES:
[1038] Ps. 31 (32):5, 6.
[1039] Ps. 6:7.
[1040] Is. 43:25, 26.
[1041] Ps. 24 (25):18.

CHAPTER VII.

The answer showing how far we ought to preserve the recollection of previous actions.

PINUFIUS: Your question, as has been already said above, was not raised with regard to the character of penitence, but with regard to its end, and the marks of satisfaction: to which, as I think, a fair and pertinent reply has been given. But what you have said as to the remembrance of sins is sufficiently useful and needful to men who are still doing penance, that they may with constant smiting of the breast say: "For I acknowledge my wickedness: and my sin is ever before me;" and this too: "And I will think for my sin."[1042] While then we do penance, and are still grieved by the recollection of faulty actions, the shower of tears which is caused by the confession of our faults is sure to quench the fire of our conscience. But when, while a man is still in this state of humility of heart and contrition of spirit and continuing to labour and to weep, the remembrance of these things fades away, and the thorns of conscience are by God's grace extracted from his inmost heart, then it is clear that he has attained to the end of satisfaction and the reward of pardon, and that he is purged from the stain of the sins he has committed. To which state of forgetfulness we can only attain by the obliteration of our former sins and likings, and by perfect and complete purity of heart. And this most certainly will not be attained by any of those who from sloth or carelessness have failed to purge out their faults, but only by one who by constantly continuing to groan and sigh sorrowfully has removed every spot of his former stains, and by the goodness of his heart and his labour has proclaimed to the Lord: "I have acknowledged my sin, and mine unrighteousness have I not hid;" and: "My tears have been my meat day and night;" so that in the end it may be vouchsafed to him to hear these words: "Let thy voice cease from weeping, and thine eyes from tears: for there is a reward for thy labour, saith the Lord;"[1043] and these words also may be uttered of him by the voice of the Lord: "I have blotted out as a cloud thine iniquities, and as a mist thy sins:" and again: "I even I am He that blotteth out thine iniquities for mine own sake, and thine offences I will no longer remember;"[1044] and so, when he is freed from the "cords of his sins," by which "everyone is bound,"[1045] he will with all thanksgiving sing to the Lord: "Thou hast broken my chains: I will offer to thee the sacrifice of praise." [1046]

NOTES:
[1042] Ps. 50 (51):5; 37 (38):19.
[1043] Ps. 31 (32):5; 41 (42):4; Jer. 31:16.
[1044] Is. 44:22; 43:25.
[1045] Prov. 5:22.
[1046] Ps. 115:16, 17.

CHAPTER VIII.

Of the various fruits of penitence.

FOR after that grace of baptism which is common to all, and that most precious gift of martyrdom which is gained by being washed in blood, there are many fruits of penitence by which we can succeed in expiating our sins. For eternal salvation is not only promised to the bare fact of penitence, of which the blessed Apostle Peter says: "Repent and be converted that your sins may be forgiven;" and John the Baptist and the Lord Himself: "Repent ye, for the kingdom of heaven is at hand:"[1047] but also by the affection of love is the weight of our sins overwhelmed: for "charity covers a multitude of sins."[1048] In the same way also by the fruits of almsgiving a remedy is provided for our wounds, because "As water extinguishes fire, so does almsgiving extinguish sin."[1049] So also by the shedding of tears is gained the washing away of offences, for "Every night I will wash my bed: I will water my couch with tears." Finally to show that they are not shed in vain, he adds: "Depart from me all ye that work iniquity, for the Lord hath heard the voice of my weeping."[1050] Moreover by means of confession of sins, their absolution is granted: for "I said: I will confess against myself my sin to the Lord: and Thou forgavest the iniquity of my heart;" and again: "Declare thine iniquities first, that thou mayest be justified."[1051] By afflicting the heart and body also is forgiveness of sins committed in like manner obtained, for he says: "Look on my humility and my labour, and forgive me all my sins;" and more especially by amendment of life: "Take away," he says, "the evil of your thoughts from mine eyes. Cease to do evil, learn to do well. Seek judgment, relieve the oppressed: judge the orphan, defend the widow. And come, reason with Me, saith the Lord: and though your sins were as scarlet, yet shall they be as white as snow, though they were red as crimson, they shall be as white as wool."[1052] Sometimes too the pardon of our sins is obtained by the intercession of the saints, for "if a man knows his brother to sin a sin not unto death, he asks, and He will give to him his life, for him that sinneth not unto death;" and again: "Is any sick among you? Let him send for the Elders of the Church and they shall pray over him, anointing him with oil in the name of the Lord. And the prayer of faith shall save the sick, and the Lord will raise him up, and if he be in sins, they shall be forgiven him."[1053] Sometimes too by the virtue of compassion and faith the stains of sin are removed, according to this passage: "By compassion and faith sins are purged away."[1054] And often by the conversion and salvation of those who are saved by our warnings and preaching: "For he who converts a sinner from the error of his way, shall save his soul from death, and cover a multitude of sins."[1055] Moreover by pardon and forgiveness on our part we obtain pardon of our sins: "For if ye forgive men their offences, your heavenly Father will also forgive you your sins."[1056] You see then what great means of obtaining mercy the compassion of our Saviour hs laid open to us, so that no one when longing for salvation need be crushed by despair, as he sees himself called to life by so many remedies. For if you plead that owing to weakness of the flesh you cannot get rid of your sins by fasting, and you cannot say: "My knees are weak from fasting, and my flesh is changed for oil; for I have eaten ashes for my bread, and mingled my drink with weeping,"[1057] then atone for them by profuse almsgiving. If you have nothing that you can give to the needy (although the claims of want and poverty exclude none from this office, since the two mites of the widow are ranked higher than the splendid gifts of the rich, and the Lord promises that He will give a reward for a cup of cold water), at least you can purge them away by amendment of life. But if you cannot secure perfection in goodness by the eradication of all your faults, you can show a pious anxiety for the good and salvation of another. But if you complain that you are not equal to this service, you can cover your sins by the affection of love. And if in this also some sluggishness of mind makes you weak, at least you should submissively with a feeling of humility entreat for remedies for your wounds by the prayers and intercession of the saints. Finally who is there who cannot humbly say: "I have acknowledged my sin: and mine unrighteousness have I not hid;" so that by this confession he may be able also to add this: "And Thou forgavest the iniquity of my heart."[1058] But if shame holds you back, and you blush to reveal them before men, you should not cease to confess them with constant supplication to Him from Whom they cannot be hid, and to say to Him: "I acknowledge mine iniquity, and my sin is ever before me. Against Thee only have I sinned, and have done evil before Thee;"[1059] as He is wont to heal them without any publication which brings shame, and to forgive sins without any reproaching. And further besides that ready and sure aid the Divine condescension has afforded us another also that is still easier, and has entrusted the possession of the remedy to our own will, so that we can infer from our own feelings the forgiveness of our offences, when we say to Him: "Forgive us our debts as we also forgive our debtors."[1060] Whoever then desires to obtain forgiveness of his sins, should study to fit himself for it by these means. Let not the stubbornness of an obdurate heart turn away any from the saving remedy and the fount of so much goodness, because even if we have done all these things, they will not be able to expiate our offences, unless they are blotted out by the goodness and mercy of the Lord, who when He sees the service of pious efforts offered by us with a humble heart, supports our small and puny efforts with the utmost bounty, and says: "I even I am He that blotteth out thine iniquities for Mine own sake, and I will remember thy sins no more."[1061] Whoever then is aiming at this condition, which we have mentioned, will seek the grace of satisfaction by daily fasting and mortification of heart and body, for, as it is written, "Without shedding of blood there is no remission;"[1062] and this not without good reason. For "flesh and blood cannot inherit the kingdom of God."[1063] And therefore one who would withhold "the sword of the spirit which is the word of God"[1064] from this shedding of blood certainly comes under the lash of that curse of Jeremiah's; for "Cursed," says he "is he who withholds his sword from blood."[1065] For this is the sword which for our good sheds that bad blood whereby the material of our sins lives; and cuts off and pares away everything carnal and earthly which it finds to have grown up in the members of our soul; and makes men die to sin and live to God, and flourish with spiritual virtues. And so he will begin to weep no more at the recollection of former sins, but at the hope of what is to come, and, thinking less of past evils than of good things to come, will shed tears not from sorrow at his sins, but from delight in that eternal joy, and "forgetting those things which are behind," i.e., carnal sins, will press on "to those before,"[1066] i.e., to spiritual gifts and virtues.

NOTES:

[1047] Acts 3:19; S. Matt. 3:2.
[1048] 1 Pet. 4:8.
[1049] Ecclus. 3:33.
[1050] Ps. 6:7, 9.
[1051] Ps. 31 (32):5; Is. 43:26.
[1052] Ps. 24 (25):18; Is. 1:16-18.
[1053] 1 John 5:16; S. James 5:14, 15.
[1054] Prov. 15:27.
[1055] S. James 5:20.
[1056] S. Matt. 6:14.
[1057] Ps. 108 (109):24; 101 (102):10.
[1058] Ps. 31 (32):5.
[1059] Ps. 50 (51):5, 6.
[1060] S. Matt. 6:12.
[1061] Is. 43:25.
[1062] Heb. 9:22.
[1063] 1 Cor. 15:50.
[1064] Eph. 6:17.
[1065] Jer. 48:10.
[1066] Phil. 3:13.

CHAPTER IX.

How valuable to the perfect is the forgetfulness of sin.

BUT with regard to this that you said a little way back; viz., that you of set purpose go over the recollections of past sins, this ought certainly not to be done, nay, if it forcibly surprises you, it must be at once expelled. For it greatly hinders the soul from the contemplation of purity, and especially in the case of one who is living in solitude, as it entangles him in the stains of this world and swamps him in foul sins. For while you are recalling those things which you did through ignorance or wantonness in accordance with the prince of this world, though I grant you that while you are engaged in these thoughts no delight in them steals in, yet at least the mere taint of the ancient filthiness is sure to corrupt your soul with its foul stink, and to shut out the spiritual fragrance of goodness, i.e., the odour of a sweet savour. When then the recollection of past sins comes over your mind, you must recoil from it just as an honest and upright man runs away if he is sought out in public by an immodest and wanton woman either by words or by embraces. And certainly unless he at once withdraws himself from contact with her, and if he allows himself to linger the very least in impure talk, even if he refuses his consent to the shameful pleasures, yet he cannot avoid the brand of infamy and scorn in the judgment of all the passers by. So then we also, if by noxious recollections we are led to thoughts of this kind, ought at once to desist from dwelling upon them and to fulfil what we are commanded by Solomon: "But go forth," says he, "do not linger in her place, nor fix thine eye on her;"[1067] lest if the angels see us taken up with unclean and foul thoughts, they may not be able to say to us in passing by: "The blessing of the Lord be upon you."[1068] For it is impossible for the soul to continue in good thoughts, when the main part of the heart is taken up with foul and earthly considerations. For this saying of Solomon's is true: "When thine eyes look on a strange woman, then shall thy mouth speak wickedly, and thou shalt lie as it were in the midst of the sea, and as a pilot in a great storm. But thou shalt say: They have beaten me, but I felt no pain; and they mocked me, but I felt not."[1069] So then we should forsake not only all foul but even all earthly thoughts and ever raise the desires of our soul to heavenly things, in accordance with this saying of our Saviour: "For where I am," He says, "there also shall My servant be."[1070] For it often happens that when anyone out of pity is in thought going over his own falls or those of other faulty persons, he is affected by the delight and assent to this most subtle attack, and that which was undertaken and started with a show of goodness ends with a filthy and damaging termination, for "there are ways which appear to men to be right, but the ends thereof will come to the depths of hell." [1071]

NOTES:
[1067] Prov. 9:18.
[1068] Ps. 128 (129):8.
[1069] Prov. 23:33-35.
[1070] S. John 12:26.
[1071] Prov. 16:25.

CHAPTER X.

How the recollection of our sins should be avoided.

WHEREFORE we must endeavour to rouse ourselves to this praiseworthy contrition, by aiming at virtue and by the desire for the kingdom of heaven rather than by dangerous recollections of sins, for a man is sure to be suffocated by the pestilential smells of the sewer as long as he chooses to stand over it or to stir its filth.

CHAPTER XI.

Of the marks of satisfaction, and the removal of past sins.

BUT we know, as we have often said, that then only have we made satisfaction for past sins, when the very motions and feelings, through which, we were guilty of what we have to sorrow for, have been eradicated from our hearts. But no one should fancy that he can secure this, unless he has first with all the fervour of his spirit cut off the opportunities and occasions, owing to which he fell into those sins; as for instance, if through dangerous familiarity with a woman he has fallen into fornication or adultery, he must take the utmost pains to avoid even looking on one; or if he has been overcome by too much wine and over-eating, he should chastise with the utmost severity his craving for immoderate food. And again if he has been led astray by the desire for and love of money, and has fallen into perjury or theft or murder or blasphemy, he should cut off the occasion for avarice, which has allured and deceived him. If he is driven by the passion of pride into the sin of anger, he should with all the virtue of humility, remove the incentive to arrogance. And so, in order that each single sin may be destroyed, the occasion and opportunity by which or for which it was committed should be first got rid of. For by this curative treatment we can certainly attain to forgetfulness of the sins we have committed.

CHAPTER XII.

Wherein we must do penance for a time only; and wherein it can have no end.

BUT that description of the forgetfulness spoken of only has to do with capital offences, which are also condemned by the mosaic law, the inclination to which is destroyed and put an end to by a good life, and so also the penance for them has an end. But for those small offences in which, as it is written, "the righteous falls seven times and will rise again"[1072] penitence will never cease. For either through ignorance, or forgetfulness, or thought, or word, or surprise, or necessity, or weakness of the flesh, or defilement in a dream, we often fall every day either against our will or voluntarily; offences for which David also prays the Lord, and asks for purification and pardon, and says: "Who can understand sins? from my secret ones cleanse me; and from those of others spare Thy servant;" and the Apostle: "For the good which I would I do not, and the evil which I would not, that I do." For which also the same man exclaims with a sigh "O wretched man that I am! who shall deliver me from the body of this death?"[1073] For we slip into these so easily as it were by a law of nature, that however carefully and guardedly we are on the lookout against them, we cannot altogether avoid them. Since it was of these that one of the disciples, whom Jesus loved, declared and laid down absolutely saying: "If we say that we have no sin we deceive ourselves, and His word is not in us."[1074] Further for a man who is anxious to reach the heights of perfection it will not greatly help him to have arrived at the end of penitence, i.e., to restrain himself from unlawful acts, unless he has always urged himself forward in unwearied course to those virtues whereby we come to the signs of satisfaction. For it will not be enough for a man to have kept himself clear from those foul stains of sins which the Lord hates, unless he has also secured by purity of heart and perfect Apostolical love that sweet fragrance of virtue in which the Lord delights.

Thus far Abbot Pinufius discoursed on the marks of satisfaction and the end of penitence. And although he pressed us with anxious love to decide to stay in his coenobium, yet when he could not retain us, as we were incited by the fame of the desert of Scete, he sent us on our way.

NOTES:
[1072] Prov. 24:16.
[1073] Ps. 18 (19):12; Rom. 7:19, 24.
[1074] 1 John 1:8, 10.

CONFERENCE 21.

The First Conference of Abbot Theonas
on the Relaxation During the Fifty Days [1075]

CHAPTER. I.

How Theonas came to Abbot John.

BEFORE we begin to set forth the words of this Conference held with that excellent man Abbot Theonas,[1076] I think it well to describe in a brief discourse the origin of his conversion because from this the reader will be able to see more clearly both the excellence and the grace of the man. He then while still very young was by the desire and command of his parents joined in the tie of marriage, for as with pious anxiety they were careful about his chastity, and were afraid of a critical fall at a dangerous age, they thought that the passions of youth might be anticipated by the remedy of a lawful marriage. When then he had lived for five years with a wife, he came to Abbot John, who was then for his marvellous sanctity chosen to preside over the administration of the alms.[1077] For it is not anyone who likes who is of his own wish or ambition promoted to this office, but only he whom the congregation of all the Elders considers from the advantage of his age and the witness of his faith and virtues to be more excellent than, and superior to, all others. To this blessed John then the aforesaid young man had come in the eagerness of his pious devotion, bringing gifts of piety among other owners who were eager to offer tithes and first-fruits of their substance to the old man I mentioned,[1078] and when the old man saw them pouring in upon him with many gifts, and was anxious to make some recompense in return for their offerings, he began, as the Apostle says, to sow spiritual things to them whose carnal gifts he was reaping.[1079] And finally thus began his word of exhortation.

NOTES:

[1076] Nothing further is known of this Theonas than what Cassian here tells us: he is clearly a different person from the one mentioned by Rufinus, Hist. Mon. c. vi. Cf. Palladius, Lausiac History, c. l.

[1077] Diaconia. Cf. the note on XVIII. vii.

[1078] This is noteworthy as being the earliest instance on record of the payment of tithes to a monastery. The language of the Conference, it will be noted, shows that they were not regarded as legally due or in any way compulsory, but as a free-will offering on the part of the faithful. Cf. Bingham, Antiquities, Book VII. ciii. S: 19; and the Dictionary of Christian Antiquities, Vol. ii. p. 1964.

[1079] Cf. 1 Cor. 9:11.

CHAPTER II.

The exhortation of Abbot John to Theonas and the others who had come together with him.

I AM indeed delighted, my children, with the duteous liberality of your gifts; and your devout offering, the disposal of which is entrusted to me, I gratefully accept, because you are offering your firstfruits and tithes for the good and use of the needy, as a sacrifice to the Lord, of a sweet smelling savour, in the belief that by the offering of them, the abundance of your fruits and all your substance, from which you have taken away these for the Lord, will be richly blessed, and that you yourselves will according to the faith of His command be endowed even in this world with manifold richness in all good things: "Honour the Lord from thy righteous labours, and offer to Him of the fruits of thy righteousness; that thy garners may be full of abundance of wheat, and thy vats may overflow with wine."[1080] And as you are faithfully carrying out this service, you may know that you have fulfilled the righteousness of the old law, under which those who then lived if they transgressed it inevitably incurred guilt, while if they fulfilled it they could not attain to a pitch of perfection.

NOTES:

[1080] Prov. 3:9, 10.

CHAPTER III.

Of the offering of tithes and firstfruits.

FOR indeed by the Lord's command tithes were consecrated to the service of the Levites, but oblations and firstfruits for the priests.[1081] But this was the law of the firstfruits; viz., that the fiftieth part of fruits or animals should be given for the service of the temple and the priests: and this proportion some who were faithlessly indifferent diminished, while those who were very religious increased it, so that the one gave only the sixtieth part, and the other gave the fortieth part of their fruits. For the righteous, for whom the law is not enacted, are thus shown to be not under the law, as they try not only to fulfil but even to exceed the righteousness of the law, and their devotion is greater than the legal requirement, as it goes beyond the observance of precepts and adds to what is due of its own free will.

NOTES:
[1081] Cf. Numb. 18:26; 5:9, 10.

CHAPTER IV.

How Abraham, David, and other saints went beyond the requirement of the law.

FOR so we read that Abraham went beyond the requirement of the law which was afterwards to be given, when after his victory over the four kings, he would not touch any of the spoils of Sodom, which were fairly due to him as the conqueror, and which indeed the king himself, whose spoils he had rescued, offered him; and with an oath by the Divine name he exclaimed: "I lift up my hand to the Lord Most High, who made heaven and earth, that I will not take from a thread to a shoe's latchet of all that is thine."[1082] So we know that David went beyond the requirement of the law, as, though Moses commanded that vengeance should be taken on enemies,[1083] he not only did not do this, but actually embraced his persecutors with love, and piously entreated the Lord for them, and wept bitterly and avenged them when they were slain. So we are sure that Elijah and Jeremiah were not under the law, as though they might without blame have taken advantage of lawful

461

matrimony, yet they preferred to remain virgins. So we read that Elisha and others of the same mode of life went beyond the commands of Moses, as of them the Apostle speaks as follows: "They went about in sheepskins and in goatskins, they were oppressed, afflicted, in want, of whom the world was not worthy, they wandered about in deserts and in mountains, and in caves and in dens of the earth."[1084] What shall I say of the sons of Jonadab the son of Rechab, of whom we are told that, when at the Lord's bidding the prophet Jeremiah offered them wine, they replied: "We drink no wine: for Jonadab the son of Rechab, our father, commanded us, saying: Ye shall drink no wine, ye and your sons forever: and ye shall build no house, nor sow any seed, nor plant vineyards nor possess them: but ye shall dwell in tents all your days"? Wherefore also they were permitted to hear from the same prophet these words: "Thus saith the Lord God of hosts, the God of Israel: there shall not fail a man from the stock of Jonadab the son of Rechab to stand in My sight all the days;"[1085] as all of them were not satisfied with merely offering tithes of their possessions, but actually refused property, and offered the rather to God themselves and their souls, for which no redemption can be made by man, as the Lord testifies in the gospel: "For what shall a man give in exchange for his own soul?" [1086]

NOTES:
[1082] Gen. 14:22, 23.
[1083] Cf. Exod. 21:24.
[1084] Heb. 11:37, 38.
[1085] Jer. 35:6, 7, 19.
[1086] S. Matt. 16:25.

CHAPTER V.

How those who live under the grace of the Gospel ought to go beyond the requirement of the law.

WHEREFORE we ought to know that we from whom the requirements of the law are no longer exacted, but in whose ears the word of the gospel daily sounds: "If thou wilt be perfect, go and sell all that thou hast and give to the poor, and thou shalt have treasure in heaven, and come follow Me,"[1087] when we offer to God tithes of our substance, are still in a way ground down beneath the burden of the law, and not able to rise to those heights of the gospel, those who conform to which are recompensed not only by blessings in this present life, but also by future rewards. For the law promises to those who obey it no rewards of the kingdom of heaven, but only solaces in this life, saying: "The man that doeth these things shall live in them."[1088] But the Lord says to His disciples: "Blessed are the poor in spirit, for theirs is the kingdom of heaven;" and: "Everyone that leaveth house or brothers or sisters or father or mother or wife or children or field for My name's sake, shall receive an hundredfold, and shall inherit eternal life."[1089] And this with good reason. For it is not so praiseworthy for us to abstain from forbidden as from lawful things, and not to use these last out of reverence for Him, Who has permitted us to use them because of our weakness. And so if even those who, faithfully offering tithes of their fruits, are obedient to the more ancient precepts of the Lord, cannot yet climb the heights of the gospel, you can see very clearly how far short of it those fall who do not even do this. For how can those men be partakers of the grace of the gospel who disregard the fulfilment even of the lighter commands of the law, to the easy character of which the weighty words of the giver of the law bear testimony, as a curse is actually invoked on those who do not fulfil them; for it says: "Cursed is everyone that does not continue in all things that are written in the book of the law to do them."[1090] But here on account of the superiority and excellence of the commandments it is said: "He that can receive it, let him receive it."[1091] There the forcible compulsion of the lawgiver shows the easy character of the precepts; for he says: "I call heaven and earth to record against you this day, that if ye do not keep the commandments of the Lord your God ye shall perish from off the face of the earth."[1092] Here the grandeur of sublime commands is shown by the very fact that He does not order, but exhorts, saying: "if thou wilt be perfect go" and do this or that. There Moses lays a burden that cannot be refused on those who are unwilling: here Paul meets with counsels those who are willing and eager for perfection. For that was not to be enjoined as a general charge, nor to be required, if I may so say, as a regular rule from all, which could not be secured by all, owing to its wonderful and lofty nature; but by counsels all are rather stimulated to grace, that those who are great may deservedly be crowned by the perfection of their virtues, while those who are small, and not able to come up to "the measure of the stature of the fulness of Christ,"[1093] although they seem to be lost to sight and hidden as it were by the brightness of larger stars, may yet be free from the darkness of the curses which are in the law, and not adjudged to suffer present evils or visited with eternal punishment. Christ therefore does not constrain anyone, by the compulsion of a command, to those lofty heights of goodness, but stimulates them by the power of free will, and urges them on by wise counsels and the desire of perfection. For where there is a command, there is duty, and consequently punishment. But those who keep those things to which they are driven by the severity of the law established escape the punishment with which they were threatened, instead of obtaining rewards and a recompense.

NOTES:
[1087] S. Matt. 19:21.
[1088] Lev. 18:5.
[1089] S. Matt. 5:3; 19:29.
[1090] Deut. 27:26.
[1091] S. Matt. 19:12.
[1092] Deut. 4:26.
[1093] Eph. 4:13.

CHAPTER VI.

How the grace of the gospel supports the weak so that they can obtain pardon, as it secures to the perfect the kingdom of God.

AND as the word of the gospel raises those that are strong to sublime and lofty heights, so it suffers not the weak to be dragged down to the depths, for it secures to the perfect the fulness of blessing, and brings to those who are overcome through weakness pardon. For the law placed those who fulfilled its commands in a sort of middle state between what they deserved in either case, severing them from the condemnation due to transgressors, as it also kept them away from the glory of the perfect. But how wretched and miserable this is, you can see from comparing the state of this present life, in which it is considered a very poor thing for a man to sweat and labour only to avoid being regarded as guilty among good men, not also to be esteemed rich and honourable and renowned.

CHAPTER VII.

How it lies in our own power to choose whether to remain under the grace of the gospel or under the terror of the law.

WHEREFORE it lies today in our own power whether we choose to live under the grace of the gospel or under the terrors of the law: for each man must incline to one side or the other in accordance with the character of his actions, for either the grace of Christ welcomes those who go beyond the law, or else the law keeps its hold over the weaker ones as those who are its debtors and within its clutches. For one who is guilty as regards the precepts of the law will never be able to attain to the perfection of the gospel, even though he idly boasts that he is a Christian and freed by the Lord's grace: for we must not only regard as still under the law the man who refuses to fulfil what the law enjoins, but the man as well who is satisfied with the mere observance of what the law commands, and who never brings forth fruits worthy of his vocation and the grace of Christ, where it is not said: "Thou shalt offer to the Lord thy God thy tithes and firstfruits;" but: "Go and sell all that thou hast and give to the poor, and come follow Me;"[1094] where, owing to the grandeur of perfection, to the request of the disciple there is not granted even the very short space of an hour in which to bury his father,[1095] as the offices of human charity are outweighed by the virtue of Divine love.

NOTES:
[1094] Exod. 22:29; S. Matt. 19:21.
[1095] Cf. S. Matt. 8:21, sq.

CHAPTER VIII.

How Theonas exhorted his wife that she too should make her renunciation.

AND when he had heard this the blessed Theonas was fired with an uncontrollable desire for the perfection of the gospel, and, committed, as it were, the seed of the word, which he had received in a fruitful heart, to the deep and broken furrows of his bosom, as he was greatly humiliated and conscience-stricken because the old man had said not only that he had failed to attain to the perfection of the gospel, but also that he had scarcely fulfilled the commands of the law; since though he was accustomed every year to pay the tithes of his fruits as alms, yet he mourned that he had never even heard of the law of the firstfruits; and even if he had in the same way fulfilled this, he humbly confessed that still he would in the old man's view have been very far from the perfection of the gospel. And so he returned home sad and filled with that sorrow which worketh repentance unto salvation,[1096] and of his own will and determination turns all his wife's care and anxiety of mind towards salvation; and began to stir her up to the same eager desire with which he himself had been inflamed, with the same sort of exhortations, and with tears day and night to urge her that together they might serve God in sanctity and chastity, telling her that their conversion to a better life ought not to be deferred because a vain hope in their youth would be no argument against the inevitableness of a sudden death, which carries off boys and youths and young persons equally with old men.

NOTES:
[1096] Cf. 2 Cor. 7:10.

CHAPTER IX.

How he fled to a monastery when his wife would not consent.

AND when his wife was hard and would not consent to him as he constantly persisted with entreaties of this kind, but said that as she was in the flower of her age she could not altogether do without the solace of her husband, and further that supposing she was deserted by him and fell into sin, the guilt would rather be his who had broken the bonds of wedlock: to this he, when he had for a long while urged the condition of human nature (which being so weak and uncertain, it would be dangerous for it to be any longer mixed up with carnal desires and works), added the assertion that it was not right for anyone to cut himself off from that virtue to which he had learnt that he ought by all means to cleave, and that it was more dangerous to disregard goodness when discovered, than to fail to love it before it was discovered; further that he was already involved in the guilt of a fall if when he had discovered such grand and heavenly blessings he had preferred earthly and mean ones. Further that the grandeur of perfection was open to every age and either sex, and that all the members of the Church were urged to scale the heights of heavenly goodness when the Apostle said: "So run that ye may obtain;"[1097] nor should those who were ready and eager for it hang back because of the delays of the slow and dawdlers, as it is better for the sluggards to be urged on by those running before than for those who are doing their best to be hampered by the slothful. Further that he had determined and made up his mind to renounce the world and to die to the world that he might live to God, and that if he could not attain this happiness; viz., to pass with his wife into union with Christ, he would rather be saved even with the loss of one member, and enter into the kingdom of heaven as one maimed rather than be condemned with his body whole. But he also added and spoke as follows: If Moses suffered wives to be divorced for the hardness of their hearts, why should not Christ allow this for the desire of chastity, especially when the same Lord among those other affections; viz., for fathers and mothers and children (all due regard to which not only the law but He Himself also charged to be shown, yet for His name's sake and for the desire of perfection He decreed that they should not simply be disregarded but actually hated)--to these, I say, He joined also the mention of wives, saying: "And everyone that hath left house, or brethren or sisters or father or mother or wife or children for My name's sake, shall receive an hundredfold and shall inherit eternal life."[1098] So far then is He from allowing anything to be set against that perfection which He is proclaiming, that He actually enjoins that the ties to father and mother should be broken and disregarded out of love for Him, though according to the Apostle it is the first commandment with promise; viz., "Honour thy father and thy mother, which is the first commandment with promise, that it may be well with thee and that thy days may be long upon earth."[1099] And as the word of the gospel condemns those who break the chains of matrimony where there has been no sin of adultery, so it clearly promises a reward of an hundredfold to those who have cast off a carnal yoke out of love for Christ and the desire for chastity. Wherefore if it can be brought about that you may listen to reason and be turned together with me to this most desirable choice; viz., that we should together serve the Lord and escape the pains of hell, I will not refuse the affection of marriage, nay I will embrace it with a still greater love. For I acknowledge and honour my helpmeet assigned to me by the word of the Lord, and I do not refuse to be joined to her in an unbroken tie of love in Christ, nor do I separate from me what the Lord joined to me by the law of the original condition,[1100] if only you yourself will be what your Maker meant you to be. But if you will not be a helpmeet, but prefer to make yourself a deceiver and an assistance not to me but to the adversary, and fancy that the sacrament of matrimony was granted to you for this reason that you may deprive yourself of this salvation which is offered to you, and also hold me back from following the Saviour as a disciple, then I will resolutely lay hold on the words which were uttered by the lips of Abbot John, or rather of Christ Himself, so that no carnal affection may be able to tear me away from spiritual blessings, for He says: "He that hateth not father and mother and children and brothers and sisters and wife and lands, yea and his own soul also, cannot be My disciple."[1101] When then by these and such like words the woman's purpose was not moved and she persisted in the same obstinate hardness, If, said the blessed Theonas, I cannot drag you away from death, neither shall you separate me from Christ: but it is safer for me to be divorced from a human person than from God. And so by the aid of God's grace he at once set about the execution of his purpose and suffered not the ardour of his desire to grow cool through any delay. For at once he stripped himself of all his worldly goods, and fled to a monastery, where in a very short time he was so famous for the splendour of his sanctity and humility that when John of blessed memory departed this life to the Lord, and the holy Elias, a man who was no less great than his predecessor, had likewise died, Theonas was chosen by the judgment of all as the third to succeed them in the administration of the almsgiving.

NOTES:
[1097] 1 Cor. 9:24.
[1098] S. Matt. 19:29.
[1099] Eph. 6:2, 3.
[1100] Cf. Gen. 2:18.
[1101] S. Luke 14:26.

CHAPTER X.

An explanation that we may not appear to recommend separation from wives.

BUT let no one imagine that we have invented this for the sake of encouraging divorce, as we not only in no way condemn marriage, but also, following the words of the Apostle, say: "Marriage is honourable in all, and the bed undefiled,"[1102] but it was in order faithfully to show the reader the origin of the conversion by which this great man was dedicated to God. And I ask the reader kindly to allow that, whether he likes this or no, in either case I am free from blame, and to give the praise or blame for this act to its real author. But as for me, as I have not put forward an opinion of my own on this matter, but have given a simple narration of the history of the facts, it is fair that as I claim no praise from those who approve of what was done, so I should not be attacked by the hatred of those who disapprove of it. Let every man therefore, as we said, have his own opinion on the matter. But I advise him to restrain his censure in considering it, lest he come to fancy that he is more just and holy than the Divine judgment, whereby the signs even of Apostolic virtue were conferred upon him (viz., Theonas), not to mention the opinion of such great fathers by whom it is clear that his action was not only not blamed, but even so far praised that in the election to the office of almoner they preferred him to splendid and most excellent men. And I fancy that the judgment of so many spiritual men, uttered with God as its author, was not wrong, as it was, as was said above, confirmed by such wonderful signs.

NOTES:
[1102] Heb. 13:4.

CHAPTER XI.

An inquiry why in Egypt they do not fast during all the fifty days (of Easter) nor bend their knees in prayer.

BUT it is now time to follow out the plan of the promised discourse. So then when Abbot Theonas had come to visit us in our cell during Eastertide[1103] after Evensong was over we sat for a little while on the ground and began diligently to consider why they were so very careful that no one should during the whole fifty days either bend his knees in prayer[1104] or venture to fast till the ninth hour, and we made our inquiry the more earnestly because we had never seen this custom so carefully observed in the monasteries of Syria.

NOTES:
[1103] Quinquagesima.
[1104] The 20th Canon of the Council of Nicaea (A.D. 325) alludes to diversities of custom with regard to posture for prayer on Sundays and from Easter to Pentecost, and ordered that for the future prayer should be made standing at these times. Cassian's language in the text would seem to show that in his day the Canon in question, though kept in Egypt, was not strictly observed in Palestine, but that the ancient diversity of customs still to some extent prevailed.

CHAPTER XII.

The answer on the nature of things good, bad, and indifferent.

TO this Abbot Theonas thus began his reply. It is indeed right for us, even when we cannot see the reason, to yield to the authority of the fathers and to a custom of our predecessors that has been continued through so many years down to our own time, and to observe it, as handed down from antiquity, with constant care and reverence. But since you want to know the reasons and grounds for this, receive in few words what we have heard as handed down by our Elders on this subject. But before we bring forward the authority of Holy Scripture, we will, if you please, say a little about the nature and character of the fast, that afterwards the authority of Holy Scripture may support our words. The Divine Wisdom has pointed out in Ecclesiastes that for everything, i.e., for all things happy or those which are considered unfortunate and unhappy, there is a right time: saying: "For all things there is a time, and a time for everything under the heaven. A time to bring forth and a time to die; a time to plant and a time to pull down what is planted; a time to kill and a time to heal; a time to destroy and a time to build; a time to weep and a time to laugh; a time to mourn and a time to dance; a time to cast away stones and a time to gather stones; a time to embrace and a time to refrain from embracing; a time to get and a time to lose; a time to keep and a time to send away; a time to scatter and a time to collect; a time to be silent and a time to speak; a time to love and a time to hate; a time for war and a time for peace;" and below: "For there is a time," it says, "for everything and for every deed."[1105] None therefore of these things does it lay down as always good, but only when any of them are fittingly done and at the right time, so that these very things which at one time, when done at the right moment, turn out well, if they are ventured on at a wrong or unsuitable time, are found to be useless or harmful; only excepting those things which are in their own nature good or bad, and which cannot ever be made the opposite, as, e.g., justice, prudence, fortitude, temperance and the rest of the virtues, or on the other hand, those faults, the description of which cannot possibly be altered or fall under the other head. But those things which can sometimes turn out with either result, so that, in accordance with the character of those who use them, they are found to be either good or bad, these we consider to be not absolutely in their own natures useful or injurious, but only so in accordance with the mind of the doer, and the suitableness of the time.

NOTES:
[1105] Eccl. 3:1-8, 17.

CHAPTER XIII.

What kind of good fasting is.

WHEREFORE we must now inquire what we ought to hold about the state of fasting, whether we meant that it was good in the same sort of way as justice, prudence, fortitude and temperance, which cannot possibly be made anything else, or whether it is something indifferent which sometimes is useful when done, and may be sometimes omitted without condemnation; and which sometimes it is wrong to do, and sometimes laudable to omit. For if we hold fasting to be included in that list of virtues, so that abstinence from food is placed among those things which are good in themselves, then certainly the partaking of food will be bad and wrong. For whatever is the opposite of that which is in its own nature good, must certainly be held to be in its own nature bad. But this the authority of Holy Scripture does not allow to us to lay down. For if we fast with such thoughts and intentions, so as to think that we fall into sin by taking food, we shall not only gain no advantage by our abstinence but shall actually contract grievous guilt and fall into the sin of impiety, as the Apostle says: "Abstaining from meats which God has created to be received with thanksgiving by the faithful and those who know the truth. For every creature of God is good, and nothing to be refused if it is partaken of with thanksgiving." For "if a man thinks that a thing is common, to him it is common."[1106]

And therefore we never read that anyone is condemned simply for taking food, but only when something was joined with it or followed afterwards, for which he deserved condemnation.

NOTES:
[1106] 1 Tim. 4:3, 4; Rom. 14:14.

CHAPTER XIV.

How fasting is not good in its own nature.

AND so that it is a thing indifferent is very clearly shown from this also; viz., because as it brings justification when observed, so it does not bring condemnation when it is broken in upon; unless perhaps the transgression of a command rather than the partaking of food brings punishment. But in the case of a thing that is good in its own nature, no time should be without it, in such a way as that a man may do without it, for if it ceases, the man who is careless about it is sure to fall into mischief. Nor again is any time given for what is bad in its own nature, because what is hurtful cannot help hurting, if it is indulged in, nor can it ever be made of a praiseworthy character. And further it is clear that these things, for which we see conditions and times appointed, and which sanctify, when observed without corrupting us when they are neglected, are things indifferent, as, e.g., marriage, agriculture, riches, retirement into the desert, vigils, reading and meditation on Holy Scripture and fasting itself, from which our discussion took its rise. All of which things the Divine precepts and the authority of Holy Scripture decreed should not be so incessantly aimed at, or so constantly observed, as for it to be wrong for them to be for a time intermitted. For anything that is absolutely commanded brings death if it be not fulfilled: but whatever things we are urged to rather than commanded, when done are useful, when left undone bring no punishment. And therefore in the case of all or some of these things our predecessors commanded us either to do them with consideration, or to observe them carefully with regard to the reason, place, manner, and time, because if any of them are done suitably, it is fit and convenient, but if incongruously, then it becomes foolish and hurtful. And if at the coming of a brother in whose person he ought to refresh Christ with courtesy and to embrace him with a most kindly welcome, a man should choose to observe a strict fast, would he not rather be guilty of incivility than gain the praise or reward of devoutness? or if when the failure or weakness of the flesh requires the strength to be restored by the partaking of food, a man will not consent to relax the rigour of his abstinence, is he not to be regarded as a cruel murderer of his own body rather than as one who is careful for his salvation? So too when a festival season permits a suitable indulgence in food and a necessarily liberal repast, if a man will resolutely cling to the strict observance of a fast he must be considered as not religious so much as boorish and unreasonable. But to those men also will these things be found bad, who are on the lookout for the praises of men by their fasts, and by a foolish show of paleness gain credit for sanctity, of whom the word of the Gospel tells us that they have received their reward in this life, and whose fast the Lord execrates by the prophet. In whose person he first objected to himself and said: "Wherefore have we fasted and Thou hast not regarded: wherefore have we humbled our souls, and Thou hast not known it?" and then at once he answered and explained the reasons why they did not deserve to be heard: "Behold," he says, "in the days of your fast your own will is found and you exact of all your debtors. Behold you fast for debates and strife, and strike with the fist wickedly. Do not fast as ye have done unto this day, to make your cry to be heard on high. Is this such a fast as I have chosen, for a man to afflict his soul for a day? Is it this, to wind his head about like a circle, and to spread sackcloth and ashes? Will ye call this a fast and a day acceptable o the Lord?" Then he proceeds to teach how the abstinence of one who fasts may become acceptable, and clearly lays down that fasting cannot be good of itself alone, but only when it has the following reasons which are added: "Is not this," he says, "the fast that I have chosen? Loose the bands of wickedness, undo the bundles that oppress, let them that are broken go free, and break asunder every burden. Deal thy bread to the hungry, and bring the needy and the harbourless into thine house: and when thou shalt see one naked cover him, and despise not thine own flesh. Then shalt thy light break forth as the morning and thy health shall speedily arise, and thy righteousness shall go before thy face and the glory of the Lord shall gather thee up. Then shalt thou call, and the Lord shall hear: thou shalt cry, and He shall say, Here am I."[1107] You see then that fasting is certainly not considered by the Lord as a thing that is good in its own nature, because it becomes good and well-pleasing to God not by itself but by other works, and again from the surrounding circumstances it may be regarded as not merely vain but actually hateful, as the Lord says: "When they fast I will not hear their prayers." [1108]

NOTES:
[1107] Isa. 58:3-9.
[1108] Jer. 14:12.

CHAPTER XV.

How a thing that is good in its own nature ought not to be done for the sake of some lesser good.

FOR we ought not to practise pity, patience and love, and the precepts of the virtues mentioned above, wherein there is what is good in its own nature, for the sake of fasting, but rather fasting for the sake of them. For our endeavour must be that those virtues which are really good may be gained by fasting, not that the practice of those virtues may lead to fasting as its end. For this then the affliction of the flesh is useful, for this the remedy of abstinence must be employed; viz., that by it we may succeed in attaining to love, wherein there is what is good without change, and continually with no exception of time. For medicines, and the goldsmith's art, and the systems of other arts which there are in this world are not employed for the sake of the instruments which belong to the particular work; but rather the implements are prepared for the practice of the art. And as they are useful for those who understand them, so they are useless to those who are ignorant of the system of the art in question; and as they are a great help to those who rely on their aid for doing their work, so they cannot be of the smallest use to those who do not know for what purpose they were made, and are contented simply with the possession of them; because they make all their value consist in the mere having of them, and not in the performance of work. That then is in its own nature the best thing, for the sake of which things indifferent are done, but the very chiefest good is done not for the sake of anything else but because of its own intrinsic goodness.

CHAPTER XVI.

How what is good in its own nature can be distinguished from other things that are good.

AND this may be distinguished from those other things which we have termed indifferent, in these ways: if a thing is good in itself and not by reason of something else: if it is useful for its own sake, and not for the sake of something else: if it is unchangeably and at all times good, and always keeps its character and can never become anything different: if its removal or cessation cannot fail to produce the greatest harm: if that which is its opposite is in the same way evil in its own nature, and can never be turned into anything good. And these descriptions by which the nature of things that are good in themselves can be distinguished, cannot possibly be applied to fasting, for it is not good of itself, nor useful for its own sake because it is wisely used for the acquisition of purity of heart and body, that the pricks of the flesh being dulled the soul may be pacified and reconciled to its Creator, nor is it unchangeably and at all times good, because often we are not injured by its intermission, and indeed sometimes if it is unreasonably practised it becomes injurious. Nor is that which seems its opposite evil in its own nature, i.e., the partaking of food, which is naturally agreeable, which cannot be regarded as evil, unless intemperance and luxury or some other faults are the result; "For not that which entereth into the mouth, defileth a man, but that which cometh out of the mouth, that defileth a man."[1109] And so a man disparages what is good in its own nature, and does not treat it properly or without sin, if he does it not for its own sake but for the sake of something else, for everything else should be done for the sake of it, but it should be sought for its own sake alone.

NOTES:
[1109] S. Matt. 15:11.

CHAPTER XVII.

Of the reason for fasting and its value.

SO then let us constantly remember this description of the character of fasting, and always aim at it with all the powers of the soul, in such a way as to recognize that then only is it suitable for us if in it we preserve regard for time, its character and degree, and this not so as to set the end of our hope upon it, but so that by it we may succeed in attaining to purity of heart and Apostolical love. Therefore from this it is clear that fasting, for which not only are there special seasons appointed at which it should be practised or relaxed, but conditions and rules also laid down, is not good in its own nature, but something indifferent. But those things which are either enjoined as good by the authority of a precept, or are forbidden as bad, are never subject to any exceptions of time in such a way that sometimes we should do what is forbidden or omit what is commanded. For there is no limit set to justice, patience, soberness, modesty, love, nor on the other hand is a licence ever granted for injustice, impatience, wrath, immodesty, envy, and pride.

CHAPTER XVIII.

How fasting is not always suitable.

WHEREFORE as we have premised this on the conditions of fasting, it seems well to subjoin the authority of Holy Scripture, by which it will be more clearly proved that fasting neither can nor should be always observed. In the Gospel when the Pharisees were fasting together with the disciples of John the Baptist, as the Apostles, as friends and companions of the heavenly Bridegroom, were not yet keeping the observance of a fast, the disciples of John (who thought that they acquired perfect righteousness by their fasts, as they were followers of that grand preacher of repentance who afforded a pattern to all the people by his own example, as he not only refused the different kinds of food which are supplied for man's use, but actually altogether did without eating the bread which is common to all) complained to the Lord and said: "Why do we and the Pharisees fast oft but thy disciples fast not?" to whom the Lord in His reply plainly showed that fasting is not suitable or necessary at all times, when any festival season or opportunity for love intervenes and permits an indulgence in food, saying: "Can the children of the bridegroom mourn while the bridegroom is with them? But the days will come when the bridegroom shall be taken away from them; and then shall they fast;"[1110] words which although they were spoken before the resurrection of His Body, yet specially point to the season of Eastertide, in which after His resurrection for forty days He ate with His disciples, and their joy in His daily Presence did not allow them to fast.

NOTES:
[1110] S. Matt. 9:14, 15.

CHAPTER XIX.

A question why we break the fast all through Eastertide.

GERMANUS: Why then do we relax the rigour of our abstinence in our meals all through the fifty days, whereas Christ only remained with His disciples for forty days after His resurrection?

CHAPTER XX.

The answer.

YOUR pertinent question deserves to be told the perfect true reason. After the Ascension of our Saviour which took place on the fortieth day after His Resurrection, the apostles returned from the Mount of Olives, on which He had suffered them to see Him when He was returning to the Father, as the book of the Acts of the Apostles also testifies, and entered Jerusalem and are said to have waited ten days for the coming of the Holy Ghost, and when these were fulfilled on the fiftieth day they received Him with joy. And thus in this way the number of this festival was clearly made up, which as we read was figuratively foreshadowed also in the Old Testament, where when seven weeks were fulfilled the bread of the firstfruits was ordered to be offered by the priests to the Lord:[1111] and this was indeed shown to be offered to the Lord by the preaching of the Apostles which they are said on that day to have addressed to the people; the true bread of the firstfruits, which when produced from the instruction of a new doctrine, consecrated the firstfruits of the Jews as a Christian people to the Lord, five thousand men being filled with the gifts of the food. And therefore these ten days are to be kept with equal solemnity and joy as the previous forty. And the tradition about this festival, transmitted to us by Apostolic men, should be kept with the same uniformity. For therefore on those days they do not bow their knees in prayer, because the bending of the knees is a sign of penitence and mourning. Wherefore also during these days we observe in all things the same solemnities as on Sunday, on which day our predecessors taught that men ought not to fast nor to bow the knee, out of reverence for the Lord's Resurrection.

NOTES:
[1111] Cf. Deut. 16:9.

CHAPTER XXI.

A question whether the relaxation of the fast is not prejudicial to the chastity of the body.

GERMANUS: Can the flesh, attracted by the unwonted luxuries of so long a festival fail to produce something thorny from the incentives to sin although they have been cut down? or can the soul weighed down by the consumption of unaccustomed feasts fail to mitigate the rigour of its rule over its servant the body, especially when in our case our mature age can excite our subject members to a speedy revolt, if we venture to take our usual food in larger quantities, or unaccustomed food more freely than usual?

CHAPTER XXII.

The answer on the way to keep control over abstinence.

THEONAS: If we weigh everything that we do, by a reasonable judgment of the mind, and on the purity of our heart always consult not the opinions of other people but our own conscience, that interval for refreshment is sure not to interfere with our proper strictness, if only, as was said, our pure mind impartially considers the right limits of indulgence and abstinence, and fairly checks excess in either, and with real discrimination discerns whether the weight of the delicacies is a burden upon our spirits, or whether too much austerity in abstaining weighs down the other side, i.e., that of the body, and either depresses or raises that side which it sees to be raised or weighed down. For our Lord would have nothing done to His honour and glory without being tempered by judgment, for "the honour of a king loveth judgment,"[1112] and therefore Solomon, the wisest of men, urges us not to let our judgment incline to either side, saying: "Honour God with thy righteous labours and offer to Him of the fruits of thy righteousness."[1113] For we have residing in our conscience an uncorrupt and true judge who sometimes, when all are wrong, is the only person not deceived as to the state of our purity. And so with all care and pains we should preserve a constant purpose in our circumspect heart for fear lest if the judgment of our discretion goes wrong, we may be fired with the desire for an ill-considered abstinence, or allured by the wish for an excessive relaxation, and so weigh the substance of our strength in the tongue of an unfair balance; but we should place in one of the scales our purity of soul, and in the other our bodily strength, and weigh them both in the true judgment of conscience, so that we may not perversely incline the scale of fairness to either side, either to undue strictness or to excessive relaxation, from the preponderating desire for one or the other, and so have this said to us by reason of excessive strictness or relaxation: "If thou offerest rightly, but dost not divide rightly, hast thou not sinned?"[1114] For those offerings of fasts, which we thoughtlessly extort by violently tearing our bowels, and fancy that we rightly offer to the Lord, these He execrates who "loves mercy and judgment" saying: "I the Lord love judgment, but I hate robbery in a burnt offering."[1115] Those also who take the main part of their offerings, i.e., their offices and actions, to benefit the flesh for their own use, but leave the remains of them and a tiny portion for the Lord, these the Divine Word thus condemns as fraudulent workmen: "Cursed is he that doeth the work of the Lord fraudulently."[1116] It is not then without reason that the Lord reproves him who thus deceives himself by unfair considerations, saying: "But vain are the children of men: the children of men are liars upon the balances that they may deceive."[1117] And therefore the blessed Apostle warns us to keep hold of the reins of discretion and not to be attracted by excess and swerve to either side, saying: "Your reasonable service."[1118] And the giver of the law similarly forbids the same thing, saying: "Let the balance be just and the weights equal, the bushel just and the sextarius equal,"[1119] and Solomon also gives a like opinion on this matter: "Great and small weights and double measures are both unclean before the Lord, and one who uses them shall be hindered in his contrivances."[1120] Further not only in the way in which we have said, but also in this must we strive not to have unfair weights in our hearts, nor double measures in the storehouse of our conscience, i.e., not to overwhelm those, to whom we are to preach the word of the Lord, with precepts that are too strict and heavier than we ourselves can bear, while we take for granted that for ourselves those things which have to do with the rule of strictness are to be softened by a freer allowance of relaxation. For when we do this, what is it but to weigh and measure the goods and fruits of the Lord's commands in a double weight and measure? For if we dispense them in one way to ourselves and in another to our brethren, we are rightly blamed by the Lord because we have unfair balances and double measures, in accordance with the saying of Solomon which tells us that "A double weight is an abomination to the Lord, and a deceitful balance is not good in His sight."[1121] In this way also we plainly incur the guilt of using a deceitful weight and a double measure, if out of the desire for the praise of men, we make a show before the brethren of greater strictness than what we practice in private in our own cells, trying to appear more abstinent and holier in the sight of men than in the sight of God, an evil which we should not only avoid but actually loathe. But meanwhile as we have wandered some way from the question before us, let us return to the point from which we started.

NOTES:
[1112] Ps. 98 (99):4.
[1113] Prov. 3:9.
[1114] Gen. 4:7 (LXX).
[1115] Ps. 32 (33):5; Isa. 61:8.
[1116] Jer. 48:10.
[1117] Ps. 61 (62):10.
[1118] Rom. 12:1.
[1119] Lev. 19:36.
[1120] Prov. 20:10, 11.
[1121] Prov. 20:23.

CHAPTER XXIII.

Of the time and measure of refreshment.

SO then we should keep the observance of the days mentioned in such a way that the relaxation allowed may be useful rather than harmful to the good of body and soul, because the joy of any festival cannot blunt the pricks of the flesh, nor can that fierce enemy of ours be pacified by regard for days. In order then that the observance of the customs appointed for festival seasons may be kept and that the most salutary rule of abstinence be not at all exceeded it is enough for us to allow the permitted relaxation to go so far, as for us out of regard for the festival season to take the food, which ought to be taken at the ninth hour, a little earlier; viz., at the sixth hour, but with this condition, that the regular allowance and character of the food be not altered, for fear lest the purity of body and uprightness of soul which has been gained by the abstinence of Lent be lost by the relaxation of Eastertide, and it profit us nothing to have acquired by our fast what a careless satiety causes us presently to lose, especially as the well-known cunning of our enemy assaults the stronghold of our purity then chiefly when he sees that our guard over it is somewhat relaxed at the celebration of some festival. Wherefore we must most vigilantly look out that the vigour of our soul be never enervated by seductive flatteries, and we lose not the purity of our chastity, gained, as was said, by the continuous efforts of Lent, by the repose and carelessness of Eastertide. And therefore no addition at all should be made to the quality or the quantity of the food, but even on the highest festivals we should similarly abstain from those foods, by abstinence from which we preserve our uprightness on common days, that the joy of the festival may not excite in us a most deadly conflict of carnal desires, and so be turned to grief, and put an end to that most excellent festival of the heart, which exults in the joy of purity; and after a brief show of carnal joy we begin to mourn our lost purity of heart with a lasting sorrow of repentance. Moreover we should strive that this warning of the prophetic exhortation may not be uttered against us to no purpose: "Celebrate, O Judah, thy festivals, and pay thy vows."[1122] For if the occurrence of festival days does not interfere with the continuity of our abstinence, we shall continually enjoy spiritual festivals and so, when we cease from servile work, "there shall be month after month and Sabbath after Sabbath." [1123]

NOTES:
[1122] Nah. 1:15.
[1123] Isa. 66:23.

CHAPTER XXIV.

A question on the different ways of keeping Lent.

GERMANUS: What is the reason why Lent is kept for six weeks, while in some countries a possibly more earnest care for religion seems to have added a seventh week as well, though neither number when you subtract Sunday and Saturday, gives the total of forty days? For only six and thirty days are included in these weeks. [1124]

NOTES:

[1124] On the different uses in regard to the Lenten fast Socrates (H. E. V. xxii.) writes as follows: "Those at Rome fast three successive weeks before Easter, excepting Saturdays and Sundays. The Illyrians, Achaians, and Alexandrians observe a fast of six weeks, which they call the forty days' fast. Others commencing their fast from the seventh week before Easter, and fasting for fifteen days by intervals, yet call that time the forty days' fast." There are difficulties in the way of accepting the statement about the custom at Rome (see below), but the great variety of customs is fully confirmed by Sozomen (H. E. VII. xix.): "In some churches the time before Easter, which is called Quadragesima, and is devoted by the people to fasting, is made to consist of six weeks: and this is the case in Illyria, and the western regions, in Libya, throughout Egypt, and in Palestine: whereas it is made to comprise seven weeks at Constantinople, and in the neighbouring provinces as far as Phoenicia. In some churches the people fast three alternate weeks during the space of six or seven weeks; whereas in others they fast continuously during the three weeks immediately preceding the festival." The statement here made with regard to the West is true except as regards Milan, where Saturday was kept (as in the East) as a festival: while for the Constantinopolitan practice Chrysostom (Hom. xi. in Gen. S: 2) confirms what Sozomen says: while Cassian's language in the text bears witness to the fact that both Egypt and Palestine agreed with the Roman practice. In either case, whether the fast began seven or six weeks before Easter, the number of days observed in the fast was the same; Saturdays (with the exception of Easter Eve which was always regarded as a fast) being excluded in the former case, while they were all included in the latter. Cf. below, c. xxvi.

CHAPTER XXV.

The answer to the effect that the fast of Lent has reference to the tithe of the year.

THEONAS: Although the pious simplicity of some folks would put aside a question on this subject, yet because you are more scrupulous in your examination of those things which another would consider unworthy to be asked about, and want to know the whole truth of this observance of ours and the secret of it, you shall have a very clear reason for this also, that you may still more plainly be convinced that our predecessors taught nothing unreasonable. By the law of Moses the command propounded to all the people generally was this: "Thou shalt offer to the Lord thy God thy tithes and firstfruits."[1125] And so, while we are commanded to offer tithes of our substance and all our fruits, it is much more needful for us to offer tithes of our life and ordinary employments and actions, which certainly is clearly arranged for in the calculation of Lent. For the tithe of the number of all the days included in the revolving circle of the year is thirty-six days and a half. But in seven weeks, if Sundays and Saturdays are subtracted, there remain thirty-five days assigned for fasting. But by the addition of Easter Eve when the Saturday's fast is prolonged to the cock-crowing at the dawn of Easter Day, not only is the number of thirty-six days made up, but in regard to the tithe of the five days which seemed to be over, if the bit of the night which was added be taken into account nothing will be wanting to the whole sum.

NOTES:
[1125] Exod. 22:29.

CHAPTER XXVI.

How we ought also to offer our firstfruits to the Lord.

BUT what shall I say of the firstfruits which surely are given daily by all who serve Christ faithfully? For when men waking from sleep and arising with renewed activity after their rest, before they take in any impulse or thought in their heart, or admit any recollection or consideration of business consecrate their first and earliest thoughts as divine offerings, what are they doing indeed but rendering the firstfruits of their produce through the High Priest Jesus Christ for the enjoyment of this life and a figure of the daily resurrection? And also when roused from sleep in the same way they offer to God a sacrifice of joy and invoke Him with the first motion of their tongue and celebrate His name and praise, and throwing open, the first thing, the door of their lips to sing hymns to Him they offer to God the offices of their mouth; and to Him also in the same way their bring the earliest offerings of their hands and steps, when they rise from bed and stand in prayer and before they use the services of their limbs for their own purposes, take to themselves nothing of their services, but for His glory advance their steps, and set them in His praise and so render the first fruits of all their movements by stretching forth the hands, bending the knees, and prostrating the whole body. For in no other way can we fulfil that of which we sing in the Psalm: "I prevented the dawning of the day and cried;" and: "Mine eyes to Thee have prevented the morning that I might meditate on Thy words;" and: "In the morning shall my prayer prevent Thee;"[1126] unless after our rest in sleep when, as we said above, we are restored as from darkness and death to this light, we have the courage not to begin by taking any of all the services both of mind and body for our own uses. For there is no other morning which the prophet "prevented," or which in the same way we ought to prevent, except either ourselves, i.e., our occupations and feelings and earthly cares, without which we cannot exist--or the most subtle suggestions of the adversary, which he tries to suggest to us, while still resting and overcome with sleep, by the phantoms of vain dreams, with which, when we presently awake, he will fill our minds and occupy us, that he may be the first to seize and carry off the spoils of our firstfruits. Wherefore we must take the utmost care (if we want to fulfil in act the meaning of the above quoted verse) that an anxious watchfulness takes regard of our first and earliest morning thoughts, that they may not be defiled beforehand being hastily taken possession of by our jealous adversary, and thus he may make our firstfruits to be rejected by the Lord as worthless and common. And if he is not prevented by us with watchful circumspection of mind, he will not lay aside his habit of miserably anticipating us nor cease day after day to prevent us by his wiles. And therefore if we want to offer firstfruits that are acceptable and well pleasing to God of the fruits of our mind, we ought to spend no ordinary care to keep all the senses of our body, especially during the hours of the morning, as a sacred holocaust to the Lord pure and undefiled in all things. And this kind of devotion many even of those who live in the world observe with the utmost care, as they rise before it is light or very early, and do not at all mix in the ordinary and necessary business of this world before hastening to church and striving to consecrate in the sight of God the firstfruits of all their actions and doings.

NOTES:
[1126] Ps. 118 (119):147, 148; 87 (88):14.

CHAPTER XXVII.

Why Lent is kept by very many with a different number of days.

FURTHER, as for what you say; viz., that in some countries Lent is kept in different ways, i.e., for six or seven weeks, it is but one system and the same manner of the fast that is preserved by the different observance of the weeks. For those who think one ought to fast also on the Saturday, have determined on the observance of six weeks. They therefore fast for six days out of the seven, and this being six times repeated makes up the six and thirty days. It is therefore, as we said, but one system and the same manner of the fast, although there seems to be a difference in the number of the weeks.

CHAPTER XXVIII.

Why it is called Quadragesima, when the fast is only kept for thirty-six days.

BUT further, as man's carelessness dropped out of sight the reason of this, this season when, as was said, the tithes of the year are offered by fasts for thirty-six days and a half, was called Quadragesima,[1127] a name which perhaps they thought ought to be given to it for this reason; viz., that it is said that Moses and Elijah and our Lord Jesus Christ Himself fasted for forty days. To the mystery of which number are not unsuitably applied those forty years in which Israel dwelt in the wilderness, and in like manner the forty stations which they are said to have passed through with a mystic meaning. Or perhaps the tithe was properly given the name of Quadragesima from the use of the custom-house. For so that state tax is commonly called, from which the same proportion of the increment is assigned for the king's use, as the legal tribute of Quadragesima, which is required of us by the King of all the ages for the use of our life. At any rate, although this has nothing to do with the question raised, yet I think that I ought not to omit the fact that very often our elders used to testify that especially on these days the whole body of monks was attacked according to the ancient custom of the people opposed to them, and was more vehemently urged to forsake their homes, for this reason, because in accordance with this figure, whereby the Egyptians formerly oppressed the children of Israel with grievous afflictions, so now also the spiritual Egyptians try to bow down the true Israel, i.e., the monastic folk, with hard and vile tasks, lest by means of that peace which is dear to God, we should forsake the land of Egypt, and for our good cross to the desert of virtues, so that Pharaoh rages against us and says: "They are idle and therefore they cry saying: Let us go and sacrifice to the Lord our God. Let them be oppressed with labours, and be harassed in their works, and they shall not be harassed by vain words."[1128] For certainly their folly imagines that the holy sacrifice of the Lord, which is only offered in the desert of a pure heart, is the height of folly, for "religion is an abomination to a sinner." [1129]

NOTES:

[1127] Cassian here gives three suggestions why the fast of thirty-six days' duration was called Quadragesima. (1) As roughly corresponding to the forty days fast of Moses, Elijah, and the Lord Himself; (2) because "forty" is the number associated with a time of probation in Scripture; and (3) because of the analogy of a legal tribute of "Quadragesima" paid to the Sovereign. It is certainly a curious and difficult question why the name Quadragesima should have been so universally applied to the fast, when there is no evidence of its having been kept for forty days till sometime after the date of Gregory the Great, when Ash Wednesday and the three following days were prefixed to the six weeks expressly for the purpose of making up the number forty. The name however, had as we see from Socrates, Sozomen, Cassian himself, and many other writers, existed long before this; and on the whole it appears probable that it originated in none of the reasons given above by Cassian, but that in the first instance it was connected "with the period during which our Lord yielded to the power of death, which was estimated at forty hours; viz., from noon on Friday till 4 a.m. on Sunday." See Dictionary of Christian Antiquities, Vol. ii. p. 973; and cf. Irenaeus Ep. ad Victor. in Euseb. V. xxiv.; and Tertullian De Orat. c. 18; and De Jejuniis c. ii. and xiii.

[1128] Exod. 5:8, 9.

[1129] Ecclus. 50:24.

CHAPTER XXIX.

How those who are perfect go beyond the fixed rule of Lent.

BY this law of Lent then the man who is upright and perfect is not restrained nor is he content with merely submitting to that paltry rule which the heads of the church have established for those who all the year round are involved in pleasure or business, that they may be bound by this legal requirement and forced at any rate during these days to find time for the Lord, and dedicate to Him the tithe of the days of their life, all of which they would have consumed as their profits. But the righteous, for whom the law is not appointed, and who devote to spiritual duties not a small part; viz., the tenth, but the whole time of their life, because they are free from the burden of tithes according to law, for his reason, if any worthy and pious occasion happening to them constrains them, are ready to relax their station fast[1130] without any hesitation. For in their case it is no paltry tithe that is diminished, as they offer all that they have to the Lord equally with themselves. And this certainly a man could not do without being guilty of a grievous wrong, who, offering nothing of his own free will to God, is forced to pay his tithes by the stern compulsion of the law which takes no excuse. Wherefore it is clearly established that the servant of the law cannot be perfect, who only shuns those things which are forbidden and does those things which are commanded, but that those are really perfect who do not take advantage even of those things which the law allows. And in this way, though it is said of the Mosaic law that "the law brought nothing to perfection,"[1131] we read that some of the saints in the Old Testament were perfect because they went beyond the commands of the law and lived under the perfection of the Gospel: "Knowing that the law is not appointed for the righteous but for the unrighteous and disobedient, for the ungodly and sinners, for the wicked and defiled, etc." [1132]

NOTES:

[1130] Statio. Cf. the note on the Institutes V. xx. and the notes on the Institutes V. xxiv.

[1131] Heb. 7:19.

[1132] 1 Tim. 1:9, 10.

CHAPTER XXX.

Of the origin and beginning of Lent.

HOWBEIT you should know that as long as the primitive church retained its perfection unbroken, this observance of Lent did not exist. For they were not bound by the requirements of this order, or by any legal enactments, nor confined in the very narrow limits of the fast, as the fast embraced equally the whole year round. But when the multitude of believers began day by day to decline from that apostolic fervour, and to look after their own wealth, and not to portion it out for the good of all the faithful in accordance with the arrangement of the apostles, but having an eye to their own private expenses, tried not only to keep it but actually to increase it, not content with following the example of Ananias and Sapphira, then it seemed good to all the priests that men who were hampered by worldly cares, and almost ignorant, if I may say so, of abstinence and contrition, should be recalled to the pious duty by a fast canonically enjoined, and be constrained by the necessity of paying the legal tithes, as this certainly would be good for the weak brethren and could not do any harm to the perfect who were living under the grace of the gospel and by their voluntary devotion going beyond the law, so as to succeed in attaining to the blessedness which the Apostle speaks of: "For sin shall not have dominion over you; for ye are not under the law but under grace."[1133] For of a truth sin cannot exercise dominion over one who lives faithfully under the liberty of grace.

NOTES:
[1133] Rom. 6:14.

CHAPTER XXXI.

A question, how we ought to understand the Apostle's words: "Sin shall not have dominion over you."

GERMANUS: Because this saying of the Apostle, which promises freedom from care not only to monks but to all Christians in general, cannot lead us wrong, it seems to us somewhat obscure. For whereas he maintains that all those who believe the gospel are at lib-

erty and free from the yoke and dominion of sin, how is it that the dominion of sin holds vigorous sway over almost all the baptized, in
accordance with the Lord's words, where He says: "Every one that
doeth sin is the servant of sin"? [1134]

NOTES:
[1134] S. John 8:34.

CHAPTER XXXII.

The answer on the difference between grace and the commands of
the law.

THEONAS: Your inquiry once more raises before us a question
of no small extent. The explanation of which though I know that it
cannot be taught to or understood by the inexperienced, yet as far as I
can, I will try to set forth in words and briefly to explain, if only your
minds will follow up and act upon what we say. For whatever is
known not by teaching but by experience, just as it cannot be taught by
one without experience, so neither can it be grasped or taken in by the
mind of one who has not laid the foundation by a similar study and
training. And therefore I think it necessary for us first to inquire
somewhat carefully what is the purpose or meaning of the law, and
what is the system and perfection of grace, that from this we may succeed in understanding the dominion of sin and how to drive it out. And
so the law chiefly commands men to seek the bonds of wedlock, saying: "Blessed is he that hath seed in Sion and an household in
Jerusalem;"[1135] and: "Cursed is the barren that hath not borne."[1136] On
the other hand grace invites us to the purity of perpetual chastity, and
the undefiled state of blessed virginity, saying: "Blessed are the barren,
and the breasts which have not given suck;" and: "he that hateth not
father and mother and wife cannot be my disciple;" and this of the
Apostle: "It remaineth that they that have wives be as though they had
them not."[1137] The law says: "Thou shall not delay to offer thy tithes
and firstfruits;" grace says: "If thou wilt be perfect, go and sell all that
thou hast and give to the poor:"[1138] The law forbids not retaliation for
wrongs and vengeance for injuries, saying" "An eye for an eye and a
tooth for a tooth." Grace would have our patience proved by the injuries and blows offered to us being redoubled, and bids us be ready to

endure twice as much damage; saying: "If a man strike thee on one cheek, offer him the other also; and to him who will contend with thee at the law and take away thy coat, give him thy cloak also."[1139] The one decrees that we should hate our enemies, the other that we should love them so that it holds that even for them we ought always to pray to God.

NOTES:
[1135] Isa. 31:9 (LXX).
[1136] Cf. Job 24:21.
[1137] S. Luke 23:29; 14:26; 1 Cor. 7:29.
[1138] Exod. 22:29; S. Matt. 19:21.
[1139] Exod. 21:24; S. Matt. 5:39, 40.

CHAPTER XXXIII.

Of the fact that the precepts of the gospel are milder than those of the law.

WHOEVER therefore climbs this height of evangelical perfection, is at once raised by the merits of such virtue above every law, and disregarding as trivial all that is commanded by Moses, recognizes that he is only subject to the grace of the Saviour, by whose aid he knows that he attained to that most exalted condition. Therefore sin has no dominion over him, "because the love of God, which is shed abroad in our hearts by the Holy Ghost which is given to us,"[1140] shuts out all care for everything else, and can neither desire what is forbidden, or disregard what is commanded, as its whole aim and all its desire is ever fixed on divine love, and to such an extent is it not caught by the delights of worthless things, that it actually does not take advantage of those things which are permitted. But under the law, where lawful marriages are observed, although the rovings of wantonness are restrained, and bound down to one woman alone, yet the pricks of carnal lust cannot help being vigorous; and it is hard for the fire, for which fuel is expressly supplied, to be thus shut in within prearranged limits, so as not to spread further and burn up anything it touches. As even if this objection occurs to it that it is not allowed to be kindled beyond these limits, yet even while it is kept in check, it is on fire because the will itself is in fault, and its habit of carnal intercourse hurries it into too speedy excesses of adultery. But those whom the grace of the Saviour has fired with the holy love of chastity, so consume all the thorns of carnal desires in the fire of the Lord's love, that no dying embers of sin interfere with the coldness of their purity. The servants of the law then from the use of lawful things fall away to unlawful; the partakers of grace while they disregard lawful things know nothing of unlawful ones. But as sin is alive in one who loves marriage, so is it also in one who is satisfied with merely paying his tithes and firstfruits. For, while he is dawdling or careless, he is sure to sin in regard to either their quality or quantity, or the daily distribution of them. For as he is commanded unweariedly to minister to those in want of what is his, although he may dispense it with the fullest faith and devotion, yet it is hard for him not to fall often into the snares of sin. But over those who have not set at naught the counsel of the Lord, but who, disposing of all their property to the poor, take up their cross and follow the bestower of grace, sin can have no dominion. For no faithless anxiety for getting food will annoy him who piously distributes and disperses his wealth already consecrated to Christ and no longer regarded as his own; nor will any grudging hesitation take away from the cheerfulness of his almsgiving, because without any thought of his own needs or fear of his own food running short he is distributing what has once for all been completely offered to God, and is no longer regarded as his own, as he is sure that when he has succeeded in stripping himself as he desires, he will be fed by God much more than the birds of the air. On the other hand he who retains his goods of this world, or, bound by the rules of the old law, distributes the tithe of his produce, and his firstfruits, or a portion of his income, although he may to a considerable degree quench the fire of his sins by this dew of almsgiving, yet, however generously he gives away his wealth, it is impossible for him altogether to rid himself of the dominion of sin, unless perhaps by the grace of the Saviour, together with his substance he gets rid of all love of possessing. In the same way he cannot fail to be subject to the bloody sway of sin, whoever chooses to pull out, as the law commands, an eye for an eye, a tooth for a tooth, or to hate his enemy, for while he desires by retaliation in exchange to avenge an injury done to himself, and while he cherishes bitter hatred against an enemy, he is sure always to be inflamed with the passion of anger and rage. But whoever lives under the light of the grace of the gospel, and overcomes evil by not resisting it, but by bearing it, and does not hesitate of his own free will to give to one who smites his right cheek, the other also, and to one who wants to raise a lawsuit against him for his coat, gives his cloak also, and who loves his enemies, and prays for those who slander him, this man has broken the yoke of sin and burst its chains. For he is not living under the law, which does not destroy the seeds of sin (whence not without reason the Apostle says of it: "There is a setting aside of the former commandment because of the weakness and unprofitableness thereof: for the law brought nothing to perfection;" and the Lord says by the prophet: "And I gave them commands that were not good, and ordinances, whereby they could not live"[1141] , but under grace which does not merely lop off the boughs of wickedness, but actually tears up the very roots of an evil will.

NOTES:
[1140] Rom. 5:5.
[1141] Heb. 7:18, 19; Ezek. 20:25.

CHAPTER XXXIV.

How a man can be shown to be under grace.

WHOEVER then strives to reach the perfection of evangelical teaching, this man living under grace is not oppressed by the dominion of sin, for to be under grace is to do those things which grace commands. But whoever will not submit himself to the complete requirements of evangelical perfection, must not remain ignorant that, although he seems to be baptized and to be a monk, yet he is not under grace, but is still shackled by the chains of the law, and weighed down by the burden of sin. For it is the aim of Him, who by the grace of adoption accepts all those by whom He has been received, not to destroy but to build upon, not to abolish but to fulfil the Mosaic requirements. But some knowing nothing about this, and disregarding the splendid counsels and exhortations of Christ, are so emancipated by the carelessness of a freedom too hastily assumed, that they not only fail to carry out the commands of Christ as if they were too hard, but actually scorn as antiquated, the commands given to them as beginners and children by the law of Moses, saying in this dangerous freedom of theirs that which the Apostle execrates: "We have sinned, because we are not under the law but under grace."[1142] He then who is neither under grace, because he has never climbed the heights of the Lord's teaching, nor under the law, because he has not accepted even those small commands of the law, this man, ground down beneath a twofold rule of sin, fancies that he has received the grace of Christ, simply and solely for this, that by this dangerous liberty of his he may make himself none of His, and falls into that state, which the Apostle Peter warns us to avoid, saying: "Act as free, and not having your liberty as a cloak of wickedness." The blessed Apostle Paul also says: "For ye, brethren, were called to liberty," i.e., that ye might be free from the dominion of sin, "only use not your liberty for an occasion of the flesh,"[1143] i.e., believe that the doing away with the commands of the law is a licence to sin. But this liberty, the Apostle Paul teaches us is nowhere but where the Lord is dwelling, for he says: "The Lord is the Spirit, but where the Spirit of the Lord is there is liberty."[1144] Wherefore I know not whether I could express and explain the meaning of the blessed Apostle, as those know how, who have experience; one thing I do know, that it is very clearly revealed even without anyone's explanation to all those who have perfectly acquired praktikh, i.e., practical training. For they will need no effort to understand in discussion what they have already learnt by practice.

NOTES:
[1142] Rom. 6:15.
[1143] 1 Pet. 2:16; Gal. 5:13.
[1144] 2 Cor. 3:17.

CHAPTER XXXV.

A question, why sometimes when we are fasting more strictly than usual, we are troubled by carnal desires more keenly than usual.

GERMANUS: You have very clearly explained a most difficult question, and one which, as we think, is unknown to many. Wherefore we pray you to add this also for our good, and carefully to expound why sometimes when we are fasting more strictly than usual, and are exhausted and worn out, severer bodily struggles are excited. For often on waking from sleep, when we have discovered that we have been defiled[1145] we are so dejected in heart that we do not even venture faithfully to rise even for prayer.

NOTES:
[1145] Cum deprehenderimus nos sordidi liquoris contagius pertulisse.

CHAPTER XXXVI.

The answer, telling that this question should be reserved for a future Conference.

THEONAS: Your zeal indeed, whereby you desire to reach the way of perfection, not for a moment only but fully and perfectly, urges us to continue this discussion unweariedly. For you are anxiously inquiring not about external chastity or outward circumcision, but about that which is secret, as you know that complete perfection does not consist in this visible continence of the flesh which can be attained either by constraint, or by hypocrisy even by unbelievers, but in that voluntary and invisible purity of heart, which the blessed Apostle describes as follows: "For he is not a Jew which is so outwardly, nor is that circumcision which is outward in the flesh, but he is a Jew which is one inwardly, and the circumcision is that of the heart, in the spirit not in the letter, whose praise is not of men but of God,"[1146] who alone searches the secrets of the heart. But because it is not possible for your wish to be fully satisfied (as the short space of the night that is left is not enough for the investigation of this most difficult question,) I think it well to postpone it for a while. For these matters, as they should be propounded by us quietly and with an heart entirely free from all bustling thoughts, so should they be received into your minds; for just as the inquiry ought to be undertaken for the sake of our common purity, so they cannot be learnt or acquired by one who is without the gift of uprightness. For we do not ask what arguments of empty words, but what the inward faith of the conscience and the greater force of truth can persuade. And therefore with regard to the knowledge and teaching of this purification nothing can be brought forward except by one who has had experience of it, nor can anything be committed except to one who is a most eager and very earnest lover of the truth itself, who does not hope to attain it by asking questions with mere vain words, but by striving with all his might and main, with no wish for useless chattering but with the desire to purify himself internally.

NOTES:
[1146] Rom. 2:28, 29.
[1075] On Quinquagesima see the note on the Institutes II. vi.

CONFERENCE 23.

The Third Conference of Abbot Theonas
on Sinlessness

CHAPTER I.

Discourse of Abbot Theonas on the Apostle's words: "For I do not the good which I would."

AT the return of light therefore, as the old man was forced by our intense urgency to investigate the depths of the Apostle's subject, he spoke as follows: As for the passages by which you try to prove that the Apostle Paul spoke not in his own person but in that of sinners: "For I do not the good that I would, but the evil which I hate, that I do;" or this: "But if I do that which I would not, it is no longer I that do it but sin that dwelleth in me;" or what follows: "For I delight in the law of God after the inner man, but I see another law in my members opposing the law of my mind, and bringing me into captivity to the law of sin which is in my members;"[1148] these passages on the contrary plainly show that they cannot possibly fit the person of sinners, but that what is said can only apply to those that are perfect, and that it only suits the chastity of those who follow the good example of the Apostles. Else how could these words apply to the person of sinners: "For I do not the good which I would, but the evil which I hate that I do"? or even this: "But if I do what I would not it is no longer I that do it but sin that dwelleth in me"? For what sinner defiles himself unwillingly by adulteries and fornication? Who against his will prepares plots against his neighbour? Who is driven by unavoidable necessity to oppress a man by false witness or cheat him by theft, or covet the goods of another or shed his blood? Nay rather, as Scripture says, "Mankind is diligently inclined to wickedness from his youth."[1149] For to such an extent are all inflamed by the love of sin and desire to carry out what they like, that they actually look out with watchful care for an opportunity of committing wickedness and are afraid of being too slow to enjoy their lusts, and glory in their shame and the mass of their crimes, as the Apostle says in censure,[1150] and seek credit for themselves out of their own confusion, of whom also the prophet Jeremiah maintains that they commit their flagitious crimes not only not unwillingly nor with ease of heart and body, but with laborious efforts to such an extent that they come to toil to carry them out, so that they are prevented even by the hindrance of arduous difficulty from their deadly quest of sin; as he says: "They have laboured to do wickedly."[1151] Who also will say that this applies to sinners: "And so with the mind I myself serve the law of God, but with the flesh the law of sin," as it is plain that they serve God neither with the mind nor the flesh? Or how can those who sin with the body serve God with the mind, when the flesh receives the incitement to sin from the heart, and the Creator of either nature Himself declares that the fount and spring of sin flows from the latter, saying: "From the heart proceed evil thoughts, adulteries, fornications, thefts, false witness, etc."[1152] Wherefore it is clearly shown that this cannot in any way be taken of the person of sinners, who not only do not hate, but actually love what is evil and are so far from serving God with either the mind or the flesh that they sin with the mind before they do with the flesh, and before they carry out the pleasures of the body are overcome by sin in their mind and thoughts.

NOTES:
[1148] Rom. 7:18, 19.
[1149] Gen. 8:21.
[1150] Cf. Phil. 3:19.
[1151] Jer. 9:5.
[1152] S. Matt. 15:19.

CHAPTER II.

How the Apostle completed many good actions.

IT remains therefore for us to measure its meaning and drift from the inmost feelings of the speaker, and to discuss what the blessed Apostle called good, and what he pronounced by comparison evil, not by the bare meaning of the words, but with the same insight which he showed, and to investigate his meaning with due regard to the worth and goodness of the speaker. For then we shall be able to understand the words, which were uttered by God's inspiration, in accordance with his purpose and wish, when we weigh the position and character of those by whom they were spoken, and are ourselves clothed with the same feelings (not in words but by experience), in accordance with the character of which most certainly all the thoughts are conceived and opinions uttered. Wherefore let us carefully consider what was in the main that good which the Apostle could not do when he would. For we know that there are many good things which we cannot deny that the blessed Apostle and all men as good as he either have by nature, or acquire by grace. For chastity is good, continence is praiseworthy, prudence is to be admired, kindness is liberal, sobriety is careful, temperance is modest, pity is kind, justice is holy: all of which we cannot doubt existed fully and in perfection in the Apostle Paul and his companions, so that they taught religion by the lesson of their virtues rather than their words. What if they were always consumed with the constant care of all the churches and watchful anxiety? How great a good is this pity, what perfection it is to burn for them that are offended, to be weak with the weak![1153] If then the Apostle abounded with such good things, we cannot recognize what that good was, in the perfection of which the Apostle was lacking, unless we have advanced to that state of mind in which he was speaking. And so all those virtues which we say that he possessed, though they are like most splendid and precious gems, yet when they are compared with that most beautiful and unique pearl which the merchant in the gospel sought and wanted to acquire by selling all that he possessed, so does their value seem poor and trifling, so that if they are without hesitation got rid of, the possession of one good thing alone will enrich the man who sells countless good things.

NOTES:
[1153] Cf. 2 Cor. 11:29.

CHAPTER III.

What is really the good which the Apostle testifies that he could not perform.

WHAT then is that one thing which is so incomparably above those great and innumerable good things, that, while they are all scorned and rejected, it alone should be acquired? Doubtless it is that truly good part, the grand and lasting character of which is thus described by the Lord, when Mary disregarded the duties of hospitality and courtesy and chose it: "Martha, Martha, thou art careful and troubled about many things: but there is but need of but few things or even of one only. Mary hath chosen the good part which shall not be taken away from her."[1154] Contemplation then, i.e., meditation on God, is the one thing, the value of which all the merits of our righteous acts, all our aims at virtue, come short of. And all those things which we said existed in the Apostle Paul, were not only good and useful, but even great and splendid. But as, for example, the metal of alloy which is considered of some use and worth, becomes worthless when silver is taken into account, and again the value of silver disappears in comparison with gold, and gold itself is disregarded when compared with precious stones, and yet a quantity of precious stones however splendid are outdone by the brightness of a single pearl, so all those merits of holiness, although they are not merely good and useful for the present life, but also secure the gift of eternity, yet if they are compared with the merit of Divine contemplation, will be considered trifling and so to speak, fit to be sold. And to support this illustration by the authority of Scripture, does not Scripture declare of all things in general which were created by God, and say: "And behold everything that God had made was very good;" and again: "And things that God hath made are all good in their season"?[1155] These things then which in the present time are termed not simply and solely good, but emphatically "very good" (for they are really convenient for us while living in this world, either for purposes of life, or for remedies for the body, or by reason of some unknown usefulness, or else they are indeed "very good," because they enable us "to see the invisible things of God from the creatures of the world, being understood by the things that are made, even His eternal power and Godhead,"[1156] from this great and orderly arrangement of the fabric of the world; and to contemplate them from the existence of everything in it), yet none of these things will keep the name of good if they are regarded in the light of that world to come, where no variation of good things, and no loss of true blessedness need be feared. The bliss of which world is thus described: "The light of the moon shall be as the light of the sun, and the light of the sun shall be sevenfold as the light of seven days."[1157] These things then which are great and wondrous to be gazed on, and marvellous, will at once appear as vanity if they are compared with the future promises from faith; as David says: "They all shall wax old as a garment, and as a vesture shall Thou change them, and they shall be changed. But Thou art the same, and Thy years shall not fail."[1158] Because then there is nothing of itself enduring, nothing unchangeable, nothing good but Deity alone, while every creature, to obtain the blessing of eternity and immutability, aims at this not by its own nature but by participation of its Creator, and His grace, they cannot maintain their character for goodness when compared with their Creator.

NOTES:
[1154] S. Luke 10:41, 42. Cf. the note on I. viii.
[1155] Gen. 1:31; Ecclus. 39:16.
[1156] Rom. 1:20.
[1157] Isa. 30:26.
[1158] Ps. 101 (102):27, 28.

CHAPTER IV.

How man's goodness and righteousness are not good if compared with the goodness and righteousness of God.

BUT if we want also to establish the force of this opinion by still clearer proofs, is it not the case that while we read of many things as called good in the gospel, as a good tree, and good treasure, and a good man, and a good servant, for He says: "A good tree cannot bring forth evil fruit;" and: "a good man out of the good treasure of his heart brings forth good things;" and: "Well done, good and faithful servant;"[1159] and certainly there can be no doubt that none of these are good in themselves, yet if we take into consideration the goodness of God, none of them will be called good, as the Lord says: "None is good save God alone"?[1160] In whose sight even the apostles themselves, who in the excellence of their calling in many ways went beyond the goodness of mankind, are said to be evil, as the Lord thus speaks to them: "If ye then being evil know how to give good gifts to your children, how much more shall your Father which is in heaven give good things to them that ask Him."[1161] Finally as our goodness turns to badness in the eyes of the Highest so also our righteousness when set against the Divine righteousness is considered like a menstruous cloth, as Isaiah the prophet says: "All your righteousness is like a menstruous cloth."[1162] And to produce something still plainer, even the vital precepts of the law itself, which are said to have been "given by angels by the hand of a mediator," and of which the same Apostle says: "So the law indeed is holy and the commandment is holy and just and good,"[1163] when they are compared with the perfection of the gospel are pronounced anything but good by the Divine oracle: for He says: "And I gave them precepts that were not good, and ordinances whereby they should not live in them."[1164] The Apostle also affirms that the glory of the law is so dimmed by the light of the New Testament that he declares that in comparison with the splendour of the gospel it is not to be considered glorious, saying: "For even that which was glorious was not glorified by reason of the glory that excelleth."[1165] And Scripture keeps up this comparison on the other side also, i.e., in weighing the merits of sinners, so that in comparison with the wicked it justifies those who have sinned less, saying: "Sodom is justified above thee;" and again: "For what hath thy sister Sodom sinned?" and: "The rebellious Israel hath justified her soul in comparison of the treacherous Judah."[1166] So then the merits of all the virtues, which I enumerated above, though in themselves they are good and precious, yet become dim in comparison of the brightness of contemplation. For they greatly hinder and retard the saints who are taken up with earthly aims even at good works, from the contemplation of that sublime good.

NOTES:
[1159] S. Matt. 7:18; 12:35; 25:21.
[1160] S. Luke 18:19.
[1161] S. Matt. 7:11.
[1162] Isa. 64:6.
[1163] Gal. 3:19; Rom. 7:12.
[1164] Ezek. 20:25.
[1165] 2 Cor. 3:10.
[1166] Ezek. 16:52, 49; Jer. 3:2.

CHAPTER V.

How no one can be continually intent upon that highest good.

FOR who, when "delivering the poor from the hand of them that are too strong for him, and the needy and the poor from them that strip him," who when "breaking the jaws of the wicked and snatching their prey from between their teeth,"[1167] can with a calm mind regard the glory of the Divine Majesty during the actual work of intervention? Who when ministering support to the poor, or when receiving with benevolent kindness the crowds that come to him, can at the very moment when he is with anxious mind perplexed for the wants of his brethren, contemplate the vastness of the bliss on high, and while he is shaken by the troubles and cares of the present life look forward to the state of the world to come with an heart raised above the stains of earth? Whence the blessed David when laying down that this alone is good for man, longs to cling constantly to God, and says: "It is good for me to cling to God, and to put my hope in the Lord."[1168] And Ecclesiastes also declares that this cannot be done without fault by any of the saints, and says: "For there is not a righteous man upon earth, that doeth good and sinneth not."[1169] For who, even if he be the chief of all righteous and holy men, can we ever think could, while bound in the chains of this life, so acquire this chief good, as never to cease from divine contemplation, or be thought to be drawn away by earthly thoughts even for a short time from Him Who alone is good? Who ever takes no care for food, none for clothing or other carnal things, or when anxious about receiving the brethren, or change of place, or building his cell, has never desired the aid of man's assistance, nor when harassed by scarcity and want has incurred this sentence of reproof from the Lord: "Be not anxious for your life what ye shall eat, nor for your body what ye shall put on"?[1170] Further we confidently assert that even the Apostle Paul himself who surpassed in the number of his sufferings the toils of all the saints, could not possibly fulfil this, as he himself testifies to the disciples in the Acts of the Apostles: "Ye yourselves know that these hands have ministered to my need, and to the needs of those who were with me," or when in writing in the Thessalonians he testifies that he "worked in labour and weariness night and day."[1171] And although for this there were great rewards for his merits prepared, yet his mind, however holy and sublime it might be, could not help being sometimes drawn away from that heavenly contemplation by its attention to earthly labours. Further, when he saw himself enriched with such practical fruits, and on the other hand considered in his heart the good of meditation, and weighed as it were in one scale the profit of all these labours and in the other the delights of divine contemplation, when for a long time he had corrected the balance in his breast, while the vast rewards for his labours delighted him on one side, and on the other the desire for unity with and the inseparable companionship of Christ inclined him to depart this life, at last in his perplexity he cries out and says: "What I shall choose I know not. For I am in a strait betwixt two, having a desire to depart and to be with Christ, for it were much better: but to abide in the flesh is more necessary for your sakes."[1172] Though then in many ways he preferred this excellent good to all the fruits of his preaching, yet he submits himself in consideration of love, without which none can gain the Lord; and for their sakes, whom hitherto he had soothed with milk as nourishment from the breasts of the gospel, does not refuse to be parted from Christ, which is bad for himself though useful for others. For he is driven to choose this the rather by that excessive goodness of his whereby for the salvation of his brethren he is ready, were it possible, to incur even the last evil of an Anathema. "For I could wish," he says, "that I myself were Anathema from Christ for my brethren's sake, who are my kinsmen according to the flesh, who are Israelites,"[1173] i.e., I could wish to be subject not only to temporal, but even to perpetual punishment, if only all men, were it possible, might enjoy the fellowship of Christ: for I am sure that the salvation of all would be better for Christ and for me than my own. That then the Apostle might perfectly gain this chief good, i.e., to enjoy the vision of God and to be joined continually to Christ, he was ready to be parted from this body, which as it is feeble and hindered by the many requirements of its frailties cannot help separating from union with Christ: for it is impossible for the mind, that is harassed by such frequent cares, and hampered by such various and tiresome troubles, always to enjoy the Divine vision. For what aim of the saints can be so persistent, what purpose can be so high that that crafty plotter does not sometimes destroy it? Who has frequented the recesses of the desert and shunned intercourse with all men in such a way that he never trips by unnecessary thoughts, and by looking on things or being occupied in earthly actions falls away from that contemplation of God, which truly alone is good? Who ever could preserve such fervour of spirit as not sometimes to pass by roving thoughts from his attention to prayer, and fall away suddenly from heavenly to earthly things? Which of us (to pass over other times of wandering) even at the very moment when he raises his soul in prayer to God on high, does not fall into a sort of stupor, and even against his will offend by that very thing from which he hoped for pardon of his sins? Who, I ask, is so alert and vigilant as never, while he is singing a Psalm to God, to allow his mind to wander from the meaning of Scripture? Who is so intimate with and closely joined to God, as to congratulate himself on having carried out for a single day that rule of the Apostle's, whereby he bids us pray without ceasing?[1174] And though all these things may seem to some, who are involved in grosser sins, to be trivial and altogether foreign to sin, yet to those who know the value of perfection a quantity even of very small matters becomes most serious.

NOTES:
[1167] Ps. 34 (35):10; Job 29:17.
[1168] Ps. 72 (73):28.
[1169] Eccl. 7:21.
[1170] S. Matt. 6:23.
[1171] Acts 20:34; 2 Thess. 3:8.
[1172] Phil. 1:22-24.
[1173] Rom. 9:3, 4.
[1174] Cf. 1 Thess. 5:17.

CHAPTER VI.

How those who think that they are without sin are like purblind people.

AS if we were to suppose that two men, one of whom was clear sighted with perfect vision, and the other, one whose eyesight was obscured by dimness of vision, had together entered some great house that was filled with a quantity of bundles, instruments, and vessels, would not he, whose dullness of vision prevented his seeing everything, assert that there was nothing there but chests, beds, benches, tables, and whatever met the fingers of one who felt them rather than the eyes of one who saw them, while on the other hand would not the other, who searched out what was hidden with clear and bright eyes, declare that there were there many most minute articles, and what could scarcely be counted; which if they were ever gathered up into a single pile, would by their number equal or perhaps exceed the size of those few things which the other had felt. So then even saints, and, if we may so say, men who see, whose aim is the utmost perfection, cleverly detect in themselves even those things which the gaze of our mind being as it were darkened cannot see, and condemn them very severely, to such an extent that those who have not, as it seems to our carelessness, dimmed the whiteness of their body, which is as it were like snow, with even the slightest spot of sin, seem to themselves to be covered with many stains, if, I will not say any evil or vain thoughts creep into the doors of their mind, but even the recollection of a Psalm which has to be said takes off the attention of the kneeler at the time for prayer. For if, say they, when we ask some great man, I will not say for our life and salvation, but for some advantage and profit, we fasten all our attention of mind and body upon him, and hang with trembling expectation on his nod, with no slight dread lest haply some foolish or unsuitable word may turn aside the pity of our hearer, and then too, when we are standing in the forum or in the courts of earthly judges, with our opponent standing over against us, if in the midst of the prosecution and trial any coughing or spitting, or laughing, or yawning, or sleep overtakes us, with what malice will our ever watchful opponent stir up the severity of the judge to our damage: how much more, when we entreat Him who knows all secrets, should we, by reason of our imminent danger of everlasting death, plead with earnest and anxious prayer for the kindness of the judge, especially as on the other side there stands one who is both our crafty seducer and our accuser! And not without reason will he be bound by no light sin, but by a grievous fault of wickedness, who, when he pours forth his prayer to God, departs at once from His sight as if from the eyes of one who neither sees nor hears, and follows the vanity of wicked thoughts. But they who cover the eyes of their heart with a thick veil of their sins, and as the Saviour says, "Seeing see not and hearing hear not nor understand,"[1175] hardly regard in the inmost recesses of their breast even those faults which are great and deadly, and cannot with clear eyes look at any deceitful thoughts, nor even those vague and secret desires which strike the mind with slight and subtle suggestions, nor the captivities of their soul, but always wandering among impure thoughts they know not how to be sorry when they are distracted from that meditation which is so special, nor can they grieve that they have lost anything as while they lay open their mind to the entrance of any thought as they please, they have nothing set before them to hold to as the main thing or to desire in every way.

NOTES:
[1175] S. Matt. 13:13.

CHAPTER VII.

How those who maintain that a man can be without sin are charged with a twofold error.

THE reason however which drives us into this error is that, as we are utterly ignorant of the virtue of being without sin,[1176] we fancy that we cannot contract any guilt from those idle and random vagaries of our thoughts, but being rendered stupid by dullness and as it were smitten with blindness we can see nothing in ourselves but capital offences, and think that we have only to keep clear of those things which are condemned also by the severity of secular laws, and if we find that even for a short time we are free from these we at once imagine that there is no sin at all in us. Accordingly we are distinguished from the number of those who see, because we do not see the many small stains, which are crowded together in us, and are not smitten with saving contrition, if the malady of vexation overtakes our thoughts, nor are we sorry that we are struck by the suggestions of vainglory, nor do we weep over our prayers offered up so tardily and coldly, nor consider it a fault if while we are singing or praying, something else besides the actual prayer or Psalm fills our thoughts, nor are we horrified because we do not blush to conceive many things which we are ashamed to speak or do before men, in our heart, which, as we know, lies open to the Divine gaze; nor do we purge away the pollution of filthy dreams with copious ablutions of our tears, nor grieve that in the pious act of almsgiving when we are assisting the needs of the brethren, or ministering support to the poor, the brightness of our cheerfulness is clouded over by a stingy delay, nor do we think that we are affected by any loss when we forget God and think about things that are temporal and corrupt, so that these words of Solomon fairly apply to us: "They smite me but I have not grieved, and they have mocked me, but I knew it not." [1177]

PART 3

NOTES:
[1176] Anamarteti id est impeccantae.
[1177] Prov. 23:35.

CHAPTER VIII.

How it is given to but few to understand what sin is.

THOSE on the other hand who make the sum of all their joy and delight and bliss consist in the contemplation of divine and spiritual things alone, if they are unwillingly withdrawn from them even for a short time by thoughts that force themselves upon them, punish this as if it were a kind of sacrilege in them, and avenge it by immediate chastisement, and in their grief that they have preferred some worthless creature (to which their mental gaze was turned aside) to their Creator, charge themselves with the guilt (I had almost said) of impiety, and although they turn the eyes of their heart with the utmost speed to behold the brightness of the Divine Glory, yet they cannot tolerate even for a very short time the darkness of carnal thoughts, and execrate whatever keeps back their soul's gaze from the true light. Finally when the blessed Apostle John would instill this feeling into everybody he says: "Little children, love not the world, neither the things which are in the world. If any man love the world, the love of God is not in him: for everything that is in the world is the lust of the flesh and the lust of the eyes and the pride of life, which is not of the Father but of the world. And the world perisheth and the lust thereof: but he that doeth the will of God abideth forever."[1178] The saints therefore scorn all those things on which the world exists, but it is impossible for them never to be carried away to them by a brief aberration of thoughts, and even now no man, except our Lord and Saviour, can keep his naturally wandering mind always fixed on the contemplation of God so as never to be carried away from it through the love of something in this world; as Scripture says: "Even the stars are not clean in His sight," and again: "If He puts no trust in His saints, and findeth iniquity in His angels," or as the more correct translation has it: "Behold among His saints none is unchangeable, and the heavens are not pure in His sight." [1179]

NOTES:
[1178] 1 John 2:15-17.

[1179] Job 25:5; 15:15.

CHAPTER IX.

Of the care with which a monk should preserve the recollection of God.

I SHOULD say then that the saints who keep a firm hold of the recollection of God and are borne along, as it were, with their steps suspended on a line stretched out on high, may be rightly compared to rope dancers, commonly called funambuli, who risk all their safety and life on the path of that very narrow rope, with no doubt that they will immediately meet with a most dreadful death if their foot swerves or trips in the very slightest degree, or goes over the line of the course in which alone is safety. And while with marvellous skill they ply their airy steps through space, if they keep not their steps to that all too narrow path with careful and anxious regulation, the earth which is the natural base and the most solid and safest foundation for all, becomes to them an immediate and clear danger, not because its nature is changed, but because they fall headlong upon it by the weight of their bodies. So also that unwearied goodness of God and His unchanging nature[1180] hurts no one indeed, but we ourselves by falling from on high and tending to the depths are the authors of our own death, or rather the very fall becomes death to the faller. For it says: "Woe to them for they have departed from Me: they shall be wasted because they have transgressed against Me;" and again: "Woe to them when I shall depart from them." For "thine own wickedness shall reprove thee, and thy apostasy shall rebuke thee. Know thou and see that it is an evil and a bitter thing for thee to have left the Lord thy God;" for "every man is bound by the cords of his sins."[1181] To whom this rebuke is aptly directed by the Lord: "Behold," He says, "all you that kindle a fire, encompassed with flames, walk ye in the light of your fire and in the flames which you have kindled;" and again: "He that kindleth iniquity, shall perish by it." [1182]

NOTES:
[1180] Substantia.
[1181] Hos. 7:13; 9:12; Jer. 2:19; Prov. 5:22.
[1182] Isa. 50:11; Prov. 19:9.

CHAPTER X.

How those who are on the way to perfection are truly humble, and feel that they always stand in need of God's grace.

WHEN then holy men feel that they are oppressed by the weight of earthly thoughts and fall away from their loftiness of mind, and that they are led away against their will or rather without knowing it, into the law of sin and death, and (to pass over other matters) are kept back by those actions which I described above, which are good and right though earthly, from the vision of God; they have something to groan over constantly to the Lord; they have something for which indeed to humble themselves, and in their contrition to profess themselves not in words only but in heart, sinners; and for this, while they continually ask of the Lord's grace pardon for everything that day by day they commit when overcome by the weakness of the flesh, they should shed without ceasing true tears of penitence; as they see that being involved even to the very end of their life in the very same troubles, with continual sorrow for which they are tried, they cannot even offer their prayers without harassing thoughts. So then as they know by experience that through the hindrance of the burden of the flesh they cannot by human strength reach the desired end, nor be united according to their heart's desire with that chief and highest good, but that they are led away from the vision of it captive to worldly things, they betake themselves to the grace of God, "Who justifieth the ungodly,"[1183] and cry out with the Apostle: "O wretched man that I am! Who shall deliver me from the body of this death? Thanks be to God through our Lord Jesus Christ."[1184] For they feel that they cannot perform the good that they would, but are ever falling into the evil which they would not, and which they hate, i.e., wandering thoughts and care for carnal things.

NOTES:
[1183] Rom. 4:5.

[1184] Rom. 7:24, 25.

CHAPTER XI.

Explanation of the phrase: "For I delight in the law of God after the inner man," etc.

AND they "delight" indeed "in the law of God after the inner man," which soars above all visible things and ever strives to be united to God alone, but they "see another law in their members," i.e., implanted in their natural human condition, which "resisting the law of their mind,"[1185] brings their thoughts into captivity to the forcible law of sin, compelling them to forsake that chief good and submit to earthly notions, which though they may appear necessary and useful when they are taken up in the interests of some religious want, yet when they are set against that good which fascinates the gaze of all the saints, are seen by them to be bad and such as should be avoided, because by them in some way or other and for a short time they are drawn away from the joy of that perfect bliss. For the law of sin is really what the fall of its first father brought on mankind by that fault of his, against which there was uttered this sentence by the most just Judge: "Cursed is the ground in thy works; thorns and thistles shall it bring forth to thee, and in the sweat of thy brow shalt thou eat bread."[1186] This, I say, is the law, implanted in the members of all mortals, which resists the law of our mind and keeps it back from the vision of God, and which, as the earth is cursed in our works after the knowledge of good and evil, begins to produce the thorns and thistles of thoughts, by the sharp pricks of which the natural seeds of virtues are choked, so that without the sweat of our brow we cannot eat our bread which "cometh down from heaven," and which "strengtheneth man's heart."[1187] The whole human race in general therefore is without exception subject to this law. For there is no one, however saintly, who does not take the bread mentioned above with the sweat of his brow and anxious efforts of his heart. But many rich men, as we see, are fed on that common bread without any sweat of their brow.

NOTES:
[1185] Rom. 7:22, 23.
[1186] Gen. 3:17, 19.
[1187] S. John 6:33; Ps. 103 (104):15.

CHAPTER XII.

Of this also: "But we know that the law is spiritual," etc.

AND this law the Apostle also calls spiritual saying: "But we know that the law is spiritual, but I am carnal, sold under sin."[1188] For this law is spiritual which bids us eat in the sweat of our brow that "true bread which cometh down from heaven"[1189] but that sale under sin makes us carnal. What, I ask, or whose is that sin? Doubtless Adam's, by whose fall and, if I may so say, ruinous transaction and fraudulent bargain we were sold. For when he was led astray by the persuasion of the serpent he brought all his descendants under the yoke of perpetual bondage, as they were alienated by taking the forbidden food. For this custom is generally observed between the buyer and seller, that one who wants to make himself over to the power of another, receives from his buyer a price for the loss of his liberty, and his consignment to perpetual slavery. And we can very plainly see that this took place between Adam and the serpent. For by eating of the forbidden tree he received from the serpent the price of his liberty, and gave up his natural freedom and chose to give himself up to perpetual slavery to him from whom he had obtained the deadly price of the forbidden fruit; and thenceforth he was bound by this condition and not without reason subjected all the offspring of his posterity to perpetual service to him whose slave he had become. For what can any marriage in slavery produce but slaves? What then? Did that cunning and crafty buyer take away the rights of ownership from the true and lawful lord? Not so. For neither did he overcome all God's property by the craft of a single act of deception so that the true lord lost his rights of ownership, who though the buyer himself was a rebel and a renegade, yet oppressed him with the yoke of slavery; but because the Creator had endowed all reasonable creatures with free will, he would not restore to their natural liberty against their will those who contrary to right had sold themselves by the sin of greedy lust. Since anything that is contrary to goodness and fairness is abhorrent to Him who is the Author of justice and piety. For it would have been wrong for Him to have recalled the blessing of freedom granted, unfair for Him to have by His power oppressed man who was free, and by taking him captive, not to have allowed him to exercise the prerogative of the freedom he had received, as He was reserving his salvation for future ages, that in due season the fulness of the appointed time might be fulfilled. For it was right that his offspring should remain under the ancient conditions for so long a time, until by the price of His own blood the grace of the Lord redeemed them from their original chains and set them free in the primeval state of liberty, though He was able even then to save them, but would not, because equity forbade Him to break the terms of His own decree. Would you know the reason for your being sold? Hear thy Redeemer Himself proclaiming openly by Isaiah the prophet: "What is this bill of the divorce of your mother with which I have put her away? Or who is My creditor to whom I sold you? Behold you are sold for your iniquities and for your wicked deeds have I put your mother away." Would you also plainly see why when you were consigned to the yoke of slavery He would not redeem you by the might of His own power? Hear what He added to the former passage, and how He charges the same servants of sin with the reason for their voluntary sale. "Is My hand shortened and become little that I cannot redeem, or is there no strength in Me to deliver?"[1190] But what it is which is always standing in the way of His most powerful pity the same prophet shows when he says: "Behold the hand of the Lord is not shortened that it cannot save, neither is His ear heavy that it cannot hear: But your iniquities have divided between you and your God and your sins have hid His face from you that He should not hear." [1191]

NOTES:
[1188] Rom. 7:14.
[1189] S. John 6:33.
[1190] Isa. 50:1, 2.
[1191] Isa. 59:1, 2.

CHAPTER XIII.

Of this also: "But I know that in me, that is in my flesh, dwelleth no good thing."

BECAUSE then the original curse of God has made us carnal and condemned us to thorns and thistles, and our father has sold us by that unhappy bargain so that we cannot do the good that we would, while we are torn away from the recollection of God Most High and forced to think on what belongs to human weakness, while burning with the love of purity, we are often even against our will troubled by natural desires, which we would rather know nothing about; we know that in

our flesh there dwelleth no good thing[1192] viz., the perpetual and lasting peace of this meditation of which we have spoken; but there is
brought about in our case that miserable and wretched divorce, that
when with the mind we want to serve the law of God, since we never
want to remove our gaze from the Divine brightness, yet surrounded as
we are by carnal darkness we are forced by a kind of law of sin to tear
ourselves away from the good which we know, as we fall away from
that lofty height of mind to earthly cares and thoughts, to which the
law of sin, i.e., the sentence of God, which the first delinquent received, has not without reason condemned us. And hence it is that the
blessed Apostle, though he openly admits that he and all saints are
bound by the constraint of this sin, yet boldly asserts that none of them
will be condemned for this, saying: "There is therefore now no condemnation to them that are in Christ Jesus: for the law of the spirit of
life in Christ Jesus hath set me free from the law of sin and death,"[1193]
i.e., the grace of Christ day by day frees all his saints from this law of
sin and death, under which they are constantly reluctantly obliged to
come, whenever they pray to the Lord for the forgiveness of their trespasses. You see then that it was in the person not of sinners but of
those who are really saints and perfect, that the blessed Apostle gave
utterance to this saying: "For I do not the good that I would, but the
evil which I hate, that I do;" and: "I see another law in my members
resisting the law of my mind and bringing me captive to the law of sin
which is in my members." [1194]

NOTES:
[1192] Cf. Rom. 7:18.
[1193] Rom. 8:1, 2.
[1194] Rom. 7:19.

CHAPTER XIV.

An objection, that the saying: "For I do not the good that I
would," etc., applies to the persons neither of unbelievers nor of
saints.

GERMANUS: We say that this does not apply to the persons either of those who are involved in capital offences, or of an Apostle and
those who have advanced to his measure, but we think that it ought
properly to be taken of those who after receiving the grace of God and

the knowledge of the truth, are anxious to keep themselves from carnal sins but, as ancient custom like a natural law rules most forcibly in their members, they are carried away to the ingrained lust of their passions. For the custom and frequency of sinning becomes like a natural law, which, implanted in the man's weak members, leads the feelings of the soul that is not yet instructed in all the pursuits of virtue, but is still, if I may say so, of an uninstructed and tender chastity, captive to sin and subjecting them by an ancient law to death, brings them under the yoke of sin that rules over them, not suffering them to obtain the good of purity which they love, but rather forcing them to do the evil which they hate.

CHAPTER XV.

The answer to the objection raised.

THEONAS: Your notion does not come to much; as you yourselves have actually now begun to maintain that this cannot possibly stand in the person of those who are out and out sinners, but that it properly applies to those who are trying to keep themselves clear from carnal sins. And since you have already separated these from the number of sinners, it follows that you must shortly admit them into the ranks of the faithful and holy. For what kinds of sin do you say that those can commit, from which, if they are involved in them after the grace of baptism, they can be freed by the daily grace of Christ? or of what body of death are we to think that the Apostle said: "Who s

hall deliver me from the body of this death? Thanks be to God through Jesus Christ our Lord"?[1195] Is it not clear, as truth compels you yourselves also to admit, that it is spoken not of those members of capital crimes, by which the wages of eternal death are gained; viz., murder, fornication, adultery, drunkenness, thefts and robberies, but of that body before mentioned, which the daily grace of Christ assists? For whoever after baptism and the knowledge of God falls into that death, must know that he will either have to be cleansed, not by the daily grace of Christ, i.e., an easy forgiveness, which our Lord when at any moment He is prayed to, is wont to grant to our errors, but by a lifelong affliction of penitence and penal sorrow, or else will be hereafter consigned to the punishment of eternal fire for them, as the same Apostle thus declares: "Be not deceived: neither fornicators, nor idolaters, nor adulterers, nor effeminate, nor defilers of themselves with mankind, nor thieves, nor covetous persons, nor drunkards, nor railers, nor extortioners shall possess the kingdom of God."[1196] Or what is that law warring in our members which resists the law of our mind, and when it has led us resisting but captives to the law of sin and death, and has made us serve it with the flesh, nevertheless suffers us to serve the law of God with the mind? For I do not suppose that this law of sin denotes crimes or can be taken of the offences mentioned above, of which if a man is guilty he does not serve the law of God with the mind, from which law he must first have departed in heart before he is guilty of any of them with the flesh. For what is it to serve the law of sin, but to do what is commanded by sin? What sort of sin then is it to which so great holiness and perfection feels that it is captive, and yet doubts not that it will be freed from it by the grace of Christ, saying: "O wretched man that I am! Who shall deliver me from the body of this death? Thanks be to God through Jesus Christ our Lord"? What law, I ask, will you maintain to be implanted in our members, which, withdrawing us from the law of God and bringing us into captivity to the law of sin, could make us wretched rather than guilty so that we should not be consigned to eternal punishment, but still as it were sigh for the unbroken joys of bliss, and, seeking for a helper who shall restore us to it, exclaim with the Apostle: "O wretched man that I am! Who shall deliver me from the body of this death?" For what is it to be led captive to the law of sin but to continue to perform and commit sin? Or what other chief good can be given which the saints cannot fulfil, except that in comparison with which, as we said above, everything else is not good? Indeed we know that many things in this world are good, and chiefly, modesty, continence, sobriety, humility, justice, mercy, temperance, piety: but all of these things fail to come up to that chief good, and can be done I say not by apostles, but even by ordinary folk; and, those by whom they are not done, are either chastised with eternal punishment, or are set free by great exertions, as was said above, of penitence, and not by the daily grace of Christ. It remains then for us to admit that this saying of the Apostle is rightly applied only to the persons of saints, who day after day falling under this law, which we described, of sin not of crimes, are secure of their salvation and not precipitated into wicked deeds, but, as has often been said, are drawn away from the contemplation of God to the misery of bodily thoughts, and are often deprived of the blessing of that true bliss. For if they felt that by this law of their members they were bound daily to crimes, they would complain of the loss not of happiness but of innocence, and the Apostle Paul would not say: "O wretched man that I am," but "Impure," or "Wicked man that I am," and he would wish to be rid not of the body of this death, i.e., this mortal state, but of the crimes and misdeeds of this flesh. But because by reason of his state of human frailty he felt that he was captive, i.e., led away to carnal cares and anxieties which the law of sin and death causes, he groans over this law of sin under which against his will he had fallen, and at once has recourse to Christ and is saved by the present redemption of His grace. Whatever of anxiety therefore that law of sin, which naturally produces the thorns and thistles of mortal thoughts and cares, has caused to spring up in the ground of the Apostle's breast, that the law of grace at once plucks up. "For the law," says he, "of the spirit of life in Christ Jesus hath set me free from the law of sin and death." [1197]

NOTES:
[1195] Rom. 7:24, 25.
[1196] 1 Cor. 6:9, 10.
[1197] Rom. 8:2.

CHAPTER XVI.

What is the body of sin.

THIS then is that body of death from which we cannot escape, pent in which those who are perfect, who have tasted "how gracious the Lord is,"[1198] daily feel with the prophet "how bad for himself and bitter it is for a man to depart from the Lord his God."[1199] This is the body of death which restrains us from the heavenly vision and drags us back to earthly things, which causes men while singing Psalms and kneeling in prayer to have their thoughts filled with human figures, or conversations, or business, or unnecessary actions. This is the body of death, owing to which those, who would emulate the sanctity of angels, and who long to cling continually to God, yet are unable to arrive at the perfection of this good, because the body of death stands in their way, but they do the evil that they would not, i.e., they are dragged down in their minds even to the things which have nothing to do with their advance and perfection in virtue. Finally that the blessed Apostle might clearly denote that he said this of saintly and perfect men, and those like himself, he in a way points with his finger to himself and at once proceeds: "And so I myself," i.e, I who say this, lay bare the secrets of my own not another's conscience. This mode of speech at any rate the Apostle is familiarly accustomed to use, whenever he wants to point specially to himself, as here: "I, Paul, myself beseech you by the mildness and modesty of Christ;" and again: "except that I myself was not burdensome to you;" and once more: "But be it so: I myself did not burden you;" and elsewhere: "I, Paul, myself say unto you: if ye be circumcised Christ shall profit you nothing;" and to the Romans: "For I could wish that I myself were Anathema from Christ for my brethren."[1200] But it cannot unreasonably be taken in this way, that "And so I myself" is expressly said with emphasis, i.e., I whom you know to be an Apostle of Christ, whom you venerate with the utmost respect, whom you believe to be of the highest character and perfect, and one in whom Christ speaks, though with the mind I serve the law of God, yet with the flesh I confess that I serve the law of sin, i.e., by the occupations of my human condition am sometimes dragged down from heavenly to earthly things and the height of my mind is brought down to the level of care for humble matters. And by this law of sin I find that at every moment I am so taken captive that although I persist in my immovable longing around the law of God, yet in no way can I escape the power of this captivity, unless I always fly to the grace of the Saviour.

NOTES:
[1198] Ps. 33 (34):9.
[1199] Jer. 2:19.
[1200] 2 Cor. 10:11; 12:13, 16; Gal. 5:2; Rom. 9:3.

CHAPTER XVII.

How all the saints have confessed with truth that they were unclean and sinful.

AND therefore with daily sighs all the saints grieve over this weakness of their nature and while they search into their shifting thoughts and the secrets and inmost recesses of their conscience, cry out in entreaty: "Enter not into judgment with Thy servant, for in Thy sight shall no man living be justified;" and this: "Who will boast that he hath a chaste heart? or who will have confidence that he is pure from sin?" and again: "There is not a righteous man upon earth that doeth good and sinneth not;" and this also: "Who knoweth his faults?"[1201] And so they have recognized that man's righteousness is weak and imperfect and always needs God's mercy, so that one of those whose iniquities and sins God purged away with the live coal of His word sent from the altar, after that marvellous vision of God, after his view of the Seraphim on high and the revelation of heavenly mysteries, said: "Woe is me! for I am a man of unclean lips, and I dwell in the midst of a people of unclean lips."[1202] And I fancy that perhaps even then he would not have felt the uncleanness of his lips, unless it had been given him to recognize the true and complete purity of perfection by the vision of God, at the sight of Whom he suddenly became aware of his own uncleanness, of which he had previously been ignorant. For when he says: "Woe is me! for I am a man of unclean lips," he shows that his confession that follows refers to his own lips, and not to the uncleanness of the people: "and I dwell in the midst of a people of unclean lips." But even when in his prayer he confesses the uncleanness of all sinners, he embraces in his general supplication not only the mass of the wicked but also of the good, saying: "Behold Thou art angry, and we have sinned: in them we have been always, and we shall be saved. We are all become as one unclean, and all our righteousnesses as filthy rags."[1203] What, I ask, could be clearer than this saying, in which the prophet includes not one only but all our righteousnesses and, looking round on all things that are considered unclean and disgusting, because he could find nothing in the life of men fouler or more unclean, chose to compare them to filthy rags. In vain then is the sharpness of a nagging objection raised against this perfectly clear truth, as a little while back you said: "If no one is without sin, then no one is holy; and if no one is holy, then no one will be saved."[1204] For the puzzle of this question can be solved by the prophet's testimony. "Behold," he says, "Thou art angry and we have sinned," i.e., when Thou didst reject our pride of heart or our carelessness, and deprive us of Thine aid, at once the abyss of our sins swallowed us up, as if one should say to the bright substance of the sun: Behold thou hast set, and at once murky darkness covered us. And yet though he here says that the saints have sinned, and have not only sinned but also have always remained in their sins, he does not altogether despair of salvation but adds: "In them we have been always, and we shall be saved." This saying: "Behold Thou art angry and we have sinned," I will compare to that one of the Apostle's: "O wretched man that I am! Who shall deliver me from the body of this death?" Again this that the prophet subjoins: "In them we have been always, and we shall be saved," corresponds to the following words of the Apostle: "Thanks be to God through Jesus Christ our Lord." In the same way also this passage of the same prophet: "Woe is me! for I am a man of unclean lips and I dwell in the midst of a people of unclean lips," seems to agree with the words quoted above: "O wretched man that I am! Who shall deliver me from the body of this death?" And what follows in the prophet: "And behold there flew to me one of the Seraphim, having in his hand a coal (or stone) which he had taken with the tongs from off the altar. And he touched my mouth and said: Lo, with this I have touched thy lips, and thine iniquity is taken away and thy sin is purged,"[1205] is just what seems to have fallen from the mouth of Paul, who says: "Thanks be to God through Jesus Christ our Lord." You see then how all the saints with truth confess not so much in the person of the people as in their own that they are sinners, and yet by no means despair of their salvation, but look for full justification (which they do not hope that they cannot obtain by virtue of the state of human frailty) from the grace and mercy of the Lord.

NOTES:
[1201] Ps. 142 (143):2; Prov. 20:9; Eccl. 7:21; Ps. 18 (19):13.
[1202] Isa. 6:5.
[1203] Isa. 64:5, 6.
[1204] Cf. XXII. viii.
[1205] Isa. 6:6, 7.

CHAPTER XVIII.

That even good and holy men are not without sin.

BUT that no one however holy is in this life free from trespasses and sin, we are told also by the teaching of the Saviour, who gave His disciples the form of the perfect prayer and among those other sublime and sacred commands, which as they were only given to the saints and perfect cannot apply to the wicked and unbelievers, He bade this to be inserted: "And forgive us our debts as we also forgive our debtors."[1206] If then this is offered as a true prayer and by saints, as we ought without the shadow of a doubt to believe, who can be found so obstinate and impudent, so puffed up with the pride of the devil's own rage, as to maintain that he is without sin, and not only to think himself greater than apostles, but also to charge the Saviour Himself with ignorance or folly, as if He either did not know that some men could be free from debts, or was idly teaching those whom He knew to stand in no need of the remedy of that prayer? But since all the saints who altogether keep the commands of their King, say every day "Forgive us our debts," if they speak the truth there is indeed no one free from sin, but if they speak falsely, it is equally true that they are not free from the sin of falsehood. Wherefore also that most wise Ecclesiastes reviewing in his mind all the actions and purposes of men declares without any exception: "that there is not a righteous man upon earth, that doeth good and sinneth not,"[1207] i.e., no one ever could or ever will be found on this earth so holy, so diligent, so earnest as to be able continually to cling to that true and unique good, and not day after day to feel that he is drawn aside from it and fails. But still though he maintains that he cannot be free from wrong doing, yet none the less we must not deny that he is righteous.

NOTES:
[1206] S. Matt. 6:12.
[1207] Eccl. 7:21.

CHAPTER XIX.

How even in the hour of prayer it is almost impossible to avoid sin.

WHOEVER then ascribes sinlessness to human nature must fight against no idle words but the witness and proof of his conscience which is on our side, and then only should maintain that he is without sin, when he finds that he is not torn away from this highest good: nay rather, whoever considering his own conscience, to say no more, finds that he has celebrated even one single service without the distraction of a single word or deed or thought, may say that he is without sin. Further because we admit that the discursive lightness of the human mind cannot get rid of these idle and empty things, we thus consequently confess with truth that we are not without sin. For with whatever care a man tries to keep his heart, he can never, owing to the resistance of the nature of the flesh, keep it according to the desire of his spirit. For however far the human mind may have advanced and progressed towards a finer purity of contemplation, so much the more will it see itself to be unclean, as it were in the mirror of its purity, because while the soul raises itself for a loftier vision and as it looks forth yearns for greater things than it performs, it is sure always to despise as inferior and worthless the things in which it is mixed up. Since a keener sight notices more; and a blameless life produces greater sorrow when found fault with; and amendment of life, and earnest striving after goodness multiplies groans and sighs. For no one can rest content with that stage to which he has advanced, and however much a man may be purified in mind, so much the more does he see himself to be foul, and find grounds for humiliation rather than for pride, and, however swiftly he may climb to greater heights, so much more does he see above him whither he is tending. Finally that chosen Apostle "whom Jesus loved,"[1208] who lay on His bosom, uttered this saying as if from the heart of the Lord: "If we say that we have no sin we deceive ourselves and the truth is not in us."[1209] And so if when we say that we have no sin, we have not the truth, that is Christ, in us, what good do we do except to prove ourselves by this very, profession, criminals and wicked among sinners?

NOTES:
[1208] S. John 13:23.
[1209] 1 John 1:8.

CHAPTER XX.

From whom we can learn the destruction of sin and perfection of goodness.

LASTLY if you would like to investigate more thoroughly whether it is possible for human nature to attain sinlessness, from whom can we more clearly learn this than from those who "have crucified the flesh with its faults and lusts," and to whom "the world is really crucified"?[1210] Who though they have not only utterly eradicated all faults from their hearts, but also are trying to shut out even the thought and recollection of sin, yet still day after day faithfully maintain that they cannot even for a single hour be free from spot of sin.

NOTES:
[1210] Gal. 5:24; 6:14.

CHAPTER XXI.

That although we acknowledge that we cannot be without sin, yet still we ought not to suspend ourselves from the Lord's Communion.

YET we ought not to suspend ourselves from the Lord's Communion because we confess ourselves sinners, but should more and more eagerly hasten to it for the healing of our soul, and purifying of our spirit, and seek the rather a remedy for our wounds with humility of mind and faith, as considering ourselves unworthy to receive so great grace. Otherwise we cannot worthily receive the Communion even once a year, as some do, who live in monasteries and so regard the dignity and holiness and value of the heavenly sacraments, as to think that none but saints and spotless persons should venture to receive them, and not rather that they would make us saints and pure by taking them. And these thereby fall into greater presumption and arrogance than what they seem to themselves to avoid, because at the time when they do receive them, they consider that they are worthy to receive them. But it is much better to receive them every Sunday for the healing of our infirmities, with that humility of heart, whereby we believe and confess that we can never touch those holy mysteries worthily, than to be puffed up by a foolish persuasion of heart, and believe that at the year's end we are worthy to receive them. Wherefore that we may be able to grasp this and hold it fruitfully, let us the more earnestly implore the Lord's mercy to help us to perform this, which is learnt not like other human arts, by some previous verbal explanation, but rather by experience and action leading the way; and which also unless it is often considered and hammered out in the Conferences of spiritual persons, and anxiously sifted by daily experience and trial of it, will either become obsolete through carelessness or perish by idle forgetfulness.

CONFERENCE 24.

Conference of Abbot Abraham
on Mortification

CHAPTER I.

How we laid bare the secrets of our thoughts to Abbot Abraham.

THIS twenty-fourth Conference of Abbot Abraham[1211] is by the favour of Christ produced, which concludes the traditions and decisions of all the Elders; and when by the aid of your prayers it has been finished, as the number mystically corresponds to that of the four and twenty Elders who are said in the holy Apocalypse[1212] to offer their crowns to the Lamb, we think that we shall have paid the debt of all our promises. And henceforth if these four and twenty Elders of ours have been crowned with any glory for the sake of their teaching, they shall with bowed heads offer it to the Lamb who was slain for the salvation of the world: for He it was Who vouschafed for the honour of His name to grant to them such exalted feelings and to us whatever words were needful to set forth such profound thoughts. And the merits of His gift must be referred to the Author of all good, to whom the more is owed, as the more is paid. Therefore with anxious confession we laid before this Abraham the impulse of our thoughts, whereby we were urged by daily perplexities of our mind to return to our country and revisit our kinsfolk. For from this the greatest reason for our desire sprang, because we remembered that our kinsfolk were endowed with such piety and goodness that we felt sure that they would never interfere with our purpose, and we constantly reflected, that we should gain more good out of their earnestness, and should be hampered by no cares about bodily matters, and no trouble in providing food, as they would gladly minister abundantly to the supply of all our wants, and besides this we were feeding our souls on the hope of empty joys, as we thought that we should gain the greatest good from the conversion[1213] of many, who were to be turned to the way of salvation by our example and instructions. Then besides this the very spot, where was the ancestral possession of our forefathers, and the delightful pleasantness of the neighbourhood was painted before our eyes, how pleasantly and suitably it stretched away to the desert, so that the recesses of the woods would not only delight the heart of a monk, but would also furnish him with a plentiful supply of food.[1214] And when we explained all this to the aforesaid old man, in a straightforward way, according to the faith of our conscience, and showed by our copious tears that we could no longer resist the violence of the impulse, unless the grace of God came to our rescue by the healing which he, could give, he waited for a long time in silence and at last sighed deeply and said:

NOTES:
[1211] Cf. the note on XV. iv.
[1212] Rev. 4:4.
[1213] Petschenig's text reads conversione, others conversatione.
[1214] On the bearing of this passage on the question of Cassian's nationality, see the Introd.

CHAPTER II.

How the old man exposed our errors.

THE feebleness of your ideas shows that you have not yet renounced worldly desires nor mortified your former lusts. For as the wandering character of your desires testifies to the sloth of your heart, this pilgrimage and absence from your kinsfolk, which you ought rather to endure with your heart, you do endure only with the flesh. For all these things would have been buried and altogether driven out of your hearts, if you had got hold of the right method of renunciation, and the main reason for the solitude in which we dwell. And so I see that you are labouring under that infirmity of sluggishness, which is thus described in Proverbs: "Every sluggard is always desiring something;" and again: "Desires kill the slothful."[1215] For in our case too these supplies of worldly conveniences, which you have described, would not be wanting, if we believed that they were appropriate to our calling, or thought that we could get out of those delights and pleas-

523

ures as much profit as that which is gained from this squalor of the country and bodily affliction. Nor are we so deprived of the solace of our kinsfolk, that those who delight to support us with their substance should fail us, were it not that this saying of the Saviour meets us and excludes everything that contributes to the support of this flesh, as He says: "He who doth not leave (or hate) father and mother and children and brethren cannot be My disciple."[1216] But if we were altogether deprived of the protection of our parents, the services of the princes of this world would not be wanting, as they would most thankfully rejoice to minister to our necessities with prompt liberality. And supported by their bounty, we should be free from the care of preparing food, were it not that this curse of the prophet terribly frightened us. For "Cursed," he says, "is the man that putteth his hope in man;" and: "Put not your trust in princes."[1217] We should also at any rate place our cells on the banks of the river Nile and have water at our very doors, so as not to be obliged to carry it on our necks for four miles, were it not that the blessed Apostle rendered us indefatigable in enduring this labour, and cheered us by his words, saying: "Every one shall receive his own reward according to his labour."[1218] Nor are we ignorant that there are even in our country some pleasant recesses, where plenty of fruits, and pleasant gardens, and fertile ground would furnish the food we need with the slightest bodily efforts on our part, were it not that we were afraid lest that reproach might apply to us, which is directed against the rich man in the gospel: "Because thou hast received thy consolation in this life."[1219] But as we despise all these things and scorn them together with all the pleasures of this world, we delight only in this squalor, and prefer to all luxuries this dreadful and vast desert, and cannot compare any riches of a fertile soil to these barren sands, as we pursue no temporal gains of this body, but the eternal rewards of the spirit. For it is but little for a monk to have once made his renunciation, i.e., in the early days of his conversion to have disregarded the present world, unless he continues to renounce it daily. For to the very end of this life we must with the prophet say this: "And I have not desired the day of man, Thou knowest."[1220] Wherefore also the Lord says in the gospel: "If any man will come after Me, let him deny himself and take up his cross daily and follow Me." [1221]

NOTES:
[1215] Prov. 13:4; 21:25.
[1216] S. Luke 14:26.

[1217] Jer. 17:5; Ps. 145 (146):2.
[1218] 1 Cor. 3:8.
[1219] S. Luke 16:25.
[1220] Jer. 17:16.
[1221] S. Luke 9:23.

CHAPTER III.

Of the character of the districts which anchorites ought to seek.

AND therefore by him who is exercising anxious care over the purity of his inner man, those districts should be sought, which do not by their fruitfulness and fertility invite his mind to the trouble of cultivating them, nor drive him forth from his fixed and immovable position in his cell, and force him to go forth to some work in the open air, and so, his thoughts being as it were poured forth openly, scatter to the winds all his concentration of mind and all the keenness of his vision of his aim. And this cannot be guarded against or seen by anyone at all however careful and watchful, except one who continually keeps his body and soul shut up and enclosed in walls, that, like a splendid fisherman, looking out for food for himself by the apostolic art, he may eagerly and without moving catch the swarms of thoughts swimming in the calm depths of his heart, and surveying with curious eye the depths as from a high rock, may sagaciously and cunningly decide what he ought to lure to himself by his saving hook, and what he can neglect and reject as bad and nasty fishes.

CHAPTER IV.

What sorts of work should be chosen by solitaries.

EVERYONE therefore who constantly perseveres in this watchfulness will effectually fulfil what is very plainly expressed by the prophet Habakkuk: "I will stand upon my watch, and ascend upon the rock, and will look out to see what He shall say to me, and what I may answer to Him that reproveth me."[1222] And how difficult and tiresome this is, is very clearly shown by the experience of those who live in the desert of Calamus or Porphyrion.[1223] For though they are separated from all the cities and dwellings of men by a longer stretch of desert than the wilderness of Scete (since by penetrating seven or eight days' journey into the recesses of the vast wilderness, they scarcely arrive at their hiding places and cells) yet because there they are devoted to agriculture and not in the least confined to the cloister, whenever they come to these squalid districts in which we are living, or to Scete, they are annoyed by such harassing thoughts and such anxiety of mind that, as if they were beginners and men who had never given the slightest attention to the exercises of solitude, they cannot endure the life of the cells and the peace and quietness of them, and are at once driven forth and obliged to leave them, as if they were inexperienced and novices. For they have not learnt to still the motions of the inner man, and to quell the tempests of their thoughts by anxious care and persevering efforts, as, toiling day after day in work in the open air, they are moving about all day long in empty space, not only in the flesh but also in heart; and pour forth their thoughts openly as the body moves hither and thither. And therefore they do not notice the folly of their mind in longing for many things, nor can they put a check upon its vague discursiveness; and as they cannot bear sorrow of spirit they think that the fact of a continuance of silence is unendurable, and those who are never tired by hard work in the country, are beaten by silence and worn out by the length of their rest.

NOTES:
[1222] Hab. 2:1 (LXX).
[1223] Cf. Institutes X. xxiv.

CHAPTER V.

That anxiety of heart is made worse rather than better by restlessness of body.

NOR is it wonderful if one who lives in a cell, having his thoughts collected together as it were in a narrow cloister, is oppressed by a multitude of anxieties, which break out with the man himself from the confinement of the dwelling, and at once dash here and there like wild horses. But while they are now roaming at large from their stalls, for the moment some short and sad solace is enjoyed: but when, after the body has returned to its own cell, the whole troop of thoughts retires again to its proper home, the habit of chronic licence gives rise to worse pangs. Those then who are unable and ignorant how to struggle against the promptings of their own fancies, when they are harassed in their cell, by accidie attacking their bosom more violently than usual, if they relax their strict rule and allow themselves the liberty of going out oftener, will arouse a worse plague against themselves by means of this which they fancy is a remedy: just as men fancy that they can check the violence of an inward fever by a draught of the coldest water, though it is a fact that by it its fire is inflamed rather than quenched, as a far worse attack follows after the momentary alleviation.

CHAPTER VI.

A comparison showing how a monk ought to keep guard over his thoughts.

WHEREFORE a monk's whole attention should thus be fixed on one point, and the rise and circle of all his thoughts be vigorously restricted to it; viz., to the recollection of God, as when a man, who is anxious to raise on high a vault of a round arch, must constantly draw a line round from its exact centre, and in accordance with the sure standard it gives discover by the laws of building all the evenness and roundness required. But if anyone tries to finish it without ascertaining its centre--though with the utmost confidence in his art and ability, it is impossible for him to keep the circumference even, without any error, or to find out simply by looking at it how much he has taken off by his mistake from the beauty of real roundness, unless he always has recourse to that test of truth and by its decision corrects the inner and outer edge of his work, and so finishes the large and lofty pile to the exact point.[1224] So also our mind, unless by working round the love of the Lord alone as an immovably fixed centre, through all the circumstances of our works and contrivances, it either fits or rejects the character of all our thoughts by the excellent compasses, if I may so say, of love, will never by excellent skill build up the structure of that spiritual edifice of which Paul is the architect, nor possess that beautiful house, which the blessed David desired in his heart to show to the Lord and said: "I have loved the beauty of Thine house and the place of the dwelling of Thy glory;"[1225] but will without foresight raise in his heart a house that is not beautiful, and that is unworthy of the Holy Ghost, one that will presently fall, and so will receive no glory from the reception of the blessed Inhabitant, but will be miserably destroyed by the fall of his building.

NOTES:
[1224] Unius puncti lege.
[1225] Ps. 35 (36):8.

CHAPTER VII.

A question why the neighbourhood of our kinsfolk is considered to interfere with us, whereas it does not interfere in the case of those living in Egypt.

GERMANUS: It is a very useful and needful rule that is given for the kind of works that can be done within the cells. For we have often proved the value of this not only by the example of your holiness, based on the imitation of the virtues of the apostles, but also by our own experience. But it is not sufficiently clear why we ought so thoroughly to avoid the neighbourhood of our kinsfolk, which you did not reject altogether. For if we see you, blamelessly walking in all the way of perfection, and not only dwelling in your own country but some of you having not even retired far from their own village, why should that which does not hurt you be considered bad for us?

CHAPTER VIII.

The answer that all things are not suitable for all men.

ABRAHAM: Sometimes we see bad precedents taken from good things. For if a man ventures to do the same thing as another, but not with the same mind and purpose, or not with equal goodness, he will immediately fall into the snares of deception and death through the very things from which others gain the fruit of eternal life: As that strong armed lad matched with the warlike giant in the combat would certainly have found, if he had been clad in the heavy armour of Saul fit only for men; and that by which one of stronger age would have laid low countless hosts of foes, would only have brought certain danger to the stripling, had he not with prudent discretion chosen the sort of weapons suitable to his youth, and armed himself against his foul foe not with breastplate and shield, with which he saw that others were equipped, but with those weapons with which he was able to fight. Wherefore it is right for each one of us first to consider carefully the measure of his powers and in accordance with its limits, to choose what system he pleases, because though all are good, yet all things cannot be fit for all men. For we do not assert that because the anchorite's life is good, it is therefore suited for everybody: for by many it is felt to be not only useless, but even injurious. Nor because we are right in taking up the system of the coenobium and the pious and praiseworthy care of the brethren, do we therefore consider that it ought to be followed by everybody. So also the fruits of the care of strangers are very plentiful, but this cannot be taken up by everybody without loss of patience. Further, the systems of your county and of this must first be weighed against each other; and then the powers of men gathered from the constant occurrence of their virtues or vices must be severally weighed in the opposite scales. For it may happen that what is difficult or impossible for a man of one nation in the case of others is somehow turned by ingrained habit into nature: just as some nations, separated by a wide difference of region, can bear tremendous force of cold or heat of the sun without any covering of the body, which certainly others who have no experience of that inclement sky, could not possibly endure, however strong they may be. So also do you who with the utmost efforts of mind and body are trying in this district to get the better of the nature of your country in many respects, diligently consider whether in those regions which, as report says, are frozen, and bound by the cold of excessive unbelief, you could endure this nakedness, if I may so term it. For to us the fact that our holy life is of long standing has almost naturally imparted this fortitude in our purpose, and if we see that you are our equals in virtue and constancy, you in like manner need not shun the neighbourhood of your kinsfolk and brethren.

CHAPTER IX.

That those need not fear the neighbourhood of their kinsfolk, who can emulate the mortification of Abbot Apollos.

BUT that you may be able fairly to measure the amount of your strength by a certain test of strictness I will point out to you what was done by a certain old man; viz., Abbot Apollos[1226] that if your secret scrutiny of your heart decides that you are not behind this man in purpose and goodness, you may venture on remaining in your country and living near your kinsfolk without detriment to your purpose or injury to your mode of life, and be sure that neither the feeling of nearness nor your love for the district can interfere with the strictness of this humble lot,[1227] which not only your own will but the needs also of your pilgrimage enforce upon you in this country. When then his own brother had come to this old man, whom we have mentioned, in the dead of night, begging him to come out for a little while from his monastery, to help him to rescue an ox, which as he sadly complained had stuck in the mire of a swamp a little way off, because he could not possibly rescue it alone, Abbot Apollos stolidly replied to his entreaties: "Why did you not ask our younger brother who was nearer to you as you passed by than I?" and when the other, thinking that he had forgotten the death of his brother who had been long ago buried, and that he was almost weak in his mind from excessive abstinence and continual solitude, replied: "How could I summon one who died fifteen years ago?" Abbot Apollos said: "Don't you know that I too have been dead to this world for twenty years, and that I can't from my tomb in this cell give you any assistance in what belongs to the affairs of this present life? And Christ is so far from allowing me ever so little to relax my purpose of mortification on which I have entered, for extricating your ox, that He did not even permit the very shortest intermission of it for my father's funeral, which would have been undertaken much more readily properly and piously." And so do ye now search out the secrets of your breast and carefully consider whether you also can continually preserve such strictness of mind with regard to your kinsfolk, and when you find that you are like him in this mortification of soul, then at last you may know that in the same way the neighbourhood of your kinsfolk and brothers will not hurt you, when, I mean, you hold that though they are very close to you, you are dead to them, in such a way that you suffer neither them to be benefited by your assistance, nor yourselves to be relaxed by duties towards them.

NOTES:
[1226] Cf. the note on II. xiii.
[1227] Cf. the note on XIX. iii.

CHAPTER X.

A question whether it is bad for a monk to have his wants supplied by his kinsfolk.

GERMANUS: On this subject you have certainly left no room for any further uncertainty. For we are sure that we cannot possibly keep up our present wretched garb, or our daily going barefoot in their neighbourhood, and that there we should not even procure with the same labour what is necessary for our sustenance, as here we are actually obliged to fetch our water on our necks for three miles. For shame on our part as well as on theirs would not in the least allow us to do this before them. However how will it hurt our plan of life if we are altogether set free from anxiety on the score of preparing our food, by being supplied by them with all things, and so give ourselves up simply to reading and prayer, that by the removal of that labour with which we are now distracted we may devote ourselves more earnestly to spiritual interests alone?

CHAPTER XI.

The answer stating what Saint Antony laid down on this matter.

ABRAHAM: I will not give you my own opinion against this, but that of the blessed Antony, whereby he confounded the laziness of a certain brother (overcome by this lukewarmness which you describe) in such a way as also to cut the knot of your subject. For when one came as I said to the aforesaid old man, and said that the Anchorite system was not at all to be admired, declaring that it required greater virtue for a man to practise what belongs to perfection living among men rather than in the desert, the blessed Antony asked where he lived himself, and when he said that he lived close to his relations, and boasted that by their provision he was set free from all care and anxiety of daily work, and gave himself up ceaselessly and solely to reading and prayer without any distraction of spirit, once more the blessed Antony said: "Tell me, my good friend, whether you grieve with their griefs and misfortunes, and in the same way rejoice in their good fortune?" He confessed that he shared in them both. To whom

531

the old man: "You should know," said he, "that in the world to come also you will be judged in the lot of those with whom in this life you have been affected by sharing in their gain or loss, or joy or sorrow." And not satisfied with this statement the blessed Antony entered on a still wider field of discussion, saying: "This mode of life and this most lukewarm condition not only strike you with that damage of which I spoke (though you do not feel it now, when somehow you say in accordance with that saying in Proverbs: 'They strike me but I am not grieved: and they mocked me but I knew it not;' or this that is said in the Prophet: 'And strangers have devoured his strength, but he himself knew it not'[1228]), because day after day they ceaselessly drag down your mind to earthly things, and change it in accordance with the variations of chance; but also because they defraud you of the fruits of your hands and the due reward of your own exertions, as they do not suffer you to be supported by what these supply, or to procure your daily food for yourself with your own hands, according to the rule of the blessed Apostle, as he when giving his last charge to the heads of the Church of Ephesus, asserts that though he was occupied with the sacred duties of preaching the gospel yet he provided not only for himself, but also for those who were prevented by necessary duties with regard to his ministry, saying: 'Ye yourselves know that these hands have ministered to my necessities and to the necessities of those who were with me.' But to show that he did this as a pattern to be useful to us he says elsewhere: 'We were not idle among you; neither did we eat any man's bread for nothing, but in labour and in toil we worked night and day lest we should be chargeable to any of you. Not as if we had not power; but that we might give ourselves a pattern unto you, to imitate us.'" [1229]

NOTES:
[1228] Prov. 23:35 (LXX); Hos. 7:9.
[1229] Acts 20:34; 2 Thess. 3:7, 9.

CHAPTER XII.

Of the value of work and the harm of idleness.

AND so though we also might have the protection of our kinsfolk, yet we have preferred his abstinence to all riches, and have chosen to procure our daily bodily sustenance by our own exertions rather than rely on the sure provision made by our relations, having less inclination for idle meditation on holy Scripture of which you have spoken, and that fruitless attendance to reading than to this laborious poverty. And certainly we should most gladly pursue the former, if the authority of the apostles had taught us by their examples that it was better for us, or the rules of the Elders had laid it down for our good. But you must know that you are affected by this no less than by that harm of which I spoke above, because though your body may be sound and lusty, yet you are supported by another's contributions, a thing which properly belongs only to the feeble. For certainly the whole human race, except only that class of monks, who live in accordance with the Apostle's command by the daily labours of their own hands, looks for the charity of another's compassion. Wherefore it is clear that not only those who boast that they themselves are supported either by the wealth of their relations or the labours of their servants or the produce of their farms, but also the kings of this world are supported by charity. This at any rate is embraced in the definition of our predecessors, who have laid down that anything that is taken for the requirements of daily food which has not been procured and prepared by the labour of our own hands, ought to be referred to charity, as the Apostle teaches, who altogether forbids the help of another's bounty to the idle and says: "If a man does not work, neither let him eat."[1230] These words the blessed Antony used against some one, and instructed us also by the example of his teaching, to shun the pernicious allurements of our relations and of all who provide the needful charity for our food as well as the delights of a pleasant home, and to prefer to all the wealth of this world sandy wastes horrid with the barrenness of nature, and districts overwhelmed by living incrustations, and for that reason subject to no control or dominion of man, so that we should not only avoid the society of men for the sake of a pathless waste, but also that the character of a fruitful soil may never entice us to the distractions of cultivating it, whereby the mind would be recalled from the chief service of the heart, and rendered useless for spiritual aims.

NOTES:
[1230] 2 Thess. 3:10.

CHAPTER XIII.

A story of a barber's payments, introduced for the sake of recognizing the devil's illusions.

FOR as you hope that you can save others also, and are eager to return to your country with the hope of greater gain, hear also on this subject a story of Abbot Macarius, very neatly and prettily invented, which he also gave to a man in a tumult of similar desires, to cure him by a most appropriate story. "There was," said he, "in a certain city a very clever barber, who used to shave everybody for three pence and by getting this poor and wretched sum for his work, out of this same amount used to procure what was required for his daily food, and after having taken all care of his body, used every day to put a hundred pence into his pocket. But while he was diligently amassing this gain, he heard that in a city a long way off each man paid the barber a shilling as his pay. And when he found this out, `how long,' said he, `shall I be satisfied with this beggary, so as to get with my labour a pay of three pence, when by going thither I might amass riches by a large gain of shillings?' And so at once taking with him the implements of his art, and using up in the expense all that he had got together and saved during a long time, he made his way with great difficulty to that most lucrative city. And there on the day of his arrival, he received from everyone the pay for his labour in accordance with what he had heard, and at eventide seeing that he had gained a large number of shillings he went in delight to the butcher's to buy the food he wanted for his supper. And when he began to purchase it for a large sum of shillings he spent on a tiny bit of meat all the shillings that he had gained, and did not take home a surplus of even a single penny. And when he saw that his gains were thus used up every day so that he not only failed to put by anything but could scarcely get what he required for his daily food, he thought over the matter with himself and said: `I will go back to my city, and once more, seek those very moderate profits, from which, when all my bodily wants were satisfied, a daily surplus gave a growing sum to support my old age; which, though it seemed small and trifling, yet by being constantly increased was amounting to no slight sum. In fact that gain of coppers was more profitable to me than is this nominal one of shillings from which not only is there nothing over to be laid by, but the necessities of my daily food are scarcely met.'" And therefore it is better for us with unbroken continuance to aim at this very slender profit in the desert, from which no secular cares, no worldly distractions, no pride of vainglory and vanity can detract, and which the pressure of no daily wants can lessen (for "a small thing that the righteous hath is better than great riches of the ungodly"[1231]) rather than to pursue those larger profits which even if they are procured by the most valuable conversion of many, are yet absorbed by the claims of secular life and the daily leakage of distractions. For, as Solomon says, "Better is a single handful with rest than both hands full with labour and vexation of mind."[1232] And in these allusions and inconveniences all that are at all weak are sure to be entangled, as while they are even doubtful of their own salvation, and themselves stand in need of the teaching and instruction of others, they are incited by the devil's tricks to convert and guide others, and as, even if they succeed in gaining any advantage from the conversion of some, they waste by their impatience and rude manners whatever they have gained. For that will happen to them which is described by the prophet Haggai: "And he that gathereth riches, putteth them into a bag with holes."[1233] For indeed a man puts his gains into a bag with holes, if he loses by want of self control and daily distractions of mind whatever he appears to gain by the conversion of others. And so it results that while they fancy that they can make larger profits by the instruction of others, they are actually deprived of their own improvement. For "There are who make themselves out rich though possessing nothing, and there are who humble themselves amid great riches;" and: "Better is a man who serves himself in a humble station than one who gains honour for himself and wanteth bread." [1234]

NOTES:
[1231] Ps. 36 (37):16.
[1232] Eccl. 4:6.
[1233] Hag. 1:6.
[1234] Prov. 13:7; 12:9.

CHAPTER XIV.

A question how such wrong notions can creep into us.

GERMANUS: Very aptly has your discussion shown the error of these illusions by this illustration: but we should like in the same way to be taught its origin and how to cure it, and we are equally anxious to learn how this deception has taken hold of us. For everybody must see that no one at all can apply remedies to ill health except one who has already diagnosed the actual origin of the disease.

CHAPTER XV.

The answer on the threefold movement of the soul.

ABRAHAM: Of all faults there is one source and origin, but different names are assigned to the passions and corruptions in accordance with the character of that part, or member, if I may so call it, which has been injuriously affected in the soul: As is sometimes also shown by the case of bodily diseases, in which though the cause is one and the same, yet there is a division into different kinds of maladies in accordance with the nature of the member affected. For when the violence of a noxious moisture has seized on the body's citadel, i.e., the head, it brings about a feeling of headache, but when it affects the ears or eyes, it passes into the malady of earache or ophthalmia: when it spreads to the joints and the extremities of the hands it is called the gout in the joints or hands; but when it descends to the extremities of the feet, its name is changed and it is termed podagra: and the noxious moisture which is originally one and the same is described by as many names as there are separate members which it affects. In the same way to pass from visible to invisible things, we should hold that the tendency to each fault exists in the parts and, if I may use the expression, members of our soul. And, as some very wise men have laid down that its powers are threefold, either what is logikon, i.e., reasonable, or qumikon, i.e., irascible, or epi qumhtikon, i.e., subject to desire, is sure to be troubled by some assault. When then the force of noxious passion takes possession of anyone by reason of these feelings, the name of the fault is given to it in accordance with the part affected. For if the plague of sin has infested its rational parts, it will produce the sins of vainglory, conceit, envy, pride, presumption, strife, heresy. If it has wounded the irascible feelings, it will give birth to rage, impatience, sulkiness, accidie, pusillanimity and cruelty. If it has affected that part which is subject to desire, it will be the parent of gluttony, fornication, covetousness, avarice, and noxious and earthly desires.CHAPTER XVI.

That the rational part of our soul is corrupt.

AND therefore if you want to discover the source and origin of this fault, you must recognize that the rational part of your mind and soul is corrupt, that part namely from which the faults of presumption and vainglory for the most part spring. Further this first member, so to speak, of your soul must be healed by the judgment of a right discretion and the virtue of humility, as when it is injured, while you fancy that you can not only still scale the heights of perfection but actually teach others, and hold that you are capable and sufficient to instruct others, through the pride of vainglory you are carried away by these vain rovings, which your confession discloses. And these you will then be able to get rid of without difficulty, if you are established as I said in the humility of true discretion and learn with sorrow of heart how hard and difficult a thing it is for each of us to save his soul, and admit with the inmost feelings of your heart that you are not only far removed from that pride of teaching, but that you are actually still in need of the help of a teacher.

CHAPTER XVII.

How the weaker part of the soul is the first to yield to the devil's temptations.

YOU should then apply to this member or part of the soul which we have described as particularly wounded, the remedy of true humility: for as, so far as appears, it is weaker than the other powers of the soul in you, it is sure to be the first to yield to the assaults of the devil. As when some injuries come upon us, which are caused either by toil laid upon us or by a bad atmosphere, it is generally the case in the bodies of men that those which are the weaker are the first to give in and yield to those chances, and when the disease has more particularly laid hold of them, it affects the sound parts of the body also with the same mischief, so also, when the pestilent blast of sin breathes over us the soul of each one of us is sure to be tempted above all by that passion, in the case of which its feebler and weaker portion does not make so stubborn a resistance to the powerful attacks of the foe, and to run the risk of being taken captive by those, in the case of which a careless watch opens an easier way to betrayal. For so Balaam[1235] gathered that God's people could be by a sure method deceived, when he advised, that in that quarter, wherein he knew that the children of Israel were weak, the dangerous snares should be set for them, as he had no doubt that when a supply of women was offered to them, they would at once fall and be destroyed by fornication, because he was aware that the parts of their souls which were subject to desire were corrupted. So then the spiritual wickednesses tempt with crafty malice each one of us, by particularly laying insidious snares for those affections of the soul, in which they have seen that it is weak, as for instance, if they see that the reasonable parts of our soul are affected, they try to deceive us in the same way that the Scripture tells us that king Ahab was deceived by those Syrians, who said: "We know that the kings of Israel are merciful: And so let us put sackcloth upon our loins, and ropes round our heads, and go out to the king of Israel, and say to him: Thy servant Benhadad saith: I pray thee, let my soul live." And thereby he was affected by no true goodness, but by the empty praise of his clemency, and said: "If he still liveth, he is my brother;" and after this fashion they can deceive us also by the error of that reasonable part, and make us incur the displeasure of God owing to that from which we were hoping that we might gain a reward and receive the recompense of goodness, and to us too the same rebuke may be addressed: "Because thou hast let go from thy hand a man who was worthy of death, thy life shall be for his life, and thy people for his people."[1236] Or when the unclean spirit says: "I will go forth, and will be a lying spirit in the mouth of all his prophets,"[1237] he certainly spread the nets of deception by means of the reasonable feeling which he knew to be exposed to his deadly wiles. And this also the same spirit expected in the case of our Lord, when he tempted Him in these three affections of the soul, wherein he knew that all mankind had been taken captive, but gained nothing by his crafty wiles. For he approached that portion of his mind which was subject to desire, when he said: "Command that these stones be made bread;" the part subject to wrath, when he tried to incite Him to seek the power of the present life and the kingdoms of this world; the reasonable part when he said: "If Thou art the Son of God cast Thyself down from hence."[1238] And in these his deception availed nothing for this reason because he found that there was nothing damaged in Him, in accordance with the supposition which he had formed from a false idea. Wherefore no part of His soul yielded when tempted by the wiles of the foe, "For lo," He saith, "the prince of this world cometh and shall find nothing in Me." [1239]

NOTES:
[1235] Cf. Numb. 24.

[1236] 1 Kings 20:31, 32, 42.
[1237] 1 Kings 22:22.
[1238] S. Matt. 4:3, 6.
[1239] S. John 14:30.

CHAPTER XVIII.

A question whether we should be drawn back to our country by a proper desire for greater silence.

GERMANUS: Among other kinds of illusions and mistakes on our part, which by the vain promise of spiritual advantages have fired us with a longing for our country (as your holiness has discovered by the keen insight of your mind), this stands out as the principal reason, that sometimes we are beset by our brethren and cannot possibly continue in unbroken solitude and continual silence, as we should like. And by this the course and measure of our daily abstinence, which we always want to maintain undisturbed for the chastening of our body, is sure to be interfered with on the arrival of some of the brethren. And this we certainly feel would never happen in our own country, where it is impossible to find anyone, or scarcely anyone who adopts this manner of life.

CHAPTER XIX.

The answer on the devil's illusion, because he promises us the peace of a vaster solitude.

ABRAHAM: Never to be resorted to by men at all is a sign of an unreasonable and ill-considered strictness, or rather of the greatest coldness. For if a man walks in this way, on which he has entered, with too slow steps, and lives according to the former man, it is right that none--I say not of the saints--but of any men should visit him. But you, if you are inflamed with true and perfect love of our Lord, and follow God, who indeed is love, with entire fervour of spirit, are sure to be resorted to by men, to whatever inaccessible spot you may flee, and, in proportion as the ardour of divine love brings you nearer to God, so will a larger concourse of saintly brethren flock to you. For, as the Lord says, "A city set on an hill cannot be hid,"[1240] because "them that love Me," saith the Lord, "will I honour, and they that despise Me shall be contemned."[1241] But you ought to know that this is the subtlest device of the devil, this is his best concealed pitfall, into which he precipitates some wretched and heedless persons, so that, while he is promising them greater things, he takes away the requisite advantages of their daily profit, by persuading them that more remote and vaster deserts should be sought, and by portraying them in their heart as if they were sown with marvellous delights. And further some unknown and non-existent spots, he feigns to be well-known and suitable and already given over to our power and able to be secured without any difficulty. The men also of that country he feigns to be docile and followers of the way of salvation, that, while he is promising richer fruits for the soul there, he may craftily destroy our present profits. For when owing to this vain hope each one separates himself from living together with the Elders and has been deprived of all those things that he idly imagined in his heart, he rises as it were from a most profound slumber, and when awake will find nothing of those things of which he had dreamed. And so as he is hampered by larger requirements for this life and inextricable snares, the devil will not even allow him to aspire to those things which he had once promised himself, and as he is liable no longer to those rare and spiritual visits of the brethren which he had formerly avoided, but to daily interruptions from worldly folk, he will never suffer him to return even to the moderate quiet and system of the anchorite's life.

NOTES:
[1240] Cf. S. Matt. 5:14.
[1241] 1 Sam. 2:30.

CHAPTER XX.

How useful is relaxation on the arrival of brethren.

THAT most refreshing interlude also of relaxation and courtesy, which sometimes is wont to intervene because of the arrival of brethren, although it may seem to us tiresome and what we ought to avoid, yet how useful it is and good for our bodies as well as our souls you must patiently hear in few words. It often happens I say not to novices and weak persons but even to those of the greatest experience and perfection, that unless the strain and tension of their mind is lessened by the relaxation of some changes, they fall either into coldness of spirit; or at any rate into a most dangerous state of bodily health. And therefore when there occur even frequent visits from the brethren they should not only be patiently put up with, but even gratefully welcomed by those who are wise and perfect; first because they stimulate us always to desire with greater eagerness the retirement of the desert (for somehow while they are thought to impede our progress, they really maintain it unwearied and unbroken, and if it was never hindered by any obstacles, it would not endure to the end with unswerving perseverance), next because they give us the opportunity of refreshing the body, together with the advantages of kindness, and at the same time with a most delightful relaxation of the body confer on us greater advantage than those which we should have gained by the weariness which results from abstinence. On which matter I will briefly give a most apt illustration handed down in an old story.

CHAPTER XXI.

How the Evangelist John is said to have shown the value of relaxation.

IT is said that the blessed John, while he was gently stroking a partridge with his hands suddenly saw a philosopher approaching him in the garb of a hunter, who was astonished that a man of so great fame and reputation should demean himself to such paltry and trivial amusements, and said: "Can you be that John, whose great and famous reputation attracted me also with the greatest desire for your acquaintance? Why then do you occupy yourself with such poor amusements?" To whom the blessed John: "What is it," said he, "that you are carrying in your hand?" The other replied: "a bow." "And why," said he, "do you not always carry it everywhere bent?" To whom the other replied: "It would not do, for the force of its stiffness would be relaxed by its being continually bent, and it would be lessened and destroyed, and when the time came for it to send stouter arrows after some beast, its stiffness would be lost by the excessive and continuous strain, and it would be impossible for the more powerful bolts to be shot." "And, my lad," said the blessed John, "do not let this slight and short relaxation of my mind disturb you, as unless it sometimes relieved and relaxed the rigour of its purpose by some recreation, the spirit would lose its spring owing to the unbroken strain, and would be unable when need required, implicitly to follow what was right." [1242]

NOTES:
[1242] The story is quoted by S. Francis de Sales, The Devout Life, and by Dean Goulbourn, Personal Religion, Part III. c. x.

CHAPTER XXII.

A question how we ought to understand what the gospel says: "My yoke is easy and My burden is light."

GERMANUS: As you have given us a remedy for all delusions, and by God's grace all the wiles of the devil by which we were harassed, have been exposed by your teaching, we beg that you will also explain to us this that is said in the gospel: "My yoke is easy, and My burden is light."[1243] For it seems tolerably opposed to that saying of the prophet where it is said: "For the sake of the words of Thy lips I kept hard ways;" while even the Apostle says: "All who will live godly in Christ suffer persecutions."[1244] But whatever is hard and fraught with persecutions cannot be easy and light.

NOTES:
[1243] S. Matt. 11:30.
[1244] Ps. 16 (17):4; 2 Tim. 3:12.

CHAPTER XXIII.

The answer with the explanation of the saying.

ABRAHAM: We can prove by the easy teaching of our own experience that our Lord and Saviour's saying is perfectly true, if we approach the way of perfection properly and in accordance with Christ's will, and mortifying all our desires, and cutting off injurious likings, not only allow nothing to remain with us of this world's goods (whereby our adversary would find at his pleasure opportunities of destroying and damaging us) but actually recognize that we are not our own masters, and truly make our own the Apostle's words: "I live, yet not I, but Christ liveth in me."[1245] For what can be burdensome, or hard to one who has embraced with his whole heart the yoke of Christ, who is established in true humility and ever fixes his eye on the Lord's sufferings and rejoices in all the wrongs that are offered to him, saying: "For which cause I please myself in my infirmities, in reproaches, in necessities, in persecutions, in distresses, for Christ: for when I am weak, then am I strong"?[1246] By what loss of any common thing, I ask, will he be injured, who boasts of perfect renunciation, and voluntarily rejects for Christ's sake all the pomp of this world, and considers all and every of its desires as dung, so that he may gain Christ, and by continual meditation on this command of the gospel, scorns and gets rid of agitation at every loss: "For what shall it profit a man if he gain the whole world, but lose his own soul? Or what shall a man give in exchange for his soul?"[1247] For the loss of what will he be vexed, who recognizes that everything that can be taken away from others is not their own, and proclaims with unconquered valour: "We brought nothing into this world: it is certain that we cannot carry anything out"?[1248] By the needs of what want will his courage be overcome, who knows how to do without "scrip for the way, money for the purse,"[1249] and, like the Apostle, glories "in many fasts, in hunger and thirst, in cold and nakedness"?[1250] What effort, or what hard command of an Elder can disturb the peace of his bosom, who has no will of his own, and not only patiently but even gratefully accepts what is commanded him, and after the example of our Saviour, seeks to do not his own will, but the Father's, as He says Himself to His Father: "Nevertheless not as I will, but as Thou wilt"?[1251] By what wrongs also, by what persecution will he be frightened, nay, what punishment can fail to be delightful to him, who always rejoices together with apostles in stripes, and longs to be counted worthy to suffer shame for the name of Christ?

NOTES:
[1245] Gal. 2:20.
[1246] 2 Cor. 12:10.
[1247] S. Matt. 16:26.
[1248] 1 Tim. 6:7.
[1249] S. Matt. 10:9, 10.
[1250] 2 Cor. 11:27.
[1251] S. Matt. 26:39.

CHAPTER XXIV.

Why the Lord's yoke is felt grievous and His burden heavy.

BUT the fact that to us on the contrary the yoke of Christ seems neither light nor easy, must be rightly ascribed to our perverseness, as we are cast down by unbelief and want of faith, and fight with foolish obstinacy against His command, or rather advice, who says: "If thou wilt be perfect, go sell (or get rid of) all that thou hast, and come follow Me,"[1252] for we keep the substance of our worldly goods. And as the devil holds our soul fast in the toils of these, what remains but that, when he wants to sever us from spiritual delights, he should vex us by diminishing these and depriving us of them, contriving by his crafty wiles that when the sweetness of His yoke and lightness of His burden have become grievous to us through the evil of a corrupt desire, and when we are caught in the chains of that very property and substance, which we kept for our comfort and solace, he may always torment us with the scourges of worldly cares, extorting from us ourselves that wherewith we are tortured? For "Each one is bound by the cords of his own sins," and hears from the prophet: "Behold all you that kindle a fire, encompassed with flames, walk in the light of your fire, and in the flames which you have kindled." Since, as Solomon is witness, "Each man shall thereby be punished, whereby he has sinned."[1253] For the very pleasures which we enjoy become a torment to us, and the delights and enjoyments of this flesh, turn like executioners upon their originator, because one who is supported by his former wealth and property is sure not to admit perfect humility of heart, not entire mortification of dangerous pleasures. But where all these implements of goodness give their aid, there all the trials of this present life, and whatever losses the enemy can contrive, are endured not only with the utmost patience, but with real pleasure, and again when they are wanting so dangerous a pride springs up that we are actually wounded by the deadly strokes of impatience at the slightest reproach, and it may be said to us by the prophet Jeremiah: "And now what hast thou to do in the way of Egypt, to drink the troubled water? And what hast thou to do with the way of the Assyrians, to drink the water of the river? Thy own wickedness shall reprove thee, and thy apostasy shall rebuke thee. Know thou and see that it is an evil and a bitter thing for thee to have left the Lord thy God, and that My fear is not with thee, saith the Lord."[1254] How then is it that the wondrous sweetness of the Lord's yoke is felt to be bitter, but because the bitterness of our dislike injures it? How is it that the exceeding lightness of the Divine burden becomes heavy, but because in our obstinate presumption we despise Him by whom it was borne, especially as Scripture itself plainly testifies to this very thing saying: "For if they would walk in right paths, they would certainly have found the paths of righteousness smooth"?[1255] It is plain, I say, that it is we, who make rough with the nasty and hard stones of our desires the right and smooth paths of the Lord; who most foolishly forsake the royal road made stony with the flints of apostles and prophets, and trodden down by the footsteps of all the saints and of the Lord Himself, and seek trackless and thorny places, and, blinded by the allurements of present delights, tear our way with torn legs and our wedding garment rent, through dark paths, overrun with the briars of sins, so as not only to be pierced by the sharp thorns of the brambles but actually laid low by the bites of deadly serpents and scorpions lurking there. For "there are thorns and thistles in wrong ways, but he that feareth the Lord shall keep himself from them."[1256] Of such also the Lord says elsewhere by the prophet: "My people have forgotten, sacrificing in vain, and stumbling in their ways, in ancient paths, to walk in them in a way not trodden."[1257] For according to Solomon's saying: "The ways of those who do not work are strewn with thorns, but the ways of the lusty are trodden down."[1258] And thus wandering from the king's highway, they can never arrive at that metropolis, whither our course should ever be directed without swerving. And this also Ecclesiastes has pretty significantly expressed saying: "The labour of fools wearies those who know not how to go to the city;" viz., that "heavenly Jerusalem, which is the mother of us all."[1259] But whoever truly gives up this world and takes upon him Christ's yoke and learns of Him, and is trained in the daily practice of suffering wrong, for He is "meek and lowly of heart,"[1260] will ever remain undisturbed by all temptations, and "all things will work together for good to him."[1261] For as the prophet Obadiah says the words of God are "good to him that walketh uprightly;" and again: "For the ways of the Lord are right, and the just shall walk in them; but the transgressors shall fall in them." [1262]

NOTES:
[1252] S. Matt. 19:21.
[1253] Prov. 5:22; Isa. 50:11; Wisd. 11:17.
[1254] Jer. 2:18, 19.
[1255] Prov. 2:20.

[1256] Prov. 22:5.
[1257] Jer. 18:15.
[1258] Prov. 15:19.
[1259] Eccl. 10:15 (LXX); Gal. 4:26.
[1260] S. Matt. 11:29.
[1261] Rom. 8:28.
[1262] Micah 2:7; Hos. 14:10.

CHAPTER XXV.

Of the good which an attack of temptation brings about.

AND so by the struggle with temptation the kindly grace of the Saviour bestows on us larger rewards of praise than if it had taken away from us all need of conflict. For it is a mark of a loftier and grander virtue to remain ever unmoved when hemmed in by persecutions and trials, and to stand faithfully and courageously at the ramparts of God, and in the attacks of men, girt as it were with the arms of unconquered virtue, to triumph gloriously over impatience and somehow to gain strength out of weakness, for "strength is made perfect in weakness." "For behold I have made thee," saith the Lord, "a pillar of iron and a wall of brass, over all the land, to the kings of Judah, and the princes and the priests thereof, and all the people of the land. And they shall fight against thee and shall not prevail: for I am with thee to deliver thee, saith the Lord."[1263] Therefore according to the plain teaching of the Lord the king's highway is easy and smooth, though it may be felt as hard and rough: for those who piously and faithfully serve Him, when they have taken upon them the yoke of the Lord, and have learnt of Him, that He is meek and lowly of heart, at once somehow or other lay aside the burden of earthly passions, and find no labour but rest for their souls, by the gift of the Lord, as He Himself testifies by Jeremiah the prophet, saying: "Stand ye on the ways and see, and ask for the old paths, which is the good way, and walk ye in it: and you shall find refreshment for your souls." For to them at once "the crooked shall become straight and the rough ways plain;" and they shall "taste and see that the Lord is gracious,"[1264] and when they hear Christ proclaiming in the gospel: "Come unto Me all ye that labour and are heavy laden, and I will refresh you," they will lay aside the burden of their sins, and realize what follows: "For My yoke is easy, and My burden is light."[1265] The way of the Lord then has refreshment if it is kept to according to His law. But it is we who by troublesome distractions bring sorrows and troubles upon ourselves, while we try even with the utmost exertion and difficulty to follow the crooked and perverse ways of this world. But when in this way we have made the Lord's yoke heavy and hard to us, we at once complain in a blasphemous spirit of the hardness and roughness of the yoke itself or of Christ who lays it upon us, in accordance with this passage: "The folly of man corrupteth his ways, but he blames God in his heart;"[1266] and as Haggai the prophet says, when we say that "the way of the Lord is not right" the reply is aptly made to us by the Lord: "Is not My way right? Are not your ways rather crooked?"[1267] And indeed if you will compare the sweet scented flower of virginity, and tender purity of chastity to the foul and fetid sloughs of lust, the calm and security of monks to the dangers and losses in which the men of this world are involved, the peace of our poverty to the gnawing vexations and anxious cares of riches, in which they are night and day consumed not without the utmost peril to life, then you will prove that the yoke of Christ is most easy and His burden most light.

NOTES:
[1263] Jer. 1:18, 19.
[1264] Jer. 6:16; Isa. 40:4; Ps. 33 (34):9.
[1265] S. Matt. 11:28-30.
[1266] Prov. 19:3 (LXX).
[1267] Ezek. 18:25 (LXX)

CHAPTER XXVI.

How the promise of an hundredfold in this life is made to those whose renunciation is perfect.

FURTHER also that recompense of reward, wherein the Lord promises an hundredfold in this life to those whose renunciation is perfect, and says: "And everyone that hath left house or brethren or sisters or father or mother or wife or children or lands for My name's sake, shall receive an hundredfold in the present time and shall inherit eternal life,"[1268] is rightly and truly taken in the same sense without any disturbance of faith. For many taking occasion by this saying, insist with crass intelligence that these things will be given carnally in the millennium, though they must certainly admit that age, which they say will be after the resurrection cannot possibly be understood as present. It is then more credible and much clearer that one, who at the persuasion of Christ has made light of any worldly affections or goods, receives from the brethren and partners of his life, who are joined to him by a spiritual tie, even in this life a love which is an hundred times better: since it is certain that among parents and children and brothers, wives and relations, where either the tie is merely formed by intercourse, or the bond of union by the claims of relationship, the love is tolerably short lived and easily broken. Finally even good and duteous children when they have grown up, are sometimes shut out by their parents from their homes and property, and sometimes for a really good reason the tie of matrimony is severed, and a quarrelsome division destroys the property of brothers. Monks alone maintain a lasting union in intimacy, and possess all things in common, as they hold that everything that belongs to their brethren is their own, and that everything which is their own is their brethren's. If then the grace of our love is compared to those affections where the bond of union is a carnal love, certainly it is an hundred times sweeter and finer. There will indeed also be gained from conjugal continence a pleasure that is an hundred times greater than that which arises from the union of the sexes. And instead of that joy, which a man experiences from the possession of a single field or house, he will enjoy a delight in riches a hundred times greater, if he passes over to the adoption of sons of God, and possesses as his own all things which belong to the eternal Father, and asserts in heart and soul after the fashion of that true Son: "All things that the Father hath are mine;"[1269] and if no longer tried by that criminal anxiety in distractions and cares, but free from care and glad at heart he succeeds everywhere to his own, hearing daily the announcement made to him by the Apostle: "For all things are yours, whether the world, or things present, or things to come;" and by Solomon: "The faithful man has a whole world of riches."[1270] You have then that recompense of an hundredfold brought out by the greatness of the value, and the difference of the character that cannot be estimated. For if for a fixed weight of brass or iron or some still commoner metal, one had given in exchange the same weight only in gold, he would appear to have given much more than an hundredfold. And so when for the scorn of delights and earthly affections there is made a recompense of spiritual joy and the gladness of a most precious love, even if the actual amount be the same, yet it is an hundred times better and grander. And to make this plainer by frequent repetition: I used formerly to have a wife in the lustful passion of desire: I now have one in honourable sanctification and the true love of Christ. The woman is but one, but the value of the love has increased an hundredfold. But if instead of distrusting anger and wrath you have regard to constant gentleness and patience, instead of the stress of anxiety and trouble, peace and freedom from care, instead of the fruitless and criminal vexation of this world the salutary fruits of sorrow, instead of the vanity of temporal joy the richness of spiritual delights, you will see in the change of these feelings a recompense of an hundredfold. And if we compare with the short-lived and fleeting pleasure of each sin the benefits of the opposite virtues the increased delights will prove that these are an hundred times better. For in counting on your fingers you transfer the number of an hundred from the left hand to the right and though you seem to keep the same arrangement of the fingers yet there is a great increase in the amount of the quantity.[1271] For the result will be that we who seemed to bear the form of the goats on the left hand, will be removed and gain the reward of the sheep on the right hand. Now let us pass on to consider the nature of those things which Christ gives back to us in this world for our scorn of worldly advantages, more particularly according to the Gospel of Mark who says: "There is no man who hath left house or brethren or sisters or mother or children or lands for My sake and the gospel's sake, who shall not receive an hundred times as much now in this time: houses and brethren and sisters and mothers and children and lands, with persecutions, and in the world to come life eternal."[1272] For he who for the sake of Christ's name disregards the love of a single father or mother or child, and gives himself over to the purest love of all who serve Christ, will receive an hundred times the amount of brethren and kinsfolk; since instead of but one he will begin to have so many fathers and brethren bound to him by a still more fervent and admirable affection. He also will be enriched with an increased possession of lands, who has given up a single house for the love of Christ, and possesses countless homes in monasteries as his own, to whatever part of the world he may retire, as to his own house. For how can he fail to receive an hundredfold, and, if it is not wrong to add somewhat to our Lord's words, more than an hundredfold, who gives up the faithless and compulsory service of ten or twenty slaves and relies on the spontaneous attendance of so many noble and free born men? And that this is so you could prove by your own experience, as since you have each left but one father and mother and home, you have gained without any effort or care, in any part of the world to which you have come, countless fathers and moth-

ers and brethren, as well as houses and lands and most faithful servants, who receive you as their masters, and welcome, and respect, and
take care of you with the utmost attention. But, I say that deservedly
and confidently will the saints enjoy this service, if they have first
submitted themselves and everything they have by a voluntary offering
for the service of the brethren. For, as the Lord says, they will freely
receive back that which they themselves have bestowed on others. But
if a man has not first offered this with true humility to his companions,
how can he calmly endure to have it offered to him by others, when he
knows that he is burdened rather than helped by their services, because
he prefers to receive attention from the brethren rather than to give it
to them? But all these things he will receive not with careless slackness and a lazy delight, but, in accordance with the Lord's word, "with
persecutions," i.e., with the pressure of this world, and terrible distress
from his passions, because, as the wise man testifies: "He who is easy
going and without trouble shall come to want."[1273] For not the slothful,
or the careless, or the delicate, or the tender take the kingdom of
heaven by force, but the violent. Who then are the violent? Surely they
are those who show a splendid violence not to others, but to their own
soul, who by a laudable force deprive it of all delights m things present, and are declared by the Lord's mouth to be splendid plunderers,
and by rapine of this kind, violently seize upon the kingdom of
heaven. For, as the Lord says, "The kingdom of heaven suffereth violence and the violent take it by force."[1274] Those are certainly worthy
of praise as violent, who do violence to their own destruction, for, "A
man," as it is written, "that is in sorrow laboureth for himself and does
violence to his own destruction."[1275] For our destruction is delight in
this present life, and to speak more definitely, the performance of our
own likes and desires, as, if a man withdraws these from his soul and
mortifies them, he straightway does glorious and valuable violence to
his own destruction, provided that he refuses to it the pleasantest of its
wishes which the Divine word often rebukes by the prophet, saying:
"For in the days of your fast your own will is found;" and again: "If
thou turn away thy foot from the Sabbath, to do thy will on My holy
day, and glorify him, while thou dost not thy own ways, and thy own
will is not found, to speak a word." And the great blessedness that is
promised to him is at once added by the prophet. "Then," he says,
"shalt thou be delighted in the Lord, and I will lift thee up above the
high places of the earth, and will feed thee with the inheritance of
Jacob thy father. For the mouth of the Lord hath spoken it."[1276] And
therefore our Lord and Saviour, to give us an example of giving up our

own wills, says: "I came not to do My own will, but the will of Him that sent Me;" and again: "Not as I will, but as Thou wilt."[1277] And this good quality those men in particular show who live in the coenobia and are governed by the rule of the Elders, who do nothing of their own choice, but their will depends upon the will of the Abbot. Finally to bring this discussion to a close, I ask you, do not those who faithfully serve Christ, most clearly receive grace an hundredfold in this, while for His name's sake they are honoured by the greatest princes, and though they do not look for the praise of men, yet become venerated in the trials of persecution whose humble condition would perhaps have been looked down upon even by common folk, either because of their obscure birth, or because of their condition as slaves, if they had continued in their life in the world? But because of the service of Christ no one will venture to raise a calumny against their state of nobility, or to fling in their teeth the obscurity of their origin. Nay rather, through the very opprobrium of a humble condition by which others are shamed and confounded, the servants of Christ are more splendidly ennobled, as we can clearly show by the case of Abbot John who lives in the desert which borders on the town of Lycus. For he sprang from obscure parents, but owing to the name of Christ has become so well known to almost all mankind that the very lords of creation, who hold the reins of this world and of empire, and are a terror to all powers and kings, venerate him as their lord, and from distant countries seek his advice, and entrust to his prayers and merits the crown of their empire, and the state of safety, and the fortunes of war.[1278]

In such terms the blessed Abraham discoursed on the origin of and remedy for our illusion, and exposed to our eyes the crafty thoughts which the devil had originated and suggested, and kindled in us the desire of true mortification, wherewith we hope that many also may be inflamed, even though all these things have been written in a somewhat simple style. For though the dying embers of our words cover up the glowing thoughts of the greatest fathers, yet we hope that in the case of very many who try to remove the embers of our words and to fan into a flame the hidden thoughts, their coldness will be turned into heat. But, O holy brethren, I have not indeed been so puffed up by the spirit of presumption as to give forth to you this fire (which the Lord came to send upon the earth, and which He eagerly longs to kindle[1279]) in order that by the application of this warmth I might set on fire your purpose which is already at a white heat, but in order that your authority with your children might be greater, if in addition the precepts of the greatest and most ancient fathers support what you are teaching not by the dead sound of words but by your living example. It only remains that I who have been till now tossed about by a most dangerous tempest, should be wafted to the safe harbour of silence by the spiritual gales of your prayers.

NOTES:
[1268] S. Matt. 19:29.
[1269] S. John 16:15.
[1270] 1 Cor. 3:22; Prov. 17:6 (LXX).
[1271] The passage alludes to the practice of counting on the fingers, in which all the tens up to ninety were reckoned on the fingers of the left hand, but with the number of a hundred the reckoning began with the same arrangement of the fingers, on the right hand. S. Jerome has a similar allusion to the practice in his work against Jovinian I. i. and compare also Juvenal Satire. X. l. 247, 248.
[1272] S. Mark 10:29, 30.
[1273] Prov. 14:23 (LXX).
[1274] S. Matt. 11:12.
[1275] Prov. 14:26 (LXX).
[1276] Isa. 58:3, 13, 14.
[1277] S. John 6:38; S. Matt. 26:39.
[1278] Cf. the note on the Institutes IV. xxiii.
[1279] Cf. S. Luke 12:49.

Also from Benediction Books ...
Wandering Between Two Worlds: Essays on Faith and Art
Anita Mathias
Benediction Books, 2007
152 pages
ISBN: 0955373700

Available from www.amazon.com, www.amazon.co.uk

In these wide-ranging lyrical essays, Anita Mathias writes, in lush, lovely prose, of her naughty Catholic childhood in Jamshedpur, India; her large, eccentric family in Mangalore, a sea-coast town converted by the Portuguese in the sixteenth century; her rebellion and atheism as a teenager in her Himalayan boarding school, run by German missionary nuns, St. Mary's Convent, Nainital; and her abrupt religious conversion after which she entered Mother Teresa's convent in Calcutta as a novice. Later rich, elegant essays explore the dualities of her life as a writer, mother, and Christian in the United States-- Domesticity and Art, Writing and Prayer, and the experience of being "an alien and stranger" as an immigrant in America, sensing the need for roots.

About the Author

Anita Mathias is the author of *Wandering Between Two Worlds: Essays on Faith and Art.* She has a B.A. and M.A. in English from Somerville College, Oxford University, and an M.A. in Creative Writing from the Ohio State University, USA. Anita won a National Endowment of the Arts fellowship in Creative Nonfiction in 1997. She lives in Oxford, England with her husband, Roy, and her daughters, Zoe and Irene.

Visit Anita's website
   http://www.anitamathias.com,
and Anita's blog
   http://dreamingbeneaththespires.blogspot.com, (Dreaming Beneath the Spires).

The Church That Had Too Much
Anita Mathias
Benediction Books, 2010
52 pages
ISBN: 9781849026567

Available from www.amazon.com, www.amazon.co.uk

The Church That Had Too Much was very well-intentioned. She wanted to love God, she wanted to love people, but she was both hampered by her muchness and the abundance of her possessions, and beset by ambition, power struggles and snobbery. Read about the surprising way The Church That Had Too Much began to resolve her problems in this deceptively simple and enchanting fable.

About the Author

Anita Mathias is the author of *Wandering Between Two Worlds: Essays on Faith and Art.* She has a B.A. and M.A. in English from Somerville College, Oxford University, and an M.A. in Creative Writing from the Ohio State University, USA. Anita won a National Endowment of the Arts fellowship in Creative Nonfiction in 1997. She lives in Oxford, England with her husband, Roy, and her daughters, Zoe and Irene.

Visit Anita's website
　　http://www.anitamathias.com,
and Anita's blog
　　http://dreamingbeneaththespires.blogspot.com (Dreaming Beneath the Spires).

Printed in the USA
CPSIA information can be obtained
at www.ICGtesting.com
LVHW041033231023
761876LV00001B/1